DAMMING THE FLOOD

DAMMING THE FLOOD

Haiti and the Politics of Containment

PETER HALLWARD

VERSO

London • New York

First published by Verso 2007
This paperback edition first published by Verso 2010
© Peter Hallward 2007
Afterword © Peter Hallward 2010

1 3 5 7 9 10 8 6 4 2

Verso
UK: 6 Meard Street, London W1F 0EG
US: 20 Jay Street, Suite 1010, Brooklyn, NY 11201
www.versobooks.com

Verso is the imprint of New Left Books

ISBN-13: 978-1-84467-466-4

British Library Cataloguing in Publication Data
A catalogue record for this book is available from the British Library

Library of Congress Cataloging-in-Publication Data
A catalog record for this book is available from the Library of Congress

Typeset in Bembo by Hewer Text UK Ltd, Edinburgh
Printed in the US by Maple Vail

Lè yo vle touye chen yo di'l fou.
When people want to kill a dog they say it's rabid.

Contents

Acknowledgments

Some of the many people who helped me to research and write this book include Lisius Orel, Reed Lindsay, Georges Honorat, Sasha Kramer, Anne Sosin, Paul Christian, David Adams, Maude Leblanc, Anthony Fenton, Isabel Macdonald, Charles Arthur, Rea Dol, Frantz Gabriel, Kevin Pina, Eléonore Senlis, Paul Farmer, Katherine Kean, Tom Reeves, Chantal Regnault, Ben Dupuy, Jeb Sprague, Mildred Trouillot Aristide, Laura Flynn, Guy Delva, Marcus Garcia, Gérard Lehmann, Michelle Karshan, Jean-Marie Samedy, Ira Kurzban, Nicolas Rossier, Robert Fatton, Father Gérard Jean-Juste, Lucie Tondreau and Sinéad Rushe.

I'm especially grateful to Patrick Elie, Kim Ives and Brian Concannon Jr.

I have assumed that most of the likely readers of this book will find French rather than Kreyol spellings more familiar – *Port-au-Prince* rather than *Pòtoprens*.

Chronology

1697	The treaty of Ryswick divides the island of Hispaniola into Saint-Domingue (French) and Santo Domingo (Spanish).
14 August 1791	A slave uprising begins in northern Saint-Domingue.
4 February 1794	Abolition of French colonial slavery.
1 January 1804	Saint-Domingue is renamed Haiti, and declares itself independent of France.
17 October 1806	Dessalines is assassinated; civil war then divides Haiti between a monarchy in the north (ruled by Henri Christophe) and a republic in the south (led by Alexandre Pétion).
1818–43	Pierre Boyer re-unifies Haiti.
1825	France recognizes Haitian independence in exchange for the payment of 150 million francs (later reduced to 90 million) as compensation for lost property.
1915–34	The United States invades and occupies Haiti.
1946–50	Dumarsais Estimé is president.
22 September 1957	François Duvalier ('Papa Doc') becomes president.
22 June 1964	François Duvalier declares himself president for life.
21 April 1971	François Duvalier dies and is succeeded by his son Jean-Claude ('Baby Doc').
7 February 1986	Jean-Claude Duvalier is pushed out of Haiti by a popular uprising; General Henry Namphy takes power.
16 December 1990	Jean-Bertrand Aristide is elected with 67 percent of the vote.

6 January 1991	Macoute leader Roger Lafontant attempts a pre-emptive coup d'état against Aristide, but is overwhelmed by popular resistance.
7 February 1991	Inauguration of Aristide's first administration; his prime minister is René Préval.
30 September 1991	General Raoul Cédras and police chief Michel François overthrow Aristide, who goes into exile first in Venezuela and then in the US; over the next few years several thousands of Aristide's supporters are killed.
3 July 1993	The Governors Island Agreement brokered by UN and OAS officials between Cédras and Aristide is signed (and later ignored by Cédras).
Summer 1993	The paramilitary death squad FRAPH is formed, led by Toto Constant and Jodel Chamblain.
11 September 1993	Lavalas activist Antoine Izméry is assassinated.
21–22 April 1994	FRAPH and Haitian army troops kill dozens of people in the Gonaïves slum of Raboteau.
19 September 1994	US soldiers occupy Haiti for the second time.
15 October 1994	Aristide returns from exile, with businessman Smarck Michel as his prime minister.
Early 1995	Aristide disbands Haiti's armed forces (FAdH).
June/September 1995	Legislative elections are won by members of the Plateforme Politique Lavalas; Evans Paul is heavily defeated by Manno Charlemagne in the Port-au-Prince mayoral election.
16 October 1995	Prime minister Smarck Michel resigns.
17 December 1995	René Préval is elected with 88 percent of the vote.
7 February 1996	Inauguration of Préval's first administration, with the OPL's Rosny Smarth as his prime minister.
late 1996	Formation of Fanmi Lavalas political organization, led by Aristide, in opposition to the ex-Lavalas faction the Organisation du Peuple en Lutte (OPL), led by Gérard Pierre-Charles.
6 April 1997	Fanmi Lavalas wins several seats in Senate elections; the results are not accepted by the

	OPL, and parliamentary deadlock ensues.
9 June 1997	Prime minister Rosny Smarth resigns.
8–9 October 1999	Jean Lamy is assassinated, and under pressure from Dany Toussaint, Préval's security minister Bob Manuel flees into exile.
11 January 1999	Parliamentary terms expire.
3 April 2000	Journalist Jean Dominique is assassinated.
21 May 2000	Legislative and local elections: Fanmi Lavalas wins landslide victories at all levels of government; opponents of Fanmi Lavalas form a US-backed coalition called the Convergence Démocratique.
2 June 2000	The OAS disputes the validity of the vote-counting method used in the Senate elections.
October 2000	PNH commanders Guy Philippe, Jackie Nau and Gilbert Dragon flee into exile after being implicated in plans for a coup.
26 November 2000	Aristide is re-elected president with 92 percent of the vote.
7 February 2001	Inauguration of Aristide's second administration, with Jean-Marie Chérestal as his prime minister; simultaneous inauguration of a parallel government led by the Convergence Démocratique's Gérard Gourgue.
28 July 2001	The first of many commando raids on police stations and other government facilities by ex-soldiers based in the Dominican Republic and led by Guy Philippe and Ravix Rémissainthe (later known as the FLRN).
17 December 2001	Ex-soldiers attack the presidential palace, provoking popular reprisals against the offices of parties belonging to the Convergence Démocratique.
21 January 2002	Prime minister Chérestal resigns.
4 September 2002	OAS adopts resolution 822.
December 2002	The Group of 184 (led by Andy Apaid, supported by the IRI) is formed at a meeting of Aristide's opponents in the Dominican Republic.
April 2003	Aristide asks France to repay the money it extorted from Haiti as compensation for lost

	colonial property in the nineteenth century.
July 2003	Inter-American Development Bank promises to disburse frozen loans and aid to Haiti.
21 September 2003	Amiot 'Cubain' Métayer is assassinated in Gonaïves; Buteur Métayer and Jean Tatoune take over Cubain's gang and turn it against Aristide.
5 December 2003	Anti-government students clash with government supporters at the State University in Port-au-Prince.
1 January 2004	Haiti celebrates the bicentenary of its independence from France.
5 February 2004	Full-scale insurgency begins in Gonaïves, led by Jean Tatoune, Buteur Métayer and Winter Etienne; they are soon joined by Guy Philippe, Jodel Chamblain and FLRN troops based in the Dominican Republic.
22 February 2004	Chamblain overruns Cap Haïtien.
29 February 2004	Aristide is forced onto a US jet and flown to the Central African Republic.
March 2004	US troops occupy Haiti for the third time, and an interim government is formed, with Gérard Latortue as prime minister; hundreds of Aristide supporters are killed.
June 2004	The US-led occupation force is replaced by a UN stabilization mission (MINUSTAH).
30 September 2004	A long campaign of violence against Lavalas supporters in Port-au-Prince begins, notably in Bel Air and Cité Soleil.
6 July 2005	A major UN assault on Cité Soleil kills at least twenty people, including the militant leader Dred Wilme.
7 February 2006	Préval wins delayed presidential elections in the first round, with 51 percent of the vote.
14 May 2006	Inauguration of Préval's second administration.
22 December 2006	UN incursion into Cité Soleil leaves around a dozen residents dead.
January–February 2007	UN military incursions into Cité Soleil continue.

Acronyms

AHP	Agence Haïtienne de Presse
AI	Amnesty International
ALAH-MPSN	Mouvement Patriotique pour le Sauvetage National (a neo-Duvalierist political party led by Reynold Georges)
ANMH	National Association of Haitian Media
AP	Associated Press
APN	Autorité Portuaire Nationale (National Port Authority)
AUMOHD	Association des Universitaires Motivés pour une Haiti de Droit (a human rights group directed by Evel Fanfan)
BO	Batay Ouvriye (Worker's Struggle)
CARICOM	Caribbean Community and Common Market
CARLI	Comité des Avocats pour le Respect des Libertés Individuelles (Committee of Lawyers for the Respect of Individual Liberties)
CD	Convergence Démocratique
CDS	Centres pour le Développement et la Santé (Centers for Development and Health), a Cité Soleil-based medical organization run in the 1990s by Reginald Boulos.
CEDH	Centre Oecuménique des Droits Humains (Ecumenical Human Rights Center), led by Jean-Claude Bajeux.
CEP	Conseil Électoral Provisoire (Provisional Electoral Council)
CIDA	Canadian International Development Agency
CIIR	Catholic Institute for International Relations
CIMO	Corps d'Intervention et de Maintien de l'Ordre (Intervention Corps for the Maintenance of Order, a special-weapons unit of the National Police)
COHA	Council on Hemispheric Affairs

CONAP	Coordination Nationale de Plaidoyer pour les Droits des Femmes (National Coordination for Advocacy on Women's Rights)
CREDDO	Coalition Réformiste pour le Développement d'Haïti (a pro-army party led by ex-general Prosper Avril)
CRESFED	Centre de Recherche et de Formation Économique et Sociale (Center for Economic and Social Research and Development Training, an NGO directed by the OPL's Suzy Castor)
CSHR	Center for the Study of Human Rights, at the University of Miami
CTH	Confédération des Travailleurs Haïtiens (Confederation of Haitian Workers)
DDR	Disarmament, demobilization and re-integration
DEA	(US) Drug Enforcement Administration
DIA	(US) Defense Intelligence Agency
DOJ	(US) Department of Justice
EIU	Economist Intelligence Unit
ENFOFANM	An organization that provides information and support for women's rights
EU	European Union
FAdH	Forces Armées d'Haïti (the Haitian army, modernized during the US invasion of 1915–1934 and disbanded by Aristide in 1995)
FEUH	Fédération des Étudiants de l'Université d'État d'Haïti (a student group supported by the G184)
FL	Fanmi Lavalas (the Lavalas Family political organization)
FLRN	Front pour la Libération et la Reconstruction Nationale (anti-Aristide insurgency force led by Jodel Chamblain and Guy Philippe).
FNCD	Front National pour le Changement et la Démocratie (National Front for Change and Democracy)
FRAPH	Front Révolutionnaire Pour l'Avancement et le Progrès Haïtien (Revolutionary Front for the Advancement and Progress of Haiti, a paramilitary group established 1993, led by Toto Constant and Jodel Chamblain)
FTAA	Free Trade Area of the Americas
FTZ	free trade zone
G184	Group of 184, established in December 2002 with support from the IRI, led by Andy Apaid

GIPNH	Groupe d'Intervention de la Police Nationale d'Haïti (a SWAT-style unit)
GRAFNEH	Grand Front National des Étudiants Haïtiens (a student group supported by the G184)
HAC	Haiti Action Committee (San Francisco)
HDP	Haiti Democracy Project (a Washington-based pressure group, founded in 2002 by Rudolph Boulos, James Morrell, Tim Carney and Lawrence Pezzullo)
HIP	Haiti Information Project, directed by Kevin Pina
HRDF	Haitian Resources Development Foundation, a Miami-based NGO directed by Gérard Latortue
HRW	Human Rights Watch
HSG	Haiti Support Group, a UK-based NGO directed by Charles Arthur
IC	international community
ICG	International Crisis Group
ICITAP	International Criminal Investigative Training Assistance Program (US DOJ)
IDB	Inter-American Development Bank
IFES	International Foundation for Election Systems
IFIs	international financial institutions
IGH	Interim Government of Haiti (2004–2006)
IJDH	Institute for Justice & Democracy in Haiti, directed by Brian Concannon, Jr.
IMF	International Monetary Fund
IRI	(US) International Republican Institute
ISC	Initiative de la Société Civile, a pro-business NGO led by Rosny Desroches
JPP	Jeunesse Pouvoir Populaire (Youth/People's Power), a pro-Lavalas group led by René Civil
KONAKOM	Congrès National des Mouvements Démocratiques (National Congress of Democratic Movements), a social-democratic party led by Victor Benoît
KOREM	Kombit Rezistans Mas Yo, a pro-Lavalas popular organization
KOZEPEP	Komite Zafè Elektoral Peyizan pou Eleksyon Pwop (a peasant organization led by Charles Suffrard, associated with René Préval and Jean Dominique, allied with LESPWA)
LESPWA	A political alliance formed in late 2005 to support

	Préval's presidential campaign, made up of two minor political parties, the Parti Louvri Barye (PLB) and the Efò ak Solidarite pou Konstwi yon Altènativ Nasyonal Popilè/Koordinasyon Resistans Grandans (ESKANP-KOREGA)
MDN	Mobilisation pour le Développement National, a Duvalierist party led by Hubert de Ronceray
MICIVIH	Mission Civile Internationale en Haïti (UN/OAS-led International Civilian Mission to Haiti (1993–2000)
MINUSTAH	Mission des Nations Unies pour la Stabilization en Haïti (UN Stabilization Mission in Haiti, initiated in the spring of 2004)
MOCHRENA	Mouvement Chrétien pour une Nouvelle Haïti (Christian Movement for a New Haiti, an evangelical political party by Pastor Luc Mésadieu)
MOJSIPD-CUD	Mouvement des Jeunes Simon/Pélé pour la Défense de la Culture et du Développement Social (a Port-au-Prince popular organization)
MPP	Mouvman Peyizan Papaye (Peasant Movement of Papaye, a peasant organization based in the Central Plateau and led by Chavannes Jean-Baptiste)
MSF	Médecins Sans Frontières (Doctors without Borders)
NACLA	North American Congress on Latin America
NCHR	National Coalition for Haitian Rights (formerly Haitian Refugees). In 2004 the New York branch of NCHR (led by Jocelyn McCalla) dissociated itself from the Haiti-based branch (led by Pierre Espérance); the latter then renamed itself the Réseau National pour la Défense des Droits Humains (RNDDH)
NDI	(US) National Democratic Institute
NED	(US) National Endowment for Democracy
NGO	non-governmental organization
OAS	Organization of American States
OPDR	Organisation Populaire Démocratique de Raboteau (a Gonaïves-based popular organization led by Amiot "Cubain" Métayer).
OPL	Organisation du Peuple en Lutte (Organization of People in Struggle), a political party led by Gérard Pierre-Charles; from 1995 to 1997 the OPL called itself the Organisation Politique Lavalas

OPs	*organisations populaires*
PANPRA	Parti National Progressiste Révolutionnaire Haïtien (National Progressive Revolutionary Party, led by Serge Gilles)
PAPDA	Platfom Ayisyen pou Pledwaye pou yon Devlopman Alternatif (Haitian Platform to Advocate for an Alternative Development, an NGO led by Camille Chalmers)
PIRED	Programme Intégré pour le Renforcement de la Démocratie (a USAID programme led by Ira Lowenthal)
PNH	Police Nationale d'Haïti (Haitian National Police, established 1995)
PPN	Parti Populaire National (National Popular Party), a leftwing party led by Ben Dupuy
RAMICOS	Rassemblement des Militants Conséquents de la Commune de Saint-Marc, an anti-Lavalas popular organization
RFI	Radio France Internationale
RNDDH	Réseau National pour la Défense Des Droits Humains (National Network for the Defense of Human Rights, formerly NCHR-Haïti)
SAP	structural adjustment plan
SIN	National Intelligence Service
SOFA	Solidarité Fanm Ayisyen (Haitian Women's Solidarity)
SOPUDEP	Société de Providence Unie pour le Développement de Pétionville (a pro-Lavalas popular organization led by Rea Dol)
TKL	Ti Kommunauté Legliz St Jean Bosco (a pro-Lavalas popular organization led by Paul Raymond)
UDMO	Unité Départemental pour le Maintien de l'Ordre (Departmental Unit for the Maintenance of Law and Order; regional branches of CIMO)
UN	United Nations
UNDP	United Nations Development Program
USAID	United States Agency for International Development
USGPN	Unité de Sécurité Générale du Palais National (the Presidential Guard, an elite unit of the PNH)
USP	Unité de Sécurité Présidentielle (the President's personal, "secret service" style security detail)
WSWS	World Socialist Web Site

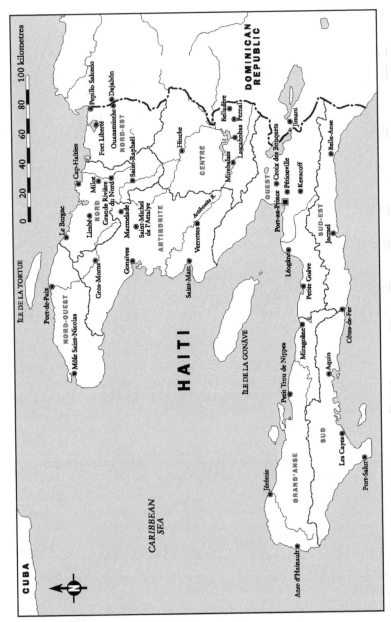

Maps by ml-design.co.uk

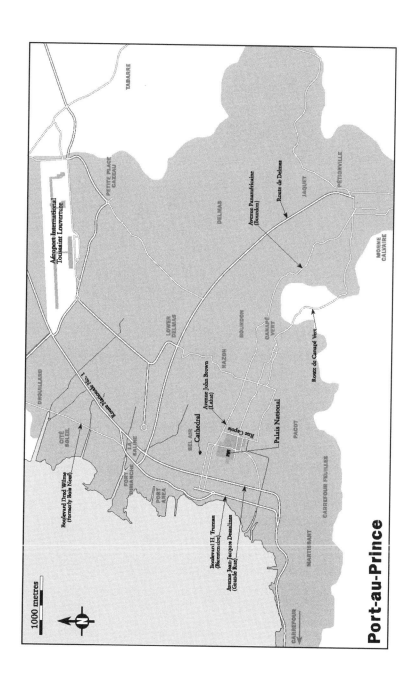

1000 metres

N

Aéroport International
Toussaint Louverture

PETITE PLACE
GAZEAU

TABARRE

DELMAS

Route de Delmas

Avenue Panaméricaine
(Bourdon)

PÉTIONVILLE

JAQUET

MORNE
CALVAIRE

LOWER
DELMAS

BOURDON

MAZON

CANAPÉ
VERT

Route de Canapé Vert

DROUILLARD

Route Nationale No 1

CITÉ
SOLEIL

Boulevard Dred Wilme
(formerly Bois Neuf)

FORT
DIMANCHE

LA SALINE

Avenue John Brown
(Lalue)

Cathedral

SEL AIR

Rue Capois

Palais National

PACOT

CARREFOUR FEUILLES

PORT
AREA

Boulevard H. Truman
(Bicentenaire)

Avenue Jean-Jacques Dessalines
(Grande Rue)

MARTISSANT

CARREFOUR

Port-au-Prince

Introduction

Ravèt pa janm gen rezon devan poul
(Roaches are never right when facing chickens)

True political freedom is as limited in Haiti as it is anywhere on the planet. It is limited by the fragility of an economy that remains profoundly vulnerable to international pressure. It is limited by a rigid and highly polarized social structure that isolates a small and very concentrated elite from the rest of the population. It is also limited by a whole range of strategic and institutional factors: the persistence of neo-imperial intervention, of elite and foreign control over the military or paramilitary security forces, of elite and foreign manipulation of the media, of the judiciary, of non-governmental organizations, of the educational and religious establishments, of the electoral and political systems, and so on. Taken together these things make it extremely difficult to sustain any far-reaching challenge to the status quo.

The prospects for such a challenge declined still further when the dictatorial François Duvalier became president of Haiti in the late 1950s. With the help of a fearsome new paramilitary force known as the *Tontons Macoutes*, Duvalier established the most violently repressive regime in the island's history. Thanks in part to the support of Haiti's most powerful neighbor, the United States, the essential features of this regime survived François Duvalier's death and replacement by his son Jean-Claude in 1971.

In spite of many obstacles, however, in the mid-1980s a remarkable political movement emerged in opposition to the Duvalierist dictatorship. Pressure from this movement forced the hopelessly decadent Jean-Claude into exile in early 1986; in an attempt to limit any more far-reaching changes the army then returned Haiti to direct military rule. The next few years were witness to a dramatic struggle for power. Against the army and the elite, a broad coalition of progressive forces waged a courageous and inventive campaign for democratic reform. Like Duvalier before them, a succession of military rulers could only suppress growing demands for change by resorting to unacceptably public levels of violence. In the late 1980s unrelenting repression brought Haiti to the brink of revolution.

In 1990 this protracted struggle culminated in a watershed election victory for the popular anti-Duvalierist movement that became known as *Lavalas* – a Kreyol word meaning "avalanche" or "flood", as well as "the mass of the people" or "everyone together" – and its presidential candidate, the liberation theologian and grassroots activist Jean-Bertrand Aristide. Aristide's election signaled an end to decades of authoritarian rule. Inaugurated in February 1991 in an atmosphere of exuberant collective enthusiasm, his government began to implement a number of desperately needed reforms and started to dismantle the structures of military and paramilitary oppression that had dominated life on the island all through the twentieth century. The campaign for the democratic liberation of Haiti was now well and truly underway.

But so was the elite's drive to contain and reverse this liberation. In September 1991, just seven months after Aristide took power, the army overthrew his government and killed many hundreds of its supporters. Nine long years later, in the autumn of 2000, Aristide was again elected president with another landslide majority. Although it cost the elite and its allies more time and effort to get rid of him a second time, a further coup duly followed in February 2004. Whereas the first coup was widely condemned as a major political crime, the second was largely ignored. Whereas the coup of 1991 triggered an international campaign for the restoration of Haitian democracy, the disastrous consequences of 2004 met and continue to meet with widespread resignation or indifference, if not approval.

I

This book began as a response to the striking difference between the international reactions to the two anti-Aristide coups of 1991 and 2004. When the Haitian army deposed Aristide in 1991, much of the world was appalled; when members of this same army helped the US and France to oust him in 2004, no-one seemed to care. What had changed? Although twice elected with massive majorities, by 2004 most mainstream international analysts had begun to denounce Aristide as an enemy of democracy. Although political violence declined dramatically during his years in office, by 2004 he was regularly condemned as an enemy of human rights. Although still immensely popular among the poor, he was attacked as aloof and corrupt. Although he was prepared to make far-reaching compromises with his opponents, he was derided as intractable and intolerant of dissent. By 2004, in other words, many international observers concluded that Aristide's own administration had turned into a version of the oppressive dictatorship it had initially sought to abolish.

The removal of such an administration, according to this logic, could then hardly be more objectionable than Jean-Claude Duvalier's expulsion in 1986. The potted history of events provided in a recent report by one of Haiti's most powerful international donors, the Inter-American Development Bank, provides a diplomatic illustration of the prevailing view. After winning "disputed elections" in 2000, Aristide's government failed to reach agreement with an "opposition coalition, preventing the organization of legislative elections. On 12 January 2004, the term of Haiti's parliament expired, and President Aristide then ruled by decree. The upheaval culminated in a change of government in March 2004, following the departure of President Aristide in February 2004."[1] What could be simpler? An illegitimate government failed to cooperate with a democratic opposition: as a result there was upheaval, Aristide then "departed" and his government was replaced.

This conveniently straightforward version of events conceals a major victory for the Haitian elite and its Franco-American sponsors. In fact it conceals a quite spectacular achievement. The effort to weaken, demoralize and then overthrow Lavalas in the first years of the twenty-first century was perhaps the most successful exercise of neo-imperial sabotage since the toppling of Nicaragua's Sandinistas in 1990. In many ways it was much more successful, at least in the short-term, than previous international triumphs in Iraq (2003), Panama (1989), Grenada (1983), Chile (1973), the Congo (1960), Guatemala (1954) or Iran (1953). Not only did the coup of 2004 topple one of the most popular governments in Latin America but it managed to topple it in a manner that wasn't widely criticized or even recognized as a coup at all.

This book tries to explain how it was done. After considering the achievements and limitations of the democratic movement that coalesced around Aristide, it pays particular attention to the way this movement was contained and repressed by a mixture of systematic media misrepresentation, foreign-sponsored "democracy promotion" and direct military intervention. It tries to explain how and why, by the time it took place in February 2004, the second coup was widely seen as a blow struck *for* rather than against Haitian democracy.

II

There was nothing inevitable about this outcome. Back in 1991, Aristide and Lavalas were among the most potent symbols for progressive political change in the entire world. As anyone who lived through them will recall, the late 1980s and early 1990s were an especially discouraging and reactionary time. Reagan and Thatcher had secured the foundations of their "new world order". Nicaragua's Sandinistas had been crushed, Cuba's Castro was marginalized, Jamaica's Manley was subdued, the national-liberation movements had been deflected. Just about every-where, leftwing parties were rapidly becoming indistinguishable from their traditional opponents. Hugo Chávez and Evo Morales were nowhere in sight. Apart from popular mobilizations in South Africa and the Philippines, in the late 1980s the Haitian struggle against military rule began in a context of almost total isolation.

In the late 1980s this struggle united a wide range of social groups who shared a common desire to break with the stifling grip of the military regime. Lavalas brought together the urban poor and the peasantry, of course, but also some influential members of the liberal elite: cosmo-politan political dissidents, journalists, academics, a few business leaders. Journalists who witnessed it described Aristide's 1990 election victory as "one of the most joyous periods in Haitian history."[2] After the army deposed him in 1991, Aristide's cause was endorsed by prominent members of the US Congress and by the president of France, as well as by many thousands of political activists all across North America. Celebrities like Steven Spielberg and Robert de Niro signed petitions calling for his restoration to power. Haitian émigrés and African-Amer-ican militants were particularly active in the campaign. In the mid-1990s, even US military analysts still regularly referred to "Aristide's enormous moral authority" and his "resemblance to Nelson Mandela"[3], and no less respectable an institution than the US Department of Justice could still recognize the essential simplicity of the conflict at issue:

> On one side are the vast majority of citizens, mostly poor and poorly educated, who have traditionally been denied participation in the political, economic, and social decisions which affect their lives; they

have been the primary targets of government-ordered or government-supported violence. On the other side are the groups that participated in the Duvalier political system and benefited from its repression of the disenfranchised majority. These include landholders who have used the political system to gain control of Haiti's limited supply of fertile land; business owners who have benefited from a submissive workforce and enjoyed monopoly control over various segments of the country's economy; and armed soldiers, section chiefs, militia, and *Tontons Macoutes* who wish to retain the trappings of their power and fear the accountability for past abuses that a new political order might impose on them. Since Jean-Claude Duvalier's flight from Haiti in 1986, the struggle has been played out openly and with brutal repression of the Haitian masses.[4]

The story of how this struggle then developed over the following decade is usually presented in terms of betrayal and fatigue. Most commentators describe the decade of Lavalas rule in Haiti from 1994 to 2004 as defined by populist deviation and criminal corruption. An initially broad-based democratic movement was perverted by Aristide's willingness to make disastrous compromises in order to secure his own increasingly tyrannical grip on power; a credulous population was deluded by a charismatic and eventually bloodthirsty demagogue who led them astray. By the time of his re-election in 2000, this interpretation had already been enthusiastically adopted by the governments of US, France and Canada, as well as most sectors in Haiti's little ruling class, including virtually all of the cosmopolitan intellectuals and liberal politicians who had tried to ride the Lavalas bandwagon ten years before.

The evolution of editorial policy at the *Washington Post* is typical of the more general trend. Back in 1996, the *Washington Post* provided a glowing assessment of Aristide's first term in office: "Elected overwhelmingly, ousted by a coup and reseated by American troops, the populist ex-priest abolished the repressive army, virtually ended human rights violations, mostly kept his promise to promote reconciliation, ran ragged but fair elections and, though he had the popular support to ignore it, honored his pledge to step down at the end of his term. A formidable record."[5] Eight years later, however, the day after his second term had been brought to its premature end, another editorial in this same newspaper concluded that "history will likely judge that Mr. Aristide was mostly responsible for his own downfall. He presided over a corrupt government that regularly used violence against its opponents and eventually provoked a violent uprising [. . .]. He bitterly disappointed Haitians who hoped he would bring democracy and development to the hemisphere's poorest country," and in the end he made only one "right decision: rather than make a last stand in his capital, he accepted the offer of an American plane trip to exile and opened the way for a US-led international force to end the anarchy overtaking the country."[6] Reporting from Port-au-Prince, the *Post* explained Aristide's sudden expulsion as the combined result of his "increasingly authoritarian style" and the emergence of "a broad-based civic opposition" that accused him of "ruining the economy, and of corruption and political intimidation."[7]

Most other newspapers were less charitable. Haiti's "little priest", the UK's *Independent* declared on 21 February 2004, has "become a bloody dictator like the one he once despised."[8] According to the *Christian Science Monitor* of 27 February, Aristide had become nothing less than "a pariah confronting total rejection by his country."[9] "After once being revered as the hope of Haiti's poor," observed *Time Magazine* a couple of days later, "Aristide has become widely reviled as a corrupt autocrat."[10] "Authoritarian and egomaniacal," noted *Le Monde*, since 2001 a "defrocked" Aristide had "governed through violence, depending on his armed gangs to create a reign of terror [and] to hunt down the opposition."[11] Publications ranging from the *Miami Herald* to *Libération* took a very similar line. So did every significant book-length analysis of the period to appear between 2003 and mid-2007. Perhaps the most balanced and persuasive of these books, Alex Dupuy's *The Prophet and Power* (2007), sets out to show that "Aristide's second term of office was disastrous on all fronts [. . .]. When he left in February 2004, Aristide had become a discredited, corrupted and increasingly authoritarian president who had betrayed the trust and aspirations of the poor majority." In particular, argues Dupuy, by 2000 Aristide could only satisfy his tyrannical thirst for power through reliance on "armed gangs, the police, and authoritarian practises to suppress his opponents."[12] On the model of Duvalier's *Tontons Macoutes*, Aristide's critics claim that he created a new and equally brutal popular militia, the so-called "*chimères*." By using armed gangs of "*chimères* as a *force de frappe* against his opponents," Dupuy concludes, "Aristide 'chimerized' Lavalas and betrayed his mass base."[13]

Unlike 1991, in 2004 a version of this interpretation wasn't only adopted by the great powers and the Haitian elite. It's also the interpretation embraced by much of the traditional left. Ashley Smith, writing in the *International Socialist Review* in May 2004, summarized a widely held view when he acknowledged that Aristide "had been the pivotal voice of the mass movement against the Duvalier dictatorship, neo-liberalism, and American imperialism. But once in office, he cut deals with the US and demoralized his mass base. As a result, the US was able to regroup its favored neo-liberal technocrats, the Haitian bourgeoisie, and death squads to impose its wish for a client state on a resigned country."[14] Although the argument sets out from different premises, it reaches a similar conclusion. Demoralized and disillusioned, by 2004 Aristide's original supporters were unwilling to defend his discredited government once it came under paramilitary attack, and when push came to shove, Aristide could only "flee" into the safety of exile.

By the first years of this century, the argument goes, the most fearless critic of Duvalier's dictatorship had turned himself into a Macoute. Writer Lyonel Trouillot summed up the international consensus in the spring of 2004 when he concluded that "everything about Aristide was anticipated by François Duvalier."[15] By the time US Assistant Secretary of State Roger Noriega came to explain some of the reasons for US support for Aristide's expulsion he clearly felt entitled to present his main argument as self-evident: "The Aristide regime bore too much of a resemblance to the Duvalier regime."[16]

There could be no more damning a verdict on a man and a movement whose entire political existence was dedicated to the dismantling of Duvalierism and its legacy.

III

This book will argue that there is a better way to understand what happened between the two coups of 1991 and 2004. It will argue that what happened during these years is best understood as the progressive clarification of one and the same basic struggle, the struggle between Haiti's poor majority and the wealthy few. What really happened after 1990 needs to be seen, first and foremost, in terms of the polarization of a far-reaching class conflict, a conflict that for obvious reasons crystallized around control of the army and the police.

A tiny and paranoid minority of Haiti's population, the rich dominate the poor through a combination of direct military coercion and transnational economic power, in close collaboration with parallel interests in the US. The privileges of the rich, and the exploitation of the poor, can persist only so long as the rich maintain an unchallenged grip on the available instruments of violent coercion. Aristide challenged that grip.

"Whether they like it or not," he warned in his inaugural speech of 7 February 1991, "the [comfortable] stones in the water will come to know the pain of the [impoverished] stones in the sun."[17]

Aristide was overthrown in 1991 because the movement that he led posed an intolerable threat to Haiti's comfortable ruling class; this book aims to show that in 2004 he was overthrown again for much the same reason.

Aristide wasn't a threat to the status quo because he sought to abolish it in a single stroke. As we shall see, the Haitian elite is well-placed to protect itself against conventionally revolutionary demands. Aristide was a threat because he proposed modest but practical steps towards popular political empowerment, because he presented widely shared popular demands in terms that made immediate and compelling sense to most of the Haitian population, because he formulated these demands within the constraints of the existing constitutional structure, because he helped to organize a relatively united and effective political party that quickly came to dominate that structure – and in particular, because he did all this after eliminating the main mechanism that the elite had relied upon to squash all previous attempts at political change: the army. Aristide was a threat because by the year 2000, for the first time in modern Haitian history, he raised the prospect of genuine political change in a context in which there was no obvious extra-political mechanism – no army – to prevent it.

Rather like the ANC in South Africa, by 2000 Aristide's Fanmi Lavalas organization could present itself as Haiti's natural party of government. Ordinary Haitian people were beginning to get a sense of their collective political strength; as Aristide's ally Father Gérard Jean-Juste put it in November of that year, "The Haitian people have finally realized that the voting card is power."[18] Lavalas activists were finally in a position to oversee sustained and durable political change. In May 2000 they won overwhelming and unprecedented majorities in both houses of parliament and at all levels of government, gaining on average more than 75 percent of the vote.

Since none of several foreign-sponsored vehicles for a "democratic opposition" ever stood the slightest chance of defeating Lavalas in an election, to get rid of their nemesis after the elections of 2000 the elite was obliged to follow a somewhat involved and laborious path. Although in 1990 some sectors of the elite that resented the repression that accompanied direct military rule were prepared to align themselves with the popular mobilization against dictatorship, a year later many of these sectors had already begun to desert this mobilization when they started to perceive it as a threat to their privileged position. As far as these sectors were concerned, Lavalas was "broad-based" when it opposed neo-Duvalierism, but it became "sectarian" when it began to pose modest challenges to the supremacy of the elite itself; it became "criminal" when it threatened *both* to dilute elite influence and to dismantle the military's grip on the country. By the time of Fanmi Lavalas' May 2000 electoral victories, virtually all of the elite politicians who had allied themselves with Aristide's *anti-macoutisme* in 1990 had switched sides. They had all joined a US-funded pro-army opposition group known as the Convergence Démocratique. Together with its allies in Haitian civil society and in the governments led by Bush and Chirac, this little posse of unelectable politicians (who collectively never enjoyed the support of more than perhaps 15 percent of the people) was then able to mount a remarkably effective campaign to deprive Aristide's government of funds and to demonize it as violent and corrupt. In one of the most impressive propaganda exercises in modern times, they were able to make the equation of Aristide and Duvalier look like a self-evident cliché. This effort required considerable amounts of money and ingenuity: according to the best available estimates, supporters of Aristide's Fanmi Lavalas organization may be responsible for around a tenth of 1 percent of the number of political killings usually attributed to François Duvalier and his Macoutes.[19]

One of the most revealing measurements of the actual threat that Lavalas posed (and still poses) to the status quo in Haiti is provided by a comparison of the numbers and kinds of military personnel required to contain it. In the late 1980s, the army could still rule the country with around 7,000 poorly equipped domestic troops, backed up by several thousand local police and paramilitary auxiliaries or *attachés*. Twenty years on, the violent pacification of post-Aristide Haiti would require some 9,000 or so international soldiers armed with state-of-the-art equipment, reinforced by some 6,000 internationally trained police and an eclectic (and rapidly expanding) array of around 10,000 private security guards.

Combined with the still more eclectic array of their counterparts in "civil society" (business leaders, NGO consultants, human rights analysts, media specialists . . .) today's new soldiers of imperial democracy are helping Haiti's people to remember a lesson that they were reckless enough to forget two decades ago. Speaking in the immediate aftermath of the first coup, the Duvalierist prelate Monseigneur Dorélien understood the true lesson of such democracy very well when he tried to remind his listeners that before you speak of the will of the majority you must "be careful, you must remember there are two kinds of majority: the qualitative majority [i.e. the intellectual and political elite] and the quantitative majority – the ignorant rabble, the *populace* that acts blindly, not understanding what it is choosing."[20] The rabble's inability to retain this lesson has delayed their political education by at least twenty years.

IV

Presented by George Bush, Jacques Chirac and Paul Martin as a "new day for democracy" in Haiti, in reality the coup that removed Aristide in 2004 marked the beginning of one of the most violent and disastrous periods in recent Haitian history. The repression that followed the second coup was almost as intense as that which followed the first (and on a par, in several respects, with that which accompanied the coup in Chile in 1973). The veteran Lavalas activist Patrick Elie is not the only person who will remember 2004–2006 as "the most difficult and terrible years for the country I've ever seen."[21] The coup of 2004 did not simply disrupt the Lavalas organization and kill thousands of its supporters. It was also intended to complete a task that began back in 1991: the task of reversing Lavalas' achievements and of inverting their significance. It didn't serve merely to put an end to the "threat of a good example," but also to discredit it beyond repair. Haiti's mobilization had proved that "the poorest people in the hemisphere", Elie goes on, "can know more about democracy than the people who are pretending to be beacons of civilization [. . .]. The movement that you see now in Latin America, the new large social movements that are sweeping away the traditional political parties, that also started in a way in Haiti. For the US, Haiti is an example that must be crushed, that must be made to fail."[22]

Haiti's poverty, together with its alleged lack of natural resources and strategic significance, is often cited by analysts who prefer to understand US intervention in Haiti along more altruistic lines. Why would the US or France want to intervene in such an apparently barren and unprofitable place? It's quite true that economic issues played less of a motivating role in Haiti 1991 or 2004 than they did in Chile 1973 or Iraq 2003. A manufacturing sector in which sweatshop wages hover around $2 a day has obvious transnational uses, but the preservation of such a place is not by itself enough to warrant such assiduous imperial attention. The prospect of a social revolution that might look west to Cuba for inspiration and then spread east into the rather more profitable canefields and hotels of the Dominican Republic is perhaps another matter, especially for a government that is beholden to the South Florida lobby. Combine the prospect of such a revolution with the peculiar legacy of militant anti-slavery and the radical promise of liberation theology – arguably the greatest single challenge to US strategic interests in Latin America in the entire post-war period – and as far as the American empire is concerned you are talking about a specter that warrants exorcism by any and all available means. Throw in Aristide's unsettling request that France should help Haiti celebrate its bicentennial in 2004 by repaying the enormous amount of money that it extorted from its old slave colony during the nineteenth century, and you are dealing with little less than a menace to postcolonial civilization itself.

There is nothing unfamiliar about the basic issues at stake in this sequence. As Noam Chomsky and others have argued for many years, "it is only when the threat of popular participation is overcome that democratic forms can be safely contemplated."[23] Back in the 1970s and 80s, in Haiti as elsewhere the prospect of popular political participation typically provoked an overtly coercive response: the general goal of the "bureaucratic–authoritarian" regimes that emerged with US support in much of Latin America during those years was "to destroy permanently a perceived threat to the existing structure of socioeconomic privilege by eliminating the political participation of the numerical majority."[24] Today we live in slightly more sophisticated times. Our rulers, notes Aristide's prime minister Yvon Neptune, still "want a democracy without the people," but rather than simply exclude them from politics today's goal is instead "to reduce the people to puppets or clowns."[25]

The priorities haven't changed, and nor have the principal means of achieving them. The way these means are presented and understood, however, has become more complex and more subtle, and thus more difficult to confront. It is one thing to oppose a military dictatorship, it is another to confront a neo-military polyarchy. It is one thing to denounce the blatant injustice of racial apartheid – it is another to resist an apartheid based on the "consensual domination" of hegemony and class.[26]

Since their development by the CIA and the State Department in the 1970s, never have the well-worn tactics of "democracy promotion" been applied with more devastating effect than in Haiti between 2000 and 2004. The implications reach far beyond the immediate threat posed to governments led by people like Castro, Morales or Chávez.[27] Anyone concerned about the power of such tactics to shape the course of our political future should pay careful attention to their recent deployment in Haiti. Ever since it began fighting for its independence back in 1791,

Haiti has been singled out for exceptionally punitive treatment by the powers that be. In 1791 and again in 1991, Haiti is the place where people broke the chains of imperial domination not at their weakest but at their *strongest* link. On both occasions, Haitians have been obliged to pay the sort of price that anyone familiar with these chains would expect.

V

This is not a book motivated by any personal association with Haiti, its government or its people, and nor has it emerged from a long familiarity with its history or culture. A philosopher and a literary critic by training, I have visited Haiti only twice, and make no claim to the sort of insider or anthropological knowledge that authorizes much published work on the country. I have no special interest in the peculiarities of Haitian society, of its (remarkable) language or (even more remarkable) religions. I have assumed the reader would have still less interest in an account of my own (altogether unremarkable) travels or experience.[28]

Instead this is purely and simply a political book. In what follows I will assume that politics doesn't concern things that make people different but things that they hold in common. I will assume that true political action is animated by collective principles that concern *everyone* by definition – principles of freedom, equality, solidarity, justice. Politics is oriented by principles like Aristide's insistence that *tout moun se moun*: every person is indeed a person, regardless of their race, background or class. I will assume that the collective action required to apply such a principle requires the self-emancipation of the oppressed, in keeping with the presumption (common to Marx, Gandhi, Freire, Gutiérrez . . .) that it is the oppressed who will "liberate themselves and their oppressors as well."[29] I will assume that such self-emancipation requires forceful engagement with the dominant forms of institutional and coercive power, and that it is this engagement – more than its social motivation or economic determination – that makes politics a matter of divisive rather than consensual universality.[30] I will also assume that the persistence of emancipatory politics demands discipline and unity, and that it depends on a capacity to resist the various kinds of fragmentation and betrayal that its very existence is bound to provoke.

Haitian political activists have always known that *l'union fait la force*, and there is perhaps no better summary of Aristide's basic political strategy than the mantra of his 1990 election campaign: "Alone we are weak, together we are strong; all together we are Lavalas, the flood [*yon sèl nou fèb, ansanm nou fò, ansanm ansanm nou se Lavalas*]." It is no accident, likewise, that the counter-mobilization that has weakened Lavalas over the past decade can best be described as an exercise in division and disintegration, a process marked among other things by the multiplication of disjointed NGOs, evangelical churches, political parties, media outlets, private security forces, and so on, along with the relentless demonization of the one individual who to this day remains most capable of uniting the popular movement: Jean-Bertrand Aristide.

The fact that Aristide and some of his supporters play a prominent role in this book is simply an acknowledgement of their place in the development of the popular mobilization that has shaped the course of Haitian political history over the past two decades – this book is an exercise in anti-demonization, not deification. During these pivotal years of Haiti's history, the most decisive *political* question did not concern the evils of neo-liberalism or the urgency of human rights but instead a matter of collective and strategic affiliation: for or against Lavalas and Aristide? The fact is that from 1990 to 2006, and no doubt beyond, there is no other politician who had anything like Aristide's capacity to mobilize the poor (and to antagonize the rich). No other modern political figure has or has had a remotely comparable stature. Back in 2001–2002, for instance, Aristide's one-time ally Senator Dany Toussaint was widely considered to be "the second most influential figure in Haiti" and a leading contender to replace him as president.[31] When Toussaint ran for president a couple of years after betraying Aristide in 2003, however, he won a grand total of 0.4 percent of the vote.

"We have become the subjects of our own history," Aristide said in 1987, and "we refuse from now on to be the objects of that history."[32] Twenty years on, what remains unique about Aristide is his relation with the great majority of ordinary Haitian people who continue to share in this refusal. It's the threatening potential of this relation that his enemies cannot forgive. As a rule, recognizes the head of Europe's most prominent Haiti Support Group, Charles Arthur, foreign commentators find it "hard to credit the strength of emotion that Aristide elicited and continues to provoke in Haiti."[33] As one of the editors of the newspaper *Haïti Progrès* put it in April 2006, "For the time being, the future of the mass movement in Haiti remains profoundly connected to the destiny of Jean-Bertrand Aristide. This is something that many people, particularly foreigners, fail to understand. There is a profound, *direct* link between the masses and Aristide, and it remains very powerful."[34] The social activist Bobby Duval makes a similar point: "Aristide's got nothing to do with the establishment, personally, ideologically, institutionally. He remains hugely popular. When he speaks, he touches a chord in the people like no-one else, it's unbelievable. He wasn't perfect, but he was the only politician who was from the people, and the only one who worked with the people."[35] The *New York Times* probably did more to discredit Aristide than any other newspaper, but even the *Times* never found it easy to deny his enduring appeal. Back on 20 September 1995 the paper admitted that "Aristide has retained his almost mystical bond with the millions of Haitians who live in want." As of 9 September 1996 "Jean-Bertrand Aristide's hold on the imagination and aspirations of his countrymen seems as strong as ever." And then: "Aristide remains the most popular political figure in this country" (29 March 1997); "Aristide remains Haiti's leading political figure" (10 November 1999); "Aristide remains the central figure in Haitian politics" (24 November 2000); "There is no other politician with Mr. Aristide's popular standing" (13 December 2002).[36]

Although he is a more controversial figure now than he used to be, there is no doubt, as Haiti's most widely respected political scientist, Robert Fatton, confirmed in November 2006, that "Aristide still remains the most popular politician in Haiti today. If he could stand for re-election tomorrow he would easily win."[37] Carol Joseph is not the only minister in the current government who insists on this same point – "It is undeniable that Jean-Bertrand Aristide is still the most popular man in Haiti, and if he could run for office again he would be re-elected tomorrow."[38] The moment Aristide is allowed to come back to Haiti, insists Cap-Haïtien journalist Alinx Albert Obas, "three or four million people will turn out to welcome him home."[39]

This is why Aristide's return to power in 2001 provoked such a hysterical reaction from the Haitian ruling class and from a US government controlled by Dick Cheney and Roger Noriega: he represented a modest threat to a fragile and indefensible status quo. If "there was a massive campaign against Aristide," Elie insists, this is "not because his government was worse than any other, but because his power came from the people."[40] By the same token, the real target of the repression aimed at Aristide was not his government but its supporters. The real targets were the people who cheered Aristide in 1991 when he insisted, for instance, that "only a complete revolution can change Haiti" – a revolution that could not depend on centralized planning or massive levels of investment, but that would have to proceed through "consciousness-raising campaigns that will entail the participation and mobilization of the entire people."[41]

If you ask residents of the poorer neighborhoods of Port-au-Prince why they still support Aristide today they are far from uncritical. They readily admit that his government made mistakes. They accept that he was too reluctant to crack down on reactionary dissent and too tolerant of the corrupt opportunists who forced their way into his entourage. Aristide was not a saint, and nor should he be assessed as one.[42] But they also insist that no other political leader had or has anything like his respect for the people themselves. Aristide was the first politician to stand alongside people from the *quartiers populaires*, to share the dangers they faced, to affirm their language, their religion and their values, to affirm them as genuinely political actors. He was the only prominent politician of his time to address the realities of class struggle and injustice in terms that made compelling sense to those who suffer their effects. Aristide helped us to organize ourselves, his supporters say: of course his own freedom of movement was limited, but he helped us to gain the measure of our strength. Again and again, they will tell you that they believed in Aristide less as a leader or "saviour" than as a representative or *spokesman*. Aristide provided them with a voice to assert their own dignity and equality. If in 2007 you ask ordinary people why they still respect Aristide, they are likely to tell you what they told Amy Wilentz almost two decades ago: rather than the usual *blah-blah-blah* we expect of politicians, "He tells the truth [. . .]. Father Aristide says aloud in front of everyone what we have the courage to say only among ourselves."[43]

The real target of the anti-Aristide campaign that began a few years ago was not the man or his government but these people and that courage. As far as Haiti's political struggle is concerned what matters is not Aristide himself but the excess of popular courage and determination he continues to inspire. "The people adopted Aristide as a spokesman," continues Duval, and in doing so "they also went way beyond him."[44]

This book aims to explain why the Haitian people's investment in and beyond Aristide remains so strong. It aims to affirm the mobilization of Lavalas as the decisive event of contemporary Haitian politics. It also aims to explain how and why a small handful of powerful people, both in Haiti and abroad, undertook to contain the consequences of this event.

1

1791–1991: From the First Independence to the Second

"We don't go around sticking our nose into democracies and trying to tell people what to do"

(US Secretary of State Colin Powell, 3 March 2004).

Although Haiti is routinely described as "the poorest country in the western hemisphere," most such descriptions neglect to point out that this poverty is the product of a long and deliberate history. As Aristide never tired of explaining, Haiti's exceptional poverty is the result of an exceptional history, one that extracted an equally exceptional wealth. "Haiti is poor *because* of the rich," he pointed out in 1988, and it's a point that he had to keep on making. In a typical speech during his last year in office he reminded his listeners that "poverty today is the result of a 200-year plot [. . .]. In 1803 and in 2003, this is the same plot. Do you understand my message?"[1]

REALITY CHECK

The message isn't complicated. Throughout both its colonial and post-colonial history, all significant social and economic power in Haiti has been concentrated in its tiny ruling class. No other country in the western hemisphere is structured along such dramatically polarized lines. Haiti isn't only the poorest country in the Latin American region, its distribution of wealth is also the most unequal in a region that is itself the most unequal in the world.[2] Just 1 percent of Haiti's population controls more than half of its wealth, while the great majority of the people endure harrowing levels of poverty. The most recent study concludes that "three quarters of the population live on less than $2 per day and over half (56

percent) – four and a half million people – live on less than $1 per day."[3]
Around 75 percent of the arable land is held by just 5 percent of its
inhabitants.[4] A tiny transnational clique of wealthy and well-connected
families continues to dominate the economy, the media, the universities
and professions, along with what remains of the state. They alone dispose
of the country's disposable income. They speak French and often English,
in a country where the vast majority speak only Kreyol. They have
university degrees, in a country where most children have little chance of
getting to secondary school. They travel and often live abroad, in a
country where most can move only as far as they can walk. They are
mindful and protective of their human rights, in a country where most
people have virtually no rights at all. They tend to live in well-guarded
villas in the heights above Haiti's crowded slums, in exclusive neighborhoods like upper Pétionville or Morne Calvaire. They have more in
common with their corporate, diplomatic or intellectual colleagues in
France and North America than they do with their compatriots in the
countryside or the slums.

These are the people who interact with the UN and with foreign
embassies, who are hired by and who profit from the chaotic and growing
profusion of national and international NGOs that now provide around
three quarters of Haiti's basic services. The most powerful among them –
the Mevs, the Brandts, the Tippenhauers, the Bakers, the Apaids, the
Boulos . . . – maintain an oligopolistic grip on industrial production and
international trade. Over the last couple of decades, the more Haiti's
economy has slid from an impoverished self-sufficiency toward outright
destitution and dependency, the richer and more powerful these few
comprador magnates have become. Whatever government is elected or
imposed, as Major Louis Kernisan of the US Defense Intelligence Agency
explained in 1994, it's "going to end up dealing with the same folks as
before, the five families that run the country, the military and the
bourgeoisie [. . .]. The bottom line is you know that you're going to
always end up dealing with them because they speak your language, they
understand your system, they've been educated in your country. It's not
going to be the slum guy from Cité Soleil."[5] The phrase coined by the
writer Herbert Gold has stuck: these are the leaders of the MRE, or
"morally repugnant elite."

Haiti's elite is far from homogeneous, but its various components tend
to gravitate towards one of only two poles. There is on the one hand a
deeply conservative, neo-feudal pole, dominated by the largest rural
landowners (the *grandons*) and their allies in the armed forces. These are

people who owe their power to the services they have rendered to the various dictatorships that have ruled Haiti over most of the past two centuries, and many of them still proclaim a more or less undisguised loyalty to the most recent and most brutal of these dictatorships, the governments of François and Jean-Claude Duvalier (1957–1986). On the other hand there is an apparently more differentiated bourgeois pole, made up of a small handful of importers, exporters, merchants, industrialists, professionals, intellectuals, academics, journalists, and so on. These people tend to be more liberal and more cosmopolitan than the Duvalierists. Occasionally – as in the late 1980s – the gap between these two poles of the Haitian elite can widen to the point that the stability of the basic social edifice is itself called into question. The invariable consequence – as in the 1990s – is then a reassertion of the basic solidarity of the ruling class, confronted by the threatening mass of the people they rule. As the political scientist Robert Fatton points out, it is almost impossible to exaggerate "the dominant class's utterly reactionary contempt for the masses; in their private as well as public utterances, members of the dominant class hold *le peuple* in nothing but disdain, scorn, and ridicule."[6] The human rights advocate Ronald Saint-Jean agrees. "Although it is more carefully hidden from public view, there is a more cruel system of apartheid in Haiti than there was in South Africa."[7]

This then is the first basic fact of Haitian political life. The country is dominated by a small and well-integrated group of privileged families, surrounded by millions of impoverished people.[8] To describe the resulting social tension in terms of class struggle would be much too benign: in Haiti class differences are preserved through nothing less than full-on warfare or assault. The elite owes its privileges to exploitation and violence, and it is only violence – the violence of radical inequality and destitution, backed up when necessary by the violence of an army or the equivalent of an army – that allows it to retain them. The poor live in a world of radical and permanent insecurity, on the very edge of survival and with nothing to fall back on; such vulnerability means that their loyalty can occasionally be bought. By contrast, with incomes guaranteed through international connections, local monopolies or "flexible" NGO contracts, members of the elite inhabit a parallel but very different sort of insecurity; barricaded behind walls of paranoia and contempt, they have generally already sold their services and allegiances to whatever might best preserve the status quo. Although racism profoundly inflects the international perception of Haiti, it is indeed *class* rather than race that exerts the most powerful influence on Haitian society. The preoccupation with skin color typical of much elite and foreign scholarship on Haiti itself serves to obscure the real power dynamics at issue, and to distract attention from the point that Jacques Roumain's Communist Party of Haiti understood long ago: "color is nothing, class is everything."[9] Whenever the elite finds itself threatened from "below," the routine tensions between mulattos and blacks that normally compound petty political rivalries between Duvalierists and anti-Duvalierists vanish immediately, eclipsed by a more fundamental class unity.[10]

Violence is what created and what preserves this world, and further violence is unlikely to change it. As an unusually candid member of the US–Haitian business community explained in 1995, his associates live in a permanent state of siege. They live in fear of the fact that

> there are six million peasants that basically could rise up and tear your house down some night [. . .]. This is always in the mind of the elite Haitians. They ride around in their armoured vehicles, they have their Uzis in their house. It's not uncommon to hear machine gun fire when you're in Port-au-Prince just because there's a thief trying to break in somewhere. And you'd better believe these rich people have got machine guns. The poorest Haitians cannot rise up. There will not be a revolution in Haiti because you cannot fight these machine guns with sticks and rocks and machetes. There's only so far you can fight.[11]

According to the best available estimate, for every battered gun that might have found its way into the hands of a Lavalas militant there are many hundreds of much better guns stashed in mainly "upper-middle-class households," to say nothing of the military weapons retained by thousands of ex-army soldiers.[12] The majority of the Haitian people understand this point all too well. Not since Péralte's uprising against the Marines in 1917–18 has conventional armed struggle had a central part to play in the renewal of a preferential option for the Haitian poor. "We don't have many weapons and we cannot win with weapons," says Bel Air Lavalas activist Samba Boukman. "We are determined to wage a nonviolent struggle because it's the only way we can win."[13]

The second basic fact of Haitian political life is inextricably bound up with the first. Pending a dramatic revolution in the global economy, pending in particular a revolution in the wealthy nations that alone have the power to influence this economy, there is very little that any Haitian government can do to address local inequalities and injustices in directly economic terms. At least for the foreseeable future, Haiti is deeply and unavoidably dependent on foreign aid and investment. This means that it is dependent on financial flows and policies designed to turn the country into the sort of place that international investors tend to like – a place with low costs, high yields, few rules and no long-term commitments. In Haiti as in most other heavily exploited parts of the world, international aid is meant to develop a space open to foreign penetration and manipulation, a place free from intrusive government regulations, a place where people are prepared to work for starvation wages, a place where private property and profits receive well-armed protection but where domestic markets, state assets and public services do not. As several well-documented studies show, the development of such a place has been the explicit goal of the foreign donors (the US, the EU, the IMF and other unaccountable international financial institutions) who have usurped much of Haiti's sovereignty over the past thirty-five years.[14]

Since the early 1970s and especially since the mid-1980s, every Haitian government has been constrained, with variable degrees of enthusiasm or reluctance, to adhere to the neo-liberal economic orientation that locals tend to deride as the "American plan" or "death plan." Successive structural adjustment programmes imposed by the IMF and other inter-national financial institutions (IFIs) have forced dramatic cuts in wages and in the size of the public sector workforce, along with the elimination of import tariffs, the ongoing privatization of public utilities and state assets and the reorientation of domestic production in favor of cash crops popular in North American supermarkets. In both theory and practice, the effect of these programs is to undermine the public sector, to do away with institutions and policies that might empower the poor majority, and to consolidate at all levels the grip on the economy of the dominant transnational class. Before trade liberalization began in the early 1980s, Haiti could meet most of its own food needs; today around half the food that Haitians eat is imported, mostly from the US. The case of rice – the staple food for most of the population – is particularly striking and significant. By 1995 the subsidies provided by the US to its domestic rice industry had risen to around 40 percent of its retail value, but in that same year the Haitian government was forced to cut the tariff on foreign rice to just 3 percent. Previously self-sufficient in rice, Haiti is now flooded with subsidized American rice that trades at around 70 percent of the price of its indigenous competition. From just 7,000 tons in 1985, annual Haitian rice imports from the US rose to 220,000 tons by 2002, out of a total market of around 350,000 tons.[15] Domestic production is undercut even more by the vast amounts of additional "free" American rice that are dumped on Haiti every year through the ministry of USAID grantees, in particular the Baptist, Seventh-Day Adventist and other rightwing evangelical churches that have multiplied with spectacular speed in Haiti in recent years.[16] A similar sequence has decimated much of Haiti's poultry sector, at the cost of around 10,000 jobs. Similar sequences, in fact, have affected most of those agricultural sectors in which Haiti might otherwise enjoy a slender "comparative advantage." According to the IMF's "trade restrictiveness index," Haiti's economy is four times more open than that of Canada or the US; Haiti, Oxfam notes, "now has one of the most liberal trade regimes in the world."[17] Haitian farmers tend to associate these and related developments with one of the most bitterly resented of all the international community's many punitive interventions in their domestic economy – the 1982 extermination, to allay the fears of American importers concerned by an outbreak of swine fever, of virtually the entire creole pig population, and their subsequent replacement with animals from Iowa that required living conditions rather better than those enjoyed by most of the island's human population.[18]

As a result of these and related economic reforms, gross domestic product per capita fell from around $750 in the 1960s to $617 in 1990 (before plummeting, as a result of the embargo imposed during the first coup, to just $470 by 1994).[19] Agricultural production fell from around 50 percent of GDP in the late 1970s to just 25 percent in the late 1990s. By driving wages down from an average of around $3 or $4 a day in the early 1980s to a mere $1 or 2$ a day in the early 2000s, structural adjustment was supposed to compensate for this agrarian collapse with increases in the light manufacturing and assembly sector. For a little while, the lowest wages in the hemisphere (combined with a virtual ban on trade unions) encouraged mainly American companies or contractors to employ around 80,000 people in this sector, and through to the mid-1990s companies like K-Mart and Walt Disney continued (via local subcontractors) to pay Haitian workers around 11 cents an hour to make pyjamas and T-shirts.[20] These companies, Charles Arthur notes, benefit from tax exemptions lasting "for up to 15 years and are free to repatriate all profits; the nature of assembly operations also means that as a rule there is no significant investment in machinery, plant, or infrastructure."[21] Nevertheless, despite the steady decline in Haitian wages over the 1980s and '90s, still more profitable rates of exploitation encouraged many of these companies to relocate in places like China and Bangladesh. Employment in the sector had already fallen to around 40,000 by 1991, before collapsing almost entirely with the introduction of post-coup sanctions in 1992. Only around 20,000 people were still employed in the Port-au-Prince sweatshops by the end of the millennium, earning wages that the *Economist* measured as "less than 20 percent of 1981 levels."[22]

Today, the official minimum wage in Haiti (in the few places where any sort of minimum is enforced at all) amounts to no more than $1.80 a day. People lucky enough to have regular jobs in the factories, schools or hospitals of Haiti's cities now survive on the brink of destitution. One of the longer-serving employees of the state hospital in the capital's Cité Soleil, for instance, is a laundrywoman called Marie Joseph. Her situation is typical. She has worked full-time in the hospital for 25 years, and still lives with her eight children in a flimsy two-room tin shack with mud floors and no furniture, no electricity and no running water.[23] The great majority of her neighbors have no wages at all. Without the remittances that Haitian emigrants send back to their families (currently worth a full third of Haiti's GDP), the only option open to most people living in places like Cité Soleil would be starvation or crime. As of 2006, says the IMF, 55 percent of Haitian households survive on a daily income equal to 44 American cents.[24]

As for Haiti's government, around 70 percent of its operating budget (and fully 90 percent of its capital projects budget) comes from foreign aid and loans.[25] Aristide was simply stating the obvious when he recognized that "If the international community is not for us, one thing is sure: we will fail."[26] As Aristide would discover in 2001 when he became president for the second time, the withholding of foreign revenues can have a catastrophic effect. The conditional disbursement of these grants gives Haiti's international donors enormous if not irresistible leverage – even the governments of wealthy nations, needless to say, cannot easily accommodate the loss of around half of their available income. Left to its own devices, the Haitian government can hardly begin to meet the basic needs of its people. As of 1999 per capita annual health spending was only $21, compared with $38 in sub-Saharan Africa.[27] Only around 35 percent of students are able to complete primary school, and just 4 percent graduate from secondary school. More than one in twenty people are HIV-positive, and perhaps one in five children die before their sixth birthday; the rate of child mortality is four times higher than it is in the Latin American and Caribbean region as a whole.[28] More than a third of the population has no regular access to safe drinking water, and a similar proportion of children suffer from what the UN World Food Program describes as "chronic malnutrition."[29] Most of Haiti's people live in conditions that are hardly more comfortable than the slavery they escaped two centuries ago, gleaning subsistence crops from tiny plots of land on hillsides long devastated by deforestation, soil erosion and over-use. The national debt, meanwhile, has grown from $300 million in 1980 to four times that amount today: nearly half of this debt was inherited from loans granted to the corrupt Duvalier dictatorships, and annual debt repayments now consume around 20 percent of the government's tiny operating budget. "In sum," concluded a prescient analyst writing for the US Army's Strategic Studies Institute in 1996,

> the Haitian government is trapped. On the one hand, it must please foreign donors or risk losing the aid it needs to jump start the economy and avoid a further sharp decline in living conditions. On the other, it must satisfy the aspirations of the poor majority of Haitians for a better life. Unfortunately, whatever its purely economic merit, the USAID/ World Bank/IMF prescription will almost certainly lead to more hardship in the short run, and probably a lot longer than that [. . .]. As a result, one should expect growing frustration and probably rising violence. While most of the latter will take the form of common crime, some will be political. There will continue to be a large pool of unemployed Haitians willing and able to hire themselves out as gunmen . . .[30]

As things stand, simple financial necessity means that "no Haitian government can survive without American support."[31] As things stand, insists Aristide's 2002–2004 prime minister Yvon Neptune, "No respon-sible Haitian leader can afford to alienate the US. We have to work with the world as it is, and deal with the balance of forces as they are, not as we would like them to be."[32] Equally simple imperatives encourage many if not most Haitian politicians to exploit their limited access to state revenues for their own personal gain. Under current conditions, the development of what Robert Fatton and Alex Dupuy describe as a structurally corrupt and "predatory" form of democracy will be very difficult to reverse.[33] The cumulative effect of neo–liberal structural adjustment policies, says Lisa McGowan, has been to lock the Haitian national economy in a "financial straightjacket" that benefits "a few creditors, some foreign investors and consumers, and a small class of Haitian elites," all at the expense of the Haitian people themselves.[34] Too many powerful interests – international lenders and entrepreneurs, US agribusiness, charitable NGOs, the employers who exploit thousands of desperate Haitian migrants in the Dominican Republic, Florida, New

York, Montréal, Paris . . . – have a stake in Haitian poverty to allow it to change anytime soon.

The fact is, in short, that Haiti's economy is too poor and its government is too fragile to afford much frontal resistance to its donors' demands. The fact is that "Haiti's material well-being is utterly dependent on the whims of the world economy and the demands of foreign financial organizations."[35] Pending a revolution in first-world priorities, this is a reality that any politician in Haiti is more or less obliged to accept. Without foreign aid and assistance, as Zanmi Lasante's Paul Farmer knows from long experience, Haiti's "misery will just increase, and thousands will die of AIDS, malaria and other diseases without any hope of treatment. Those who say the aid is not worth what Haiti has to do to get it do not live daily with the reality of poverty and suffering."[36] Indignant talk about the (uncontroversial) economic evils of neo–liberalism amounts in this context to little more than hot air. As we shall see, the real question, the divisive question, concerns the *political* empowerment of the people who for the time being are doomed to suffer their effects.

COLONIZATION AND REVOLUTION

The structural basis both of Haiti's social polarization and its economic vulnerability is a direct legacy of colonial slavery and its aftermath. Recognized as a French territory from the late seventeenth century, by the 1780s Saint-Domingue (as Haiti was then called) had become far and away the most profitable colony in the world. "On the eve of the American Revolution," Paul Farmer writes, "Saint-Domingue – roughly the size of the modern state of Maryland – generated more revenue than all thirteen North American colonies combined." On the eve of the French Revolution it had become the world's single largest producer of coffee and the source for around 75 percent of its sugar.[37] This exceptional productivity was the result of an exceptionally cruel plantation economy. Haiti's slaves were worked to death so quickly that even rapid expansion of the transatlantic trade over these same years was unable to keep up with demand. "Slaves in Haiti," William Robinson observes, "were kept down by perhaps the most extreme and arbitrary terror known in modern history."[38] Eric Williams suggests that by 1789 this "pearl of the Caribbean" had become, for the vast majority of its inhabitants, "the worst hell on earth."[39]

Rapid economic growth put significant strains on the colony's social structure. Coercive power was divided between three increasingly antagonistic groups – the white plantation-owning elite, the representatives of French imperial power on the island, and an ever more prosperous but politically powerless group of former slaves (*affranchis*) and mulattos. With the outbreak of the French Revolution in the summer of 1789, tensions between these factions of the colonial ruling class led to open conflict and when a massive and well-organized slave rebellion began in August 1791 the regime was unable to cope. Sent to restore order, the French commissioner Léger Sonthonax was soon confronted by another rebellion, that of the white planters seeking greater independence from republican France and withdrawal of the civic rights recently granted to the island's *affranchis*. He only managed to deal with the planters by offering permanent freedom to the slave armies who still controlled the countryside, in exchange for their support. Over the next few years, the army of emancipated slaves led by Toussaint L'Ouverture slowly gained control of the colony. In a series of brilliant military campaigns, Toussaint defeated the planters, the Spanish, the British, and his own rivals among the black and mulatto militias. By the turn of the century he had become the effective ruler of Saint-Domingue.

Toussaint never wavered in his public declarations of loyalty to republican France, but was determined above all to ensure that the abolition of slavery remained permanent. "The same hand which has broken our chains," he warned the French Directory in November 1797, "will never enslave us anew."[40] Four years later Toussaint felt secure enough to enshrine abolition in a new constitution for the island. France's own revolution, however, had since taken a very different course. Influenced by the post-Thermidor revival of the powerful colonial lobby, in late 1801 Napoleon dispatched the largest expeditionary force that had ever yet crossed the Atlantic, ostensibly to strengthen the colonies' defenses in case of further foreign attack, actually to deport Toussaint and to restore slavery.

Napoleon's general Charles Leclerc was at first successful and after some initial resistance managed to win over most of the black generals and undo Toussaint's constitution, before tricking him into a meeting that led to his arrest and imprisonment in France (where he died some months later). But once Toussaint's troops learned of his deportation and heard that slavery had been re-established in the French colony of Guadeloupe, war broke out again with new force. One by one the other black generals abandoned Leclerc, and together with most of the mulatto militias joined up under the ferociously effective leadership of Toussaint's former lieutenant Jean-Jacques Dessalines. Calling for immediate independence from France and the expulsion of all whites, Dessalines forced Leclerc's army to retreat. By September 1802, already dying of the yellow fever that would kill off many of his soldiers, Leclerc told Napoleon that only "a war of extermination" could break his opponent's resistance.[41] After a further year of gruesome fighting the French gave up; like Pitt before him, Napoleon lost more than 50,000 troops in his campaign to return the people of Saint-Domingue to slavery.[42] As C.L.R. James wrote in his classic account of Haiti's revolution, "for self-sacrifice and heroism, the men, women and children who drove out the French stand second to no fighters for independence in any place or time. And the reason was simple. They had seen at last that without independence they could not maintain their liberty."[43]

By late 1803, to the universal astonishment of contemporary observers, the armies led by Toussaint and Dessalines had thus broken the chain of colonial slavery at "what had been, in 1789, its strongest link."[44] Renamed Haiti, the new (and utterly devastated) country celebrated its independence in January 1804. Of the three great revolutions that began in the final decades of the eighteenth century – American, French, and Haitian – only the third forced the unconditional application of the principle that inspired each one: affirmation of the natural, inalienable rights of all human beings. Only in Haiti was the declaration of human freedom universally consistent. Only in Haiti was this declaration sustained *at all costs*, in direct opposition to the social order and economic logic of the day. Only in Haiti were the consequences of this declaration – the end of slavery, of colonialism, of racial inequality – upheld in terms that directly embraced the world as a whole.[45] The declaration of Haitian independence thereby dealt the myth of white supremacy a mortal and thus unforgivable blow. (As you might expect, the bicentenary celebration of this independence, in 2003–04, would prove scarcely more welcome than the original achievement itself.)

Arguably, there is no single event in the whole of modern history whose implications were more threatening to the dominant global order of things. The mere existence of an independent Haiti was a reproach to the slave-trading nations of Europe, a dangerous example to the slave-owning US, and an inspiration for successive African and Latin American liberation movements. Much of Haiti's subsequent history has been shaped by efforts, both internal and external, to stifle the implications of this event and to preserve the essential legacy of slavery and colonialism – that spectacularly unjust distribution of labor, wealth and power which has characterized the whole of the island's post-Columbian history.[46]

THE ENDLESS COUNTER-REVOLUTION

The deeply subversive success of Haiti's revolution provoked both at home and abroad a counter-revolution that in many ways continues to this day. Outside Haiti, the slave-owning world immediately closed ranks and locked the island in a state of economic isolation from which it has never recovered. "The existence of a Negro people in arms, occupying a country it has soiled by the most criminal acts," the French foreign minister Charles Talleyrand wrote to US Secretary of State James Madison in 1805, "is a horrible spectacle for all white nations."[47] An understandably horrified US government refused to recognize the country until it finally began to address the status of its own slaves half a century later, in 1861. France initially contented itself by preserving a crippling embargo on its ruined ex-colony, and by maintaining a level of hostility sufficient to induce Haiti's new leaders to devote much of their limited resources to building a series of extravagant fortresses in anticipation of further assault. France only re-established the trade and diplomatic relations essential to the new country's survival after Haiti agreed, in 1825 (and under the watchful gaze of the entire French Atlantic fleet), to pay its old colonial master a "compensation" of some 150 million francs for the loss of its slaves – an amount roughly equal to the French annual budget at the time. The signing of this agreement, Paul Farmer recognizes, "was to prove the beginning of the end for any hope of autonomy."[48] With its economy still shattered by the colonial wars, Haiti could only begin paying this debt by borrowing, at extortionate rates of interest, 24 million francs from private French banks. Though the French demand was eventually cut from 150 to 90 million francs, by the end of the nineteenth century Haiti's payments to France still consumed around 80 percent of the national budget. France received the last instalment in 1947. Haitians have thus had to pay their original oppressors three times over – through the slaves' initial labor, through compensation for the French loss of this labor, and then in interest on the payment of this compensation. No other single factor played so important a role in establishing Haiti as a systematically indebted country, a condition which in turn served to justify a long and debilitating series of international raids on the Haitian treasury.[49] (The prescient reader may be able to guess at the consequences of Aristide's decision, in April 2003, to ask France to give this money back . . .)

Inside Haiti itself, meanwhile, it took only two years for what was left of the colonial elite – the *affranchis* – to secure their grip on the country's future. Fresh from one of the bloodiest wars in history and determined at all costs to prevent its renewal, in the spring of 1804 Dessalines had taken a step that would confirm Haiti's exclusion from "civilized society" and his own demonization in the annals of white historiography: he ordered the execution of many of the several thousand French settlers who remained on the island, sparing those who had fought against Leclerc or who were prepared to renounce slavery, together with physicians, priests, and artisans.[50] He also introduced taxes on foreign trade that made him unpopular with Haiti's nascent elite, tried to eliminate privileges that favored mulattos over blacks, and after nationalizing French-owned lands (around 75 percent of the arable total) took dramatic steps towards its more equitable distribution. "Negroes and mulattos," he announced, "we have all fought against the whites; the properties which we have conquered by the spilling of our blood belong to us all; I intend that they be divided with equity."[51] Dessalines' plans struck a chord with the great majority of the population, whose priority was to block any return to the plantation economy. (Sure enough, unlike most other Latin American and Caribbean countries, the development of export-oriented latifundia was limited in post-independence Haiti by the widespread survival of small peasant proprietorship; today around 80 percent of rural households still have at least *some* access to their own land.[52]) In October 1806, however, before Dessalines' proto-socialist policies could have much practical effect, he was assassinated by a conspiracy led by prominent members of the emerging *affranchi* elite. As soon as the colonial race war with France was over, Haiti's postcolonial class war began.

So long as their small farms were fertile enough to support them, the life of Haiti's small farmers compared favorably with that of their counterparts in Europe. The same sort of comparison is less favorable to Haiti's bourgeoisie. Since it was unable to drive or induce sufficient numbers of peasants off their land to create an exploitable proletariat, rather than try to invest in domestic agricultural or industrial production Haiti's ruling class became in the nineteenth century what it remains to this day – a parasitic clique of medium-sized and authoritarian land-owners on the one hand, combined in uneasy alliance with an equally parasitic though more "outward-looking" assemblage of importers, merchants and professionals.[53]

So impotent an elite and so dispersed a population could offer little significant resistance to the foreign raids on the Haitian economy that became more common towards the end of the nineteenth century, at a time when the imperial ambitions of countries like Germany, France and the US were expanding fast. The most consequential of these raids was launched by Woodrow Wilson in 1915, as a counterpart to his punitive assaults on the Mexican Revolution. The US occupation lasted for nearly twenty years, and it helped to shape the course of much of Haiti's subsequent political history. The American military regime proceeded to institute a kind of structural adjustment programme *avant la lettre*: they abolished an "undemocratic" clause in the constitution that had barred foreigners from owning property in Haiti, took over the National Bank, reorganized the economy to ensure more regular payments of foreign debt, expropriated land to create new plantations, and trained a brutal military force designed to fight against one and only one enemy – Haiti's own domestic population. With the enthusiastic support of the media back home, rebellions against the occupation and the land appropriations and forced labor that accompanied it (in particular the revolt led by Charlemagne Péralte during the early years of the occupation) were savagely repressed. By the time they pulled out in 1934, US troops had gone a long way towards discouraging peasant resistance to what was only the first of repeated doses of such imported "modernization," killing anywhere between 15,000 and 30,000 people in the process.[54] In suggestive anticipation of their future commitment to Haitian democracy, the US validated their occupation through a plebiscite that apparently won 99.2 percent of the vote.

The army the US had modernized became the dominant power after the Marines departed, keeping both the population and the politicians in check. As the US Department of Justice acknowledged in 1993, "Nothing in a Haitian soldier's background prepares him to respect the rule of law."[55] When they felt threatened (as they did following the election of a mildly progressive government led by Dumarsais Estimé in 1946) there was little to stop the generals from taking over the presidency for themselves. Coup followed upon coup. It was both to counter and then to complement the influence of the army that the amateur anthropologist and country-doctor François Duvalier organized his own murderous militia, the *Tontons Macoutes*, after winning a rigged presidential election in 1957. Building on the network of hundreds of army barracks and outposts established by US Marines, Duvalier granted more than 10,000 petty thugs, organized in some 500 regional "sections" (the smallest administrative unit in Haiti), the right to extract a living from the local population in return for preserving its docility. For the next fourteen years, as "Papa Doc" declared himself the divine incarnation of the Haitian nation, his Macoutes and his *chefs de sections* held the country in an iron grip. Perhaps 50,000 people were killed.[56] Along with the peasantry and the urban poor, the liberal wing of the elite also suffered. The seminaries were closed, the press muzzled, dissidents murdered, jailed or forced into exile. Patrick Bellegarde-Smith estimates that by the mid-1960s around 80 percent of Haiti's professional and political class had left the country.[57] At all levels, political life was drowned in a mixture of superstition and fear.

Initially wary of his *vaudouiste* nationalism, the US soon embraced Duvalier's staunchly anti-communist regime. When François Duvalier died in 1971, his son Jean-François ("Baby Doc") was declared Haiti's new President for Life and enjoyed still more enthusiastic US support, in exchange for providing the sort of investment climate his patrons had come to expect – minimal taxes, a virtual ban on trade unions, the preservation of starvation wages, the removal of any restrictions on the repatriation of profits. In the mid-1980s these measures were supplemented by the beginning of the structural adjustments that would soon reduce Haiti's public sector to a bare-boned shell while stripping its markets of protective tariffs. There were just seven foreign firms in the light assembly sector in 1967; twelve years later there were 51, and by 1986 there were over 300 US corporations working in Haiti. In real terms, average wages fell by around 50 percent between 1980 and 1990, and as import controls were removed, the value of US agricultural exports to Haiti almost tripled during the last years of the decade.[58]

In order for the US/IMF's structural adjustment plan for Haiti to work properly, however, its authors required a government capable of managing its unavoidable social effects. Then as now, the donors needed a client government capable of dealing with the transition from mere poverty to abject misery in ways that reduced the potential risks to the few who stood to profit from this transition. By the mid-1980s the Duvalier regime could no longer provide the international community with the kind of security it required. The undiluted brutality and venality of Jean-Claude's regime provoked a political movement that not even the network of Macoutes could contain. Resistance to Duvalier's predatory thugs grew steadily over the 1980s, nurtured by small, informal organizations – *organisations populaires* – which emerged to defend their communities and to help arrange some of the basic social services that the state was unwilling or unable to provide. Many hundreds of these vibrant organizations developed in tandem with new community-based church groups, the *ti legliz* – groups which, via the inspiration of liberation theology, began in the late 1970s to break with the traditional conservatism of the Catholic Church. Charismatic priests like Father Antoine Adrien, Father Jean-Marie Vincent, Father Jean-Bertrand Aristide, and Bishop Willy Romélus openly denounced the regime and demanded social justice. Millions of Haitian people rallied to their call. Crucially, so did some sections of Haiti's liberal elite – exiled politicians, journalists, academic, entrepreneurs, students. As street protests that began in the town of Gonaïves grew in scope and intensity over the course of 1985, leading members of the army also came to share the conclusion already reached by the US embassy, the Church hierarchy and the business community: Jean-Claude had become more of a liability than an asset. In Gonaïves, the army killed three schoolboys during a demonstration on 28 November 1985, and all over the country poor neighborhoods boiled over in anger. When massive anti-Macoute rallies finally started in Port-au-Prince itself, in January 1986, even the elite Haitian Industrialists Association grew concerned about the resulting threat to property and the "chances for attracting future investment". They too called for Jean-Claude to step down.[59] In the same month the US suspended aid payments. As the US army officer with responsibility for strategic planning in the region explained, in order to avoid "massive internal uprisings" and to "maintain the military as an institution, Duvalier had to be eased out."[60] The army finally decided to cut its losses and to return the country to direct military rule. On 7 February 1986 Jean-Claude was escorted into a comfortable retirement on the French Riviera, and General Henry Namphy assumed control of a National Governing Council (CNG).

For another few weeks, crowds of anti-Duvalier protestors would continue to shout "Long live the army." For a brief moment of confusing euphoria, it seemed as if the entire country – peasants, workers, business leaders, political dissidents, Catholic prelates, populist generals, ordinary soldiers – had united in a common cause.

THE ARMY OR LAVALAS

It took five (if not fifteen) full years for the confusion of 1986 to dissolve, and for it to become clear that in post-Duvalier Haiti there were, in a sense, just two viable political positions.

On the one hand, there was the ongoing mobilization of the great majority of the people via the *organisations populaires* and *ti legliz*, a mobilization inspired by the modest though revolutionary principles of liberation theology's preferential option for the poor – an affirmation of the dignity and equality of the people, and a critique of the wealth, corruption and brutality of the elite. Since the dominance of this elite rests in the end on the army or the paramilitary substitute for an army, the logic of this first position was very simple: the ongoing mobilization of the people would require the lasting demobilization of the army. An anonymous Aristide supporter cited by the New York *Guardian* on the day after the 1990 election captured the gist of this position when he said "We know Father Aristide has been elected because neither the Macoutes nor the Army were able to stop the elections. Those were the only threats to Aristide, not any of the other candidates."[61]

The only genuine alternative amounted to an inversion of this first position. To preserve the status quo and the privileges of the elite, the mobilization of the people would have to be countered by the ongoing remobilization of an army, or its equivalent. According to someone like General Namphy, for instance, Haiti "is not ready for full democracy, but needs the army to gradually lead to a more open way"[62]; Namphy's successor General Cédras would later tone this down, preferring to say instead that "the army is an apolitical institution that guarantees freedom."[63] Cédras' ally Michel François summed up the whole neo-Macoute approach when he insisted in 1993 that "the military controls Haiti, and it always will."[64] In particular, this pro-army or anti-people position involved the preservation of the crucial repressive mechanism inherited from the US occupation of the country in 1915–34 and retained in all essentials by both Duvalier and Namphy: the power invested in Haiti's five hundred *chefs de section*. As the US Department of Justice noted in 1993, "Understanding the role of the rural section chiefs is critical to fully appreciating the power of the Forces Armées d'Haïti (FAdH) in rural Haiti." Although in theory they are meant to refrain from acting as a judge or extracting fines,

in practice, section chiefs have unlimited authority over the residents in their communities. The section chief often serves as de facto executive, legislature, and judiciary for his section. Section chiefs occupy the lowest official rung of the historic power structure in Haiti and consequently are the most visible – and notorious – instruments of repression and violence against the rural population [. . .]. Section chiefs appointments are normally given to friends and associates of the military commanders [and] in turn direct an average of 50 "police" [. . .] Section chiefs are appointed in exchange for payments or promises of sharing in the money and goods which they will receive from the peasants in their jurisdictions. The section chiefs, in turn, extract similar payments or promises from the members of their rural militia. The unrestrained power of the section chiefs as agents of the State combined with their need to make money creates a system that runs on extortion and corruption [. . .]. The identities of the victims of this corruption and extortion are clear. Those who act in opposition to the military, or in ways that can be viewed as threatening to its continued control, are most vulnerable. Since the September 1991 coup, all those engaged in the development of Haiti's civil society have been placed at risk. They have no connection to the military and have no link to the existing institutions of power.[65]

After he was elected in 1990, nothing that Aristide did was more subversive than his attempt to tackle this network of violent extortion and intimidation head on.[66] In 1991, continues this same DOJ report, "the Aristide government ordered the elimination of the section chief system, which was under military control, and its replacement by a rural police accountable to the Ministry of Interior. Following the 1991 coup, this reform was quickly reversed" – only to be re-reversed when Aristide eventually returned in late 1994. Nothing that Aristide then did following this return was more important than his decision, in the face of powerful domestic and international opposition, to get rid of the army in early 1995. As Brian Concannon recognized in 2004, "It is impossible to overestimate the impact of this accomplishment on the lives of average Haitians. It has been called the greatest human rights development in Haiti since emancipation, and is wildly popular. For once in their troubled history, Haitians are free to speak their minds and travel freely." For almost all Haitians, he goes on, "the army's return means a return of brutality, spies, theft, corruption, coups and the dictatorships. So it is no surprise that the vast majority of voters oppose it. It should also not be a surprise that Haitians fear and distrust anyone purportedly running for office on such an unpopular platform."[67]

More than anything else, what happened in Haiti during the tumultuous years between 1986 and 2001 is the progressive clarification of this basic antagonism – *Titid ou lame*. Aristide or the army. One by one, almost all of the elite groups that in the mid-1980s had aligned themselves temporarily with Aristide and popular *anti-Macoutisme* broke away and returned to a direct or indirect approval of military rule. First the church hierarchy and the foreign embassies, then the comprador magnates and entrepreneurs, then the liberal politicians, then the ex-socialist politicians,

then the liberal theologians, then most professionals, academics, intellectuals and journalists, finally some "progressive" charities and NGOs –
over time they would all turn against the popular movement and fall back
upon positions that were more or less enthusiastically in line with that of
the army and its imperial patrons.

If in 1986–87 Father Jean-Bertrand Aristide emerged as the leading
figure in the popular mobilization it is because he understood the nature
and depth of this antagonism as clearly as other members of the *peuple*
themselves. It is because he understood that this mobilization could only
proceed in direct confrontation with the army and with the elite that the
army protects. It is because he had the courage to speak and act in keeping
with this confrontation and all its implications, in the face of constant
intimidation. It is because he stood with and by the militants of the
organisations populaires (OPs) and the *ti legliz* as they struggled to defend
themselves against successive waves of paramilitary assault. It is because,
OP members explain, he was "willing to listen to us, to discuss things
with us."[68] It is because he was prepared to endure the same sort of
sacrifices as those suffered by most members of the OPs – repeated
attempts on his life, demonization in the press, the implacable hatred of
the elite.

Above all, Aristide emerged as the crystallization of Haitian demands
for social transformation because he managed to combine a concrete
strategy for acquiring practical political power with the uncompromising
inspiration of liberation theology. This is a crucial though often neglected
aspect of the Lavalas story, and its neglect isn't accidental. Liberation
theology is entirely organized around the active self-liberation of the
oppressed; grounded in a refusal to tolerate the scandalous "iniquity" of
poverty and injustice, it "emerges as the strategy of the poor themselves,
confident in themselves and in their instruments of struggle."[69] As
Chomsky points out, liberation theology marked "a very significant
change in modern history. For most of its history, the Catholic church
had been the church of the wealthy, the church of the oppressors. There
was a very dramatic change in the 1960s and the 1970s, when large
segments of the church committed themselves to working for the needs
and interests of the vast majority of the population who are impoverished
and suffering, and living in semi-slavery. And that had big effects, it led to
very significant organizing efforts, led by people of real nobility."[70] In the
words of its leading proponent, Gustavo Gutiérrez, liberation theology
combined a critique of dependency and merely reformist "development"
with a transnational drive for "social revolution."[71] Fidel Castro is not

alone in considering liberation theology "one of the most important events of modern times."[72]

US army intelligence officers also understood exactly what was at stake, and all through the 1980s and early 90s recognized that "the most serious threat to US interests was not secular Marxism–Leninism or organized labor but liberation theology."[73] Nowhere did the counter-insurgency measures that the US and its allies devised in order to deal with liberation theology in the 1980s and early 90s fall more heavily than they did on the Haiti of Lavalas and the *ti legliz*. It's no coincidence that the most notorious assassin hired to terrorize Lavalas from 1990 to 1994, Toto Constant, first began working for the CIA on a course designed to explain and contain the "extreme leftwing" implications of "The Theology of Liberation," which Constant understood as an attempt " 'to convince the people that in the name of God everything is possible' and that, therefore, it was right for the people to kill soldiers and the rich."[74]

Haiti is the only country in Latin America that had the temerity to choose a liberation theologian as its president – twice. If Aristide still remains the defining political figure in Haiti to this day it's not because he represents a utopian alternative to the economic status quo, or because he embodies a demagogic charisma that threatens to stifle the development of democracy, or because his followers believe that he made no strategic mistakes. It's because in the eyes of most people he is *not a politician*, precisely, but an organizer and an activist who remains dedicated to working within what he famously affirmed as "the parish of the poor." It was as such an activist that Aristide disbanded the army in 1995, and it was as such an organizer that he dedicated the rest of his political life to helping the popular mobilization deal with the new threats and the old antagonisms that soon emerged as a result.

WHY ARISTIDE?

Back in 1986, no-one could have imagined that Haiti's lethal army would one day be abolished by the young priest of Saint-Jean Bosco and his enthusiastic followers in the impoverished Port-au-Prince slums of La Saline, Bel Air and Cité Soleil. Born in 1953 to a poor family and educated at the Salesian church school in Cité Soleil, Jean-Bertrand Aristide belonged to the same world as the people who attended mass at his La Saline church. As he grew up he was inspired by liberation theologians like Leonardo Boff and Jon Sobrino, and at a young age committed himself to the empowerment of the poor. A brilliant student and orator, after studying for some years in Jerusalem and Montréal, he returned to Haiti in January 1985, as the anti-Duvalier movement gathered strength. He founded a militant youth programme, *Solidarité Ant Jen* (Solidarity among Youth). His sermons were soon being recorded, distributed and heard all over the country. "Aristide is exactly what the Haitian people have been waiting for," said his supporter Antoine Izméry, and the people responded to Aristide's call for a "popular revolutionary government" with fervent enthusiasm.[75]

Five themes characterize what Aristide said and did during these years.

First and foremost, Aristide's approach is affirmative and egalitarian, based on the self-evident but explosive principle that *tout moun se moun*. Everyone counts as one, every person is endowed with the same essential dignity. That Aristide prefers to assert this principle in primarily theological terms is an indication of its unconditional quality, not of its dependence on any sort of supernatural domain. What he calls "God" is simply a name for an uncompromising commitment to equality and justice. "There is no force superior to humankind" and "There is no Messiah other than the people."[76] Theology as Aristide conceives it is nothing other than "a liberating force which pushes toward a better world," and "what the Haitian people call God is a force of resistance, resistance against the Macoutes and against all evils."[77] It is "better not to believe than to believe in a miracle from heaven." The only sort of miracle that Aristide is prepared to accept occurs when collectively "women and men take control of their own future."[78] Such is the lesson that Aristide retains from Freire and Boff: "The essential point is that the poor themselves should be the actors."[79] In perhaps the most famous of his many speeches, an address broadcast on Radio Haiti-Inter on 22 November 1988, Aristide proclaimed his basic message in quasi-apocalyptic terms:

> Alone we are weak, together we are strong, together we are the flood [*Lavalas*]. Let the flood descend, the flood of poor peasants and poor soldiers, the flood of the poor jobless multitudes [. . .]. And then God will descend and put down the mighty and send them away, and He will raise up the lowly and place them on high.[80]

The second theme is in line with the first. The only agent or actor adequate to the declaration *tout moun se moun* are the people themselves – the people united in a collective project of social transformation. Haiti's history isn't short of material that illustrates the national motto *l'union fait la force*. Aristide had an exceptionally keen understanding of this principle, in line with the liberationist assumption that unity is never given in advance but remains a task to be achieved – unity, as Gutiérrez explains, is a "task and a victory that we win in history," through the concrete struggle of the oppressed.[81] "We have the steering wheel of Haiti's history in our hands," Aristide told a packed Port-au-Prince Cathedral on 20 August 1987, "and we must make a turn to the left. We must build a socialist Haiti," and we can only build it *together*.[82] Aristide always understood that "the political strategy of our enemies favors the multiplication of diverse political tendencies" in order to divide and rule the electorate, and that "the only solution is unity: the unity of all those who say no to the Macoutes and yes to democracy."[83]

The third theme extends this egalitarian logic to the domain of political organization. In keeping with his affirmation of an unconditional equality, Aristide rejects any conventional hierarchy of the leader and the led. When Lavalas activists affirm the equality of the people, notes Haitian journalist Guy Delva, this has "immediate and very practical effects: it means that people, the masses, feel they are somebody, that they can stand up in front of anybody, in front of a businessman like Andy Apaid or anyone else, and say *I don't agree with you. I too am somebody*."[84] Yes there must be organization, there must be leaders; not everyone can speak at once. But for Aristide as for Mirabeau, "the assembled people take no orders."[85] If there are leaders, they lead only as the voice or instrument of a collective power that leads through them – "although it seems that you can choose, in reality you have no choice."[86] As Paul Farmer points out, "Aristide's main inspiration comes directly from the poor themselves. He has worked with disaffected and unemployed urban youth, and with the street children and beggars and homeless inhabitants of a city of well over a million people."[87]

If then as Aristide admits "I have often been criticized for lacking a programme," if he has often been accused of being too simplistic or superficial, this is a result of the obvious "fact [that] the people had their own program." The people have their own program, and "it did not require a wizard to formalize it after years of struggle against neo-Duvalierism." The people's program called for "dignity, transparent simplicity, participation."[88] For Aristide, simplicity is an essential political virtue. If politics is not clear and inclusive it is not politics at all. This isn't a trivial point, in a country where most political discourse is spoken in a language that the majority of people don't understand. One of the most highly educated politicians of his day, Aristide seldom forgets who he is talking to. "At the risk of annoying certain technocrats, I have always avoided the jargon of the social sciences. One does not set oneself to listen to the people in order to reply to them in incomprehensible terms."[89] With his every Kreyol sermon and his every Kreyol speech, Aristide sets about breaking up the monopoly of discourse that has long served to protect the "natural" dominance of the cosmopolitan class. This deliberately inclusive simplicity is another priority of a theology that likes whenever possible to refer things back to a question that *any* parishioner can understand:

> In what we call theology of liberation, we look at what is going on and we ask ourselves, What would Jesus do? What would Jesus say confronted with this situation: people are hungry, people have no job. Jesus would say, I don't agree with this situation, I'm going to change it. And he would do something. All of us trying to do something for the poor are doing what Jesus did. And now, if a bishop can tell us we are wrong – then who is wrong?[90]

In such a situation there are indeed only two positions: right, and wrong. This is a fourth theme. To unconditional affirmation corresponds unconditional critique. Aristide's first sermon as an ordained priest, in 1982, set a pattern that continues to this day. "We must end this regime where the donkeys do all the work and horses prance in the sunshine, a regime of misery imposed on us by the people in charge. They are voracious and insatiable dogs, who go their own way, each one looking out for himself."[91] Three years later, Aristide took the unprecedented step of openly denouncing the Duvalier regime in the capital's cathedral: "The path of those Haitians who reject the regime is the path of righteousness and love, and that is what the Lord requires."[92] His cry of 2 January 1986, "*Va-t'en, Satan!*" needed no decoding. Three years and four assassination attempts later he issued another warning to Duvalier's military replacement of the day, Prosper Avril. "General Avril," he said on radio in November 1988, "the people's court is right: your government is guilty and powerless [. . .]. The matter is in your hands. The people will write their own fate. The blessing of God is upon them. Thus grace will descend until the flood brings down all Duvalierists, all Macoutes, all criminals."[93] Though he would learn to be more careful and diplomatic once he was elected president – he had become less "candid," he said in 1994, after "years of dealing with certain sharks and vultures" – Aristide never stopped believing that the "deadly economic infection called capitalism" was the source of profound social harm, if not a "mortal sin."[94] Though his experience of the concrete obstacles to social change made him more cautious, he never lost his conviction that the political revolution which began in 1990 could only continue through its extension into a "social revolution."[95] Only revolutionary change, he told Mark Danner in 1987, could shift Haiti "from the Duvalierist structure to a de-Duvalierized structure."[96] Only revolutionary change could address the basic fact of Haiti's class polarization. As Aristide put it in one of his most famous metaphors,

> The rich of my country, a tiny percentage of our population, sit at a vast table covered in white damask and overflowing with good food, while the rest of my countrymen and countrywomen are crowded under that table, hunched over in the dirt and starving. It is a violent situation, and one day the people under that table will rise up in righteousness, and knock the table of privilege over, and take what rightfully belongs to them. It is our mission to help them stand up and live as human beings.[97]

In this struggle between oppressor and oppressed there is no middle ground. When necessary, Aristide did not mince his words. He reminded Haiti's bishops (and the rest of Haiti's elite) that "if they do not wish to share fraternally with those whom, before the world, they call brother and sister, then they must accept the fate that they have chosen. They must accept the simple fact that it is they, and not I and my colleagues, who are advocating war."[98]

Hence the fifth and no doubt most contentious principle. Since it is violence that preserves injustice, those who fight for justice must protect themselves against violence. Aristide invariably condemned violence that was either aggressive or vindictive. No less than the Gandhi or Martin Luther King whom he often quotes, Aristide insisted and insists on the primacy of a principled and "active non-violence," a "non-violent revolution."[99] Nothing did more to condemn him as a "firebrand psychotic" in the eyes of the elite at home and in the US, however, than his pointed refusal to condemn all forms of *defensive* violence. Aristide never reviled the anti-Macoute violence of *déchoukaj*, in circumstances where it was "authorized" (if not demanded) by the imperatives of self-defense.[100] After quoting *Luke* 22:36 ("he that hath no sword, let him sell his garment and buy one"), he did not hesitate to remind his listeners that "a machete is useful in almost any situation."[101] Aristide's critics were quick to equate the speaker of such words with a militant of the Shining Path; following an example first set by Jean-Jacques Honorat, one of Haiti's most distinguished intellectuals, the anthropologist Laënnec Hurbon, would later equate Aristide and Pol Pot.[102] Not for the first time, the priest had a more perceptive understanding of the situation than the academic. "I did not invent class struggle any more than Karl Marx did," wrote Aristide in 1993. "I would even prefer never to have seen it. Perhaps that is possible, if one never leaves the squares of the Vatican or the heights of Pétionville. But who can avoid encountering class struggle in the heart of Port-au-Prince? It is not a subject of controversy, but a fact, a given."[103] Given this fact, sustainable participation in the struggle requires self-defense. As he said to Amy Wilentz in 1987, you can't "tell your people to struggle against power and give them no means to defend themselves. If you do, you end up with what we've had so far, which is dead bodies."[104]

To this day there is nothing more controversial about Aristide than his apparent willingness to condone, on a couple of notorious occasions, the most fearsome of these means of popular self-defense – *Père Lebrun*. Most notably in a speech of 4 August 1991, Aristide advised an enthusiastic audience not to forget about Père Lebrun, and to remember "when to use it, and where to use it" – always with the proviso that "you may never use it again in a state where law prevails."[105] Based on the name of a local tire-dealer, Père Lebrun is a notorious euphemism that came into currency during the *déchoukaj* of Duvalierism in the late 1980s. If you ask a sample of Haitian people what the phrase "Père Lebrun" meant in 1990/91 most of them will readily admit that its range of meanings included "necklacing Macoutes" – a local version of the method adopted by South Africa's anti-apartheid militants for killing police assassins or informants with a burning tire. US human rights and intelligence analysts would quickly simplify its meaning, until it became a synonym for "murder" pure and simple.[106] Though politically convenient, this interpretation remains crucially incomplete. As Kim Ives explains, when Aristide spoke of *petit Père Lebrun* in the summer of 1991 he was using "code, or shorthand, for 'popular power,' 'street power' or 'popular vigilance.'"[107] Such power certainly included, *in extremis*, recourse to necklacing, but it was not reducible to it. For the thousands of impoverished people who in 1991 came out into the streets to protest against the enemies of the government they had elected, the real meaning of Père Lebrun was very simple: given their lack of weapons, resources, or international friends, it meant resistance by all means necessary to prevent a further coup d'état and further aggression from the Macoutes. In the context of 1990–91, if not Père Lebrun, if not some form of intimidating popular pressure, who or what might keep the army at bay once it had decided to suspend the rule of law and remove the people's government by force? Like its poorest supporters, the head of this government knew that to insist on a *blanket* condemnation of Père Lebrun in the circumstances of either January or September 1991 would have been tantamount, in practise, to an insistence on mass submission to the Macoutes.[108]

Since he lived in Port-au-Prince rather than Paris or New York, Aristide couldn't dodge the issue of popular violence, and in the process he gave his enemies a considerable supply of damaging propaganda. As Patrick Elie point out, however, "It is utterly hypocritical to condemn Aristide's occasionally inflammatory *words* unless you first condemn the *weapons* that provoked them."[109] It is even more hypocritical to condemn these words without remembering that they were spoken as part of a long and remarkably effective call for non-violent social change. Given the long history of systematic oppression that structures Haitian society, what is most extraordinary about the events of 1990–91 is surely the *lack* of popular violence that accompanied them. Douglas Perlitz has been working with street kids in Cap-Haïtien for more than a decade, and makes sense of the situation of 1991 with a helpful analogy:

> The way I see it, it's as if the poor had been suffocated for decades, in fact for centuries; the rich, and their army, were like a hand keeping their heads under water, and they couldn't breathe. Aristide was the person who removed that hand. But when the people could finally lift their heads from out of the water they didn't just gasp for breath, they also tried to lash out at the hand that had oppressed them for so long. *Some* popular violence in the wake of Aristide's election victory in 1990 was inevitable; Gandhi himself would have been powerless to stop it. What's remarkable is that things never got out of hand. Under the circumstances the level of discipline in the popular movement was very impressive.[110]

Despite endless provocations, there were just two or three occasions during the whole of Aristide's first administration in which outraged crowds attacked and killed notorious enemies of their government. Not a single incidence of popular violence can be fairly blamed on the government itself.

Although people like Laënnec Hurbon or Jesse Helms would soon do their best to present him as an advocate of indiscriminate terror and mob rule, the fact is that Aristide always refused – to the dismay of a few of his more militant supporters – to sanction calls for armed struggle. In reality it was Bush and Clinton who calmly and deliberately sanctioned recourse to violence in Haiti during these years, not Aristide. Unlike his American counterparts, the Haitian president always "recognize[d] that institutionalized violence is stronger than any we could unleash. We are not armed. And I do not believe that we will ever have the means to compete with the enemy on that key terrain. But they cannot count on me to condemn acts of despair or of legitimate defense by the victims of aggression."[111] Anyone living in places like La Saline or Cité Soleil knew exactly what he meant. Do not attack the army but if the army attacks you then defend yourselves, Aristide told them, because nobody else will.

THE PERSISTENCE OF DUVALIERISM

In 1986–87 this was good advice. After tolerating a brief wave of popular reprisals against a few of the most hated Macoutes in the immediate aftermath of Duvalier's departure (the *déchoukaj* or uprooting of Duvalierism), the army quickly turned back to business as usual.[112] On 26 April 1986, less than three months after Jean-Claude's expulsion, tens of thousands of demonstrators converged on the notorious prison and torture chamber of Fort Dimanche, the place that for Aristide as for everyone else was "a symbol of the Army and the police and the Tontons Macoutes, of all the forces organized to destroy us".[113] To disperse the crowd the army opened fire, killing at least eight (if not twenty) people and wounding many more.[114] Seven months later, more than 100,000 people marched in Port-au-Prince to protest against a government they blamed for a rising number of political killings. In all essentials General Namphy presided over a version of what came to be known as "Duvalierism without Duvalier." Many Macoutes were integrated into the army or maintained as informal paramilitaries, and used to crack down on peasant activists, trade unionists and other members of the OPs. Fear returned to the countryside, and all through 1987 there were nightly incursions into the poorer neighborhoods of Port-au-Prince. Scores if not hundreds of people were killed. In the bloodiest single incident, in July 1987, three or four hundred members of the peasant collective Tet Ansamn were butchered in the north-western district of Jean-Rabel, after organizing a march to protest recent land appropriations by the local *grandons*.[115] A few weeks later, Aristide and three other priests narrowly escaped death when the army opened fire on a public meeting at Port-Sondé; Macoutes attacked their car again at a checkpoint on the way home.

The US DIA and CIA meanwhile, were busy developing alternative sources of social control, in case another round of popular mobilization forced the Macoutes back into more permanent hiding. As the US Army's former Caribbean planning chief explained a few years after the fact, when the *déchoukaj* put the Macoutes on the defensive in 1986 it left a sudden and "total vacuum" in internal security. "In that year and a half to two years after Duvalier fell, things were in such a flux. Democracy, freedom, people were suddenly publishing – writing in Creole for the first time – everybody was very enthusiastic, and really thought something was going to change, and so there were a lot of strange people coming and going, and we didn't know who they were. And nobody had a handle on it, particularly in the outback, because the Tontons Macoutes had had total control in the interior and now they were gone."[116] The US hastened to fill the void by helping the army to create a new National Intelligence Service (SIN), ostensibly to keep tabs on drug traffickers, actually to spy on and intimidate dissidents. The CIA's Donald Terry helped set it up, and recruited versatile allies like Emmanuel "Toto" Constant to the cause.

By late 1987 it might have seemed that the army could afford to relax. After presiding over the approval in March 1987 of a new constitution designed to dilute executive power and to preserve the status quo,[117] the army cancelled elections scheduled for November 1987 on polling day – but not before it had engineered the slaughter of perhaps another 150 people. At one voting station, a school on the capital's ruelle Vaillant, more than thirty men and women were struck down as they waited to cast their ballots, in full view of the world's media.[118] The selection of a new puppet president (Leslie Manigat) in January 1988 did nothing to change the underlying situation, and Namphy resumed control four months later. In a day of violence that was exceptional even by Namphy's standards, on 11 September 1988 hundreds of petty thugs were hired to storm Aristide's crowded church. They killed at least a dozen members of the congregation and destroyed the building; Aristide was again snatched to safety by his supporters, his aura of righteous invincibility growing with each new attack.[119] In the protests that followed the 11 September massacre, General Prosper Avril manipulated the frustration of rank-and-file troops to oust and replace Namphy, before throwing some of these *ti soldats* in jail. The autumn of 1989 brought more mass strikes and mobilizations against Avril's regime, a further bloody crackdown and further protests. As human rights advocate Brian Concannon notes, a US District Court subsequently found that "Avril's regime had engaged in 'a systematic pattern of egregious human rights abuses.' It found him personally responsible for enough 'torture, and cruel, inhuman or degrading treatment' to award six of his victims $41 million in compensation."[120] In March 1990, General Avril too was driven from power. Haiti's elite was now finally obliged to accept that it was time to try something else.

Back in 1986, the American plan for Haiti after Duvalier had rested on the assumption that, as Under-Secretary of State Elliott Abrams put it, the army offered the "best chance for democracy."[121] In the eighteen months that followed Jean-Claude's departure, Namphy's government received no less than $200 million in direct US aid. The army was indeed willing to accelerate the pace of privatization and neo-liberal reform that began under Duvalier. In the end Namphy and Avril were no more capable than Jean-Claude, however, of keeping a lid on social unrest. Unrest is bad for business. Although no-one cared to keep precise records, by the end of their first year in office Namphy and the generals had already "openly gunned down more civilians than Jean-Claude Duvalier's government had done in fifteen years."[122] The relentless violence was starting to attract some unwelcome attention. Over the space of four years, eleven unstable administrations had come and gone. By the middle of 1990 there was nothing for it: the old strategy of reliance on straight military repression would have to be supplemented by a new and less abrasive strategy of democratic deflection. The army would be better able to play its essential role – to protect the property and interests of the ruling class – if it stepped back into the shadows. In Haiti as in various other parts of what George Bush was starting to call the "new world order," the time had come to replace a pro-democratic military with a pro-military democrat.

THE ELECTION OF 1990

By the end of 1980s, US policy makers already had plenty of experience of promoting democracy and running elections in various parts of the exploited world. Bush could rely on subservient clients in the Dominican Republic, in Jamaica, in El Salvador, in Guatemala, and indeed in most of Latin America. In February 1990, US policy makers had even managed to engineer the electoral defeat of the socialist Sandinista government in Nicaragua, the culmination of a political re-education program that had cost at least 50,000 lives. When US diplomats and most of the Haitian business elite picked the neo-liberal economist and former World Bank official Marc Bazin as their preferred candidate for December 1990, then, they anticipated an easy ride.

1990 remains the single most important date in modern Haitian history. In a sense, the election campaign which dominated that year is still going on to this day. From 1990, the Haitian people could no longer simply be excluded from the political scene; from now on, they would at least have to be given some choice in the form and management of their exclusion. The basic range of such choice that was determined in Haiti's first "free and fair" election would again define the political field in 1995, 2000 and 2006: Lavalas on the left (i.e. slow movement towards social change), the Macoutes on the right (i.e. rapid movement back to *Duvalierisme*), and an uncertain mix of neo-liberal technocrats in the "center" (i.e. no movement at all).

Ever since 1990 the US strategy has never changed. The goal has been to preserve the status quo by making sure that the "center" is always in charge. The simplest way to do this, of course, would be directly to engineer the election of a suitable centrist, i.e. pro-US candidate – Marc Bazin and Serge Gilles in 1990, Evans Paul or Victor Benoît in 1995, Gérard Pierre-Charles in 2000, Evans Paul again in 2006 . . . At least a few voters can sometimes be induced to opt for such uninspiring candidates if confronted with the prospect of a marginal but much less palatable option on the right. In Haiti as in a few other places, however, the absolute priority was and remains to prevent victory for the left. Since the Haitian electorate consistently prefers Lavalas activists over centrist (KID, KONAKOM, OPL, PANPRA . . .) careerists by a factor of around 10 if not 20 to 1, this priority presents US democracy promoters with a serious challenge. If outright electoral victory isn't often possible, however, the promoters can at least demonize the undesirable candidate and cast doubt on the legitimacy of the electoral process itself. If the wrong candidate still accedes to the presidency then it may yet be possible to force him to accept the right sort of prime minister, and thereby turn him into a semi-acceptable candidate after the fact: the attempt to tame Aristide and then Préval by coercing them into an alliance with this or that "centrist" representative of the status quo (Victor Benoit, René Théodore, Robert Malval, Smarck Michel, Rosny Smarth . . .) would consume a great deal of US diplomatic energy all through the 1990s.

As far as the international donors are concerned, all through their carefully supervised transition to democracy Haiti's people should have voted for Bazin (or the equivalent of Bazin), but instead they kept voting for Aristide (or a *marassa d'Aristide*). They should have embraced the status quo, but persisted in their determination to change it. Confronted by the Haitians' unfathomable refusal to identify with the class interests of their oppressors, the US responded by doing everything in their power to convert the objectionable Aristide into a version of the acceptable Bazin, with the proviso that when this conversion began to run out of democratic steam (in the summer of 1991 and the autumn of 2003) they might then accelerate the process with a little extra-democratic assistance.

It would have been so much simpler if the Haitian people had made the right choice in the first place! Back in 1990 the US did what they could to make them see the light. They invested a staggering $36 million in Bazin's campaign, and they also invited the outlawed Macoute chief Roger Lafontant to return to Haiti and pose as an ultra-right candidate.[123] But this plan backfired in spectacular fashion. Rather than encourage the Haitian electorate to make the sensible and moderate choice, it provoked the candidacy of the anti-Macoute par excellence – Jean-Bertrand Aristide. The day after Aristide announced his candidacy, remembers one of his supporters, "the people rushed to get their voting cards. That day the people suddenly understood what elections could mean for Haiti."[124] Up until then the electorate had remembered the violence of November 1987 and had kept their heads down. Many in the popular movement advised against participation in the elections. During the run-up to the 1987 fiasco, while the CIA was busy channeling money and funds to various pro-US candidates, Aristide had instead urged a popular boycott, arguing that the army would only use the occasion as a mechanism to identify and kill its opponents. "The army is our first enemy," he insisted, and in "Haiti like anywhere else in Latin America elections are in the hands of the oligarchy who use them to undermine popular demands."[125] Non-participation in 1990, however, risked marginalizing the popular sector within a more respectable version of the status quo, the development of a less criminal but purely "formal system that would exclude all the lower classes."[126] After weeks of hesitation, on 18 October 1990 Aristide bowed to intense pressure from fellow priests and his supporters in the slums, and reluctantly accepted an invitation to replace the hapless reformist Victor Benoît as the candidate for a loose coalition of small liberal-democratic parties that called itself the National

Front for Change and Democracy (FNCD). (A resentful Benoît repaid the favor by becoming the first in the interminable line of liberal politicians to turn against Aristide; five years later, Benoît got his chance to run in a presidential election, and won 2 percent of the vote.)

It was as obvious to Aristide as to anyone else that the elections were designed to pacify the Lavalas movement by forcing it to operate on its enemy's terrain. In 1990 as in 1994, Aristide gambled that a process which was initially forced on the country from the outside could be turned to the people's advantage, and threw himself into the task. "If we're going to participate in elections," he said in November, "we must take them over entirely."[127] Despite the lack of any organized party or campaign, Aristide's participation transformed a lackluster ritual into an electrifying event, and on 16 December no less than 80 percent of the electorate turned out to participate in Haiti's first free and meaningful election. As Patrick Elie remembers, the 1990 electoral campaign "was done with nothing. Aristide was running around the country in my car, in a borrowed car. His security at the time was me with a little .38 pistol. It was ridiculous."[128] Though on 5 December yet another assassination attempt killed eight people at a pro-Aristide rally and wounded a further fifty, voters were not intimidated. Thanks to the energetic mobilization of hundreds of *organisations populaires* and *ti legliz* congregations, the turnout was massive and Aristide won an overwhelming 67 percent of the vote, compared to just 14 percent for Bazin and 3 percent for the leading Duvalierist Hubert de Ronceray. As the US Department of Justice recognized, "The circumstances of Aristide's election revealed the power of the numerous grassroots 'popular' organizations which had developed in Haiti",[129] and when he won poor neighborhoods all over the country erupted in jubilant celebration. Nobody caught the promise of the moment better than radio journalist Jean Dominique: "To feel linked, intricated, with *millions* of people, millions of people who could feel for one second – one second in a century, one second in light-years, but still for one precious and wonderful second – this sense of being *together*, of doing things together, of moving forward together with them: I think it was a wonderful experience, the most wonderful experience of my life."[130] For the first time in their country's history, the president had been chosen by the people themselves, rather than imposed by the army, by the US or by a faction of the ruling elite. "For us," remembers Bel Air activist Samba Boukman, "16 December 1990 was an historic date, a great achievement. We the impoverished people of Haiti, we who are the great majority of the people in Haiti, we believe in elections, they are our greatest weapon."[131]

The US and its allies were astonished and dismayed by this outcome. Rarely has elite democracy promotion gone so disastrously wrong. The New York *Guardian* described Aristide's inauguration as "one of history's truly great displays of mass catharsis, [as] hundreds of thousands of jubilant Haitians from all over the country and the world filled the streets of the capital."[132] In the days that followed his inauguration, Mark Danner notes, "the new president performed one feat after another. He flung open the doors of Fort Dimanche, the dreaded Duvalier prison, and let the people wander through to gaze at the torture chambers where so many thousands had died. He invited the poorest of the poor to come to the Palace, where on the vast green lawns he served them a copious meal of rice and beans. Or rather, he had his soldiers serve them – soldiers, serving the poor!"[133] These soldiers and their backers were still more dismayed when Aristide's government, rather than try directly to legislate for the "social revolution" he had advocated (which would have ensured its automatic demonization as extremist and undemocratic) or fall into the traditional patterns of political corruption (which would have allowed for its co-option within the status quo), instead set about briskly implementing a sensible and cautious set of policies. Although he inherited a bankrupt and chaotic state apparatus, Aristide won promises of new loans from international lenders by balancing the budget and trimming the bureaucracy. He enforced the collection of import fees, and increased tax revenues from the rich. He kept direct conflict with the army to a minimum but sent a clear signal on the day of his inauguration, by purging the officer corps of most of its top commanders. He initiated the process that would replace the army's hated section chiefs with elected officials and an apolitical police. Political violence and state-sanctioned repression came to an abrupt halt. He appointed a presidential commission to investigate the extra-judicial killings of the previous few years. He took tentative steps towards the redistribution of some fallow land, began a literacy programme aimed at the poorer neighborhoods, cracked down on drug-trafficking, lowered the price of food and imposed a modest increase in the minimum wage. The ambition was not to implement an unattainable socialism, but simply to move from destitute misery to "poverty with dignity."[134]

Aristide had good reason to be cautious. Modest though they were, Aristide's tentative measures antagonized almost every vested interest in the country. The rich were concerned about higher taxes and wages, the army about an end to impunity, the police about their dissociation from the army, the bishops about the erosion of their influence in the church, the technocrats about cuts in government jobs. Although some of Aristide's more militant followers were disappointed by the pragmatic inflection of his administration, in reality its very existence was an intolerable challenge to the status quo. Although in the late 1980s the liberal wing of the elite had been happy to use the popular mobilization as an instrument in their struggle against their neo-feudal Duvalierist rivals, they had no intention of allowing this movement to exercise genuine power on its own right. No less than the Duvalierists themselves, Fatton insists, the liberal "reformists and the middle sectors have always resisted the ascendancy of popular forces," and when Aristide came to power the two wings of the elite quickly closed ranks in a united opposition.[135] The simple presence of Lavalas in government terrified a large portion of the ruling class. Long before he became president, Fatton continues, "the dominant classes despised Aristide, they engaged in plotting maneuvers immediately after his election, and they never entertained the idea of compromise. Only surrender would have satisfied them [. . .]. They abhorred the president who came to embody everything they feared from the *populace*."[136]

For both his supporters and his enemies, what Aristide did was less important than what he symbolized. What he actually accomplished was less significant than what his words seemed to promise. "Panic seized the dominant class. It dreaded living in close proximity to *la populace* and barricaded itself against Lavalas."[137] With Lavalas in power, many observers noted a "new confidence among the poor people of Haiti."[138] For the first time in living memory the distribution of private property seemed vulnerable, as occasional instances of land invasion and squatting went unopposed. For all his pragmatic caution, moreover, Aristide was occasionally required or willing to strengthen his hand in government by encouraging his supporters to be vigilant in the face of provocative action taken by "bourgeois thieves."[139] During the summer of 1991, some of these thieves, led by the most powerful families in the country – the Brandts, the Mevs, the Apaids, the Nadals – began collecting the millions of dollars they would need in order to pay the army to conduct another coup.[140]

As the pressure from the establishment grew more intense, so did the force of Aristide's class-conscious rhetoric. In the last days of September the government's enemies closed in for the kill, and Aristide found himself trying "to fight bullets with words."[141] On 27 September, in an impassioned speech that appalled a small fraction of its audience and thrilled the rest, he called on his supporters to rally in their self-defense. He warned the bourgeoisie that the time of reckoning was drawing near –

"You earned your money in thievery, under an evil regime, it is not really yours." He encouraged the poor, "Whenever you are hungry, to turn your eyes in the direction of those people who aren't hungry." If you catch a thief, he told his listeners, or a Macoute, or a "false Lavalassian, don't he-si-tate-to-give-him-what-he-deserves! [. . .]. Alone, we are weak. Together we are strong! Together, together, we are the flood! Do you feel proud? Do you feel proud!?"[142]

The elite was acutely sensitive to the threat of such words, not to mention such pride. Many of Haiti's business leaders have from the beginning considered Aristide "a cross between Ayatollah and Fidel."[143] Under Aristide, as one rightwing US analyst put it (discreetly glossing over the dramatic reduction in political violence he initiated), "rather than the indigents it was the elites who were terrorized; under Aristide-style repression, the socioeconomic pyramid was inverted."[144] As a result, Fatton concludes, "Among the Haitian elite hatred for Aristide was absolutely incredible, an obsession. It's the way he talked. He had that very calm, cold way of putting it: 'We've waited very long, we the poor; it's our time to take over . . .' "[145] Ever since 1990, gated communities have multiplied in the more comfortable suburbs of Port-au-Prince. The provision of private security became one of Haiti's fastest growing industries, and the visceral sympathy for such measures among western elites who over these same years began to perceive themselves as similarly "terrorized" both at home and abroad goes a long way towards explaining the recent international perception of the Lavalas project.

In the autumn of 1991, several factors transformed the likelihood of an anti-Aristide coup into an inevitability. In the first place, despite the clarity of his own presidential mandate, Aristide didn't have anything like a working majority in parliament. The FNCD was too diffuse and disorganized to win enough seats in the legislative elections that took place in January 1991, and Aristide was obliged to compromise every step of the way. More to the point, Aristide didn't govern in the way that the FNCD and other members of the liberal elite had expected. When they asked him to stand in the election of 1990, they assumed they could use his popularity with the poor as a tool for advancing their own long-frustrated ambitions. They assumed he would be willing to act as the moral figurehead of a government staffed by members of the traditional political class, along with wealthy exiles who had returned to post-Duvalier Haiti in the expectation that they were now free to inherit their proper political place. They didn't anticipate that Aristide meant to be "the president of the people, even if this means confronting the very government I am creating."[146] It never seems to have occurred to them that Aristide might *already* have a well-developed political base that would allow him to operate at a principled distance from the usual practice of parliamentary opportunism. They were outraged, then, when rather than hand out government jobs to career politicians or elite intellectuals like the FNCD's Victor Benoît or PUCH's René Théodore, Aristide appointed a mixture of competent administrators and activists from within the popular movement itself, people like the agronomist René Préval (prime minister) or the leftwing dissident Patrick Elie (security).[147] Like the vast majority of his constituents, Aristide had little confidence in career politicians. "For the great mass of the people," insists FL activist Ramilus Bolivar, "political parties have always represented only the elite and the imperialists."[148] The politicians had nothing to do with the organization of the real popular movement in the slums and countryside. They belonged to a different world. They contributed nothing to Aristide's political popularity, and he knew it.

Over the course of 1991, as they realized that Aristide might become an obstacle to their own ambitions, much of the original FNCD coalition turned against him. "Because FNCD reformists could not control the alliance, they became Aristide's most bitter enemies, and many actively participated in destabilizing his government."[149] This was the start of a process that would last as long as Aristide's own political career: although the vast majority of Aristide's active supporters continue to back him to this day, most members of the liberal elite who thought they could use him for their own purposes found themselves, sooner or later, in the opposition's pro-army camp. His critics would later refer to this development as proof of Aristide's megalomania. As we shall see, by 2000, scores of these embittered schemers – such as Evans Paul, Paul Denis, Gérard Pierre-Charles, Gérard Gourgue, Serge Gilles – had all become members of a US-funded front that called itself the "Democratic Convergence," and that adopted the restoration of the army as one of its first and most insistent demands.

From the beginning, of course, Aristide had been heading on a collision course with the creator and patron of that same army, the United States. Shortly before the September coup, Bush's ambassador Alvin Adams – a veteran of the Kissinger school of US diplomacy – met with Aristide's prime minister René Préval, and asked him to replace some of his ministers and policies with more conservative alternatives. Préval's refusal marked a point of no-return.

US disapproval of the Aristide–Préval government didn't come out of nowhere. On the very day of the election, in December 1990, a high-level US delegation fronted by ex-president Jimmy Carter tried to persuade Aristide "to renounce his success in favor of the candidate [Bazin] that he had beaten by more than 50 percent of the vote".[150] A US official spoke for a more general Washington consensus when he said that "Aristide – slum priest, grassroots activist, exponent of liberation theology – represents everything that the CIA, DOD, and FBI think they have been trying to protect this country against for 50 years."[151] As Aristide's government took shape a few weeks later, another worried diplomat described it as the successor to "Paris 1968 and the Cultural Revolution in China."[152] The millions that USAID had spent to promote Namphy's Haiti as a low-cost investment zone for American companies were suspended almost immediately. Although US and IFI officials approved of Aristide's relatively moderate macro-economic policy, USAID observed that his government was making some regrettable decisions, "decisions that could be highly detrimental to economic growth, for example in the areas of labor and foreign-exchange controls."[153] USAID was particularly concerned about the government's decision to increase the minimum wage by a few cents a day, and to regulate the price of basic foodstuffs. A substantial fraction of the $26.7 million that USAID funneled to the Haitian business sector in 1991, according to the National Labor Committee, was used "actively to oppose a minimum wage increase from 33 to 50 cents an hour proposed by the Aristide government."[154] The US was also able, in 1991 as in 2001–04, to put pressure on Haiti via its altogether more subservient clients across the border, in the Dominican Republic. The DR's dictatorial president Joaquín Balaguer was incensed when Aristide dared to criticize his country's (notoriously scandalous) treatment of migrant Haitian workers, and deported thousands of them back to their over-crowded slums. The DR was glad to be rid of Aristide in September 1991, and would be just as glad to contribute military resources to destabilize him when he returned to power ten years later.

The combination of domestic and foreign opposition backed Aristide into a corner. So long as the US supported it, the army was too powerful to dislodge; without an armed wing of its own, the popular movement could not confront it directly. In 1991, Patrick Elie later recognized, "Aristide came to power too early and too fast. We were not ready. We came to power through a *coup de peuple*; the mobilization of the people was strong enough to bring us to power, but not yet strong enough to keep us there."[155] As it became clear that the new administration would never be able to win over either the army or its American creators, Aristide's advisors turned to the Swiss government for help in training a new and more reliable security service for the National Palace.[156] But there was nothing that either this tiny force or the vast multitudes in the slums could do when Cédras and the generals, with unofficial but unequivocal US support, moved against the regime on the night of 30 September 1991.

2

1991–1999: The First Coup and its Consequences

Se nan chimen jennen yo kenbe chwal malen
(If you want to catch a wild horse, find a tight corral).

By the time it turned on Aristide in September 1991, the army had learned the single most valuable tactical lesson in its long campaign against Lavalas. It's a lesson that continues to guide its paramilitary and international replacements to this day: in order to contain the popular mobilization, you must seal off and then terrorize the slums where its most determined partisans live.

The importance of this lesson was brought home with dramatic effect when on 7 January 1991, a month before Aristide's inauguration, some of the more reactionary elements of the army jumped the gun and launched a pre-emptive coup to install the embittered Macoute Roger Lafontant as president in his place. The assault was rushed and poorly planned. Although Lafontant was able to occupy the National Palace for a few hours and proclaim a new government, he failed to anticipate the full strength of the popular reaction. Port-au-Prince erupted in fury, the Palace was surrounded by tens of thousands of people, and his unprepared troops proved reluctant to shoot into the crowds. By the end of the day, Lafontant was forced to back down and give himself up to the police. Popular reprisal attacks left some twenty to thirty Macoutes dead.

In the last days of September, therefore, just before they abducted Aristide, General Raoul Cédras and police chief Michel François were careful to deploy large numbers of better-prepared troops to strategic positions in the capital. Reliable officers had spent the preceding months persuading their men that "Aristide and the people who supported him were a danger to the army and to their own livelihood, and that he threatened to deliver the country to mob rule."[1] The millions collected from families like the Brandts and Mevs were doled out as necessary; to steady their nerves, ordinary soldiers received up to $5000 apiece.[2] As crowds tried to gather in defense of the government, the army opened fire, and kept firing. "Having learned their lesson in January," says a veteran US intelligence monitor, "the soldiers shot everything in sight. They ran out of ammunition so fast that it seems the US had to re-supply them with night-time helicopter flights from Guantanamo."[3] At least 300 people were killed in the first night of the coup, probably many more; the *Washington Post* reported that 250 people died in Cité Soleil alone.[4] Another US analyst described the coup as an exercise in "pre-emptive butchery," as a harsh but understandable response to Aristide's "un-ambiguous call for mob violence."[5] It was the beginning of a reign of terror that would kill around four or five thousand Lavalas supporters over the next three years. As the Heinls explain, once Aristide was gone, "The officers handed back the weapons that had been confiscated from the section chiefs and re-established their reporting line to the Army. The chiefs lost little time in re-asserting their authority, taking good care to avenge slights, perceived or real, that they had suffered during the past eight months."[6] Churches and community organizations were invaded, peasant and labor activists were murdered. Perhaps 300,000 people went into hiding or internal exile; another 60,000 fled in makeshift boats, only to be intercepted and returned (or interned) by the US Coast Guard.[7] "I was in Haiti at the time," remembers Chomsky, "and I don't think I've ever seen such terror."[8] Drawing on a logic that would return with a vengeance in 2004, Cédras defended the putsch as a "correction of the democratic process."[9]

Covert US support for the 1991 coup has been well-documented by Allan Nairn, Kim Ives, Jane Regan and several other investigators.[10] In public, the Bush administration maintained an apparently ambivalent position. Two days after Aristide was ousted, US Secretary of State James Baker condemned the Cédras junta and promised that it would be "treated as a pariah, without friends, without support, and without a future. This coup must not and will not succeed." A few days later, Bush's spokesman clarified the meaning of success when he explained that the restoration of constitutional rule might not include the return of a president who had relied on "mob rule:" "We don't know [if Aristide will return to power] in the sense that the government of his country is changing and considering any number of different possibilities."[11] A few months after that, the CIA's leading Latin American analyst told Congress that Cédras belonged to "the most promising group of Haitian leaders to emerge since the Duvalier family dictatorship was overthrown in 1986," and declared that there was "no evidence of oppressive rule' by Cédras' regime.[12] As far as the US was concerned, a blanket amnesty for the coup leaders immediately became a non-negotiable precondition for any diplomatic discussion about an eventual return to constitutional democracy. Later, after giving the generals the green light to decimate the popular movement for several years, the US took good care of them when in October 1994 – their mission accomplished – they were eventually induced to step down. After arranging to lease three of his houses, the US flew Cédras into a luxurious retirement; Michel François and his hatchet-man "Toto" Constant found safety in the DR and Puerto Rico. (US treatment of the still serviceable ex-general Prosper Avril is perhaps more telling. When in November 1995 Avril was implicated in plans for what US intelligence itself described as a "harassment and assassination campaign directed at the Lavalas Party and Aristide supporters" and whose victims included Aristide's cousin Jean Hubert Feuillé, US troops intervened to prevent Haitian police from arresting him and US officials facilitated his subsequent flight to Israel. When he returned to Haiti in the late 1990s he received financial assistance from the US International Republican Institute to establish a fake political party, CREDDO. CREDDO has never yet contested an election, but as a member of the US-brokered "Conference of Political Parties" it served as a useful intermediary linking the interests of the old army to those of a new "democratic opposition" to Lavalas. Once US troops had left Haiti and Aristide was at last able to arrest Avril, in May 2001, the event was applauded as a victory for justice at home but condemned as an "arbitrary" arrest by the IRI and the US embassy.[13])

Behind the scenes, however, there was nothing ambiguous about US policy. It's perfectly clear that neither Cédras nor his associates Michel François and Philippe Biamby would have so much as contemplated overthrowing Aristide without US approval and support. Shortly after the coup began in 1991, Haiti's CIA station-chief John Kambourian privately admitted to the *LA Times* Caribbean correspondent that he hoped the coup-regime would last longer than Aristide's presidential term.[14] The real power behind the throne in Haiti 1991–94, Michel François, was a longtime CIA asset, as was one of the most notorious of his "Anti-Gang" attachés, Marcel Morissaint (who would become the chief suspect in the 1993 assassination of Aristide's justice minister Guy Malary).[15] Thanks to the National Intelligence Service (SIN) that the CIA's Donald Terry had helped the army to establish in 1987, by 1991 both Haitian commanders and US officials could draw on an extensive network of paid informants and compliant military personnel. Along with several other dedicated members of this network, in the months that followed the 1991 coup SIN veteran Emmanuel "Toto" Constant began working with Kambourian and US colonel Collins to form a new "Haitian Resistance League" that might "balance the Aristide movement" and conduct "intelligence work against it."[16] Constant began to receive monthly CIA payments, and his League slowly grew in brutality and size until, in the summer of 1993, it was rebranded and launched as a public "political organization" – FRAPH (Front Révolutionnaire Pour l'Avancement et le Progrès Haïtien).

FRAPH was responsible for most of dirty work required to keep the first coup-regime in place, and the organization received thousands of military-style weapons from US authorities in Miami, often via Michel François' brother Evans, in flagrant violation of a (notoriously selective) "embargo" against the coup-regime.[17] In November 1993 a DIA analyst observed with satisfaction that FRAPH was now in a commanding political position, and that its members were starting to enjoy "the perception of power derived from being able to walk the streets of a town carrying an automatic weapon with total impunity."[18] Unsurprisingly, when US troops later arrived to "uphold democracy" one of the first things they did was to sequester and then censor some 160,000 pages of FRAPH-related documents. Not that US support for FRAPH was secret. Although they briefly detained some of them, US soldiers were instructed to protect FRAPH personnel as if they were members of a legitimate political organization, and even provided security for a press conference announcing Constant's plans to run for office.[19] A little later, in December 1995, in order to give himself some legal leverage with his old US patrons, Constant himself told *60 Minutes* about his close financial and tactical relations with the CIA. Despite repeated Haitian demands for his extradition, he would spend the next decade living in a peaceful exile in New York.[20]

In the meantime, as popular resistance to the coup-regime increased so did the violence designed to discourage it. In late 1993 and early 1994 Toto Constant's FRAPH led a series of increasingly brutal incursions into the pro-Lavalas slums.[21] In Cité Soleil (the largest slum of Port-au-Prince) FRAPH assassins murdered their opponents more or less on a nightly basis. Aid worker Eléonore Senlis remembers that ten years later, after a second coup which owed much to the contribution of FRAPH deputy commander Jodel Chamblain, "People in Cité Soleil were living in constant fear that FRAPH would return: there was a lot of talk that Toto Constant would come back, and it was if they were talking about the devil incarnate!"[22] According to Amnesty International, a 27 December 1993 FRAPH raid on Cité Soleil left at least seventy people dead.[23] A different sort of threshold was crossed when in September 1993 Constant's deputy Jodel Chamblain himself reportedly killed, in broad daylight, one of the few prominent Aristide supporters who had not gone into hiding – the well-connected businessman and philanthropist Antoine Izméry. Aristide's Justice Minister Guy Malary was killed in similar circumstances the next month; Father Jean-Marie Vincent's turn would follow in August 1994. "Haiti's 'old guard,'" noted the US Department of Justice in 1993, "appears to have united behind the *de facto* government to brutally punish not only those who work to return Aristide to power but also anyone engaging in even the most basic kinds of political activity."[24]

Slowly but surely FRAPH intimidation began to have its desired effect. A few years after the event, Colin Granderson, head of the joint United Nations/Organization of American States' mission monitoring human rights, acknowledged that "by early 1994, the repression had forced the resistance to stop making public protests everywhere, except in Raboteau [a slum in the port city of Gonaïves]."[25] In April 1994, therefore, FRAPH paramilitaries under the local leadership of Jean Tatoune descended upon Gonaïves to conduct the single most notorious operation in this phase of the long war against Lavalas. The lawyer who later helped to prosecute those responsible for the Raboteau massacre has described what happened. After some initial incursions on 18–19 April,

the main attack started before dawn on the 22nd of April 1994. Army troops and paramilitaries approached Raboteau from several angles, and started shooting. They charged into houses, breaking down doors, stealing and destroying possessions. They terrorized the occupants. The onslaught forced many to take the familiar route to the harbor. The attackers were ready, with an ambush. Armed men waiting on the beach and in boats shot at those trying to flee. Many were killed; some were wounded, on the beach, in the water and in boats [. . .]. The death total will never be known, because the attackers prevented relatives from claiming the bodies. Several were buried by paramilitaries in shallow graves or left to rot on the beach. Others floated out to sea. A total of eight murders were documented. Dozens of people were assaulted, arrested, imprisoned and/or tortured. Thousands were terrorized into leaving their homes for a few days, as the bustling neighborhood cleared out.[26]

As for Aristide himself, the CIA had already begun undermining him in a covert campaign launched back in 1987.[27] The continuation of this campaign became anything but covert in the wake of the 1991 coup. In October 1993 the CIA's Brian Latell testified before Congress to defend a 1992 Agency profile that diagnosed Aristide (in the tradition of other "irrational" political leaders like Patrice Lumumba and Nelson Mandela) as a "psychotic manic depressive with proven homicidal tendencies." As a Bush administration official admitted, Latell deliberately set out to present his report as "the most simplistic, one-dimensional message he could [make] – murderer, psychopath."[28] Much of Latell's profile was based on information provided by Lynn Garrison, an advisor to the Cédras regime who invented a good deal of his material out of thin air.[29] It didn't matter. Brent Scowcroft, President Bush's national security adviser, could now say that Aristide was "probably a certifiable psychopath." Powerful US senators like Jesse Helms were free to denounce him as a "killer" and a "grave human rights abuser," in spite of the fact that during Aristide's brief tenure as president human rights abuses had come to an immediate and altogether exceptional stop.[30]

THE POLITICS OF *MARRONAGE*, 1991–94

The Lavalas movement never fully recovered from the wave of repression that followed the 1991 coup. "In 1994 people said that Lavalas had lost 3 years," recalls Patrick Elie: "in fact we lost more like 30 years, because when we came back we'd lost so much momentum, so many people. It wasn't just the thousands who were killed but also the thousands who had returned from the diaspora in early 1991, and who now would never come back."[31] Most of the visible Lavalas leaders died or were driven into exile. Given the lack of a neutral police force or system of justice, moreover, some of the Lavalassians who survived did so by organizing defensive gangs whose growing radicalism was not always easy to align with the development of a non-violent movement. An article in the *International Herald Tribune* of 10 May 1994 summed up the situation in a single headline – "Grassroots of democracy in Haiti: all but dead."

As the Raboteau massacre and other FAdH/FRAPH atrocities made clear, François and Cédras were prepared to counter the popular movement by any means necessary. One of the arguments that most divided the survivors of this repression concerned the viability of an armed response. Should Aristide have accepted the militarization of Lavalas, and given his blessing to a guerrilla war that might engage the army on its own terrain? Some people on the left of the movement, including Ben Dupuy's APN (later PPN), urged Haiti's president to abandon his diplomatic dependence on the US and to sanction an armed liberation struggle. "The Haitian people has no choice," said the APN's Harry Numa in early 1994, "we have to fight, whatever the means, whatever the price."[32] Longtime PPN ally Kim Ives recalls the force of this argument:

> In Haiti, in the countryside and city, there was an overwhelming desire to fight the coup. It is difficult to overstate the degree of outrage and anger that the 1991 coup provoked among Haitians, both in Haiti and in the diaspora. The Haitian masses were in an extremely revolutionary state of mind, and thousands of Haitian men and women were ready to leave their jobs and dedicate themselves to any form of army that Aristide might have formed. Others were ready to pay for that army. The official army that opposed them, moreover, was extremely weak. It had spotty discipline, poor morale, inadequate equipment, and a divided command structure. It might not have taken much of a "liberation force" to send them running for the hills.[33]

Other Lavalassians were more cautious. The vast majority of guns in Haiti lie in the hands of its jittery ruling class. If threatened, Haiti's armed forces could rely on the tactful but vigorous support of allies in the US and the Dominican Republic; in the early 1990s, neither Cuba nor Venezuela were in a position to offer much help. If necessary, François and Constant knew that thousands of semi-employed Macoutes were available for recruitment into a more organized version of FRAPH. Even if Lavalas won the short-term battle against François, Nicaragua's recent experience demonstrated that the prospects for winning a longer war against the ruthless people behind François were far from encouraging.[34] One sympathetic US analyst who had close links to the Clinton administration is convinced that the advocates of violent uprising in Haiti "were very much mistaken: the attempt would have led to immense bloodshed without a victory. In my opinion their wish was the father of their thought."[35] In 1992–94 as in 2004–06, notes Yvon Neptune, Lavalas leaders had to come to terms with "the plain fact that we live in a world dominated by a single hyper-power, a power that is quite prepared to overrule the UN security council and to wage unilateral war for its own purposes."[36] More importantly, Lavalas' fundamental if not definitive commitment to non-violence would have been compromised. Aristide himself never seems to have wavered in his rejection of armed struggle, and had long ago decided on his answer to the question he had asked in the late 1980s: "Who wants to be proved right by the blood of the people?"[37] "You're kidding yourself," Aristide says, "if you think that the people can wage an armed struggle. We need to look the situation in the eye: the people have no weapons, and they will never have as many weapons as their enemies. It's pointless to wage a struggle on your enemies' terrain, or to play by their rules. You will lose."[38]

As far as most Haitians people are concerned, the fact that their liberation movement crystallized around a priest rather than a soldier was an obvious strength, not a weakness. So long as it enjoyed sufficiently ruthless international support, however, neither non-violent crowds nor violent struggle could overcome the army on their own. Knowing that Haiti's reliance on foreign imports and in particular on foreign oil meant that "the putchists would have no answer to a real and efficient embargo,"[39] Aristide had to find ways of pressuring the US to turn against the army it had created. He had to make a compelling moral and political case to attract alternative sources of international protection, in the hope that he could then use the cover provided by such protection to disband the army altogether.

This alternative was at the heart of Aristide's strategy in 1992–94, and it eventually paid off. The question that has divided Lavalas supporters ever since is whether this success was worth its very considerable cost. Aristide's critics say that in order to persuade the US and the UN to return him to power in October 1994 he had to abandon most of his own political principles. They say that he had to adopt precisely those neo-liberal policies that as an activist in the slums he had so fiercely opposed. They say that after disbanding the army in 1995, in order to forestall its remobilization the Lavalas governments were obliged to politicize the police. The remainder of this chapter will consider these three accusations in turn.

Perhaps no criticism of Aristide's first government is more common than the assertion that in 1993–94 it made too many compromises in order to return to power. The leader of the regional peasant organization the MPP, Chavannes Jean-Baptiste, spoke for many of Aristide's 1990 fellow-travellers when he said in 2005 (years after Chavannes had allied himself and his Central Plateau organization with the most reactionary pro-army groups in the country) that "Aristide completely changed in the US. He had become unrecognizable, a monster, obsessed with money and power."[40] Another early Aristide ally, the anti-globalization economist Camille Chalmers (an aide to Aristide during the first coup, but a scourge of Lavalas in the run-up to the second coup) described his second administration as one that "completely submits itself to the order given by the United States; [it is] a government ready to do whatever it takes as long as it can remain in power."[41]

There is no doubt that when Aristide came back in 1994 he was less confrontational and more diplomatic.[42] The people who accuse him of selling out to Uncle Sam forget, however, two rather significant things. First, they forget that by the spring of 1994 there was no compelling alternative to reliance on US assistance. Given the actual balance of power in the region, Fatton is probably right to argue that in order "to restore his presidency Aristide had no choice but to depend, and depend utterly, on massive US military assistance [. . .]. In spite of its huge ambiguities and contradictions, the US intervention was the only means capable of ending the military dictatorship."[43] Even a superficial review of the "negotiations" that eventually allowed Aristide to return is enough to show that the junta's own willingness to cooperate varied directly with the apparent urgency of the US military threat.[44] They forget, second, the immense obstacles that stood in the way of acquiring US assistance. The army that Lavalas opposed was to all intents and purposes a direct extension of US power, and to persuade the US to abandon the long-standing instrument of its hegemony required considerable diplomatic finesse. To persuade the US to do this at a time when it was governed by people like James Baker and Jesse Helms required little less than a miracle. The people who accuse Aristide of selling out forget what he was up against.

Instead of a miraculous conversion, Aristide's overtures to Washington were received with an all too familiar mixture of hypocrisy, racism and deceit. As *New York Times* reporter Howard French repeatedly explained, US policy makers never lost their "deep-seated ambivalence about a leftward-tilting nationalist" whose "erratic style" was marked by a "tendency toward ingratitude." Since Aristide's "class-struggle rhetoric [. . .] threatened or antagonized traditional power centers at home and abroad," so then his calls for punitive measures against the coup leaders could only confirm his reputation as an "inflexible and vindictive crusader."[45] Faced with such a fearsome antagonist, the basic strategy of Aristide's American hosts was very simple: Haiti's elected government would be permitted to go back when and only when its unelected replacement was satisfied that this return would no longer pose a threat to the status quo. Aristide was required, then, to accept the coup-regime as an equal and legitimate party to negotiations, to accord its leaders an unconditional amnesty, and to replace Préval with the sort of "moderate," Bazin-style prime minister that the US had been pressing for all along. With Bazin himself busy running the country on behalf of Cédras and François, Aristide was instead encouraged to consider alternative moderates like René Théodore (January 1992), Robert Malval (August 1993), finally Smarck Michel (September 1994), each more enthusiastically pro-US and pro-business than the last. To induce Aristide to accept these things and to placate the army that had overthrown him the Bush and Clinton administrations had an equally simple strategy – they colluded in the killing of his supporters. All through the interminable negotiations between Aristide and Cédras, explains Allan Nairn, "the US had a very clear, systematic policy of supporting the forces of terror in Haiti while at the same time, back in Washington, twisting Aristide's arm. He had a gun to his head, figuratively, just as his supporters had guns to their heads literally. It was outright political extortion."[46]

All through 1992 and 1993, remembers Patrick Elie, an incredulous Aristide was "confronted with the reality of American power."[47] Nothing of substance changed when Clinton came to power in January 1993. Although Clinton had strengthened his presidential campaign in the autumn of 1992 by references to the "cruelty" of Bush's policy towards Haiti and the naked racism of its illegal treatment of Haitian refugees, as soon as he got into the White House he promptly picked up where Bush had left off. Like Bush, Clinton officially supported the restoration of constitutional rule and seemed willing to tighten (flagrantly selective) trade sanctions against the junta, but in private "many officials" continued to brief journalists that "Aristide is so politically radical that the military and the island's affluent elite will never allow him to return to power."[48] So long as US policy makers held on to the view that the Haitian army provided a "vital counterweight" to Aristide's erratic extremism there was little the elected government could do.[49] A first US plan to broker his return fell apart in February 1992 when a "vindictive" Aristide restated his determination to punish the leaders of the army that was guilty of killing many hundreds of his supporters.[50] Stalemate ensued. By June 1993 he reluctantly came to the conclusion that he would have to accept most of the army's terms, and then try to undo the worst of their consequences once he was back in Haiti. On 3 July 1993 Aristide signed the so-called Governors Island accords, which gave Cédras almost everything he wanted in exchange for a promise to restore democratic rule before the end of October. Cédras then calmly ignored the agreements, and the pretense that was US "pressure" on his army finally collapsed altogether when on 11 October 1993 the USS *Harlan County* (carrying an advance party of soldiers and engineers who were meant to prepare the way for Aristide's return) decided to turn back when it was confronted on the jetty by a few dozen machete-wielding thugs – thugs organized by none other FRAPH's own Toto Constant, who arranged the entire stunt with the CIA.[51] The following week, rather than ask questions about how the US navy had been forced to retreat by a made-for-television charade, US Senator Bob Dole voiced a broad Pentagon consensus when he said that "the return of Aristide to Haiti is not worth even one American life."[52] A few weeks on, an adviser to Cédras acknowledged that the army had just been going through the motions all along. "The whole thing was a smokescreen. We wanted to get the sanctions lifted [. . .]. But we never had any intention of really agreeing to Governors Island, as I'm sure everyone can now figure out for themselves. We were playing for time."[53] Back in Washington, Aristide could do little more than condemn the situation as "grotesque, futile, ridiculous, nauseating."[54]

During the next year the situation in Haiti went from bad to worse. FRAPH violence peaked in the first half of 1994, and Clinton's envoy Lawrence Pezzullo began to warn Aristide that unless he made more far-reaching compromises there would be nothing to stop "FRAPH [from] taking over" and becoming "the dominant force on the ground."[55] Rather than step up the pressure on the army, in February 1994 Clinton's Secretary of State Warren Christopher endorsed a plan put forward by "moderate" Haitian legislators which again involved an unconditional pardon for the perpetrators of the coup and required Aristide to participate in a coalition government with his opponents, pending further negotiations to decide the date of his own eventual return to office. Christopher presented the plan as if it was indigenous, spontaneous, and consistent with previously agreed negotiating principles, when in fact it was conceived and prepared by US negotiators in open violation of guidelines agreed just the previous month, in Miami, during a meeting chaired by Senate leader Firmin Jean-Louis (who promptly quit the parliamentarians' delegation in disgust). As with the Governors Island agreement Aristide himself was never consulted. When after hours of futile negotiation he rejected this "Parliamentarians' Proposal" as tantamount to an unconditional surrender to Cédras, his interlocutors in both

Washington and Port-au-Prince regretted such "intransigence" and the US threatened to lift their leaky sanctions regime.[56]

FROM ONE ARMY TO ANOTHER

As the spring of 1994 dragged into summer, however, even Clinton finally started to lose patience with Cédras. Clinton's reputation as a statesman still hadn't recovered from his army's humiliation in Somalia the previous autumn, and if he was to avoid Carter's political fate he couldn't afford to humor the junta indefinitely. Unlike Bush, Clinton also couldn't afford indefinitely to ignore black voters. As thousands of people went on trying to escape FRAPH violence in Haiti only to be repatriated by the Coast Guard or incarcerated in the de-facto concentration camp that was Guantanamo Bay, relentless criticism of Clinton's hypocrisy from influential African-American leaders like Jesse Jackson, Randall Robinson and Maxine Waters (along with Hollywood supporters like Danny Glover and Jonathan Demme) finally started to have some significant political effect. Haiti became an unwelcome *cause célèbre* in church halls and on university campuses.

Although fundamental US priorities hadn't changed – the consolidation of an elite, neo-liberal, and US-friendly regime in Haiti, securely protected from any sort of popular democratic threat – for the time being they couldn't be pursued in so literal a fashion as a military coup. In any case, with Lavalas in tatters, the army's historical mission was coming to an end. So long as the US was confident that it could retain a free hand to develop alternative and more efficient forms of economic and paramilitary coercion, it was at last prepared to abandon the old-fashioned version of Haiti's army, for the same sorts of reasons that led it to abandon Duvalier a few years before. Aristide's return would stem the flow of refugees, bolster Clinton's "humanitarian" credentials, and provide impressive televisual proof of the fact that US Marines still knew how to invade small Caribbean islands. So long as he remained dependent on the US, a newly "pragmatic" Aristide might promise international investors a more stable business climate than an army that was now disgraced beyond repair.

This was the context in which, under immense pressure and with great reluctance, in August 1994 Aristide signed a new agreement with the US and the IFIs that guaranteed his return, in exchange for significant new concessions. The so-called "Paris Plan" again obliged Aristide to agree to an amnesty for the coup-makers. He had to concede US control over the development and training of a new police force. He had to share power with the opponents that he had defeated so convincingly in 1990, and to adopt most of their highly conservative policies. In particular, he was required to implement a drastic new structural adjustment programme, in line with the measures already adopted by Duvalier and Namphy during the previous decade (I'll come back to this in a moment). Satisfied that an Aristide who accepted these conditions could pose no serious threat to the status quo, Clinton then permitted himself one of the more memorable indulgences of his political life. Cloaked in the ardor of moral rectitude, in September 1994 he authorized the deployment of some 20,000 Marines in order to remove "the most brutal, the most violent regime anywhere in our hemisphere," a regime guilty of "executing children, raping women, killing priests" and of "slaying orphans."[57]

Dispatched to negotiate the terms of their exile (so as to ensure that the "invasion" remained a bloodless PR exercise), Clinton's envoys Jimmy Carter and Colin Powell sent Cédras and François a rather different signal, praising them as "honorable" partners and arranging one of the most outrageously generous asylum packages that the US has ever provided to a client regime.[58] On arrival in Haiti, US troops cooperated closely with leading pro-coup families in the business elite like the Mevs and the Boulos, renting their facilities, investing in their infrastructure, hiring their personnel.[59] As of October 1994 tens of thousands of small arms still remained in military or Macoute hands, and upon arriving back in Haiti Aristide knew full well that "the focal point of the entire operation is the disarmament of the Haitian paramilitary and the neutralization and reformation of the Haitian army. The entire success of the mission is linked to the process of disarmament, because if the forces that have reigned over the past three violent years are not neutralized, we will have little to build on."[60] Rather than disarm the FRAPH paramilitaries, however, the Marines went out of their way to protect them. To the dismay of an initially enthusiastic Haitian population, rather than exclude or punish them the Marines proceeded to treat Haitian soldiers with what one US officer described as "courtesy" and "respect."[61] As the US embassy put it in November, a strong Haitian army remained an "essential part of the 'iconography' of nationhood."[62] No action was taken to reverse the inestimable damage of the army's assault – as we will see, covert steps were instead being taken to prepare for a similar assault in the future.

It is perfectly clear that, as far as its architects were concerned, this new US occupation was designed to disarm not Haiti's army but its people. After speaking to a range of high-level military planners, Allan Nairn reached the unavoidable conclusion that the main purpose for the occupation was "to prevent the Haitian population from taking politics into its own hands and to forestall the danger of radical mass mobilization [. . .]. The United States intends to contain Haiti's popular movement, by force if necessary. The objective, in the words of one US Army Psychological Operations official, is to see to it that Haitians 'don't get the idea that they can do whatever they want.' "[63] According to Captain Lawrence Rockwood (who was later court-martialed for violating orders instructing US soldiers to ignore the plight of Haitian political prisoners), all US intelligence officers and reports "were very much anti-Aristide [. . .]. We only received anti-Aristide information."[64]

It is more than likely that the occupation that began in September 1994 may prove, in the long run, to have been just as damaging to the interests of Haitian democracy as the first US occupation of 1915–34. It gave the occupying power profound and temporarily irreversible influence over the reconfiguration of a state apparatus more compatible with its own priorities. As the soldiers themselves began to leave over the course of 1995, a whole swathe of para-civilian advisors, trainers and consultants remained behind to administer the consequences of their work – and to prepare the ground for future doses of that "humanitarian intervention" which has come to replace traditional forms of military action as the primary means of neo-imperial control. "The nefarious consequences of Aristide's choice to return in the company of US troops debilitate Haiti to this day," notes Kim Ives; "the political and cultural degeneration that the 1994–2000 occupation wrought on Haiti cannot be overemphasized."[65] It may even be that the occupation of 1994–2000 did as much political damage to the popular movement as did the 1991–94 coup itself.

It may also be, however, that there is little or nothing that the Haitian people could have done to avoid this occupation, sooner or later. If they had opted to depend on their own arms, rather than those of the US, it is a virtual certainty that the US would have done everything necessary to justify international "pacification" in due course. When Aristide was elected in 1990 he knew very well that only some sort of "marriage between the people and the army" offered his government any chance of survival.[66] Occupation by the patron of that army may have been a necessary price to pay for a still more necessary divorce.

THE POLITICS OF NEO-LIBERALISM

When Aristide finally returned to the national palace on 15 October 1994, the situation he inherited was extremely delicate. Lavalas was back in power, the people were delighted and relieved, and the presence of foreign troops now served to protect them, up to a point, from further domestic aggression.[67] Though some leftwing intellectuals who had supported Lavalas in 1991 were dismayed to see Aristide return in the company of US troops, journalists who bothered to consult his supporters in the slums received a different reaction. When in November 1994 Xabier Gorostiaga "asked the impoverished but happy residents of Cité Soleil the same question I had put to everyone else I encountered," he received a "completely unanimous answer: 'The gringos didn't bring Aristide. Aristide brought the gringos, to free us from Cédras and the Tontons Macoutes. This is a victory for Aristide.'"[68] Eighteen months after Aristide's return, an analyst at the US Army War College was impressed by both the "lack of large-scale revenge-motivated violence" and the "extraordinary flowering of political participation."[69] Around the same time the *New York Times* recorded that ordinary Haitians "say they are living without fear for the first time in decades. 'We walk freely,' said Amson Jean-Pierre, 35, an unemployed father of five children who joined a pro-Aristide rally today in front of the National Palace. 'We sleep quietly. There are no men who come for us in the night.'"[70]

There was an obvious reason for this decline in political violence. After slowly demobilizing most of its soldiers (and all but one of its superior officers) over the course of the preceding months, on 28 April 1995 Aristide took the dramatic step of dissolving the army altogether. As a leading member in today's grassroots Lavalas movement puts it, "As a result of its brutality during the coup the army had lost all legitimacy; when it then tolerated the US occupation it abandoned its very raison d'être, and all Aristide had to do was to finish it off."[71] Even so, it would be hard to exaggerate the significance of this move, which was made in the face of determined powerful US and elite opposition. It was precisely this outcome that the US backers of Haiti's army had been determined to avoid all along. In September 1992, the *New York Times* cited a comment from a "senior [Bush administration] official has been repeatedly echoed in American diplomatic circles: 'Aristide wants us to get rid of his enemies for him so that he can have a free hand to mop up, and we're just not going to do that for him.'"[72] Two years later Clinton's administration accepted that the army should be reduced in size, but insisted that a nucleus of at least 1500 well-equipped troops should be retained under close international supervision; preservation of such a force would then continue to provide that "vital counterweight" required to keep any transition to democracy on a reliable political track. Aristide's supporters, however, had a different priority. Some of the many thousands of people who came out to listen to listen to Aristide on his first day back in the country told reporters that "before the foreigners leave, they have to destroy the army [. . .]. Every night, they break into our houses and rape our daughters and wives. Don't leave any of them."[73] Despite US pressure, Aristide did exactly what such people asked, and promptly reduced the army to nothing more than its marching band. All by itself, this was a major victory in the long struggle of the poor against the rich – perhaps the single most promising development in the whole history of that struggle since the assassination of Dessalines in 1806. Although the backlash it provoked wouldn't be long in coming, Lavalas had at least bought itself a little time.

In every other respect Aristide's position in late 1994 was even weaker than it had been three years before. Basic administrative structures were in ruins, and would take months to repair.[74] His enemies were neither marginalized nor disarmed, and divisions had emerged among some of his leading supporters. Still lacking any disciplined parliamentary support, he was now obliged to cooperate yet more directly with members of the traditional political elite, people like Gérard Pierre-Charles and a new business-oriented prime minister Smarck Michel – people whose loyalty to the Lavalas project would soon be exposed as paper-thin. With US troops in total control of Haiti's security, he was obliged to preside over the constitution of a new security force (the Haitian National Police) under conditions that threatened to allow the old army to endure in a new "civilian" guise. Above all, he was obliged to enforce neo-liberal economic measures that were sure to provoke the resentment of the poor, particularly in the countryside. The austerity programme that in the summer of 1994 Aristide was obliged to accept in exchange for an end to military rule and FRAPH intimidation was designed, "in the words of one of the main authors of that program, to redistribute some wealth from the poor to the rich."[75]

Now the notion that a Haitian politician could be "for or against neo-liberalism" in the 1990s is even more abstract than similar questions addressed to the politicians who came to power during these same years in significantly less dependent countries like Jamaica or South Africa, to say nothing of countries like France or the UK. Although US officials and newspapers might routinely decry Aristide as a "fiery leftist" to this day, in reality he always understood that given the current balance of forces, no Haitian government can afford to adopt anything like an openly socialist set of priorities.[76] Better than many of his critics, he knows that a country like Haiti cannot afford to "plan a political economy that would turn the entire world against it."[77] As things stand, Haiti is confronted with a "choice between death and death: either we enter a global economic system in which we know we cannot survive, or, we refuse, and face death by slow starvation." The only alternative is slowly to open up "some room to maneuver, some open space simply to survive."[78] Aristide understands as well as anyone that "neo-liberalization is a kind of colonialism," that the "neo-liberal strategy is to weaken the state in order to have the private sector replace it."[79] But acceptance of basic neo-liberal rules is for the time being part of the air that every Haitian politician is obliged to breathe, and the power to change this does not lie within Haiti itself.

Anyone concerned with public welfare, let alone popular empower-ment, can only be outraged by the effects neo-liberalism has had in Haiti, as in most other heavily exploited countries – but to blame these effects on the victims who suffer them is not helpful. As UN envoy Lakhdar Brahimi candidly explained on Haitian radio in 1996, there was never any question that either the US or the UN would tolerate even limited attempts to dilute the elite's monopoly of economic power.[80] The only pertinent political question to ask about enforcement of IFI dictates in Haiti in the mid-1990s was simply this: should the government accept unconditional compliance with IFI requirements, or insist on a combination of com-pliance and compensation? Aristide and his supporters (the group that would soon establish the organization *Fanmi Lavalas*) chose the second path; his prime minister Smarck Michel, Paul Denis, Gérard Pierre-Charles (the group that would soon rename their faction the *Organisation du Peuple en Lutte*) chose the first, as did virtually all other members of the liberal elite and its traditional political class. It doesn't require much in-depth knowl-edge of Haitian political life to guess which group came to receive the enthusiastic backing of the US and its allies. According to the only appropriate frame of reference, far from being too subservient to the US Aristide was as independent as he could feasibly be – "He was the only politician with any actual responsibility," Bobby Duval recognizes, "who stood up to the US."[81] It's this stubborn independence that would eventually condemn Lavalas to absolute international isolation. As the Haiti Action Committee pointed out in 2003, most left-leaning critics of Aristide's alleged neo-liberal turn "completely disregard Haiti's reality":

> Haiti is the poorest country in the Western Hemisphere, has a 70 percent unemployment rate and now confronts a brutal US-orchestrated em-

bargo. Haiti, like every other developing nation in the world, has no choice but to negotiate with international lenders to secure investment, release loans and create new jobs. The fact remains: the United States is attacking Haiti's government and popular organizations not because Haiti is a compliant partner, but precisely because it represents an alternative to globalization and corporate domination.[82]

It's undeniably true that the 1994 Paris Plan forced Aristide to make some very painful decisions. In exchange for some $770 million in promised aid and loans, the list of concessions appears calamitous: tariffs were to be "drastically" reduced, wages frozen, around half of the civil service to be laid off, and all nine of Haiti's remaining public utilities (telephone, electricity, port, airport, cement, flour, a cooking oil plant and two state banks) were to be sold off. Aristide's critics on the left often point to his acceptance of this Plan as a decisive moment in his apparent evolution from grassroots idealist to Machiavellian dictator. Like the US and IMF officials that Aristide and Préval would soon have to deal with, however, these critics don't often read the text of what was actually agreed in Paris (and nor do they appreciate the relative continuity between these 1994 agreements and what one World Bank official described as the "rather conservative financial approach" of Aristide's 1991 administration[83]). Yes tariffs on rice were to be slashed, but only "concurrently" with substantial new investment in a "rice sector support package" to improve water management, drainage, provision of fertilizers, pesticides, tools, financial services, etc. Yes the accords asked the government to lay off some 22,000 civil servants, while stipulating that "the objective is to secure the *voluntary* [italics in the original] departure of about half of the 45,000 civil servants; to reach this goal, a generous severance package will be offered." (In reality, Aristide managed to avoid all but a cosmetic number of redundancies, and even when Préval was obliged to implement this part of the SAP in early 1997 it had been watered down to the point that it involved laying off around 7,000 government workers over an 18 month period[84].) Yes the utilities would be sold – but not simply to the highest bidder. The plan called instead for the "democratization" of public assets, and specified that their sale "must be implemented in a way that will prevent increased concentration of wealth within the country." The sale must

transfer part of the ownership to traditionally excluded segments of society, with particular attention given to the families of the victims of

the recent political turmoil [. . .]. To further strengthen the redis-
tributive objectives, the Government will invest half of the proceeds
from the divestiture into infrastructure investments in the poorest areas
and low-cost urban and rural housing. The other half will be invested
in a permanent trust fund whose annual proceeds will be used to
subsidize education and health for the rural poor.

The plan further stipulated that some of the donors' $770m will be
invested in the provision of a "social safety net" and promised that "as a
major priority, [the government] will invest in basic education for the
poor, the rural segment of the population, with a special attention to
young women's schooling and an adult literacy program." The plan also
affirmed the government's determination to "empower labor unions,
grassroots organizations, cooperatives, community groups." It pledged to
"demilitarize public life" and to exclude from the armed forces anyone
guilty of human rights violations.[85] Even the amnesty that Aristide agreed
to provide the coup leaders was – very discreetly – framed in such a way as
to apply only to the 30 September assault itself, and not the crimes that
followed it: prosecutions for at least some of these atrocities would
eventually follow in due course.[86]

The Paris Plan involved regrettable compromises, in short, but not
unconditional surrender. As Elie puts it, "Yes, Aristide negotiated, and he
was obliged to negotiate. The problem was that the people he negotiated
with did not negotiate in good faith."[87] What then happened when
Aristide returned to the presidency in October 1994 is predictable
enough. The US and the IFIs put huge pressure on his government
to abandon all of the social conditions and compensations that had just
been agreed in Paris, and threatened to suspend the disbursement of the
promised funds unless he moved forward with the immediate and
unadulterated privatization of state assets. The dilemma split his government. Prime minister Smarck Michel, Gérard Pierre-Charles and their
associates argued that the government had no choice but to proceed in
line with US demands, and began to take steps to implement them;
Michel's appointment as prime minister, after all, "was aimed at appeasing
the nation's powerful business elite" and had been welcomed in Washington "as a crucial step in winning support from foreign investors and
attaining international development funds."[88] During the summer of
1995 popular resentment of the structural adjustment and privatization
measures increased, and protests were organized all over the country.
Aristide wore himself out with futile calls on the US/IMF to respect the

terms of the "democratization" agreed in Paris, before pushing Smarck Michel out of office on 16 October 1995. He replaced him with the person who had been his own preferred candidate for the position all along, Claudette Werleigh (a woman who the previous year was denounced in US government circles for her "leftist bent").[89] Aristide warned that any official who tried to proceed with the untrammeled privatization of state assets would be jailed. The US and the IFIs responded by suspending the disbursement of most of the promised aid and loans; almost overnight the gourde lost 20 percent of its value, and the price of basic foodstuffs began to rise. An exasperated Aristide lashed out against this foreign interference. "The game of hypocrisy is over," he said in a speech on 11 November 1995. "We don't have two, or three heads of state, we have one."[90]

The stage was now set for one of the defining political conflicts of the subsequent decade. The stakes were high. "These guys will take a major hit" if they stall on privatization, an unnamed diplomat warned the NYT in October 1995.[91] Sure enough, in an interview he gave ten years after the fact, Aristide explained that there were three reasons behind the intensification of US hostility to Lavalas during the mid-1990s: "privatization, privatization and privatization."[92] The issue had been high on the transnational agenda for Haiti ever since the intensification of structural adjustment in the mid-1980s. In 1987 (under Namphy) the state-run sugar mill had been privatized in exactly the manner that Aristide was determined to avoid. It was bought by a single wealthy family (the Mevs) who promptly closed it, laid off its staff and began importing cheaper sugar from the US and the Dominican Republic so as to sell it on at prices that undercut the domestic market. Once the world's most profitable sugar exporter, by 1995 Haiti was importing 25,000 tons of American sugar and most people could no longer afford to buy it.[93] The state assets and utilities not only earn significant revenues while providing local goods and services under equitable conditions, they also offer (through the recruitment of thousands of public sector employees) one of the only significant ways a cash-strapped government can make limited progress towards affirmative action and the redistribution of wealth. The ports and telecommunications company alone employ around 8,000 people, and account for a substantial portion of what little leverage the government still retains in its permanent struggle with a predatory private sector. On 10 May 1996 Aristide echoed what his supporters had been saying for months when he openly denounced the IMF's version of privatization, arguing that such moves have never "improved the lot of citizens of any country."[94]

Aristide refused to privatize any of the state enterprises, Préval was prepared to privatize a couple of them, and Smarck Michel/Pierre-Charles, all of them – in a nutshell, this defines the political spectrum of 1994–2004. What complicates the picture is the fact that a new round of parliamentary elections took place in June 1995, before the conflict over privatization and the political orientation of the Lavalas government had fully broken out into the open. As you might expect, these elections were won, and won easily, by the group associated with Aristide and the Lavalas movement – the Plateform Politique Lavalas (PPL). Ninety percent of people eligible to vote registered for the elections, which took place in circumstances that bore no resemblance to the violence of November 1987.[95] Despite technical failings, recognized a professor at the US Army War College, "no serious observer doubts that Lavalas would have won an overwhelming victory even under the most pristine conditions."[96]

Once the tally of second-round run-offs was completed in September, the PPL held 17 of 27 Senate seats and 67 of 83 seats in the chamber of Deputies. The problem was that by mid-1995, most members of the largest single faction in the Lavalas Platform (a party that called itself the Organisation Politique Lavalas or OPL, which was led by the career politician and economics professor Gérard Pierre-Charles) were no longer Aristide supporters.[97] Pierre-Charles exemplified the "cosmopolitan" wing of the political elite, people who had been forced into exile under Duvalier, and who after returning to Haiti in the mid-to late 1980s were concerned above all to adapt their principles so as to fit with the prevailing balance of power; in the case of someone like Pierre-Charles, this would involve a progressive shift in affinities from Fidel Castro to Jean-Bertrand Aristide to Jesse Helms.[98]

From the beginning, therefore, there was a tension between the purely party-political or opportunistic configuration of this OPL – which oriented it, as a group of career politicians, towards the interests of the business sector, bourgeois civil society, the universities and the liberal elite – and the basis of its electoral success, i.e. its perceived association with Aristide, the *organisations populaires* and the rest of the grassroots Lavalas mobilization. After June 1995, Pierre-Charles' OPL had a strong position in parliament, and the conservative prime minister that the US had imposed on Aristide, Smarck Michel, was one of its leading members. The anti-presidential bias of the 1987 constitution ensured that at least for a year or two, Michel, Pierre-Charles and the rest of the OPL would retain considerable leverage.

Two further developments shaped the course of 1995. On the one hand, US pressure on privatization and other forms of structural adjustment intensified, a renewal of old USAID priorities with a newly humanitarian face. Following fast on the heels of the Marines came the shock troops of what Jane Regan accurately described as a "more permanent, less reversible invasion" – the IFIs, USAID, the US National Endowment for Democracy and a plethora of liberally funded technocrats and NGOs. All these divergent agencies were authorized by their donors to bypass the elected government and to invest directly in a wide range of development projects designed

> to impose a neo-liberal economic agenda, to undermine grassroots participatory democracy, to create political stability conducive to a good business climate, and to bring Haiti into the new world order appendaged to the US as a source for markets and cheap labor. As in other countries, this democracy promotion industry will support those projects and people willing to go along with its agenda and will mold them into a center. In the crude old days, grassroots organizers unwilling to be co-opted would have been tortured or killed. Now, they will simply be marginalized by poverty and lack of political clout.[99]

In this way, most of the international money that Aristide had fought so hard to secure during his Washington exile was in fact used in 1994–95 to undermine his government and much of what it sought to achieve. Most of it went straight to pro-elite, pro-US, pro-business private sector groups whose political opposition to Lavalas was already explicit. In anticipation of a development that would play a crucial role in the destabilization campaign of 2002–03, the political affiliation of many of these groups was carefully managed through a US-funded network known as the Programme Intégré pour le Renforcement de la Démocratie (PIRED). PIRED was directed by Ira Lowenthal, an American anthropologist with seemingly limitless connections in the Haitian business community. It remained in operation all through the coup years, and was instrumental in helping to guarantee the basic continuity of elite control before and after 1994. Under PIRED's generously funded tutelage, Regan notes, "scores of labor unions and neighborhood groups went from demanding higher wages and denouncing US imperialism to thanking Bill Clinton and promoting reconciliation." PIRED played a crucial role in brokering "power-sharing arrangements with the military regime," and in preparing the ground for the convergence in a new "civil society" of pro-military and pro-business interests. PIRED money also helped secure the allegiance of Aristide's old political rival Evans Paul, who during the last two years of the coup was embraced by the US and by prominent pro-coup industrialists like Gregory Mevs as a reliable frontman for the elite.[100] With undisguised US encouragement and in order to strengthen his position as a candidate in the presidential elections planned for December 1995, in the municipal elections of June Evans Paul stood against Aristide's preferred candidate Manno Charlemagne for mayor of Port-au-Prince. In spite (or because) of US help, like Bazin before him Paul could only win 14 percent of the vote; Aristide had gained himself another bitter enemy. Although Paul would never again come close to winning an election, he would play a leading role in the development of the democratic opposition to Aristide. (The true extent of his political support is probably best measured by his tally in the presidential election of 2006: 2.5 percent.)

In early 1995, Clinton's Deputy Secretary of State Strobe Talbot explained his government's basic strategy: "Even after our [military] exit in February 1996 we will remain in charge by means of the USAID and the private sector."[101] This defined the context in which Aristide had to negotiate even for very modest components of his social program, for instance to increase a minimum wage that had remained frozen at around 15 gourdes (around $1) a day since 1983. Aristide pressed for a new 45 gourde rate; USAID official Brian Atwood was adamant that Haiti's economy wasn't "ready to consider" any increase at all.[102] Atwood's Haitian interlocutors remembered that "when Aristide first came in he said, 'There's going to be a mandatory $5 minimum [daily] wage' – it was just so outlandish that nobody even took it seriously."[103] By 1994 the IFIs were more sanguine. Fears of wage hikes in Haiti were softened by a recognition that, as World Bank official Axel Peuker put it, "in a country like Haiti the government's enforcement capacity is nil."[104] Although reluctant to accept any increase in the minimum wage and insistent that the government maintain a three-year public sector wage freeze, the IMF observed with satisfaction that even the new 36 gourde rate agreed in May 1995 "falls well short of the real and US dollar equivalent minimum wage of ten years ago, and should not affect the good prospects for the export sector."[105] (In any case, noted the Campaign for Labor Rights in 1998, "more than half of the approximately 50 assembly plants producing in Haiti for the US market pay less than the legal minimum wage".)[106]

The second development was more narrowly political, but dovetailed perfectly with the first. Over the course of 1995, ambitious OPL parliamentarians and their allies became alarmed as popular support grew for demands made by Aristide loyalists, that he be allowed to extend his presidential term in order to recover the three years usurped by Cédras. Determined to avoid such an extension at all costs, Pierre-Charles and his friends were more than willing to go along with the US when in late 1995, as Kim Ives explains, it "turned to the OPL to push Aristide out."[107]

This was a decisive moment in the political evolution of the Lavalas movement. The case for an extension of Aristide's mandate was hardly unreasonable, and as an unnamed diplomat told the *New York Times* in September, Aristide was in a commanding position: "There is no competition for him, it's all his."[108] Aristide himself hesitated. The issue had been ostensibly resolved on the eve of the invasion, noted an analyst for the NED, "when Aristide promised that he would leave office at the end of his term and make way for a democratically elected successor (although, cleverly, he never did say when he thought the term should end)."[109] The clear majority of the Haitian people thought it should end in 1999, rather than 1996. The mobilization of people clamouring to allow Aristide to serve out his full term in office became so intense, Laura Flynn remembers, that when he gave a speech in Bel Air in the autumn of 1995 "He was unable to say anything for around an hour, because the thousands of people who had turned out to listen to him kept chanting 'Three more years!' "[110] The leaders of what was still an informal Lavalas political coalition – notably Father William Smarth and Gérard Pierre-Charles – also hesitated, but decided that the organization should fall into line with the insistence of the US and the rest of the IC, and that Aristide should make way for a more pliable successor. Both career politicians and the international advocates of privatization and structural adjustment had a common interest in replacing a man with unrivalled popularity and unimpeachable moral authority with a more conciliatory and pragmatic administrator. The OPL opted to allow Aristide's mandate to expire "on schedule," and to run his old prime minister René Préval as his successor. Under pressure to maintain the unity of the Lavalas coalition (and following a visit by former US national security advisor Anthony Lake) Aristide reluctantly agreed to toe the party line, but resentment lingered on both sides of the dispute. Disappointment among the Lavalas OPs was palpable. After telling reporters in late November that he was so close to Préval that "they used to call us twins," Aristide only announced his official support for the Préval campaign in the closing days of the race.[111] As a Latin-American diplomat explained, "This is really an election that no one in Haiti except the international community has wanted. Aristide's supporters would prefer to see him remain in office, and his opponents know they don't have the slightest chance of winning."[112] Préval won with 88 percent of a relatively low turnout, and his inauguration duly took place in February 1996.

An accomplished administrator and conciliator, Préval then tried to steer a middle course between the Aristide loyalists and an increasingly anti-Aristide OPL. This proved to be an impossible task. Obliged by the constitution to work with a prime minister from the largest party in parliament, he chose the OPL's Rosny Smarth (rather than its leader Pierre-Charles). With the IMF and other IFIs Préval and Smarth negotiated a new $1.2 billion Emergency Economic Recovery Plan in October 1996, which re-affirmed most of the principles and priorities of the 1994 Paris accords. Like Smarck Michel before him, Smarth was another advocate for IMF-style privatization, and in spite of Préval's reluctance in 1997 and 1999 the two smallest and least profitable state enterprises (flour and cement) were duly sold. Although the sale was relatively well-managed and kept a 30 percent stake in public ownership, the flour mill went for just $9 million, at a time when its potential annual profits were estimated at around $25 million per year.[113] "Circumstances have forced Mr. Préval into an alliance" with the OPL, its leader Pierre-Charles observed in March 1997 – while regretting that Préval continued to "identify himself ideologically with Aristide" and "doesn't really like political parties or having to count on one [for support]."[114]

As in the summer of 1995, however, protests against OPL policy grew in intensity in the first half of 1997.[115] Tensions between the OPL and Préval grew as well. The split between the committed and opportunistic Lavalassians became irreversible. "A lot of traditional politicians and intellectuals endorsed the original Lavalas coalition in 1990," remembers Yvon Neptune (FL prime minister 2002–04), "but as they began to realize that things weren't going to play out in the traditional way, that they wouldn't be rewarded in the traditional way, then they drifted away or turned against it. They wanted access to power, and they worked with Lavalas only so long as they considered it as useful vehicle for their own ambitions. They never really accepted the idea that uneducated people could elect a president or play a leading role in the development of a political organization – in other words, they never wanted to be part of an organization that they themselves couldn't dominate."[116] Dismayed by the OPL's political re-orientation and the divisive multiplication of competing political factions (FNCD, KID, KONAKOM, PLB, KOR-EGA, PANPRA . . .), over the course of 1996 Aristide and his closest allies both in parliament and among the *organisations populaires* resolved to create an alternative political organization – L'Organisation Politique Fanmi Lavalas. Fanmi Lavalas (FL) was designed to re-establish direct links between local branches of the Lavalas mobilization and its parliamentary representation. "Aristide never wanted to lead a political party," explains Yvon Neptune,

> or to devote much of his time to developing a party organization. But eventually he realised that if he wanted to be part of a movement to build popular democracy in Haiti it would have to be done through a party, there was no choice. And he had to participate in this himself, once his former allies in the OPL started to move in a different direction. Fanmi Lavalas was created at the right time. It was the first time that a significant political organization was created, or created itself, in a non-traditional way, from the bottom up. It was grounded in scores of local cells, or *ti fanmis*, and we spent many months working on our collective programme, *Investir dans l'humain*.[117]

When another set of legislative elections took place in 1997, this new party was set to win back control of parliament from the OPL (which in order to clarify its relation to Lavalas renamed itself the *Organisation du Peuple en Lutte*). Although the turnout was low, the outcome of a first round of voting in April resulted in what the *New York Times* called "decisive victories for several candidates closely aligned with Mr. Aristide."[118] An indignant Pierre-Charles and the OPL insisted the results were fraudulent, refused to accept them and blocked (or rather persuaded the UN to block) the organization of the second round needed to complete the process. After failing to bludgeon Préval into line on the elections and on privatization, in June 1997 Rosny Smarth and most of his ministers resigned. Further privatization legislation was shelved, but Préval's government was left in political limbo. "Lavalas had imploded," notes Bellegarde-Smith, "and the elites rejoiced."[119]

By hanging on to their seats, by refusing to accept any of Préval's several nominees for a new prime minister, by obstructing all of his initiatives and freezing the disbursement of hundreds of millions of dollars in unspent international aid, the OPL deputies were able to paralyze Préval's government for a full eighteen months, until their terms finally expired in January 1999.[120] They then delayed the arrangement of another set of elections until May 2000, forcing Préval to govern by decree. Working in conjunction with members of Fanmi Lavalas, from January 1999 through to the end of his mandate in February 2001 Préval was at last able to re-activate and extend the sort of policies he had helped to initiate back in 1991 – limited land reform, modest improvements in public infrastructure, investments in education and health, and so on. He was also able to maintain a fragile grip on an institution whose political affiliation would prove decisive in the run-up to the 2004 coup – the new Haitian National Police (PNH) that Aristide established in the first part of 1995 to fill the security void left by the demobilization of the army.

FROM THE ARMY TO THE POLICE

The struggle to control the orientation of this new police force proved to be one of the critical political issues of the post-coup era. Since the army had been the only thing standing between Haiti's system of socio-economic apartheid and open revolution, its elimination by Aristide over the course of 1995 provoked something close to panic within the ranks of the ruling class. As Préval's police chief Pierre Denizé explained in 1999, up until 1994 members of the elite had always been "well protected by the army that served them and the repressive, dysfunctional system that went with it." While actual levels of criminal and political violence remained "inexplicably low," nevertheless now that the rich had lost their military protection they had started to fall "prey to criminality like everyone else."[121] The possibility that one day the poor might "give them what they deserved" had never seemed more imminent. The elite responded in the only way it knew how. As one of the dozens of US police trainers that Clinton sent to help "professionalize" the new PNH told the *New York Times* in 1997, "Almost every middle-class Haitian family has automatic weapons. The middle class are all sympathizers with the former army and the Tontons Macoutes. If they didn't know Big Brother was watching over them, they would probably stage a coup."[122]

The opportunity for a further coup would come in due course. In the meantime, the elite and its ex-army pawns threw themselves into a pitched battle for control of the new security force. Although first Préval and then Aristide (together with many hundreds of loyal PNH recruits) put up a remarkably strong fight, four factors helped ensure an eventual victory for the elite.

First of all, from 1994 through to 1999 the funding, training and development of the new force all depended on the US. Officially, despite its initial resistance the US embassy soon came to accept "Mr. Préval's position that the armed forces have been legally abolished."[123] Future US investment in Haitian security would have to work through slightly more discreet channels. But if the style changed, the substance did not. The first thing that US troops and intelligence officers did on arrival in Haiti in 1994 was take steps to protect and retain its most important FAdH and FRAPH assets.[124] The US thwarted every attempt by the new government to prosecute crimes committed during the Cédras regime, and made sure that the National Commission for Truth and Justice which Aristide established in March 1995 was restricted to the mere documentation of cases – some 8,652 in total – of human rights abuse undertaken between 1991 and 1994. (Justice for some of the coup victims would have to wait until the altogether exceptional Raboteau trial in 2000, which effectively served as an indictment of the entire coup regime.) During the last year of the coup, a select group of around a dozen young Haitian soldiers led by Guy Philippe, Jacky Nau and Gilbert Dragon had already been hustled off to Ecuador's military academy to receive special training. As Steven Dudley explained some years later, Philippe and his team became known as the "Ecuadorians" because they "stuck together" after their training. "We lived in the same house for years [said Dragon], and we were loyal to the military institution." When the coup ended Philippe and his friends came back to Haiti and were fast-tracked into leadership positions in the new police force. All through the late 1990s, Dudley continues, Philippe's men "maintained their *esprit de corps*. 'We're not former military; we *are* military,' Philippe said. 'We are soldiers.'"[125]

In addition to nurturing these future freedom fighters, the State Department and the CIA oversaw the crucial stages of the initial PNH recruitment, and in line with an entrenched tradition that had helped maintain its working relationship with the Haitian army, ensured that many police units received training at Fort Leonard Wood in Missouri.[126] Retired US sergeant Stan Goff led a special forces team in Haiti in the autumn 1994, and confirms that the CIA was actively recruiting sympathetic members of the former military and the new civilian police all through 1994 and 1995. By the time it was formally established in the middle of 1995, the Haitian National Police already "had untold numbers of people who were on the US payroll, or being prepared to be on the payroll."[127] As Dan Coughlin wrote in the spring of 1999, "a multi-agency US group selected each recruit and determined the design, training and financing of the 6,500-strong PNH. More than

50 percent of the top police commissioners are recycled Haitian Army personnel" and "United States trainers placed soldiers they considered reliable in a number of key units, and systematically purged a group of reformist army officers who had refused to support the 1991 coup."[128] In particular, the US helped ensure that the most powerful units of the new police force – the 500-strong member Presidential Guard (USGPN) and two 60–80 member SWAT-style units (GIPNH and CIMO) were all staffed largely by ex-army personnel. These were the only PNH units capable of something resembling military combat, and the effort to control them is one of the most significant pieces in the whole post-coup puzzle. Under the auspices of its International Criminal Investigative Training Assistance Program (ICITAP), the US funneled hundreds of military-style weapons to selected units of the PNH at least through to 1998.[129] In September 1996 the *New York Times* noted that while most of its troops had left Haiti, "the United States continues to be deeply involved in the day-to-day management of this country – and reliant on the unilateral application of force to achieve its objectives [. . .]. The United States seems to be mounting a parallel security and support system, with Haiti's reluctant compliance," in order to turn the country into what one diplomat described as "an American protectorate."[130] When Préval's security chief Bob Manuel organized a purge of the presidential guard after exposing coup and assassination plans in the summer of 1996, for instance, some forty State Department security agents were sent to Haiti in order to help shape the inflection of the USGPN and to limit the influence of Aristide loyalists within the security forces.[131] In February 1999, no less a person than the director of the Justice Department's ICITAP in Haiti (Jan Stromsem) was forced out of her job, after denouncing repeated CIA efforts to recruit police trainees.[132]

Second, around one in four members of the new force were eventually transferred into the PNH from the army itself.[133] Once again, Aristide had little choice: if it was unable to incorporate and win over a large fraction of the former army then the new civilian police stood no chance at all. Nevertheless, the transition was fraught with predictable difficulties. Most of the army's 7,000 soldiers were demobilized in late 1994, but around 3,400 were temporarily retained to man an (understandably unpopular) interim police force, pending the establishment of the PNH proper in July 1995. By February 1995, Aristide felt secure enough to dismiss the whole of the army's senior officer corps, leaving the chief of this interim police force, Major Dany Toussaint, as the most senior remaining officer.[134] Dany Toussaint and his associates Médard Joseph and Pierre Cherubin were among the small handful of relatively pro-gressive young army officers who had rallied to Aristide's cause in 1990. Toussaint had risked his life defending Aristide on the night of 30 September 1991, and both Toussaint and Médard had reportedly refused to carry out orders to have him killed back in 1988. In 1994–95, Aristide relied on them to supervise the transition from the army into the police. This role gave them formidable (and fateful) influence over events to come. Like everyone else in his position, Toussaint immediately became the object of careful US attention. If the US was unable to block the demobilization of the army, they could at least make sure that Aristide had little success in winning over reliable recruits among the force that was intended to replace it. Officers suspected of fidelity to Lavalas were routinely demonized as untrustworthy in public (and just as routinely wooed by representatives of the CIA, in private). Laura Flynn was Director of International Relations for the Aristide Foundation for Democracy in the late 1990s and remembers that this was a major US priority all through the decade that began in 1994:

> It was part of a consistent pattern. Whenever Aristide or his advisors tried to develop a working relationship with a member of the former military, or with anyone who might have influence among the security forces, the US or its proxies would immediately denounce these people as unreliable, if not as guilty of human rights abuses or drug offences. This was the standard operating procedure, from the false accusation of Aristide's interior minister Mondesir Beaubrun for the murder of the FRAPH leader Mireille Durocher-Bertin in March 1995 all the way through to the dismissal of Oriel Jean in 2003.[135]

Much to Aristide's horror, meanwhile, the US adamantly refused to disarm the remaining members of the FAdH and FRAPH, who took their weapons with them into an embittered retirement.[136] "US failure to disarm the paramilitary squads is absolutely disquieting," complained a UN official in late 1994.[137] According to troops interviewed by Brian Concannon in 1995, US officials "repeatedly refused to authorize operations to confiscate large caches of weapons, even though soldiers on the ground believed they had the intelligence and capacity to make safe, successful seizures."[138] In spite of a relatively generous severance package and six-month re-training program, it wasn't long before some of them started to use their weapons against the regime that had cost them their jobs. According to the programme's director, only 8 percent of the

4,500 soldiers who enrolled in the re-training programmes were able to find alternative jobs after graduation.[139] The most substantial study to date makes plain that US "efforts to disarm the paramilitary forces were never serious," and as US troops withdrew in 1995 "not only did the traditional political violence continue but random crime, a new phenomenon in Haiti, appeared on the scene. Paramilitaries began inciting street violence in an effort to undermine social order with the hope of creating political chaos."[140] Earlier that year Jane Regan noted that despite US assertions to the contrary, "The reality on the ground is that both FAdH and FRAPH forces remain armed and present in virtually every community across the country."[141]

By the summer of 1996 Préval's officials had already accumulated a mass of evidence related to "the involvement of former members of the armed forces in recent assassination plots, robberies, kidnappings and other crimes." On 16 July 1996 Préval arrested Jean-Claude Duvalier's army chief of staff ex-general Claude Raymond and three associates (political allies of ex-general Prosper Avril and Hubert de Ronceray) and charged them with committing "terrorist acts in the framework of a process to destabilize public authority and order." Another former soldier, André-Pierre Armand, was shot and killed by his co-conspirators three days after he exposed "a plot to destabilize the Government" that entailed the assassinations of Aristide and Préval.[142] A further twenty dissident ex-soldiers were arrested the following month, and on 18 August a group of around 30 of their colleagues responded with an open assault on the PNH headquarters in Port-au-Prince. Préval understood what was going on perfectly well. "The military are instruments of political destabilization," he told reporters in August 1996, "but behind them you will find the politicians who are pulling the strings, and the people who are really committing these actions: the economic sector."[143] "We are living in a moment when many demons have been set loose," Bob Manuel warned in December 1997, referring to "plots that have both a national and international dimension," perpetrated by "all sorts of old interests who are against democracy."[144] (Little had changed by the summer of 2000, when as we will see, new plans for another coup took shape around the "Ecuadorian" PNH commander Guy Philippe. A few months after Philippe's second major attempt at a coup finally succeeded, in February 2004, officers loyal to the elected government told an American human rights delegation that "almost all high command offices throughout Haiti are [now] held by former FAdH soldiers," that "almost all municipal police chiefs are former soldiers as well" and that only former soldiers were considered for promotion by the post-coup police chief Léon Charles.[145] Over time and under intense pressure, Patrick Elie observed in December 2005, the PNH started "more and more toward behaving like the old army. The corruption seeped in slowly and now, especially after 29 February 2004, what we see is the militarization of the police. If you've been around the city, you see that most police that you meet are armed with war-type weapons: assault rifles, battle rifles, and this sort of thing. It is truly a police that has its own people as the enemy."[146])

In the third place, the conditions in which the new policemen were required to work were almost guaranteed either to demoralize or corrupt them. In a substantial study published in the *New York Times* magazine in May 1997, Elizabeth Rubin explained that so long as "the army ran the criminal-justice system there [had been] no need for time-consuming tasks like gathering evidence, securing a crime scene, collecting testimony. When the military brought in a suspect, he was presumed guilty. No questions asked." An investigative model of justice in which the "burden of proof is on the accusers not the accused," Rubin continues, remained "a revolutionary idea in Haiti." There was never any chance that this idea would simply catch on overnight.[147] Most of the new policemen were rushed through an inadequate four-month training programme. "Many did not know how to drive, let alone handle a weapon or conduct investigations, and were thrust into the streets with no supervision, little or no equipment and no experienced officers to show them the ropes. Their job was made even more precarious by the fact that they were threatened by thugs of the old regime whom the American troops had failed to disarm." Armed only with .38 revolvers, PNH officers were generally reluctant to take on gangs of ex-soldiers armed with automatic weapons. Between July and September 1996 at least eight PNH officers were murdered, leaving a substantial portion of the force "so undermined and demoralized by their own resourcelessness, the deaths of their colleagues and the debilitated prosecutorial process that they are beginning to adopt a policy of equally unworkable extremes: free the criminals or execute them."[148] Others found it simpler to fall into the more familiar patterns established by their Macoute predecessors, and turned the culture of impunity to their own advantage. As early as December 1995 the *New York Times* noted that in poor neighborhoods like Cité Soleil, "general enthusiasm for the new force appears to be waning as signs of arbitrary behavior by officers have increased."[149] In

January 1997 Human Rights Watch attributed at least forty-six extra-judicial killings to the PNH in its first eighteen months of operation, including the summary execution of six men in Cité Soleil on 6 March 1996.[150] Systematic police extortion and intimidation led many communities to re-establish vigilante groups in self-defense.

In October 1998 Préval's security minister Bob Manuel admitted that the process of creating a viable police force from scratch was turning out to be a "nightmare."[151] By November 1999, around 1000 of the original 5300 members of the force had been dismissed for corruption or human rights abuses, and recruitment of sufficient numbers of reliable officers at a time when the amount of drug-related money passing through Haiti in any given year may have been something like "three or four times the total judicial/police budget" proved an impossible task.[152] The viability of the PNH was further compromised by the proliferation of new private security companies, some of which were run by leading police officers themselves (including both Aristide's Dany Toussaint and Préval's Pierre Denizé). As Charles Lane observed in September 1997, Denizé's company "Cobra provides armed protection to those with enough money to pay," and its "financial success depends upon a public perception that the Police can't do their job fully – which is precisely the perception that Denizé is supposed to be eradicating." Rather than reduce the obvious conflict of interest, the lack of viable alternatives led Préval's government to hire Cobra to guard the national telephone company.[153] In the decade that followed 1994, few things were to play more helpfully into the hands of the elite than this fragmentation and quasi-privatization of Haiti's security forces.

A fourth, more contingent but no less decisive factor also helped the elite to divide and rule the new security network – the intrusion of petty factional interests. After leading the interim police force in 1995, Dany Toussaint left the PNH in 1996 and a new security team took over, led by Préval loyalists Bob Manuel and Pierre Denizé. Préval integrated all of the various security forces under a single command structure – and provoked some predictable resistances in the process. Dany Toussaint, however, did not fade away in retirement. "After being the interim police chief," explains Frantz Gabriel (a well-connected member of Aristide's presidential security unit), "Dany had quite a lot of influence on many of the ex-military commanders in the PNH. Many ordinary policemen were afraid of him because of his influence with the ex-military."[154] Toussaint spent the last years of the decade building up his network of contacts through his successful police supplies and private security company

("Dany King"), and thanks in large part to his iconic role as Aristide's bodyguard in 1991 was able to cultivate a small but vocal group of supporters in the slums of Port-au-Prince – and, by all accounts, among the growing number of drug-runners in the PNH. Over the course of 1999, tensions between the Manuel and Toussaint factions within the police grew more intense and more violent, and contributed to lasting divisions within the broader Lavalas movement. In October 1999 Manuel's close friend ex-colonel Jean Lamy was mysteriously assassinated, and Manuel himself fled into exile.[155] In a biting editorial on 19 October 1999, Radio-Inter's Jean Dominique sent a prescient warning to Aristide, to beware of Toussaint's "ambitions," his ability and his willingness "to pay and arm his followers."[156] Although the details are likely to remain sketchy, the in-fighting between Toussaint first with Manuel and Do-minique and then with other factions within Lavalas provided the movement's enemies with endless possibilities for infiltration. At some point in the late 1990s, it seems they managed to win Toussaint and some of his associates over to their cause. Writing in early 2002, Andrew Reding surveyed the damage that his maneuvering had done to Fanmi Lavalas and concluded that "as long as Toussaint remains untouchable, no one is really safe."[157]

In spite of the in-fighting and cronyism that had begun to weaken Lavalas, when Préval's first administration drew to a close in 2000 the political situation in Haiti was clearer than it had been at any stage since 1986. The confusing tangle of opportunistic alliances that complicated matters in 1990–91 and again in 1994–95 had for the most part been resolved into relatively straight lines. Most members of the political class, including ex-Duvalierists and ex-putschists as well as the OPL, Evans Paul and other ex-social democrats, were now united in support of a pro-US, pro-army coalition that called itself the Democratic Convergence. Most of their allies from Haiti's "civil society" – industrialists, bankers, importers, media leaders, intellectuals, NGO administrators – were soon to band together to oppose Lavalas in another US-funded umbrella group, dubbed the Group of 184. The Church hierarchy had long since turned its back on the *ti legliz*, which found themselves facing increasingly hostile competition from many hundreds of new aggressively anti-Catholic and generally US-funded sects.[158] Lavalas was no longer an informal and eclectic movement that could include just about anyone opposed to Duvalier. Led by the Fanmi Lavalas organization, it had become a relatively disciplined movement, one capable of winning and retaining political power at all levels of government. Already beset by opportunists and demonized by the elite, the organization was far from perfect, but as a mechanism for popular political empowerment it has no rival in the whole of Haiti's history.

The essential question was now exposed for all to see: to move forward with Lavalas, or to retreat with the army? In the elections that decided on Préval's successor, the great majority of the Haitian people made one choice but the elite made another.

3

2000–2001: Aristide and the Crisis of Democracy

"I think, unfortunately, that the last ten years were all about Aristide. It was all about making apologies for his mistakes, excuses for his violations, and compensating, accommodating his pathological behavior, quite frankly. He's not a typical Haitian, thank God"
(Roger Noriega, US Assistant Secretary of State, 1 March 2004).[1]

Aristide was elected president for the first time in 1990 and for a second time in 2000. On both occasions he won a clear and decisive mandate. The circumstances of these two elections, however, were very different.

In 1990, Aristide was backed by an informal and eclectic coalition that included peasant organizations and the urban poor, together with progressive members of the church and the liberal elite. This fragile alliance held together only briefly, and for partly negative reasons: although it was his popularity with the poor that won the election, the result was embraced by some members of the political class less in order to launch a distinctive legislative programme than as an opportunity to limit the stifling influence of the Duvalierists and the Macoutes. Some elite members of this original coalition then acquiesced in the September 1991 overthrow of Aristide's government, once it became clear that it posed a modest but genuine threat to the status quo. Many more of them later came actively to oppose both Aristide and Préval, once it became still more clear that the enduring popularity of the Lavalassians threatened to limit their own political influence.

The legislative elections of 2000, by contrast, were won by a relatively disciplined and united organization, Fanmi Lavalas, with a clear political profile and programme. The electoral mandate was not simply unambiguous but overwhelming. For the first time, a Lavalas administration was poised to take office with a workable majority in parliament, and *without* an extra-parliamentary army that might get in its way. For the first time in Haitian history, a political organization had emerged that, somewhat like the ANC in South Africa, could plausibly present itself as the natural party of popular government. For members of the traditional elite, including erstwhile members of the early anti-Duvalier coalition, this development was nothing short of catastrophic. It was no longer possible to deny the fact that so long as Aristide was around, Lavalas would remain in power for the foreseeable future. Despondent opponents of Fanmi Lavalas told journalist Venel Remarais that they expected it to remain the dominant party "for the next sixty years."[2]

The year 2000, in other words, is the pivotal moment of the Lavalas political sequence to date. It's the year that Aristide was finally in a position to harness his principles and popularity to a systematic program of significant social change. It's also the year that it became clear to the enemies of the Lavalas movement that narrow parliamentary maneuverings would no longer suffice to divide and divert it. By 2000, Aristide's opponents both in Haiti and abroad realized they needed to develop a new and more active program of destabilization and counter-mobilization. In keeping with a familiar formula, this program included four distinct though mutually reinforcing components: (a) the preparation, on the model of Nicaragua's Contras, of a force for paramilitary intervention so as to create a climate of fear and insecurity and undermine government authority, obliging it to take costly measures of self-defense; (b) intensified forms of economic pressure and assault, so as to bankrupt the government and limit its capacity to deliver on its promises to alleviate poverty and inequality; (c) the recruitment of suitably "pluralist" representatives of the business sector and civil society, including members of internationally validated non-governmental organizations, which might be presented as a legitimate opposition to the government; (d) the management of a media disinformation campaign to characterize the government as corrupt, authoritarian and undemocratic. All of these measures were designed to provoke the government or at least some of its more frustrated supporters into responding in ways that might plausibly be presented as brutal and dictatorial, which might then recruit new members to the "democratic" opposition and motivate new forms of "popular" protest, in turn soliciting renewed bursts of "brutality." Once the cycle started to spiral out of control, the foreign allies of the local elite would get their chance to step in and save the day.

As it happened, Lavalas resistance was strong enough to keep them waiting for four long years.

THE MAY 2000 ELECTIONS

The May 2000 legislative elections were arguably the most remarkable exercise in representative democracy in Haiti to date. Since for most Haitians to cast a vote involves considerable effort and sacrifice, legislative elections rarely solicit a large turnout, compared to presidential elections (which the IC prefers to schedule separately, to avoid giving a popular president an "unfair" parliamentary advantage). Even in 1990/91 only around a quarter of those who participated in the presidential election voted in the legislative elections as well. But despite massive logistical challenges and a lack of promised support from the OAS and the foreign donors, unprecedented numbers of people (in excess of 4 million) were registered to vote and unprecedented numbers of polling stations were provided for them to cast their ballots. As the most comprehensive study of the elections concluded, "free, fair and peaceful elections" were held after "months of struggle and intimidation." Turnout was nearly on a par with the presidential election of December 1990, estimated at around 65 percent.[3] At many polling stations, crowds waited patiently over several hours to make their choice. The day after the election, OAS spokeswoman Mary Durran confirmed that "we observed no major (voting) irregularities," and as CNN reported, even the US government "congratulated Haiti on the elections" and "praised the people of Haiti for holding legislative and local elections 'in a pervasive atmosphere of non-violence and high voter participation.'"[4]

That was before the results came in. The 1995 elections had already "completely discredited the so-called traditional political parties – especially those that collaborated with the military regime between 1991 and 1994 – and rendered them inconsequential in Haitian politics."[5] In 2000, members of the original Lavalas coalition who had turned against Aristide suffered the same fate. Pierre-Charles' OPL was utterly wiped out, winning just a single seat in the chamber of Deputies. Fanmi Lavalas won overwhelming majorities at both the local and national levels of government. Once all the votes had been counted (including the second-round ballots that were held in July), Aristide's organization had won 89 of 115 mayoral positions, 72 of 83 seats in the chamber of Deputies and 18 of the 19 Senate positions contested. If Haitian elections were run according to a first-past-the-post system like those in the US or UK then in May 2000 Fanmi Lavalas would have won more than 95 percent of the seats in both houses of parliament.

According to Charles Arthur – one of FL's most forceful critics – FL won these elections because it was the only party to propose a detailed and "coherent political program" (improvements in infrastructure, health and education, investment in micro-financing and peasant cooperatives) and to wage an active campaign based on the "mobilizing efforts of young party activists across the country."[6] It was also now the only party that could benefit from Aristide's largely undiminished popularity among the poor. Apart from the MPP (which turned out several thousand people for an anti-FL rally at Hinche in September 2000), none of the political groups or parties opposed to Lavalas in 2000 made any effort to organize mass meetings or demonstrations.[7] If Haitian elections were run according to a first-past-the-post system like those used in the US or the UK then in May 2000 Fanmi Lavalas would have won more than 95 percent of the seats in both houses of parliament.

No more than the election victory of 1990, such an outcome was not at all part of the IC's plan for Haitian democracy. For obvious reasons, both the domestic elite and its foreign patrons have a vested interest in the weakness of the state and the instability of its government. A weak government means minimal taxes or tariffs, minimal regulations, minimal interference in the exploitation of labor, trade or contraband. "As soon as any poor country begins to win a struggle for real autonomy," notes FL deputy Ramilus Bolivar, "the imperial nations immediately do everything they can to undermine it."[8] In 2000, in the last months of the Clinton administration, US policy-makers were entitled to worry that all the good work they had accomplished in 1993–94 might now start to come unstuck.

In the immediate aftermath of their defeat, local anti-Aristide politicians could do little more than wring their hands in the face of what they denounced as an "electoral coup d'état." The OPL immediately called for the "entire electoral process to be annulled,"[9] and CD spokesman Professor Micha Gaillard declared that "We will never, ever accept the results of these elections."[10] But nor did he need to: since the results were obviously unacceptable, France and the US never accepted them either. In what must rank as one of the most impressive and improbable propaganda exercises in contemporary politics, an alliance of Aristide's foreign and domestic enemies soon managed to persuade most of the independent media to present the government elected in 2000 as undemocratic and illegitimate. The awkward fact that this government had an electoral mandate incomparably more powerful than that enjoyed by leaders like Bush or Chirac was never allowed to interfere with the essential point: in 2000 as in 1990, the Haitian people had again misunderstood the true meaning of democracy. They had failed to choose the leader that the great powers had chosen for them. A few years down the line, US Assistant Secretary of State Roger Noriega would deride May 2000 as a "farcical electoral exercise."[11] By that stage, international dismissal of this farce had become one of the single most insistent features of mainstream reporting on Haitian politics – nothing was to become more common in Reuters and Associated Press dispatches during the years running up to the 2004 coup than recognition of the fact that Aristide's country had "failed to hold credible elections."[12]

Since the May 2000 elections confirmed that there was no short-term chance of defeating FL at the polls, the decision to cast doubt on their credibility was indeed the opposition's only alternative option. A minor technical complaint made by observers from the US-sponsored Organization of American States (OAS) provided the pretext. Like every other observer, the OAS actually described the May 2000 elections as "a great success for the Haitian population, which turned out in large and orderly numbers to choose both their local and national governments." An estimated "60 percent of registered voters went to the polls," and "very few incidents" of either violence or fraud were reported. "Voters were able to cast their ballots free of pressure and intimidation," and "most voters were able to find their polling stations with relative ease."[13] Even the staunchly anti-Lavalas Center for International Policy agreed that the May 2000 elections were Haiti's "best so far."[14] If OAS spokesman Orlando Marville subsequently characterized the elections as "flawed," in a letter of 2 June, it wasn't because he disputed the fairness of the vote or the overwhelming clarity of its result but because, once the Lavalas victories were recorded, he claimed that the methodology which Haiti's Provisional Electoral Council (CEP) had "used to calculate the vote percentages for Senate candidates is not correct."[15]

Since the subsequent political impact of this objection would be hard to overstate, it's worth explaining what it amounted to. Unlike first-past-the-post electoral systems, in Haiti a candidate needs to gain an absolute majority (50 percent + 1) of the votes cast in order to win a seat in a single round of voting. Because OPL obstruction had served to cancel the 1997 legislative elections, in 2000 an unusually large number of Senate seats were contested – two (and in one case three) for each department. As in 1990 and 1995, the CEP put all the candidates for a given department on a single ballot, and electors were free to pick the two (or three) candidates of their choice. However, because many voters preferred to vote for only one candidate, and because some other voters spoiled part of their ballot,

there was no mathematically perfect way of calculating absolute majorities for any given seat. The CEP decided to simplify and resolve the issue
by counting only the actual votes cast for the top four candidates in each
departmental district (or the top six, in the department contesting three
seats). "This practice followed the precedents of the 1990 and 1995
elections," Concannon points out, and "in those two contests, no
candidate complained about the calculation method, nor did the OAS
observers," who met regularly with the CEP all through the 2000 pre-
election period.[16] By counting the votes this way, the CEP converted
several large Lavalas pluralities into majorities. (In the North-East department, to take one of the examples least favorable to Lavalas, a total of
132,613 votes were cast for two Senate seats. If all twelve candidates' votes
were counted, 33,154 votes would be needed to win a seat on the first
round, and in that case, in 2000 both seats would have had to be decided
in a run-off. But with only the top four candidates' votes counted, FL
candidates went through with comfortable majorities, even though they
had garnered only 32,969 and 30,736 votes respectively; their closest rival
polled less than 16,000.) Calculated by this method, Lavalas candidates
won 16 of the 19 contested Senate seats in the first round of voting, taking
an average 74 percent of the vote.[17] The OAS conceded that "since one
political party [Fanmi Lavalas] won most of the elections by a substantial
margin, it is unlikely that the majority of the final outcomes in local
elections have been affected" by the calculation method, but it argued
that if all the votes were counted, eight of the Senate contests should still
have gone to a second round of voting.[18] Seven of these contests had been
won by FL candidates. Leading members of FL came under immediate
pressure to encourage the CEP to revise their procedures. Although all
seven of these FL senators reluctantly agreed to step down a couple of
months after Aristide's inauguration in 2001, the refusal to buckle
immediately to this pressure is regularly cited as the single most important
tactical error of Aristide's later political career.

The CEP, however, is an independent institution. A crucial component of Haiti's 1987 constitution, the CEP is a sovereign body which acts
as the exclusive and final arbiter in all electoral matters. From the day it
was established, its autonomy and then its very existence came under
attack by Namphy and the Duvalierists.[19] Politicians like Préval or
Aristide have no authority to interfere in its operation, and in any case
the 2000 CEP included no FL representatives. The CEP made its
decision. Its head, Léon Manus, responded angrily to Marville's demand.
He accused the OAS of "reckless" interference, of trying to "induce the

Haitian people to error and to discredit the CEP in the eyes of the nation."[20] The OAS had itself been closely involved in the development of the vote-counting protocol in the months leading up to the election, and had made no complaints. There is no reason to believe that the balance of power in the Senate would have been any different whatever method was used. The results were consistent both with the undisputed returns registered in the Chamber of Deputies ballot held at the same time and with a US-commissioned Gallup poll taken in October 2000, to say nothing of Aristide's own election as president in November 2000.

Nevertheless, two weeks after his initial response to Marville, on 16 June Léon Manus was abruptly whisked out of the country, courtesy of the US embassy. Once safely in the US, Manus had a mysterious change of heart. In a declaration dated 21 June, he confessed that after "reflection and study" he had come to realize the counting method he had previously approved was incorrect. He now denied the validity of the results *tout court*, claiming they were tainted by "massive electoral fraud." He also gave a compelling reason for his initial denial of these facts: Préval and Aristide had both pushed him to endorse the results, he said, and unless he approved their immediate publication, had threatened to "engulf the capital and provincial cities in fire and blood, destroying everything in their path."[21] (Two and a half years later, Manus would reappear among the fifty or so anti-Aristide luminaries and IRI-grantees who met to launch the rightwing "Group of 184" in Santo Domingo.[22]) Why exactly a government that was already guaranteed an overwhelming parliamentary majority might want thus to "snatch defeat from the jaws of victory" was left unexplained. It didn't matter. In the eyes of the independent and international press the elections were forever "tainted" and "flawed," and the parties that had fared so dismally at the polls now had the crucial argument they needed in order to re-brand themselves as the genuine democratic opposition to dictatorship. It wouldn't be long before newspapers like the *New York Times* had become so used to this interpretation of May 2000 that they could even explain rising political tensions in Haiti as a result of the startling fact that "Aristide had failed to compromise with his opponents and has ruled by decree since disputed elections in 2000."[23]

Meanwhile the dictator in question went ahead and won his own second mandate in the presidential elections held in November 2000. Many of the other contestants boycotted a ballot they had no chance of winning, and Aristide was returned with 92 percent of the votes cast. Once again there was a minimum of violence and fraud, and voter turnout was again estimated (by the International Coalition of Independent Observers and thousands of volunteers from the KOZEPEP peasant organization) at around 60 percent – though much less, of course, by members of the opposition.[24] Lavalas candidates had now won three landslide presidential elections in a row. Fonkoze's Anne Hastings was in Port-au-Prince in November 2000, and was struck above all by the "tremendous energy that went into cleaning up the city before election day. It was as if everybody was mobilized, everywhere, to get rid of all the trash, to make everything spotless. There was a lot of excitement about Aristide's return."[25]

THE COST OF VICTORY

Some of this initial excitement wore off rather quickly. US foreign policy makers have long known, of course, that the most efficient means of containing even limited forms of popular empowerment are economic. Like most of the other components of the anti-Lavalas campaign, in 2001 these means would involve less a break with than a refinement of Cold War tactics: back in the 1970s the CIA already knew that "the incredibly low standard of living and the backwardness of the Haitian masses work against communist exploitation, in that most Haitians are so completely downtrodden as to be politically inert."[26] The downtreading had already increased dramatically all through the 1990s, starting with the 1991–94 embargo, and some of the desired inertia followed in due course. Lavalas was contained, first and foremost, by one of the most concerted campaigns of deliberate impoverishment of recent years. By 2003, annual per capita incomes in Haiti had fallen to less than half of those of Bolivia, Latin America's next poorest country.[27]

Rather like the Palestinians when they voted for an inappropriate party in January 2006, the Haitian people were straight away forced to pay a high price for their failure to elect a suitably moderate and broad-based government. The US seized on the OAS accusation of fraudulent elections to justify a crippling embargo on all further foreign aid. The US hadn't seemed particularly concerned about democratic legitimacy when it funneled millions of dollars to the Duvaliers and the juntas which followed them (to say nothing of the much larger sums it continues to invest in the authoritarian regimes of countries like Saudi Arabia, Pakistan or Colombia). In the summer of 2000, however, democratic legitimacy quickly rose to the top of the agenda, and by the time Jesse Helms and Benjamin Gilman described Aristide's "sham" election in November as "a tragic day in Haiti's long and troubled quest for pluralism and representative democracy" they were only echoing a well-established motif.[28] During the last years of Préval's administration, levels of international aid had already dropped to a fraction of 1995 levels, and just weeks before the May 2000 vote, Helms managed to overcome State Department resistance and chop $30 million in US aid after Préval's government had the audacity to accuse a US-owned rice company of fraud.[29] But after May, *all* US aid to the Haitian government was suspended, and the new US ambassador, Dean Curran, was instructed to tell Aristide on the eve of his inauguration that the US would not normalize relations until the "problems with the May elections are resolved."[30] A year into Aristide's second administration – and long after Aristide had duly resolved these "problems" – USAID official Sharon Bean admitted to Timothy Pershing and other journalists that Aristide's administration "would never receive a dime of American aid."[31] (USAID continued, meanwhile, to funnel considerable sums of money to suitably complicit NGOs: an average of $68 million a year from 2000 to 2003.) In April 2001, the US further blocked the release of $145 million in previously agreed loans from the Inter-American Development Bank, and of another $470 million scheduled for the following years. Incredibly, the IDB also required the FL government to continue paying millions of dollars in interest on some of these frozen loans, even though it could make no use of the money it had "borrowed" and had already set aside for approved investments in health, education and infrastructure.[32] As lawyer Marguerite Laurent notes, all this was in "total violation of these international lending agencies' charters, which commit them to provide financing for social and economic development irrespective of the political character of the requesting government."[33] The prominent macro-economist Jeffrey Sachs was indignant. "When I spoke with President Aristide in 2001, he laid out a very sensible, responsible economic vision and wanted to work with the Inter-American Development Bank, the International Monetary Fund, and the World Bank. Thus, I was particularly shocked to come back to Washington to find a US-imposed freeze on all of those institutions."[34]

It would be hard to exaggerate the impact of these measures. Haiti's profound dependency on foreign assistance gives its donors massive if not irresistible leverage. Back in 1995 the Haitian government had received close to $600 million in aid; by 2003 the total government budget had been reduced to the risible sum of just $300 million. To put this in context, this amount is roughly equal to the municipal budget of a small

US city with around 100,000 inhabitants; the 2007 municipal budget for New York City was $52 billion. Aristide's $300 million had to cover, among other things, the annual $60 million payment on the national debt, 45 percent of which was incurred by the Duvalier dictatorships.[35] The effect of the US aid embargo, in short, was to slice Aristide's minuscule spending-power roughly in half. The cuts didn't just interrupt the provision of basic public services. As Sachs explains, the US embargo further drained Haiti's government "of foreign exchange reserves. As Aristide continued to service the debts to the international institutions, the exchange rate collapsed, the inflation rose, and the economy collapsed – and that was the deliberate result of the strangulation of aid."[36] Public expenditure was further constrained by another round of agreements reached with the IMF before Aristide himself came to power, on 6 November 2000. New public sector investment became a practical impossibility. Among other things, the IMF obliged Aristide's government to reduce the subsidies it provided for sensitive commodities like fuel, contributing to a 40 percent rise in the consumer price index during 2002–03.[37] In spite of this increase in the cost of living, Michel Chossudovsky notes, the IMF continued to require cuts in public sector wages (including those paid to teachers and health workers), as a means of "controlling inflationary pressures."[38]

Few governments could survive such sustained financial assault. The combined effect of these measures was to overwhelm an already shattered economy. Haiti's gross domestic product fell from $4 billion in 1999 to just $2.9 billion in 2003. From a level of around $810 in 1980 (measured in constant US dollars for the year 2000), by 2000 GDP per capita income had fallen to just $468, bottoming out at $425 in 2004.[39] In its review of the socioeconomic situation in 2002, the United Nations Development Programme concluded that mass destitution had become so severe "Haiti will need more than 50 years, or the equivalent of two generations, to recover from its current state if the process of recovery were to start now."[40] Two months before the 2004 coup, a survey of economic indicators carried out by Oxfam, Christian Aid and several other NGOs came to the conclusion that "at the close of 2003, Haiti is living in a crisis without precedent."[41]

Before he took office, in February 2001, Aristide's government was already bankrupt and so long as the aid embargo lasted all meaningful control over the economy was out of its hands.

All that Aristide's enemies in the US now had to do in order to ensure that this bankruptcy remained permanent was to make the resumption of international aid depend upon a negotiated settlement with the parties that Fanmi Lavalas had virtually wiped out in the last elections. During his first months in office Aristide had little choice but to agree to most of the compromises demanded by his opponents since their defeat the previous May: he accepted resignations from the winners of the disputed Senate seats, approved the participation of several anti-Lavalas politicians (notably Marc Bazin and Stanley Théard) in his new government, agreed to convene a new and more opposition-friendly CEP and to hold another round of legislative elections several years ahead of schedule. In the spring of 2001, OAS secretary general César Gaviria promised FL negotiator Jonas Petit an end to the embargo in return for these concessions.[42]

As it turned out, the embargo was never lifted. Arguably, by trying to negotiate with the opposition Aristide made a serious mistake. Negotiation was never its real purpose.

THE DEMOCRATIC OPPOSITION

The actual strategic function of the political opposition to Fanmi Lavalas soon became clear enough. It was intended to extract, through interminable discussion, the maximum number of crippling concessions without ever yielding on an essential and non-negotiable goal: the removal of Aristide's government by any means necessary. All of the losers of May 2000 – former allies like ex-communist Gérard Pierre-Charles, ex-Lavalassian Paul Denis, ex-social democrat Serge Gilles and ex-anti-Duvalierist Evans Paul, as well as Duvalierists, rightwing evangelicals and conservative business leaders – had a common interest in getting rid of the winner. Almost as soon as the May results were announced, the leaders of most of the vanquished parties formed a loose made-for-media coalition called the *Convergence Démocratique* (CD).[43] As we shall see, this alliance of far-right and ex-far-left opportunists was held together by something rather more forceful than simply a shared hatred of Aristide. Devised and supervised by the most reactionary wing of the US foreign policy establishment, the CD's strategy was based on recognition of a single and self-evident principle: the futility of electoral politics so long as Aristide's FL remained an organized and coherent force. With a touch of poetry, CD leaders Evans Paul and Gérard Pierre-Charles named their alternative *option zéro*.

"At every turn," notes Amy Wilentz, this "US-backed opposition tried to bring political life under Aristide to a halt."[44] The US used its leverage in the OAS to ensure that any solution to the so-called electoral crisis would depend on the CD's approval, thereby handing a minority group supported by a small fraction of the population an effective veto over the elected government.[45] Between June 2000 and February 2004, the Democratic Convergence would reject each and every FL offer of new elections and of new forms of power-sharing. Max Blumenthal estimates that by the end of its second year in existence, the Democratic Convergence had already rejected "over twenty internationally sanctioned power sharing agreements."[46] In 2003, Evans Paul tried to get at the heart of the problem. "It will be difficult to create the peaceful conditions necessary for the holding of credible elections in the country with Jean-Bertrand Aristide in power," he said, since as far as the opposition was concerned "the electoral experiences with Aristide have all proven disastrous."[47] When the negotiations duly entered their terminal phase in early February 2004, Evans Paul indicated with perfect frankness what had been at stake all along: the only thing that the opposition was "willing to negotiate [is] the door through which Aristide will leave the palace – the front door or the back door."[48]

Unconditional and unwavering intransigence is the defining feature of the civilian opposition to Lavalas during Aristide's second administration. As we have seen, most of the leading figures in the CD were already well versed in the ways of obstruction long before Aristide took office. Refusal to compromise with the Préval government had become the sole *raison d'être* of Pierre-Charles' OPL in the years leading up to its annihilation in the 2000 ballot. When Aristide invited members of the CD to join his new government in early 2001, they refused point blank.[49] When in November 2002 he agreed to name opposition members to a new CEP, they refused to take their seats; when he then agreed to give them a majority of seats on the CEP, they refused this as well. Again and again, FL would propose a date for new elections and the CD would reject it. In each case, the basic strategy was almost comically straightforward: *option zéro* would always require precisely those demands that even the most pliable government couldn't possibly meet. In the aftermath of May 2000, these included an insistence on the immediate resignation of Préval's administration, the formation of an interim government of "national unity," the nomination of a new CEP, and the arrangement of a new set of legislative elections.[50] In January 2001 the CD insisted that it be able to nominate one of its own members as prime minister, that this prime minister be granted the authority to govern by decree, and that Aristide effectively stand down to allow a three-member presidential council to act as head of state in his place.[51] Just before Aristide's own inauguration on 7 February 2001, the opposition's demands – greatly strengthened, the previous month, by the fateful selection of George W. Bush as US president – were reformulated in a ten-point plan that met with the enthusiastic approval of French and American diplomats. Perusal of just a few of these points sheds a little light on what FL was up against. Point two refers to "the ten years (1991–2001) during which the Lavalas government has choked Haiti's national economy, undermined democracy, and imposed the rule of a single political party." Point three derides the elections of 1997 and 2000 as fraudulent and illegal. Point four notes the "full adhesion of the Haitian population to the efforts undertaken by Convergence Démocratique." Point eight declares a refusal to cooperate with "any attempt to inaugurate the illegal and illegitimate presidency of Jean-Bertrand Aristide," and point nine announces a plan to establish an alternative provisional government.[52]

With a flair for the absurd that was to characterize every stage of option zero, on the same day that Aristide was sworn in as president the CD duly went ahead with the inauguration of this parallel government, under the democratic leadership of ex-human-rights lawyer Gérard Gourgue. Evans Paul compared the establishment of Gourgue's administration to "loading a cannon" in the ongoing battle with Aristide.[53] After issuing strident calls for the re-establishment of the army and pretending to exist for a few months, it quietly faded away later that spring. It is perhaps a sign of how extreme things had become that in the months before the formation of Aristide's administration even his old opponent Marc Bazin, the very incarnation of traditional US interests in Haiti, came to side with FL against the "unreasonable" and "counterproductive" position of the CD.[54]

The CD negotiators, however, had little incentive to be reasonable. When thirty-four North and South American heads of state met at a major summit in Québec two months after the inauguration of Gourgue's parallel government they agreed on a statement that singled out FL as solely responsible for the failure "to end the deadlock in negotiations with opposition parties that followed last years' elections, which were widely condemned as flawed." A BBC report on the summit went on to acknowledge that "The presence of Mr. Aristide at the summit has been an embarrassment to some of the leaders, who agreed that only democratic countries would be included in the [new] Free Trade Zone of the Americas" that the summit was intended to establish.[55]

On the first anniversary of Aristide's administration CD spokesman Paul Denis was relieved to find that Roger Noriega, Otto Reich and their colleagues in the Bush administration remained "very receptive to the views of the Convergence."[56] Haiti's dependence on foreign aid, relentless diplomatic pressure and appropriate media management ensured that interminable negotiation with Denis and the other Convergence leaders was to remain one of the defining stories of Aristide's whole second term in office. In a rare (and quickly regretted) moment of candor, the OAS official responsible for overseeing these discussions, Luigi Einaudi, explained on Canadian radio the logic behind the CD's approach: the democratic opposition "groups are afraid of elections, because if free and fair elections were to take place in the country, it is certain that the party in power would win."[57] Given such well-founded fears, the CD's basic strategy never changed. It endured right through to the final attempt at a peaceful resolution of the conflict, a proposal officially approved by Colin Powell and Roger Noriega themselves in mid-February 2004. Like previous proposals, this one centred on major and debilitating government concessions: Aristide would have to work with one of his opponents as his prime minister, hold early legislative elections and serve out the remainder of his term with severely limited powers. In keeping with a pattern that became more marked with the passage of time, Aristide accepted the deal immediately and the CD refused it just as immediately, before somehow persuading its imperial patrons to follow suit.

Again and again, the international and independent media would present the FL-CD impasse as a simple deadlock between two equally legitimate and equally stubborn negotiating parties. A November 2003 overview in the *Economist* is typical. After coming to power through elections that "many observers regarded as fraudulent," the *Economist* observed, "Mr. Aristide has been locked in a three-year-long standoff with his domestic political opposition. The two sides have repeatedly failed to come to agreement over when, and how, to conduct new legislative elections. This has stalled critical international financial aid as well as contributed to a breakdown in law and order and an increase in misery in the country, the poorest in the hemisphere."[58] In an article written on the day of Aristide's expulsion in 2004, Jeffrey Sachs was one of few people with access to the mainstream press who recognized what had really happened:

By saying that aid would be frozen until Aristide and the political opposition reached an agreement, the Bush administration provided

Haiti's un-elected opposition with an open-ended veto. Aristide's foes merely had to refuse to bargain in order to plunge Haiti into chaos. That chaos has now come. It is sad to hear rampaging students on BBC and CNN saying that Aristide "lied" because he didn't improve the country's social conditions. Yes, Haiti's economic collapse is fuelling rioting and deaths, but the lies were not Aristide's. The lies came from Washington.[59]

4

2000–2003: Investing in Pluralism

Ti chen gen fòs devan kay mèt li
(A little dog is really brave in front of his master's house).

Back in the autumn of 1994 Clinton's special envoy to Haiti, Lawrence Pezzullo, argued strongly against using the US army to restore Aristide to power. Aristide had "failed politically when he was in there," Pezzullo explained, and he deserved no second chance. Blinded by his popularity among the poor and his overwhelming electoral mandate, he had proved "unwilling to make political compromises to broaden his political base." Rather than pander to the elite's parliamentary representatives, Aristide had preferred to represent the people who elected him. According to Pezzullo, "It was precisely Father Aristide's estrangement from the elected Parliament, coupled with his chilly relationship with business leaders and the military, that led to his overthrow" in 1991.[1]

This wasn't an easy way to account for the first coup, and the revival of a version of this same argument in order to justify a second coup would require considerable dexterity. Nevertheless, this is precisely what the new Washington foreign policy establishment managed to pull off in the early years of this century. Pezzullo himself moved along with the times, and in 2002 was a prominent founder-member of a new conservative think-tank, the aptly named Haiti Democracy Project. Whereas in 1994 Pezzullo had merely argued against helping to restore Aristide to power, in late 2002 he argued in favor of active intervention so as to drive him from office. All of Pezzullo's worst fears had apparently come true. A ruthless Aristide had "used US support to impose a repressive regime that bears a strong resemblance to that of Papa Doc Duvalier, the former dictator of Haiti." He had manipulated Clinton to "destroy the Haitian army, the only public institution in the country," leaving "democracy all but dead." Flushed with the "arrogance that comes from absolute power," Aristide's "sordid regime" had become little more than a parody of the repugnant Somoza dictatorship in Nicaragua. Now that "political repression is rampant" and "Aristide has lost his legitimacy to rule," the only "critical question is what or who would replace Aristide if he could be induced to resign?"[2]

The question was indeed critical. The democratic alternative to Aristide always suffered from one unfortunate limitation: it had no significant links with its own *demos*. All of the innumerable opposition parties combined could scarcely count on 15 percent of the popular vote. When the Convergence Démocratique held its first major conference in January 2001, they announced it might draw up to 20,000 people; Stan Goff, who witnessed the event, noted that a figure of "three hundred would be much closer to the mark."[3] That the main purpose of the democratic opposition was indeed merely to oppose (rather than actually to replace) Aristide is further borne out by the fact that once their nemesis had at last been overthrown, none of the prominent figures in the CD were rewarded with a significant role in the 2004 post-coup government.[4] None of them would fare any better, either, in the next round of presidential elections, in February 2006. Democratic opposition is one thing, the actual running of a client state is occasionally something else. Lacking any significant popular support or domestic political base, without sustained financial and strategic support from abroad the CD could never have existed at all. Happily for the CD, plenty of both kinds of support was on offer, courtesy of Aristide's enemies in Europe and the US. The more the "CD's electoral support plummeted," Concannon notes, the more "its international support skyrocketed."[5]

As we have seen, Clinton's administration (1993–2000) was always profoundly hostile to Aristide. When Clinton was replaced by Bush II, however, this hostility was replaced by nothing less than a genuine hatred. The team of people that Aristide was doomed to deal with during his last three years in Haiti reads like a who's who of reactionary American foreign policy. Jesse Helms' former aide Roger Noriega served as Bush II's Assistant Secretary of State for Western Hemisphere Affairs, after a stint as ambassador to the OAS: as the former US ambassador to El Salvador Robert White said in February 2004, "Roger Noriega has been dedicated to ousting Aristide for many, many years, and now he's in a singularly powerful position to accomplish it."[6] Noriega was assisted by the bitterly anti-Castro and anti-Chávez Cuban-American Otto Juan Reich (Special Representative for Hemispheric Initiatives) and flanked by

Elliot Abrams (National Security Council) and John Negroponte (ambassador to the UN). Among other things, these veterans of the Cold War were the main architects of the 1980s Contra insurgency that eventually overthrew the socialist Sandinista government in Nicaragua – a destabilization campaign that bears an unmistakable resemblance to what happened in Haiti 2000–04. These are people who, as Fatton observes, "would have done anything they could to undermine Aristide."[7] They are people who resented the fact that the good work they had done in Latin America in the 1980s had been partly undone during the flaccid and indulgent 1990s. "The United States had squandered a good deal of its credibility by its support for Aristide during the Clinton years," Roger Noriega told the *New York Times* in January 2006. "The crime is that the Clinton administration supported him as long as it did [. . . They] essentially held his coat while stuffing millions of dollars in it, while he terrorized the opposition."[8]

The new Republican policy makers were not subtle about their priorities. A year and a half into Aristide's second administration Timothy Carney, an influential former US ambassador to Haiti and another founder-member of the Haiti Democracy Project, summed up the prevailing US/elite view with a single "big question." "The big question is whether Aristide is going to understand that he has no future."[9] The outline of an alternative future for Haiti was agreed by US, French and Canadian diplomats in January 2003, if not before, when Noriega's Canadian counterpart Denis Paradis hosted a two-day meeting at Meech Lake. As Paradis would later explain, the consensus reached at Meech Lake was that "The international community wouldn't want to wait for the five-year mandate of President Aristide to run its course through to 2005." Instead "Aristide should go," and the international community should prepare for a new round of humanitarian intervention and military occupation in keeping with its democratic "responsibility to protect" the vulnerable inhabitants of a "failed state."[10]

When they turned their attention to Haiti early in 2001, Roger Noriega and his team inherited the makings of what would soon become a fine Contra-style destabilization force (more on this in the next chapter). More immediately, however, they had a green light to make newly intensive use of the tried and tested tactics of democracy promotion. In Haiti as elsewhere, the main vehicles for delivering the policy were USAID, the International Foundation for Electoral Systems (IFES) and the International Republican Institute (IRI). Altogether, from 1994 to 2002 Washington would contribute some $70 million – a staggering sum by Haitian standards – to organize and "train" an appropriate political opposition to Aristide.[11] Fanmi Lavalas, by contrast, has no regular operating budget at all, and the vast majority of its members are too poor to pay any sort of membership dues; the organization can't even afford to pay for regular office space, let alone provide training for its new recruits.[12]

The political bias of USAID funding is one of the great constants of Haitian politics over the last couple of decades. After helping establish an investor-friendly business environment under Jean-Claude Duvalier, from 1986 until Aristide's election in 1990 US democratization funding supported the various junta governments, along with corporate organizations associated with the elite. Once Aristide came to power in 1991 these organizations continued to receive USAID funds, but the democratization money shifted abruptly away from the government and towards the anti-Lavalas opposition. This anti-Lavalas orientation didn't change when Aristide returned to Haiti in 1994. A decade on, from 2000 to 2003, USAID supplemented its various development projects with a new "Democracy and Governance Program" for Haiti. In the financial year that ended in September 2003, the budget for this program – just one of a number of overlapping US programs dedicated to the promotion of "civil society, the media, human rights organizations and political parties" – exceeded three million dollars. The official description of this program begins with the assumption that "continued deterioration of Haiti's economic, security, and human rights situation can be tied directly to a failure of democratic governance in Haiti." It proposes to remedy this failure by "developing political parties, helping non-governmental organizations resist Haiti's growing trend toward authoritarian rule, and strengthening the independent media."[13] In other words: by giving money to anyone and anything that might criticize and undermine the elected government. A revealing glimpse of USAID priorities is provided by its own description of one of the minor social projects it began funding, in the summer of 2005, to sweeten the pill of "transition" after the removal of that government – a so-called "Play for Peace summer camp." The camp was established in Petit Place Cazeau, a place USAID describes as

> the Port-au-Prince stronghold of Lavalas party presidential candidate Father Gérard Jean-Juste [. . .]. The fruits of these efforts were seen during a recent demonstration attended by 200 people. At the same time that the demonstration was taking place, 300 people were

enjoying the summer camp. It is believed that the camp prevented the demonstration from being larger and giving greater legitimacy to the protesters. The coming weeks will see a deepening of [USAID] activities in Petit Place Cazeau, where events like the summer camp will become increasingly important now that Father Jean-Juste has been arrested. His imprisonment has inflamed pro-Lavalas fires in the area and made him a martyr to some Haitians.[14]

One of USAID's main contractors during the Aristide years was the International Foundation for Electoral Systems (IFES).[15] IFES involvement in Haiti began in 1990, and was scaled back dramatically after Aristide's expulsion in 2004. IFES personnel and priorities overlap to a considerable extent with those of the IRI – the chairman of its board of directors, for instance, William J. Hybl, is also on the board of the International Republican Institute (IRI) and is a close associate of US vice-president Dick Cheney. The main IFES program that ran during Aristide's second administration was a "Civil Society Strengthening Project for Judicial Independence and Justice." In November 2004, investigators from the University of Miami Law School spoke to IFES officials at length about the program. The officials explained that it began sometime around 2001 with a starting budget of around $3.5 million. Its original purpose was "to advocate for the independence of judges from the executive branch via the formation of a range of coalitions from various societal institutions." It organized meetings and seminars to "sensitize" influential civil society groups. High-profile beneficiaries of the program included several of the people who would come to power in the post-coup interim government of 2004–06, in particular justice minister Bernard Gousse. As the Miami Law report explains,

> The premise of IFES' justice program was that President Aristide "controlled everything" and therefore controlled the judges in Haiti in contravention of the constitutional separation of powers. Because the judicial system was corrupt, so went the premise, Aristide must be the most corrupt. IFES initially undertook to form a network of organizations that could concentrate opposition to the perceived corruption of the judiciary by the Aristide government. IFES formed new associations and established relationships with existing ones, making them more cohesive with a formally planned program of "sensitization" – what the administrators called "opening their eyes" to IFES' viewpoint

that Aristide was corrupting the justice system. Through various programs – that included catered meals, accommodations, entertainment, and payment of a cash "per diem" – IFES "sensitized" attendees to the problems with the justice system under Aristide and insisted that they act as a united group for greatest effect.[16]

At the same time, the IFES also helped found and then consolidate a range of suitably receptive professional associations – a Coalition for Reform of the Law and Judiciary, a National Association of Haitian Magistrates, and a Haitian Bar Association. Some of the many other groups sensitized by the IFES included Rosny Desroches' Initiative de la Société Civile, Carlos Hercule's Center Toussaint L'Ouverture pour la Défense des Droits Humains et le Développement, Marylin Allien's La Fondation Héritage pour Haïti, and Marie-Claude Bayard's Association des Industries d'Haïti. IFES officials explained to the Miami Law investigators that they then "used the same formula to establish formal associations of 'private sector' and 'business sector' groups in order to 'provide economic force' to the opposition movement. IFES included a program to 'sensitize' media and journalist groups, and to 'use all the radio stations in Haiti' to publicize Aristide's corruption." Later, IFES extended its reach to include human rights campaigning and student politics. Asked why Aristide didn't simply expel the IFES officials from Haiti, they explained that "IFES was bootstrapped to USAID, and that Aristide had to allow IFES to operate or else he would have had to forego humanitarian and other assistance from USAID. [. . .] The administrators further stated that IFES/USAID workers in Haiti want to take credit for the ouster of Aristide, but cannot 'out of respect for the wishes of the US government.'"[17]

The International Republican Institute (IRI) embraced an almost identical set of tactics and priorities, with a distinctive neo-con twist. A front for establishment interests in the US, the IRI's work in Haiti is characterized by what COHA describes as its "consistent backing for the most regressive, elitist, pro-military factions in Haitian politics and its steadfast alliance with the elite opposition coalitions Group 184 and Democratic Convergence, which from the day of their inception devoted themselves entirely to derailing the administration of President Aristide."[18] The IRI is an affiliate of the Republican Party, and receives much of its funding from the National Endowment for Democracy and USAID. Reagan launched the NED in 1983, and some of the people who helped set it up would later make no secret of the fact that "a lot of what [it] does today was done covertly 25 years ago by the CIA."[19] The

NED funds programs in strategically sensitive countries all over the world. In Latin America its particular obsession is Cuba, of course, though it also plays a vital role in promoting opposition to Hugo Chávez in Venezuela and to Evo Morales in Bolivia. The official aim of the IRI is to provide money, advice and logistical support for political parties and democratic procedures like civic education, campaigning and election monitoring. In April 2002, the IRI revealed something of its actual priorities when it issued a press release applauding the attempted over-throw of Hugo Chávez.[20] In 2003, the Institute's overall budget was $26m; two years later it had risen to $75m.

The IRI campaign to destabilize the Lavalas regime in Haiti began in earnest in 1998 with a $2 million grant, largely from USAID. The program was run by the arch-reactionary Stanley Lucas, a member of one of the large, neo-feudal land-owning families whose dominance was threatened when Duvalier was overthrown. According to witnesses and an Amnesty International report, Stanley Lucas' cousins Leonard and Remy were involved in the Jean-Rabel massacre of 1987, and Lucas himself has longstanding links with rightwing elements in the Haitian military.[21] The day after Aristide's second inauguration, Lucas evoked the prospect of his assassination on Haitian radio.[22]

Lucas began working for the IRI in Haiti back in 1992, ostensibly in order to help the Cédras regime with the important business of mid-coup "election monitoring." The job of presenting elite Duvalierist and pro-army groups as democrats during the Cédras coup years and their immediate aftermath wasn't easy, even for so congenial a fellow as Lucas. It wasn't until the late 1990s that prominent and outspoken pro-coup members of the elite like businessman Olivier Nadal or ex-general Prosper Avril could risk an overt return to the political stage. As the Heinls note, "it would be hard to imagine a more thoroughly Duvalierist product" than Avril, and it took some time before the political class was prepared to welcome him and his ex-army colleagues back into the fold.[23] Only by 1999 did Nadal and his friends feel confident enough to start publicly organizing "civil society" demonstrations in league with anti-Lavalas members of the OPL and other members of an incipient "democratic opposition." In May 1999 (on Radio Métropole) Nadal derided Lavalas partisans and Préval's officials as "uneducated cretins." By that stage the IRI had helped to broker a crucial rapprochement between General Avril and his erstwhile victims Evans Paul and Serge Gilles. This was perhaps the single most important development in the emergence of a suitably "broad-based" anti-Lavalas opposition. Although always more pro-US than Aristide, Evans Paul had also been active in the democracy movement of the late 1980s, and became something of a celebrity when in 1989 Avril arrested him and Serge Gilles and four other anti-Duvalierists, tortured them and then broadcast images of the bloody results on national television. In 1990 Paul had endorsed Aristide's election campaign, and was then himself elected mayor of Port-au-Prince. Almost lynched by pro-Cédras auxiliaries or *attachés* soon after Aristide was overthrown in 1991, he went into hiding when the first coup began; before it was over, however, he was already being groomed by the US to take over from Aristide. In 1994 Paul and Gilles were both due to receive several million dollars in damages from Avril after winning their case against him in a Miami court. Before the decade was out, IRI had somehow managed to coax a written apology to Paul from Avril and to persuade Paul and Gilles to drop their lucrative lawsuits. Paul then joined with Avril in the creation of a new Haitian Conference of Political Parties, smoothing the way for a tactical alliance of both far-right and centrist opposition to Aristide that would endure all the way through to the dénouement of 2004.[24]

When the various parties representing this opposition were crushed in the May 2000 elections, Lucas and the IRI helped to rebrand it as the so-called Convergence Démocratique. Fronted by a charismatic ex-Lavalassian like Evans Paul, the CD provided the instrument that would finally allow members of the old hard-line elite, Duvalierist and ex-military opposition to Aristide to present themselves with a pluralist and democratic face. As Kim Ives explains, the CD provided a suitably respectable institutional form for a perverse "macouto-bourgeois" alliance, in which members of the liberal bourgeoisie represented by civil society grouplets like the Association of Haitian Industries or the Haitian Chamber of Commerce (along with self-styled social-democratic political parties like the OPL, PANPRA and KONAKOM) could temporarily throw in their lot with the neo-Macoute "forces of their age-old rival, the landed oligarchy or *grandons*," represented by openly Duvalierist or neo-feudal parties like Prosper Avril's CREDDO, Hubert de Ronceray's MDN, Reynold Georges' ALAH-MPSN and Pastor Luc Mésadieu's MOCHRENA.[25] The point that Wilentz made back in 1989 was still more true a decade later: typically made up of around twenty-five core supporters and another 100-odd hangers-on, "There is hardly any difference in structure between political parties of the democratic opposition and the groups that attached themselves to various Duvalierist figures like retired general Claude Raymond or Franck Romain, the mayor of Port-au-Prince. All are based on attachment to the *gwo nèg*, the big man."[26]

The CD provided a forum, in short, in which respectable US clients like Evans Paul and Pierre-Charles could share a platform with putchists like ex-general Avril or the ex-colonel Himmler Rébu, and make common cause both for the return of the army and the expulsion of the president who disbanded it. When the CD installed ex-human rights lawyer Gérard Gourgue as Haiti's "parallel President" in February 2001, his first speech included a promise to re-establish the army that Aristide dissolved in 1995. The army has an essential role to play, he explained, in "protecting life and property" and for "imposing order [*pour imposer un ordre de choses . . .*]. Soldiers both at home and abroad should know," he declared, that "our Provisional Government wants you to come home; you have spent too long in purgatory for sins that, perhaps, you did not commit."[27] A few weeks after Gourgue's inaugural speech, hundreds of ex-army personnel held the first of what would become a regular series of public meetings, demanding their immediate reinstatement. When in late 2002 the CD began to organize demonstrations in Cap-Haïtien and various other parts of the country that called for the violent overthrow of the Lavalas government, people like ex-colonel Himmler Rébu played a prominent role in the rallies.

Stanley Lucas' job was to manage the internal rivalries that might otherwise have divided this new Convergence, and to keep his recruits focused on the business at hand. In January 2006, the *New York Times* published a substantial and revealing (albeit belated) analysis of the IRI's role in the Haiti destabilization campaign, which is worth drawing on at some length.[28] As the *Times* reporters discovered, Lucas' loathing for Aristide was so extreme that it sometimes worried his local contractors. Evans Paul himself, for instance, told them that "Mr. Lucas's stand against negotiating was 'a bit too harsh' even for some in the opposition"; Lucas always made it plain that "negotiations would be a bad idea."[29] Lucas was even too hardline for the US ambassador in Haiti 2000–03, Dean Curran, a Clinton appointee who found himself increasingly at odds with the new Republican foreign policy. Curran told the *Times* that while he was urging "the opposition in Haiti 'to show flexibility,' Mr. Lucas was sending the opposite instructions: 'Hang tough. Don't compromise. In the end, we'll get rid of Aristide.'" To the astonishment of Curran and embassy officials, Lucas actively undermined the ambassador's position, threatening his staff and spreading malicious rumors about Curran's personal life, all with the apparent approval of his masters in Washington.[30] Curran was finally pushed out of the embassy in September 2003 because, Otto Reich admitted, "We did not think the ambassador was carrying out the new policy in the way we wanted it carried out." (Curran's replacement, James Foley, cut his diplomatic teeth in another momentous experiment in democracy promotion – the conversion, in the late 1990s, of the Kosovo Liberation Army into a "respectable" political force.[31]) In his unusually undiplomatic final speech, Curran denounced the covert action of Lucas and the other *"chimères* of Washington," claiming they had been deliberately trying to forestall any viable settlement between the government and its foes. The point has since been amply confirmed by veteran OAS diplomat Luigi R. Einaudi, who regularly dealt with the IRI during the second Aristide adminis-tration. He remembers "attending the IRI's 2001 fund-raising dinner, and being surrounded by a half-dozen Haitian businessmen sounding a common cry: 'We were foolish to think that we could do anything with Aristide. That it was impossible to negotiate with him. That it was necessary to get rid of him.' " This would become the leitmotif of the next three years.

Towards the end of Préval's first administration IRI activity was already so provocative that in 1999 he encouraged it to close its Haiti office. When Lucas set to work re-enhancing the democratic opposition in 2002, therefore, he had to train its members over the border, in the more congenial environs of the Dominican Republic. Training sessions took place at the Fanjul family's Hotel Santo Domingo. Owners of a giant sugar-cane business, the Fanjuls were refugees from Castro's Cuba and had little love for Aristide. IRI officials told the *Times* that "there were perhaps a dozen sessions, spread over a year" and that "hundreds of opposition members came," though no FL members or allies were invited. The IRI's Georges Fauriol explains that "this was because the opposition parties were less powerful and needed more help. The goal, Mr. Fauriol said, 'was to broaden, if you will, the ability of various actors to participate in the political process.' "[32]

This broadening of participation didn't stop with a few lacklustre political parties. Young researchers like Anthony Fenton, Yves Engler and Jeb Sprague have investigated the IRI's role in Haiti, and shown how in the years leading up to the 2004 coup it organized meetings and training sessions for hundreds of other people belonging to a wide range of conservative civil society organizations, business groups, human rights groups, NGOs, and so on. A very partial list of the recipients of USAID, IFES and/or IRI support during these years includes: a new coalition of the main "independent" media outlets, the Association Nationale des Médias Haïtiens (more on this below); human rights organizations like Pierre Espérance's National Coalition for Haitian Rights (rebranded in 2005 as the Réseau National pour la Défense Des Droits Humains), Renan Hédouville's Comité des Avocats Pour le Respect des Libertés Individuelles, and Jean-Claude Bajeux's Center Ecuménique des Droits Humains; student groups like the Fédération des Étudiants Universitaires d'Haïti, professional organizations like the Association Nationale des Magistrats or the Fondation Haïtienne de l'Enseignement Privé, as well as new fronts for the internationally-oriented business sector like Rosny Desroches' Initiative de la Société Civile and Andy Apaid's Fondation Nouvelle Haiti.[33]

One of the IRI's most prominent and influential partners was the so-called Haiti Democracy Project, an organization launched with great fanfare at the Brookings Institute in Washington in November 2002. The HDP provided reactionary Haitian civil society groups with an impeccably well-connected international public relations team. The list of its members and associates includes many of the big-hitters of the rightwing American and Haitian-American political establishment. Much of its funding comes from its founder, industrialist Rudolph Boulos. Like his brother Reginald (head of the Haitian Chamber of Commerce), Dr Rudolph Boulos has long been a dominant figure in the Haitian business community. His various commercial interests include Pharval Pharmaceuticals (responsible for the manufacture in 1996 of contaminated medicines which led to the deaths of some 70 children) and his political connections extend backwards to FRAPH and the post-Duvalier military, and forwards to the 2003–04 recruitment of anti-Lavalas gangs in Cité Soleil. Other founding members of the HDP include Timothy Carney (US ambassador to Haiti 1998–99 and again in 2005–06), Lawrence Pezzullo (Clinton's special envoy to Haiti 1993–94), Orlando Marville (chief of the OAS electoral mission that tried to discredit the May 2000 elections), Lionel Delatour (of the aggressively neo-liberal Center for Free Enterprise and Democracy, a prominent USAID grantee), and Boulos' old friend Ira Lowenthal (a leading figure in the early development of the democratic opposition to Lavalas via PIRED and several other USAID-funded democracy enhancement programs, including Associates in Rural Development, the Americas Development Foundation and the obscure but influential United Nations Office for Project Services). The general tenor of HDP activities can be guessed from the guest-list of its inaugural dinner: along with Roger Noriega,

Stanley Lucas, and OAS go-between Luigi Einaudi, the list of VIPs included another luminary of the far-right business establishment, Miami-based entrepreneur Olivier Nadal. A former president of the Haitian Chamber of Commerce and a key player in the renewal of civil society opposition in the late 1990s, Nadal was widely accused (by Antoine Izméry, among others) of being one of the main financial backers of the 1991 coup, and was eventually indicted, fourteen years after the event, for his role in the 1990 Piatre massacre of eleven farmers in the Montrouis region.[34]

Like other partners of the IRI, the HDP understands very well that in order to replace the unruly threat of "popular democracy" with appropriately docile forms of "liberal democracy" it's helpful to work in several constituencies at once. The values associated with "democratization," "pluralism" and "moderation" have for some time now been indistinguishable from those of the transnational elite, and are perfectly compatible with the preservation if not intensification of global inequalities.[35] A particular USAID and IRI priority, consequently, was to foster opposition to Aristide among Haitian youth, student and women's groups. One of the US grantees and G184 leaders in Haiti, for instance, was the suave, English-speaking Hans Tippenhauer, a man whom Michael Deibert describes as "an economic advisor at the consulting firm Groupe Croissance and scion of one of Haiti's most respected families." Tippenhauer is also the director of an NGO called Fondation Espoir, and heads what one free-thinking website describes as "Haiti's most important youth platform": *Jeune Ayiti*.[36] In mid-2005, Tippenhauer's uncle was rewarded with an appointment as Haiti's new interim "ambassador" to Canada[37]; Tippenhauer junior would later play a prominent role in Charles Baker's 2006 far-right presidential campaign.[38] For reasons that will become obvious in chapter eight, in 2003 student groups like the Fédération des Étudiants de l'Université d'État d'Haïti (FEUH) came to receive particularly assiduous favors and attention from the IRI and its various intermediaries. FEUH leader Hervé Saintilus attended the December 2002 meeting in the Dominican Republic that inaugurated the G184[39], and scores of other anti-Lavalas "student leaders" make no secret of the financial and logistical support they received from the IRI.[40] Members of a human rights delegation organized by the Quixote Center in April 2004 met numerous "students, women and union organizers who had formed specifically anti-Aristide groups to demand the ouster of Aristide earlier this year. They proudly asserted their connection to USAID, the State Department Democracy Enhancement program and the NDI. 'They trained us and taught us how to organize, and we organized the groups you see here to demand the corrupt government of Aristide be brought down.' "[41] Overlapping women's groups like SOFA, ENFOFANM, and CONAP were all on the IRI/USAID/CIDA payroll, and all were to play an important role in the disinformation campaign.

During one of the more momentous Santo Domingo meetings, Lucas and his clients came up with a new civil society vehicle to gather all these independent recruits as part of a still more pluralist coalition. The meeting took place shortly after the dismal failure of a CD-sponsored "general strike" that had been planned for early December 2002. The IRI invited some 50 businessmen and CD members for a three-day session to discuss alternative destabilization strategies. They gave what emerged the eye-catching name "The Group of 184."[42] Combining representatives of the elite, the business sector, independent media outlets and CD politicians, G184 was designed to coordinate the cultural and political opposition to Aristide in a single mechanism. Better, like the Civil Society Initiative which preceded it, it was designed both to represent the opposition and to serve as a "neutral" arbiter between itself and the government. Reich and his team knew what they were doing: the US had encouraged similar sorts of business/civil society opposition before it turned on Manuel Noriega in Panama, and has long been making similar investments in Cuba, Jamaica, Venezuela, and Bolivia.

Virtually all of the groups that received USAID or NED/IRI money, including all of the organizations listed in the preceding pages, became G184 members, as did various other CD spin-offs or allies like Chavannes Jean-Baptiste's MPP and Suzy Castor's CRESFED. So did dozens of obscure if not simply fictional "popular" associations. In addition to support from the IRI, G184 received generous subsidies from IFES and the European Union. Over the course of 2003 it became the loudest and most influential voice in the growing chorus of anti-FL opposition groups. Newspapers like the *New York Times* and *Libération* would regularly refer to G184 simply as "a civil society organization," if not as a progressive coalition of "trade unions, socio-professional organizations, NGOs and human rights groups."

Together with his fellow businessman and ultra-reactionary brother-in-law Charles Baker, the leading figure in the G184 was the brash industrialist André Apaid junior. Apaid inherited Alpha Industries, one of the largest and oldest sweatshop chains in Haiti, from his enthusiastically pro-Duvalier father. Among other things, back in the late 1980s Andy Apaid senior was president of USAID's Prominex project, which when

Aristide came to power in 1991 received more than $7 million "to develop a consensus in the business community on key economic requirements for sustainable economic growth and develop an approach for policy dialogue with the government." A couple of months after the September 1991 coup, Apaid senior explained what this meant when he told a meeting of around a thousand Caribbean business leaders in Miami that if Aristide tried to come back he would "strangle him."[43] Like his father, Apaid junior opposed Aristide's return to power in 1994, before opposing his moves to increase the minimum wage (in 1995 and again in 2003) and corporate tax revenues. As of 2006, Apaid's main factory employs several thousand workers on the edge of Cité Soleil, mostly women who sew T-shirts and jeans for companies like Gildan Active-wear, Hanes and Fruit of the Loom; they also make military uniforms for the US. According to journalists who interviewed several dozen Apaid employees, the women generally work 11-hour shifts, making anything from $1.50 to $3 a day; needless to say they can be fired without notice, have no meaningful trade union representation and are not eligible for any overtime-, maternity-, sick- or vacation-pay.[44] Repeatedly accused of tax evasion, in 1999 Apaid was fined two million gourdes for fraudulent manipulation of international telephone services.[45]

An American citizen born in New York, Apaid had no obvious credentials to act as the spokesman for the Haitian opposition, even one as democratic as that promoted by the IRI. Back in the US, however, Boulos and Morrell's Haiti Democracy Project helped ensure that Apaid would become perhaps the most frequently cited figure in the "grass-roots" and "civil society" opposition to Aristide during the last decisive months of 2003. Tom Reeves reckons that the HDP was behind "every public event or press release about the G184 in the United States, and many in Haiti."[46] In Canada, federally-funded NGOs Alternatives and Rights & Democracy performed a similar function; in September 2003, for instance, the latter issued a report on Haiti which characterized G184 as a "grassroots" coalition and "promising civil society movement."[47]

Staffed by affluent and well-connected members of the elite, in reality the CD, G184 and various other incarnations of civil society made little pretence to be anything other than pitifully blunt instruments of Haiti's tiny ruling class. The regular flow of foreign money paid to its members absolved them of the need to collude in one of the most familiar features of mainstream Haitian politics – the temptation to make temporary compromises and tactical alliances in order to gain profitable access to state revenues and power. Thanks mainly to US subsidies, people whose active political career had hitherto consisted of little more than one compromise after another – CD leaders Gérard Pierre-Charles and Evans Paul are a case in point – could suddenly afford to become paragons of principled consistency. They now enjoyed a democratic autonomy rather more resilient than any mere electoral mandate. (A similar luxury extends to people fortunate enough to be employed by an internationally-connected NGO, a good many of whom were included in or associated with the G184.)

There was no material reason, then, to discourage members of the democratic opposition from giving full expression to the remarkably intense personal bitterness most of them came to feel for President Aristide. In order to make sense of CD priorities and tactics it's essential to remember (from chapter two) that its leading figures were not just opponents but former "allies" of Aristide. It's also important to remember the primarily tactical basis of these old alliances. From the beginning, career politicians like Pierre-Charles had seen Aristide mainly as a useful tool in the development of a new political party which they themselves expected to control; what Pierre-Charles retained from his earlier in-carnation as an underground Communist was less a specific set of principles than a sort of Popular Front-style cynicism. Once it became clear that in the mid-1990s Aristide himself was central to the develop-ment of a genuinely mass-based party, relations with the career "experts" quickly soured. With too many ambitious politicians competing for the very limited number of profitable posts, the originally broad Lavalas alliance soon split into several resentful factions. As Fatton explains, "The utter lack of resources characterizing Haitian society has meant that the top membership of the original Lavalas coalition was too large to enjoy fully the fruits of power."[48] After a few months' futile maneuvering, by the end of 1995 most of the 1991 fellow-travellers already found themselves back on the sidelines, and their resentment of Aristide's popularity left them with only one alternative route – one that would lead, via the likes of Stanley Lucas and Roger Noriega, straight back to the Macoutes. Along with Evans Paul, Pierre-Charles's coterie switched their allegiances away from Aristide and towards his enemies in the US just months after his return in October 1994. Paul's humiliating defeat at the hands of a pro-Aristide candidate in the municipal elections of 1995 turned rivalry into enmity. Once they had settled into their permanent and comfortably funded oppositional role, Fatton notes, these erstwhile allies proved remarkably receptive to "the most virulent anti-Aristide propaganda that they had themselves rejected until recently. They came to share Lynn Garrison's extravagant and bizarre portrayal of Aristide as a demented psychopath responsible for virtually all the murders that have taken place in the country since 1990."[49] For people in delicate positions like those occupied by Pierre-Charles and Evans Paul, such a portrayal had its uses. It's easier to justify a convergence with violent Duvalierists if you can persuade yourself that you are opposed by still more bloodthirsty bandits. It's easier to take money and instructions from people like Noriega and Lucas if it is in order to get rid of dictators like Préval and Aristide, whom the CD would routinely describe as mere "putchists, no different from Raoul Cédras and Michel François."[50] In interview after interview, OPL leaders Suzy Castor and Pierre-Charles stuck to their main theme: thanks to Aristide's personal lust for power and wealth, FL had become indistinguishable from the dictatorial regimes it had originally sought to replace.

The political evolution of Aristide's former ally MPP leader Chavannes Jean-Baptiste is typical of many of the more "progressive" members of the democratic opposition to Lavalas. The two men were close in 1990–91 and shared a commitment to grassroots organization. Unlike any other anti-Lavalas group, the MPP retains to this day a substantial though purely regional following around its headquarters in Hinche, sustained in large part by the regular and growing flow of NGO patronage that passes through Chavannes' hands. Like his more militant supporters in the Quixote Center, in October 1994 Chavannes opposed Clinton's military intervention, arguing that Aristide should remain in exile rather than compromise with the Americans.[51] Chavannes campaigned on behalf of Aristide's supporters in the June 1995 elections, but then turned against him a few months later once it became clear that Aristide would endorse Préval rather than Chavannes himself as his successor.[52] Chavannes and some of his rivals in the Lavalas coalition then began trading accusations of corruption and greed, and by the end of the 1990s ugly confrontations between MPP and Lavalas activists in and around Hinche had become a fairly regular occurrence. By 2000, this former scourge of imperialism was willing to align himself with the Duvalierists in the Convergence Démocratique, having reached the conclusion that "It wasn't Cédras but Aristide who almost eliminated the popular movements."[53] A couple of years later he joined the G184 and endorsed its unapologetically conservative "Social Contract," and in the 2006 presidential campaign, Chavannes was even prepared to back the campaign of far-right industrialist Charles Baker. Chavannes' hostility to Aristide makes more sense in the light of such affiliations. "For me," Jean-Baptiste told a sympathetic Michael Deibert in 2001, "Aristide is nothing but a political cadaver who will pass like garbage through the history of Haiti."[54] When anti-government guerrilla attacks in the Central Plateau began in 2001 Chavannes kept quiet, before effectively endorsing them in a statement released 24 February 2004: "Aristide is a criminal, an assassin, a thief, a liar, a traitor, a gang leader, a dictator. There is no hope with him. All sectors of national life are finished with him. No compromise with him is possible. Democracy is not possible with Aristide. It is over [. . .]. We must cut out this cancer."[55] Insurgent leader Guy Philippe would later admit that he was grateful to Chavannes and the MPP for their "good advice and logistical help."[56] When Tom Reeves visited the Central Plateau shortly after the 2004 coup he was told by farmers, union organizers and priests that "most of the weapons and men that moved from the Dominican Republic to start the rebellions in Gonaïves and Cap-Haïtien in early February, came through Chavannes' turf. 'There's no way that could have been done without his active support.' "[57]

For many years a favorite in progressive US media and NGO circles, in April 2005 Chavannes was awarded a prestigious Goldman Environmental Prize.

TANGLING THE STRINGS

Members of the CD not only had no incentive to compromise with FL, they clearly didn't have permission to negotiate at all. The exceptionally strident tone that was duly adopted by the CD negotiators further allowed their North American employers to play, in public, an ostensibly moderate conciliatory role. So long as progressive democrats like Chavannes Jean-Baptiste were on hand to deny the legitimacy of "any person nominated by Lavalas at any level of government" and to urge "the political parties and the civil society initiative not to enter into negotiations with Aristide because it makes no sense to negotiate with a thief,"[58] so then Colin Powell and his spokesmen could safely keep up the pretence of trying to reason with a well-intentioned though somewhat stubborn opposition. At the height of the February 2004 crisis, OAS mediator Einaudi finally persuaded some opposition leaders to meet with Aristide at the US ambassador's house. The intention was to discuss his last-ditch power-sharing arrangement. Aristide had already accepted the deal and agreed to give up much of his power, and Powell went on television to say that he expected the CD to follow suit. At the last minute, Einaudi was apparently "stunned" to learn that American officials had unilaterally canceled the meeting. They "pulled the rug out," he said, killing off "what was in fact my last move."[59] By that stage, at least one lie had become untenable – the assertion, which had been a constant of US and French diplomacy from the first days of Aristide's administration, that responsibility for the failure to find a compromise with the opposition lay exclusively with FL.[60]

Exposure to these and related lies is made more difficult by one of the most immediately striking features of the USAID/IRI democracy enhancement programme – its labyrinthine convolution. As the reader may have already gathered, the funding streams are so contorted, the chain of command is so diffuse, the number and diversity of grantors and grantees are so bewildering and complex, that it is almost impossible to reconstruct the actual sequence of events. In the case of Haiti 2000–04, the task is made more difficult by the fact that, as Fenton and Engler have documented at some length, much of the more delicate destabilization work was sub-contracted out to an ostensibly neutral if not benign hemispheric partner – Canada. Rarely has Canada executed its client functions in so exemplary a fashion. Canada's foreign minister Pierre Pettigrew reportedly met with leading figures in the anti-Aristide opposition and insurgency shortly before the February coup, and as we have seen his deputy Denis Paradis was instrumental in coordinating the international community's "responsible" plan for regime change. CIDA (Canada's equivalent to USAID) provided significant financial assistance to pro-coup pressure groups like NCHR and SOFA. Other Canadian government funded NGOs such as " 'Development and Peace,' 'Rights and Democracy,' and 'FOCAL,' helped foment the demonization and destabilization campaign against the elected government," before "aiding and abetting the massive cover-up" that followed it.[61] France and the European Union also made significant financial contributions to democracy promotion in Haiti. The French Socialist Party is the main financial backer of a few of the more prominent grouplets in the CD, and in 2002–03, Rosny Desroches' Initiative de la Société Civile and André Apaid's Fondation Nouvelle Haiti were contracted to funnel €773,000 from the European Commission to various "human rights groups," including the Chamber of Commerce and half a dozen other organizations belonging to the G184.[62] (I will return to the crucial role France played in the February 2004 coup in chapter nine.)

This transnational multiplicity of groups, actors and agendas helps conceal any "underlying" imperialist motive or plan, beyond the seemingly innocent promotion of pluralism itself. Calling an organization the "Group of 184" helps conceal the fact that in most respects that number would be more appropriately used to count individuals rather than organizations. What its members lacked in terms of popularity and depth, however, they made up for in terms of connections and influence. Technically, the CD was itself made of scores of groups, most of which had little more than a nominal existence. But like the G184, the Convergence also had a suggestive name; however contorted the rivulets of the funding stream, virtually all of them lead back to a single source.

THE INDEPENDENT MEDIA

A similar unity of purpose and dependency characterizes the work of perhaps the most strategically significant sector to receive IFES/IRI funding: the anti-government or "independent" media. In a country with such poorly developed transportation (and such high levels of illiteracy), the media and in particular the radio play a very important role in shaping public perceptions of what's going on. As the director of Haiti's largest micro-credit association explains, "It's very difficult to find any significant evidence for the things that people say about Aristide, but my experience is that there's a real pattern in Haiti, and no doubt in some other countries as well, that things *become* reality once they're articulated enough times; after a while you're never going to change the view that people have, no matter what evidence you put in front of them. It's very strange around here, how things that seem totally illogical and without merit come to be taken as the God's truth!"[63] If over several years you can keep on referring to Aristide's election as "fraudulent," to his regime as a "dictatorship" and to his supporters as "bandits," sooner or later the words start to sink in. There was nothing to stop the democratic opposition from referring to things this way: although one of the great leitmotifs of its disinformation campaign was the claim that an authoritarian Aristide had stifled all dissent, in reality it took place during a time of respect for freedoms of speech and assembly without precedent in the whole of Haitian history.

Anyone who tries to make sense of the campaign against Lavalas is immediately confronted by what Patrick Elie describes as "the total monopoly of the press, and especially of the radio, by the bourgeoisie and sectors which are under the control of the US."[64] The development of this monopoly was one of the most significant achievements of the Haitian political elite in the decade following the 1991 coup. As suggested by a document leaked in October 1993 by a security guard at the US embassy in Haiti (who was assassinated a few days later), US officials had long understood the need for a "broad, sustained, and very discrete approach from the US policy makers and the media which will counteract and nullify the propaganda of the Lavalas organization."[65] Ten years later there was less need for discretion. "There are about 50 radio stations broadcasting to the Port-au-Prince area," noted the Catholic Institute for International Relations in 2004, and "all of the most important ones are now firmly in the anti-Aristide camp; of those that broadcast news their coverage is consistently anti-government."[66] By 2003 most independent newspapers and radio stations were either members or associates of the G184, and the most powerful of them belonged to the bitterly partisan National Association of Haitian Media (ANMH), an organization of elite media owners that received plenty of enthusiastic international support. Haiti's most widely read newspapers – the center-right "paper of record" *Le Nouvelliste*, along with the far-right *Le Matin* – are members of the ANMH, as are around a dozen of the highest-profile radio stations, including Radio Kiskeya, Radio Vision 2000, Radio Signal FM, and Radio Métropole. By the end of 2004, according to the human rights organization CARLI (itself a recipient of IFES funds in the run-up to the February coup), of the main twenty-five radio and print outlets, twenty were owned by members of the Group of 184 and served to "uncritically disseminate the anti-Lavalas propaganda of the interim government."[67] Even before Aristide was re-elected president in 2000, these news organizations sustained an extraordinarily vehement campaign of lies and distortion to demonize Fanmi Lavalas and to amplify the size and significance of the opposition. The chapter on Haiti in the 2005 edition of *World Press Freedom Review* (whose author cannot be accused of being a FL partisan) notes that throughout the year following the 2004 coup

> the main, Port-au-Prince-based media houses – grouped in the National Association of Haitian Media (Association Nationale des Médias Haïtiens, ANMH) – continued to take an open position of support for the ouster of the Lavalas Family government and of extreme hostility to the large swathes of the poor population who continued to voice support for the exiled President Jean-Bertrand Aristide. The ANMH radio stations in particular exercised a clear editorial line favoring the Group of 184, a political platform led by the

country's small private sector. At the same time, these stations' news broadcasts consistently described opponents of the [post-coup] interim government, living in shanty-towns, such as Bel Air and Cité Soleil, as "outlaws" and "terrorists."[68]

Readers without access to Haitian radio can get a sense of the often farcical flavour of much of this coverage via the prominent *We Haitians* website, a self-described "scholarly journal of democracy and human rights" which makes regular reference to a certain "hell-sent totalitarian dictator Jean-Bertrand Aristide."[69]

The political affiliation of the ANMH outlets should come as no surprise, given the impressively concentrated character of the democratic opposition. The wealthy and well-connected Boulos family, for instance, owns the *Le Matin* newspaper and is one of the principal owners of the station Radio Vision 2000. RV2000's director is Leopold Berlanger, who is a prominent member of the rightwing Fondation Nouvelle Haiti. The Foundation's spokesman used to be Andy Apaid, who founded Tele-Haiti, and the Foundation is itself a member of Rosny Desroches' Initiative de la Société Civile; both the Foundation and the Initiative, like the ANMH, are dominant members of the G184. Radio Métropole is owned by Herbert Widmaier, and is directed by his son Richard Widmaier along with a couple of other members of the family. Liliane Pierre-Paul directs Radio Kiskeya; her husband Anthony Barbier was the executive secretary of the G184, and her sister is one of the leaders of the anti-Lavalas women's group SOFA. The co-founder and director of Radio Signal FM, Anne-Marie Issa, was chosen to represent the Chamber of Commerce in the "Council of Sages" put in place to select a post-Aristide government in March 2004; she later became president of the ANMH.[70]

Towards the end of 2003, notes Isabel Macdonald, "The ANMH publicly announced that it had banned the President of the Republic of Haiti from its member stations' airwaves."[71] Macdonald has interviewed many of the leading figures in the Haitian media and anti-Aristide opposition, and demonstrated the quite remarkable integration of the one with the other. Back in the days when the Arbenz government was destabilized in Guatemala, Elie remembers, democratic oppositions "had to organize their own radio to poison the mind of the people. Now they can count on all those radio stations that belong to the Haitian bourgeoisie to do the job for them."[72]

Their job was made infinitely easier when one of the country's only genuinely independent journalists, Jean Dominique, was mysteriously murdered in April 2000, a few weeks before the decisive legislative elections in May. A member of the progressive wing of the liberal elite, Dominique had been a thorn in the side of his more reactionary colleagues for many years. He had played a decisive role in the campaign against Duvalier and the juntas of the late 1980s, and in the 1990 election of Aristide. In 2000 he remained the most widely respected and influential voice on Haitian radio, and he never tired of attacking the blatant class bias of the mainstream media. Although he was occasionally critical of Lavalas compromises after 1994, everyone knew where his political sympathies lay. Everyone knew that he was, in Gérard Jean-Juste's words, a supporter of "Lavalas, he was strong Lavalas, helping the peasants, helping the poorest ones. And who should profit off the killing of Jean? Who should profit off getting rid of such a great journalist?"[73] Jean-Juste and Patrick Elie are not alone in their speculation that Dominique's outspoken criticism of the pro-business and anti-government bias of his profession during Préval's first presidency may have been one of the several factors that led to his assassination.[74]

With Dominique out of the way (and with the leftwing press reduced to a few embattled organizations like Ben Dupuy's *Haïti Progrès* and Venel Remarais' Radio Solidarité), the independent media were more or less free to present the news in line with the political priorities of their backers in the IRI and USAID. Anti-Aristide demonstrations like those held on 28 May 1999 or 14 November 2003 received round-the-clock coverage, to give the impression of a growing "tide of dissent." Small meetings attended by perhaps a couple of hundred members of the anti-Lavalas elite were reported as major protests attended by thousands of people. As one ANMH media owner explained to Macdonald, "we always support the pro-democracy demonstrations," and "sometimes we advance fantastical numbers because we don't want the public to draw the wrong conclusion. If a group has 10 people but they want you to say 2000 or 300,000, if you say 10 [. . .] you can make enemies, you can damage the group and their credibility. It can create animosity, so it's better not to talk about it."[75] While much larger FL demonstrations like those which took place on 25 November 2002 or 7 February 2004 were downplayed or ignored, generally minor confrontations with indignant FL supporters were turned into highly charged scenes of brutal intimidation. No story was too far-fetched, so long as the appropriate "bandits" were responsible. Student demonstrators were given sinister injections by police, Aristide had sacrificed children in a vaudou ceremony, Lavalas kidnappers had torn out the eyes of a baby . . . Though no such students, children or babies ever materialized, the independent media faithfully reported an endless stream of such fictions as fact. During these same years, as *Haïti Progrès* points out, "a media campaign was also launched in the United States to split the Haitian community and to undermine the support of the Congressional Black Caucus" and other pro-Lavalas advocacy groups. Radio stations like Vision 2000 provided additional programing for sympathetic stations in Florida and New York. In these same states, US ambassador Curran became a regular voice on anti-Aristide radio, as did still more independent analysts from the Haiti Democracy Project.[76] "Here's the way it works," Kevin Pina explains: "Métropole reports a fabrication; AP and *RFI* pick it up for their wire services, then Kiskeya and the others report it again in Haiti backed by the credibility of the international press. The positive feedback loop of disinformation for the opposition is now complete."[77] A nice example of just how far the US disinformation campaigners were prepared to go was provided by US Attorney General John Ashcroft on 23 April 2003, when he stumbled upon a useful though surreal way of connecting the twin terrors of Haitian migration and Islamic extremism. Ashcroft asserted "an increase in third country nations (Pakistanis, Palestinians, etc.) using Haiti as a staging point for attempted migration to the United States." Although he never provided any evidence for the premise, Ashcroft knew how to draw the obvious conclusion: there was now a compelling "national security interest" to take further steps to "cure use of this migration route." It fell to State Department spokesman Stuart Patt to try to explain Ashcroft's comments. "We are all scratching our heads," he confessed to reporters. "We are asking each other, 'Where did they get that?' "[78]

As anyone even vaguely familiar with the way the mainstream media works might expect, in 2001–04 the international press generally wasn't very concerned by this sort of question. Most international correspondents know very little about Haiti and tend to spend a large part of their very occasional visits to the country at just one or two media-friendly elite hotels – hotels which during the crisis of 2003–04 were literally staked out by Evans Paul, Andy Apaid and a whole team of other talking heads from the G184 and the CD. It is scarcely possible to find an article about Haiti during Aristide's second administration in newspapers like the *New York Times*, the *Guardian, Le Monde* or *Libération* that doesn't emphasize its apparent corruption, autocracy and complicity in the abuse of human rights. Confronted by a sustained string of allegations along these lines, the casual consumer of mainstream commentary was encouraged to believe that what was at stake had nothing to do with a protracted battle between a poor majority and a wealthy elite but was instead just a convoluted free-for-all in which both sides were equally at fault. Rather than a *political* struggle, rather than a battle of principles and priorities, the fight for Haiti became just another instance of the petty corruption and mass victimization that is widely assumed to characterize public life beyond the heavily guarded confines of western democracy. Rather than conditioned by radical class polarization or the mechanics of systematic exploitation, Aristide's demise has most often figured as yet another demonstration of perhaps the most consistent theme of the profoundly racist first-world commentary on the island: that poor non-white people remain incapable of governing themselves.

As usual, this element of the second coup had been anticipated, in diluted form, the first time around. All through 1991, the US press regularly referred to Aristide as "flaky," "volatile," "confrontational," "demagogic," "unpredictable," "anti-American" and (therefore) "anti-democratic." Lally Weymouth sounded a characteristic note in her 1992 op-ed for the *Washington Post*, in which she derided Aristide as an "extremely radical anti-American priest" who "condoned violence and mob terror."[79] Important contributions to these early efforts were made by the influential *New York Times* reporter Howard French[80] – the headline of his 22 October 1991 article, "Aristide's Autocratic Ways Ended Haiti's Embrace of Democracy," speaks for itself. So does the title of the editorial published in this same newspaper to mark the occasion of Aristide's re-election in November 2000: "Haiti's Disappearing Democracy."

Since this editorial anticipates in concentrated form the wave of propaganda that was soon to overwhelm Aristide's second administration it's worth lingering for a moment to examine its argument. The *New York Times* begins on the sort of upbeat note typical of most liberal critics of Aristide's subsequent "degeneration." Aristide's "election as president of Haiti the first time, ten years ago, was hailed as a triumph for democracy in a land that had known little but dictatorship." Aristide began his career, the *Times* concedes, "as a courageous priest, championing the rights of Haiti's poorest and most abused citizens." But ever since handing power over to his associate René Préval in 1996, "Aristide has maneuvered to assure his own return to the Presidential Palace, at great cost to Haiti's extremely fragile democratic institutions and its economy." Although in November 2000 he was indeed re-elected with 90 percent of the vote, this new victory was only achieved by "trampling on democratic procedures." Aristide trampled on democracy, the *Times* explains, because "the weeks before the voting were marred by bombings and other politically motivated violence, and all serious opposition candidates boycotted the race, citing doubts about its fairness." Worse, the legitimacy of legislative elections won by Aristide's power a few months earlier (in May 2000) "has been widely disputed," and "the constant turmoil has estranged many former Aristide allies and contributed to a climate of violence." As a result, "most international aid to Haiti has been suspended." The *Times*' conclusion follows as a matter of course: since Aristide's "tolerance for political violence raises concerns that he might one day lead Haiti back to dictatorship [. . .], Washington should make clear that a resumption of American aid depends on a return to the democratic ways that Mr. Aristide once symbolized."[81] (Although this was precisely the conclusion that Washington, Ottawa and Paris had already reached, its plausibility required the reader to overlook a few inconvenient facts: the violence which marred the weeks leading up to the November presidential election was instigated by Aristide's opponents, not his supporters; Aristide was immeasurably less tolerant of political violence than any previous Haitian politician; Aristide's rivals were only concerned about the "fairness" of the presidential election in November because they knew they had no chance of beating the most popular politician in Haiti's history; the only people who "disputed" the unequivocal outcome of the May legislative elections were the losers who saw it as signalling the end of their political careers; Aristide's "former allies" were never genuine allies so much as opportunistic fellow-travelers, and they were not estranged by but rather mainly responsible for both the "constant turmoil" and the "climate of violence" that paralyzed most of Préval's administration; the reason why international aid to Haiti was suspended had nothing to do with Aristide's trampling of democratic procedures but everything to do with the fact that the Haitian electorate had once again dared to vote for someone that Washington didn't like.)

It would be an instructive albeit redundant exercise to track the consolidation of this new Washington consensus in the mainstream press over the next few years. Virtually without exception, all through February 2004 western newspapers adopted versions of the same basic story: "although beloved when elected in 1990," wrote the *Los Angeles Times* on the day he was abducted, "Aristide is now widely resented for dashing fervent hopes of lifting this country out of the misery, repression and corruption that have defined it throughout its 200 years of independence."[82] It may be enough to cite the titles of a couple of representative tirades published in the *Independent*: "Haiti's Despot Aristide Stirs Up People's Revolution" (13 January 2004) and "The Little Priest Who Became a Bloody Dictator Like the One He Once Despised" (21 February 2004). A brief exchange in early March on the BBC's flagship news program further illustrates the impressively flexible stance adopted by the world's media during the second coup. After a short interview with a now-exiled Aristide, in which he repeated his claim that he been forced out of office under US pressure, the program anchor turned to BBC correspondent Daniel Lak in Port-au-Prince to sort out the confusion. "So it's not completely made up, Aristide does have people who support him, it's not just a handful of thugs who are paid by him?" Lak replied: "Oh absolutely. The people who support him are the poor of this country, the vast majority. There are 8 million Haitians, and probably 95 percent of them are desperately poor. It's the rich and the small middle class who support Aristide's opponents, and the poor who generally support Aristide." What then about the conflicting explanations of Aristide's departure: was it effectively a coup, or a voluntary resignation? "Is it possible to peer through and establish any truth about this," asked the anchor, "or is it just too difficult, from where you're standing?" Lak's answer speaks volumes. "I think it's just too difficult, um . . . The two options are pretty stark. But it's clear that the Americans did want to see the back of Mr. Aristide."[83]

For reasons we'll come back to in chapter nine, the French press played an especially important role in developing a suitably nuanced and multilateral approach to the 2004 coup. Of all the journalists who took up the role assigned to them by an obsessively anti-Aristide French embassy in Port-au-Prince, none made such an important contribution as *Le Monde*'s Jean-Michel Caroit. Drawing almost exclusively on a tiny section of Haiti's ruling elite – anonymous members of the French diplomatic corps (Eric Bosc, Yves Gaudeul, Thierry Burkard), unelectable members of the democratic opposition (Serge Gilles, Evans Paul, Micha Gaillard), rightwing industrialists and leaders of civil society (Andy Apaid, Charles Baker), francophiliac intellectuals and artists (Laënnec Hurbon, Raoul Peck), anti-Lavalas human rights observers (Pierre Espérance, the "tireless" Jean-Claude Bajeux) – it's difficult to see how Caroit could plausibly have done more to shore up French strategic requirements of the day. Well before Aristide's re-election, Caroit had established the leitmotif that would inflect all his coverage of the Fanmi Lavalas administration: its apparent revival of neo-Duvalierist *macoutisme*, i.e. its decision to allow, "in complete impunity, the 'chimères' to impose a reign of terror."[84] Since a corrupt and incompetent FL organization apparently owed its "surprise" victory in the 2000 elections to the "violent intimidation" of its rivals, when Aristide returned to the National Palace in February 2001 he already suffered from a self-evident "lack of legitimacy". With only the "disastrous legacy of five years of Lavalas government" to build on, on the day of his inauguration Caroit's Aristide could promise his country nothing more nor less than the "Calvary of absolute misery."[85]

A little later in the story of Haiti's crucifixion, as the destabilization campaign began to accelerate in the autumn of 2003, it wouldn't have been difficult to deduce the general strategy of the French diplomatic offensive conducted by Dominique de Villepin and his new ambassador Thierry Burkard directly from the titles of Caroit's dispatches. On 7 October 2003, Caroit noted the ominous fact that Haiti was busy "preparing for the bicentenary of its independence," adding that it planned to link this bicentenary to a claim for "financial reparations from France." The next day, however, Caroit observed that "political violence and protests are on the increase."[86] On 11 October, drawing mainly on discussions with the head of the internationally sponsored ANMH (Hérold Jean-François), Caroit explained that the government's responses to such protest included the "harassment of the independent press," and compared the government's own "propaganda" (including its demand for reparations from France) to that of North Korea.[87] On 12 October, in an article that consisted largely of a glowing biography of G184 leader Andy Apaid ("a businessman who has managed to win the confidence of trade unionists and peasant leaders"), Caroit celebrated the welcome fact that Haiti's broad-based "civil society is organizing itself in opposition to president Aristide."[88] Then on 5 November Caroit filed the longest of his 2003 dispatches from Haiti, showing how the country was once again "terrorized by armed gangs, the descendants of Duvalier's Tontons Macoutes."[89]

The next time Caroit mentions Haiti's bicentenary it's in a story of 4 December 2003, headlined "Haiti sinks into chaos."[90] The erstwhile "prophet of the slums," Caroit added a fortnight later, had succeeded only in "uniting all sections of Haitian society against him. The demands of the opposition, of civil society and of the student movement are now in unanimous agreement: declared 'beyond the pale' [*hors la loi*] by a coalition of socio-professional organizations, the president must go."[91] In its editorial survey of 18 December 2003 *Le Monde* was entitled to be proud of its own contribution to the portrayal of Haiti as a "country in agony, a country in rebellion," one led by a "despised president" whose name was now synonymous with "fiasco" and "martyrdom" – a country which, as it prepared for this fateful bicentenary, was finding that it had "only bad news to celebrate."[92]

Shortly after *Le Monde* came to the conclusion already reached by Chirac and de Villepin regarding France's "obligation to help a population in danger,"[93] it chose to celebrate some more of Haiti's bad news by commissioning CNRS professor Laënnec Hurbon to write a substantial review of Aristide's second administration. Hurbon duly described it as an "an avalanche of assassinations, rapes, and illegal arrests," and cited 17 December 2001 as one of the "culminating points" of Lavalas violence. As we shall see in chapter five, this was the day when "armed chimères burned the offices of the opposition parties and killed two followers of a political leader." So as not to confuse his readers, however, Hurbon chose to omit the fact that this (quite exceptional and endlessly misrepresented) outburst of popular anger was in fact a response to an altogether more violent coup attempt mounted by ex-soldiers acting in direct collusion with the leaders of these opposition parties.[94] A few days after Hurbon's characteristically hysterical diatribe – Hurbon is the anthropologist who would later compare Aristide to Pol Pot – Jean-Michel Caroit added perhaps the most substantial of his contributions to Haitian regime change, a "portrait" of Aristide's transition from "prophet to dictator," complete with references to his "thirst for absolute power", his "incapacity to negotiate honestly," his "fracticidal" hatred for his former political allies, his reliance on "the old Latin-American recipe of clientelism, corruption and extra-judicial violence," and in particular, of course, his dependence on "the 'chimères,' armed gangs that have taken the place of Duvalier's 'Tontons Macoutes.' "[95]

Most if not all other French newspapers embraced the task at hand with a quite extraordinary unanimity of purpose. Few did so with more enthusiasm than the purportedly left-of-center French daily *Libération*. Like other French papers, on the eve of Haiti's bicentenary *Libération*'s Jean-Hebert Armengaud uncritically embraced the G184 as a progressive and pluralist alternative to a "despotic" though thankfully "isolated" regime.[96] *Libération*'s editorialist Patrique Sabatier repeatedly vilified Aristide as a "defrocked priest turned tyrant millionaire" and identified his violent "turn towards despotism as the primary cause for the growing chaos."[97] Along the same lines, when the ex-communist daily *L'Humanité* ran a portrait of Aristide on the day after his expulsion it presented his political career as an evolution from "liberation theology to dictatorship," and accused the "paranoid defrocked priest" of relying on his "Cannibal Army militias" and of "necklacing his adversaries."[98] As for the right-of-center *Le Figaro*, it assumed that Aristide was nothing less than "one of the worst dictators in the whole of Haiti's long history."[99]

In the weeks leading up to the climax of foreign intervention in Haiti in February 2004, the less blinkered wing of the international press fell back on another well-worn editorial tactic. The real problem in Haiti, papers like the *Washington Post*, the *Guardian* or the *Globe & Mail* would decide, was the international community's reluctance to get involved. The *Washington Post* blamed the Bush administration for "feckless" inactivity and "minimalist diplomacy." It accused it of "ignoring" the crisis in Haiti, and failing to do enough to help the country "build democratic institutions."[100] The day of the coup, a *Guardian* leader bemoaned the fact that "at this moment of dire need" the great powers had done "nothing much" about it. "For all their doctrines and declarations, they have dithered and debated, ducked and dodged, and danced that old, slow diplomatic shuffle."[101] The best that can be said for this assessment is that it offered a slight grammatical improvement on US defense secretary Donald Rumsfeld's own inimitable presentation of his government's policy at the height of the insurgency:

> Needless to say, everyone's hopeful that the situation, which tends to ebb and flow down there, will stay below a certain threshold and that there's – we have no plans to do anything. By that I don't mean we have no plans. Obviously, we have plans to do everything in the world that we can think of. But we – there's no intention at the present time, or no reason to believe that any of the thinking that goes into these things day – year in and year out – would have to be utilized.[102]

Once the last of these non-existent plans had been put into effect by the end of February 2004, the mainstream press performed its appointed task with aplomb. *Libération* gloated over the dissolution of "the pathetic carnival over which Aristide had proclaimed himself king."[103] For the *New York Times* the joint French–US restoration of proper democracy to Haiti on 29 February was a fine example of how old allies can "find common ground and play to their strengths."[104]

It would be difficult indeed to describe most of the *Times'* coverage of the 2004 coup as anything other than anti-Lavalas propaganda pure and simple.[105] More intriguing is the fact that during these years much of the alternative press toed a very similar line. Groups like NACLA and

Grassroots International adopted (and subsequently maintained) an openly pro-coup stance that agreed in all essentials with the angle promoted by the IRI and the Haiti Democracy Project.[106] A pair of articles published by Peter Dailey in the *New York Review of Books* are typical of what many American and European readers were learning about Aristide in the "progressive mainstream" press in 2003–04. Dailey's main theme is Aristide's "betrayal" of his original ideals. As early as "1999, it seemed to many Haitians that Aristide, who once personified Haitian aspirations for democracy, now represented Haitian democracy's biggest obstacle." Discreetly glossing over US interference in Haitian affairs, Dailey somehow manages to present the CD as the "social democratic-constitutionalist wing of the Lavalas movement", a hard-pressed grass-roots movement confronted with an increasingly "violent," "corrupt" and "authoritarian" Aristide. Since only "gross electoral fraud" brought Aristide to power in 2001, Dailey argues, so only systematic violence and intimidation had been able to keep him in office.[107]

Dailey was right about one thing, at least: violence would indeed decide the fate of Aristide's regime, though not exactly in the way Dailey himself anticipated.

5

2001–2003: The Return of the Army

"We can't be called upon, expected or required to intervene every time there is violence against a failed leader. We can't spend our time running around the world and the hemisphere saving people who botched their chance at leadership"
(State Department spokesman Richard Boucher, 5 March 2004).

Economic constraints paralyzed the Lavalas administration and political pressure backed it into a corner. In the end, however, only old-fashioned military coercion on the Contra model could dislodge it from power. Leading figures in the Convergence Démocratique declared their ambitions to the world at the time of Aristide's reinauguration as president in February 2001. They openly called for another US invasion, "this time to get rid of Aristide and rebuild the disbanded Haitian army." Failing that, they told the *Washington Post*, "The CIA should train and equip Haitian officers exiled in the neighbouring Dominican Republic so they could stage a comeback themselves."[1]

Their northern friends, it seems, obeyed these instructions to the letter. Although definitive proof may remain hard to find, there has long been little doubt that while the IRI and USAID was funding the democratic opposition and the independent media in Haiti, less visible elements in the US government arranged for the establishment of the small Contra-style group of "rebels" that was initially dubbed the *Armée sans maman* (the motherless army) and that eventually came to be known under the still more absurd name of the *Front pour la Libération et la Reconstruction Nationale* (FLRN).

US policy makers realized long ago that democracy is best enhanced if its opponents are first compelled to take patently undemocratic steps to combat acts of sabotage and insurgency. A regime that was imprudent enough to disband its own army makes itself particularly vulnerable to this sort of pressure. In a country like Haiti, a small but properly equipped paramilitary force can easily overwhelm isolated rural police stations and terrorize rural populations; the effort to develop some means of defending itself can then easily ruin an already impoverished regime. Better still, if paramilitary provocation manages to goad some of the more militant and frustrated supporters of that regime into vigilante-style forms of mobilization or reprisal, a large part of the script for humanitarian intervention begins to play out all by itself. What was first just a struggle between an unscrupulous dictator and his democratic opponents intensifies to become a pitched battle between brutal thugs and the partisans of law, order and the "responsibility to protect." In the midst of such regrettable insecurity, moreover, how could a democratic opposition reasonably be expected to negotiate a new date for elections?

On its own, a non-violent destabilization campaign against FL had little or no chance of success. As with the Sandinistas before them, nothing short of military pressure could compromise and then undermine the Lavalas project. Although the IFES and its associates managed to put a dent in Aristide's popularity, on the eve of the 2004 coup he remained, by every available measure, far and away the most popular and most trusted politician in Haiti. As Fatton notes, "It's clear that Aristide would never have been toppled had it not been for the armed insurgents. I don't think that the civil opposition, although it became larger and broader in its appeal, was in any way capable of forcing Aristide out of power. It's only when you had the armed insurgents that you have the opportunity for the so-called 'civil society' to force the issue."[2]

Contingency plans for such an insurgency were in all likelihood already at an advanced stage by the late 1990s. As we have seen, in 1994–95 the CIA was careful to leave US options open, and took steps to preserve the valuable paramilitary structures it had built up during the first coup. According to Allan Nairn, in the weeks following the October 1994 invasion CIA agents accompanying US troops began a new recruitment drive for the agency; Nairn learned from US officials involved with the operation that "those placed or continued on the payroll include FRAPH leaders and *attachés*."[3] As we have seen, the US pointedly refused to take steps to disarm or otherwise compromise the power of their employees, and their insistence on a full amnesty for the coup leaders, coupled with the structural weakness of Haiti's fledgling judicial system, allowed them to weather Aristide's dissolution of the army and of the *attaché* network with a minimum of disruption. As

Andrew Reding noted in a prescient 1996 report, once the time was right and the UN occupation force was safely out of the way there would be little to stop a reactivated paramilitary force from "overwhelming the country's inexperienced and lightly armed police."[4]

When the time for this reactivation came, in late 2000, there were two obvious places to look for new recruits. A first option was to enlist one or more of the various armed groups operating in the slums of Port-au-Prince, Gonaïves and other destitute cities. Some of these groups were little more than impoverished criminal gangs; perhaps a few of their members could be bought. The problem with this option was that most if not all of these groups remained stubbornly loyal to Aristide. Aristide's opponents would have to wait until the middle of 2003 before they managed to induce a couple of them (Labanye's gang in Cité Soleil, Cubain's gang in Gonaïves) to switch camps. Their time would come. Meanwhile the second option was more immediately compelling, and much more familiar. Aristide's dissolution of the army in 1995 had created a large pool of eligible and resentful ex-military labor. Many of these soldiers had been trained in or by the US. Many hundreds of them were later integrated into the (consequently) volatile and unreliable police force. No doubt the best and most efficient option would have been a single coordinated uprising by the PNH itself, preferably before Aristide's official return to power. As we have seen, in the early 1990s a small group of ex-army personnel (Guy Philippe, Gilbert Dragon, Jean-Jacques Nau . . .) were awarded scholarships by Cédras for special training in Ecuador in anticipation of precisely this purpose. Over the course of 2000 a number of disgruntled officers led by Philippe and Nau duly began making the necessary preparations. Things came to a head in October, when on the day that Aristide officially announced his candidacy for re-election Nau – the right-hand man of ex-general and soon-to-be interior minister Hérard Abraham – clashed with an angry group of FL demonstrators led by Ronald Cadavre. Later that month an FL senator was assaulted and gunmen opened fire on a meeting of the militant Lavalas organization JPP, wounding eight people.[5] Although Philippe would later remember, "We were in control of almost all the police at that time," his move in the autumn of 2000 was premature and won over only a handful of conspirators.[6] By the time Préval and his prime minister denounced the incipient coup, on 18 October, Philippe and several other plotters had already fled to the safety of the Dominican Republic, apparently with the connivance of the US embassy.[7]

Guy Philippe would soon become the most public face of the FLRN.

With a penchant for luxury hotels and a media-friendly smile, Philippe was regularly profiled in the US press as a disinterested, well-educated and rather sexy patriot.[8] After quickly rising through the ranks of the Haitian army, his career began in 1992 in Ecuador's military academy, where he spent three years on a scholarship from the Cédras government, and reportedly trained with US special forces; he would later use his fluent Spanish to good effect in another client state of the US, Haiti's old enemy the Dominican Republic, where he spent most of the years 2000–04. He joined the new Haitian National Police in 1995. After a posting at Ouanaminthe on the Dominican border, from 1997–99 he served as police chief in the Port-au-Prince district of Delmas. During his Delmas tenure, his squad was implicated in the summary execution of "dozens of suspected gang members."[9] In May 2003 Philippe publicly admitted that he "would support a coup: we have to get rid of the dictator."[10] A year later he told the *Miami Herald* that the person he most admired was another anti-dictatorial strongman, Augusto Pinochet, the man who "made Chile what it is".[11]

After the debacle of October 2000, Philippe followed the familiar ex-military route of exile in the Dominican Republic, where he soon became a regular guest of the Santo Domingo hotel. (Philippe frustrated journalists by refusing to answer how a poorly-paid ex-policeman could afford such accommodation.) Understandably, while staying at the hotel, Philippe would meet from time to time with his old friend and ping-pong partner, the IRI's Stanley Lucas. "I was living in the hotel, sleeping in the hotel," Philippe told the *New York Times*, "so I saw him and his friends and those guys in the opposition, but we didn't talk politics." Paul Arcelin, a professor at Montréal's Université de Québec in the 1960s, one of the FLRN's main strategists and a man often described as Philippe's "political advisor," was another regular guest of the hotel: "I used to meet Stanley Lucas here in this hotel, alone, sitting down talking about the future of Haiti."[12] By coincidence, Arcelin also happened to be the CD's representative in the DR. Ten days after the completion of the February 2004 coup, Arcelin freely admitted that for at least two years he and Philippe had spent "10 to 15 hours a day together, plotting against Aristide. From time to time we'd cross the border through the woods to conspire against Aristide, to meet with the opposition and regional leaders to prepare for Aristide's downfall."[13]

Detailed reconstruction of the early development of the FLRN insurgency will have to wait for the declassification of the relevant CIA files (if not forever), but the general outlines of what happened have now been fairly well established – if not as incontrovertible fact then at least, in Fatton's words, as "very, very, very, very likely."[14] First of all, in 2001 Philippe started collaborating with Louis Jodel Chamblain, who was in exile in the DR and would later emerge as the operational commander of the FLRN. It is hard to imagine a more sinister combination. A prominent Macoute in the 1980s, in 1993/94 Chamblain served under Emmanuel Constant as deputy leader of the FRAPH death squad – at the time, a US intelligence official intimately connected to FRAPH tried to distinguish the urbane, "pro-Western" Constant from his deputy Chamblain, "a cold-blooded, cutthroat, psychopathic killer."[15] Implicated in numerous atrocities, he was convicted in absentia both for the 1993 murder of Antoine Izméry and for a role in the Raboteau massacre of April 1994. Despite these convictions, neither the US nor the Dominican Republic ever sought to extradite him to Haiti. On at least one occasion during the run-up to Aristide's expulsion, Chamblain appeared on a TV newscast in the uniform of a Dominican policeman.[16] Another prominent figure in the insurgency, Jean Tatoune (a.k.a. Jean-Pierre Baptiste), was also an active member of FRAPH. As the insurgency gained momentum Tatoune was in a Gonaïves prison serving part of the life-sentence he was given in 2000 for his own part in the Raboteau massacre. Tatoune escaped from prison in August 2002, and there is good reason to think that he played an instrumental role in developing what would in early 2004 become a crucial link between the FLRN rebels based in the Dominican Republic and newly anti-Aristide gang-leaders in Gonaïves.

Then, in the spring of 2001, Philippe (or Chamblain) enlisted a number of disgruntled ex-FAdH personnel, including Ravix Rémissainthe and Jean-Baptiste Clotaire, and began preparing a small anti-Lavalas force in the Dominican Republic. For the DR this was business as usual. The DR had provided refuge to former Haitian army officers and FRAPH commanders in the 1990s, and barbaric treatment of Haitian migrant workers has been standard DR policy for decades. As journalist David Adams points out, ever since Aristide had done away with the Haitian military in 1995 "some Dominican generals were worried about their own job security. Without an army next door in Haiti, the traditional enemy of the Dominican Republic, calls were growing in Santo Domingo to slash the size of their own notoriously bloated and corrupt armed forces. [Philippe's] rebels exploited this to the full. They set up a small guerrilla base near the border," at Pernal, which they used as a staging post for a series of incursions into Haiti that began in the summer of 2001.[17] Robert Muggah's 2005 report for the *Small Arms Survey* summarizes what everyone knows but that no-one has yet been able to prove: "It is widely rumored that US Special Forces were involved in the training of a number of former FAdH headed by Guy Philippe in the Dominican Republic. Military equipment and supplies were believed to have been transferred via Dominican police and military authorities to members of the former Haitian military stationed in the Dominican Republic."[18] By 2003, this small rebel force probably consisted of some 50 to 100 men. The Dominican Republic is a thoroughly cooperative client state of the United States and, and it is hard to imagine that any of these things could have happened without the active cooperation of its patron. As Elie notes, the Dominican Republic is a "very policed society and the idea that 80 to 100 men could be armed and trained in the DR without the assent of the government or the army there is totally preposterous. This was done with the complicity of the Dominican services, and they are but the proxies for the US."[19]

The rebels' first significant incursion into Haiti took place in July 2001. The timing is significant. After breaking down back in February, "negotiations" between the government and the CD had started up again in the spring of 2001. As it became more and more obvious that Aristide was willing to make substantial compromises in order to proceed with his legislative agenda, it became more and more difficult for the negotiators to sustain their *option zéro*. By July it looked as if Aristide's new administration might finally be making some political progress. Shortly after promising talks were held in mid-July at the Hotel Montana in Port-au-Prince, Pierre-Charles and other leaders of the CD acknowledged that they were close to achieving a "total agreement" with Fanmi Lavalas. Less than a fortnight later, however, on 28 July, the FLRN launched its first major operation. Separate groups of insurgents dressed in military uniform and shouting "Long live the army!" simultaneously attacked the Haitian National Police Academy in Port-au-Prince and three police stations near the Dominican border in the Central Plateau. The insurgents killed five police officers and wounded fourteen others.[20] After raiding the Police Academy's arsenal, the assailants were chased out of Port-au-Prince and back to their base in the Dominican Republic by a combination of police and members of the local population.[21] Rather than condemn the attacks, members of the CD like Himmler Rébu and José Jacques Nicolas used the occasion to remind people that "in all countries the military has a role: ensuring stability in the country. Haiti needs a military: the real security of the country is the army."[22]

What happened next is typical of the pattern that persisted right through to the completion of *option zéro* on 29 February 2004. The government briefly held thirty-five suspects linked to the attacks, including some CD supporters. With the approval of US ambassador Curran, the CD leaders responded by breaking off further negotiations with FL, claiming that Aristide had staged the attacks himself in order to justify a crackdown on his opponents. Future "negotiations" would stumble over similar hurdles.[23] From now on, the dangerous prospect of a political solution to the crisis could always be kept at a safe military distance. The government's failure to prosecute any of the attackers also set a demoralizing precedent, and did nothing to reassure rattled members of the PNH.[24]

The next major attack was a brazen assault on the presidential palace on 17 December 2001. With 50mm calibre machine-gun support, around thirty heavily armed commandos seized the palace for several hours, announcing on radio that "Aristide was no longer President and that Guy Philippe was the new commander of the National Police of Haiti." A detailed OAS report on the incident noted that "the assailants took the principal building without resistance from the guards," and that the whole operation relied on "complicity within the National Police"; the operational commander seems to have been Chavre Milot, one of the USGPN officers dismissed by Aristide earlier in the year.[25] Five or six people died in the attack, including Milot himself. In response, all over Haiti thousands of people stormed out to protest the attempted coup, and in both Gonaïves and Port-au-Prince crowds of indignant Lavalas supporters converged on the headquarters of a couple of parties in the CD and set them on fire. Speaking for the CD, Evans Paul said: "This was no coup d'état, it was a coup de théâtre."[26]

Further FLRN assaults on rural police stations took place the following year. On the night of 23 June 2002, a detachment of Philippe's troops led by Ravix Rémissainthe descended on Belladère in search of the local FL activist Cleonor Souverain; when they discovered he wasn't at home they laid out five members of his family on the ground and shot them instead (one of the victims, 17-year-old Nathalie Souverain, died from the blast of a shotgun inserted into her vagina).[27] Belladère was hit at least three other times that same year, first on 30 April and again on 28 November; the town hall was torched and FL activist Jean Bronchette and judge Christophe Lozama were killed. In a follow-up attack on 10 December, rebels emptied the Belladère jail and killed a further four civilians. On 19 December 2002, a group of these same insurgents held a brief press conference in Pernal, near Belladère, and announced their intention to "overthrow Aristide in a military manner." They called on "all the military men who have gone into hiding and all the competent citizens in the country to come out, to return and join us so we may fight" Aristide's government together with the popular organizations and gangs that supported it. In the remote areas of the Central Plateau, incursions by groups of ex-soldiers calling for the restoration of the army and the violent overthrow of the government soon became a regular occurrence. After being pushed out of Pernal by a police SWAT team, insurgents attacked the Plaisance police station in January 2003 and the Baptiste police station in February. Also in February they killed a couple of FL activists in Petit Goâve, policeman Patrick Samedi near Belladère, and presidential security agent Irandal Pierre-Louis in Port-au-Prince.[28] In May 2003 around 20 insurgents attacked the country's largest power station, the Peligre hydroelectric plant in the Central Plateau, killing two security guards. (On 6 May, the Dominican authorities briefly complied with a Haitian request to arrest five people suspected of involvement in these attacks, including Philippe and Arcelin, before releasing them almost immediately.) On 18 June, Ravix Rémissainthe executed FL supporter Marais Pierre in Belladère. On 25 July 2003 rebels killed four members of an Interior Ministry delegation to the Central Plateau. Further attacks took place off and on through the summer and autumn of 2003. By the time rebels murdered Amorgue Cléma (the deputy mayor of Savanette-Baptiste) on 14 December, it brought "the total number of Lavalas Family members and supporters killed in the Pernal-Belladère area over the last twelve months to 30."[29]

When the full-scale military uprising against Aristide finally began in February 2004, in other words, police and Lavalas activists based in the more isolated parts of the country had good reason to be nervous. Before the end of that month, Chamblain felt strong enough to declare that he had already achieved his main goal: "The army was demobilized. Now the army has been remobilized."[30] Asked on 24 February whether the rebels were cooperating with the CD and the rest of the democratic opposition, Chamblain's colleague Guy Philippe "smiled and said 'not officially.' He refused to elaborate [but] said he was on his way to a Western Union office to pick up donations being sent by Haitians in the United States and Canada. He said his rebellion was also being funded by businessmen in Haiti."[31]

Needless to say, US policy makers have always denied any knowledge of Philippe's little band of insurgents. Noriega told a Senate hearing in 2004 that there was no link of any sort between Philippe, Lucas and the

IRI. If any such connection existed, he declared, "we would certainly stop it. We knew who Guy Philippe was and that he had a criminal background."[32] A decent democratic organization like the IRI could have nothing to do with crooks like Philippe. Stanley Lucas maintains to this day that "I do not know Guy Philippe" and that he can only recall meeting him once, back during Philippe's time in Delmas. (Philippe himself is rather more forthcoming, acknowledging "Mr. Lucas as 'a good friend' whom he has known much of his life" and saying that they met repeatedly not only at the Santo Domingo Hotel but on a couple of occasions in 2000 and 2001, while he was still in exile in Ecuador.[33])

Since it was democratic, the democratic opposition also denied any links with the military opposition. Once the FLRN incursions began in the summer of 2001, members of the CD regularly claimed that the government itself was behind the attacks, staging them in order to whip up public sympathy and a pretext to crack down on the democratic opposition. Reports in the independent press both in Haiti and the US almost invariably presented the paramilitary attacks as doubtful or "difficult to verify," despite the fact that on several occasions, groups of these paramilitaries stepped up to the microphone (for instance at Pernal on 19 December 2002) to introduce themselves as the armed wing of the opposition and to broadcast a call to other ex-military personnel to help them organize attacks against the government, the police, Lavalas supporters and *organisations populaires*.[34]

By the time such attacks had grown into the open insurgency of February 2004, the CD took a rather different position. CD spokesman ex-colonel Himmler Rébu told Radio Métropole on 9 February that "Aristide has no choice but to resign after losing control of towns in different parts of the country." After noting that "the police had received insufficient training to deal with the situation they face in Gonaïves," Rébu called on "police officers to defect rather than take actions to the detriment of the wider population." Like their foreign financial backers, G184 leaders like Andy Apaid and Hans Tippenhauer were slightly more discreet than Rébu and other openly pro-army factions of the opposition, but made little attempt to hide their approval of the "freedom fighters" (see below, page 221).[35] Their G184 colleague Charles Baker took the same line: "The rebels are heroes in Gonaïves and they are heroes throughout Haiti, whether you like it or not."[36]

In reality, relations between the opposition's democratic and military wings had been rather less equivocal all along. Philippe himself says that he began to "make serious plans with leading members of the CD for a military project against the government [in] December 2000," and explains that "the Haitian elite and the political parties in the Convergence helped us with money and weapons. Some leading Haitian businessmen met with us, and in Cap-Haïtien for instance they donated around $50,000 (US) [. . .]. The businessmen seemed keen to help us at all costs. Getting hold of money was not a problem."[37] By the end of 2003, Philippe continues, since "everyone knew that Aristide wouldn't resign as a result of peaceful protests," a broad coalition of anti-Aristide groups including "representatives from most of the political parties, three representatives of the private sector, and leaders of student groups" met at the Santo Domingo hotel on 13 December 2003 to help plan the launch of an armed insurgency under Philippe's command.[38] The neo-Macoute director of Cap- Haïtien's Radio Maxima Jean-Robert Lalanne played an important mediating role in both the logistical planning and media representation of the campaign. In exchange for toppling the tyrant, Philippe was promised that in a post-Aristide Haiti he and his men "would be responsible for the country's security."[39] A more detailed sense of the deal that was struck between the military and political wings of the opposition is indicated by the actions and expectations of Philippe and his followers in the immediate aftermath of the February coup. In early March 2004, Philippe made public assurances to the rebels based in Cap-Haïtien that "They will be able to join the National Police," telling them that "The procedures are multiplying for them to advance in a legal framework for the Haitian population's benefit"; sure enough, many hundreds of his men were later integrated into the PNH. In the summer of 2004, Ravix Rémissainthe and other ex-military members of the FLRN started to claim (and receive) ten years' back-pay as compensation for the jobs they lost when Aristide disbanded the army in 1995.

As the summer drew to a close, however, Ravix and his followers drew more insistent attention to the promises they said they had been given, before the coup, of post-coup promotions in a reconstituted version of the Haitian army. These alleged promises were never kept. As a frustrated Ravix began to outlive his usefulness, in the autumn of 2004 he made ever more incriminating claims on public radio about his pre-coup association with leading figures in the CD and the G184. According to Ravix, all of the most notorious incidents that opposition leaders tried to pin on a tyrannical government – the attack on the National Palace of 17 December 2001, the hit-and-run raids in and around Belladère in 2002–03, the sabotage of the Boutilliers radio transmitters on 13 January 2004, etc. – were in fact commissioned by these very opposition leaders themselves.[40] Ravix would soon pay a high price for his indiscretion: members of the newly "depoliticized" PNH, with UN support, gunned him down in April 2005. Gonaïves-based insurgent Winter Etienne has likewise briefed international journalists about the close financial and logistical links between the military and the political (Himmler Rébu, Evans Paul, Jean-Renel Latortue, Hérard Abraham . . .) wings of the opposition.

Guy Philippe played his cards more prudently than Ravix. Nevertheless, once it was clear that his old allies had no further use for his services, Philippe too went on radio to acknowledge the crucial role played by leading figures of political opposition in the paramilitary attacks on the government that began in July 2001. In 2006 he even admitted that no less a person than PANPRA's Serge Gilles ordered one of the FLRN's most high profile attacks, the May 2003 assault on the Peligre dam.[41] A few months later it seems that an exasperated US government decided to reduce the risk of still more damaging revelations, and in July 2007 Philippe was indicted by the DEA.

The FLRN campaign finally restored to the US a version of the behind-the-scenes leverage it had enjoyed in Haiti before 1995. On the one hand the US was (secretly) behind both a political and a paramilitary opposition that sought to generate maximum levels of insecurity and tension. On the other hand, the US and the OAS could now (openly) blame the FL administration for failing to create the "climate of security" necessary for continued negotiation with that same opposition. When Roger Noriega called on Aristide to take steps to "heal the wounds" caused by the 17 December 2001 attack on the presidential palace, for instance, he made it clear that in the opinion of the US it was the *government* (rather than those who attacked it) that was mainly responsible for causing these wounds. As further rebel attacks against it multiplied over the following year, rather than help it confront these mysterious new aggressors Noriega demanded instead that "the Haitian government make difficult and unpopular decisions, and call on local officials, especially mayors, and so-called popular organizations to lay down arms and refrain from their use."[42] Thanks to the FLRN, in other words, the US was able to set in motion a process that was designed to negotiate for one and only one objective: the unconditional surrender of Lavalas.

All through 2003, Yvon Neptune and members of the FL government regularly and rightly insisted that the groups of armed men causing havoc in the Central Plateau represented "the armed branch" of the Democratic

Convergence. "The people who were involved in the attacks on the police academy in July 2001 and the National Palace in December 2001, on Pernal and the surrounding villages in 2002–2003, the demonstrations and unrest in Gonaïves in the autumn of 2003 – this was all the same network of people."[43] By contrast, when CD leader Pierre-Charles was asked about these rebel incursions in March 2003, he said "We consider this whole thing a fake. The Lavalas government is doing this to justify its permanent and institutionalized violence against the Haitian people. We do not believe in violence."[44] A year later, the UN would be scarcely less dismissive. When the Security Council finally got round to passing a resolution on the crisis in Haiti, on 29 February 2004, it drew attention to regrettable levels of violence and insecurity but made no mention of the role or even the existence of the rebels. The IFES and IRI had invested their money to good effect: from 2001–04, the independent and democratic media both at home and abroad made sure that what was most prominent in the public domain was not the assault against government institutions or Lavalas personnel so much as the occasional and altogether less violent acts of retaliation that this assault was designed to provoke.

6

2001–2004: Aristide's Second Administration

Piti, piti, zwazo fè nich li
(Little by little the bird builds its nest).

In the run-up to the bicentenary celebrations planned for January 2004, grounds for discouragement were easy to find. Even before Aristide's inauguration in February 2001, Haiti's government was already verging on bankruptcy. Its social and economic programmes were already compromised by concessions extorted by the US, the IMF and the domestic elite. From July 2001, it was also obliged to govern under more or less constant paramilitary pressure, pressure that contributed to a demoralizing sense of tension and insecurity. The atmosphere was further poisoned by the constant barrage of anti-Lavalas propaganda in the US-funded press, and as we shall see, some opportunistic members or associates of Fanmi Lavalas would soon provide the anti-government media with at least a little of the incriminating material it was looking for, through their complicity in a series of damaging scandals and mistakes. "It's as if Aristide was put in charge of a house that was falling apart," says Patrick Elie, "and was expected to fix it. But then his enemies start setting fire to the back door, they send people with guns to attack the front door, and when these people finally manage to break in they said 'Look! He didn't wash the dishes in the sink! He never repaired that leak in the roof!' They made him spend all his time trying to put out the fire and to protect the door, and then once they got rid of him they said he was pushed out *because* he'd failed to repair the house."[1]

All things considered, however, one of the more remarkable things about the Lavalas administrations – especially now that we can compare them with the infinitely better-funded, better-equipped and better-armed Latortue government that was to follow it, to say nothing of the Duvalier,

Namphy or Cédras dictatorships that preceded it – is how much they managed to accomplish with the desperately limited means at their disposal. Cap-Haïtien businessman Steve MacIntosh was critical of what he considered Aristide's socially divisive rhetoric, but acknowledges that during 2001–04 "there was a lot of social investment in and around the Cap; new schools were built, irrigation canals were dug, literacy centers opened, that kind of thing. This all stopped in 2004, and the UN has done nothing to restart them."[2] In spite of the pressure they were under, agrees Elie, "in spite of the fact that they had no money and were under siege from the get-go, the Lavalas governments still have the best record of any Haitian government to date."[3] A 2006 IMF report recognized that Haiti's Human Poverty Indicator (a rough measurement of quality of life, which takes into account levels of mortality, nutrition, illiteracy, access to basic health services, and so on) "appears to have dropped from 46.2 percent in 1987 to 31.8 percent in 2000," which under the circumstances is a rather remarkable feat. ("It remains to be seen," the report continues, "if that improvement has diminished or even been erased in the wake of conditions of violence and insecurity from 2004 to 2006".)[4] "If the people still cry '*Vive Aristide*' today," notes the veteran broadcaster Marcus Garcia, "it's not because they are stupid or deluded, it's because he did things they appreciate, he responded to some real needs."[5] In occasional moments of lucidity even a mainstream paper like the *Washington Post* could see (in November 2003) that what had happened since Aristide's re-election in 2000 was not that Aristide had become a cynical tyrant but that he had sought to apply "with mixed success a populist agenda of higher minimum wages, school construction, literacy programs, higher taxes on the rich and other policies that have angered an opposition movement run largely by a mulatto elite that has traditionally controlled Haiti's economy."[6]

Aristide's final prime minister still regrets the fact that as result of all sorts of pressures and constraints, "Lavalas has never yet been given the opportunity to prove itself."[7] It is understandable, perhaps, that this chapter is the shortest in the book. Nevertheless, from 1994 to 2004 Aristide and Préval were at least able to build on their various achievements, maintaining a level of continuity that is itself exceptional in recent Haitian politics. Small but helpful steps were taken in the fields of education and health, supplemented by initiatives in social and urban policy.

ACHIEVEMENTS OF THE
LAVALAS ADMINISTRATIONS[8]

Education provides the main means of escaping the socio-economic penitentiary in which most Haitian people live. Between them, Préval and Aristide built some 195 new primary schools, together with 104 new secondary schools (building on an initial total of just 34). Haiti's public schools operate free of charge but remain few and far between, and fees for books and uniforms still serve as an effective barrier to wider participation; as a stopgap, Lavalas also provided thousands of scholarships to allow children to attend private or church-run schools, and between 2001 and 2004, primary school enrolment rates rose slightly, from 68 percent to 72 percent. Hundreds of thousands of children benefited from a school-lunch program. Hundreds of thousands of adults, meanwhile, benefited from a major literacy campaign, launched in May 2001. Millions of literacy booklets were printed and many hundreds of literacy centers were established. Most classes were taught, after-hours, on local school premises. A total of perhaps 300,000 people attended such classes, many of them traveling to and from class in specially designated buses. Although estimates vary, between 1990 and 2003 illiteracy probably fell from something like 65 percent to something closer to 45 percent. Aristide himself took particular pride in the establishment of a new university in Tabarre, one of the largest in the country. Designed and staffed with Cuban assistance, Tabarre's medical school was a major new investment in equitable health care: unlike the state university, Tabarre offered students scholarships and room and board in exchange for a commitment to work for several years in remote parts of the country. (The university was shut down after the coup, and the complex was appropriated as a base for US troops; as of 2007 it remains closed and partly occupied by MINUSTAH soldiers, forcing the staff to relocate the medical training to Cuba itself.)

When Aristide came to power in 1990, health care in urban areas remained extremely limited, and in many rural areas – i.e. in most of the country – it was more or less non-existent. Aristide's second administration built or renovated a number of health clinics and hospitals, including, in Port-au-Prince, the substantial Hôpital de Delmas 33 and major clinics based in Bel Air and at Lafanmi Selavi. (After February 2004, the Lafanmi complex was gutted, and material from Delmas 33 was stolen and distributed to private health clinics.) Cooperative ventures with Zanmi Lasante (a remarkable international healthcare programme founded in the early 1980s by the American doctor Paul Farmer) led to major improvements of government facilities in several parts of the country. Parallel cooperation with Cuba enabled that country to send some 800 hundred doctors and nurses to Haiti, a country with less than 1000 doctors of its own. Significant steps were taken to improve maternity wards and ante-natal programs. New programs were launched to combat infectious diseases like tuberculosis and HIV, and were so successful that Haiti was one of the first three countries to win grants from the new UN Global Fund for AIDS, TB and malaria. During the 1990s, the rate of HIV infection – a legacy from the sex tourism industry of the 1970s and '80s – was frozen and then slightly reduced, to a level of 5 percent. As the Catholic Institute for International Relations recognized in 2004, the "incredible feat of slowing the rate of new infections in Haiti has been achieved despite the lack of international aid to the Haitian government, and despite the notable lack of resources faced by those working in the health field."[9] Under the Lavalas administrations, says Laura Flynn, "infant mortality declined from 125 deaths per 1000 to 110, and the percentage of underweight newborns dropped from 28 percent to 19 percent."[10]

Bearing in mind the circumstances in which they were obliged to work, the achievements of the Préval-Aristide governments in other domains are no less impressive. Most obviously and importantly, an end to systematic repression meant that incidents of political violence dropped to a tiny fraction of pre- and post-Aristide levels (see below, page 155). Impunity remained a problem under Aristide, and the independence and efficiency of the woefully under-funded legal system were often criticized – as US military experts acknowledged in 1998, reform of Haiti's judicial system represented a "mind-boggling" challenge, since as a result of structural neglect "Haitian justice lacks everything: financial resources, materials, competent personnel, independence, stature and trust."[11] Nevertheless, the overall provision of legal services improved. Most defendants were brought before a judge with a speed that bears little comparison to the pre-1991 or post-2004 regimes, and many proceedings took place in Kreyol rather than French. In the last year of Préval's first administration, the elaborate and successful trials of those responsible for the Carrefour-Feuilles and Raboteau massacres marked a watershed in Haitian legal history – the first real demonstrations that the law might be used on behalf of the victims rather than the perpetrators of state-sanctioned violence. The Raboteau trial held in November 2000 not only convicted sixteen former FRAPH and FAdH members for their participation in the 1994 massacre, it also served as a belated indictment for the entire 1991 coup-regime. In the wake of the army's dissolution in 1995, more general respect for basic political freedoms like freedom of speech, association and assembly rose to unprecedented levels. Between 1996 and 2003, around 100 judges and prosecutors were trained at a new school for magistrates. Significant measures were adopted to limit the widespread exploitation of children, including a 2003 law designed to end the often dramatic abuse of the estimated 400,000 thousand *restaveks* (children sent, mainly from the countryside, to work as unpaid servants in wealthier homes). Breaking with a long and shameful history, under Aristide children began to receive meaningful legal protection. Special children's courts were established, and a dedicated child protection unit was attached to the national police. Thanks to the creation of the extraordinary child-run station Radio Timoun at the Lafanmi Selavi center for street kids that Aristide founded in the late 1980s, children and children's issues gained access to the public sphere for the first time.[12] Also for the first time, women were named to the posts of prime minister, finance minister and foreign affairs minister, and chief of police, and unprecedented numbers of women were elected to parliament. A new Ministry of Women's Affairs was created in 1995, to coordinate policy on issues like violence against women, pre-natal care, post-natal education, conditions of work, and so on.

As we have seen, no more than the ANC in South Africa or Michael Manley's last administration in Jamaica – no more, in fact, than any government of an impoverished country during the 1990s – the Lavalas governments were not in a position to pursue anything like socialist forms of redistribution or economic policy.[13] Although the ongoing effects of the structural adjustment plan imposed on Haiti after 1994 led inexorably to increased hardship for the poor majority, still the Lavalas governments did what they could to soften the blow. They maintained subsidies for sensitive consumer goods. They pushed through some limited land reform in the country's most fertile region, the Artibonite valley, with around 1500 peasant families each receiving access to a couple of new acres of land. A major road linking the capital to towns in the hitherto remote south-western part of the country was built, irrigation infra-structure was repaired, and thousands of new Caribbean pigs were reintroduced across the country, undoing some of the damage caused by the 1982 extermination program. Under Aristide, for the first time the Haitian government began to participate in regular discussions with Venezuela, Cuba and other Caribbean islands in order to develop economic strategies for limiting US influence in the region, including hemispheric trading agreements to offset the neo-liberal effects of the FTAA and other hegemonic initiatives.[14] At the same time, and in the face of vigorous opposition, Aristide managed to extract and raise tax contributions from the elite. Despite further and similar opposition, in April 2003 Aristide again managed to double a woefully inadequate minimum wage. More importantly, in what was left of the state sector he managed to create thousands of new jobs for people in the poorer neighborhoods. Perhaps four to five thousand people found work, often for the first time in their lives, as public sector employees in the state-owned telephone, port-authority and water companies; hundreds of others were hired as security guards or as members of the PNH. Although critics of the government claimed that many of these jobs were corrupt – and some undoubtedly were[15] – the sharing out of these small salaries helped maintain at least a minimal standard of living in neighborhoods like Solino, Bel Air, La Saline and Cité Soleil (a situation that would come to an abrupt end in March 2004, when all of these "political" employees would be fired en masse and replaced with more "appropriately quali-fied" personnel). Although the poverty of a district like Cité Soleil remains as flagrant as that of any slum on the planet, Aristide left the neighborhood in considerably better shape than he found it, with a large new public square and playground in its center, flanked by a refurbished market space and a serviceable port. Similar public squares were built in some fifty other over-crowded areas of Port-au-Prince, along with a substantial number of new low-cost houses (a total of around 1000 new units in 2002–03 alone).

LAVALAS AND POPULAR ORGANIZATION

The Aristide-Préval years were an exceptional period by every pertinent standard. For the first time in its history, Haiti's people were ruled by a government of their choosing, one that adopted their priorities as its own. There are good reasons why so many of its supporters remain unwilling to this day to abandon their calls for Aristide's return, why they refuse US and NGO calls simply to "move forward" and "look ahead" to a future that the international community has chosen for it. More than its concrete achievements, perhaps the most important reason why a majority of the Haitian poor remains sympathetic to Lavalas in general and to Aristide in particular is the fact that, despite its limitations and mistakes, they could affirm them as vehicles for their *own* empowerment.

"Everyone who is anyone is against Aristide," a Haitian businessman told a reporter shortly before the September 1991 coup, "except the people."[16] In 1991 as in 2001 (and in all likelihood as in 2011), it is the *peuple*, the people who traditionally have been treated not as anyone but as no-one, who have always stubbornly supported Aristide. If you ask FL activists like Jean-Marie Samedy or John Joseph Jorel why they still support him, the first thing they say is, "He was close to the people from the poorer neighborhoods, and he always worked alongside us"; "He gave us a lot of respect, he was the only politician ever to treat us with dignity, to value us, to help us confront the obstacles that we face."[17]

This popular investment in Aristide and his legacy remains the single most decisive and divisive element of Haitian politics. "Aristide is always at the heart of the contradiction," Bobby Duval recognizes, "he's always there where things are going to blow up. You've got to give him credit for that!"[18] Aristide's opponents, including left-leaning members of the intelligentsia who also oppose the US, the IMF and the status quo, tend to frame their critique in terms of delusion and betrayal: a manipulative and self-serving demagogue, Aristide wasn't worthy of the people's trust; he didn't focus on institutions and procedures; he was more of a priest than an administrator; he made too many compromises with the imperialists. If you confront people in places like Cité Soleil or Bel Air with this sort of objection, they tend to smile or shrug. Aristide helped us to organize ourselves, they say. Of course his own freedom of movement was limited, but he helped us to mobilize for the first time as active participants in national politics.

The close affiliation of a mass movement with a particular leader is always a mixed blessing, of course, and there is no denying that part of the popular enthusiasm for Aristide is a legacy of the ambiguous authority of the Catholic church. Aristide himself (a relentless critic of this authority) is the first to admit that he remains more of a priest than a conventional politician. It's also obvious that this is one reason why this particular electorate – an electorate that has had very little positive experience of either politicians or political parties – prefers leaders like Aristide and Gérard Jean-Juste over people like Bazin, Pierre-Charles or Evans Paul, let alone Baker or de Ronceray. Dawn Raby makes a point about Venezuela's popular enthusiasm for Hugo Chávez that applies equally well to Haiti's Aristide: in both cases, NGO administrators and left-leaning academics are often uneasy with what they see as a merely populist deviation. Loath to admit even the possibility of radical change, conventional academic scepticism "refuses to consider the possibility that the charismatic leadership and chiliastic enthusiasm which it so despises may fulfil a necessary symbolic function in popular mobilization and in the real, effective construction of a new and more just social system."[19] At least at this stage in their mobilization, most Haitians clearly feel that a shared allegiance to a single well-known figure does more to strengthen and consolidate rather than divide or weaken the popular movement. It's no less obvious that if Aristide himself has little interest in developing a political party in the narrow sense, he is the only major figure in Haitian politics to sustain a genuine interest in popular organization in the broader sense. As even his less dogmatic rivals on the left of the political spectrum will admit, he is the only prominent political leader to maintain close and sympathetic links with a broad range of grassroots militants.[20] If his supporters continue to this day to insist on his immediate return to Haiti this is not because they want him to become president once again (an option forbidden by the constitution) but because they refuse to accept the coup of 2004, and because they know "he can help us strengthen Fanmi Lavalas and the popular struggle."[21]

Popular support for Aristide, in other words, is anything but passive. Much of this support has for more than two decades now been channeled through the informal but resilient network of *organisations populaires* (OPs), which have played a central role in the collective mobilization since the demise of Jean-Claude Duvalier (if not, as many OP members will tell you, since the development of mass resistance to the US occupation 1915–34). In a country in which state services are so weak and intermittent, OPs provide an instrument for all kinds of social programs – schooling, construction, youth projects, cultural projects, sports and athletic activities, street cleaning and waste management, and so on. Leaders like Gérard Jean-Juste and Jean-Marie Samedy are good examples of the way Lavalas authority emerges from local commitment: they owe their prominence as political spokesmen primarily to their constancy as social activists and advocates for the poor inhabitants of the neighborhoods where they live. Jean-Juste's church runs a range of social programs, including a soup kitchen that now feeds several thousand people a day. In Bel Air, Jean-Marie Samedy has been active in the Lavalas movement since he was a teenager, and has paid for his willingness to act as a spokesman first for his neighborhood (and then for a national network of popular organizations) with repeated police beatings and incarcerations. Pro-Lavalas OPs like SOPUDEP (Société de Providence Unie pour le Développement de Pétionville), KOREM (Kombit Rezistans Mas Yo) or MOJSIPD-CUD (Mouvement des Jeunes Simon/

Pélé pour la Défense de la Culture et du Développement Social) provide, in addition to valuable work in education and legal advice, highly engaged forums for political discussion and debate.

Most of the older OPs developed out of the pro-democracy movement of the mid-1980s, at a time when poor neighborhoods also formed *comités de vigilance* to defend themselves against the military's increasingly regular incursions. Following the transformative mobilization around Aristide's first election in 1990, many of these committees later evolved in tandem with the grassroots organization of Fanmi Lavalas. Fanmi Lavalas is derided by its critics as little more than an ad hoc association of ambitious and unprincipled schemers, grouped submissively around their charismatic chief. Many opportunists certainly did worm their way into the organization, once it became clear that it offered an almost guaranteed pathway to political power; I'll come back to this point in the following chapter. Critics of FL who harp on about the scoundrels that jumped on its electoral bandwagon downplay, however, the genuine popular force that lends this wagon its momentum in the first place. As Ramilus Bolivar (a rural activist elected as a FL deputy in May 2000) puts it, "Fanmi Lavalas is the only political organization that has ever tried systematically to formulate and implement the people's demands, and to do this in direct confrontation with Haiti's old imperial enemies. This is why I'd guess that around 75 percent of the peasantry still supports Fanmi Lavalas."[22]

On the model of the *ti legliz* and the *organisations populaires* before it, FL draws its power from many hundreds of local *cellules* or *ti fanmis*, small groups of dedicated, grassroots militants. This national network of *militants de base* – the *baz*, for short – is what distinguishes FL from any other Haitian political party or organization. As things stand, FL is by far the most inclusive and participative of Haitian political organizations. Its organization is cohesive enough to win a national election, but elastic enough to stretch over a diffuse network of semi-autonomous groups. Each neighborhood or district has its own informal committee whose members meet regularly to discuss local issues, engage with local problems, maintain the integrity of the local organization, and agree on feedback to be communicated to the wider regional cell. This cell is further represented at the municipal and national levels through participation in steering committees like the Cellule de Réflexion Nationale, and the Cellule Nationale de Base de Fanmi Lavalas. Unlike the great majority of Haitian politicians, the leading figures in the FL grassroots – people like Jean-Charles Moïse, Jean-Marie Samedy, John Joseph Jorel, Gérard Jean-Juste, Samba Boukman – are people who have acquired political influence (and in some cases political salaries) not through manipulation of a few elite connections but through their daily work in the midst of the people.[23] They have emerged through the mobilization of a particular neighborhood or region, through an endless series of meetings, demonstrations, encounters with the police, occasional discussions with the media, and if they attain a certain prominence it is because they retain broad approval as *spokesmen*, precisely, for their particular district.

For the time being, at least, Fanmi Lavalas remains the single most important organized political force in the country. Its leaders may decide to adopt a different name and formal configuration, but as things stand it remains Haiti's central political actor. Fanmi Lavalas is the main obstacle to the elite's political agenda. More than any other political organization or institution, it stands in the way of elite attempts to turn the clock back, to undo the revolution of 1990. Rather than Aristide per se it was this organization's enduring strength in the poorer neighborhoods that was the real target of pro-coup forces in and after 2004.

7

2001–2004: The Winner Loses?

Di dyab bonjou l ap manje ou, pa di l bonjou l ap manje ou
(If you don't greet the devil he will eat you,
but if you do greet him he will still eat you).

For all its resilience and strength, during its years in office Fanmi Lavalas suffered from undeniable faults. No doubt it relied too much on Aristide's charisma, and no doubt it could have done more to formalize its procedures and organization. More importantly though, following the victories of 2000 it suffered from the effects of its own popularity.

SUBVERSION FROM WITHIN

The emergence of Fanmi Lavalas as a dominant political force had at least three problematic consequences.

First of all, the combination of its power, its novelty and its relative informality made it an obvious target for infiltration by opportunistic members of the conventional political class, as well as by some former Macoutes, some former soldiers, and some criminal gang leaders. As a leader of the peasant group Tet Kole explained in late 2000, "it is difficult to have confidence in the government when murderers are at large. Many of these people, including former military, are opportunists who have aligned themselves with whatever party is in power, and now consider themselves to be Lavalas supporters. When it became clear that Aristide's party was going to be the most powerful, former section chiefs became FL partisans as a way of riding Aristide's coattails into power. It would be virtually impossible for Lavalas to prevent this kind of behavior."[1] The defense of emergent popular organizations against opportunists is never easy – consider for instance Lenin's obsessive meditations on the problem, which even Bolshevik forms of discipline were unable to solve. Groups in somewhat similar circumstances, like the ANC and the PLO, have also been prey to somewhat similar difficulties. Fanmi Lavalas, however, was especially vulnerable to this sort of manipulation. Duvalier's repression discouraged the local emergence of a progressive middle class in Haiti, and unlike the OPL or Communist Party before it, FL lacked systematic ties with members of the close-knit professional and intellectual circles who provide most of the "liberal" wing of the elite with its political personnel. Few leading members of FL had significant administrative experience, and the recruitment and retention of effective administrators was not one of Aristide's particular skills. Many of the people who assumed formal leadership positions within the upper echelons of the organization in 2001–04 – people like Louis-Gérald Gilles and Leslie Voltaire – have more in common with their political opponents and counter-parts among the elite than they do with their own *baz*. Other Lavalas politicians, again in line with conventional practice, were perfectly willing to use their positions for their personal gain, implicating the government in a series of damaging scandals (more on this below). Too many Lavalas big-wigs started to behave, as Elie acknowledges, "in a traditional Haitian way, vying for power, vying for money." They provoked a lot of resentment among Aristide's poorer supporters.[2] It wasn't long before the first prime minister of Aristide's second administration, Jean-Marie Chérestal, was bogged down in debilitating parliamentary squabbles with other ambitious members of FL like Prince Pierre Sonson or ex-FAdH officer Fourel Célestin.[3]

Second, by demonstrating so starkly the weakness of the existing vehicles for the anti-Lavalas opposition and the short-term futility of any further electoral challenge to Lavalas, Aristide's success at the polls ensured that the opposition would instead seek to undermine the organization from within. Since they were unable to blunt popular support for Aristide in places like Cité Soleil in any other way, elite businessman Andy Apaid and his associates Charles Baker and Reginald Boulos began offering money and weapons to gangs who were willing to turn against Lavalas – a strategy that began to pay dividends by mid-2003. At the same time, Aristide's enemies were well-placed to turn the state's own security forces against him. As Aristide's former security advisor Patrick Elie explains, from the day he arrived in the presidential palace to the day he left, Aristide was living in "enemy territory [. . .]. Everyone is totally wrong about how much control he had."[4] Six weeks after his inauguration, Aristide named his former security advisor Nesly Lucien as police chief; the string of further police appointments that continued through to the summer of 2003 is one of several symptoms of the protracted battle between FL and the IC for control of the PNH.[5]

The top commanders of the national police were not the only people Aristide had to worry about: even the specialized force attached to the presidential palace itself (the USGPN) was anything but reliable. Soon after his inauguration in February 2001, Aristide replaced some of the more overtly hostile USGPN commanders, and a document circulated by the IRI's Stanley Lucas (and written by bitterly anti-Aristide ex-Senator Rosny Mondestin) in April 2001 helps explain why. "This specialized PNH unit is almost exclusively made up of former members of the Haitian Army. It has discipline and is well equipped. Aristide does not trust it anymore."[6] With good reason: lawyers working for the government to prosecute human rights abuses carried out by the *de facto* dictatorship received reports of plotting by police, including USGPN members, throughout Aristide's second term.[7] One of the leading officers in the USGPN during the late 1990s was Youri Latortue. A veteran of François' notoriously brutal Anti-Gang Unit during the first coup, Youri was widely accused of involvement in the assassination of the grassroots activist Father Jean-Marie Vincent (1994) and the embezzlement of many thousands of dollars from the USGPN payroll. He was also a good friend and "comrade in arms" of future FLRN chief Guy Philippe.[8] In February 2001 Latortue was included among the handful of officers that Aristide transferred out of the force.[9] The July and December 2001 attacks soon provided a stark indication of the unreliability and ineffectiveness of the PNH, and especially of the USGPN; after December 2001, notes Frantz Gabriel, the USGPN "became totally untrustworthy."[10] From that moment on, if not before, Aristide was a virtual prisoner in the midst of his own security apparatus.

Unlike Castro or Chávez, unlike Mandela or Arafat, Aristide and his immediate entourage had no experience of war or armed struggle, and virtually no links with the former military. For reasons considered in chapter two, many leading figures in the USGPN and other quasi-military units of the PNH were loyal to the army or to its main international patron. Many others owed their position to the mediation of a small number of army officers that Aristide had picked to oversee the creation of an interim police force in early 1995, most notably the charismatic ex-major Dany Toussaint and his associate ex-captain Médard Joseph. A veteran of several courses of US training (including CIA instruction in surveillance that made him "the best clandestine photographer in Haiti"), in March 2004 Toussaint was still regularly described as "the great specialist in everything to do with security and armed force in Haiti."[11] Though nominally a member (and later a senator) in Aristide's Fanmi Lavalas party, it seems that at some point in the late 1990s – if not as early as his 1997 detention in Miami – Toussaint began actively working against the interests of Lavalas in general and of Aristide in particular. His rivalry with other Lavalassians like Bob Manuel, Charles Suffrard or Jean Dominique helped drive a wedge between the associates of Préval on the one hand and the supporters of Aristide on the other. As far as the US itself was concerned, it was always obvious that Toussaint might be useful as a weapon to use against Aristide but never tolerable as an alternative to replace him.[12] Nevertheless, although his official break with Aristide's government came only in December 2003, many people in Aristide's circle believe that Toussaint had been working for their opponents for years. Toussaint himself told journalist Michael Deibert that "he and Aristide had been in a 'cold war' since the May 2000 elections, when Aristide had put word out among the young political militants in the slums who had supported Toussaint's 2000 senatorial campaign to no longer rally for the senator in public."[13]

In September 2003, Dany Toussaint used his position in the Senate to veto Aristide's last-ditch attempt to eliminate the constitutional basis for the army. Over the next few months Toussaint was well-placed to help the ex-soldiers and gang-members who turned against the government in Gonaïves, and to provide useful advice to Guy Philippe and Paul Arcelin as they waited to join them across the border in the DR.[14] When the time came, Toussaint also helped convince leading members of the USGPN, SWAT and CIMO units to rally in support of Chamblain and Philippe, rather than Aristide. Given his apparently detailed knowledge of the names and locations of hundreds of "pro-Aristide chimères" in the slums of Port-au-Prince, Toussaint was also well-placed to spread rumors that these "chimères [. . .] got their guns from the National Palace," and no doubt also to assist Youri Latortue and ex-general Hérard Abraham in tracking some of them down when they took over responsibility for security on behalf of the post-Aristide government.[15] The day that Toussaint publicly denounced the FL government as a "fascist regime," in December 2003, he added that "he could guarantee security within 48 hours of Aristide's departure."[16]

As time went on, the more Aristide tried to rein in rogue elements of Fanmi Lavalas the more he ran into conflict with interested parties in the security services. Apart from Dany Toussaint's clique, there was no other substantial faction in the security forces to which he could appeal. When the CIA and DEA began to accuse high level police officers of drug smuggling and corruption Aristide was initially reluctant to believe it, thinking – with good reason – that "such accusations were mainly designed to isolate the government from the (very) few allies it still had in the security forces."[17] Soon after Aristide appointed him head of Palace security in March 2001, his veteran bodyguard Oriel Jean became the subject of a DEA investigation. In the summer of 2003 Aristide was reluctantly obliged to dismiss him (along with several commanding officers of the PNH) on the basis of vague suspicions of complicity in drug smuggling – "to get at the king," as Oriel said after the fact, "they needed to take down the rooks who protected him."[18] Rightly or wrongly, Aristide decided against another risky purge of the palace guard, but systematic infiltration of the police forced the government on several occasions (e.g. at Belladère in the summer of 2003, or in Gonaïves that autumn) to rely on informal auxiliaries in confrontations with its enemies; some observers insist that a few of these pro-government enforcers were as thuggish as the insurgents they were meant to suppress. When in the summer of 2001 the government called for "zero tolerance" of criminals and insurgents, a few members of a population exasperated by police incompetence and the persistence of impunity responded in the usual way, by taking matters into their own hands. Aristide's apparent willingness to condone the increasingly volatile behavior of a small minority of his supporters left other Lavalas activists confused and dismayed, and as it turned out his attempt to placate rather than confront unreliable PNH leaders managed only to delay an eventually disastrous defection.

By the end of 2003, notes Yvon Neptune, it was all too obvious that "very few members of the national security forces deserved to be trusted. They had been corrupted by members of civil society, and by representatives of some foreign governments. There can be no doubt about this. G184 leaders André Apaid and Charles Baker themselves made public statements about this at the time, saying that they had people in the police force who were working with them."[19] A well-placed PNH source told me in March 2007 that in the months before Aristide's expulsion "there were scores if not hundreds of policemen who had aligned themselves with Guy Philippe." Members of Aristide's inner circle suspect that the prominent PNH officer Wilson Casséus, for instance, was working in concert with Guy Philippe at least several months before the government fell; Casséus certainly cooperated with

Philippe's men when they moved into Port-au-Prince on 1 March 2004, and shortly afterwards was promoted to lead the post-Aristide USGPN.

There were good reasons, in short, why after December 2001 Aristide's advisors decided to increase the small number of foreign bodyguards (contracted through the California-based Steele Foundation) responsible for his personal security.[20] Long before the eventual coup, remembers a senior member of this Steele detachment, "it was clear that the President's Haitian security forces were not reliable. There were perhaps 7 members of his 25-man personal security detail that I genuinely trusted, and we were always worried about treachery inside the USGPN; frankly we were expecting some sort of incident well before February 2004."[21] So were many FL supporters in the slums, who as the pressure grew on their government urged Aristide to organize some sort of popular militia in response.

Aristide's indecisive handling of the security situation was compounded by a third problem associated with FL popularity: in spite of its international isolation, the extent of its obvious electoral advantage and popular support encouraged a degree of complacency. Disappointed by Aristide's forced collusion in the IMF's punitive structural adjustment plan, some of his supporters began to feel that they were being taken for granted. Rather like Toussaint L'Ouverture before him, in his last years in office Aristide did not make enough of an effort to keep critical groups of his constituency on board, especially in the countryside and in the more remote towns. Secure in the knowledge that the bulk of the people continued to back him, Aristide was also remarkably tolerant of the opposition's campaign to unseat him. He allowed the G184 to organize strident and occasionally armed demonstrations calling for his government to be overthrown. He allowed groups of ex-FAdH soldiers to participate in similar demonstrations, openly advocating the reconstitution of the army and a new coup d'état. Meanwhile, as the IFES-funded media campaign against him intensified in 2002–03, Aristide's public relations team sometimes handled the chorus of accusations with what one long-time Lavalas loyalist describes as a "lethargy and incompetence characteristic of Arafat's Palestinian Authority." Later, when the insurgency finally broke out into the open in February 2004, Aristide's government failed to develop a sufficiently assertive strategy to deflect or defeat it. Unwilling to risk the bloodshed that might accompany armed resistance on a massive scale, the Lavalas administration hesitated during the crucial weeks of mid-February 2004, and persisted in its vain strategy of negotiation with the opposition. Aristide and his entourage underestimated what they were up against. Right up until a day or two before it happened, it never seems to have occurred to them that their foreign enemies might actually be prepared to go in and seize them by force.

SCANDAL AND CORRUPTION

Needless to say, the democratic opposition together with their friends and relations in the independent press were quick to make the most of the government's weakness and mistakes. They didn't have long to wait. The combination of systematic destitution and long-standing tendencies in Haitian politics (which underlie what Fatton calls a "predatory" relation to state power) together with the exceptional pressures imposed on the FL administration (which reduced the spoils available for predation) encouraged a certain amount of corruption in parts of the rapidly expanding Lavalas hierarchy. The fact that this corruption paled in comparison to both the "officially sanctioned piracy"[22] typical of the earlier Duvalier regime and the ruthless exploitation that underpins the very existence of the elite – to say nothing of the obvious fact that a certain amount of corruption is an automatic if not deliberate conse-quence of the punitive trade and structural adjustment policies imposed on severely impoverished nations by their wealthier neighbours – made no difference to the real political point. The real point was to demonstrate that Lavalas was just another group of profiteers in the long line of state predators, that Titid's people were no better than the *grands mangeurs* they sought to replace. The real point was to show that there could be no genuine alternative to the status quo, and that the political process could offer no prospect of genuine change. The fact that Lavalas in general and the "saintly" Aristide in particular was always bound to be judged by standards quite different to those applied to other Haitian governments (not to mention other nations' governments) only made the point that much easier to make. So did the apparently obnoxious fact that many of the Lavalassians who gained some access to money and power during the Aristide years did so for the first time: it's much easier to notice and denounce the fact that a resident of a poor neighborhood has acquired a government car or a house than it is to keep track of the benefits accumulated by politicians who are already members of the elite.

Perhaps it's not surprising that after the long years of struggle in the 1990s, by 2001 the main priority for some Lavalas activists was now to acquire and retain a reliable source of income. "Our determination to create an inclusive organization," says Neptune, means that "we had to make some risky alliances. It was inevitable that some people would try to exploit Aristide's popularity. Genuine discipline takes time to emerge, there are no shortcuts."[23] The persistence of petty cronyism, combined with routine forms of opportunism and corruption, helped FL's many (often more securely funded) critics to paint a lurid picture of a government mired in drugs, embezzlement and the abuse of human rights. Drug-running in particular had become a lucrative sideline for some government officials and police officers under Jean-Claude Duvalier, before blossoming into a major industry during the embargoed years of the Cédras coup.[24] Several members or associates of Aristide's government carried on the tradition in the same sort of style, and several eventually wound up in the hands of the US Drug Enforcement Administration. Rudy Therassan, a senior member of the PNH, apparently began to act as an informer for the DEA in the final year of Aristide's administration. Several other high-ranking members of the security services, including Fourel Celestin, Jean Nesly Lucien, Romaine Lestin and Evintz Brillant, were later indicted in Miami (Brillant was acquitted; Therassan and Lestin pled guilty to charges of drug trafficking and got fourteen and nine years respectively; Lucien and Fourel pled guilty to charges of money laundering and both received three years).[25]

More damaging for Aristide were the accusations leveled at the leading member of his personal security team, Oriel Jean, who was arrested in Canada a week after the February 2004 coup. Many critics (as well as some allies) of Lavalas accuse Oriel of profiting from his position, and under pressure from the DEA he admitted to accepting gifts from drug-traffickers like Jacques Kétant and Serge Edouard. Oriel was flown to Miami in March 2004 after waiving his right to extradition proceedings, and although US investigators couldn't find the evidence they needed to prosecute him for drug offenses (he too was sentenced to three years for money laundering) he was expected to play an important role in proceedings planned against the president himself.[26] Much the biggest such role was reserved for the recklessly flamboyant Kétant, a man who had ingratiated himself with several leading members of Aristide's security forces and who was alleged by his brother, once he was put on trial in the US, to be the godfather of Aristide's own daughter (a claim that is still widely believed in Haiti, even though it was denied by both Jean-Bertrand and Mildred Aristide, as well as their lawyer Ira Kurzban, their pilot Frantz Gabriel, their press attaché Michelle Karshan, and then eventually by Kétant himself).[27] Kétant was first indicted on drug charges in the US back in 1997, and Aristide eventually handed him over to the

DEA in June 2003. Some reports suggest that by the time he was arrested Kétant oversaw the movement of around half of all the cocaine smuggled into Florida. The day of his capture, the US embassy's Judith Trunzo told the AHP she was "delighted by the Haitian authorities' collaboration in the operation," and commended their "strong efforts to fight drug trafficking."[28] Kétant's trial came to a timely end just a few days before Aristide's own truncated term in office, and on the day he was sentenced in late February 2004 Kétant was given twenty minutes to denounce "Haiti's biggest druglord" to the court and the attendant press. The day after Aristide's expulsion on 29 February, US embassy officials in Haiti told reporters that Kétant's accusation the previous week "gave the United States more leverage to persuade Aristide to leave the country."[29] Surely it was now only a matter of time before a Noriega-style indictment of Aristide would rid the US of their turbulent priest once and for all.

Talk of an indictment duly continued for as long as it was useful, through the spring of 2004.[30] The so-called war on drugs emerged as a routine instrument of US foreign policy in Latin America at a time when for obvious reasons it became more expedient to vilify un-American interests as criminal rather than communist. Combined with appropriate forms of economic pressure, it offers endlessly versatile opportunities to infiltrate a vulnerable government's security apparatus and to undermine its credibility. Notorious SIN-era drug-runners like Michel François were actively used and later protected by their American backers. Once an enemy of democracy came to power, however, the war on drugs became a much more principled and assiduous affair. Ramilus Bolivar isn't the only FL activist to insist that the only abnormal thing about drug smuggling under Aristide was simply the determination of the US and the elite to use it as an overt rather than merely covert mechanism of destabilization – "if corruption in the PNH was worse under Aristide than under Préval it's because the imperialists went to more trouble to make it so," by doing more to ensnare officers in contraband or protection rackets. As it turns out, Bolivar says, the enemies of the government went after people like Oriel Jean and Dany Toussaint, but "anyone in their position would have been either corrupted or elimi-nated, that's almost guaranteed."[31] The "laboratory" that still wields significant behind-the-scenes power in Haiti (and in a few other places) knows very well that if you want to demonize an immensely popular elected president then the easiest way to get to him is through his close associates. If these associates cooperate with the demonization campaign they will be rewarded; the less uncooperative ones may have to be punished. So long as Dany Toussaint pretended to be loyal to Aristide, for instance, the US and the elite denounced him as a thug and a drug-dealer; as soon as he changed camps the talk of drugs and murder came to an abrupt stop, and in 2006 he was allowed to stand for president alongside other law-abiding democrats like Guy Philippe and Franck Romain.

Far from refusing to cooperate with US officials, Préval and Aristide were the first presidents to grant DEA officers a wide range of powers to intervene directly in Haitian affairs. DEA staff appear to have devoted considerable effort to the cause, and there can be little doubt that if the US had any proof that Aristide or his leading ministers were complicit in the drug trade they would already be sitting in a Miami jail. The problem is that there is no such proof. Some prominent members of Aristide's security forces (Fourel, Chérubin, Oriel . . .) occasionally accepted money from Kétant but the judge in Kétant's case proved to be some-what less credulous than US diplomats, and found his claim to have paid Aristide a monthly $500,000 fee to land drug flights from Colombia on a highway near his Tabarre home no more convincing than his portrayal of Haiti as a "narco-country" in which "you either pay Aristide or you die."[32] Rather than lighten his sentence in exchange for such useful information, Kétant's judge condemned him to 27 years in prison and a $15 million fine. Having served his political purpose, Kétant has had no further public part to play in prosecuting the case against Aristide. To all intents and purposes that case collapsed altogether in the summer of 2005, once it became clear that neither Rudi Therassan nor Oriel Jean could provide any evidence that might incriminate senior members of Aristide's cabinet, let alone Aristide himself. (Alleged post-Aristide-era drug smug-glers, such as Youri Latortue, Dany Toussaint and Jean-Claude Louis Jean, meanwhile, were no doubt relieved to discover that as soon as Aristide was out of the picture the DEA quickly lost interest in further extradition proceedings.)

American prosecutors had a back-up plan. As hopes for a drug conviction began to fade, old charges of corruption and embezzlement were revived. For years, Aristide's opponents had accused him of appropriating vast sums from Haiti's treasury and telephone companies, and of manipulating the charitable Foundation for Democracy and Lafanmi Selavi for his private gain. They did their best to present him as someone living in decadent luxury, barricaded behind the defensive walls of his allegedly "palatial" house in Tabarre. With appropriate fanfare, in November 2005 Latortue's de facto government filed a dramatic lawsuit that accused Aristide of stealing tens of millions of dollars. Few people familiar with the "detail" of the allegations were surprised, however, that the indictment was filed in a US rather than a Haitian court, effectively reducing the move to an empty political stunt. The attempt to portray the ascetic Aristide as an idle playboy on the model of Jean-Claude Duvalier is no easy trick. As people like Patrick Elie or Georges Honorat will tell you, "The people who accuse Aristide of embezzling money from drugs, Teleco, etc., know nothing about him. He has absolutely no interest in luxury or money. He is a peasant, a priest! He hasn't the slightest notion of what to do with money."[33] Aristide's house was built for him by an enthusiastic benefactor back in 1990, and when he was forced out of Haiti in 2004 he retired not to a golden exile on the French Riviera but a modest academic post in South Africa. "He has no money," insists his attorney: "he left with the clothes on his back."[34] The embezzlement suit was never served on its defendants, and in July 2006 it too was quietly withdrawn, once the Chicago-based lawyers hired to prosecute the case had come to the conclusion that they were wasting their time.[35]

Although Lavalas detractors had little luck pinning corruption charges on Aristide, they did manage to score a few points against some members of his government and organization. Once in office, some of the more overtly opportunistic Lavalas *cadres* like Jean-Marie Chérestal, Prince Pierre Sonson or Louis-Gerald Gilles began flaunting a suspiciously comfortable lifestyle, as did some regional FL leaders. In January 2002, several FL deputies were denounced by rivals within FL for collusion in the sale of around $4.7 million worth of ostensibly charitable (and thus tax-exempt) rice.[36] More people, and in particular more middle-income people, were affected when over the summer of 2002 thousands of families in both Haiti and the diaspora lost the savings they had invested in privately-launched "cooperative" banks. As the anti-Lavalas journalist Cali Ruchala explains, "The program was seen by many international experts as an ingenious form of 'micro-credit loans,'"[37] and though his government urged investors to be cautious, the expansion of the new co-ops no doubt owed something to Aristide's well-known commitment to genuinely cooperative ventures in agriculture, education and health.[38] Designed to cash in on a loophole in the domestic financial services industry (which in order to ensure some exchange-rate stability prevents ordinary banks from lending substantial amounts of money), some of the new co-ops grew very rapidly to become no more than an unregulated variation on the sort of pyramid scheme that had already come to grief in Albania a few years before. Aristide promised to reimburse investors as the banks began to fail in July but by that stage his government was itself on the verge of financial ruin, and in some quarters the fiasco left a lasting sense of betrayal and anger.

Although they tarnished its image, the rice and banking scandals were not government policy. More damaging in its effects on Lavalas' own core constituency was Préval and Aristide's continued acquiescence in neo-liberal structural adjustment. Although neither president ever had much more than symbolic room for maneuver on this front, there is no denying that during his second administration Aristide paid a high price for his forced collusion with the sort of neo-liberal policies he otherwise continued to denounce. Peasant groups like KOZEPEP and Tet Kole Ti Peyizan complained bitterly about the ongoing impact of subsidized US imports on domestic agricultural production, particularly in the rice-growing Artibonite region. In 2001–02 rival leftwing groups like the PPN and Batay Ouvriye sometimes found themselves on the same side of the argument, as they criticized FL compromises with the private sector and the World Bank. As the OPL had learned in the mid-1990s, in Haiti this sort of criticism is more easily made in opposition rather than in government, and the Préval who in 2006 was re-elected in the face of implacable resistance from the business elite has once again been obliged to carry on in much the same old neo-liberal vein. As things stand, no Haitian government can function without some sort of cooperation from leading families like the Mevs or Vorbes. Even someone as critical of Aristide as Alex Dupuy knows that that since "rich Haitians and their foreign allies will do everything they can to prevent any significant tampering with the status quo," Aristide therefore "needed to win some of these actors over to his side to have the slightest chance of success."[39] Nevertheless, Aristide's 2002 decision to "placate the imperialists" (as he put it in a private meeting with representatives of the PPN) by establishing free trade zones along the border with the Dominican Republic was opposed by some members of his own entourage. Subsidized by a $20 million World Bank grant and designed for the benefit of foreign investors like the Dominican contractor Grupo M, creation of the first FTZ at Ouanaminthe promised to generate several thousand new light-assembly jobs, but it came at the expense of dozens of peasant evictions.[40] "Aristide thought he could walk down the middle of the road," remembers Ben Dupuy: "I used to tell him that that's where accidents happen. I told him that sooner or later he would have to choose the left sidewalk, or the right sidewalk. It seemed to me that he never really made up his mind, and he paid a high price for his hesitation."[41]

The growing impression that some members of FL were prepared to disregard the interests of its more disadvantaged supporters in favor of their traditional class enemies was compounded by accusations from Batay Ouvriye and the PPN during the spring and summer of 2001 that FL mayor Fernand Sévère was actively encouraging repressive anti-union measures at the Guacimal (Rémy Cointreau) orange plantation at Saint Raphaël in northern Haiti.[42] HSG's Charles Arthur argues that when Sévère was later shot dead by gunmen working for one of his local rivals in Fanmi Lavalas. Aristide's reaction "clearly signaled that the mayor's brutal anti-union activities accurately reflected national party policy." Sévère's brother became mayor in his place, and then on 27 May 2002, says Arthur, "the full extent of the Lavalas Family Party's determination to crush independent workers' activity was revealed with [a] horrific and murderous attack on a peasant/worker rally at Guacimal" which left two elderly demonstrators dead and several others injured, including two journalists.[43] For reasons that were never properly explained, the journalists were also detained in prison after the demonstration, along with nine protestors; the journalists were released on 8 June but two of the trade unionists were held without charge until 2 December. According to Robert Fatton, although "Aristide didn't instigate the crackdown at Guacimal, he tolerated it. He was in a very difficult position. The fear was that if the union didn't back down then the whole project there would have collapsed, and with it the negotiations for the new Free Trade Zone near the DR border."[44] Enemies of the government, confirms Neptune, "manipulated issues like the free trade zones and the claims of some trade unions to keep it on the defensive, at a time when we were under immense pressure to placate foreign donors and the international financial institutions." The popular mayor of Milot Moïse Jean-Charles likewise insists that Batay Ouvriye's main priority was always to embarrass and destabilize the government, and that "all the local farmers opposed the demonstrators" they bussed in to demonstrate at Guacimal.[45] (I'll come back to these and related criticisms from the leftwing opposition to Lavalas early in the next chapter.)

THE POLITICS OF HUMAN RIGHTS

Not all of FL's critics shared the priorities of embattled trade unions, of course, but from 2001–04 all sectors of the democratic opposition were united by a profound concern for what the independent media would invariably describe as a "worsening human rights situation." Human rights work has been controversial in Haiti ever since the CIA began running training courses, in the late 1980s, about how to manipulate such work for political effect – in a spectacular early demonstration of just how far such manipulation can go, the person that Cédras picked as prime minister in the immediate aftermath of the first coup was Haiti's most prominent human rights activist in 1990–91, Jean-Jacques Honorat, the man who did more than anyone to present the rights record of Aristide's government as comparable to that of Idi Amin or Pol Pot.[46] Ten years later, no claim did more to facilitate the converging of the Convergence Démocratique than the assertion that since Aristide's return to power, "human rights abuses [were] on the rise" (to quote the title of an October 2003 Amnesty International report).[47]

Reports published by the most frequently cited human rights groups of the 2001–04 period, NCHR, CARLI and CEDH, read just the way their IFES backers wanted them to – as the moral justification for imminent regime change. Six weeks after the February coup, as the morgues were overflowing with bodies, these same groups had failed to identify let alone investigate a single case in which a Lavalassian was the victim rather than the perpetrator of violence.[48] Less blatantly biased but still perfectly representative samples of the genre are provided by the short summaries that preface Human Rights Watch (HRW) annual reports for the years 2000–03. In its 2001 report, HRW described 2000 as a year of "mounting political violence" and claimed that "Increasing political intolerance was apparent in several violent protests by supporters of former President Jean-Bertrand Aristide, as well as armed attacks on political figures and a leading human rights activist." In 2002, HRW noted that "Police and government passivity in the face of intimidation and violence by supporters of the Fanmi Lavalas party raised serious human rights concerns." In 2003, HRW said that "worsening human rights conditions, mounting political turmoil, and a declining economy marked President Jean-Bertrand's Aristide first year back in office [. . .]. After more than two years of political impasse, anti-government protests gained strength, with many thousands of Haitians taking to the streets in mid-November. Human rights conditions remained poor, characterized by frequent allegations of police violence, arbitrary arrest, and wrongful detention, among other problems."[49] HRW's 2004 World Report didn't include a section on Haiti, but the organization made its priorities clear when on 14 February, as US-backed insurgents were rampaging their way through much of northern Haiti, it issued a press release blaming the government itself for the worst of the violence. Since "the violence in

Haiti is threatening to spiral out of control," HRW argued, so then "President Aristide must take immediate, constructive steps to re-establish the rule of law and rebuild the country's democratic institutions."[50] Once Aristide's puzzling failure to do these things had facilitated his removal from office, rather than call for the immediate restoration of the elected government or even press for an inquiry into the circumstances of its removal, HRW urged, instead, the speedy dispatch of more foreign troops.[51] When subsequent AI and HRW reports later began to pay attention to the atrocities committed by the post-coup regime they chose to frame their distinctly muted criticisms in terms of the essential *continuity* of the "cycle of violence and impunity that has plagued the Caribbean republic for so many years."[52]

Here we reach the crowning achievement of the disinformation campaign, a propaganda coup as brazen and astonishing as anything yet accomplished by the IRI and its acolytes anywhere in the world. Remember the basic numbers: perhaps 50,000 dead under the Duvaliers (1957–86), perhaps 700 to 1,000 dead under Namphy/Avril (1986–90), 4,000 dead under Cédras (1991–94) and then at least another 3,000 killed under Latortue (2004–06). And under Aristide? What sort of numbers might warrant claims of "continuity" or even "deterioration"? After the first coup, Jesse Helms spoke for much of the US political establishment when on 20 October 1993 he denounced Aristide as a "psychopath and grave human rights abuser" – but although after Lafontant's failed coup attempt of January 1991 some Macoutes were indeed lynched in popular reprisals, neither Helms nor anyone else could pin a single political killing on the 1991 administration. In the run-up to the second coup, incomparably more insistent versions of the same charge would resurface at every turn, but even the long years of economic aggression and FLRN provocation failed to goad FL "bandits" into taking the sort of retaliatory measures their enemies seemed to expect, if not desire. Of course under Aristide there was gang violence in places like Cité Soleil and Raboteau, as there was before Aristide and after Aristide (more on this in the next section). But if reports from Amnesty International can be trusted – and it's telling that as far as I know neither AI nor any human rights organization has yet risked an estimate of the total numbers of people killed under Aristide – then from 2001 to 2004 perhaps thirty political killings can be attributed to the PNH (whose political affiliation was often *anti*-government) or to groups with (often tenuous) links to FL.[53] Less or differently biased analysts like Ronald Saint-Jean, Kim Ives and Laura Flynn put the real total closer to 10.[54]

In early 2004, Brian Concannon spelled out what should have been the obvious conclusion: yes there were some human rights violations during the decade following Aristide's 1994 return, but they were

> neither quantitatively nor qualitatively comparable to those of the dictatorship. The prisons are overcrowded, and prisoners' procedural rights are not always respected. But there is nothing like the horrors of Fort Dimanche, the political prison that Duvalier opponents rarely left alive. There are too many killings, some by police officers, but none of the systematic massacres organized under the Duvalier, CNG, Avril and *de facto* dictatorships. In that sense, Haiti has undergone a democratic transition: the human rights violations of a dictatorship – peasant massacres and other large-scale killings, political prisons, and official censorship of the media, the courts and political dissent – have been left behind, but have been replaced by the human rights violations of democracy – non-systematic police brutality, judicial corruption and inefficiency, and difficulty protecting citizens from acts of other citizens. Although there have been some notable successes [. . .], Haiti has struggled in this area. It has struggled about as much as one would expect of a new democracy with no tradition of democratic policing or justice and little money to invest in them.[55]

Under these circumstances, instructions to present the dramatic and exceptional decline in political violence under Aristide as the symptom of a "worsening human rights situation" must at first have struck even the most hard-nosed IFES propagandist as a virtually impossible task. Happily, however, in our age of responsible and humanitarian intervention what passes for the defense of human rights has long been one of the most openly ideological categories of political analysis. As writers ranging from Alain Badiou to Chidi Anselm Odinkalu have argued, the neo-liberal insistence on certain human rights is now a well-established facet of benevolent or post-colonial imperialism. The supervision of human rights in the most heavily exploited parts of the planet, Odinkalu notes, "appears almost by design to exclude the participation of the people whose welfare it purports to advance."[56] Most of the "neutral," affluent and well-connected supervisors live at an immeasurable distance from the world endured by the people they supervise, and at a still greater distance from the sort of militant, unabashedly *political* mobilization that can alone offer any meaningful protection for truly universal rights. In a place as saturated with internationally funded NGOs as Haiti, human rights work is more often than not an ostentatiously privileged profession. Everyone can see, after all, that the propertied, the well-educated and the civilized have more rights to protect than do the penniless or illiterate. And since everyone can indeed see this, in order to sustain the equation of Aristide with Duvalier there was no need to draw attention to what might actually be taking place in Aristide's Haiti. All that needed to be done was to allow people to see what they already knew. The IFES/IRI just needed to trigger recognition of a familiar pattern, the pattern of "degeneration" whereby a once-principled populist sets about assaulting the property, the speech and occasionally the person of the still-principled few.

Rather than a set of tiresome statistics or comparative analyses, all you really need to trigger such recognition is a couple of suitably resonant examples, set against an atmosphere of rising tensions and growing "insecurity." The democratic opposition to Lavalas found all it needed in the killings of two very different journalists: Jean Dominique (3 April 2000) and Brignol Lindor (3 December 2001).

Long a prominent scourge of Duvalierism and the predations of the elite, Jean Dominique was a strong though never uncritical ally of Lavalas, and after Aristide himself was perhaps the most widely respected democracy advocate in the country. Dominique's fearless denunciation of *Macoutisme* in all its forms had alienated him from most members of his own social class, and by 2000 he had many enemies among the Duvalierist and the business elite. Perhaps the most prominent of these enemies was the magnate Rudolph Boulos, who along with Pezzullo and Carney in 2002 would become the founder of the Haiti Democracy Project (a group for whom "justice for Jean" would become something of a sacred quest). Boulos' company Pharval Pharmaceuticals was responsible for concocting poisoned cough syrups which killed over 70 children in 1996, and Dominique stubbornly kept the story at the forefront of the news. Just as stubbornly, Dominique implicated both the Boulos and the Mevs families in another scandal, the manufacture of contaminated alcohol which poisoned dozens of peasants in the southern part of the country.[57] Again, when the Duvalierist general Claude Raymond died in prison in February 2000, rather than collude with speculation that he'd been killed by agents of FL, Dominique added a whole new set of enemies to his list when he pointed out the obvious but still deeply scandalous truth – that Raymond had died of AIDS. In the spring of 2000, Dominique was also working to expose the US contribution to the sabotaging of the coming elections (electoral card manipulation, vote observation maneuvering, etc.). By April 2000, in short, "many people had an interest in killing Jean Dominique."[58] As far as the elite and the enemies of Lavalas were concerned, the most prominent of these people was Dany Toussaint, whom Dominique had once attacked in a biting radio address, back in October 1999.[59] After his election to the Senate Toussaint drew on his parliamentary immunity to evade the protracted and ultimately inconclusive murder enquiry conducted by the controversial judge Claudy Gassant. As the investigation dragged on, NCHR and its allies in the independent media presented the story as self-evident proof that Toussaint's apparent patron Aristide had become a murderous dictator, presiding over a culture of lawless impunity. A clear verdict may never emerge. What *is* perfectly clear, however, is that the anti-Lavalas partisans who from 2000 to 2004 gained the most from the campaign for justice for Jean suddenly lost all interest in this campaign once people from among their own ranks came to power. Unsatisfactory under Aristide, the inquiry into Dominique's death was simply non-existent under Latortue. Still more striking is the fact that the same democrats who had so insisted on bringing Dany Toussaint to trial when he was an apparent ally of Aristide quietly dropped this demand when he announced his shift of allegiance in December 2003. From March 2004 the democratic opposition was at last free to take the reigns of justice into their own hands – and they did nothing about it.

Although the circumstances of Brignol Lindor's death in Petit Goâve were very different the political manipulation of its consequences was very similar. On 2 December 2001 Joseph Duverger, a member of the local pro-Lavalas group Domi Nan Bwa, was attacked and left for dead by a group of pro-CD militants. The following day a group of Duverger's enraged friends went looking for revenge and stumbled by chance upon Brignol Lindor, who as the newsroom director for the local Radio Echo 2000 was a flamboyant and well-known figure in the anti-Lavalas media. His murder was denounced by people across the political spectrum, and Lindor's cause was immediately taken up by every organized media group in the country– the Haitian Journalists' Association, the Haitian Press Association, the National Press Workers' Union of Haiti and the National Association of Haitian Media, with the energetic support of the Paris-based watchdog Reporters Without Borders, NCHR, Amnesty International, HRW, the State Department and the rest of the "human rights community."

The issue here isn't one of guilt or innocence, but of balance. Rituals of mourning for Lindor would soon become a familiar exercise on Haitian radio, and as the Haiti Action Committee points out, "The case eventually received so much international attention that the OAS included progress on its investigation as a precondition for the release of aid."[60] By contrast, none of the dozens of FL members or sympathizers who were killed not through febrile retaliation but by calculated paramilitary assault – including for instance the November 2002 execution of Justice of the Peace Christophe Lozama and the December 2003 murder of Savanette-Baptiste's deputy mayor Amorgue Cléma – received anything like the same amount of attention. By way of an approximate indication, a Google search conducted 26 September 2006 turned up 35,400 hits for Lindor but only 303 for Lozama and just 2 for Cléma.

This dramatic bias in mainstream human rights work would persist right through to the last days of Aristide's administration. A few days after the insurgency started in Gonaïves, a clash between pro- and anti-government gangs in the town of Saint-Marc offered NCHR and its backers their last and best chance to illustrate the main point it had been trying to make over the previous few years. On 7 February 2004, the insurgent gang RAMICOS took control of Saint-Marc. They were dislodged a couple of days later by the combined forces of CIMO police and a pro-Lavalas OP known as Bale Wouze. Then on 11 February there was a violent clash between RAMICOS and Bale Wouze members which, according to Le Nouvelliste, Agence France-Presse and other media reports from mid-February, resulted in three to five deaths, with casualties on both sides.[61] So the matter lay, until, a couple of days after Aristide's expulsion, members of the ex-democratic opposition and their international backers were relieved to learn that the difficult moral case for that expulsion had just been bolstered by startling new facts exposed by Pierre Espérance's NCHR, Haiti's highest profile human rights group. NCHR had conducted an enquiry into the 11 February confrontation, and now chose to describe violence it attributed exclusively to Bale Wouze as a "cruel, horrific, savage and barbaric [. . .] crime against humanity" that had resulted in the deaths of at least fifty people and the destruction of several dozen houses. In the days following the alleged massacre, NCHR continued, pro-FL forces subjected the people of Saint-Marc to the "overwhelming and systematic practice of summary executions, kidnappings, torture and/or inhumane acts."[62] In a subsequent statement, NCHR concluded that the Saint-Marc "genocide constitutes the largest massacre perpetrated against the civilian population by the Lavalas regime."[63] It certainly constituted the single most important piece of evidence in the case that Latortue's government and allies would soon construct in order to provide a retrospectively humanitarian justification for the coup, together with legal justification for the persecution of several leading members of the previous administration (including Aristide's prime-minister Yvon Neptune and his interior minister Jocelerme Privert). Canada's CIDA promptly allocated $100,000 to NCHR to prosecute the genocide and provide support to its survivors.[64]

The problem with this particular genocide, as Ronald Saint-Jean was quick to demonstrate in convincing detail, is that NCHR wasn't able to provide much evidence that it ever took place.[65] No credible news organization or human rights group was prepared to corroborate Espérance's story, not even NCHR's own parent organization in New York (which soon cut its links with the discredited Espérance, obliging him to rename himself as the RNDDH). Espérance made no attempt to interview members of the Bale Wouze gang, and tried to explain away the lack of incriminating corpses by suggesting that the bodies might have been "eaten by dogs." By the time the UN's human rights officer Louis Joinet finally came to consider the case in April 2005 he rejected the term "massacre" in favor of the account of a "confrontation" originally proposed in the press.[66] Thierry Fagart, MINUSTAH's human rights director, later condemned the RNDDH's investigation of La Scierie as a "real failure". Rather than any sort of massacre, "It was just a fight between two different gangs." Nevertheless, Neptune and Privert were kept in jail until the summer of 2006, even though Fagart himself admitted in March 2006 that "it is clear that they have never had any legal grounds to prosecute him [Neptune]," and that "from the very beginning until today, all the proceedings against [Neptune] were illegal."[67]

By 2006, however, the need for humanitarian justification was no longer so acute. By 2006, in fact, the whole question of human rights in Haiti had more or less dropped off the political radar. If media concern is a reliable measure of these things, the deliberate and systematic killing of several thousand Lavalassians represents an infinitely less serious infringement of human rights than does the death (in controversial circumstances) of a couple of journalists, the injury of a small handful of students and the damage done to some buildings owned by wealthy members of the CD. In a telling indication of what is really at stake here, a recent *Media Lens* study found that the two most significant reports documenting human rights violations in the post-coup period of 2004–06 passed through the western media almost without trace. The University of Miami CSHR's devastating February 2005 report on criminal violations carried out by the Latortue regime "received literally no coverage in the mainstream press." A still more damning report published in the *Lancet* in August 2006 (which implied that the coup may have killed almost 4000 people in the capital alone) was only mentioned in a newspaper like the *Guardian* once a trivial controversy about the impartiality of one of the report's authors enabled the paper to cast doubt on its credibility.[68] In the US, apart from a single editorial by Aristide's lawyer Ira Kurzban in the *Miami Herald*, the *Lancet* study came and went without any mainstream acknowledgement at all.[69]

LAVALAS VIOLENCE: A NEW REIGN OF TERROR?

Although it undoubtedly adds up to no more than a small fraction of the bloodbath imagined by the anti-government press, the actual amount of violence that can be attributed to FL partisans during Aristide's years in office is a matter of ongoing debate. In the period 2000–04, in tandem with concerns about the "worsening human rights" situation, no single accusation was more common or more damaging than the State Department's claim that as the "years passed, Aristide increasingly relied on *chimères*, violent gangs, to maintain his authority, intimidate opponents, and control the streets."[70] Like Duvalier and Cédras before him, argued NCHR in September 2003, Aristide was apparently building up his own private army of murderous auxiliaries, threatening to turn Haiti "into a bandit-State living on the fringe of the civilized world."[71]

The prototype for this sort of criticism again lies in the aftermath of the September 1991 coup when, in order to justify its reservations about Aristide, the Bush administration reiterated rumors that he had relied upon "mob rule."[72] The second time around, however, it wasn't just the State Department and its proxies like the NCHR, HDP or the G184 who insisted on this point. Newspapers from across the political spectrum ran versions of the story that was published in *The Independent* on 13 February 2004, at the very height of the rebellion: "Aristide's Thugs Crush Hopes of People's Revolution with Beatings and Intimidation." In the eyes of most elite and foreign observers, by 2004 Lavalas had become just another paymaster to the same lumpen proletariat that had provided Duvalier with his Macoutes and Namphy with his *attachés*. MPP leader Chavannes Jean Baptiste spoke for most of the democratic and international opposition when he argued that "because Aristide recognized he has no popular base he decided to make a series of gangs his power base," and that he then "armed all these gangs" and instructed them "to 'sow the peace of the cemetery' throughout the country."[73] Journalist Michael Deibert devotes much of his 2005 book to an expanded version of this same argument, claiming that the arming and deployment of murderous pro-Lavalas gangs was deliberate government policy, that it was coordinated by local PNH boss Hermione Léonard and veteran Aristide loyalist Jean-Claude Jean-Baptiste along with others in the presidential security team, all with Aristide's active encouragement.[74] Erstwhile Lavalas sympathizers like Jane Regan, Charles Arthur, Alex Dupuy and Christophe Wargny have made similar allegations in less frenzied form.[75] One way or another, the argument amounts to a claim that in the decade following 1994 Aristide reinvented himself as a Macoute.

Now it's certainly true that as elite opposition to Aristide's administration became more provocative and more violent, popular resentment of this opposition in both in its political and paramilitary forms also became more emphatic and more organized. It's clear that members of the elite (including the charitable elite) who were accustomed to easy access to the corridors of power and to getting their own way became increasingly frustrated during 2001–04. Prominent FL militants like René Civil (leader of the Jeunesse Pouvoir Populaire [JPP]) and Paul Raymond (of the Ti Kommunauté Legliz St Jean Bosco [TKL]) undeniably sought to challenge the heads of elite political parties that were trying to destabilize the regime – as when in January 2001 they denounced the CD leaders who were then busy with their plans to set up their own extra-legal parallel government.[76] There's also no denying the fact that opposition demonstrations led by pro-coup and pro-army figures like Himmler Rébu and Andy Apaid were regularly met by vigorous counter-demonstrations, and that noisy confrontations between pro- and anti-government forces became an increasingly regular occurrence. Once opposition rallies ceased to *protest* against a given aspect of government policy in order to call instead for the immediate and unconditional *elimination* of the government, so then many of the more militant and vulnerable supporters of the government began to treat engagement with the opposition as a matter of survival pure and simple. On a couple of isolated occasions, such confrontations left one or two protesters dead on both sides. On every such occasion, the violence was reported by the independent media as additional proof of Aristide's drift towards dictatorship if not "totalitarianism."

A fair assessment of this "rising tide of violence" needs, I think, to bear at least six things in mind.

First and foremost, we need to remember that the basic forms of social exclusion and economic exploitation which allow Haitian society to survive themselves depend on violence, and always have done. The only way that Haiti's factory owners can sustain production with starvation-level wages in plants located on the edge of slums as poor as Cité Soleil is through reliance on direct intimidation. Insecurity discourages invest-ment. Back in the happy days of Duvalier and Namphy, army com-manders like Jean-Claude Paul used to rent out their soldiers to bourgeois properties in the industrial belt. "There have always been gangs in the 'hot' neighborhoods," explains Jean-Marie Samedy, "but as long as the army was around the elite found them easy to control or manipulate."[77] Kim Ives agrees: "The bourgeoisie has been recruiting lumpen thugs to defend its interests since the fall of the Duvalier regime in 1986. The recruitment has grown in size and sophistication as the old forces that used to protect them – the Macoutes, then the police and the army – have gradually degenerated, dwindled or disappeared: over the past twenty years there's been a sort of gradual privatization of the security forces *à l'haïtienne*."[78] The result has been a corresponding diversification and "commercialization" of violence in the poorer parts of Port-au-Prince.

During the first coup, powerful and well-connected local magnates Reginald and Rudolph Boulos could operate quite successfully in a place like Cité Soleil through a combination of carrots like their USAID-funded health clinics (the Centers for Health and Development, or CDS) and sticks like FRAPH and FAdH: FRAPH provided the necessary security, while the CDS provided useful intelligence and valuable political leverage for "Mister Cité Soleil." Writing in December 1994, Jane Regan observed that "CDS has had FRAPH members including those accused of brutal murders on its payroll. CDS operates 12 health centers around the country and received at least $4 million in AID funding last year. It also has a database which includes records on most of the 180,000 residents of the poor, staunchly pro-Aristide neighborhood of Cité Soleil and is directed by Dr Reginald Boulos, a close associate of Marc Bazin, the presidential candidate the US had supported against Aristide in the 1990 election. According to residents, CDS, which offers the only health care in the area, turned away people who admitted to voting for Aristide in the 1990 elections."[79] A major threshold was crossed, then, when Aristide came back and disbanded the army. Angry Lavalas protests against CDS and FRAPH forced Boulos onto the defensive, and by the time of popular backlash against the 28 July 2001 attacks his network of clinics was reduced to a shadow of its former self. Shortly after the 17 December 2001 attack the government took over the running of its largest remaining clinic, the Saint-Catherine

Hospital. For the next couple of years, Cité Soleil was a no-go area for Boulos and other like-minded industrialists, notably Andy Apaid and Charles Baker. Pending the arrival of a more "security-conscious" government, the only solution was to try demonize pro-Lavalas groups while trying to enlist some of local gang-members to the anti-government cause. Slowly but surely this strategy began to pay off in the summer of 2003, mainly in the Boston area of the Cité; I'll come back to this in chapter 11. Although it's difficult to measure these things with any precision, such recruitment, in combination with increasingly desperate levels of poverty and demographic pressure, is one of the most important factors behind the resurgence of violence on the streets of Port-au-Prince over the course of the past few years.[80]

By any pertinent measure, however, what's remarkable about the campaign to overthrow the most popular president in Haiti's history is not how much but how *little* violence it provoked. This is the second point. No prominent opposition leaders were killed or "disappeared." Patrick Elie knows "of very few targeted political assassinations and none which were ordered at the top," though he acknowledges that Aristide's calls for "zero tolerance" in the face of rising criminality "were interpreted by elements in the police as a green light for the summary execution of some petty criminals."[81] After the only significant incidents (8 April 2000, 17 December 2001) in which property belonging to opposition parties or leaders was damaged, the government paid millions of dollars in compensation to its owners. There was nothing remotely like the sort of systematic terror that government supporters were all too familiar with. When, for instance, in conjunction with the IRI and the CD, student groups began organizing large-scale demonstrations openly calling for Aristide's expulsion in December 2003/January 2004 (see below, page 194), thousands clashed in what could easily have become pitched battles. During several of these clashes some students were indeed injured (and one student was accidentally killed when he was hit by a police tear-gas canister), but to the best of my knowledge, all through these most heated weeks of open struggle on the streets of Port-au-Prince only one other anti-government protester was killed, in a confrontation on 7 January 2004 that also claimed the life of a pro-government partisan.[82] Freelance reporter Reed Lindsay arrived in Port-au-Prince in time to witness one of the largest of these student demonstrations, at the height of the tension.

The one opposition protest that I personally witnessed, in February 2004, was as big as they got and it wasn't that big; maybe 5000 people, maximum. It proceeded down Delmas. The students and other demonstrators were doing everything possible to provoke a police reaction. Those students were very hardcore; they were quite willing to risk their lives trying to provoke the police into shooting at them. Meanwhile, every now and then from the side-streets there were some kids throwing rocks at the students. The police were in the middle, trying to keep everyone calm; I thought they were remarkably professional and did a very good job.[83]

So it went on, day after day, at a time when paramilitaries linked to these same demonstrators were killing scores of pro-government activists or police in towns and villages all over the northern half of the country. It is not easy to compare what happened in Aristide's Haiti in 2003–04 with, say, the gruesome state repression maintained by the US government's client regime in Colombia during those same years.

In the third place, in most of the cases where pro-government forces turned violent, it's obvious that such violence was largely and under-standably defensive. From the moment of its "convergence," the opposition's every move was calculated to goad their enemies into reprisals that they could then turn to their advantage – the formation of Gourgue's pro-army parallel government in February 2001 is an especially provocative case in point.[84] Many of the "bandits" who turned out to heckle the democratic allies of Avril and Chamblain were veterans of the 1986 *déchoukaj* and survivors of the 1991–94 repression, and knew exactly what they were dealing with. The stakes were very high. As Kevin Pina tried to explain, most of what the independent media presented as "the evil 'shock troops,' the *chimères* of a dictatorial Lavalas, was the righteous indignation and anger of a very, very frightened mass of poor people in this country who for the first time had a government that they felt represented their interests."[85] As anyone could have predicted, in 2004–05 they would discover they had good reason to be afraid. Critics surprised or outraged by the persistence of a degree of vigilantism in Aristide's Haiti simply haven't taken on board the legacy left by people like François, Constant and Chamblain, compounded by the lack of an independent or effective judicial process. They forget that the people who mobilized around Aristide were far and away the main targets of political violence through this period. They forget that without a certain amount of defensive counter-violence, Aristide and other Lavalas leaders would never have survived the assaults of the late 1980s and early 1990s (the November

1987 killings, the attack on Saint Jean Bosco, the Lafontant coup . . .), let alone the return of paramilitary pressure from 2001. And they forget that for most poor people in particular, notions like police protection and the rule of law are in the great majority of cases empty words.[86] In 1991–94 and in 2004–06, the only force that would protect the people from their enemies would be the people themselves. What is a "*chimère*," after all, if not someone who refuses his or her own marginalization? What is a "*chimère*" if not someone who, as Ronald Saint-Jean puts it, "confronts the forces of repression and tells them 'I am not afraid.' "[87]

It's also the case, in the fourth place, that in some instances it's difficult if not impossible to establish a clear line between political and perfectly ordinary criminal violence. There are criminal gangs in places like Gonaïves and Port-au-Prince, as there are in Sao Paulo, Johannesburg or Los Angeles. There are mafias all over the world, and Haiti is no angelic exception to this rule; the local pool of recruits has moreover grown in recent years with the massive influx of internal refugees from Haiti's devastated countryside, compounded by the deportation to the island of well over a thousand Haitian and Haitian-American convicts from the American prison system. Violent competition between thousands of desperate and generally unemployed young men in ever more crowded slums is no more surprising in Haiti than it is in Jamaica or South Africa. Anti-Lavalas writers like Alex Dupuy or Michael Deibert, however, regularly conflate inter-gang violence with deliberate government policy, and point to clashes between rival gangs like those that took place in Fort Mercredi (June 2001, which according to Deibert left thirteen people dead) or Cité Soleil (October 2003, which according to Deibert left twelve dead) as examples of the way Aristide sought to maintain a quasi-military grip on power.[88] The implication, presumably, is that because some of the people involved in these battles were indeed "pro-Lavalas," so then the government (for reasons that remain somewhat mysterious) may have incited them to declare war on their neighbors. Perhaps the fact that Aristide then tried to calm things down by speaking with all the groups involved, rather than by shooting at them, is further proof of his complicity in such violence. Since violent turf-wars between criminal gangs and drug-dealers don't seem to be confined solely to pro-Lavalas neighborhoods in Haiti's capital city, however, in the absence of any credible evidence to the contrary it could just be that Aristide and his government had nothing to do with them.

No one denies that there was violence between gangs in Aristide's Haiti, and there is nothing obscure about the correlation between destitution and crime; since many of Aristide's supporters live in destitution it's no surprise that some of them are also caught up in crime. How much crime is again a matter of debate. In poor neighborhoods in Haiti as in the US or other Latin American countries, rival gangs compete to control the few resources that may lie within their reach – a few government-sponsored jobs, control of a port or transportation route, access to contraband or extortion rackets of one sort or another. Occasionally (as in Gonaïves in 2003, for instance, or in Cité Soleil in 2004–05) such criminal/economic rivalry may coincide with political rivalry: the more destitute and politicized the neighborhood, the more likely the coincidence. Experienced investigators like Anne Sosin and Judy DaCruz readily confirm the predictable fact that some of the Cité groups that "present themselves as political are really just trying to advance an economic claim" within the severe limits of their situation.[89] So long as the army or its proxies aren't running things, however, what's again most remarkable about this unremarkable violence is its rarity. Despite truly and increasingly desperate conditions in the slums (and leaving aside coup-related killings), the average murder rate in Haiti is less than a quarter of that in Jamaica, for instance, and well below that of cities like New York or Miami.[90]

It's worth remembering, in the fifth place, that isolated acts of Lavalas violence took place at a time when police numbers, supplies and morale were all running desperately low. In February 2004 the city of New York on its own had around twenty times more police (some 40,000 officers) than the whole country of Haiti. In the autumn of 2005, even so heavily policed a country as France had some trouble controlling the inhabitants of its *banlieues*. As we have seen, the attempt to control violence in Haiti was made immeasurably more difficult, during Aristide's second administration, by the fact that substantial parts of the national police were not simply beyond government control but were actively working *against* the government. Despite this lack of control, under Lavalas (as opposed to the IGH/MINUSTAH), when abuses were committed there was at least some attempt to investigate the incident and punish those responsible; the Carrefour-Feuilles trial of 2000 is the most notable case in point.

The violence attributed to Lavalas, such as it is, might have been either defensive or criminal or both, but it was almost never offensive or deliberate. This is the sixth and most important point. Despite repeated assertions to the contrary, there is simply no convincing proof that political violence was initiated and guided by Aristide's government. Veteran reporter Guy Delva is one of the most neutral and balanced observers of the period, and in 2001–02 he drew strong criticism from Lavalas activists irritated by his association with anti-government NGOs like Reporters Without Borders. Delva knows of no deliberate campaign of violence and of no coordinated effort to arm the "chimères." "There's no evidence of it. Of course it's *possible* that in 2004 some weapons were handed out to gangs loyal to the regime: there was an armed insurgency going on, after all, and it's possible that the government wanted to strengthen itself against the rebels. But the government had very few weapons, in fact, and the supply of police munitions was very low."[91] The most that can plausibly be said, according to Professor Robert Fatton (on the basis of what he admits is only rumors and speculation), is that in its last months, as the full extent of police unreliability became clear, some members of Aristide's security team *may* have handed out a total of perhaps 100 battered handguns to sympathetic gang-members in Port-au-Prince.[92] Source close to Kim Ives have told him that "Some government security officials – possibly acting on their own initiative – did send a few, very few, arms to popular organizations in parts of Haiti in the lead-up to the coup," as part of belated, "half-hearted and anarchic attempt to create a civil defense force."[93] But Lavalas partisans like Belizaire Printemps or Elias Clovis (members of the Port-au-Prince *organisation populaire* Konbit Rezistans Mas Yo) insist that there was no effort to arm government supporters or to mount a campaign of political intimidation. "Never in my life did I witness Aristide call people from the slums to violence, never."[94] Aristide's pilot and confidant Frantz Gabriel is adamant: "There weren't enough guns to arm the USGPN, let alone members of pro-FL popular organizations."[95]

It's true that once G184 demonstrations demanding Aristide's expulsion started in November 2003 some of the group leaders in the Cité received occasional calls from Aristide's departmental police chief Hermione Léonard and his interior minister Jocelerme "Miss" Privert encouraging them to stage counter-demonstrations. Local Lavalas activists like John Joseph Jorel insist, however, that the main purpose for government communications with popular leaders in Cité Soleil was to try to keep the peace among rival gangs in the most desperately impoverished parts of the city. "Hermione was the local police chief," says Jorel, "and it was her job to maintain order, to keep conflicts to a minimum. To do this of course she had to remain in contact with the various gangs, and try to work with them as best she could, to talk to the appropriate people, and so on. I imagine police have to do the same thing in Miami or Johannesburg. It's precisely because Hermione had links with local leaders like Colobri and Billy that she was appointed to her position in the first place, and people like her helped to defuse a lot of the violence that you're always going to find in a place as poor as Cité Soleil – just look at how bad things got once Aristide was overthrown."[96]

Eléonore Senlis ran the largest international NGO outpost in Cité Soleil from June 2003 till July 2004. She befriended leaders of the Cité's armed groups and was as well-placed as any outsider to assess claims that the government set out to arm groups of its poorest supporters in order to intimidate its (generally less poor) opponents. The main reason for contacts between government representatives and leaders of armed groups in Cité Soleil, Senlis confirms, wasn't to turn the latter into a quasi-military force that might intimidate the opposition, but simply to keep a lid on social conflict in an acutely unstable part of town. From time to time Hermione Léonard would arrange "a meeting with the various group leaders, a sort of peace would last for a while, and then sooner or later new groups would push their way onto the scene, begin to interfere with another group's activities, the leaders would start fighting amongst themselves, and the process had to start all over again." As for claims that the government set out to arm such groups in order to intimidate its opponents, Senlis knows of only one unambiguous case, in an emergency triggered by a combination of open paramilitary assault and police weakness:

> After the trouble started in early February 2004, some of the group leaders in Cité Soleil, along with some of their men, were sent up to Gonaïves, and there they were given weapons by the government, to confront the insurgents. The rest of the time it wasn't at all clear that the government was deliberately trying to arm groups from Cité Soleil. Members of these groups generally seemed to steal their guns from the police or security guards or from other residents of the Cité. The bigger guns were always bought, often from the DR, with money stolen from shops or occasionally donated by various interested parties as "contributions to the security of Cité Soleil." But as far as I know there was never any large-scale distribution of weapons from the government to their supporters.

Of course, it may be that such distribution was not necessary. Perhaps the *chimères* were already so well-armed that they could "stifle dissent" in

Aristide's Haiti without the government's help. What sort of weaponry did they actually have at their disposal? Eléonore Senlis is again one of the most reliable foreign witness available.

> As for the actual number of guns, at least until mid 2004 there weren't very many of them to go round. As of February 2004, there were three well-armed groups, led by Dred Wilme, Labanye, and Amaral Duclona. Each of these three leaders had several automatic weapons at his disposal, maybe half a dozen high calibre pistols and several dozen .38 revolvers, most of which were loaned out to their followers. I think I saw most of them, and I'd guess that there was a grand total of around 250 guns in the hands of groups from Cité Soleil during the turmoil of February 2004, and considerably less before then.[97]

In the context of a country blessed with an estimated 210,000 firearms (the vast majority of which remain securely in the hands of its ruling families and businesses),[98] it may be that this *chimère* arsenal of around 250 handguns never posed a very worrying threat.

In reality, Aristide had nothing to gain from violence, and he repeatedly denounced it. In reality, despite its lack of resources and the uncertain loyalties of the police in general and the USGPN in particular, on several occasions Aristide's government courted vehement popular protest by arresting pro-FL activists (e.g. Amiot Métayer, Franco Camille, Ronald Camille) when they were accused of crimes. In reality, Aristide insisted on peaceful negotiation and reconciliation with his enemies, even when this insistence did little more than weaken his own position. Had Aristide given the order for a popular uprising there can be little doubt that opposition calls for a coup would have been instantly drowned in blood. Had he issued a call to arms, opposition rallies would have ended overnight. As an increasingly exasperated Patrick Elie pointed out a few months after the coup, "had President Aristide created an armed militia the ex-military and the death squads would not have stood a chance. All we're seeing [now] is the violence being visited upon the partisans of President Aristide and it is obvious that this 'army' of '*chimères*' that they were talking about doesn't exist and is being proven a total, total lie. Every day you read in the newspapers about the Aristide militia, the bandits armed by Aristide, the *chimères*: that is a total urban legend."[99]

As with any dispute that rests largely on rumor and hearsay, the best way to deal with this point is to focus on the indisputable bigger picture. It's not hard to find a gun in Haiti, and no-one denies that some Aristide supporters had guns. What has always been just as obvious to anyone in Cité Soleil or Bel Air is that their enemies have bigger guns, more of them, and more ways of getting hold of them. As we've seen, after 1994 military and FRAPH personnel were never disarmed, and they had powerful friends both in the moneyed hills above Port-au-Prince and across the border in the Dominican Republic. To compare the firepower of the ruling class with the weaponry of the average *Lavalassian* would be a truly ludicrous exercise. It's hardly reasonable to equate the defensive struggle waged by Lavalas militants with the outright warfare launched by the CD's "freedom fighters." It's still more unreasonable, finally, to skirt the most obvious question of all: who had the most to gain by shifting this particular political struggle onto military terrain? A mass movement of the poor and the dispossessed, inspired by the principles of liberation theology and mobilized through cooperatives, popular organizations and the *ti legliz*? Or a disgruntled tactical alliance of rightwing businessmen and ex-army officers, backed up by the most powerful military machine on the planet?

In 2004, who stood to profit by generating widespread anarchy and fear? Was it perhaps people who actively sought the restoration of the army, the elite and the old "forces of order"? Or else those people who had easily won the last election and who knew that if they able to cast them again, their votes would win them the next few elections as well?

There is no doubt that the combination of genuine and imagined grievances undermined support for Lavalas over the course of Aristide's second administration. A couple of years after Aristide's return in 1994, some members of the original Lavalas coalition who were unhappy with the concessions he had made in order to restore democracy were growing increasingly restive. "These days Lavalas is starting to show signs of wear and tear," Jane Regan wrote in 1997, as she noted a rise in popular protests against "rising prices, high taxes, the lack of services, empty promises, invasion of foreign products, and the greed and corruption of politicians."[100] By 2002, even strong Lavalas loyalists were wrestling with what Ottawa-based activist Jean Saint-Vil acknowledged as "the multiple errors, faults, concessions and outright disappointments caused by a weakened and overwhelmed Aristide government."[101] Elite NGOs like PAPDA and SOFA presented themselves as the spokespeople of an apparently broad-based disaffection with the government (more on this in a moment). A quasi-vocational distrust of Aristide's "demagogic populism" alienated many of the foreign or exiled intellectuals – René

Depestre, James Morrell, Christophe Wargny, Amy Wilentz . . . – who had once supported him.[102] More importantly, as the effects of structural adjustment took their toll on Haitian farmers, a couple of the country's higher-profile peasant organizations (Tet Kole Ti Peyizan and KOZE-PEP) grew increasingly hostile to FL. Although they stopped short of the pro-coup position embraced by Chavannes Jean-Baptiste and the MPP, they condemned FL along with the rest of Haiti's main political parties for cooperating with the imperialists and for becoming *anti-populaire*. Clément François of Tèt Kole speaks for many critics of Lavalas when he argues that Aristide should not have agreed to the US conditions that allowed him to return from exile. "He should have stayed outside and let us continue the struggle for democracy; instead, he agreed to deliver the country on a platter so that he could get back into office."[103]

No less than the MPP itself, however, Tèt Kole and KOZEPEP were certainly weakened by their opposition to Aristide, and today none of these groups remain a significant political force.[104] The militancy of their followers has long been dulled, as Stan Goff notes, "by the steady trickle of project dollars flowing through the almost interminable list of non-governmental organizations that infest every corner of Haiti."[105] In its regional stronghold of Hinche, the MPP decided to run its own candidates in the May 2000 elections; Charles Arthur, who observed these elections as part of the OAS mission, noted that the MPP candidates "polled very poorly, below the OPL and the Espace de Concertation and far below FL."[106] Anti-Lavalas intellectuals like Camille Chalmers, Marc-Arthur Fils-Aimé or Micha Gaillard, meanwhile, no longer have a substantial domestic audience; were it not for the funding and the sympathy they receive from abroad they would probably no longer have any public voice at all. The OPL, led by the career politicians Gérard Pierre-Charles and his wife Suzy Castor, was no doubt the party which most closely resembles that elite "civic" alternative to Fanmi Lavalas so dear to liberal commentators both in Haiti, France and North America,[107] but after its years of sterile parliamentary maneuvering it was wiped out in the 2000 elections. No OPL politician had any significant support among the Haitian poor. Long before the CD's strategic purpose had been fulfilled it too had stopped pretending to be a significant actor on the political stage.

For all its faults, the fact is that to this day Aristide's Fanmi Lavalas remains the most significant force for popular mobilization in Haiti. It is the only group that can mobilize large numbers of demonstrators and voters via well-organized cells located in every part of the country. It is often said that over time Aristide managed to alienate most of his initial supporters. This isn't true. Most of the fellow-travelers and tactical allies fell away, certainly, but the committed local activists – Gérard Jean-Juste, John Joseph Jorel, Jean-Charles Moïse, Belizaire Printemps, Samba Boukman, Rea Dol . . . – have remained loyal to Aristide from the beginning.

So have, by every available indicator, a large majority of the Haitian people. By 2003–04 relentless destabilization and FL mistakes had taken their toll on support for FL, but as the most detailed—and by no means uncritical—study of the recent period concludes, there was no doubt that Aristide still enjoyed "undisputed and overwhelming popularity" among the mass of Haitians.[108] In a US-commissioned Gallup poll of October 2000, FL was thirteen times more popular than its closest competitor, and over half of those polled identified Aristide as their most trusted leader. According to the last "neutral" measure before the 2004 coup, a further Gallup poll conducted in March 2002, FL remained four times more popular than all its significant competitors combined; 60 percent of respondents again picked Aristide as the leader they trusted most, while his nearest rival, Convergence leader Gerard Gourgue, won the backing of just 3.7 percent of respondents.[109] Based on her experience and assessment of the situation in Port-au-Prince over 2003–04, Eléonore Senlis thinks that "At no point during its last year in office would any serious political poll have shown support for Fanmi Lavalas to be less than 60 percent; Aristide's electoral base remained solidly behind him, even if they still hoped that the government would do more."[110] Based on her assessment of the situation in the countryside, Jean Dominique's widow Michèle Montas observed the month before the coup that "the peasantry has always been very loyal to Aristide," and that "for now their loyalty appears intact; they legitimately fear a return to the Duvalier-style dictatorship they lived under for so long."[111] The less biased elements of the international press also acknowledged the point from time to time. When the BBC covered Aristide's re-election campaign in November 2000, for instance, it had to admit "Mr. Aristide's massive support from Haiti's vast underclass of poor makes it hard to imagine anyone who could seriously challenge him for the job."[112] Reporting from Port-au-Prince three and a half years later, BBC correspondent Daniel Lak had to concede much the same argument.[113] So did Professor Robert Fatton, despite his reservations about Fanmi Lavalas: "I'm convinced that Aristide is still the most popular individual in Haiti [. . .]. If you had elections – so-called 'free and fair' elections – I'm sure that he would win, in spite of all the corruption and all of the problems that he has."[114] The plain fact of the matter, as Stan Goff understood very well, is that in 2003–04 Aristide remained capable of mobilizing the Haitian people like no-one else. "Aristide had established a rapport with the Haitian masses, with the poor, the peasants, the slum dwellers, and that's what made him a threat" – a threat that no amount of insistence on "reconciliation" could do anything to disarm.[115]

Despite all the effort and the energy of the destabilization campaign, in other words, by mid-2003 Fanmi Lavalas still remained the dominant political force in Haiti. Its elimination would require new weapons and a new willingness to use them.

8

2003–2004: Preparing for War

Ou wè sa w genyen, ou pa konn sa w rete
(You know what you've got, but you don't know what's coming).

Looking back at the period 2000–04 a couple of years after the fact, the sequence of events that culminated in Aristide's abduction by US troops on 29 February 2004 can be read in one of three ways.

In the first place, many if not most people seem to think that there wasn't a coup at all but just a local variation on the sort of "Orange Revolutions" that became popular during the height of a global war on terror, evil and dictatorship. This was the official line, of course, put out by the US State Department, the Haiti Democracy Project, the Group of 184 and their allies. Confronted with a corrupt and tyrannical regime, the Haitian people rose up and liberated themselves from their oppressor, and the US only intervened, once things started to get out of control, to protect Aristide and his family from harm. This was also the version parroted by much of the mainstream press. There was no coup, said *The Times* on 1 March 2004, but rather a "popular revolution" inspired by "the resentment left by Aristide's flawed victory [in 2000], his increasingly despotic and erratic rule, and the wholesale collapse of the local economy."[1]

Some other people remember what happened to Arbenz in 1954, to Allende in 1973, to Manley in 1980, to Ortega in 1990, to Chávez in 2002 – and to Aristide himself in 1991 – and recognize an obvious pattern. From this perspective, the whole destabilization campaign looks all too familiar and all too predictable, and it was indeed predicted. February 2004 was one of the most widely anticipated "surprises" of contemporary world politics. In 2001, Stan Goff could already see the writing on the wall, and knew that the "reactionary wing of the

Republican Party will settle for nothing less than Aristide's political neutralization" and the "surrender of [Haitian] sovereignty."[2] Writing in 2002, Robert Fatton observed that "Rightwing US policymakers have already condemned Aristide for being a dangerous radical and an intransigent man who surrounds himself with 'narco-traffickers' and encourages 'thuggish violence'. These accusations, which have never been substantiated, could easily become the basis for a major campaign of systematic denigration," and prepare the way for Aristide's "surgical removal" on the Panama-Noriega model.[3] In several searing articles published over the course of 2003, writer-activists like Kim Ives, Georges Honorat and Kevin Pina documented the machinations of the impending coup in compelling detail.[4] In speech after speech, the PPN's Ben Dupuy made the same point. The prescience of these analyses speaks for itself.

It is a short step, however, from predicting such an outcome to accepting it as almost inevitable. This is the risk run in Fatton's pessimistic version of events, as it is in some leftwing analyses preoccupied with the diabolical machinations of the CIA and the IRI, along with the stifling malevolence of the IMF or the World Bank. The trap laid by the enemy for Aristide and for Lavalas was too powerful, the argument goes, and the more they tried to resist their fate the weaker and more compromised they became; in the end, all that is left is *fate* itself. What then is to stop us from drawing the conclusion that the sequence that led to February 2004 should be understood in terms of closure and defeat, as the *end* of the emancipatory project that began with the *déchoukaj* of 1986?

A third interpretation (which informs the present book) agrees with much of the second. Yes the assault on Lavalas was consistent with the long-standing pattern and priorities of imperial foreign policy in Latin America and the rest of the world. For this assault to succeed in 2004, however, it was obliged to go to quite exceptional lengths. The coup of 2004 was far more difficult to achieve than that of 1991. It took much longer and cost much more. It required the coordination of many more people, and the deployment of a vastly more elaborate and varied range of strategies. The sheer labor and intensity of the destabilization campaign (together with the amount of foreign money and troops required to cope with its aftermath) is itself a measure of the strength of its target. It is an indication of the fact that the outcome was never inevitable – though hardly an accident, February 2004 was indeed a surprise. It is better understood as *scandal* than as fate.

February 2004 was a scandal, it was never inevitable, and its effects are not irreversible. Despite its violence and atrocity, moreover, the coup was itself a failure. As we shall see in our final chapter, its authors failed to accomplish their main objective – the elimination of Lavalas as an organized political force. February 2004 was less a defeat than a setback. The military coup of February 2004 would be reversed in due course by the popular anti-coup of February 2006, which itself opened the door to a new phase in the Lavalas project.

We are already familiar with the routine features of the destabilization campaign: crippling economic aggression, forced structural adjustment, the mobilization of rightwing civil society, paralyzing negotiations with an invented opposition, systematic media manipulation, repeated allegations of corruption, violence and the abuse of human rights, and so on, all backed up with the pressure of naked paramilitary force. To get their coup in 2004, however, the US, France and Canada, together with the domestic elite, would have to do three things that they hadn't needed to do back in 1991: (a) they would need to nourish ideological support for regime change not only on the right but also on the *left* of the political spectrum, via the collusion of "progressive" NGOs and pressure groups like PAPDA, Batay Ouvriye and Grassroots International, together with a stage-managed student protest movement; (b) they would need to win over not just merely tactical fellow-travelers of Lavalas (Pierre-Charles, Evans Paul, Paul Denis . . .) but also some militants and organizations who were once sympathetic to Aristide himself (Dany Toussaint and his coterie, as well as Labanye's gang in Cité Soleil and Amiot Métayer's gang in Gonaïves); (c) when push came to shove, the *coup de grace* would have to be delivered not by Haitian proxies like the FLRN and the former military but by imperial troops themselves.

PREPARING THE GROUND:
NGOS AND POLITICS OF BENEVOLENCE

Few things are more urgently needed for a better understanding of contemporary Haitian politics than a detailed analysis of the precise economic and ideological role of the non-governmental organizations (NGOs) that now play such a big part in the administration of the country. There's no space for such an analysis here, but it is well worth drawing some attention to the most salient aspects of the question.

First of all, there are *a lot* of NGOs in Haiti. According to several estimates, there are more NGOs per capita in Haiti than anywhere in the world. In 1998, the World Bank guessed that there are anything between 10,000 and 20,000 NGOs working in the country.[5] Something like 80 percent of basic public services (the provision of water, health care, education, sanitation, food distribution . . .) are undertaken by NGOs; the largest organizations have budgets bigger than those of their corresponding government departments.[6] The vast majority of the $1.2 billion promised to Haiti's post-coup regime by international donors as part of the 2004 Interim Cooperative Framework was pledged via USAID, USAID's Office of Transition Initiatives, or more independent-seeming NGOs, rather than to government agencies. Usually managed by well-connected members of the elite in conjunction with international parent companies or partners, much of what they do is effectively independent of government scrutiny. Most of what they do, moreover, is extremely fragmented. All by itself, the complex multiplicity of the NGO sector discourages incisive evaluation. The fact that there are so many NGOs, each with their own priorities and projects (which are often quite foreign to actual Haitian requirements), makes it almost impossible to develop a coordinated policy in any given field. There are some exceptions – the medical project Zanmi Lasante (Partners in Health), for instance, works closely with Haitian government medical authorities in various parts of the country, as well as with international donors and experts.[7] More often than not, however, the power and multiplicity of NGOs serves to undercut if not simply to replace government initiatives, and in doing so helps reinforce the prejudice that aid or development money is better funneled through "reliable" NGOs than through corrupt or inefficient departments of state.

The mainstream press has a ready explanation for the recent growth in NGO funding. "The United States is Haiti's largest donor," observed a *Washington Post* editorial in January 2004, "and to ensure that assistance gets to those Haitians most in need, it is channeled principally through nongovernmental organizations."[8] No further explanation is required. There is another reason, though, why the vast majority of aid money flows through non-governmental rather than governmental organizations: it's easier, that way, for the people giving the money to take it back. USAID itself "boasts that 84 cents of every dollar of its funding in Haiti goes back to the US in the form of salaries, supplies, consultant fees, and services."[9] The international donors set strict political and economic conditions for the charity they provide. As we have seen, the bulk of USAID money that goes to Haiti and to other countries in the region is explicitly designed to pursue US interests – the promotion of a secure investment climate, the nurturing of links with local business elites, the preservation of a docile and low-wage labor force, and so on.[10] Only a tiny fraction (perhaps 5 percent of the total) of aid money is aimed where it is most needed – towards a *lasting* reinvigoration of Haitian agriculture and the rural economy.[11] Rather than strengthen Haiti's capacity to resist the foreign manipulation of its economy, USAID initiatives like PIRED or the Pan-American Development Foundation combine with IMF-driven structural adjustment to enhance US penetration of the local market and to reinforce the economic basis of Haiti's rigid class structure. Some of the more devastating consequences of such policies are then softened (but also exacerbated) by secondary initiatives like the distribution of food aid through agencies like CARE or aggressively pro-US evangelical churches like the Baptists and Seventh Day Adventists. Distribution of this "free" food further undercuts domestic agricultural production and creates new cycles of economic and ideological dependency.

Since a minimum of around 70 percent of NGO funding is distributed by USAID and its sibling organizations in client states (notably Canada's CIDA), NGOs would in many respects be better described not as non-governmental but as *other*-governmental – the government that funds and directs most of what they do is not the government of Haiti but that of its benevolent neighbor to the north. NGOs provide rich countries a morally respectable way of subcontracting the sovereignty of the nations they exploit.[12] Some indication of the impact of USAID policies in Haiti is provided by the organization's assessment of its own Democracy and Governance Program: "In 2001, USAID and its partners trained nearly 11,000 people in almost 1,000 organizations with total membership exceeding 200,000 people throughout the country. As a result of this training, civil society organizations made over 500 attempts to engage government and advocate their interests or defend their rights. Well over one-third of these attempts were successful in leveraging assistance, resources, or services from the government."[13] There are good reasons why many Haitians see the provision of democratization funds, development grants and food aid as part of a more general process of subversion, facets of a single integrated programme that has long been denounced as the "American plan" or the "death plan" (see above, page 5).

A third and related problem with many NGO programs is that they tend to disrupt and then disempower the lives of the people they are supposed to support. Many programs are run on a short-term basis, and provide relatively well-paid but temporary employment. This has the perverse effect of luring farmers and agricultural workers away from their fields, thereby reducing the amount of food harvested, of land cultivated and of time spent on the collective work projects (*kombits*) which are integral to the rural economy; when the development scheme then comes to an end there is nothing to take up the slack, and the ex-employees are soon worse off than before.[14] The same thing can happen in urban areas, when NGOs like Médecins Sans Frontières or the International Organization for Migration sweep into an area, double the wages of a few local people for several months and then move on, without leaving permanent programs or facilities in their wake.[15] Again there are some exceptions – Oxfam's work with coffee-growing co-operatives in northern Haiti may be a case in point – but given the priorities of their own donors, charity-oriented NGOs are generally less interested in helping to enhance what may be strong and assertive in Haitian society than in offering services to the vulnerable and the weak. As a rule, NGOs do not provide resources to strengthen government initiatives like the FL literacy program of 2001–03, let alone to help empower or organize a militant popular movement. They prefer to help look after the ill, the orphaned, or the under-nourished. While such services are indeed urgently needed, the way they are provided reinforces the prevailing balance of political power. The great majority of those few North Americans who visit Haiti travel as part of carefully supervised religious missions, and engage in a sort of charity-tourism. Compared even to very basic state investment in say education or public health, many NGO programs have very little to show for the millions they spend (other than the very considerable proportion that they lavish on them-selves). The poorest region of Haiti, the North-West department, is also the zone most intensely penetrated by NGOs. "The NGOs need the situation to continue," the director of the Cité Soleil hospital points out, "since otherwise they have no reason to be here."[16] As for its ideological impact, the provision of white enlightened charity to destitute and allegedly "superstitious" blacks is part and parcel of an all too familiar neo-colonial pattern. Wealthy nations have an obvious interest in pre-serving the image of poorer nations as "failed states" that need generous outside help to survive, just as the charities have an interest in preserving the structural conditions of Haitian poverty, while raising money to alleviate a few of its most unsightly effects.

There is another structural side-effect of NGO infiltration in Haiti. Employment and promotion in an internationally oriented NGO is fast becoming a well-trodden path towards power and influence within Haiti itself – the configuration of the G184 is an obvious case in point.

Expansion of an inter-connected NGO sector serves to consolidate rather than challenge the hegemony of the cosmopolitan elite. As Nicolas Guilhot points out in a helpful study, one of the reasons why "NGOs have become key regulatory actors of globalization" is because they effectively enable the renewal, with democratic terminology and credentials, of a quasi-"aristocratic" approach to politics. Apparently preoccupied with civic virtue, political neutrality and institutional stability, most NGO administrators understand that "civic virtue is best served by those whose already dominant social status is a guarantee that their motives are pure and disinterested." Like the *notables* described by Montesquieu or the *honoratiores* described by Weber, NGO personnel tend to be people whose already privileged status allows them to pose as if they "live *for* politics, without living *from* politics."[17] By definition, surely, such principled people cannot be bought. Nothing is more obnoxious in their eyes than the spectacle of "corrupt" or "extremist" members of a lower-income petty-bourgeois class who might dare to seek inclusion within their exclusive ranks – a description which fits a large fraction of the new Lavalas cadres, if not (in the eyes of many of his rivals) Aristide himself. Suitably staffed and oriented, many NGO consultants operate in practice as what Guilhot calls "double agents." Although their influence is ostensibly derived from their grassroots links, in reality they are ever more smoothly integrated with IFIs and other transnational agencies, to the point that "their identity has been dissolved in a seamless web of 'global governance' where they interact and sometimes overlap with government agencies, international organizations and corporations."[18]

Rather than the army or state bureaucracies, NGOs now provide the main institutional and ideological mechanism for the reproduction of Haiti's ruling class. As even the casual visitor to Port-au-Prince will immediately gather, foreign aid-workers and their local colleagues, like other members of their class, have access to vehicles, houses and meeting-places that set them sharply apart from the great majority of the population.[19] Many NGO employees or consultants tend to treat the country they're working in as enemy territory.[20] The people who work for elite advocacy groups like PAPDA and SOFA come from much the same affluent, well-educated, French- and/or English-speaking milieu as does the rest of the political set. Rather than organize with and among the people, rather than work in the places and on the terms where the people themselves are strong, groups like PAPDA, SOFA and NCHR organize trivial made-for-media demonstrations against things like the uncontroversial evils of neo-liberalism or the high cost of living.[21] Such protests are usually attended by tiny groups of 30 or 40 people – which is to say, by nobody outside the organizers' own inter-connected circles.

PAPDA AND BATAY OUVRIYE

One of the most striking things about the 2004 coup is the vigorously *political* role played by some of these same advocacy groups – not least because NGOs, charities and human rights groups so often disguise their political impact behind an ostensibly neutral and principled if not moral façade. If you can't trust a non-governmental charity then what can you trust? This is again something that operatives working for the IRI and NED understood very well. They knew that, given the chance, groups like PAPDA and many similar organizations, together with their international allies like Christian Aid, Catholic Institute for International Relation, Catholic Relief Services, Action Aid, and so on, could provide some of the most trustworthy and media-friendly ammunition to the destabilization campaign. By the end of the 1990s, most of the anti-neo-liberal NGOs had much closer links with Suzy Castor's OPL than they did with FL, despite the fact that in reality the OPL was more aggressively neo-liberal than FL. By the end of 2003, most of these same NGOs had rallied around a version of the CD's *option zéro*, again in spite of the fact that, under the circumstances, such an option could only lead to one outcome – the *untrammeled* triumph of neo-liberal imperialism in Haiti.

Anyone unsure of the actual ideological function of the charitable NGOs should look closely at the way they responded to events in Haiti in early 2004. Christian Aid is a representative example. A recipient of UK and Canadian government development money, Christian Aid is the main financial backer of Charles Arthur's Haiti Support Group, shares the perspective of conservative G184 intellectuals like Lyonel Trouillot, and has long-standing links with CD politicians like Suzy Castor. A couple of days after the coup, Christian Aid's Helen Spraos spoke for most of the international-charitable NGOs when rather than call for the restoration of the elected government, or even for new elections, or even for an inquiry into the circumstances of Aristide's abduction, she claimed instead that Aristide had got what he deserved. He was no "champion of the poor. Instead, his regime was little different from Haiti's other rulers when power was exercised in the personal interests of previous presidents. Christian Aid's Haitian partner organizations have ample evidence of serious human rights abuses and misrule committed by Aristide and his supporters."[22] Together with these independent partners (NCHR, PAPDA, GARR, SOFA . . .), Christian Aid went on to repeat the US/CD version of the sequence that led to Aristide's departure more or less word for word. "An intractable crisis has marked the political landscape for several years, because of human rights' and civil liberties' abuses, and a dispute about the validity of the electoral process in 2000. It is this that has led, in recent months, to the political and civil unrest that has become increasingly violent."[23] After endorsing opposition claims about "the destruction wrought by Aristide's foot soldiers, the *chimè*," on 4 March Helen Spraos went on to note without further comment that these "*chimè* are now being pursued for their own brutality." Happily the path towards reconciliation is clear. "Now that former Haitian president Aristide has left Port-au-Prince," she writes, "the voice of the poor needs to be heard if Haiti is to find peace and prosperity."[24] There was no need to enquire into the circumstances of his leaving or to listen to what the poor had *already* said in their own voices and with their own votes, because like the IRI and the CD, Christian Aid and its partners already knew what so many of these poor people didn't yet seem to know – that Aristide had "become a tyrant," that together with Duvalier, Namphy and Cédras he had trapped the country in a continuous "cycle of terror and misrule," and that the "armed insurrection" which somehow emerged in February 2004 was simply an extension of popular "protests" against Aristide's corruption and his "repression of dissent."[25]

Whatever else you might say about Christian Aid, its position was indeed a faithful reflection of that held by its Haitian partners. Veteran activist Tom Reeves has met with members of SOFA, NCHR and other like-minded groups repeatedly over the past fifteen years, and in 2004 was bemused by SOFA's insistence that the "Aristide government after 2000 was 'worse than Cédras or Duvalier.' I met these women in hiding during the previous coup period and found them terrorized. I saw them last year [2003], under Aristide, openly functioning from their office in down-town Port-au-Prince," operating with a freedom unimaginable under any pre-Aristide regime.[26] Guy Delva also finds the hostility of elite women's groups like SOFA and CONAP hard to fathom, noting that Aristide did far more for women, and for children, than any other Haitian politician.[27] Women's rights activist Anne Sosin confirms what you might expect, that what is at stake is a form of class rivalry. Foreign observers underestimate, she explains, the massive gap between elite (wealthy, French-speaking, internationally oriented) NGO professionals and grassroots (poor, Kreyol-speaking, neighborhood-oriented) activists. As the pressure on the FL administration increased after 2000, "there was a growing split between the two kinds of organizations, with the grass-roots remaining pro Lavalas and Aristide, and the NGOs mostly opposed." Soon the leaders of groups like SOFA and CONAP became "hysterical in their opposition to anything associated with Lavalas and Aristide, including now Préval and the Lespwa platform."[28]

These days SOFA and NCHR are perhaps too discredited to warrant further discussion. PAPDA, on the other hand, still retains a certain following on the fringes of the international left, and US- or UK-based allies like Grassroots International and the Haiti Support Group ensure that its opinions receive considerable attention.[29] PAPDA emerged as an ostensibly significant voice on Haitian affairs in an age when the very institutions it appears to attack – the US State Department, USAID, the World Bank and other IFIs – all came to embrace a broad human rights and "civil society" agenda. PAPDA began to receive international attention and funding at a time when all these hegemonic actors began pretending to embrace "'bottom-up' methodologies and 'grass-roots' approaches" that might "widen participation" while ensuring good governance and encouraging the development of neutral and stable political institutions.[30] Fronted by the affable and cosmopolitan economist Camille Chalmers, PAPDA's main purpose is to compile trenchant though politically inconsequential analyses of the damage inflicted upon Haiti's rural economy by more than twenty years of structural adjustment.[31] From 2001–04, it also produced a steady stream of press releases denouncing the irredeemable depravity of the Lavalas government. Three quotations should be enough to illustrate the basic point. In 2001, after the short burst of vigilante violence that followed FLRN's attempted coup of 17 December, PAPDA joined with SOFA (itself a member of PAPDA) and ENFOFANM (another small elite women's group) to issue statements saying "No, No, No. This coup mustn't happen! This plot to destroy the democratic aspirations of the people mustn't happen!" The "coup" at issue, however, was *not* the actual assault just attempted by ex-army paramilitaries allied to the CD but rather the popular reprisals that it provoked, i.e. the "appalling" attacks carried out by "bands of fascists" against properties belonging to leading members of the CD[32] (who were themselves busy making the absurd but widely repeated claim that the government had staged the coup-attempt itself). A couple of years later, just days before the full FLRN insurgency took off and under the guise of condemning his "immorality, corruption, and systematic violations of the most elementary rights of Haitian citizens," PAPDA issued a ringing call for Aristide's immediate departure. It insisted in particular that no-one should interfere in the persecution of Lavalas partisans that this departure was sure to trigger. "PAPDA IS OPPOSED TO THE INTERVENTION OF ANY MULTINATIONAL POLICE OR MILITARY FORCE ON HAITIAN SOIL UNDER THE PRETEXT OF RE-ESTABLISHING ORDER."[33] Finally, two months after getting rid of their nemesis and in the midst of the most brutally violent wave of repression in recent Haitian history, PAPDA joined with NCHR, CONAP and a handful of their friends in a characteristically tiny public protest – not against the killing of hundreds of Lavalas supporters in the slums, but exclusively against the alleged crooks of the previous regime. The aim of their demonstration was to censure Latortue for "being too slow in the process of arresting all those accused of committing crimes under the Aristide government." According to the *Agence Haïtienne Presse* reporter who covered the event, PAPDA and its co-protestors "did not comment on the issues of confirmed criminals still walking the streets and former rebels who committed serious crimes during the events of recent months." Instead they called for the arrest of ex-prime minister Yvon Neptune, on account of his apparent complicity in the so-called "massacre" at La Scierie in Saint-Marc on 11 February 2004 (see above, page 159).[34] Ronald Saint-Jean speaks for many exasperated allies of Lavalas when he derides PAPDA as nothing other than "the humanitarian face of the CIA."[35]

When the London-based Haiti Support Group came to present its interpretation of the February 2006 election result, by contrast, PAPDA was the one and only Haitian voice it chose to cite, in a newsletter that managed to explain Préval's re-election without so much as mentioning the main reason for his success: his endorsement *en masse* by the very same Lavalas activists whose repression Chalmers had tacitly endorsed back in 2004.[36]

When it comes to anti-Lavalas bias, however, no Haitian NGO can rival the small, quasi-clandestine network of labor activists known as Batay Ouvriye (BO). In recent years BO has helped organize several trade union campaigns, notably in Guacimal 2001–02 and in factories in the new free trade zone near Ouanaminthe 2003–05.[37] Although they have no significant presence in the country's largest and most exploitative sweatshops (in Port-au-Prince), in the new and marginally less exploitative situation at Ouanaminthe BO helped the SOKOWA union of garment workers sustain a protracted struggle to win an important though as yet un-implemented wage deal with their Dominican employers, the contractor Grupo M.[38] Some mainstream commentators like Marcus Garcia and Guy Delva acknowledge that BO is doing important work in the free trade zone, and given the likely growth in this sector of the economy, believe that the organization may eventually play a significant role in Haiti's future. BO leaders Didier Dominique (a.k.a. Paul Philomé, and brother of the bitterly anti-Aristide priest Max Dominique) and Yvonne Castera (a.k.a. Yannick Etienne, and the owner of the Ife Hotel) have a forceful understanding of Haitian class dynamics and the workings of US imperialism.[39] They were perfectly aware that the G184 is a front for ruling class interests. More controversial are BO's secrecy (it has no membership and no clear organizational structure or operational continuity, making collaboration with other unions difficult[40]), its highly orthodox workerism (which confines its influence to parts of Haiti's tiny industrial sector), its vehemently sectarian style (which underlies its contempt for just about every other left-leaning organization in the country, including the PPN and the CTH[41]), and its apparent lack of any presence or support in the countryside and the poorer urban neighborhoods (which limits its political influence to what Patrick Elie describes as a PAPDA-like irrelevance[42]). OP activist Belizaire Printemps acknowledges that "BO adopted the right sort of positions in the free trade zones, but their influence is and will remain severely limited by the people's profound resentment of the position they took against Lavalas and Aristide. BO say they are on the left but the actual, practical effect of what they do serves to defend the right."[43] BO, in short, is perhaps the most useful of the organizations that some Lavalassians dismiss as members of the "useless left".

Unfortunately for Aristide, his enemies found a very compelling use for Batay Ouvriye in the run-up to 2004. Apart from the G184 and the CD themselves, perhaps no other organization attacked him with the same venom and zeal. BO activist Mario Pierre's rant, in January 2006, against the "corrupt, immoral, thieving, charlatan, incompetent, bankrupt, criminal [. . .], putrid, pro-imperialist, and anti-worker Lavalas government" may give you some idea of the rhetorical inflation typical of BO's contribution to the disinformation campaign.[44] At the height of the crisis, in December 2003, BO issued a statement adding its voice to the chorus of those already crying "DOWN WITH THE BLOODTHIRSTY LAVALAS THIEVES!" After denouncing the "outright criminal" Aristide government as "the main agent of corruption" in Haiti, BO went on to insist that Lavalas had "always taken sides against the peoples' struggles," that it pursued "everywhere, indistinctly, always the same objective: to dismantle the demanding peoples' struggles, to annihilate free speech!" Lavalas sought only "to fight the working classes' interests, those of the poor peasants, workers, and popular masses in general."[45] Hysterical polemic is something of a BO speciality. Their various online statements and clarifications are peppered with references to the "puppets of imperialism" and "yellow, rotten, collaborationist unions." Their critics are dismissed as "nitwits" and "quacks." The death of two protestors at Guacimal becomes a "massacre," compromises with the IMF an unforgivable "crime." "During all of its administration," says BO, "Lavalas accomplished nothing. Quite the opposite, if they did [anything], all they did was negative: theft, corruption in general."[46]

It would be wrong to condemn Batay Ouvriye's opposition to Lavalas in 2003–04 as opportunistic. According to the then-incipient BO, Aristide's first election as president back in 1990 was already a disastrous "deviation" and "legalization" of the radical movement, to say nothing of Aristide's unholy alliance with Clinton in 1994. BO insists to this day that "there was never any popular mobilization under Aristide" and that he served only to "demobilize" the people before consigning them to "untrammeled capitalist exploitation." For BO, Fanmi Lavalas represents nothing more than a new petit-bourgeois phase of capital accumulation and the emergence of a new set of enemies for what should be a permanently revolutionary working class.[47] Paul Philomé explained a month after the 2004 coup that BO had always "worked to denounce all of the plans that the Fanmi Lavalas government had, we denounced them and fought to make sure those plans were not successful, and we also took positions so the government can leave the country because we felt that the Aristide government was a government that accepted impunity for the factory owners".[48] Although BO would later deny that they had actively supported the coup, the least that can be said is that they did nothing to discourage it. As Mario Pierre admitted in response to a program on WBAI radio, since FL were "traitors" and "imperialist puppets," so then "it is correct to say that the coup d'état [of 2004] did not and does not represent a loss for the Haitian People." As for the killing of Lavalas activists in the wake of the coup, this too was yet another devious Lavalas crime – "The massacre of the masses by the occupation forces and the repressive Haitian police is the continuation of the work of the Lavalas leadership to break the back of the workers."[49]

It is one thing to criticize and protest against a government elected by the great majority of the people, it is another to denounce it as an evil to be destroyed at all costs. Although it is easier to make certain criticisms when you have none of the responsibilities of power, leftwing labor groups are clearly entitled to pressure any government to adopt more progressive policies. Labor activists are clearly entitled to argue with Yvon Neptune's justification of the FTZs, to counter his claim that "even low-paying jobs and a small increase in the minimum wage are better than nothing."[50] But BO not only attacked Lavalas, they attacked it in ways that played straight into the hands of their own worst enemies, and they did so with a bitterness that can only be understood in terms of a distorted sense of betrayal and resentment. Like several other journalists, Guy Delva joined with BO in condemning FL after the bloody confrontation at Guacimal in May 2002 (see above, page 153). But just as he finds it hard to understand why a women's rights group like SOFA would denounce Aristide as worse than Duvalier or Cédras, Delva finds it puzzling that a workers' rights group like BO should dedicate so much energy to denouncing Lavalas as anti-labor and anti-poor. "Aristide certainly wanted to work on behalf of the poor, it's impossible to deny this."[51] What happened at Guacimal was a crime and it should be prosecuted as such, but it also needs to be understood in the light of entrenched local attitudes to trade unions, combined with the relentless pressure of the IFIs. In the continuum of anti-union violence that Haiti has long endured, Aristide's government again deserves to be understood more as an exception to than an instance of the norm.

One clue as to what might motivate BO's vitriol involves the funding that allows it to exist. In the autumn of 2005, the independent researcher Jeb Sprague pointed out that BO had benefited by a $3,500 grant issued by the State Department's National Endowment for Democracy (via the AFL-CIO's American Center for International Solidarity) – an amount roughly equal to the entire annual operating budget of Haiti's largest trade union confederation, the CTH. By the end of the year, Sprague had discovered that the full NED allocation to BO for 2005–06 amounted to at least $100,000 (and perhaps even as much as $450,000), which by Haitian standards is a very substantial sum.[52] BO first denied that it received any US government money, then grudgingly acknowledged the $3,500 grant in September 2005; then, after further denials, it admitted rather more defiantly to the $100,000 in January 2006. For most people working among the poor in Haiti this settles the issue once and for all – "You cannot possibly take money from USAID," says *Haïti Progrès'* Georges Honorat, "and still claim to be working for the people."[53] The

NED, however, is entitled to be happy with its investment: perhaps no other group has done as much damage to Lavalas' reputation on the international left than Batay Ouvriye.

Batay Ouvriye's foreign prominence is not an accident. Along with PAPDA, Batay Ouvriye is energetically supported by the most significant Haiti-related group in the UK, if not in Europe as a whole, Charles Arthur's Haiti Support Group. Arthur is one of the most knowledgeable international observers of Haitian affairs, and through a wide variety of publications and outlets he plays an important role in shaping international reactions to events in Haiti. He has long been outspoken both in his criticism of the US and the Haitian elite and in his defense of labor unions, grassroots activists and peasant organizations. His judgment is colored, however, by the profound contempt for Aristide and Fanmi Lavalas that he shares with his allies Yannick Etienne and Camille Chalmers. By comparison with other left-of-center analysts, Arthur and his associates seemed relatively indifferent to the fact that in 2003–04 unconditional opposition to FL could have only one outcome – the suspension of democratic rule, a new wave of repression and the disastrous return to power of the most reactionary elements in the old Haitian elite.[54] In 2006 as in 2004, Arthur sees mainly deviation and duplicity in the persistence of popular support for Aristide. Rather than pay attention to the resilience of its organization in the poorer neighborhoods of Port-au-Prince and the countryside, he derides Lavalassians for stubbornly refusing to accept the upshot of the coup, to abandon Aristide and to "move on" towards something like PAPDA's version of a progressive future. According to Arthur there is an essential "continuity" and consistency that unites the whole period from 2000 to 2006 in a single "disaster" during which nothing was achieved apart from the development of new forms of corruption and repression. The coup of 2004, though undertaken by distasteful actors, amounts from this perspective to little more than a superficial change in the identity of the oppressors.[55]

PROTESTS FROM STUDENTS AND THE G184

As is so often the case in the story of the 2004 coup, at least one thing is clear about the controversial positions taken by groups like PAPDA and BO – the identity of the interests that most benefited from them. The ideological assault on Lavalas as anti-worker and anti-poor provided invaluable propaganda for the sector of civil society that went to the greatest lengths to mobilize the opposition to Lavalas in the final months of 2003, namely the employers and the rich, and in particular the rich employers represented by the Group of 184.

Launched towards the end of 2002, apart from call a typically ineffectual "general strike" for 23 January 2003, the G184 did little of substance during most of its first year of existence. But there are several reasons why the democratic opposition to Lavalas became much more active in the autumn of 2003.

First of all, the defection of a pro-Lavalas gang in Gonaïves finally gave the paramilitary wing of the opposition an all-important foothold inside Haiti (I'll come back to this in a moment, page 202).

Second, by July 2003 a series of Lavalas concessions (coupled with a lawsuit threatened by the Robert Kennedy Memorial Human Rights Center in Washington) had finally obliged the US to back down, in principle, on its suspension of the $145m IDB loan agreed in 1997/98, for health, education, rural roads and water programs, that was so crucial to FL's social agenda. Unless some new circumstance arose, it was now only a matter of time before Aristide's government had access to this "new" money. What's more, on 13 November the IDB formally announced that it would approve "$176.9 million to Haiti to support a basic infrastructure rehabilitation program, a local development program for poor communities and a project to boost agricultural output"; the IDB also announced that it would soon begin "streamlining" disbursement of the older loans.[56] As Robert Maguire understood very well, receipt of this money would have had major and immediate consequences. Aristide's government had been bankrupt from the get-go, and receipt of even a small amount of money – let alone a sum equivalent to around 50 percent of the national budget – would have immensely strengthened Aristide "because of the ability to provide jobs and projects. The opposition was scared to death of foreign aid, which would have resulted in renewed support for Aristide. His popularity would have spiked enormously. You could argue that's why things suddenly got hot. The opposition wanted to get rid of Aristide before this happened."[57]

Third, over this same time and with the approval of the IMF and World Bank, the Lavalas government had begun taking newly effective measures to improve revenues from taxes on corporations and the wealthy. In August 2003, the IMF published a generally positive report on FL's management of public spending and tax collection.[58] Needless to say it was crucial for the elite to nip this latter development in the bud, before it became a bad institutional habit. One of the first decisions of the post-coup government, in March 2004, was to suspend corporate tax collection for three years.

Fourth, January 2004 was the bicentenary of Haitian independence and an unrivaled opportunity for Aristide to press home a number of threatening political demands, most notably a call for France to repay the huge sum of money it had extorted as post-colonial compensation from Haiti back in 1825 (I'll come back to this too, page 226). Aristide's demand for the restitution of this French debt was hugely popular, and became a regular feature of the speeches he made at mass rallies commemorating Haiti's independence. In 2003 Thabo Mbeki and the ANC linked Haiti's imminent bicentenary directly with the tenth anniversary of South Africa's own democratic revolution, and threw their full support behind Aristide's campaign to celebrate "the history and achievements of all African people, wherever they may be," hailing the bicentenary as a reminder that "the poor of the world can and must act together decisively to confront the common challenges they face – poverty, underdevelopment, discrimination and marginalization."[59] As far as the IFES/IRI was concerned, the stage was set for a major public relations disaster. Sure enough, when the time came the independence day celebrations themselves proved an uncomfortable reminder of the basic reality that to outside eyes had long been hidden by the disinformation campaign: even the normally anti-FL *Miami Herald* found it hard to denigrate the event, noting on 1 January 2004 that

> hundreds of thousands of jubilant Haitians swarmed the National Palace as they celebrated their nation's bicentennial and embraced their embattled president's vision of an improved and united Haiti. President Jean-Bertrand Aristide's appearance at the top of the steps of the palace whipped an already excited crowd into a frenzy, causing a fence to topple and a platform to break. Aristide greeted his adoring audience with "Happy New Year", repeating the wish five times and counting them on his fingers to symbolize the five-year term that he has been elected to serve.[60]

As time went by, it might become more and more difficult to present Aristide as a tyrant who had lost all popular support.

Fifth, on 12 January 2004 the parliamentary mandate of deputies elected in May 2000 was due to expire (and the constitution expressly forbids their extension). In the autumn, as the deadline drew closer, Aristide's efforts to get the opposition to agree to participate in a new round of elections became increasingly desperate. At a public meeting in

Grand Goâve on 5 October he reaffirmed yet again his insistence that "only elections can help us solve the present crisis."[61] On 21 October, the head of the CEP announced new measures to allow elections to be held on 12 January, and some lower-profile opposition parties (temporarily forgetting their actual purpose) said they might be prepared to participate in them. On behalf of the CD, Gérard Pierre-Charles, Victor Benoît, Luc Mésadieu and Hubert de Ronceray responded immediately by urging their members to keep refusing to participate in any election so long as Aristide remained president, and renewed their call for domestic and international pressure to force the government from power.[62] Since Aristide was thus "unable to agree" with the opposition on a new date for election, as the US and France liked to put it, so then once the parliamentary term ran out in January he was obliged instead to govern by "dictatorial" decree. The CD would have no better opportunity to characterize their opponent as a tyrant.

For the democratic opposition to Lavalas, therefore, the last months of 2003 were a do-or-die occasion. The G184 kicked off the final stage of the campaign to unseat Aristide with the opposition's most ambitious demonstration to date, a rally held in Port-au-Prince on 14 November 2003.[63] Alongside G184 leaders Andy Apaid and Charles Baker the list of prominent demonstrators included Paul Denis of the OPL, KONA-KOM's Victor Benoît, ex-colonel Himmler Rébu, and Jean-Claude Bajeux of the Ecumenical Human Rights Center. The *Economist Intelligence Unit* identified the rally as the "highest profile" incident in a rising wave of new anti-government protests. Since this publication cannot easily be confused with pro-FL propaganda, it's worth quoting its own description of what happened at some length:

> On the morning of the rally, a few hundred Group of 184 supporters had assembled at the designated site but found themselves heavily outnumbered by as many as 8,000 Aristide loyalists. When some government supporters threw stones and shouted threats at their opponents, the police struggled to keep order. As the situation rapidly deteriorated, the police dispersed the crowd using tear gas and firing live ammunition in the air. Meanwhile, the Group of 184's flat-bed truck with a sound system was stopped by police en route to the rally and thirty people travelling in the convoy with it were arrested when police discovered unlicensed firearms. Clearly unable to proceed as planned, the Group of 184 organizers called off the rally before it had begun. Reacting to the events, the Group's coordinator, André Apaid

[. . .] said the episode showed that the authorities would not allow opponents to assemble and thus were not contemplating fair elections.

This particular *EIU* report does not draw attention to the fact that Apaid is a wealthy international businessman who owns several factories in Haiti, is the founder of Haiti's most prominent independent television station, and was a leading figure in the spring 2003 campaign to prevent Aristide from doubling the minimum wage. The *EIU* does go on to note, however, that

> the turnout for the rally was lower than might have been suggested by the Group's claim to have more than 300 member organizations. It was scarcely able to assemble more than this number of demonstrators. The presence at the rally of many members of the more affluent sector of society reinforced a perception that the Group of 184, despite its claims to represent civil society, is an organization with little popular appeal. This interpretation was confirmed by the failure of a "general strike" called by the Group on November 17th. Although many private businesses in Port-au-Prince, including private schools and banks, did not open, the state-owned banks, government offices and public transport, as well as street markets, functioned as normal. In the rest of the country the shut-down was largely ignored . . .[64]

A reporter from *Haïti Progrès* further observed that "most of the signs held up by G184 demonstrators were written in English" and that "as if prearranged, CNN and other international television network crews, rarely seen these days in Haiti, showed up" to cover the event. Once the rally was over, Roger Noriega's newly installed Ambassador James Foley condemned the government's repression of dissent, saying that the "refusal of state authorities to let a peaceful demonstration take place has cast a shadow on the bicentennial celebrations."[65]

It wouldn't be difficult to extrapolate, from this single example, a general description of the whole civic campaign to dislodge FL. Reference to the virtues of civil society is often a vacuous distraction at the best of times; in class-riven Haiti it has rarely been more than a positive hoax. Luckily for the G184, by the autumn of 2003 a much more effective and familiar vehicle for popular protest was available, in the form of a media-friendly student movement.

According to PAPDA and many other progressive pro-coup groups, the turning point in the campaign to oust Lavalas "came in the fall of 2003 when student protests about lack of services and lack of university autonomy were met with severe repression by Haitian National Police accompanied by extra-legal armed gangs." GARR spoke for many in the democratic opposition when it said that these attacks on students and other "sectors of civil society" were "like the straw that broke the camel's back."[66] As another progressive observer put it, a protest from the students was a protest from "Haiti's youth – her most promising sons and daughters, the ones who would lift the country out of the darkness of ignorance, poverty, and an early, anonymous death. In attacking the students, Aristide's partisans essentially attacked the entire nation."[67]

Who were these representatives of the "entire nation," and what were they protesting? Although any generalization is approximate, most Haitian university students occupy a fairly distinct social position. The vast majority of Haitians never make it to secondary school, of course, let alone university, whereas the most privileged members of the elite send their children away to be educated in France or North America. The thousand or so students who manage to win a place at Haiti's own fiercely competitive (and in many ways corrupt and exclusive) state university every year often come from fairly poor backgrounds, and have generally worked extremely hard to gain their chance at a professional qualification and the social promotion that accompanies it. As the economy was pushed deep into recession by the combination of structural adjustment and the aid embargo of 2000–04, some students began to resent what they saw as restricted access to their hard-won rewards. Understandably, many were more interested in escaping poverty than in reducing it, and nothing is more valuable for an ambitious student than a visa to the US, Canada or France. Many students, moreover, were sympathetic to the political tendency that after 1994 remained heavily dominant within the university – the tendency represented by Pierre-Charles, Castor and the OPL. Most of the random sampling of students I met in April 2006 said that in the February elections of that year their preferred presidential candidate had been the conservative professor Leslie Manigat. The great majority of intellectuals and academics in Haiti are conservative as a matter of course; most joined or were sympathetic to the G184, and spurred by the energetic Eric Bosc in the French embassy some (including Lyonel Trouillot, Laënnec Hurbon, Frank Etienne, Yannick Lahens, Raoul Peck . . .) even formed a group, the *Comité du Non* (Committee of the No), whose reactionary inflection makes the G184 itself look moderate by comparison.[68] The obvious class antagonism was compounded by the fact that within established university circles, Aristide was widely considered as a genuine rival. Well-known as one of Haiti's most accomplished biblical scholars, during his second administration Aristide devoted considerable time and resources to the development of a new, public-service oriented university at Tabarre, and to encouraging the state university to fall into line with its own regulations on finances, admissions and elections. By 2003, the elimination of Aristide by fair means or foul had become for people like Castor or Hurbon a virtual crusade.

When the IRI and G184 went looking for supporters for its destabilization campaign, therefore, it wasn't difficult for them to enlist a certain number of students to the cause. Between them, the IFES and the IRI put considerable though unspecified amounts of time and money into the creation of several new student groups, including FEUH (Fédération des Étudiants de l'Université d'État d'Haïti) and GRAFNEH (Grand Front National des Étudiants Haïtiens); the latter had an office in Charles Baker's own building. As anyone who was active in the movement will readily tell you, scores of "student leaders" were offered money and visas to the US and France in exchange for their help in organizing protests against the government. "Only a fraction of the students in the system participated in the protest movement," explains Anne Sosin, "and many did so to get visas to leave Haiti; many of the so-called students were not actually students in the state university but were sent in to sow chaos in the system."[69] It is no secret that by the end of 2003 "many of the student leaders had taken workshops with the International Republican Institute."[70] In exchange for this modest investment, the IRI bought itself the perfect cover for the coup – idealistic young democrats like the quasi-student Hervé Saintilus (leader of FEUH), people that independent newspapers like the *New York Times* could then quote as demanding that "Bush and the State Department come get this toxic garbage [Aristide] out of here as fast as they can."[71]

All that was missing was a suitably clear-cut reason to protest a president who (along with Préval) had done immeasurably more for Haitian education than any other president in the country's history. FEUH found the pretext it needed when it managed to present the removal of Jean-Marie Paquiot from his position as rector of the Université d'État d'Haiti (UEH), in July 2002, as a gross violation of the university's autonomy. In reality, rector Paquiot's four-year term had expired in May 2002, and his academic vice-rector Jean-Reynold Elie had already quit. The process leading to the nomination of Paquiot's replacement should have begun in February, when students duly began protesting against the perennially poor quality of university facilities, teaching and management. By late spring, many students and professors no longer perceived the university's managerial team as legitimate. As

Paquiot continued to stall on the organization of elections for his successor, in late July Aristide's exasperated education minister, Myrtho Célestin-Saurel, tried to bring the crisis to an end by replacing him with a temporary appointee, Charles Tardieu. The intervention backfired. Critics of the government quickly organized a vocal campaign in Paquiot's defense. "Even though their own [initial] grievances had been clearly formulated against Paquiot and his colleagues," remembers UEH professor Marie Carmel Paul-Austin, "the students were furious with the way Paquiot was dismissed. The rules had been violated: the students had been hoping for an intervention by parliament, or for a decision taken in consultation with the parties concerned."[72]

In October 2002, then, a new wave of student protests turned against Paquiot's successor and the government who had appointed him. A few weeks later the government was ready to compromise, as usual, and Aristide replaced his education minister with professor Paul-Austin. She was not herself a member of FL, and was well known as a long-standing advocate of UEH independence and renewal; the day she began work, on 2 December 2002, she reinstated Paquiot in his job. Student protests then subsided, temporarily, but the independent media made sure that their listeners retained the important point: a dictatorial Aristide had trampled on one of the last independent institutions in the country.

The university returned to dominate the front pages a year later, after FL "repression" of the G184 rally in mid-November 2003. On 5 December 2003, a student rally in support of the G184 turned into a brawl between anti- and pro-government protestors. Perhaps two dozen students were injured, and Paquiot's legs were allegedly broken in the mêlée. For many critics of Fanmi Lavalas, this was the defining moment of its demise. "Most knowledgeable observers," says the left-leaning anti-Lavalas journalist Cali Ruchala, identify the 5 December 2003 clash as the single-most important incident leading to the coup of 29 February. "This was the day Aristide's partisans opened fire on demonstrating students at the University of Haiti, shocking many diehard supporters of Lavalas and some of Aristide's most committed allies [. . .] Never in the past had an assault seemed so brazen, or the roles so clearly defined."[73] The new education minister, Paul-Austin, interpreted this attack on the university premises as a premediated act of terror and aggression, condemned the apparent complicity of the police, and immediately resigned.[74] According to the democratic opposition, the assault represented the climax of "*chimère*" mayhem, the single most violent episode in a long campaign of state-sanctioned intimidation. "After December 5," G184's Hans Tippenhauer told Deibert towards the end of that month, "we told the students 'whatever you do, we are behind you.' "[75] The incident became known in opposition circles as "black Friday", and via G184 channels like Andy Apaid's Tele-Haiti and Radio Métropole, the violence received massive media attention.

In reality, however, things were not so clear-cut. "The standard media account", insists Kim Ives, "was completely false." An AHP reporter described the incident as follows:

> One member of a popular organization (OP) and one student were shot and wounded on Friday, December 5 during a confrontation between students and OP members downtown in the capital. Many other people, students and OP members, were also injured with stones and sticks. The confrontation started when students, reinforced by members of the Convergence and the Group of 184, began to throw volleys of stones on OP members who were in front of the national university premises and the social sciences faculty. That was the starting point of a demonstration with students and opposition members to demand the resignation of governmental authorities. Furious, OP members got into the university yard, which has been closed for over a week by students who demand their dean's resignation. Violent blows with sticks and stones were exchanged after, between opposition members, students and OP members. That's when an OP member named Harold was shot from the roof of the social sciences faculty, where the students and G184 were. Shooting continued to try to stop the police from evacuating the wounded OP member. The police had to shoot in the air to force students and OP members to leave. In this confusion, one student, Carlo Jean, was shot and wounded according to a Justice of the Peace. The students accuse the police of not protecting them against those they call "chimères" [but] members of the G184 and the Haitian trade union who were inside the university office, notably Josué Merilien and Montes Joseph, are accused of encouraging students to commit violent acts.[76]

Aristide and Neptune immediately and vigorously denied responsibility for the violence, and condemned it in the strongest terms. According to Neptune, PNH spokesmen, and several witnesses, it was the students who prevented the police from entering the university to defuse the situation. When the case eventually came to trial in the spring of 2006 (in the context of charges brought against FL activist So Anne), Paquiot was unable to remember the identity of his attackers and refused a court request for medical documentation of his injuries. A doctor who treated him at the hospital later confirmed that his legs were not broken after all.[77] Almost all of "the student plaintiffs ignored summons to appear before the investigating judge and never testified; none of the victims and witnesses who testified were able to identify any of the defendants as their aggressors or place them at the scene of the incident."[78]

In the meantime, however, 5 December provided the IRI/IFES with exactly the sort of publicity material they were looking for. When Tom Griffin spoke to them in November 2004, IFES administrators told him that they "believed that violence by Aristide supporters during a demonstration at the state university on 5 December 2003 was the 'mistake' that put him 'over the top' and effectively signaled the end of his government [. . .]. The administrators say that the university had been brought to the boiling point by FEUH, IFES' 'sensitized' association of university students. They said that IFES had held 'sensitization' meetings at the university that became anti-Aristide rallies." Once Paquiot was attacked, they added, "It was IFES that arranged to have the Rector flown out of Haiti within days, along with an IFES escort."[79] Paquiot stayed in the US for around six months.

The IFES and its G184 allies made sure that after 5 December there would be no going back. A protest that had its origins in a relatively trivial dispute about the university rectorship quickly snowballed into a major campaign for the unconditional elimination of Aristide. ANMH news outlets like Radio Signal FM immediately rallied in support of what its director called the students' "noble cause," and provided round-the-clock coverage of their struggle to "combat the dictatorship."[80] Under the pressure of daily confrontation, resolve hardened on both sides. It's clear that many student protestors felt that they were under attack, an impression heightened by relentlessly provocative media coverage, G184/IFES encouragement and at least some blatant manipulation of the truth.[81] Student demonstrators like those who with Himmler Rébu and Dany Toussaint led a violent march through Port-au-Prince on 11 December openly announced that "our objective is to besiege the Palace and oust the government authorities."[82] Members of pro-Lavalas OPs, on the other hand, were determined to meet this new threat head on. "We couldn't afford to remain inactive," explain Belizaire Printemps and Elias Clovis, "in the face of a movement that was seeking by all available means to overthrow the government, the government elected by the great majority of the people. When the students put 500 people on the streets, we would put 5,000 or 10,000, to indicate the real balance of forces." Of course there were some occasional clashes, Belizaire admits, "but it's ridiculous to think these were planned or coordinated by FL or the government."[83] If the student protests were intended to expose a government intent on the suppression of dissent, what they actually indicated was a tolerance verging on complacency. Apart from one or two casualties on both sides (including on the night of 11 December the shooting of a leading figure in the FL literacy campaign, SOPUDEP's André Jan-Marie), actual levels of violence were quite remarkably low, and the cycle of protest and counter-protest never spiralled out of the government's control.

The public relations damage linked to the student protests, however, was immense. The sequence of demonstrations provided the independent media with endless amounts of material with which to press home their message. Several government ministers resigned, apparently in protest of the government's handling of the crisis. On 10 December 2003, the International Development Bank's Lionel Nichol again confirmed that $200m in IDB funds were available for the Haitian government, and that their release was imminent. Just two days later, though, the US used the excuse of mounting insecurity and political tension to scale back their diplomatic presence in Haiti, and in this new atmosphere the money never materialized. Continued "security concerns" served to justify further CD refusals to contemplate participation in elections.

The damage was immense – but not fatal. Compared to the small rally of 14 November 2003, anti-government demonstrations like the one organized by the G184 outside the UN headquarters on 16 January 2004 had grown to include several thousand people. By the end of January 2004, however, it was clear that demonstrations alone would never suffice to topple the government. Pro-government rallies continued to dwarf anti-government protests – no G184 or FEUH rally came close to attracting the tens of thousands of people who turned out in support of Aristide on 26 December, let alone the estimated 100,000 or so people present at what was probably the largest rally of Aristide's entire presidency, on 7 February 2004. In spite of a severely restricted budget and the constraints of political isolation, celebrations marking the bicentenary year of Haiti's independence had begun as planned in January, and promised to bolster a president still widely associated with the country's "second independence." One month into the new year, the consensus among the usual assortment of diplomats, "observers" and "experts" cited by the *New York Times* was that Aristide would survive the protests and emerge more or less unscathed.[84]

In early February 2004, therefore, someone, somewhere, decided that the time had come to unleash the paramilitary storm that had been brewing for some time, in Gonaïves and across the border in the Dominican Republic.

9

2004: The Second Coup

"The Bush administration believes that if we all do our part and do it
right, Haiti will have the democracy it deserves"

(Roger Noriega, 14 April 2004).

From the time they began in the summer of 2001 through to the middle
of 2003, direct paramilitary attacks against Aristide's government remained mere hit-and-run affairs. Then in the autumn of 2003, FLRN
attacks became more regular and intense, spreading from the Central
Plateau to Petit Goâve and Cap-Haïtien. In several parts of the country,
reported the *Washington Post* on 19 November, "small collections of men
are attacking police stations and government buildings in the hopes of
destabilizing Aristide's administration [. . .]. The groups have increased
the tempo of their attacks in recent months, and are showing signs of
coordinating military efforts around the country," adding a "potent new
element to a civilian opposition movement that had failed to generate
much interest beyond the capital, broadening its reach for the first time
into provincial regions traditionally supportive of the president." The *Post*
also noted that "opposition political leaders have declined to condemn the
armed attacks," preferring to "blame Aristide for the deteriorating security
situation."[1] So long as they lacked a reliable neighborhood base in the
country itself, however, the ex-FRAPH and ex-FAdH troops were
mostly confined to their barracks in the DR. A genuine insurgency
would require at least one strategic foothold inside the country. One
way or another, Aristide's opponents needed to turn at least one of the
more powerful urban gangs against the government. The task had
become easier with time, as under growing economic pressure some
of the gangs became less political and more mercenary. Over the course of
2003 this strategy failed in Port-au-Prince but succeeded in Gonaïves.

The Port-au-Prince effort centered on the strategically sensitive eastern edge of Cité Soleil, a neighborhood known as Boston. Built on reclaimed land by the edge of the sea, Cité Soleil is the largest slum in Port-au-Prince, and one of the most powerfully concentrated zones of FL support in the country; whoever controls Boston is in a position to cut Cité Soleil off from the rest of the capital, depriving Lavalas of many of its most ardent supporters and effectively turning the slum into a giant political prison. Although the details remain sketchy, intermediaries working for Reginald Boulos and Andy Apaid had begun making overtures to various pro-FL gangs in Cité Soleil soon after Aristide's re-election, if not before. For a long time there were no takers, and Boulos had to wait till midsummer 2003 before he could risk a public incursion into the neighborhood. On 12 July Boulos and other G184 leaders defied instructions from the Cité mayor and tried to stage a visit of the G184's so-called "Caravan of Hope." Indignant members of the local OPs (with the informal encouragement of Aristide's interior minister) chased the Boulos motorcade off their turf, in a clash that left more than a dozen people injured. Around the same time, however, Boulos and Apaid succeeded in winning Boston gang leader Thomas "Labanye" Robinson and his lieutenant Evens Jeune to their cause. In October, Labanye had a further meeting with Apaid and in exchange for money and the promise of a visa provided him with a long list of misdeeds that he attributed to the Aristide government (see below, page 289). Members of Labanye's gang later confessed that in exchange for such services, tens of thousands of dollars were at stake; the precise sort of inducements offered are hard to verify but easy to guess, and have been confirmed by well-placed members of the elite. In a place as poor as Cité Soleil, even a little well-placed patronage goes a long way.

Well-armed, well-funded and clearly protected by some anti-FL elements in the police, Labanye's gang was able to mount a direct challenge to the pro-FL groups. In response, the latter banded together around the informal leadership of a dread-locked alumnus of Lafanmi Selavi and devoted follower of Aristide, Emmanuel "Dred" Wilme, backed up by Amaral and Billy. The conflict intensified after the shooting on 31 October 2003 of Rodson Lemaire (a.k.a. Colibri), an ally of Labanye.[2] Although Aristide managed to broker a fragile truce during his final months in office, this local war ignited again in the autumn of 2004, and was waged with an intensity born of the fusion of competing political affiliations with issues of urgent material survival; it would prove to be one of the decisive struggles of the post-coup era, and I'll come back to it in the next chapter. So long as Aristide was in power, however, Wilme and his allies were too strong for Labanye, and the G184's influence in Cité Soleil and the rest of the poorer neighborhoods of Port-au-Prince remained weak.[3] The democratic opposition had to look for their beach-head elsewhere.

A FOOTHOLD IN GONAÏVES: THE SEIZURE OF RABOTEAU, SEPTEMBER 2003

The full story of how the democratic opposition eventually found its paramilitary foothold in Gonaïves has yet to be told, and what follows is only an abbreviated and somewhat speculative outline of what happened. Haiti's third-largest city with around 200,000 inhabitants, Gonaïves is an impoverished port-town several hours' drive north of Port-au-Prince; even this short distance from the capital is enough to ensure a dramatic drop in international media coverage and attention, which is one of the reasons why it's a good spot to undertake the sort of violent intimidation required to shift popular political loyalties. Lavalas activists in Gonaïves, concentrated in the seaside slum of Raboteau, paid a high price for their staunch support of Aristide during the first coup. Some of the FRAPH's most brutal violence was directed at Raboteau residents, most notoriously on the night of 22 April 1994 when hundreds of homes were burned down and dozens if not scores of people were killed, their bodies thrown out into the sea. As mentioned earlier, the perpetrators of the Raboteau massacre were prosecuted and convicted in a landmark trial in 2000.[4] Along with Chamblain and Constant, their number included local FRAPH agent Jean-Pierre Baptiste, a.k.a. Jean Tatoune, who first came to prominence as an anti-Duvalier activist in 1985. One of Tatoune's targets in 1994 was a local Lavalas militant called Amiot "Cubain" Métayer, leader of the organization Populaire Démocratique de Rabo-teau (OPDR).[5] As Kevin Pina explains, during the first coup Cubain played a pivotal role in the development of "clandestine networks of Aristide supporters," helping to develop the tactic of " 'flash demonstra-tions' against the dictatorship where hundreds, and sometimes thousands, of Lavalas supporters would appear out of nowhere to protest for five minutes and then disappear before the military and their henchmen arrived on the scene." After he and his family were terrorized during the Raboteau massacre, Cubain and his brother Buteur Métayer accepted an offer of asylum in the United States but Cubain soon returned to Gonaïves. Denounced as a brutal government enforcer by the democratic opposition, it seems that much of the population of Raboteau respected him as a sort of bellicose Robin Hood.[6]

By 2002, Tatoune was serving a life-sentence in the Gonaïves prison for his role in the Raboteau massacre, and Cubain's gang – commonly known as the "Cannibal Army" – had become a powerful political and economic force in the city. By all accounts Cubain's people made a little money off the trickle of trade and contraband that passed through Gonaïves' port, and they remained outspoken partisans of the Lavalas government. In the immediate wake of the 17 December 2001 coup attempt, Luc Mésadieu, leader of rightwing evangelical party MOCHRENA and a prominent member of the CD, blamed Cubain (with virtually no evidence) for leading a reprisal arson attack on his house and for killing one of his security guards. All through the early months of 2002, the US and the OAS pressured Aristide to pay full compensation to the CD parties that suffered damage in December, and to prosecute those responsible for the reprisals, most notably Métayer.[7] At the same time, Aristide was also under pressure from the US to crack down on the alleged smugglers and drug-dealers operating in Gonaïves and Saint-Marc. Reluctantly, on 4 July 2002 the FL authorities duly put Cubain behind bars pending his trial for arson, in the same penitentiary as his old enemy Tatoune. Cubain's followers were outraged. A few weeks into his incarceration, on 2 August, a group of them hijacked a bulldozer and smashed their way into the prison, liberating all 160 inmates. For a few days, Cubain and his gang organized vocal protests against Aristide's treachery. Before the opposition could capitalize on this fortuitous breach in their enemy's ranks, however, Cubain and Aristide were reconciled and by 9 August the protests had stopped as abruptly as they'd begun. Cubain told reporters that he had shouted "Down with Aristide" with only "half his heart."[8] The autumn of 2002 then saw Cubain's gang back playing its familiar role, in defense of the Lavalas government. The US renewed its insistence that Aristide prosecute Cubain, though for some reason it never called for the re-arrest of the already convicted Tatoune. On 28 November 2002 Cubain's gang clashed with an anti-Lavalas demonstration led by Tatoune, and a couple of nights later Cubain's lieutenant Evens Auguste was killed by Tatoune's gang, prompting a retaliatory attack that left 20 houses burning in Tatoune's Jubilé neighborhood. During the spring and summer of 2003, Cubain's people forced Tatoune into hiding, and in May 2003, citing a lack of witnesses and evidence, prosecutors outraged the opposition by dropping all charges against Cubain. As the summer of 2003 drew to a close, in short, Gonaïves seemed as solidly pro-Aristide as Cité Soleil.

On 19 September 2003, a day after meeting with the new US ambassador James Foley, Aristide announced that new elections would now finally take place, before the end of the year.

Opportunity missed? Maybe not: just two days after Aristide's meeting with Foley, on 21 September, Cubain Métayer was murdered with a brutality calculated to provoke maximum outrage. No-one has ever confessed to or been charged with the murder, and to this day Cubain's death remains one of the biggest mysteries of the entire coup sequence. For the opposition and the independent media, of course, the identity of the killer was a foregone conclusion. Everyone with an interest in turning Cubain's gang against the government came forward to name Aristide as the chief suspect. A day or two after his brother's death, an alcoholic Buteur Métayer emerged to claim his place as one of the leaders of the Cannibal Army. Strange as it might seem, he was joined by none other than Jean Tatoune, who emerged from hiding on 24 September to lead some of the Cannibals in violent protests against the government. Buteur and Tatoune claimed that the assassination had been organized by local FL commissioner Harold Adéclat, perhaps on the order of Jean-Claude Jean-Baptiste, and that the trigger man was a versatile local schemer, Odonel Paul. Odonel Paul, who had occasionally worked for Aristide's Minister of the Interior, was an old friend of Cubain and the last person seen with him that night; he himself disappeared almost immediately afterwards, and is presumed dead.[9]

The new French and US ambassadors who arrived in Haiti around the time of the murder made sure that the story that Aristide killed Cubain, perhaps out of jealousy or fear, or to mollify the US and the OAS, or to silence an incriminating witness, or in order to regain control of the port, soon became one of the most widely repeated claims of their whole destabilization campaign. Along with embassy officials, NCHR spokesmen and leaders of the democratic opposition, veteran reporters like Jane Regan and Amy Wilentz were (initially) quick to endorse Tatoune's version of events.[10] So did most of the independent media. When Tom Griffin spoke to IFES administrators in November 2004 they told him that along with the university incident of 5 December 2003, "Aristide's other serious mistake was the murder of Amiot 'Cubain' Métayer."[11] Needless to say, the government itself categorically denied any involvement, and on 25 September attributed the murder to paramilitary groups operating in the Central Plateau. Lavalas partisans in Milot claim that it was carried out by renegade members of the PNH, working on behalf of the French. Others – Kim Ives, Frantz Gabriel, Ronald Saint-Jean . . . –

compare Amiot's murder to that of Mireille Durocher-Bertin in 1995, and describe it as a crime carried out by the "laboratory" (as Haitians call the Pentagon–CIA machine) in order to undermine Aristide, a claim that won't surprise anyone who's glanced through Philip Agee's famous account of CIA operations.[12] "I'm convinced that the laboratory engineered the murder of Amiot Métayer," agrees Ben Dupuy, "so as then to pin it on Aristide; Métayer was the perfect target, and the consequences of his death were expertly and instantly manipulated, with devastating effect."[13] In early 2007 Amy Wilentz admitted that when she speculated in 2003 about "possible Aristide involvement in the killing of Amiot Métayer I wrote from a great distance [. . .] and I think now that I may have been played by certain anti-Aristide elements."[14] Claims that Amiot was killed on the orders of the CIA or by a National Palace insider may not be mutually exclusive, in any case, since it's perfectly clear that "the National Palace security apparatus was totally infiltrated by the Company."[15] Brian Concannon may be closest to the truth, when he suggests that "the most likely motive for the killing was not political, but drugs."[16]

Since as far as I know there's no proof either way, the only question worth considering concerns motives and consequences. Who stood to gain by this murder, in the autumn of 2003, of a tried and tested Aristide loyalist? As Haitians like to say, we must judge a tree by the fruit it bears. It's true that Aristide's government was under significant pressure to crack down on some of his more militant supporters, as a condition for the aid promised by OAS resolution 822.[17] But who had an interest in making a graphic example of a widely respected veteran of the resistance to the army and FRAPH? Who might want to get rid of the leader of local mobilizations against the incursions of the FLRN? Aristide himself? Or perhaps an embittered ally of the army and the FLRN, someone like Cubain's old enemy and rival Jean Tatoune or his ex-FRAPH associates?

If the circumstances of Cubain's death remain obscure, its consequences soon became crystal clear. Whereas in Cité Soleil Labanye would prove unable to use the killing of Colibri to turn the local gangs against the government, in Gonaïves Tatoune and his allies manipulated Cubain's assassination for all it was worth. With the help of other ex-military personnel and the usual mix of inducement and intimidation, Tatoune quickly turned the Cannibal Army into a local extension of the FLRN. From late September 2003 right through to early February 2004, the rate of minor but unnerving hit-and-run attacks on local government facilities and supporters dramatically increased. According to Reuters and AHP reports, two policemen and seven civilians were shot in demonstrations led by Tatoune on 24 and 25 September. Another policeman and a child were shot on 29 September, and a couple of houses were burned; on the same day, Buteur Métayer called for "the establishment of a united front between the Democratic Convergence, the Group of 184, the Civil Society Initiative and his own organization to oust the elected autho- rities."[18] Two days later Tatoune's men burned three government offices. Over the course of October, around thirty or so thugs under Tatoune's command took control of most of Raboteau and through sustained intimidation managed to bludgeon at least part of the population into accepting its new affiliation. Despite repeated attempts to arrest him and a $17,000 reward for his capture, the police were never able to put Tatoune back in jail. Police searches for Tatoune sparked gun battles that may have killed five or six people in early October.[19] Later in the month, Tatoune's fellow Cannibal Winter Etienne announced the gang's intention to mount attacks against all government officials in Gonaïves. By 26 October, Tatoune was strong enough to lead an open assault on the Gonaïves police station: three policemen were injured and an adolescent was killed in the crossfire. The following day independent radio station Radio Vision 2000 broadcast the Cannibal's intention to push the country towards "civil war."[20] More shootings followed on 28 November, 1 December, 2 December, and 4 December. On 2 December Tatoune's men torched the town hall; later they would burn dozens of homes and vehicles belonging to government officials or FL supporters. Another person was killed and several others wounded in a gun battle on 11 December. On 6 January 2004 Buteur announced the imminent massacre of all FL supporters in Gonaïves: "No supporter of Fanmi Lavalas will be spared by the opposition hordes."[21] In Gonaïves and throughout the surrounding area attacks on police stations and FL activists became routine events – on 1 January, for instance, the police station in Gros Morne was sacked and the inmates of the local jail set free; on 11 January the newly appointed police chief for the North (Edner Jeanty) was assassinated near Cap-Haïtien. And so it went on. Between the end of September and the end of January, the combination of Cannibal attacks in Gonaïves and FLRN raids across the Central Plateau left around forty to fifty people dead. When they started reporting on the growing unrest in Haiti in early February, newspapers like the *New York Times* and *Washington Post* would refer to the fact that "over the past few months, some 50 people have been killed in the resulting street clashes"[22] – what they didn't bother to mention was the fact that the overwhelming majority of the victims were *supporters* rather than oppo- nents of the government.

A few other pieces of the Gonaïves puzzle are equally certain, even if they do not yet add up to anything like a definitive account of events.

We already know that one of the first things that post-coup prime minister Gérard Latortue did was arrange a public meeting in Gonaïves, on 21 March 2004, to applaud Tatoune and Buteur, along with Guy Philippe and an assortment of ex-army rebels, as patriotic "freedom fighters."[23] One of the people standing at Latortue's side that day was his newly appointed minister of justice, Bernard Gousse. Shortly after Métayer's death in September 2003, while a distraught Aristide was trying to comfort Amiot's relatives at a meeting in Port-au-Prince, the IFES dispatched Bernard Gousse to Gonaïves. According to IFES officials, Gousse "wanted to be with the rebels" during this time of violence and uncertainty.[24] Although in 2004–05 the new Justice Minister Gousse went to considerable lengths to track down Lavalassians accused of the most improbable crimes, he never so much as began the process to return the *already* convicted murderer Tatoune to his prison cell. In a move that struck even NCHR and Human Rights Watch as scandalous, in early April 2004 Gousse suggested that Tatoune should be pardoned for his participation in the Raboteau massacre, and raised the prospect of a new trial for fellow convict Chamblain. Sure enough, the following year, in perhaps the most spectacular perversion of justice in Haitian history, Jodel Chamblain and his FRAPH colleagues had their convictions overturned. Tatoune is living as a free man in Gonaïves to this day, though like some other pawns in the destabilization campaign, he has found himself excluded from the post-Aristide order that he helped to create.

It's also known that IGH prime minister Gérard Latortue hails from Gonaïves, as does his nephew Youri Latortue. Youri Latortue has long exercised significant influence in the city. As we saw in chapter three (page 143), Youri was the deputy commander of the USGPN whom Aristide dismissed soon after his inauguration in 2001, after doubts emerged about his loyalty, and Youri retained close ties with Guy Philippe and other members of the police who fled Haiti after their coup plans were exposed in the autumn of 2000.[25] Youri Latortue is one of the great survivors of Haiti's repressive apparatus. During the first coup he was second-in-command of the notoriously brutal Anti-Gang unit, under Chamblain's colleague Joanis Jackson. Along with Chamblain and Jackson, he was implicated in the murders of Antoine Izméry and Jean-Marie Vincent. As the HSG explains, Jackson and Latortue's Anti-Gang squad was the "worst unit of the Haitian Army when it came to human rights," and it was also regularly accused of systematic embezzlement.[26] Like many other "reliable" soldiers, in 1994 Youri made a smooth transition from the old to the new security forces, and in 1995 he became a captain in the USGPN. Later dubbed "Mister 30 percent" on account of the return he receives in exchange for favors, Youri Latortue was implicated in the running of drugs through Port-au-Prince and Gonaïves from the mid-1990s through to 2001.[27]

After his dismissal from the USGPN in 2001, Youri says he spent a couple of quiet years out of the country, in Montreal and Miami. He says he only returned to Haiti after the 2004 coup (at which point his uncle was in a position to pay him $20,000 a month to arrange for his personal security).[28] It is reasonable to assume, however, that along with Médard Joseph and Jackie Nau, Youri played an important part in the link that was established, in the last months of 2003, between Chamblain and Philippe's rebels in the DR and Tatoune's gang in Gonaïves. Youri owns the La Chandelle hotel in his home town, which in the run-up to the February 2004 insurgency may have served as a conduit for arms between the Cannibal Army and the FLRN.[29] As Anthony Fenton confirms, "Youri Latortue and Guy Phillipe certainly were (and remain) close, and during the IGH Guy Philippe was a regular visitor to Youri's office."[30] In 2006, Youri Latortue's local influence and patronage helped him win a comfortable majority in his campaign to become senator of the department that includes Gonaïves – parliamentary immunity is especially useful for someone who has been under DEA investigation for several years. In 2006 Youri also emerged as a leading voice in the chorus of new calls to re-establish the army. "With regard to the FAdH," Youri said in November 2006, "I believe that I am an intellectual who has written books and expressed my opinions. Since I took office in the Senate, my position has been clear. I believe that the Haitian army has its role to play in the country's security [. . .]. What we believe is that for an army that existed and that is no longer, there needs to be a serious debate to get people to accept the idea of its return."[31]

That's not the end of the Latortue family's involvement in the Gonaïves uprising. A couple of years after the coup, Tatoune's colleague Winter Etienne told reporters that the chief financial backer of the Gonaïves rebels had been Youri's brother Jean-Renel Latortue, who in 2003 was in charge of the port authority of Saint-Marc. Etienne says that during the last months of 2003 the Cannibals received $20,000-worth in ammunition from Jean-Renel.[32] Once uncle Gérard became prime minister, Jean-Renel was promoted to become head of the much larger port of Cap-Haïtien. Gérard Latortue's "surprise" appointment as prime minister in March was perhaps not quite as surprising as some people seemed to find it at the time.

We know, finally, that Tatoune and Etienne's gang were working hand-in-hand with members of the disbanded army. *Washington Post* reporter Scott Wilson was one of the only foreign correspondents to pay attention to the Gonaïves group in the final months of 2003. He noted "Some of its foot soldiers [once] relied on Lavalas patronage for their livelihoods, forming a gang-like network formerly known as the Cannibal Army. But at its upper echelons the group appears to be led by former members of the Haitian military, dissolved in 1994 when Aristide returned to power, and the paramilitary group that opposed him."[33] In a revealing article published 18 November 2003, Wilson observed the increasing incidence of newly effective and "coordinated" anti-government raids in Gonaïves and the surrounding area, noting that "many of the participants are either former members of Haiti's military [. . .] or a paramilitary force that opposed the president's return [in 1994]."[34] Tatoune and other FRAPH commanders worked closely with the army back in the early 1990s, and there's no reason to suspect that these ties weakened with time. When the government was finally able to arrest some of the Gonaïves rebels in early November 2003, it had good grounds for accusing them of "working closely with the [ex-military] gang that has been terrifying the people of Pernales in the Central Plateau";[35] Guy Philippe explained, after the fact, that Tatoune's team "was helped by some soldiers that Jean Robert Lalanne and the Democratic Convergence sent to Gonaïves, to train and organize the others."[36] Residents and officials in nearby Saint-Marc would later confirm that the local insurgent gang RAMICOS was linked to Tatoune's group in Gonaïves, and that it too "contained a number of former paramilitary members."[37]

Although Etienne and Tatoune's people were understandably discreet about the precise extent of their collaboration with the widely hated army, as money, weapons and ammunition flowed into Gonaïves the need for secrecy began to dissolve. When reporters interviewed other Gonaïves rebels on 10 February 2004, they gratefully acknowledged that former soldiers "have come to lend us a helping hand." The Associated Press observed that around "50 of the ex-soldiers, heavily armed and dressed in old fatigues, have been operating for a year outside Gonaïves."[38] In another day or two they would be joined by plenty more, fresh from the

Dominican Republic, and once Philippe and Ravix arrived to bolster Buteur's group in early February 2004, says Philippe, "We had meetings with various businessmen and they helped us; via Ravix they contributed around $200,000 (US) to buy arms and ammunition."[39]

Along with Justice Minister Gousse, the other high-profile minister next to Latortue during his March 2004 "freedom fighters" speech in Gonaïves was the new Interior minister, ex-general Hérard Abraham. Abraham was the patron, among other people, of Guy Philippe's colleague Jackie Nau. Abraham had long made re-establishment of the army something of a personal crusade, and in the spring of 2004 he would personally intervene to block moves to disarm Tatoune, Philippe and their "troops."

THE FEBRUARY 2004 INSURGENCY

It was this alliance of criminals, death-squadders and former soldiers who on 5 February 2004 (five months after the initial uprising in Raboteau) launched what Winter Etienne called the final operation to "liberate Haiti from the dictator Aristide." Armed with assault weapons and aided by at least twenty former soldiers, Tatoune's gang finally managed to overwhelm the long-suffering Gonaïves police force in a three-hour gun battle, and drove them out of the city.[40] They burned the police station and, in keeping with a time-honored tactic for gaining new recruits, released the 100 or so inmates from the city jail; they also torched houses belonging to the mayor and other FL officials. Flushed with its success, the Cannibal Army renamed itself the Revolutionary Artibonite Resistance Front. Two days later (7 February), in the single most important engagement of the entire insurgency, a combination of Etienne's Gonaïves rebels and Philippe's ex-soldiers ambushed a substantial though inept police counter-attack, killing seven officers. They were now the undisputed masters of a terrified city. Winter Etienne proclaimed himself mayor of Gonaïves, and Buteur Métayer took the title of "provisional president of Haiti" (though by the end of February, as he slid further into the alcoholic stupor that would kill him in 2005, he settled for the title of "president of Gonaïves" instead). The rebels went on to take Hinche on 16 February and Cap-Haïtien on 22 February. By 27 February they appeared to control most of the northern half of the country, and parts of the south and south-west as well.

What better proof could there be that Aristide had lost the support of his people? Who now could argue with Himmler Rébu, Colin Powell, Dominique de Villepin and the rest of the democratic opposition when they called upon Aristide to resign, given his failure to control a "crisis of his own making"?

The democratic opposition and the independent media were more than happy to explain why this "sudden" February insurgency was so successful. Their explanation depended on four convergent myths, all designed to create the impression that the ousted Aristide had only himself to blame.

Myth number one: isolated abroad and under pressure from his democratic opponents at home, as Aristide tumbled towards dictatorship he bought off various criminal gangs and *organisations populaires* to prop up his regime. He gave them money and weapons (a point that, once they had turned against FL, some members of Buteur's gang appeared happy to confirm). But as the gangs became more greedy and aggressive, Aristide's attempts to rein them in pushed them to open revolt. Aristide gave the gangs guns and they turned them against him. Gonaïves, then, was the place where Aristide's neo-*Macoutisme* blew up in his face.

Myth number two: although the Gonaïves insurgents were supposedly mere criminals, their uprising nevertheless sparked a "popular liberation movement" because they sought freedom from dictatorship. The Haitian people so hated FL that they had come to the conclusion that anything would be better than Aristide. This is why members of the democratic opposition, in unguarded moments, affirmed the rebels' right to take up arms against the dictator and against the police. This is also why the rebellion was presented as an irresistible and continuous "tide of protest," an inexorable movement that could lead only to Aristide's surrender and "flight." With the cowardice of any bully, once Aristide was confronted with the full power of the people's might he abandoned ship, leaving his deluded supporters to be slaughtered in their shacks.

Myth number three: although the rebels were entitled to wage their liberating war against Aristide, the democratic opposition itself, of course, could never collude in any sort of violence. By definition, members of the Democratic Convergence would only converge with other democrats.

Myth number four follows automatically from the third: since the international allies of the Convergence were likewise determined to achieve a "political" and "democratic" solution to the crisis, they were themselves obliged to intervene once Philippe's mysterious little troop threatened to get in the way of democracy. As the ever-truthful Colin Powell would soon say, the idea that a democratic country like the US might stoop to supporting the rebels or removing an elected president from power was self-evidently "baseless" and "absurd."

What really happened in February 2004 bears about as much relation to this imaginative version of events as did the CD to "democracy" or Powell to "truth." Let's take each point in turn, starting with the characterization of the Gonaïves gang as a merely criminal affair. This was a crucial aspect of the disinformation campaign. If word got out that the people behind the violence in Gonaïves in 2003 were former members of FRAPH and the army, then the democratic opposition would face a public relations challenge that no amount of IFES sensitization could meet. Accordingly, in the run-up to February the independent media was careful to focus on Buteur Métayer – brother of the gang leader who was so obviously betrayed and murdered by Aristide – as the apparent leader of the rebellion. Since the betrayal was obvious it required no proof or explanation, and nor did Buteur's righteous revenge. The media could therefore skip over the role of the former-military and Tatoune, despite the fact that anyone who visited Gonaïves could see who was really in charge. "Tatoune's a heavyweight in this," his lieutenant Dieujuste Jeanty told the *Washington Post* in November 2003, and "this is not just a movement sitting here in Gonaïves."[41] Reporters from the *Miami Herald* and AP who covered the 5 February assault recognized Tatoune as the operational commander, though the talking heads who fed the media their lines over the next week or so remained Buteur and Winter Etienne.[42] The cat finally came out of the bag a few days later, when a smiling Guy Philippe showed up to take apparent command of the operation in Gonaïves. Philippe told the *Washington Post* that on 10 February "He and three other rebel leaders walked five hours across the border from the Dominican Republic to lead the armed effort against Aristide."[43] On 14 February, Buteur formally announced the arrival of reinforcements from the Dominican Republic, and passed the baton over to Philippe.[44] Philippe furnished a new communications "office" with statues of Alexandre Pétion and Henri Christophe looted from a public square in Gonaïves, and in an unending series of press interviews that began on 16 February, declared to the world's media that he was leading an army of national liberation designed to accomplish "one thing and one thing only: Aristide has to go. We won't settle for anything less."[45] Philippe's deputy Gilbert Dragon (who like Philippe was trained by the US military in Ecuador in the early 1990s and then fled to the DR after the failed PNH coup of October 2000) explained that their team "had been planning this for a long time, and then came an opportunity. We seized it."[46]

But in some ways Philippe too was another front. While he spent most of the next few weeks handling an international press-corps that never failed to acknowledge his boyish charm, conducting poolside interviews at Cap-Haïtien's most glamorous hotel and drinking bottles of Prestige or playing dominos with an assortment of other off-duty liberators, much of the real work of leading the insurgency was undertaken by Jodel Chamblain. Chamblain was Tatoune's erstwhile commander in the FRAPH and one of the most feared and hated figures of the 1991–94 coup (see above, page 123). On Saturday 14 February, Chamblain led a force of around 30 to 40 soldiers over to Gonaïves from the Dominican Republic, killing two Dominican soldiers en route at Dajabon. Unlike the distracting "ragtag" band posing for cameras alongside Buteur and Etienne, Chamblain's troops "were well armed, with new uniforms and flak-jackets." According to *Haïti Progrès*, "They were an obviously military-trained corps. They brought two truckloads of weapons from the Dominican Republic including M-16s, M-60s, rocket propelled grenades, and sufficient equipment to shoot down the one helicopter that the government had in its possession."[47] FRAPH was back. "The army is no longer demobilized, the army is mobilized," announced ex-sergeant Jean-Baptiste Joseph.[48] Now the insurgency could begin in earnest. On 16 February Chamblain led a force of around fifty men to invade the regional capital of Hinche, killing three of the town's ten lightly armed policemen and forcing the others to flee south to Mirebalais.[49] Over the next few days similar attacks on small northern towns would end with similarly predictable results.

Prior to Chamblain's arrival, however, the democratic liberation of Haiti was starting to look like a rather less promising affair. Contrary to the impression given by their sponsors back in Pétionville, the sacking of Gonaïves had nothing to do with a popular movement. In Gonaïves itself, it had taken Tatoune and his ex-army associates four full months to re-educate the people of Raboteau and to intimidate the local authorities. Tatoune and Buteur discussed their strategy with the *Miami Herald*, and explained their subtle plan to "'cleanse' this impoverished land of Aristide's supporters": "they embarked on their cleansing scheme by first going after members and sympathizers of Lavalas and torching just about anything they owned. They then went after police and government officials."[50] Wherever they had failed to go after Lavalas sympathizers with sufficient force – which is to say, just about everywhere in Haiti apart from Gonaïves itself, Hinche, and a few surrounding villages in the Central Plateau – the would-be liberators found themselves up against resilient and well-organized resistance. In almost every case, an alliance of police and local FL activists was enough to send even a substantial number of the aggressors packing.[51]

In the immediate aftermath of 5 February, various groups of rebels made brief incursions into ten villages and towns,[52] but by the end of 9 February a combination of police and impromptu Lavalas militia had regained control almost everywhere. Just twenty miles south of Gonaïves, Saint-Marc was the only other place in Haiti to suffer what Jane Regan called an "organized armed rebellion."[53] As in Gonaïves, in Saint-Marc ex-army troops were reinforced by a local anti-Lavalas gang, known as RAMICOS. As if in emulation of Tatoune's Cannibals to the north, RAMICOS had been waging a low-intensity war upon the population of Saint-Marc for several months. They had repeatedly burned pro-FL properties and radio stations and harassed the police; the most significant attack took place on 14 January. On 7 February a combination of RAMICOS militants and other rebels managed to dislodge the police and empty the jails. Hundreds of Saint-Marc's desperately poor inhabitants took advantage of the mayhem to loot televisions and food from the port. On 9 February, however, a police SWAT team supported by members of the local FL *organisation populaire* Bale Wouze managed to dislodge the rebels in their turn, after a firefight that killed two people. Visiting the town a couple of days after the police victory, Scott Wilson observed, "Their ability to bring Haiti's increasingly restive countryside under government control depends on the help they receive from a potent militia of eager young men loyal to President Jean-Bertrand Aristide." Amanus Mayette, a Lavalas deputy and founder of Bale Wouze explained to Wilson that "The opposition says it wants to mobilize peacefully, but they always do so with guns and shooting. If they attack the police and the population, then we will help them fight back."[54] Bale Wouze confronted RAMICOS militants again on 11 February: some three to five people died in the clash and "close to a dozen houses were burned."[55] (This was the incident that NCHR and PAPDA would soon describe as the "La Scierie Genocide," the "massacre" for which Amanus Mayette and many others would spend more than two and a half years in prison).

Forever demonized by the democratic opposition and its foreign patrons, the truth is that in February 2004 groups like Mayette and his eager young men were the only people who tried to hold the front line in the war to save constitutional democracy in Haiti. As one of them tried to explain to a skeptical *New York Times*, "We are here to defend our country from the animals. We are the only ones who can protect the people. If we go, it will be a catastrophe."[56] Catastrophe was indeed on its

way; the odds are that the unnamed militant who spoke these words
didn't live out the year. Thanks to their readiness to stand up to the ex-
army attackers, however, groups like Bale Wouze were at least able to
buy the FL regime a little time. By 10 February the rebels had been forced
to retreat back into their Gonaïves stronghold, and a couple of days later
even the *New York Times* could see that the rebel movement "appears not
to have massed enough militants to take on the police and pro-Aristide
militants in other major cities."[57] A G184/CD demonstration in Port-au-
Prince on 15 February that applauded the "goals of the Gonaïves
rebellion" drew perhaps 1,000 people; as usual, it was dwarfed by a
much larger pro-government demonstration.[58]

Far from advancing with an irresistible momentum, in other words,
Tatoune's uprising was quite quickly contained, in spite of low police
morale and dramatically inadequate firepower. As the *LA Times'* Carol
Williams observed the day before Chamblain made his move on Hinche,
the "short-lived revolts in a dozen towns and cities exposed the hair-
trigger emotions of people fed up with poverty, disease and a seemingly
bottomless downward spiral, but those outbursts – more aimed at looting
than ruling – fizzled as soon as the booty ran out. The gunmen now
bragging of an imminent assault on Cap-Haïtien and eventually Port-au-
Prince remain a ragtag faction, and their message that the time for
patience is over has mostly fallen on deaf ears."[59] Their assault on Haiti's
beleaguered police had not served to ignite the long-smoldering flames of
popular discontent. Instead, all across the Central Plateau the insurgency
was instantly recognized for what it was: not an insurgency at all, so much
as a *re*surgency of *lame* – a return of the old army. On 22 February, the
Miami Herald noticed a point that seemed to have escape general attention
– that "The gunmen behind a revolt against President Jean-Bertrand
Aristide that is terrifying Haiti are surprisingly few."[60] Even Ambassador
Foley recognized on 17 February that "the rebels have no real support";
Noriega dismissed them as "a dozen losers."[61]

If after 16 February Chamblain's DR-based troops were nevertheless
able to steamroller their way quite easily across most of northern Haiti,
this wasn't the result of popular enthusiasm but of simple military
superiority, backed up with a good dose of psychological warfare. A
handful of local policemen supported by Lavalas OPs and the general
population, though armed only with aging revolvers might well be able
to handle a dozen losers like Buteur Métayer; a series of "lightning raids
on towns and villages across the region"[62] by a coordinated team of fifty
to 100 soldiers led by Chamblain and equipped with US-made assault

weapons and communications was a different matter. Rightly or wrongly, rather than try to mount a counter-offensive in the north the government pulled most of its scattered forces back to defend Port-au-Prince. Aristide hoped that still more negotiation might help find a way out of the impasse. "In our plan, dialog is essential," he had told journalists on 12 February. "I will not give any order to the police to open fire. We prefer to go slowly."[63] Writing in *CounterPunch* a couple of days later, former US commando Stan Goff may have had a better strategic grasp of the situation:

> Aristide needs to wage a ruthless fight to retake each of those towns in turn, to acknowledge that the macouto-bourgeoisie is waging a civil war, and to state that this is war, openly, in order to do what is necessary. If not, then the rightwing paramilitaries will maintain the initiative, they will operate within the logic of war, and they will topple Aristide's government and clamp down yet again on popular sovereignty, with assistance from the hegemon to the north [. . .]. The question has been called in Haiti. Sovereignty or subjugation. This is the stark choice, and the time for conciliation is past. Now it is time for Dessalines.[64]

FROM CAP-HAÏTIEN TO PORT-AU-PRINCE

As it turned out, Aristide's refusal to issue a national call to arms and his decision to retreat back to the fortress of Port-au-Prince probably sealed the government's fate. The inhabitants of the north were abandoned to the mercies of Chamblain and Tatoune, and the resulting domino-effect did more to strengthen the hands of Aristide's enemies in Washington, Paris and Pétionville than did any number of "popular" protests. As soon as they had taken control of Gonaïves, the rebels cut off the only viable road from the capital to Haiti's second city, Cap-Haïtien. The convoys of food aid upon which around 300,000 people in northern Haiti depend were stopped in their tracks. By mid-February UN officials admitted that the situation was already desperate. Just a couple of days after the fall of Gonaïves, Cap-Haïtien had run out of fuel. Electricity failed and regional hospitals closed. Patients needing surgery in the Cap, Wilson reported on 15 February, were "forced to bring black-market fuel to the hospital to power the generator during operations."[65] Fueled by the independent radio stations, rumors of the government's imminent collapse spread like wildfire. Images of the bodies of policemen lynched and mutilated in the streets of Gonaïves received obsessive media attention.[66] By Wednesday 18 February, the Cap's few remaining police officers had "barricaded themselves inside their station, and said they would be unable to repel a threatened rebel assault."[67] Although several early rebel assaults on the Cap (starting with an initial foray on 7 February) were repulsed, by the end of the week residents started to panic.

When then on Sunday 22 February Chamblain showed up on the outskirts of a heavily barricaded Cap-Haïtien with something like 200 troops the shooting lasted only a few hours. It left eight Lavalassians and three FLRN soldiers dead.[68] Hundreds of starving looters quickly pounced on whatever food supplies remained in the city's port. "With aid stocks now gone," noted the *New York Times*, "aid agencies raised the spectre of a widespread relief crisis, as people run out of food and hospitals deplete their supplies of medicines"; the *Times* added that the newly arrived "soldiers arrested anyone suspected of being a pro-government militant."[69] Some of the rebels were more explicit about their intentions. "We're going to clean the city of all *chimères*," Dieusauver Magustin told the *Associated Press*. Another rebel, Claudy Philippe, explained that "The people show us the *chimère* houses. If they are there, we execute them."[70] Working under Chamblain's supervision, people like Claudy Philippe would have a free hand to rule Cap-Haïtien as they pleased for the next several months. By the time a token number of French troops arrived to patrol parts of the Cap in late March, they found a "very difficult situation: there is no police and all the institutions that represented the government have been destroyed."[71]

The international and independent media chose to describe the fall of Cap-Haïtien as a "stunning defeat" for Aristide. A local journalist quoted by the *Miami Herald* was more sanguine: "All the police had left. The people in charge here were simply outgunned and outmaneuvred."[72] Although papers like the *New York Times* sought to present the capture of Cap-Haïtien as proof that Aristide was rapidly losing popular support, observers of what actually took place noted simply that "hundreds of cheering people accompanied rebel units as they patrolled this port city of 500,000 on Monday, while many stunned Cap-Haïtien residents looked on from their homes and balconies."[73] American activist Doug Perlitz has lived in Cap-Haïtien since 1996 and had a more accurate sense of the popular mood. "The situation was very tense, after three or four false alarms over the previous few days. Everyone was terrified. The rebels chased away the police, burned a few houses, torched the city's most progressive radio station, and bought off a few local desperados. They executed a few people and locked others up in containers, down at the port; that was enough to cow the population in the short term, but there was no popular support for the rebels."[74] It's not hard to see why a certain number of destitute people might want to ingratiate themselves with a new set of military masters. It also isn't hard to see how, after taking the Cap, Chamblain's men were quickly able to terrorize the rest of northern Haiti into submission. What happened in the small north-western town of Port-de-Paix was typical of a more general pattern. A small group of rebels burned the abandoned police station and customs office, and ransacked the local tax office. According to foreign witnesses they then commandeered "patrol cars and uniforms from police officers who had fled, and rode around the city yelling, 'Now we are the police!'"[75]

Though hardly stunning, the loss of Cap-Haïtien was certainly a demoralizing blow for what was left of the country's official police force. This is another crucial aspect of the débacle. As we saw in chapter seven, far from ruling with tyrannical dominance Aristide's authority was severely compromised by the relative impotence and unreliability of the country's security services. The number of active-duty officers had fallen from a high of around 5,000 in the late 1990s to something between 3,000 and 2,500.[76] (New York City, by contrast, which has a population roughly equal to that of Haiti, is patrolled by some 40,000 officers.) There was only a single special-weapons or tactical unit for the entire country, staffed by around eighty well-armed men. By 20 February, at least forty policemen had already been killed by the insurgents; by the end of the month, the total number of people they had killed had risen to around 200. Outside of Port-au-Prince, the police are generally stationed in small, isolated groups – appropriate for keeping local law and order, but of no consequence in the face of military assault. In the days before it fell to the rebels, for instance, only two policemen reported for duty in the town of Gran Rivière du Nord. They shared a grand total of three clips of ammunition between them, and for lack of batteries and electricity had no radio contact with other police in the surrounding area.

It's not surprising that in many such towns, when Chamblain's noisy troupe approached, the police usually stepped out of their uniforms and melted away.[77] They had few options. As the US started to lose control of the PNH in the late 1990s (see above, page 65) it had begun to enforce an arms embargo that it had imposed (along with the OAS and the UN) back in 1993, against the coup leaders who overthrew Aristide. Incredibly, this US embargo remained in force even after Aristide's return, and then once he was re-elected president in 2000 "the restrictions were increased to include tear gas, riot shields, and other defensive equipment."[78] They also served to ground the administration's one and only helicopter in late 2003, once it ran out of spare parts.[79] By February 2004 Haiti's police had exhausted most of its supplies. The only country willing to provide Aristide's Haiti with police equipment and munitions – tear-gas, rubber bullets, bullet-proof vests . . . – was Mbeki's South Africa. It is no coincidence that a plane full of such munitions was en route to Haiti the very day that Aristide was overthrown.

By the middle of 2003, the US-driven "war on drugs" had also taken its toll on police morale, leading to the arrest of several prominent officers and a rapid turn-over of high-level commanders. Indicted by the DEA, police chief Jean Nesly Lucien was replaced by Aristide's preferred candidate Jean-Claude Jean-Baptiste on 26 March 2003, who as a result of international pressure was replaced in turn by Jean-Robert Faveur on 6 June. After Faveur mysteriously resigned and fled into exile after just two weeks on the job he was replaced by Jocelyne Pierre, the most senior judge of the civil court. While there seems to be little doubt that drug-related crime was indeed rife in parts of the police force – as it was before Aristide came to power, and as it is almost certain to remain long after his departure, pending dramatic structural changes in the Haitian economy – it isn't hard to see why, after turning a blind eye to the flagrant drugs offenses of their pro-coup clients under Raoul Cédras and Michel François, the US chose to target people like Oriel Jean and Nesly Lucien in 2003. Nor is it hard to understand why the independent media was all ears when the IFES-funded human rights group NCHR issued a report on 2 September 2003 claiming that the police had organized a new extra-legal unit of "special brigades," a quasi-military force that NCHR and its allies were quick to equate with Duvalier's Macoutes and Cédras' *attachés*.[80]

Few things were less certain in February 2004 than the reliability of the police force itself. It's clear that in early February many nervous officers stuck to their guns, literally, with great courage and professionalism.[81] It's also clear that around a quarter of PNH officers had joined the force after serving in the disbanded Haitian army, and that many of these soldiers-turned-police retained links with Philippe, Dragon and their colleagues in the Dominican Republic; that in February, Chamblain and Philippe had considerable success in winning members of the PNH over to their cause;[82] that Philippe's friends Youri Latortue and Dany Toussaint had played a pivotal role in determining the orientation of the police in Port-au-Prince, and that they had particular influence within the palace-based USGPN; that by 2003 the USGPN was already "totally unreliable;"[83]

that the deputy commander of the USGPN in February, Wilson Casseus, was active in preventing the force from responding effectively to the insurgency, and then became head of the USGPN after the coup; that Philippe was almost certainly telling the truth when he said on 25 February that "rebels are already present in Port-au-Prince, including some under cover in the National Palace"[84]; that in early 2004, Dany Toussaint played a significant though clandestine role in the destabilization of the government, at one point even broadcasting a call for 200,000 people to attack the national palace and to leave Aristide either "in prison or dead"[85]; that in the immediate aftermath of Aristide's removal, Dany Toussaint played a rather less clandestine role in the pacification of Port-au-Prince, boasting to reporters on 2 March that "when they talk about security, they talk about me."[86] It's also clear that after being beaten back by Tatoune's gang of criminals and ex-soldiers in Gonaïves on 7 February, the all-important SWAT unit took part in only one other significant engagement (the recovery of Saint-Marc on 9 February). A reporter from the *Herald* noted without further comment that the unit's "loyalty to Aristide was first questioned" during the last week of February.[87] "Don't forget," writes Aristide's security advisor Frantz Gabriel, "that the 'Company' was involved: all it takes is a few US visas along with a few dollars and presto, the commanders are no longer loyal to the commander in chief."[88] In any case, on the day that Aristide was flown out of the country most police units switched their allegiance to the opposition and the rebels more or less instantly: on Sunday 29 February it was only a matter of hours before a combination of CIMO officers, rebels and various other anti-FL vigilantes had gained control of downtown Port-au-Prince, pushing Aristide's discouraged supporters back into the surrounding slums. In Pétionville, Scott Wilson noted that on that Sunday afternoon police "returned" to take control of their station after being "largely absent in recent days."[89]

It's clear, in short, that by the end of February the only people who could be trusted to protect the regime were the Lavalas partisans who spent much of the month fortifying the city and preparing for Chamblain's assault. As we shall see, they had good reason to want to protect their neighborhoods – and protect them they did.

A NEGOTIATED SETTLEMENT

Up in Pétionville, meanwhile, the democratic opposition was scarcely able to contain its enthusiasm for its "new" military allies in the north.

Since the US and the rest of the IC kept insisting all through the February crisis "that a multinational police force can only be dispatched once the government forges some sort of an agreement with the opposition to halt the fighting,"[90] the opposition were entitled to be excited. That it was under strict instructions to contain itself is obvious from the ritual denials issued by CD leaders like Evans Paul or Micha Gaillard of any possible connection between the "legitimate" opposition and what Neptune, Aristide, Civil and other Lavalas spokesmen invariably (and correctly) identified as its "terrorist" and "paramilitary wing."[91] All through February US diplomats just as invariably poured scorn on Neptune's claims, insisting that "no one would be swayed by [FL] attempts to 'lump together' the armed rebels in Gonaïves with the mainstream opposition"[92] – this was before CD representative Paul Arcelin (to say nothing of Philippe or Ravix themselves) proudly confessed to the close working relationship between the CD and the FLRN (see above, pages 127–29). But as FLRN attacks increased in the autumn of 2003, even the independent media couldn't fail to notice that rather than condemn the attackers, "Opposition political leaders instead blame Aristide for the deteriorating security situation, which has complicated government efforts to hold new elections that are a condition for the lifting of US aid restrictions."[93] When the uprising began on 5 February, CD spokesman professor Micha Gaillard explained that "Aristide had only himself to blame for the violence in Gonaïves." An incredulous Yvon Neptune tried to remind the world that "it is not the government that is organizing the violence,"[94] but Gaillard and his academic colleagues in the democratic opposition were too sophisticated for such crude logic. A few days later Gaillard calmly announced that the CD couldn't accept even Roger Noriega's own blueprint for a negotiated settlement, since that would only be "perceived as an alliance between Jean-Bertrand Aristide and us against the rebels."[95] Rather than risk offending the patriotic rebels, CD leaders like Leslie Manigat stuck to their main theme, that "Aristide can no longer save the situation for his regime." As the rebel attacks grew in daring and significance, those opposed to the man Evans Paul denounced as a "delinquent outlaw president" grew increasingly animated.[96] On 9 February, Manigat's CD colleague ex-colonel Himmler Rébu compared the 5 February uprising with the 1985 revolt that led to the overthrow of Duvalier, and said, "We are in a situation of armed popular insurrection."[97] On 11 February G184 leader Andy Apaid clarified what this meant when, after reiterating his group's principled rejection of violence, he went on to describe Tatoune's uprising as "a legitimate insurrectional situation [. . .]. It's a struggle for people trying to take a non-violent approach, because it limits our options."[98] On 23 February Apaid's G184 colleague Hans Tippenhauer went a little further still, applauding the fact that "anti-government rebels had been greeted as 'freedom fighters' by people across Haiti."[99] On 27 February G184's Charles Baker took the same line, saying "he no longer regarded Philippe's gunmen as dangerous rebels but as 'liberators' because they are cheered by Haitians when they move in and scatter the hated *chimères*."[100]

While the opposition generally tried to keep a lid on the precise nature of their relationship to these mysterious rebels, Guy Philippe himself was a little more obliging, hinting "that the groups do have an open line of communication."[101] Asked around the same time if the opposition might yield to US pressure to accept a negotiated settlement, Philippe's answer was less ambiguous: "They won't do that, you can believe me. They are very responsible people. I don't think they will betray the people of Haiti."[102] Philippe was only slightly more cagey about who was paying the bills for his group vacation in the Cap's Mont Joli hotel. On the last day of February the hotel's managers admitted that "Philippe has paid the tab for the dozens of rebels, though they wouldn't give the amount. Philippe [. . .] said the movement is funded by Haitians in the United States and Canada, who wire money through Western Union, and businessmen in Haiti."[103] More importantly, it's clear that Philippe, Apaid and Rébu all agreed on what Philippe called the "principles of democracy," and that these principles most definitely did not include allowing the elected president to serve out "a four- or five-year term."[104] Given a principled agreement on this essential point, there was considerable room for practical collaboration. The day Aristide was thrown out, Baker told reporters that the G184 had "welcomed Philippe's offer [to commit] his troops to help maintain order amid reports of continued looting in the capital."[105] In early March Micha Gaillard said that Philippe's gang was backed up by "great popular support; we are in no way antagonistic toward it."[106] On 9 March Evans Paul publicly encouraged "Guy Philippe take up arms once again, in order to guarantee security for the population." On 17 March Paul said that Philippe and his associates should be consulted before a new government was formed. When Philippe met with Haiti's new Interior Minister ex-general Hérard Abraham in the last week of March, he happily reported that "Abraham had made no mention of the need for the rebels to disarm."[107]

No doubt the democratic opposition was sufficiently well-trained by the IRI in the Dominican Republic to keep most of its actual links with the rebels safely out of public view. (This would only change when, later in 2004 and then again in 2005, some of the more intransigent ex-rebels like Ravix Rémissainthe, disappointed with the new government's failure to make good on its initial promises to the freedom fighters, started to speak openly in the media about what had really happened back in the DR.) The least that can be said about February 2004 itself, however, is that as far as the "political process" was concerned, both of the two main rebel attacks were very conveniently timed. In the middle of January, realising that a crisis was imminent, CARICOM leaders had tried to broker a last-ditch agreement between FL and the CD. They met with opposition leaders and representatives of the Haitian business elite on 21 January, and then with Aristide on 31 January. On 2 February Aristide announced that he had agreed to the CARICOM proposal, which required him to accept a prime minister of the opposition's choosing, to hold new elections and to take further measures to disarm his supporters and to reform the police. "We will have elections and security; without elections, there is no way to have peace," he said, while noting that some members of the opposition were still "not ready to embrace democracy. Why do they refuse to go to elections? They fear that simple and important principle: one man, one vote, whereas I think we are all equal. I think the peasant and the rich man are all equal."[108] The democratic opposition's rejection of this unpalatable principle looked less unreasonable when Gonaïves suddenly went up in flames a couple of days later. The very day of Tatoune's assault, 5 February, the CARICOM mission admitted defeat and withdrew, "after key opposition leaders said they would refuse to negotiate with President Jean-Bertrand Aristide."[109]

Something very similar happened two weeks later, when Roger Noriega himself arrived in Haiti on Saturday 21 February, apparently to try to persuade the opposition to accept one last version of a negotiated settlement. This would be the final move in Noriega's long game of diplomatic charades. As with the CARICOM proposal, Noriega's plan required Aristide to replace his prime minister Yvon Neptune with a "more independent" and "broad-based" figure. It required him to accept a cabinet largely made up of his enemies in the opposition, to crack down on his more "hard-line" supporters, to yield the PNH to "international" control, and to organize new parliamentary elections "under international supervision."[110] The plan gave the opposition virtually everything they asked for, and represented little less than unconditional surrender for Aristide. Had the agreement gone through, it would have left him almost entirely powerless; Noriega's plan didn't even hold out the prospect of international assistance in disarming the rebels who by now were rampaging their way across the northern half of his country. Nevertheless, on Saturday 21 February, the ever-intransigent Aristide agreed to Noriega's terms without discussion. "Completely and entirely I have accepted," he said. "In a word: yes." (Six weeks later, Noriega would explain that Aristide's downfall was the result of his "wilful refusal to give any quarter to or compromise with political adversaries."[111])

For an anxious moment, the opposition's position looked rather delicate. On Thursday 19 February, two days before Noriega's trip, Colin Powell had appeared firm but fair: Haiti's democrats "have to come up with a political solution" he said, adding that "the opposition must recognize that whatever their legitimate complaints, 'they will not be dealt with if they fall in league – or get under the umbrella – with thugs and murderers.' "[112] Powell had been speaking this way for some time. On 12 February he had re-assured the US Senate Foreign Relations Committee that "the policy of the administration is not regime change." The next day, Powell reminded the world that "We all have a commitment to the democratic process in Haiti, and we will accept no outcome that is not consistent with the constitution. We will accept no outcome that, in any way, illegally attempts to remove the elected president of Haiti."[113] It hardly seemed surprising, then, that on the evening of 21 February, as Noriega flew back to Washington "empty-handed," a State Department spokesman announced that Colin Powell had just spoken personally with Andy Apaid by telephone, and had "urged him to accept the agreement" outlined by Noriega. That same evening, "a senior Western diplomat in Port-au-Prince" told reporters that opposition leaders "are really risking everything by refusing the helping hand of the international community. If they say no, they will have forfeited the support of the international community. It's a tremendous risk."[114] On the other hand, could the opposition risk abandoning the demand that provided it with its sole *raison d'être*? Opposition figure Rosemond Pradel grasped the problem with perfect clarity on the Saturday afternoon, when he said that "If we accept the plan without the departure of Aristide, we are going to disappear as an opposition."[115]

Mercifully, just a few hours later the prospect of this disappearance itself disappeared, when on Sunday, at the urging of Lalanne, Chamblain and Philippe amazed everyone by conquering a defenseless Cap-Haïtien. Andy Apaid breathed an audible sigh of relief: "This is all the more reason for Mr. Aristide to go. This is all the more reason to press harder for what we see as the only way out, and it is only more clear that we need to do this very, very quickly."[116] When Powell called Apaid and other opposition leaders again on Monday 23 February, supposedly to renew his insistence that they accept Noriega's proposal, somehow or other one of the most powerful men in the world "won only a promise to hold off their formal rejection until 5 p.m. Tuesday."[117] When this formal rejection was duly announced at the appointed hour, the game was finally up. Even in the hardened international press and diplomatic corps the sense of astonishment, even incomprehension, was palpable. "Given Aristide's election by popular vote," noted the *Washington Post*, Noriega's "proposal gives the opposition few options but to take its place in a power-sharing government or else lose credibility as a democratic movement."[118]

Such hard-won democratic credibility, however, is not so easily lost. Although the *New York Times* claimed that the "opposition's stubborn refusal to sign the agreement has infuriated American and other regional diplomats anxious to prevent further bloodshed in Haiti,"[119] the imperial fury had uncommonly few consequences. Was Powell really going to allow his authority to be so publicly flouted by Haiti's little gaggle of political schemers? Yes, he was. OAS diplomat Luigi Einaudi and other "mediators" would later help explain why this was so, when they revealed that it was Noriega himself who – to *their* astonishment – pulled the plug on the final phase of negotiations, canceling the meeting that was supposed to bring the two warring parties together. "If the opposition was unprepared to accompany this process," Noriega asked, "did we have some sort of obligation to put American lives at risk" to keep Aristide in power?[120] Everyone knows the sort of criteria that must be met to put American lives at risk. Because the US and the UN continued to require that Aristide reach agreement with the democratic opposition before they would contemplate sending any sort of aid or military assistance, by 5 p.m. on Tuesday 24 February international support for an outright coup – a coup that would over the next two years lead to the loss of several thousand non-American lives – was already explicit.

Whether or not Powell himself was entirely pleased with the role he had to play in Noriega's drama, the deceitful manipulation of this support was one of the more masterful diplomatic achievements of the entire Bush era. On their own, however, Noriega and Foley could never have managed it. The beauty of the 2004 coup is that – unlike 1991, and indeed unlike most other US interventions in its "own" hemisphere – it was a gloriously multilateral affair. For more than a year, Canada had helped to coordinate the semi-covert international campaign to destabilize Aristide's govern-ment and to prepare the grond for another round of "humanitarian" intervention. And at the most delicate point in the whole destabilization process, the moment when the imperial powers finally had to shift from ostensible approval of Haiti's constitutionally elected president to overt calls for his resignation, the US was more than happy to withdraw behind an occasionally erratic but most welcome ally: France.

THE FRENCH CONNECTION

One of the several under-noticed things that distinguishes Haitian coup number two from Haitian coup number one is the role played by the country's old colonial master. Back in September 1991, the French ambassador Jean-Raphaël Dufour stuck his neck out to help save Aristide from his enemies.[121] Back in 1991, France was a country in transition, one that still maintained a few residual links to the tradition of socialist internationalism. By 2003, Jacques Chirac's country had become one of the most conservative countries in a deeply paranoid "fortress Europe." It had spent the best part of the intervening decade tearing itself up over issues inherited from its imperial past. In large part it had come to define itself, politically, through its reactionary approach to issues surrounding immigration and the ramified legacies of slavery and colonialism.

Chirac, his foreign minister Dominique de Villepin and indeed most of the French population (if its purportedly progressive newspapers provide any clue of the national mood) were nothing less than scandalized, then, when in April 2003 Aristide was impudent enough to bring up the old question of the "French debt." As we saw in chapter 1, this refers to the massive sum extorted in 1825 from a destitute Haiti by French gunboats, as compensation for the loss of colonial property. No single act of imperial coercion made as dramatic a contribution to Haitian under-development. In April 2003, realising that he stood little chance of ever seeing any of the international aid his country had been promised back in 1997–98, Aristide decided to ask France to give this money back. The demand had been a long time coming – "We would never finish," he wrote back in 1993, "if we tried to recite all that France took from us."[122] In a speech he gave at the UN on 25 September 1991 Aristide included as one of "Ten Democratic Commandments" the "right of the impoverished masses to demand what they are owed." Unlike more acceptable third-world leaders, Aristide never accepted the logic of charity in lieu of justice. "The historic debt contracted by the nations to the north cannot be paid off by sending us their surplus [. . .]. We're not looking for pity, no, but for you to acknowledge that we have the right to recuperate a part of what has been stolen from us."[123]

Arguably, Aristide's 2003 demand for the recuperation of this theft is the single most threatening international demand that anyone has made on Haiti's old imperial creditor (if not on the whole ex-colonial world) since the end of its last major colonial war, in 1961. Two years before Aristide issued his request, the French parliament had itself recognized slavery as a crime against humanity. Unlike most slavery-related reparation demands currently in the air, the Haitian claim refers to a precise and well-documented sum of money extracted in hard currency by the ex-colonial power. Assuming a low return of 5 per cent in annual interest, Aristide's advisors calculated that the original sum claimed by France in 1825 as compensation for the loss of their colonial "property" was now equivalent to 21 billion American dollars. Lawyers and economists appointed to the Haiti Restitution Commission began to meet in the later part of 2003 to prepare their legal and political case, and were due to publish a substantial report in the spring of 2004. There is good reason to think that public scrutiny of Aristide's claim might well have proved very costly to France, in all kinds of ways. As NYU professor Michael Dash notes, "Aristide got a lot of support for this demand both inside and outside of Haiti," particularly in other former colonies in Africa and Latin America.[124] In the long run-up to Aristide's Independence Day speech (itself organized as a set of twenty-one points), songs and television advertisements reminded an enthusiastic audience of the 21,685,135,571 dollars and 48 cents that would soon be coming their way. Few Haitians who lived through 2003 will forget either the amount demanded nor the reasoning behind it. Writing in the *Washington Post* in November, Scott Wilson noticed the "potent hold it has over much of the population. Port-au-Prince is festooned with banners promoting the campaign. A song recorded by the *racine* band Koudjay calling for restitution is a staple on the radio, and the claim is the chief source of news and entertainment in a country where more than half the population is illiterate."[125]

Though quick to pour scorn on the claim, the French government was clearly rattled. "Before bringing up claims of this nature," Chirac warned, "I cannot stress enough to the authorities of Haiti the need to be very vigilant about – how should I put it – the nature of their actions and their regime."[126] Chirac's bitterly anti-Lavalas ambassador Yves Gaudeul added his own warning in September 2003, on the eve of his replacement by the still more hard-nosed Thierry Burkard, when he stirred up wild speculation in Port-au-Prince by warning Haiti of an imminent "political storm, even if the sky seems blue [. . .]. Hang on tight," he advised, "since it's going to blow a gale!"[127] (Several leading Lavalassians, noted *Le Monde*, were quick to assume that when Amiot Métayer was murdered in Gonaïves a couple of days after Gaudeul's departure his death marked a clear sign of change in the political weather.[128]) By September 2003, semi-covert subversion of Lavalas had long been a full-time job for intelligence officer Eric Bosc and other members of the French embassy staff. With the possible exception of their US counterparts, no other group of diplomats made such an enthusiastic contribution to the media's systematic anti-Aristide bias, or to the anti-Aristide street demonstrations that began in November 2003.[129] Visas and plane-tickets were liberally handed out to scores of new converts to the old *mission civilisatrice*. The ground for this effort had been prepared well in advance: over the two decades following Baby Doc's fall in 1986 the lion's share of French political investment in Haïti always went to the versatile "social democrat" and G184 enthusiast Serge Gilles, who in addition to serving as a senator under Cédras had allied his PANPRA "party" to anti-Aristide candidate Marc Bazin (in 1990) and the anti-Aristide insurgent Guy Philippe (from 2001).[130] On the day that Aristide re-affirmed his demand for restitution of the French debt in his bicentennial speech, Burkard invited Gilles and ten other leading members of the political opposition to a "friendly gathering" at the ambassador's house, where for their part they "re-affirmed their refusal of any compromise with Aristide."[131]

As the destabilization campaign intensified in the autumn of 2003, the French Foreign Ministry dispatched a Commission led by ex-philosopher Régis Debray to devise a suitably sophisticated rejection of Aristide's request. Debray's team concluded that, while Haiti had indeed been "impeccable" in its own payments to France, there was no "legal case" for reimbursement.[132] To general applause from the French media, the Commission's Report described the FL demand for restitution as "aggressive propaganda" based on "hallucinatory accounting." It noted with satisfaction that "no member of the democratic opposition to Aristide takes the reimbursement claims seriously." It referred to the desirable consequences of "President Aristide's resignation," while noticing that both the opposition and paramilitaries might lack sufficient "mobilizing force" to see the job through. It also noticed that the Americans, though hamstrung by domestic considerations ("*boat-people*, Black Caucus"), were looking for "an honorable way out of the crisis."[133] There was thus a rare opportunity for "audacious and resolute coordination" with this old but recently estranged ally – a chance to move past the awkward inter-imperial rivalries provoked by initial French reluctance to sign up to the American war in Iraq.[134]

On 21 November 2003 the French Socialist Party issued a formal statement accusing Aristide of establishing a "dictatorship" in Haiti and calling for him to step down. The following month, Régis Debray and Dominique de Villepin's sister Véronique Albanel repeated this demand in person.[135] Aristide's attempt to preserve diplomatic niceties in the face of such overt French contempt caused widespread consternation among his more militant adherents. (His refusal to lash out at an insufferably smug de Villepin during these months, his willingness to engage in a diplomatic charade with de Villepin's sister and other French "dignitaries," remembers the PPN's Georges Honorat, "made me want to tear my heart out."[136])

Very soon Aristide was too preoccupied with his own survival to make any further reference to the French debt. On 17 February, de Villepin gave a press conference in which he observed that France's former colony was once again "on the edge of chaos." Since Aristide "over the years has let things degenerate," he announced that France was "ready to act" with other members of the IC. With several thousand troops close at hand in its permanent colonies of Martinique and Guadeloupe, he announced that France could quickly and easily help organize an international intervention force to preserve democracy in Haiti – "We have the means and many friendly countries are mobilized."[137] There was a catch, however. De Villepin waited until 25 February – the day after the CD formally rejected the peace plan that De Villepin himself had endorsed, alongside Powell and Noriega – to explain that the condition for French military assistance was Aristide's resignation. Noting that Aristide "bears heavy responsibility for the current situation," De Villepin explained that as far as France was concerned "the regime has reached an impasse and has already shaken off constitutional legality [. . .]. Everyone sees quite well that a new page must be opened in Haiti's history," starting with the institution of a "politically neutral government of national unity."[138] Other French officials told the press that their government had "advised Aristide to step down,"[139] and the following day French Ambassador to the UN Jean-Marc de la Sablière confirmed that there was "no support 'at this time' for an official vote authorizing" any sort of international intervention force to protect Aristide's government.[140] Without a hint of irony, on 26 February the *Washington Post* argued that "Haitians can only be grateful if France proves able to fill the vacuum" left by US "neglect."[141]

On 1 March, French troops joined their US counterparts in a Haiti liberated from Aristide. The *New York Times* celebrated the multilateral invasion as a dramatic example of how "longtime allies can set aside differences, find common ground, play to their strengths and operate in an atmosphere of trust." Bush and Chirac exchanged tender words by telephone, expressing their delight at "the excellent French–American cooperation."[142] No doubt Chirac was equally delighted when Aristide's more rational and more democratic successor Latortue recognized in April 2004 that the restitution claim had been "illegal, ridiculous and was made only for political reasons. This matter is closed."[143]

With the French willing to play the role of public executioner in February, the US could afford to play its own hand a little more subtly than usual. During the first two weeks of February, while Powell made stern speeches about respecting the Haitian constitution, US officials "said privately that they would not be sorry to see Aristide go if his departure contributed to a fresh start for the hemisphere's poorest nation."[144] Even in public, the US made no secret of its real intentions. After admitting on 17 February that "There is frankly no enthusiasm right now for sending in military or police forces to put down the violence that we are seeing," on 20 February Powell added that "The United States would not object if Aristide agreed to leave office early."[145] Tim Carney, US Ambassador to Haiti in 1998–99 and a leading member of the Washington-based Haiti Democracy Project so close to Stanley Lucas, Roger Noriega and their foreign policy team was more candid: "Aristide is toast. He's gone. The only question is whether he goes out in a pine box or on an airplane."[146]

A certain amount of subtlety was expedient, given the perennial US obsession with the menace of Haitian emigration. A full-blown blood-bath might always trigger a repeat of the 1991 catastrophe, which saw more than 60,000 desperate refugees take to the seas. In early 2004, the US made plans for a similar contingency.[147] On 27 February, a group of Aristide supporters had the temerity to assault perhaps the country's only state enterprise that still enjoys undivided US attention and support – the hated Haitian Coast Guard. A group of Lavalas militants attacked the Guard's Admiral Killick base and forced its officers to flee the site. " 'Those guys had to fight for their lives' [a White House] official said of the Coast Guard employees, whom he praised as heroes. 'They had to get out to sea. It was a clear effort to shut down the repatriation [of refugees].' "[148] As far as the White House is concerned, for a Haitian government to threaten its absolute authority immediately and auto-matically to return destitute dark-skinned asylum-seekers straight back to the violence they are seeking to escape is tantamount to a declaration of war. Hours after Aristide was overthrown, US troops arrived to help repair and reinforce the Haitian Coast Guard facility. As the US dispatched extra Coast Guard resources to Haiti and readied its Guanta-namo holding pens for another exercise in humanitarian intervention, it's clear that someone, somewhere, gave Chamblain, Philippe and their associates strict instructions regarding political decorum: in the short-term, hundreds of low-profile killings would certainly be acceptable, but perhaps not thousands, or at least not all at once.

Too much subtlety, however, might be counter-productive. As Aris-tide told CNN on 26 February, even a token gesture from the inter-national community would have been enough to stop the insurgency in its tracks. "From my point of view, if we have a couple of dozen of international soldiers, police, together right now, it could be enough to send a positive signal to [Chamblain's] terrorists and to prevent them from killing more people."[149] A hundred properly equipped troops would have been more than enough. In fact there was no need for any international troops at all; the proverbial "single phone call" from Powell to his clients on the ground would have resolved the crisis there and then. Since this military solution was so easy and so obvious, it was all the more important to preserve international discipline on the need for a suitable political and humanitarian settlement. As Canadian diplomats told the *Globe & Mail* in early March, all through the crisis US officials made it "abundantly clear to their counterparts in Ottawa that Washington had a 'high tolerance' for further Haitian bloodshed and would not be pres-sured into defending Mr. Aristide in order to prevent it. 'In no way were the Bush guys going to help him out – in no way,' one diplomat said. Given that stand, Canada recognized that Mr. Aristide had to leave for the good of his own people."[150] A US government that was always so sensitive to the abuse of human rights when Préval and Aristide were in power lost interest in such trivia when people that Amnesty International described as having "abysmal human rights records" started to close in on Port-au-Prince.[151] After speaking twice with de Villepin on Wednesday 25 February, on Thursday Powell allowed the new international con-sensus to emerge at last into the open. "Whether or not Aristide is able to effectively continue as president is something he will have to examine carefully in the interests of the Haitian people," Powell said.[152] That afternoon, the Franco–US alliance had no difficulty in blocking a last-ditch CARICOM appeal to the UN Security Council for help to save Aristide's government. On Saturday 28 February, president George Bush himself signed on to the new agenda, when White House spokesman Scott McClellan blamed Aristide for "the deep polarization and violent unrest that we are witnessing in Haiti today." McClellan observed that "this long-simmering crisis is largely of Mr Aristide's making," a regrettable but predictable result of his "failure to adhere to democratic principles [. . .]. Aristide's own actions have called into question his fitness to continue to govern Haiti. We urge him to examine his position carefully [and] to accept responsibility."[153]

There was nothing remotely subtle, however, about what still had to be done to get Aristide out of Port-au-Prince.

29 FEBRUARY 2004: A RESCUE?[154]

Three years into his second administration, Aristide and FL were certainly in a weaker position than they were when it started. Structural adjustment and the aid embargo had taken their toll on a country already poised on the brink of destitution. Relentless disinformation had begun to undercut Aristide's political reputation. The persistence of corruption and opportunism, though far from exceptional, had taken much of the saintly shine off the Lavalas project. Although his mandate remained much stronger than that enjoyed by leaders like Bush, Blair or Chirac, there is no denying that by the beginning of February 2004 Aristide no longer enjoyed near-universal support. There is no denying that during the protests it organized between November 2003 and January 2004 the CD and G184 were able to tap into a frustration that had grown considerably since 2000. There is no denying, furthermore, that by the end of February Aristide's strategic options were severely limited by the combined machinations of the democratic and military opposition. As de Villepin and Powell issued their calls for his resignation on February 26, the area under the government's direct control had shrunk to little more than greater Port-au-Prince, a region home to around a third of the country's population.[155]

The US–French account of what then happened on the night of 28 February is straightforward enough. They say that as the international community began to turn its back on him, even so intractable an autocrat as Aristide could see he was doomed. They say that as Philippe's small group of rebels started to overrun the police stations of Haiti's provincial towns and cities, Aristide realised that his "bandit" militias were no match for their disciplined firepower. They say that as a few parts of Port-au-

Prince descended into anarchy on 26–27 February, his nerve cracked. They say, then, that on the evening of Saturday 28 February Aristide sent out a desperate appeal for help to the American embassy. Foley says that Aristide asked him for a way out that would "guarantee his security" and "protect his property."[156] Foley also says that he and his colleagues "were completely stunned" by Aristide's request. "We had not the slightest inkling that he would be prepared to leave, on that day," so Aristide's sudden decision to flee "caught us totally off-guard."[157] Colin Powell's Assistant Secretary of State Roger Noriega too "found it rather remarkable that Aristide decided to leave, and throughout the evening on Saturday, I wholly expected that he would change his mind because he has been proven to be erratic and unreliable."[158]

According to Ambassador Foley and his versatile deputy Luis Moreno, Aristide made a perfectly free and voluntary choice. "Aristide was not persuaded at all," remembers Foley. "He decided himself to leave. He feared he faced death if he could not get out."[159] Since Philippe's rebels were apparently ready to advance on Port-au-Prince, Foley admits that his government shared these fears. "We feared that in that confrontation the president would be killed," and therefore the US resolved to mount a last–minute operation to rescue him.[160] No doubt the US could have done a few other things to prevent such a confrontation. They could have endorsed CARICOM's appeal to the UN for the deployment of a hundred or so international peacekeepers, for instance, or they could have simply instructed Guy Philippe's men to lay down their M16s and return to their US-sanctioned exile in the DR. But as Colin Powell's chief of staff Lawrence Wilkerson later explained, rather than discourage Philippe and his "ragtag band," Foley preferred instead to talk "with President Aristide; he confronted him with the situation that he was going to meet on the morn, so to speak, confronted him with the devastation that was likely to take place, and President Aristide, to his credit, made the decision to take Ambassador Foley's offer and to leave the country." As far as the world's most powerful democracy was concerned, Wilkerson said, it was clearly the elected president rather than the extra-legal insurgent who needed to leave Haiti. "Aristide was the focal point. Aristide was the person who needed to be removed from Haiti, and even he understood that. In the conversation he had with our ambassador, he understood that. He knew that he was the lightning rod, and that if he didn't remove himself from the island, there was going to be a lot of bloodshed."[161]

Embroidering a little more on his story, Ambassador Foley says that he spoke with Aristide at least four times during that Saturday night. He says "I told him how very sad I thought it was that this was happening. It was a very sad series of conversations." Foley remembers that Aristide "never challenged our position" that there would be a bloodbath if he did not leave." He remembers that "what was surprising was Aristide's passivity and philosophical resignation. My own feeling was that Aristide had already decided to leave. He didn't need convincing." Perhaps he had come to share Foley's candid assessment of his "horrendous" legacy.[162]

Though stunned and saddened, the US government quickly arranged for Aristide's safe transport out of Haiti, on a plane that took off from an otherwise abandoned Port-au-Prince airport around 6:15 a.m. on the morning of Sunday 29 February. According to Foley, in addition to US Marines already present in Port-au-Prince, an elite six-member US army team arrived to coordinate the operation "with Aristide's security personnel, including the head of his bodyguards from the California-based Steele Foundation," David Johnson.[163] Foley's deputy Luis Moreno says that together with the newly arrived US personnel he accompanied Aristide and his wife to the airport. Like his boss, Moreno too felt sad. "I expressed sadness that I was here to watch him leave," he told the *Washington Post* on 2 March. "'Sometimes life is like that,' Aristide replied." At some point before he left, Aristide was induced to sign a letter which, as far as his US minders were concerned, appeared to provide constitutional grounds for a democratic transition. "The constitution must not be written with the blood of the Haitian people," it read. "If my resignation prevents the shedding of blood, I agree to leave." And then Moreno "shook his hand and he went away."[164]

Since the US sought only to protect him, it allowed the fugitive to pick his own destination. The US says that Aristide chose the safety of Bangui, in the Central African Republic – he would be safer there, presumably, than in a lawless place like Miami, or in openly supportive neighboring countries like Venezuela, Jamaica or the Bahamas. "We did not force him on to the airplane," Colin Powell insisted; "he went onto the airplane willingly, and that is the truth." George Bush's spokesman Scott McClellan likewise insisted that Aristide's departure was "entirely his decision," and that the decision to go to the Central African Republic was also "his choice, the choice of the country to which he would choose to travel."[165] Colin Powell explained that Aristide's chief concern had been his security and in particular his property: when he called Foley, Aristide "talked about protection of property, protection of his personal property, his – property of some of his ministers, and would he have some choice as to where he was going if he decided to leave. We gave him answers to these questions, positive answers."[166] (It may not be unreasonable to judge Powell's positive answers to Aristide's various questions according to the one that Powell himself chose to emphasize here, the question of Aristide's property. Powell's positive answer to this question is easily verified. It involved the immediate withdrawal of all security from Aristide's house, thereby allowing it to be comprehensively looted and trashed for several days. Around 7 a.m. on 29 February, the house in which Aristide's prime minister Yvon Neptune was staying suffered the same fate, obliging him to spend the next twelve days in his office.)

Despite the US having been "caught totally off guard" by Aristide's sudden decision to resign, once he was safely out of Haitian airspace the US and the rest of its international community reacted with quite astonishing speed. Aristide was dispatched around 6 a.m. Sunday morning. Before noon the US troops who already controlled the airport were bolstered by the arrival of fifty additional Canadian soldiers. Two hundred more US troops landed later that same day, a couple of hours after the UN Security Council suspended its normal 24-hour pre-vote consultation period to agree, unanimously and instantaneously, the emergency resolution (number 1529) that authorized their deployment.[167] On Monday the French started to disembark, and by Wednesday there were 600 French soldiers in Port-au-Prince, alongside 1,100 US Marines. All that remained was for Bush to call and thank Chirac, expressing his delight at the "perfect coordination" of their joint intervention.[168]

. . . A RESIGNATION?

Leaving aside the tricky question about whether it was Aristide (winner of 92 percent of the vote in 2000) or Philippe (winner of 2 percent of the vote in 2006) who might most reasonably be held responsible for the imminent prospect of a bloodbath in Haiti, there are still a few awkward problems with the US version of events.

In the first place, if Aristide's decision to resign was a simple matter of free choice, it's at least a little puzzling that he chose to exercise his freedom in such remarkable solitude and haste. All through February 2004 Aristide repeatedly insisted on his determination to serve out the remainder of his term in office. Two nights before his abduction, on Thursday 26 February, Jim Lehrer interviewed the *New York Times* reporter Lydia Polgreen. She confirmed that "Aristide has made every indication that he plans to stay in power. He has made absolutely no statement other than he plans to remain president of Haiti [. . .]. There are no signs whatsoever [that this might be negotiable] from my conversations with people close to him. He is not making any plans to exit."[169] Aristide corroborated this in an interview with CNN that same night, in which he again insisted that he would never resign nor bow to another coup d'état: "We need now to respect the constitutional order, and I will leave the palace on February 7, 2006."[170] CNN anchor Wolf Blitzer spoke with Aristide again on Friday 27 February (the day before the abduction), and saw that "It was clear he wanted to stay. Listen to what he said to me on Friday: 'I have the responsibility, as an elected president, to stay where I am protecting the people the way I am, the way I can.' "[171] The *Miami Herald* spoke to French officials, also on Friday, and was told " 'the time has come, Aristide must go, he must resign.' Aristide firmly rejected such demands. 'Out of the question,' he said."[172] Late on the Friday night he met with his de facto security chief Oriel Jean, Harold Adéclat and half a dozen or so other loyal PNH commanders and confirmed his determination to confront the insurgents and to finish his mandate.[173] Up until 1 a.m. or so on the morning of Sunday 29 February Aristide never seems to have told *anyone*, including his closest political allies and friends, that he was even prepared to consider leaving office before his term came to an end in February 2006. The last time his chief legal counsellor Ira Kurzban managed to speak with him was on the morning of Saturday 28 February, and there wasn't so much as a hint that Aristide had begun to toy with the idea of resignation.[174] His international press secretary Michelle Karshan was away in the Dominican Republic that weekend but received a note from Aristide's wife Mildred the night of 28 February, a note that simply discussed new proposals for moving forward in another round of negotiations with the political opposition – again there wasn't a whisper about resignation. "Several of us were in touch with [Aristide . . .] until very late Saturday night," confirmed Jamaican Prime Minister and CARICOM chairman P.J. Patterson. "Nothing that was said to us indicated that the president was contemplating a resignation."[175]

Without exception, Aristide's closest allies and confidants all testify to the same point. Aristide's pilot and security advisor Frantz Gabriel joined him on the plane to Africa that night, and "was at the house [in Tabarre] at 5 a.m. when Moreno came in to tell the president they were going to organize a press conference and be ready to accompany them. We boarded to go to the embassy and we ended up at the airport."[176] A couple of years later, Gabriel described what happened at greater length: "Moreno arrived with two special operations guys – obviously military, but they had beards and were carrying some serious hardware [. . .]. Aristide, Mildred and I were taken *manu militari* into Moreno's embassy car. We had no time to pack, and had to leave without bags or passports. We left with nothing."[177] This is consistent with the testimony of the senior Steele guard who was on duty outside Aristide's house that night. Around midnight the entire Steele security detail was told to "plan for a road move to the US Embassy where the President would make a TV broadcast; from there a road move would escort the President and First Lady back to the National Palace." The speculation among the team was that "the President would be making another appeal for calm, the same sort of broadcast that he had regularly made in the previous few days." From about 2 a.m. or so, remembers the Steele guard,

> we could hear that people were making preparations inside the house, and the noise and urgency from the sounds within the house made us think that something more was going to happen. The speculation was that we would relocate at the Palace and hold out there after the press conference. But then just minutes before we actually left, we were told instead that we'd be escorting the President to the international airport, and that we'd be leaving with him by plane. We had no time to prepare. We were not packed at all and most of us had to leave a considerable amount of personal possessions behind. The President and the First Lady also brought very few belongings with them; the president had a briefcase and the First Lady had her overnight bag, nothing else.[178]

Aristide's wife Mildred was as astonished as everyone else. "It was outlandish," she recalls. "Until the moment I was seated in that plane on the Saturday night, you could never have persuaded me that things could possibly arrive at that point."[179]

In the second place, given US insistence on the free and voluntary nature of this resignation, it's quite puzzling that the US itself chose to arrange it in utter secrecy, in the middle of the night, apparently in the absence of any cameras or reporters or any sort of independent witness who might later have been able to confirm its self-evidently voluntary qualities to a (predictably?) suspicious Haitian electorate. When reporter David Adams asked Foley and Moreno about this, they candidly explained that it was a simple mistake, an oversight due to the fact that the rescue operation had to be mounted at great speed and with only a skeleton staff.[180] Perhaps these same factors help account for the fact that Foley was prepared to accept such a strangely worded and enigmatic "letter of resignation." When dealing with so "momentous an event as the resignation of a President," notes lawyer Brian Concannon, "common sense would require a clear statement that demonstrates an unequivocal and freely-made decision to resign. Instead, this letter seems closer to something written by someone who did not intend to resign, but was not free to express that intention."[181]

It's still more puzzling that Aristide himself would have chosen the Central African Republic as his preferred place of refuge. CAR is a dictatorial and heavily policed client state of Aristide's bitter enemy France, and as soon as he arrived he was effectively kept under house arrest and blocked from virtually all access to the media or the telephone.[182] Powell and Noriega hastened to explain that Aristide's "first choice" had been South Africa: regrettably, however, they said that after his plane was already making its way across the Atlantic, Thabo Mbeki – Aristide's staunchest international ally – suddenly reneged on an initial promise to grant him temporary asylum, obliging the US to spend around a dozen dreary hours looking for an alternative destination. The *New York Times* and other papers dutifully reported this intriguing assertion as fact, and some reporters (on the sole basis of Foley's say-so) continue to repeat it to this day. But both Aristide and his confidant Frantz Gabriel (who accompanied the Aristides into exile on 29 February) insist that they never asked South Africa for asylum. Gabriel says that when he was led onto the plane Aristide "had no idea where he was going."[183] Aristide's friend Randall Robinson spoke with the South African foreign minister on the afternoon of Sunday 29 February, and was told "we haven't heard anything from [Aristide]. We don't know where he is, and there's been no request for asylum."[184] On 2 March Dumisani Kumalo, the South African ambassador to the United Nations, confirmed that Aristide had never asked for asylum or exile in South Africa, and that the South African government had "not denied him amnesty or exile as alleged by the US State Department and the *New York Times*."[185] A few weeks after his expulsion from Haiti, South African president Thabo Mbeki welcomed Aristide with open arms, and he continues to welcome him to this day.

It's also rather puzzling, if Aristide really did opt to flee Haiti out of fears for his own security, that his French and American friends didn't just leave his reasonably competent and well-connected team of Steele Foundation security guards to fly him out on their own. On the other hand, once the US was in charge of Aristide's security during their "rescue operation," why was every member of his Steele team, along with their families, still obliged to accompany him on the long plane trip to Bangui?

Despite the fact that neither the French and American governments have yet managed to come up with convincing answers to such questions, the mainstream media and NGOs seemed quite happy to accept their story more or less at face value. An ActionAid report published in October 2006 strikes the typical note, when it observes that after seizing Gonaïves armed insurgents "gradually worked their way through the country until they were poised to enter the capital, Port-au-Prince. This resulted in President Aristide's resignation on 29 February and his leaving the country."[186] No further explanation is required. For a sample of the press coverage it's enough to cite the *New York Times*' description of Aristide's "resignation" as a "stunning exit [. . .]. He was felled by a small but resilient coalition of political opponents and a separate group of armed insurgents who threatened to depose him by force." Since his re-election in 2000, the *Times* continued, Aristide's authority had "eroded as political corruption in his government and political anger in the streets grew out of control," forcing a reluctant US to step in and rescue Aristide from the consequences of his misrule. So long as the dictator remained in Haiti the hands of the international community had been tied; fortunately, the *Times* concluded, "Aristide's departure enables a proposed international peacekeeping force to land in Port-au-Prince, secure the capital and enable desperately needed food and economic assistance to flow to Haiti, the poorest nation in the Western hemisphere."[187] As an added bonus, Powell and de Villepin's joint "resolution of the Haiti conflict" also enabled them to put their differences on Iraq aside and "get French–American relations back on track."[188] In support of this fine version of events, the *Washington Post* cited a phone interview that an exhausted and semi-coherent Aristide gave to CNN on Monday 1 March, and added its own gloss: "'American agents talked to me. Haitian agents talked to me. And I finally realized it was true. We were going to have bloodshed. And when I asked how many people may get killed, they said thousands may get killed.' With that, Aristide told the network, he decided to resign."[189]

In fact, Aristide told the network no such thing. On the contrary, he told CNN that he was "taken by force by US military," that his house was surrounded by US and Haitian security forces, that the US used the threat of massive and immediate violence "to push me out" and to sign, against his will, a letter saying that "I have been forced to leave to avoid bloodshed." If we pick up the script of the disjointed interview where the *Washington Post* leaves off, it reads as follows: ". . . they said thousands may get killed. So using that kind of force to lead a coup d'état, it was clear. [. . .]. We had [US] military surrounding the airport, the palace, my house. And they told me in a clear and blunt way that thousands of people will get killed once they start. So I had to do my best to avoid that bloodshed. They used [unintelligible] to push me out. That's why I call it again and again a coup d'état." CNN's Anderson Cooper pressed him again on this point, later in the same programme:

> [Cooper] Are you saying that you wish you were still – that if it was up to you, you would still be on the ground in Haiti, that you did not leave of your own free will?
> [Aristide]: Exactly that. [. . .].
> [Cooper]: Mr. Aristide, I am having trouble reconciling the two statements, the statements that you have made and the statement the US government has made through Secretary Colin Powell, who, again, has said that you were not kidnapped, that we, the United States, did not force you on to the airplane, that you went on to the airplane willingly. And they say that is the truth. You say – your story is categorically the opposite of that.
> [Aristide]: Of course, because I am telling you the truth.[190]

As soon as he managed to get to a phone, around 36 hours later, this is what Aristide told everyone he could reach. (Along with the actual substance of the interview, however, the *Washington Post* neglected to mention the fact that no sooner Aristide had spoken with CNN on the Monday night than "his telephone privileges were revoked" and he was barred by the Bangui authorities from leaving his heavily guarded villa or from making any further "regrettable statements".[191])

Noriega and his colleagues rounded on the ungrateful ex-dictator with fury. Powell dismissed Aristide's accusation as "absolutely baseless" and "absurd." "We provided him an exit, a humanitarian service," said Noriega, "and his response has been to accuse us of violating his rights. It's very irresponsible."[192] White House Press Secretary Scott McClellan derided Aristide's account as "complete nonsense." On Bush's behalf, McClellan stood up in front of the world's media and said that the US had rescued Aristide at his own request, that it had simply taken "steps to protect Mr. Aristide and his family so they would not be harmed as they departed Haiti." McClellan insisted that Aristide's departure was "entirely his decision," and that the decision to go to the Central African Republic was also "his choice, the choice of the country to which he would choose to travel." McLellan had a little more to say about the Haitian people and their choices:

> Conspiracy theories do nothing to help the Haitians move forward to a better, more prosperous future [. . .]. We are working on what is in the best interest of the Haitian people, as expressed by the Haitian people [. . .]. Aristide was not adhering to his democratic principles that were enshrined in the constitution [but] we now have a democratic constitutional process that is working, that is moving forward. So we helped preserve a democratic and constitutional government by the action that we took, along with the international community.[193]

A couple of days later, Powell's spokesman reasserted the US line, in the face of muted calls for an inquiry from CARICOM and the congressional Black Caucus. "There was no kidnapping, there was no coup, there were no threats," so "there's nothing to investigate [. . .]. We did not advocate his stepping down."[194] As usual, Donald Rumsfeld managed to go one better than even Powell or Bush, and denied not only that Aristide had been abducted but also that Aristide had so much as claimed to have been abducted. "I don't believe that's true that he is claiming that. I just don't know that that's the case. I'd be absolutely amazed if that were the case [. . .]. The idea that someone was abducted is just totally inconsistent with everything I heard or saw or am aware of. So I think that – I do not believe he is saying what you are saying he is saying."[195]

When in mid-April the time came for the ritual UN rubberstamp, Kofi Annan produced a *Report on Haiti* that endorsed the Franco–US storyline in every significant respect.[196]

. . .OR AN ABDUCTION?

Claims that Aristide was abducted by the US on 29 February 2004 do not depend on the argument that soldiers literally burst into his house in a surprise attack. By the end of February, there was no longer any need for such a crude application of imperial power. Aristide's enemies had done everything necessary to make sure that the threat rather than the use of violence would be enough to lever him out of Haiti that night. Foley's claim that "Aristide 'never challenged our position' that there would be a bloodbath if he did not leave" is probably true. Although there was little chance that Philippe's men could have taken the city on their own, Aristide knew that they *might* well have managed it soon enough, in conjunction with suitable international support on the one hand and massive defections from the police on the other.

Aristide was driven from office by US insistence on the one prospect he was not prepared to confront – the imminent prospect of overwhelming violence against unarmed civilians, coupled with the longer-term prospect of a debilitating civil war. Once it became clear that he could do nothing to avoid this prospect, then it seems Aristide did indeed "agree" to leave office. Such "agreement" helps explain some of Aristide's decisions during his last hours as president. During the last days of February, although he called on the population to remain vigilant, he doesn't appear to have summoned an effective war cabinet or to have made effective plans to defend Port-au-Prince. He chose to spend the weekend of 28/29 February at his suburban house in Tabarre, rather than in the more central and more easily defended National Palace. On the night of 28 February itself, Aristide seems to have taken no steps to mobilize his supporters to protect his house against the prospect of imminent attack. Around 11 p.m., Labanye, Billy and other Cité Soleil militants who in February regularly manned barricades to protect the Tabarre residence were apparently instructed to return home.[197] A little later, it seems that someone close to Aristide dismissed at least some of his Haitian security guards. He then chose to spend the rest of that night almost alone and mainly on the phone, trying to talk a way out of the crisis. From midnight or thereabouts his prime minister and finance minister and various others were waiting for instructions just a few hundred yards away, but he didn't ask them to come over to his house.[198] By the time Moreno and his Delta-Force escort arrived at Aristide's house, after 4 a.m., it appears that Aristide had been induced to accept what was already a *fait accompli*, and had bowed to inflexible Franco–US demands that he resign before dawn. When Aristide was escorted out of the house by Moreno a little later, although it's not clear that he expected to be taken straight to the airport he was at least prepared to join the US ambassador at an early morning press conference to explain the situation to the nation.

We can only describe these decisions as based on a form of "agreement," however, if we empty this word of its usual meaning and forget the difference between freedom and compulsion. Powell and Foley are only entitled to say that Aristide freely "agreed to leave" Haiti the night of 28/29 February if they can explain how exactly an agreement prompted by the threat of an imminent bloodbath might be described as a free and voluntary one. Until Foley explains this, there can be no doubt who is lying and who is telling the truth. The truth is that Aristide chose not to commit suicide, and he decided not to lead his supporters into a war that they were ill-prepared to fight. This was indeed a decision, of a kind. But as Patrick Elie insists, "It *was* still a kidnapping, there's no doubt about that. Somebody came up with an apt comparison: it's as if you push someone back into their house, then you nail all the windows shut, and throw a Molotov cocktail inside. Then when he comes running out of the door you say he came out 'of his own free will.' That's ridiculous. He could have stayed inside and died. Instead he came out, ok – but it certainly wasn't of his own free will."[199]

In 2004 as in 1991, Aristide refused to engage his enemies directly on their chosen military terrain. But at the point where diplomatic push came to military shove, the night of 28/29 February, there was at least one thing that Aristide remained free to do: he could still oblige his enemies to come and burn down his house. Aristide did not jump to safety, he was pushed out – what complicates the picture a little, however, is that it was Aristide himself who at the last minute managed to force his foreign enemies actually and *overtly* to push him out, by refusing to bow to their demands that he simply resign and leave on his own. Although he could do nothing to save his government in the face of implacable international hostility, Aristide was still able to make sure that the world would see who had actually been responsible for its demise. Or at least, he made sure that the world might be able to see this, once it began to open its eyes.

To make proper sense of what happened on the night of 28 February we need to keep three decisive factors in mind.

First factor: the immediate source of the threat on the night of 28 February came not from Guy Philippe but from James Foley and Thierry Burkard. Philippe was at least a week away from any sort of an assault against Port-au-Prince. We have seen that Chamblain and Philippe were indeed well-equipped to overrun the defenseless towns and hamlets of northern Haiti. The capital, however, was an entirely different prospect. Once the democratic opposition refused Noriega's proposal on Tuesday 24 February, thousands of residents began to take steps to defend themselves. Barricades went up all over the city. Though he continued to insist on non-violence, in his final speeches "Aristide urged residents of the capital not to be intimidated by the rebels," and "predicted that the rebels would be met by thousands of Haitians in the streets". On Wednesday, *Washington Post* reporters noticed that "residents of the capital generally appeared unworried about the gathering political storm."[200] From Thursday through Sunday, foreign correspondents had a hard time finding any local residents who expressed anything other than an adamant determination to stand and fight. "We'll die before we let those soldiers in," a pro-Aristide militant told the *Sentinel*, "echoing the sentiments of many Aristide loyalists."[201] It isn't difficult to see why thousands of the city's residents were determined to stop Chamblain in his tracks. On Saturday a *Los Angeles Times* reporter broke with routine to consider, for a moment, why Aristide still had so much support on the city streets. Lavalas partisans told him that "The reason we're ready to die for Aristide is that he is the only one able to bring us a better future." Others said that "If Aristide leaves now, the country will fall into an abyss"; "Aristide has done a lot for the poor"; "Aristide is the only politician that we trust"; "Aristide must stay in power for five years"; "We want peace, and we're not criminals."[202]

As the militias formed to man their barricades, on Friday a few isolated incidents of violence broke out, and the press reported (without further investigation) that at least two people had been shot. White House officials spread rumors that "Aristide may have given the order to begin killing opponents and looting businesses."[203] On Friday evening Aristide went on air again to prove the Americans wrong. As the *Herald* observed, he urged his supporters to abstain from "acts of looting and violence. And they promptly did. But he also ordered followers to be alert for rebel attacks and to man roadblocks at night [. . .]: 'Our duty as a people is to be on guard so they do not catch us by surprise,' Aristide said."[204] Once again the people took him at his word. On Saturday afternoon, thousands turned out to participate in what the *Post* described as a "furious if mostly peaceful march through the capital's commercial center."[205] Thousands more kept a bleary watch on the Saturday night. Virtually everyone I spoke to in Port-au-Prince two years after the event – people from all walks of life and from a wide range of political perspectives – agreed that on their own, the rebels could never have conquered Port-au-Prince. Patrick Elie is indignant: "Port-au-Prince would never have fallen to Guy Philippe's rebels, no way."[206] It is only appropriate that when Philippe and Chamblain finally rolled into the city, on Monday 1 March, Chamblain leaned out of the window of his truck to proclaim their thanks: "We are grateful to the United States!"[207]

Far from posing an imminent threat to Port-au-Prince, on the night of Saturday 28 February Philippe's troops were nowhere near the city. They were still marking time up in Cap-Haïtien, waiting for instructions. "Nobody has tried to contact us," an exasperated Philippe told Jane Regan on Thursday, "nobody."[208] There's nothing to suggest that Philippe or Chamblain were planning an imminent attack on the city. On the contrary, Philippe told reporters that the rebels planned to blockade the city and then "wait for the right time." Speaking on Thursday, Philippe understood perfectly well that "Port-au-Prince now, it would be very hard to take it. It would be a lot of fight, a lot of death."[209] Regan herself, the chief rebel cheerleader in the US press, noticed on Friday that as it approached the capital, "the uprising appeared headed to a standoff here – one of Aristide's last remaining strongholds."[210] Philippe later admitted that his whole "rebellion" was largely a media-manipulated bluff. "We weren't that strong and we didn't have very much ammunition, but we wanted Aristide to be afraid."[211]

The truth is that Aristide was in no immediate danger from the rebels in late February, and it is perfectly plausible to assume that if he had been able to remain in office for just another week or so his government might well have been able to regain control of the situation. There was no popular revolution and there was no crisis of leadership. The month came to an end much as it began: the elected government was simply confronted by a small though well-armed and well-funded insurrection backed by a similarly small and deeply unpopular section of the country's military and business elite. In the absence of any credible political opposition, the Lavalas administration was threatened only by around 300 thugs led by notorious criminals with deeply suspicious international connections. Even token amounts of international help from Venezuela or South Africa might have been enough to allow the government to keep going indefinitely, and with a little more time it would have become harder to stop the UN or the press from taking a closer look at the situation. Any sort of standoff, however brief, was most definitely not in the imperial interest.

Foley, Noriega and the other hawks in the US knew that they couldn't afford to wait for a week, or even for a few days. This is the second point. No doubt Foley understood, as he later admitted, that by choosing to escort Haiti's president out of the country in a US plane in the middle of the night "we gave him an alibi for the scenario he's been using ever since. We clearly walked into a trap."[212] It's reasonable to assume that Foley said and did everything he could to avoid this trap, in conversations with both Aristide and his Steele team – Powell more or less admitted as much (to the intense irritation of Steele's CEO Kenneth Kurtz) when he let slip that "The first call we received was from security people of President Aristide [who had] a question about their ability to continue protecting him," and that later on it was Aristide's "bodyguards who told him it was time to leave."[213] As a leading member of the Steele detachment points out, "We were certainly capable of getting the president out of the country on our own. We could have got him out by road or boat, if not by air, no problem."[214] From the US perspective this would have been an infinitely preferable endgame. After hours of threatening phonecalls, however, by 2 a.m. or so it seems that Aristide still wouldn't budge, and Foley himself had now run out of options. Port-au-Prince was once again on the brink of revolution, and Foley knew as well as anyone that the prospect of a quick and easy and thus media-friendly victory for Philippe was far from guaranteed. Open conflict between Philippe's group and pro-Aristide militants in Port-au-Prince could have led to utter chaos, and utter chaos isn't something that Haiti's little ruling class has any reason to relish. Meanwhile a long-awaited planeload of police munitions was due to arrive from South Africa within hours,[215] and Haiti's allies in CARICOM were growing more restive by the day; it's possible that Venezuela too was getting ready to send unilateral help. Time was now desperately short. It was growing more difficult to conceal the obvious links between the political and the military wings of the US-backed opposition, in awkward contradiction of Powell's repeated refusal to condone any sort of cooperation with "murderers and thugs." According to some well-placed sources, the French in particular were starting to panic, and were now determined to force the issue at all costs.

At some point that night, then, Foley had to settle for plan B: direct US abduction. Realizing that there wasn't a moment to lose and that there was no-one else they could trust, the US had to send some of its own most discreet troops to Tabarre to take Aristide out. This is the most obvious difference between 2004 and 1991: the imperial powers didn't just condone the second coup, they had to conduct it pure and simple. Although most of the pieces required for this contingency were already in place and had probably been arranged at least a week in advance (when extra US troops arrived to take control of the airport), nevertheless it seems that some aspects of the operation had to be improvised at the last minute. From the Franco-American perspective, the main virtue of abduction was that it would allow them immediately to silence Aristide and shut him up as a virtual prisoner in their plane without access to any means of communication for around 24 crucial hours while they helped his enemies to conquer Port-au-Prince. With Aristide already out of the picture, the prospect of open-ended conflict with his supporters would rapidly recede, and in the short term the story that a terrified president came begging for US assistance would help (and still helps) to generate some demoralizing confusion within Lavalas.

Third factor: even if Philippe posed no immediate threat that night, Aristide's own room to maneuver was rapidly vanishing beneath his feet. As we saw in chapter seven, he knew that many influential figures in the security forces had already turned against him. He had good reason to suspect that the SWAT and CIMO units were poised to join Philippe and Toussaint's allies in the USGPN at any moment. He knew that Foley had successfully blocked his request for reinforcements from Steele.[216] He knew that France and the US would do everything in their power to block the deployment of international peacekeepers, and that Lavalas itself was poorly prepared to engage in a conventional military campaign with its enemies. He also knew a last-minute call to arms might easily have spiraled out of control. Even if Lavalas managed to win the immediate battle against Philippe, the prospects for winning a longer war with Philippe's domestic and international patrons were no more encouraging in 2004 than they had been ten years before. In the process, Lavalas' longstanding and fundamental commitment to non-violence would have been compromised. In 2003–04 as in 1990–91, Aristide was prepared to make many compromises with his enemy, but when faced with a military threat he remained determined to confront it with exclusively non-military means.[217]

In the long term, Aristide's unwavering insistence on non-violence may turn out to have been the right strategic decision. The immediate price to be paid for this insistence, however, was very steep. Once Foley had said whatever he needed to say to make sure that "Aristide 'never challenged our position' that there would be a bloodbath," there was only one choice left for Aristide to make. He could remain in Tabarre and effectively commit suicide: the result would have been mass upheaval and political conflagration. Or he could "choose" to leave, in such a way as to expose the real actors in command of this choice. He could choose a scenario that forced the Americans to play their hand out in the open. This way he would at least be able to clarify the situation for the resistance that was sure to follow the abduction, on the assumption that though the short-term battle was indeed already lost Lavalas would later be able to regroup and prevail in the longer-term struggle. The movement would retain its commitment to non-violence, and eventually Aristide himself would be free to return to fight another day.

Although Aristide could not prevent himself from being forced out he was at least able to oblige the Americans to come to his house with their own troops, to escort him to the airport in their own vehicle and then to fly him out into quasi-captivity on their own plane, to a destination that could only be of their own choosing. In doing so, he left all but his most blinkered countrymen in no doubt as to who was really behind this most hypocritical stage in Haiti's ongoing "transition to democracy."

There can be no minimizing, however, the shock that accompanied the first phase of this realization. On the night of Saturday 28 February Port-au-Prince stood ready to repel any rebel assault. When news broke on Sunday morning of Aristide's "resignation," consequently, it was received with utter disbelief on the city's streets. The fiction of Aristide's free and voluntary resignation was as bold and as bald a lie as any of the many lies uttered by Colin Powell and his associates, and like the lies told to prepare the way for the US occupation of Iraq the deceit of 29 February had a devastating effect. Foreign correspondents were witness to the "shock and grief shared by many in the capital."[218] Thousands gathered outside the Palace, screaming at journalists "It's not true! The president will never leave!"[219] At first, recall OP members Belizaire Printemps and Elias Clovis, "We all thought it was a joke. No-one could believe it."[220] Until he heard what had really happened, even an unwavering Aristide supporter and life-long activist like Father Gérard Jean-Juste was crushed. A reporter was with him when he heard the news "by cell phone after finishing his sermon. His jaw dropped and his eyes turned glassy. 'I can't believe it. I never thought Titid would leave. I thought he was going to stay, but he left. It's a big disappointment for his following.' "[221]

For a few hours on Sunday morning, Aristide's supporters vented their rage and their confusion on downtown Port-au-Prince. The city was full of reporters who watched the spectacle. "Almost simultaneously, smoke began billowing from barricades at dozens of spots throughout the city, and streets that had previously been quiet and safe became gauntlets of brutality."[222] Gas stations and banks belonging to members of the opposition were torched, and property belonging to USAID and CARE was stolen. Unsurprisingly, hundreds of destitute people took advantage of the anarchy to loot the downtown shops. The police response, however, was remarkably swift. During the last days of February, people like Dany Toussaint and his associates were by all accounts closely involved in discussions with members of CIMO, the USGPN and the rest of the Haitian National Police. On 2 March, Toussaint told a *Herald* reporter who confirmed his prominence "among the businessmen and former police and army officers who have emerged to take on pro-Aristide militants" that "Guy Philippe reminds me of myself in 1991 – very young, very dynamic."[223] It isn't unreasonable to assume that the US embassy provided a little moral support. Backed up by a group of around fifty ex-military rebels and pick-up trucks full of "well-dressed" young men, a convoy of police "swooped down from the hilltop upper-class Pétionville suburb to the downtown district, stopping at nearly every block and shooting in the air to chase away looters."[224] Dozens of people were shot. (One of the only rebels interviewed the following day was proud to confess that he had shot "some looters" on Sunday, but by that stage the international press was already starting to lose interest in this side of the story.[225]) Around the same time, the national penitentiary was emptied of its 1,000 inmates, many of whom promptly joined in the new business at hand. Among the people set free that day were a number of the most notorious figures of Haiti's disbanded army, including ex-general Prosper Avril, ex-general Jean-Claude Duperval, ex-Anti-Gang unit commander Jackson Joanis and several other high-profile 1991–94 putchists. While three US Coast Guard cutters idled just offshore to intercept anyone foolish enough to try to escape the violence by sea, Scott Wilson noticed how "the State University Hospital, just blocks from the suddenly unoccupied National Palace, filled steadily with bewildered victims throughout the day. Only the doctors and nurses stayed away."[226] The bullet-riddled bodies of other victims appeared in various places around the city.

Estimates of the number of Aristide supporters killed in the first few days of the coup range from 300 to 1,000, though as the *New York Times* admitted the "total death toll was impossible to ascertain."[227] It would remain so for the next several weeks (indeed for the next several months), in part because reporters and other "independent observers" were discouraged from going anywhere near the places where virtually all of the violence was carried out: the slums inhabited by Aristide's most dedicated supporters.

That the neutralization of these slums was the real reason behind the coup was something that the residents of Bel Air, La Saline and Cité Soleil were about to find out.

10

2004: Revenge of the Haitian Elite

Konstitisyon se papye, bayonèt se fè
(A constitution is made of paper, bayonets of steel).

The perpetrators of the 2004 coup sought to portray it as a regrettable but necessary strike, on behalf of constitutional democracy, against a dictatorial regime that had lost all connection with the Haitian people. Once the steps taken to undermine this regime started to look sufficiently spectacular, the international media descended upon Haiti to observe the dénouement.[1] In addition to providing largely uncritical backing to the outright lies propounded by Bush, Powell and de Villepin, the more subtle effect of this media blitz was to distort the very conflict at issue. What was at stake in the civil war of February 2004 was not simply a struggle between a weakened administration and its immediate opponents. The campaign to "get rid of Aristide" was a diversion: the real goal of the opposition, both in Haiti and abroad, was to break once and for all the movement that had mobilized through and around Aristide. Their goal was to crush the remarkably resilient and profoundly threatening mass movement sustained by many dozens of pro-Lavalas *organisations populaires*. Their goal was to make sure that whatever happened, the next presidential election would not be lost to the same sort of people as the elections of 1990, 1995 and 2000. Needless to say, the whole logic behind the 2004 coup would come crashing down if in the next round of elections the people of Haiti dared to choose yet another pro-Lavalas president.

In the short term, to avoid this outcome would require: the formation of a suitably reliable de facto government, made up exclusively of members of the ruling elite and reinforced with the requisite amounts of foreign money and military power; a campaign of direct aggression against Lavalas organizations, especially in the places where they remained most powerful and most concentrated (the slums of Port-au-Prince); the manipulation of an electoral process that might serve to divide and contain the Fanmi Lavalas party, and to discourage the majority of the population from supporting a Lavalas candidate. In the longer term, it would require intensification of the processes that might "integrate" Haiti into a suitably stable regional order: the adoption of untrammeled privatization and neo-liberal adjustment, increased reliance on foreign aid, increased penetration of the economy by foreign NGOs, increased international supervision of the national police, and so on. All of these measures would serve to reinforce the class barriers that were briefly threatened by the ad-hoc alliance of 1990 and then challenged by a united and well-organized Fanmi Lavalas in 2000.

THE IMMEDIATE AFTERMATH OF 29 FEBRUARY

Although an important part of the official logic behind the coup was that Aristide's government had become too weak and too unpopular to retain any constitutional legitimacy, once again the reality was very different. In spite of all it suffered under the impact of the long destabilization campaign, by every available measure Lavalas continued to enjoy the support of most of the population. Risky public demonstrations of enthusiasm for the government faded away, of course, in some of the places that were directly vulnerable to rebel intimidation; one of the most striking features of the international coverage of February 2004, however, is the frequency with which even pro-coup journalists bore witness to the determination of Aristide's supporters to defend their political investment and to ensure their political if not physical survival. Memories of the violence suffered in 1991–94 remained fresh in their minds. Port-au-Prince resident Willy Dumeria, cited in the *New York Times* on 11 February, spoke for thousands of Aristide loyalists when he denounced the opposition as "terrorists" who "don't respect the government. [. . .] But we will take care of them and save our power. With everything I have got I will fight them."[2] Over and over, reporters were harangued by people who told them "We will fight to the death."[3] A typical member of one of the groups manning a barricade against anti-FL demonstrators, Harold Geffrand (who described himself as a small business owner) asked an AP reporter in mid-February: "If those guys get power can you imagine what would happen? They would destroy and destroy and destroy."[4] It's no surprise then that in the slum of La Saline, for instance, news of Aristide's abduction was met in equal measure with outrage, determination and fear. "It's a violation of our constitution," said one resident: "We had a president who was elected for five years." Now that he is gone, said another, "We are worried that we will be killed, and that the guys with the guns will not put them down. We will have to fight back."[5] Ernseau Bolivar, a student living in La Saline, tried to get the *New York Times* to grasp the point that his neighbors already understood only too well. "The army and the people with money always were against the poor. Traditionally the political class used the army to oppress us. That is what we fear. President Aristide made a lot of mistakes, it is true. But he was always representing people of the poor, people of my class." Bolivar could see perfectly well what his interviewer could not. "He said he thought Mr. Aristide had been forced out by American pressure. He called the president's fall a coup. 'We elected Mr. Aristide,' Mr Bolivar said. 'How can the Americans now come and take him away? What about our Constitution? What about our laws?' "[6] Sony Aurélien, a port-inspector who lives in La Saline, made the same point a few days later. "With Aristide, for the first time we have started to live. I am the first one in my family to have a regular job. Aristide tried to lift us up, so America kidnapped him and took him away."[7]

For a brief moment on Sunday 29 February, it might have seemed that the sort of popular uprising that has long terrified the ruling elite could finally materialize. As thousands of furious young men gathered outside the empty national palace they told journalists: "If Aristide has left we're going to reduce this country to ash. We're going to burn it to the ground and chase down the bourgeoisie and burn them in their homes. They'll all be hiding in holes." With Aristide gone, it might have seemed that there was nothing to mediate the naked class antagonism that structures Haitian society. "The rich took our president, so now we're going to take everything of theirs."[8] For a few hours, the spectre of Dessalines loomed large over Port-au-Prince.

In fact, in 2004 as in 1991, overtly armed resistance to the coup was very quickly suppressed. As counter-revolutionaries have always understood, it is much easier to split and control a revolutionary movement if you can first force it onto paramilitary terrain: the political evolution of people like Jean Tatoune and Dany Toussaint provides graphic confirmation of the point. Acutely mindful of this danger, rather than seek to develop anything like an organized military wing of Lavalas, Aristide had done everything possible to discourage it. Of course he could not dissuade groups of their most vulnerable and impoverished supporters from forming informal gangs to defend themselves, but Aristide never wanted to issue, and never tried to issue, anything like a national call to arms. If he *had* issued such a call, reckons Patrick Elie, Port-au-Prince would have exploded overnight.[9] Instead, by eliminating Aristide so unexpectedly, the US and France decapitated the resistance before it began. After just a few hours of anarchy, by mid-afternoon on Sunday 29 February a combination of police, insurgents and opposition vigilantes had scattered most of the FL militants. By Monday 1 March the majority of them were already contained in the slums where they live, and for the next couple of years the main challenge for FL and OP leaders in places like Bel Air and Cité Soleil was simply to stay alive.

Despite all the talk of marauding bands of Lavalas "*chimères*," therefore, what pro-coup leaders needed to do in early March was not break the back of a quasi-military movement so much as beat a bitterly resentful population into submission. The real issue was again political, rather than military. Given the nearly unanimous support for Aristide and Lavalas in the slums, and given the massive and well-organized electoral blocs that they represent, what could be done to contain the democratic threat? What could be done to make sure that when the time finally came for another presidential election, a reliable establishment candidate would be sure to come out on top?

The first priority of the putchists of 2004 – Powell and de Villepin, along with their various Haitian accomplices (Jodel Chamblain, Himmler Rébu, Evans Paul, Hérard Abraham, Andy Apaid, Charles Baker, Dany Toussaint . . .) – was of course to take advantage of the initial confusion to deal as powerful a blow against their class enemies as political decorum allowed. Anonymous and defenseless victims were fair game; high-profile figures in the Lavalas administration, or anyone who might have international connections, generally wound up in exile or in prison, rather than dead. On this condition, for at least a few days Chamblain, Dany Toussaint and the rest of the macouto-bourgeois opposition had more or less a free hand to inflict as much damage as was compatible with another US priority, the prevention of anything resembling the unsightly exodus of refugees that accompanied the previous restoration of the status quo, back in 1991.

As they rolled into Port-au-Prince on Monday 1 March, "armed rebels said in interviews that they intended to kill suspected gang members loyal to the president,"[10] and that's exactly what they did. Over the next couple of days many hundreds of Lavalas supporters were killed, up and down the country. In the battleground that was Saint-Marc, for instance, the anti-FL gang RAMICOS took its revenge against the OP Bale Wouze, and in the first three days of March executed around twenty of their enemies.[11] In Cap-Haïtien, dozens of Aristide supporters were shot and many others were abused, intimidated or incarcerated in cargo containers. "It was chaos," remembers the director of Cap-Haïtien's Radio Africa, "and scores of people were killed."[12] All across northern Haiti, rebels would continue to wield absolute and entirely unsupervised power for several months, acting as judge and executioner with complete impunity. As even the UN had to acknowledge towards the end of March, towns like Fort Liberté were forced to live at the mercy of the murderers and other criminals freed when the rebels torched the court-houses and police stations and opened their jails. For much of the spring of 2004 Chamblain held court in Cap-Haïtien, undisturbed by any international supervision. Although reporters rarely made the long trip up to Cap-Haïtien from the capital, the *Associated Press* confirmed on 23 March that "dozens of bullet-riddled bodies have been brought to the morgue in the last month." A small detachment of French soldiers arrived in Cap-Haïtien a couple of weeks after Aristide's ouster, but "neither the French soldiers nor the police have taken any action to free Aristide supporters illegally detained by rebels, or to confiscate weapons." Down in Les Cayes, continued Reuters, "armed rebels who helped oust Haiti's first democratically elected leader carry out public executions, unchal-lenged by police or foreign troops. In the main square every morning, they shoot accused thieves before an expectant crowd" without the least semblance of any judicial process.[13] Ti Gary, a prominent anti-Lavalas militant and leader of a local group of around thirty rebels, publicly admitted to carrying out at least five executions in Les Cayes in the immediate coup aftermath. Similar legal services were provided in the town of Petit Goâve by a group of rebels led by Ti Kenley, in cooperation with ex-FAdH personnel.[14] Reporting from Haiti in mid-May, Stan Goff observed that ex-army and "ex-FRAPH paramilitaries are now basically running around doing anything they want, anywhere they want [without] being interfered with in the least by French, Canadian, or American troops, taking over town after town after town and imposing themselves as local governments."[15] The new rulers of Haiti made no effort to hide their complicity with the paramilitaries. In the Central Plateau, for instance, former army sergeant Joseph Jean-Baptiste took on the role of acting as Chamblain's deputy in Hinche and refused to disarm his growing band of ex-soldiers – perhaps several hundred men by mid-April. Around thirty Chilean troops began spending occasional days in

Hinche in late April, returning to their barracks in Port-au-Prince at night; shortly after their deployment, Tom Reeves notes, "two police stations and the Hinche FL headquarters were burned."[16]

Back in Port-au-Prince, meanwhile, as soon as the rebels arrived they promptly began punitive incursions into areas like La Saline and Bel Air that left hundreds of people dead or missing.[17] Working side by side with the newly "depoliticized" PNH, the ex-army rebels were further strengthened by scores of affluent vigilantes who descended from Pétionville to help hunt down "pro-Aristide gangs." Reporting for the *Boston Globe*, Steven Dudley accompanied one of several such "upper-class paramilitary groups" as it set to work in Cité Soleil in the immediate aftermath of the coup. Armed with M-4 or M-14 assault weapons and led by young, affluent and US-educated businessmen like Sean Saint-Remy and Peter Calixte, they waited until the initial police assault had forced FL militants to retreat back to their slums. Then "as darkness settled, Calixte and dozens of other paramilitaries went out in groups of 10 to 15 men to finish the job. 'We went down every alley, every street. We're cleaning up the neighborhoods,' said one of Calixte's colleagues."[18] Survivors of these incursions testify to the fact that "more people died after 29 February 2004 than 30 September 1991; although during the first coup many Aristide supporters were killed or disappeared, back then we didn't have to endure a systematic campaign of open shooting in the streets."[19] By 3 March 2004, the eight largest hospitals in Port-au-Prince had already stopped admitting patients.[20] The state morgue in Port-au-Prince normally dumps around 100 bodies a month – these are bodies that are never claimed by relatives, either out of fear of public association with the deceased or because they cannot afford to pay for a burial. According to the morgue's director, some 800 bodies were "dumped and buried" on Sunday 7 March. As he explained in April to a human rights delegation led by the Miami-based lawyer Tom Griffin, bodies are normally kept for twenty-two days before being dumped. By coincidence, however, the motor in the morgue's refrigerator broke down on 29 February, forcing the director to reduce this period to just four or five days. By further coincidence and in spite of the unprecedented resources that would soon be put at the disposal of the post-coup government, it apparently took a full year to fix this troublesome motor. In the meantime bodies would have to be dumped by the truckload on a regular basis, many with their hands still tied around their backs and bags over their heads. Griffin's team was able to confirm some isolated details of the bigger picture. On 23 March, between forty and sixty corpses were partially burned just off the

Piste d'Aviation near Port-au-Prince, and on 28 March, the city morgue dumped another 200 bodies.[21] It is certain, moreover, that the number of bodies collected by the morgue is itself only a fraction of the total number of people killed. Residents of the capital's slums quickly became used to the sight of bodies abandoned to the pigs that root for food on the side of city streets, or washed up on the "beaches" around Port-au-Prince; Father Rick Freshette and his group of volunteers were still collecting semi-decomposed bodies in and around Cité Soleil almost every day, right through to the end of 2005.

Neither the domestic nor the international media were encouraged to delve too deeply into what was going on. Several pro-Lavalas journalists were abducted and beaten (Lyonel Lazarre on 30 March; Jeanty André Omilert on 16 April; Charles Prosper on May 15). In May Justice Minister Gousse closed down the pro-Aristide station Radio-Télé Timoun and arrested one of its cameramen.[22] In the most high-profile incident, on 7 March 2004, unidentified marksmen killed seven people during an anti-Aristide rally, including a Spanish correspondent, Ricardo Ortega; an American photographer was badly wounded. Although the US and the IGH blamed the shootings on pro-Aristide militants (including the musician Yvon Antoine) their version of events was contradicted by some witnesses on the day and in September, when one of Ortega's Spanish colleagues went to Haiti to investigate his death, he concluded that Ortega was probably killed by US troops.[23] After the initial furore, the Haitian and international authorities soon let the matter drop.[24]

The relentless violence had an immediate political effect. For weeks after Aristide's overthrow, the names of people included in the new government's lists of "most wanted" were broadcast by pro-coup radio stations. Anyone associated with Lavalas or indeed with any sort of *organisation populaire* went into hiding or internal exile. Tom Griffin's delegation met with around thirty members of organizations involved in FL-related literacy and street-children programmes a month after the coup, and noted that "every single one of them has been in hiding since March 1st."[25] As in 1991–94, in the spring of 2004 the elaborate and fragile network of popular organization that enables so many poor Haitians to endure their destitution was smashed beyond any hope of immediate repair.

The day after Philippe's rebels arrived, the residents of Port-au-Prince were witness to a spectacle that anticipated much of the spirit and the practice of the new regime. The building that once served as the army headquarters stands near the national palace; after disbanding the army, Aristide had turned it into the new Women's Affairs Ministry, and in the weeks before the coup the building had come to serve as a temporary exhibition space for an exceptionally valuable collection of Haitian art celebrating the bicentennial of independence. On 2 March, as a small crowd of supporters cheered outside, Philippe and a group of ex-soldiers rampaged though the building, and began tossing paintings, crosses, coffins and other material from the exhibition out of the windows. A few dozen of their supporters set the wreckage on fire. The mayhem prompted one bystander to say "This is the worst thing I've ever seen in my life: they are sacrificing the new regime at its baby stage."[26] From the balcony of the ex-museum Philippe then proclaimed himself Haiti's new ruler. "I am the chief. The military chief. The country is in my hands." While he was speaking, noted the *New York Times*, Philippe's men "scoured the slums, which formed Mr. Aristide's strongest political base, seeking out Aristide loyalists."[27]

Although Philippe's patrons back in Washington were quick to remind him of the need for more discreet language, there was nothing discreet about US priorities during that first week of March. Despite the fact that hundreds of Marines were already in control of the city by the morning of Monday 1 March, it wasn't until the end of Wednesday that some of the 2,000 foreign troops began heavily armored patrols of the more public sections of downtown Port-au-Prince. The main purpose of such patrols was not to protect ordinary people from rebel reprisals but to soften up "hostile" neighborhoods by clearing away their last remaining defenses, the makeshift barricades erected to ward off rebel attacks. Foreign reporters kept a respectful distance but the *New York Times* described Wednesday as "a day of violence and fear in the capital," as "rebels and the police battled Aristide loyalists with volleys of gunfire in the squalid slums that sent thousands of people fleeing."[28] In the midst of the gunfire, US officials did their best to explain to jeering local residents why their Marines "have no instructions to disarm the rebels" and "were under orders not to use force to halt Haitian-on-Haitian violence."[29] Journalists who visited Haiti in early April 2004 learned from numerous witnesses that in the neighborhood of Bel Air, something between fifteen and fifty people were killed and then carted away in a single attack on the night of 12 March, with the connivance (if not active participation) of US troops – as Anthony Fenton observed, the idea seemed to be that "once the fear of a militarized Haitian police and a 'trigger-happy' US military are instilled in these people, they will think twice about disrupting the new political process that is being imposed on them."[30] A further US assault on Bel Air on the night of 17 March left at least another five people dead.[31] After interviewing soldiers and city residents, Tom Reeves estimated that US troops were responsible for at least forty to sixty killings in March. Many of the Marines he interviewed, "some fresh from Iraq, defended 'pre-emptive' violence, by claiming that 'every Haitian we see could be the enemy.'"[32] Eléonore Senlis was obliged to work for a short spell as a translator for the US Marines in Cité Soleil, and immediately regretted it. "They were total assholes. They were completely paranoid, incredibly scornful of the people. They were basically moronic kids. I can remember hundreds of incidents. And their officers were so arrogant, so full of themselves, it was truly horrible."[33]

Not content with direct complicity in the mass murder of Haitian civilians, the US government was careful to invest its first new instalments of foreign aid where they were most needed: in order to seal off the only practicable escape route for slum-dwellers trapped between the rebels and the sea, the US announced in early March that it would maintain its heightened Coast Guard presence off-shore, and generously offered to pay the salaries of the Haitian Coast Guard for the next three months.[34] The "hopeful new chapter in Haiti's history" that Bush announced when he authorized the dispatch of US troops back on February 29 was now well and truly underway.

Before the political disarmament of Lavalas could take a more sophis-ticated (and still more devastating) turn, however, two other immediate tasks confronted the coupsters of February 2004. If it's too blatant, foreign intervention in a place like Haiti, as in some other places, tends very quickly to become counter-productive. Some nominal Haitians would need to be involved in the creation of a suitable post-coup government; others would have to help with the reconfiguration of an equally suitable post-coup security force.

THE RESTORATION OF DEMOCRACY

Anyone curious about what the current US government and media actually mean by the term "democracy" need look no further than the "democratic and constitutional" government that Colin Powell and a few others rigged up to replace Aristide's dictatorship in 2004. The messy and patently undemocratic business of electing a leader through popular vote was replaced, in March 2004, by a more appropriately mediated process that unfolded in four steps. First of all, to fill the immediate void left by Aristide's abrupt removal, and apparently in keeping with the letter of the Haitian Constitution, the chief justice of the Supreme Court, Boniface Alexandre, was sworn in as interim president on Sunday morning 29 February. Unfortunately, the Constitution also calls for such an appointment to be ratified by the Legislature. Since the Convergence Démocratique had rejected Aristide's every attempt to hold new elections, parliamentary terms of office had run out in January and there were now no legislators on hand to ratify the transition. In a fine gesture of support for constitutional democracy in Haiti, on the morning of 29 February US Ambassador Foley stepped into the breach as a substitute for the missing Haitian parliament, and supervised Alexandre's interim appointment himself. (Further constitutional niceties, including the facts that the appointment of an interim president can only proceed after the unambiguous resignation, impeachment or impairment of the incumbent president, or that such an appointment must be followed within ninety days by the election of a new president, or that the replacement of a president does not itself authorize the replacement of a legitimate prime minister, etc. were simply ignored altogether.[35])

The next step involved the nomination, on March 3, of a temporary "Tripartite Council" made up of representatives from the Lavalas government (Leslie Voltaire, ex-minister for Haitians Living Overseas), the opposition (Paul Denis) and the international community (Adama Guindo, from the UN Development Program). Given that Denis and Guindo were sure to speak with one voice, the creation of this democratic council already served to invert the actual balance of electoral power between Lavalas and its opponents; in any case, neither the FL organization nor Neptune's administration authorized Voltaire to represent them. The Tripartite Council's job was to appoint (in a third step) yet another council, a seven-person *Conseil des Sages* – the "Council of the Wise." Described as a broad-based group "selected from different socioeconomic and religious sectors, representing the different political persuasions found in Haitian society,"[36] apart from a minor and pliable figure in Fanmi Lavalas (Paul Emil Simon) this further Council was also entirely drawn from the anti-FL elite, including USAID/IRI/CIDA-grantees Ariel Henry (CD), Anne-Marie Issa (director of the rightwing Radio Signal FM) and Danielle Magloire (director of ENFOFANM, another elite women's rights group), along with members of the anti-Aristide clergy and the anti-Aristide university sector. It fell to these sages to pick (step four) a more suitable prime minister than Aristide's Yvon Neptune. To the irritation of Paul Denis and other members of the "proper" opposition, they chose someone who had spent most of the past twenty years in Florida – Gérard Latortue. Latortue is a neo-liberal economist and former UN functionary whose chief virtue was an irreproachable loyalty to Haiti's main imperial patron, complemented by some powerful family connections among the opposition's paramilitary wing. Although in 2004 he was invariably described as a detached and neutral figure who had played no role in the destabilization of the regime, members of the CD later admitted to well-placed members of Aristide's entourage that both Gérard and his nephew Youri had played significant roles in the coordination of the political and military components of the opposition. Unlike any other prime minister in recent Haitian history, with only a symbolic president above him and no political party beneath him, Latortue would wield effectively absolute power in Haiti for the next two years. The CD's Micha Gaillard praised Latortue as "a real professional and a man of integrity"; in the slum of La Saline, noted the *New York Times*, "Mr. Latortue's name barely registered. 'We don't know who he is,' said Ernseau Bolivar, a student. 'We want Aristide back.'"[37]

Latortue's new government didn't include a single member of Fanmi Lavalas or indeed any members of any organization that enjoys popular support. "Had there been an organization that sponsored a Lavalas member," Latortue explained to reporters, "I would have been happy [to include one]. But there weren't any."[38] In order to justify its decision to exclude Haiti's most popular party from all thirteen of the ministries of state, the new government had to pretend to keep its distance from other political parties as well. Although, consequently, none of the leading members of the CD were rewarded with a ministerial post, their organization and its allies were still well represented in Latortue's cabinet. Yvon Simeon, the new Foreign Affairs Minister, had represented the CD in Europe. PAPDA's Yves André Wainwright (Environment), Adeline Magloire Chancy (Women's Affairs), and Oxfam consultant Philippe Mathieu (Agriculture) were also members of the CD or OPL. The new Justice Minister Bernard Gousse was prominent in the Group of 184, as were Danièle Saint-Lot (Commerce and Industry) and Pierre Buteau (National Education). As Reed Lindsay notes, the IGH chose the CD's Micha Gaillard, "a light-skinned member of the elite and leader of one of Haiti's myriad fervent anti-Aristide political parties, with negligible popular support, to head its national dialogue commission."[39] In a particularly ominous sign of what was to come, the Ministry of the Interior went to Latortue's old friend and fellow Floridian ex-general Hérard Abraham, who had plenty of opportunity to influence a process close to his heart – the reconstitution of the substance of the Haitian army within a newly reworked Haitian police.

Beyond its primary political purpose (the repression of Lavalas), Latortue's government is not likely to be remembered for doing a great deal. As Father Rick Freshette put it a month before the end of Latortue's administration in 2006, "It has done absolutely nothing, nothing with a capital N. It's been an absolute dead loss."[40] On the other hand, it managed *not* to do an impressive number of things. In March 2004 Aristide's literacy programme was abandoned overnight. Subsidies for schoolbooks and school meals were canceled. Agrarian reform came to a halt, as former landowners began to reclaim land that had been redistributed to peasants through legislation initiated by Préval.[41] The collection of income taxes was suspended for three years, supposedly to compensate members of the elite who had suffered property damage during the elite-sponsored insurgency (no state support, needless to say, was offered to the thousands of poorer citizens who lost property let alone relatives during the coup). As the last remaining price controls and import regulations were lifted after Aristide's departure, the handful of leading comprador families who dominate Haiti's ruling class took advantage of the decline of local agricultural production to help push food prices up by around 400 percent; the price of rice had already doubled just five months after the February coup.[42] The new university at Tabarre was shut down and remains occupied by UN troops to this day. Having outlived its strategic utility, the student movement that had earned such praise in the independent media in the last months of 2003 faded into sullen resignation.[43] Despite the injection of new international money – $1.2 billion in heavily conditional "aid" was pledged at a donors' conference in July 2004 – the president of the Haitian Association of Economists noticed that eight months into its mandate the de facto government had still "done nothing in the areas of job creation, production, public works."[44]

One of the most important things that Latortue undid was Aristide's own small contribution to job creation. Almost as soon as he took control of a country with 70 percent unemployment, Latortue fired several thousand public sector employees. Many of the people thus sacked from the municipal government, port authority or state telecommunications company lived in poor neighborhoods, and many supported a large extended family on their single paycheck. (A good many of them also found their names advertised on long lists of "*chimères*" who had been fired and barred from re-applying for their jobs; inclusion on such a list was equivalent to a death sentence, and forced hundreds of people to go into hiding.) At a stroke, the loss of these jobs without any sort of compensation or re-training reversed in many parts of Port-au-Prince Aristide's modest attempt to move from abject misery to a semi-dignified poverty. As they tumbled into utter destitution in the spring of 2004, many of these ex-employees would be left with little means of survival other than those provided through affiliation with semi-criminal/semi-political gangs. Along with this purge of public sector workers, the beginning of the Latortue government also ended the careers of many thousands of elected officials. The entire electoral system, both national, regional and municipal, was overthrown in February along with the elected president. Although in many cases (thanks to the opposition's refusal to participate in new elections) their terms had already expired in early 2004, under Latortue Haitian democratic practice was at last brought back into line with US democratic theory as locally elected leaders were replaced *en masse* by hand-picked appointees. No less importantly, notes Brian Concannon, "in 2004 and 2005 the Minister of Justice illegally pushed out trial judges appointed by Haiti's democratic governments and replaced them with people willing to do the IGH's bidding; these de facto judges remain in their posts to this day, and they will continue to wield considerable political influence in Haiti for the foreseeable future."[45]

Critics of the 2001–04 Lavalas administration may be entitled to claim that it did not do enough to benefit the poor. Nevertheless the contrast is startling between what the defenseless and cash-starved FL government managed to accomplish – small but significant advances in health and education, investment in public spaces and social housing, the creation of thousands of new jobs for residents of the poorest neighborhoods, the doubling of a grossly inadequate minimum wage – and the sheer absence of any pretence of social investment under Latortue's incomparably better armed and better funded government. By June 2005, even the little gaggle of anti-FL Sages who had appointed the new prime minister were prepared to dismiss his government as a "failure," and warned that their Council "will soon issue an ultimatum to Latortue: bring the country under control in thirty days or resign."[46]

As far as its domestic and international sponsors were concerned, perhaps the only significant benefit to emerge from the Latortue débâcle was the more or less self-imposed emasculation of a large part of the official Fanmi Lavalas leadership. With or without Aristide, the persistence of Fanmi Lavalas posed a significant challenge to any post-coup regime. Even Latortue could see that an outright ban on Haiti's only popular political party might be counter-productive, and at least in public the great powers had to keep up the pretense that in any future elections it was "absolutely necessary" that Lavalas be free to participate.[47] So long as a Lavalas politician like ex-senator Yvon Feuillé could claim that Lavalas was the "victim of a political massacre," the democratic orientation of the post-Aristide era might remain open to debate. "Without Lavalas," Feuillé said in March 2004, "there is no solution; without Lavalas, there won't be the peace we need so much."[48] This was never going to be an easy argument to evade. The only alternative to mere exclusion was a variation on the classic formula of divide and rule – a combination of carrots and sticks that might buy off a couple of mid-level FL function-aries, in the hope that their defection would embroil the party in permanently debilitating dissension. In this sense, the Latortue episode helped to accelerate a tendency that had already begun some years before, namely the progressive betrayal of the Lavalas project by a certain number of its more opportunistic functionaries. No sooner had Aristide been forced out of the country than someone somehow found the leverage to persuade his former chief of staff Leslie Voltaire to participate in the absurd "Tripartite Council" invented by the US/OAS to kick-start the post-coup process of democratic transition. Voltaire's collusion in this process seemed to lend it a degree of political legitimation. So did ex-prime minister Yvon Neptune's decision – under extreme if not irre-sistible pressure from the US embassy – to remain in Haiti as a familiar public face at a time when most of his FL colleagues were forced into hiding or exile. US Marines made a point of "protecting" Neptune for a few weeks after 29 February. As we'll see in a moment, as soon as this little gesture had served its purpose they abandoned him, along with the rest of the FL leadership that they couldn't buy off, to the tender mercies of Justice Minister Gousse and the National Penitentiary.

It's not hard to imagine the sort of pressure that was put on Voltaire and Neptune in early March 2004. What's less clear is how, over the course of 2004–05, a handful of other high-profile FL leaders (ex-senators Louis-Gérald Gilles, Louis Hériveaux, and Yvon Feuillé, along with a few others the *baz* came to dismiss as "embassy-Lavalas") were induced to sign up to an especially important part of the post-coup project: the validation of an electoral process in which Fanmi Lavalas would cease to enjoy an unfair political advantage, i.e. the advantage of having significant levels of popular support. As Ambassador Foley put it towards the end of April 2004, when he started to push what was left of Lavalas to endorse proceedings that would initiate a new round of elections, "We cannot be held hostage by a party that doesn't want to play the democratic game."[49]

It would take another year before it started to become clear what this game would involve for the FL leadership. To anticipate a little on subsequent events, in the summer of 2005 the interim government found itself under increasingly intense pressure to arrange for the election of its replacement. The official FL position, defended by exiled leaders like Jonas Petit as well as prominent *baz* members like Moïse Jean-Charles and John Joseph Jorel, was an echo of the line held by Mandela and South Africa's ANC back in the early 1990s. The organization decided to boycott the elections so long as it was obliged to fight them with both hands tied behind its back, i.e. so long as its leading potential candidates were in prison or in exile, so long as its members continued to suffer direct persecution by the state, and so on. But as the deadline for the registration of new presidential candidates approached, in late August, ex-FL-senators Feuillé and Hériveaux abruptly adopted Aristide's old opponent Marc Bazin as "their" candidate, and two other formerly influential figures in the party, Jean-Marie Chérestal and Louis-Gérald Gilles, decided to present themselves (briefly) as candidates in their own right. As shallow an opportunist as any member of Haiti's political class, Gilles is now best remembered for his apparent treachery during the crisis of February 2004.[50] When I spoke to Gilles in April 2006 he made little attempt to hide the degree to which he had come to accept a version of Ambassador Foley's own vision for Haiti's future – a vision that included much closer economic integration with the US, the compulsory teaching of English in all Haitian schools, a principled distance from Castro, Chávez and other "Latin American idiots," as well as an acceptance that certain high-profile Haitian exiles should remain permanently out of the country.[51] The participation of pseudo-FL leaders like Gilles and Hériveaux in the 2006 election appeared to give some legitimacy to the post-February transition to democracy. Their maneuvering threatened to split the party down the middle.

For a few short days in early September 2005, it might have seemed that part of the anti-Aristide dream had finally come true.

THE RE-MILITARIZATION OF
THE HAITIAN NATIONAL POLICE

Along with a suitably stable and broad-based government, the other main priority of the 2004 putschists was the re-development and re-education of a more army-friendly Haitian National Police. Here again Latortue had to tread a rather fine line. To accomplish his main objective he needed to re-organize the old death-squad network, but he had to do this in such a way as to avoid offending the new humanitarian sensibilities of his patrons. The paramilitaries and neo-Macoutes had an essential role to play in preserving the status quo, but international capitalism sometimes finds that unalloyed violence is a poor guarantee of stability.

On the one hand, then, the US made it clear that it had learned an important lesson from 1986–90 and 1991–94: a return to outright military dictatorship was not likely to provide the sort of long-term security that imperial democracy requires. Aristide's dissolution of the army in 1995 was the most popular and significant thing he ever did. Even the head of US Southern Command, General James Hill, seemed unambiguous. "There is no need for a Haitian Army," he insisted in early March 2004. "I was [in Haiti] when President Aristide disbanded it, and that was the correct thing to do at the time."[52] As far back as 1988/89, the donors had become increasingly unhappy with their main Haitian investment. In its old institutional form, the army was expensive, wasteful and incompetent, and it no longer offered either a sustainable means of controlling the domestic population or a cost-effective channel for recruiting a small number of poor black people into the governing elite. Both in public and in private, therefore, the US was careful to discourage any immediate reconstitution of the old army and to warn against any straightforward adoption of Chamblain's ex-army rebels as the nucleus of a new security force.

Latortue and Abraham were visibly disappointed.[53] Their reluctant adoption of the new international policy involved a degree of public relations finesse that escaped some of these rebels themselves, many of whom clearly believed that they were *already* part of a reconstituted army. As ex-corporal Ravix Rémissainthe would try to explain all through the middle months of 2004, "The government doesn't need to reconstitute us. We are here. We have always been here. The only thing the government has to do is pay us the 10 years they owe us and let us do our jobs."[54] The promise of getting their old jobs back seems to have been the main incentive offered to FLRN recruits. It was also a perfectly explicit ambition. When Chamblain's men overran Hinche in mid-February 2004, they announced that the army had been "remobilized"; as Philippe lounged around the pool with his men in the Mont Joli hotel he told anyone willing to listen that "they would form the nucleus of a reformed Haitian Army, which was disbanded by Mr. Aristide in 1995."[55] The US kept quiet when on 1 March Philippe announced that "We are going to remobilize the army, constitutionally."[56] Powell and Noriega quickly spoke out, however, when the following day an over-excited Philippe strayed off his script and declared himself chief and master of Haiti *tout court*. "He is not in control of anything but a ragtag band," Noriega retorted, adding that as foreign troops begin to assume direct control of the country Philippe's own role would become "less and less central in Haitian life, and I think he will probably want to make himself scarce."[57] By Wednesday 3 March Philippe's main mission was already accomplished, and Colonel Charles Gurganis (the preliminary commander of US forces in Haiti) reminded him of who was really in charge. While White House spokesman Scott McClellan assured the world that there could be "no place for thugs, criminals, and the so-called rebels in Haiti's political system," a chastened Philippe met the press later in the day to acknowledge that "We can't fight here. The US asked us to lay down our weapons [. . .]. We are dismantling the front." He announced that his troops would shortly hand their guns over to the national police and then return to Cap-Haïtien and the surrounding countryside.[58]

Over the course of 2004 a gap soon emerged between "legitimate" rebels like Philippe and Chamblain (who when asked whether he intended to take control of a reconstituted army knew enough to answer, "with a smile, 'that's my secret'"[59]) and other once-useful pawns like ex-corporal Ravix Rémissainthe. From 2001 through 2004 Ravix was a leading member of Philippe's strike force. Now that they were in power, Ravix and his friends expected their old allies in the democratic and international opposition to keep their word and to issue them new uniforms. They expected gratitude for their contributions to security and democracy in the Central Plateau over the past couple of years. In 2004 as in 1991–94, they expected to play a leading role in restoring stability to places like Bel Air and Cité Soleil. They also expected back-pay for the years of undignified unemployment they had suffered since 1995. Some of these expectations were met – around $30 million back-pay "due" to ex-soldiers was indeed paid out, in instalments that began in January 2005. As of October 2004, a semi-regular contingent of around 300 armed and uniformed ex-FAdH soldiers still remained on active and public duty in Pétionville (billeted in a housing complex owned by Jean-Claude Louis Jean), and continued to make regular armed incursions in neighborhoods like Bel Air, Martissant and La Saline. Their deputy commander, Jean-Baptiste Joseph, told human rights investigators that "a force of 5,000 of the irregular FAdH soldiers is currently on 'active duty' throughout Haiti."[60] By the autumn of 2004, however, it had finally started to dawn on poor Ravix and his men that their dream of reincorporation into a conventional army was never going to come true. As far as the elite was concerned, by the end of 2004 the combination of an enhanced PNH and limitless international firepower made lumbering old-fashioned soldiers redundant. The reckless Ravix started to denounce the Latortue government as weak and indecisive, and warned that hundreds of ex-FAdH troops under his command stood ready to intervene. Ravix also began to denounce the treachery of the CD and the US in radio interviews that must have made for uncomfortable listening in Pétionville and Washington. On Radio Solidarité and other stations, Ravix openly admitted that in the run-up to February 2004 his paramilitary squad had been armed, funded and supported by members of the G184 and the de facto government, including Gousse and Abraham.[61] In December 2004, tension between Ravix's little death-squad and UN troops boiled over into open conflict, and Ravix tried to remobilize his troops in a pathetic parody of "guerrilla war." After several months of cat and mouse, a combination of SWAT and UN troops caught up with him in April 2005, and in a couple of dramatic shoot-outs they left Ravix, his friend René "Grenn Sonnen" Anthony and five of their associates dead.[62]

Short of giving carte blanche to an embarrassing liability like Ravix, from the day he took office the most important and most pressing priority on Latortue's agenda was to reincorporate as much of the old army and death-squad structure as was compatible with his new democratic authority. Rather than the army per se, however, the US insisted that the official vehicle of national security had to remain a "civic" albeit thoroughly re-oriented Haitian National Police. As we saw in chapter two, back in the late 1990s the US and its allies had begun to lose control of the PNH – a development which more than any other contributed to their characterization of the Préval/Aristide governments as authoritarian. In 2004, with the cooperation of old hands like Youri Latortue, the new police team led by ex-Coast Guard Commander Léon Charles made political reliability and/or ex-military experience the essential criteria of promotion and recruitment. On 22 March, Latortue's new Interior Minister ex-general Abraham went public with his plans to integrate many of Chamblain's paramilitaries into the police force.

As Ira Kurzban points out, US ambassador Foley was well-qualified to assist Abraham and Latortue in their work. "Foley had integrated the death squads into the army in Kosovo and I believe he was brought in to do the same in Haiti. In the months following the coup USAID paid for three KLA members to 'assist' in the integration of former FAdH members into the Haitian police."[63] Hundreds of "political" police officers were duly laid off, and in the first post-coup months around 1,000 or so former soldiers were hired to replace them. On the last day of March Guy Philippe obligingly provided Léon Charles with a list of more than 1,500 recommended names, and "individuals with a military background made up 85 percent of the first class of post-coup police academy graduates."[64] A month after Aristide's expulsion, FL deputy Ramilus Bolivar observed that before the coup only two of the ten national "chiefs of police were former military; now they are all military."[65]

By the autumn of 2004 this "depoliticized" PNH had evolved into the domestic extension of the foreign occupation force. "What we've been seeing," Patrick Elie explained in October, is the "remilitarization of the repressive apparatus in Haiti, most especially the Ministry of the Interior [. . .]. Ex-officers of the Haitian army are quietly coming back and organizing this ministry along the lines of how it was always organized during the dictatorship."[66] Over the summer of 2004, Abraham enlisted some of the most notorious criminals of the pre-1994 era, including ex-colonel Williams Regala (implicated in the 1987 election massacres) and ex-colonel Henri-Robert Marc-Charles (implicated in the 1990 Piatre massacre).[67] In the de facto prime minister's office, meanwhile, Youri Latortue had a free hand (along with a monthly $20,000 slush fund) to develop less formal means of providing security. Well-placed sources close to the prime minister's office suggest that Youri Latortue and his assistant Jean-Wener Jacquitte were intimately involved in the creation of the Lame Timachete, for instance, which was responsible for a number of gruesome attacks in the summers of 2005 and 2006. A substantial chunk of Youri's money was also spent on police informants in Bel Air and other sensitive neighborhoods. Given the regularity of Guy Philippe's visits to Youri's office, it's reasonable to assume that some of Youri's money also found its way into the hands of people who had established their security credentials during the 2004 insurgency.[68] (By the summer of 2006, uncle Gérard himself was obliged to confess to reporters that Youri was "shady," and he was careful to "distance" himself from Youri when he ran for and won a Senate seat the previous February. " 'He did provide me first-class security,' Latortue said. 'Everybody feared him. The people who wanted to kill me confessed that, if he was not here, it would have been easy to kill me.' "[69])

Every credible human rights investigation that visited Haiti in 2004–05 confirmed the same essential point: after quickly absorbing reliable members of the former military or paramilitary, the PNH redeployed them, in conjunction with US and then with UN troops, to wage an open "campaign of terror in the Port-au-Prince slums."[70] When members of Griffin's legal team spoke with and observed police officers working in the poorer neighborhoods of Port-au-Prince, for instance, they were struck by the absence of any "preliminary intelligence or detective work; there are usually no plans laid out for the arrest of a particular subject or for entry into a suspect's house," and no attempt to keep casualties to a minimum "by luring suspects away from populated areas." Instead dozens of officers, often masked (for fear of popular reprisals) and out of uniform, would descend upon densely populated areas and launch what could only be described as "indiscriminate guerrilla attacks."[71]

Whereas it had done everything possible to deprive Haiti's police of munitions when it was under the wrong political leadership, in 2004 the enforcement of the US arms embargo on Haiti (which had been initiated as a measure against Cédras, not Aristide) became rather more selective. In the summer of 2004, US Under Secretary for Arms Control John Bolton authorized the transfer of at least 2,600 guns to the Latortue regime, and in August 2005 Foley announced another $2 million shipment, explaining that as a result of "the state of insecurity in this country, the attempts to create chaos, we have to do our best to protect the people from the forces of insecurity and criminality."[72] In early 2005, however, *Small Arms Survey* analyst Robert Muggah suggested that the actual number of weapons transferred to the PNH from the US the previous year amounted to nearly 10,000 guns (5,435 "military-style weapons" and 4,433 handguns) and around a million rounds of ammunition – a package worth some $7 million.[73] In 2004–05 the PNH (and its paramilitary allies) had only one purpose for such equipment: the suppression of pro-FL activists in the slums. "The Haitian police," admitted a UN police officer in early 2006, "are the biggest gang of all."[74]

While the US was busy re-arming their new PNH, all talk of trying to disarm the ex-rebels quickly faded into a pointed silence. Just two days after Philippe made his sober promise to lay down his arms on 3 March 2004, he announced that his fighters would not actually "disarm unless they are guaranteed they will not be prosecuted for their role in forcing former President Jean-Bertrand Aristide to resign."[75] A couple of days later, Philippe promised Radio Vision 2000 that if the foreign troops don't manage to "disarm the *chimères* I will reassemble my men and take up arms again"; in the meantime, Philippe's advisor Paul Arcelin told the

Associated Press, the rebels would simply "hide" their guns.[76] Up in Gonaïves strongman Ti-Wil (Wilfort Ferdinand) made it plain that his men would never disarm before they had got rid of their enemies in the pro-Aristide camp. His colleague Winter Etienne added that they would be happy to "put down their weapons," but explained that "when you say you lay down your arms you really have to lay them down in a place where if needed they could be taken up again by the soldiers."[77] By that stage the US had already lost interest in the rebels' arsenal. "This is a country with a lot of weapons and disarmament is not our mission," US General Ronald Coleman said on 21 March, soon after he arrived to take command of the "multinational" force. "Our mission is to stabilize the country"[78] – an objective that is perfectly compatible, after all, with the ex-military's retention of arms. The 450 Canadian soldiers who joined the Franco–US invasion force in the middle of March obeyed similar rules of engagement. "Any weapons that could potentially pose a threat to the multinational force will be confiscated," said its commanding officer, Lieutenant-Colonel Jim Davis. "We will disarm the bad guys [i.e. people unreconciled to the coup and the occupation] but those people entitled to have weapons for any number of reasons yet to be defined will have an opportunity to carry them."[79] People like Ti-Wil would remain entitled to do so for the next couple of years. A protégé of the increasingly powerful Youri Latortue, over the course of 2004–05 Ti-Wil soon managed to eclipse his rivals Jean Tatoune, Winter Etienne and Buteur Métayer in the internecine squabbles that followed the national liberation struggle of February 2004, to become (by early 2006) Youri Latortue's chief enforcer in the streets of Gonaïves.

A significant fraction of the thousands of new guns delivered to the PNH by the US in 2004/2005 clearly wound up in the hands of ex-army or ex-rebel paramilitary groups.[80] By January 2006, despite unprecedented resources and many thousands of foreign troops, the disarmament and demobilization programme launched by the UN in the summer of 2004 had only succeeded in collecting a total of around thirty guns.[81]

POLITICAL PRISONS

Needless to say, so long as the government it had ousted continued to enjoy significant popular support, disarmament of the pro-coup militias who dominated post-coup Haiti was never going to be the first priority of the international community. Once the first wave of out-and-out repression had subsided and a dependable new PNH team was in place, a more pressing concern was the systematic imprisonment of Lavalas activists. In mid-March 2004 the Haitian police began arresting – rather than simply shooting – Lavalas militants on suspicion of unidentified crimes, at the same time that it decided *not* to pursue rebel death-squad leaders, including those already convicted of specific atrocities. On 14 March the new National Police Chief Léon Charles warned that the jails "would be packed in coming weeks." He explained that while "there's a lot of Aristide supporters" to be arrested, the government "still has to make a decision about the rebels – that's over my head."[82] In fact the government had already decided what to do about the rebels (i.e. incorporate many of them into Charles' own police force), and the jails would remain packed for rather more than a few weeks.

In late 2006 Haiti's jails remained full to overflowing with Lavalas sympathizers and residents of the pro-Lavalas slums. Built to house around 500 prisoners, in the spring of 2006 the squalid national penitentiary in Port-au-Prince held more than four times that number. Of the 2,115 people imprisoned there as of mid-April 2006 – around twice the number behind bars during the last month of Aristide's administration – only 81 had been convicted of a crime.[83] A large proportion of these people were picked up by police simply because they live in the wrong sort of neighborhood, or on suspicion of association with "Lavalas bandits." Analyst Ronald Saint-Jean estimated that at a minimum, more than half of the inmates were grassroots FL militants or OP members.[84] Many were kept in indescribable conditions for a full year or more. Many remain there to this day, usually held only on the utterly indeterminate suspicion of *association de malfaiteur*, a sort of vague conspiracy charge. Most were never charged with a specific crime and never brought before a judge, let alone sentenced. One of the few human rights groups that devotes real effort to getting some of these people out of jail, Evel Fanfan's AUMOHD, says that the great majority of the 100 or so young or adolescent men it has helped to set free over the past couple of years were simply picked up during police sweeps into "hostile areas," generally in Cité Soleil or the nearby neighborhoods of Pélé and Simon.[85] During their months in prison, most have no access to any sort of legal assistance and live crammed into filthy cells so small that there is often no room to lie down. For much of the autumn of 2004, for instance, the Anti-Gang unit of the PNH kept an average of 30 to 40 people in its tiny 9-feet by 9-feet jail cell.[86]

As Latortue's government consolidated its position over the spring of 2004, the number of higher-profile and overtly political prisoners rapidly increased. Aristide's interior minister Jocelerme Privert was incarcerated on 5 April. On 10 May FL activist Annette Auguste (a.k.a. So Anne) was arrested by US Marines. A warrant for the arrest of Prime Minister Yvon Neptune was issued a few weeks later, and to pre-empt assassination he turned himself in on 28 June. He joined dozens of other political prisoners in the national penitentiary, including ex-deputy mayor of Port-au-Prince Harold Sévère, ex-Director of Sanitation Paul Keller, ex-Director of Airport Security Rospide Pétion, ex-USGPN captain Anthony Nazaire, ex-regional delegate Jacques Mathelier, and ex-parliamentary deputy for Saint-Marc, Amanus Mayette.[87] Many of these people remained in prison two years later. By the time Latortue's tenure finally came to an end in the spring of 2006, Privert, Neptune, Mayette, Mathelier, Nazaire, and Sévère were still all behind bars. They had been joined by FL activists Paul Raymond, Bob Molière (released April 2006) and Yvon Antoine. René Civil also spent much of 2006 in prison.

Brief consideration of the three highest profile cases should be more than enough to illustrate the actual purpose behind Gousse and Latortue's enforcement of the rule of law.

So Anne is a well-known singer and a familiar figure at FL demonstrations and events. Now sixty years old, in May 2004 she was recovering from an operation and confined to her bed. In flagrant violation of basic legal procedure, along with eight members of her family she was arrested without a warrant in the middle of the night by a squadron of around twenty Marines in full combat gear. To the amusement of local residents, US Colonel David Lapan said the fragile grandmother represented a threat to his troops, who proceeded to blast open the gates to her house before searching it for weapons. They found none. After also failing to find any evidence of her involvement in resistance to foreign troops, Gousse and NCHR shifted their primary accusation to one of complicity in the clash between students and FL militants at the university on 5 December 2003. Three days after her arrest, the judge in charge of her case recognized that there was no evidence to back up this accusation either, but the government's prosecutor justified her detention with the explanation that "more charges were coming." The case against So Anne didn't get any stronger with time. No one came forward to accuse her of a specific role in the December incident, and prosecutors were unable to determine if she had been so much as present on the day. As this line of inquiry grew stale, prosecutors changed tack again and accused her of the more eye-catching crime of child-sacrifice. This time the charge was based on testimony of a "friend" who had left Haiti for a more comfortable life abroad, with help from Minister Gousse. Her main piece of evidence was a HaiTel phone-number that she said provided proof of her friendship with So Anne; on closer inspection, it was shown that it was indeed So Anne's number – but that it was a number she had only acquired some months *after* the alleged sacrifice was supposed to have taken place. The company HaiTel itself didn't exist at the time.[88] So Anne understood perfectly well what was going on. She told a human rights delegation in July 2004 that "They're doing this to me because I am an organizer and I stand with the people. They know that we can bring millions into the streets and they want to prevent us from doing that."[89] She was eventually released once the immediate danger of such demonstrations had passed, after being acquitted in a trial in August 2006 – a trial in which no evidence or witnesses were presented against her and her several co-defendants.

Interior Minister Privert and Prime Minister Neptune were both arrested on suspicion of collusion in the so-called "Massacre of La Scierie" in Saint-Marc, during the height of the FLRN insurgency in mid-February 2004. As we know, Gousse and NCHR paid particular attention to this incident as the single most damning piece of evidence in the general case against the brutal Lavalas dictatorship (see above, page 159). They claimed that Privert, Neptune and local deputy Amanus Mayette had helped the OP Bale Wouze to murder at least fifty anti-FL civilians in cold blood. The case should have collapsed before it could start, when reporters and investigators were only able to find evidence that three to five people had died (in an armed confrontation between Bale Wouze and the anti-FL gang RAMICOS). Despite the implausibility of the charge, the case against the two ministers dragged on for more than two full years. Like So Anne, Privert too was arrested in the middle of the night. Although accused of conspiring to kill people in Saint-Marc, prosecutors failed to name or even count how many people he had apparently helped to kill. The main accusation against him involved a phone call he made to the inspector general of police, Jean-Robert Esther. Curiously, however, the court was never told anything about the substance of this call, and Esther himself was never arrested.[90] The case against Neptune is no more convincing.[91] He is accused of visiting Saint-Marc by helicopter on 9 February, the day CIMO police reclaimed control of the town from rebels who had previously overwhelmed the police. Gousse then tried to pin the blame for the subsequent confrontation between Bale Wouze and RAMICOS on Neptune (needless to say, no RAMICOS members were arrested for their part in the insurgency and the ensuing violence). The only evidence prosecutors could come up with was the fact that Neptune had indeed visited the town a couple of days before the "massacre" and made some phone calls to local officials – not exactly a surprising thing for a prime minister to do, in the midst of an incipient civil war. No-one came forward with anything resembling proof that Neptune had been even indirectly involved with the violence in Saint-Marc. Apart from Gousse, Latortue and Espérance themselves, virtually no-one – not even the UN's Pierre Joinet – ever thought the case against Neptune amounted to anything more than a crude political joke. His health shattered by a long hunger strike, Neptune was eventually released on 27 July 2006, six weeks after Privert; the charges against them were only dropped in April 2007.

Once again the comparison between the 2004–06 and 2001–04 administrations is revealing. Nothing remotely similar to Latortue's systematic political persecution ever took place under Aristide. Aristide's government never arrested political opponents like Evans Paul or Himmler Rébu, even as they worked openly and energetically to overthrow it. There was never any campaign of mass arrests against anti-FL protestors, nor any sort of state crackdown on the expression and organization of dissent. Nor, despite the persistence of impunity and the failings of a fledgling judiciary, was there anything comparable to Latortue's grotesquely biased application of the law. While keeping hundreds of young men in prison for simply participating in peaceful pro-Lavalas demonstrations, Latortue's government did nothing to prosecute those responsible for horrific crimes that took place in full public view, like the execution in August 2005, under police supervision, of around a dozen people during a USAID-sponsored soccer match in the Port-au-Prince district of Martissant. In early April 2004 even Human Rights Watch had to acknowledge that "the contrast between the Haitian government's eagerness to prosecute former Aristide officials and its indifference to the abusive record of certain rebel leaders could not be more stark."[92]

Latortue not only turned a blind eye to violence against FL supporters (in those cases where he or his nephew didn't help organize it themselves), he also took the remarkable step of *undoing* the most significant criminal convictions in modern Haitian history. Back in 2000, FRAPH/FLRN leader Louis-Jodel Chamblain was convicted in absentia both for the 1993 assassination of Antoine Izméry and for his part in the Raboteau Massacre and several other FRAPH atrocities. On 22 April 2004, having dealt with his most urgent business in Cap-Haïtien, Chamblain turned himself in to Latortue's police in order to have his case reconsidered. Latortue's minister of justice pondered Chamblain's "great services to the nation," and assured him that he had nothing to worry about.[93] Then in a farcical re-trial that lasted just a few hours and paid no attention to the overwhelming evidence against them, on 18 August 2004 Chamblain and his accomplice Jackson Joanis were acquitted of Izméry's murder; just one of the eight witnesses called for the trial actually showed up in court (where he could say only that he had no relevant information).[94] The rest of Chamblain's exoneration effectively came through a little later, when on 15 May 2005, on the basis of a minor and impertinent technicality, Haiti's Supreme Court overturned the convictions secured in the land-mark Raboteau Massacre trial of 2000.[95] Even US Ambassador Foley, in his last speech in Haiti, decried Chamblain's acquittal and release as "a scandal for the country and for its image in the world."[96] There was nothing that Latortue could have done to emphasize more crudely the basic continuity between the first and second post-coup governments.

Prison was an important tool in the campaign to repress Lavalas, but it had its limitations. As the number of prisoners grew over the course of 2004, the police capacity to keep them under control was stretched to the breaking point. On 1 December 2004, on a day when Colin Powell passed through town to remind Latortue that "we are with you all the way,"[97] an informal protest by hundreds of inmates got out of control when their guards opened fire. The PNH admitted that ten prisoners had died in the ensuing mêlée, with another fifty wounded; witnesses interviewed by investigators from the IJDH suggested that somewhere between 60 and 110 prisoners may have been killed.[98] A couple of months later, on 19 February 2005, a small and mysterious group of gunmen stormed the national penitentiary and allowed hundreds of prisoners to escape, including Aristide's ministers Privert and Neptune who were driven off in a car by Arnel Belizaire, an ex-FAdH veteran of Philippe's insurgency. Enemies of Lavalas immediately accused "*chimère* gangs" of being behind the operation, but as Reed Lindsay pointed out it wasn't easy to understand how just a couple of blocks from the police headquarters four or five gunmen were able to "get past dozens of guards and free more than a third of the inmates before the police and UN troops arrived." Several witnesses and escapees insisted that the attackers were themselves policemen, while a "top official in the police force [hinted that] former soldiers were responsible."[99] It soon emerged that the prison break was the work of PNH insiders contracted by a group of drug-traffickers to free some of their incarcerated associates, notably Jean-Claude Louis Jean, a financial backer of Philippe's insurgency who in the autumn of 2004 provided Pétionville housing and support for Ravix Rémissainthe's ex-FAdH troop. A few weeks after the prison break (and before he was subsequently re-captured in the Dominican Republic), Arnel Belizaire helped clear up the rest of the mystery when he confessed to reporters that members of Latortue's security team with advance knowledge of the operation had tried to use it as an opportunity to assassinate Neptune. Belizaire said that government officials offered him a gun and $10,000 US to carry out the job, but when the moment came he refused to go through with it. Although he had been a staunch adversary of Aristide, after spending some time with Neptune in prison he became reluctant to kill someone whose "true personality" didn't match "the negative image painted of him by the anti-Lavalas opposition."[100]

Few members of this opposition shared such scruples. As the prisons filled up over the summer of 2004, the Latortue government was getting ready to push the persecution of pro-Lavalas neighborhoods to unprecedented levels of intensity.

11

2004–2006: Repression and Resistance

Kreyon pèp la pa gen gòm
(The people's pencil has no eraser).

With hindsight we can divide the political pacification of Lavalas in the aftermath of the 2004 coup into three rough phases. After the initial all-out assault on Lavalas activists in early March 2004, unchecked repression was allowed to continue for another couple of months in most parts of the country. Soon, however, the combination of mild indignation in the international press and the arrival of new UN troops and resources induced the government to adopt somewhat less abrasive tactics. Public executions gave way to pseudo-legal arrests and a return to more conventional forms of punitive imprisonment. International advisors were brought in to help "professionalize" and re-militarize the PNH. New police munitions poured into the country. By early summer, most of the hated US Marines had been replaced by more "neutral" UN soldiers, mainly from Brazil, Chile and Jordan. In July and August there was a relative lull in the violence. As the summer drew to a close, however, it remained painfully obvious that Latortue's mission remained far from accomplished. As far as anyone could tell, support for Lavalas and for Aristide was as strong as ever in the Port-au-Prince slums, most obviously in neighborhoods like Bel Air and Cité Soleil. Widespread public outrage over the February coup showed no sign of abating. A new round of democratic elections could never take place in such inappropriate circumstances.

But by September 2004 Latortue was ready to move to the third phase of his program. The conditions were auspicious. The PNH had been re-trained, re-armed and reinforced. If needed, thousands of UN troops could provide quite spectacular amounts of additional firepower. The independent media kept up a steady stream of stories to demonize the Lavalas "terrorists" and "bandits" in the slums. Conveniently, the international media had long since lost interest in the story, while remaining sensitive to what was fast becoming the global obsession of the day – the ever-growing need for state-sanctioned security in the face of apparently organized terror.

THE ASSAULT ON BEL AIR

The opportunity for a new crackdown came when Lavalas OPs had the audacity to organize a mass demonstration commemorating an especially provocative event – the anniversary of the first coup, on 30 September 2004. More than ten thousand people converged on Bel Air to declare once again their loyalty to Aristide and to Lavalas. Rattled by the size of the crowd, the police responded by shooting at them; between three and ten demonstrators were killed and many others wounded. Furious protesters smashed car windows before police gunfire cleared downtown Port-au-Prince.[1] Organizers of the march insisted that CIMO agents opened fire on the march as it approached the Direction Générale des Impôts. Latortue admitted that "We shot them, some of them fell, others were injured, others ran away," and announced his intention to forbid future Lavalas demonstrations. Gousse pretended that three policemen had also died during the demonstration, a claim that appeared inconsistent with his police chief Léon Charles' explanation, that one policemen had been killed and two others wounded in a quite separate incident earlier in the day (at a wharf in La Saline).[2] Gousse went on to allege that his three dead policemen had been decapitated by Lavalas extremists, as part of what he described as a sinister new "Operation Baghdad." Immediate police reprisals (combined with attacks carried out by Labanye's auxiliaries) killed around a dozen further people, including FL activists Maxo Casséus and Wendy Manigat. altogether, no less than eighty people were killed on 30 September and the first few days of October, including, said the PNH, eleven policemen.[3] On 2 October, as they contributed to a radio debate on the implications of the violence, ex-FL senators Yvon Feuillé, Louis-Gérald Gilles and Rudy Hériveaux were arrested without warrants on suspicion of complicity in the attacks on the police; Gousse denounced them as "barbaric and violent." The day they were arrested, the pro-coup human rights analyst and Latortue-ally Jean-Claude Bajeux described Operation Baghdad as a new "urban guerrilla operation" launched by FL in order to dramatize, on the Iraqi model, "the failure of US policy in Haiti."[4]

In the autumn of 2004, when the US occupation of Iraq still commanded a certain amount of trans-imperial support, "Operation Baghdad" was a felicitous phrase. (It also happened to be the title of a regular section devoted to slum violence in Haiti's most widely read newspaper, *Le Nouvelliste*.) Calls for its suppression received an automatically sympathetic hearing in places like Washington, Paris and Ottawa. Although Gousse's original version of events was quickly abandoned, in early October press reports appeared to confirm the discovery of the decapitated bodies of two plainclothes policemen. Surely there was now only a difference of degree between Lavalas and Al-Qaeda! Lavalas leaders did their best to dismiss Bajeux's accusations as a clumsy and "calculated attempt to manipulate the media and US public opinion against us. It was the police who fired on unarmed demonstrators on September 30th that started the violence. This claim of an 'Operation Baghdad' is being used to justify continuing the slaughter and arbitrary arrests of our members."[5] Activists and analysts sympathetic to Lavalas pointed out that the organization had little to gain by picking a fight with the police, and that for the previous month the G184 and other rightwing groups had been calling for more forceful incursions into pro-Lavalas slums. They pointed out that it was far from clear who might have killed or beheaded the two policemen – the simmering conflict between the police and Ravix's disgruntled ex-soldiers had already begun to boil over (see above, page 266). They said there was no evidence that Lavalas was involved in any sort of urban guerrilla operation. They pointed out that the vast majority of the violence was suffered by rather than inflicted by Lavalas partisans.[6] Even the pro-coup human rights group CARLI soon came to the conclusion that Operation Baghdad had never existed outside of the febrile imaginations of Gousse and Bajeux. A CARLI investigation concluded that two officers, Ancelme Milfrane and Jean Janvier, were indeed decapitated – but by former soldiers on 29 September, and not by FL partisans on 30 September.[7]

It didn't matter. The useful fiction that was "Operation Baghdad" stuck in the national and international media for as long as it was required. Latortue's government was now part of an embattled vanguard in the global war against terror. In early October, with Haiti's national security on the line and cheered by G184 magnates like Reginald Boulos and Andy Apaid, Latortue ordered massive and repeated multinational incursions into Bel Air and other pro-Lavalas neighborhoods in lower Port-au-Prince.

Why Bel Air? Like the adjoining districts of La Saline and lower Delmas, Bel Air is an impoverished but remarkably resilient community. It has always been an unflinching bastion of support for Aristide and for Lavalas, and it remains so to this day. Unlike the more populous but more isolated Cité Soleil, it is situated on the very edge of downtown Port-au-Prince, adjacent to the city's commercial center and just a kilometre away from the national palace and police headquarters. Its location makes it a natural meeting place and launching pad for street demonstrations. Again unlike Cité Soleil, although Bel Air is very poor its communal structure is relatively stable. Its infrastructure is basic, but not non-existent. Most inhabitants are life-long residents, and most have spent at least some time in school. Many are long-standing members of a ramified network of diverse social and political *organisations populaires*. One of the dozen or so people I interviewed at random during several trips to Bel Air in April 2006, a man in his mid-thirties called Jean-Marie, seemed to speak for most of his neighbors when he described how he and his friends "are fighting so that our voices be heard, so that we are respected, so that our constitution is respected." In 2000 as in 1990,

> we voted for Aristide, and he was kidnapped, it's as simple as that. Did he still deserve our fidelity? That's for us to decide, on our own. And it remains intact. From 1986 to this day, there has been no other leader who defended us as he did, who affirmed our convictions as he did. Look around you, you will see that everyone here feels the same way.

Jean-Marie adamantly refused to accept the February coup as a fait accompli. "It was a crime, pure and simple. We will not allow other people to make our decisions for us." Like most people I met in Bel Air, Jean-Marie expressed a similar fidelity to the local FL representatives Jean-Marie Samedy and Samba Boukman. "All through these years of violence Samba's been here, he's spoken for us, on the radio, in the press, and said what had to be said. We respect him, for his courage. He has carried our convictions. He has done good work." Samba is one of the leaders of an OP based in Bel Air, the Mouvman Rezistans Baz Popile, which works to limit the recourse to violence in Port-au-Prince, to resist the infiltration of the popular movement by armed gangs, to call for a release of the political prisoners, to insist on the return of the political exiles and the restoration of the constitutional government. Neither Samba nor Aristide nor any representative of Aristide, Jean-Marie said, comes to Bel Air to issue unilateral instructions and commands. "No, we are all struggling together, we are all fighting for our own rights; we meet, we discuss things, we decide what we should do, together." As for traditional politicians, as for someone like ex-FL-senator Louis-Gérald Gilles, they count for nothing – "We have never seen him, we have no contact with him." Jean-Marie sees no difference between the FL opportunists and the rest of the elite. "Because we live here the elite treat us as *chimères*, as pariah; because we live in such poverty, they treat us as illiterate savages. We are dying of hunger, but the police and UN only shoot at us. This is the way it has always been. And we are determined to change it."[8]

Bel Air is also a neighborhood that knows how to defend itself. Its *comités de vigilance* were at the forefront of resistance against the military dictatorships in the late 1980s and early 1990s, and many of the same people led the movement to confront the CD, the G184 and other pro-coup groups. It is this combination of poverty, solidarity and *strength* that the elite and its backers cannot endure. When the police began their murderous incursions into pro-Lavalas neighborhoods immediately after the February coup, Bel Air fought back. The day after Aristide's over-throw, a police raid on the neighborhood was repulsed and two officers were killed; their bodies were left to burn along with their pick-up truck, on Boulevard Dessalines.[9] As the Marines arrived to reinforce the police, it was Bel Air that attracted their most lethal attention. On 6 March, bemused reporters watched a patrol of around seventy-five Marines as they were challenged and then taunted by Bel Air residents; "after a brief confrontation, they left the neighborhood."[10] Although subsequent Marine attacks may have left some forty residents dead, this was far from enough to terrorize the district into docility.

Latortue's campaign in the autumn picked up where the Marines had left off in the spring. On 6 October 2004, around 150 PNH officers supported by 200 MINUSTAH troops descended upon Bel Air and arrested some seventy-five people (a police spokesperson expressed some surprise that "not a single weapon was found in the possession of the Bel Air residents"[11]). Dozens of people were jailed or shot almost every day for the next couple of weeks; on 11 October alone, another 130 people were put in prison. By November, Samba Boukman recalls, several hundred members of the local Mouvman Rezistans had been arrested. All the way through to the spring of 2005, Latortue's government took increasingly violent measures to silence the Mouvman's demands. Day after day and night after night, remembers Samba Boukman, police and other unidentified "security forces" invaded Bel Air, shooting or arresting hundreds of people, often at random. "They did everything they could to frighten us, to prevent us from saying Aristide's name, to prevent us from defending ourselves."[12] On several well-documented occasions, the police simply laid pro-FL youths down in the street and shot them in the back of the head – a dozen people were killed this way by a PNH troupe led by René Etienne in Fort National on 25 October, and another five were executed on 27 October, in the Carrefour Péan section of lower Delmas. Griffin's report includes a description and photographs of the latter incident.

> At approximately noon on that day, according to multiple witnesses, police vehicles blocked a two-block long section of Rue St. Martin, forcing traffic and pedestrians to stop. They then brought five boys out of the vehicles and forced them to lie face down in the street. The police shot them one at a time in the back of the head. One got up and ran before he was shot, was hit in the back, and died the following day at the General Hospital. The police shouted out that the bodies should be left there. Contrary to Haitian law, no Justice of the Peace came to investigate the scene.[13]

In Bel Air as elsewhere, the paramilitaries that continued to work alongside the police paid special attention to the street-kids who are almost invariably Aristide supporters; as their outraged advocate Michael Brewer observes, "There are dump zones where the decomposing bodies of little boys can be found any day of the week."[14] By 17 October the morgue at the nearby General Hospital announced that it had already received 600 new bodies, and no longer had space for additional corpses (although when Griffin spoke to morgue workers the following month, they said that "since 30 September 2004, the PNH rarely even bring people killed by violence to the morgue [but] simply take the bodies of those they kill directly to undisclosed dumping grounds"[15]).

In November, the Latortue-appointed assistant mayor of Port-au-Prince, Jean Philippe Sassine, explained the logic behind the government's strategy. "Shoot them and ask questions later," he said. "Right now our country needs security. Unless you clean up the bad people, the gangs, there will be no progress. It will be a massacre, people will die. But let us do it, or it will be worse."[16] In the last weeks before he too would have to go into hiding, ex-army corporal Ravix Rémissainthe was only too happy to offer his troupe of 300 ex-soldiers as unofficial accomplices in such a massacre. As soon as the government gives us the order, he boasted, "We can clear Bel Air and Cité Soleil of bandits in three days." Griffin's investigative team was witness to one of their innumerable joint operations, a typical police/ex-army/UN incursion into Bel Air that took place on 18 November:

> The operation began with one or two helicopters hovering over the target neighborhood, while PNH officers gathered in trucks (pickups and SUVs) and on foot just outside. Most officers were dressed in black, with black helmets and face masks; all carried large semi-automatic rifles, or fully automatic assault rifles. Once ready, they made a sudden, high speed entry into Bel Air, with officers dismounting to spread out.
>
> Before and during the PNH incursion, MINUSTAH soldiers in APCs rumbled at high speeds down streets crowded with women and children. The peacekeepers were positioned with their heads and shoulders poking out of the tanks, holding automatic rifles in the ready position aimed in all directions. Each APC had one soldier manning a large, fixed gun on top. The APCs blocked off roads surrounding the target neighborhood, preventing entry or exit by journalists, investigators and anyone else who was not a police officer or soldier.
>
> Within seconds of the PNH incursion, gunfire began, and rattled sporadically for hours. When it ended, the forces cleared out. According to some reports, the police left some bodies behind, but transported others away.
>
> The investigators gained entry to Bel Air just after the November 18 operation, in the mid-afternoon under escort from neighborhood leaders. Dead bodies were on the street. [. . .] Neighborhood residents then escorted the investigators to several homes where victims were in their beds suffering from gunshot wounds. Hercules LeFevre, shot through the shoulder, said he was walking to work when a soldier in a MINUSTAH APC shot at him with a high-powered rifle. Another was Inep Henri, age 35, found in his bed at 3:00 p.m., having been shot at 10:00 a.m. by a bullet that entered his left eye, travelled through his brain, and exited the back of his head. [. . .]. Inep was semi-conscious when investigators reached him. Like many others, he and his family stated that the police would take him away if he went to the hospital. [He died three days later].[17]

Journalist Guy Delva is as neutral a voice as any in the Haitian media, and in 2004/5 was a regular witness to the results of such police operations. In the autumn of 2004, he explains, the de facto government was absolutely determined "to block anything that might show that Aristide still had a lot of support. That's the reason behind a lot of the police operations in the slums, in Bel Air and Cité Soleil, in which the police went in and killed a lot of people. I've seen those things: you see ten bodies here, five bodies there, bodies lying in piles of garbage . . .'' All through January and February 2005 the assault continued.[18] On 25 February for instance, according to Samba Boukman, the PNH killed fourteen youths in the street, in full view of MINUSTAH troops.[19] After the worst was over, Bel Air resident Lyonel Barthelemy took another journalist on a guided tour of the ruins of his neighborhood. "Until last year, a house had stood there, Barthelemy said, but the owner had been involved with Lavalas, and the police burned it down. He took me around the block and showed me the charred remains of another home. The police again, he said. They arrested everyone who had lived there. And he pointed down another street, Rue Montalais, where police had gathered 11 young men, all suspected of ties to Lavalas. The policemen made them lie on the ground side by side, then shot them one by one."[20]

According to Oxfam, "between September 2004 and December 2004 at least 700 people in Haiti were killed by intentional arms-related violence [and] four times that number were injured."[21] No-one really knows, though, how many people died in the police assault on Bel Air and other pro-Lavalas neighborhoods like Solino, Martissant, La Saline, Village de Dieu, lower Delmas . . . The most detailed and reliable analysis to date is a September 2006 report by Athena Kolbe and Royce Hutson published in the highly respected medical journal, *The Lancet*.[22] In keeping with another recent *Lancet* study, of casualty figures in the Iraq war, Kolbe and Hutson's report isn't based on figures passively collected by government agencies or NGOs, since these pick up only a fraction of the actual amount of violence – as the *Lancet*'s editor Richard Horton points out, "Only when you go out and knock on the doors of families, actively looking for deaths, do you begin to get close to the right number. This method is now tried and tested. It has been the basis for mortality estimates in war zones such as Darfur and the Congo."[23] In the war zone that was Port-au-Prince between 29 February 2004 and December 2005, Kolbe and Hutson extrapolate from thousands of random interviews an estimated 8,000 killings and no less than 35,000 sexual assaults. They attribute around half of the killings to the police or anti-Lavalas paramilitaries, and the other half to criminals; they blame only a tiny share of the political violence on pro-Lavalas partisans. Kolbe's impartiality has been challenged, on account of her previous (and initially undisclosed) involvement with Aristide's Radio Timoun and Foundation for Democracy, and some analysts question the credibility of her report. While 4000 political killings in Port-au-Prince during 2004–06 may be an over-estimate, the best available evidence suggests that the coup claimed several thousand victims – roughly the same number, in other words, as the coup that overthrew Chile's Allende in 1973.

All through this period, as a damning 2005 report undertaken by Harvard Law Student Advocates for Human Rights (together with members of the Brazil-based Centro de Justiça Global) demonstrates in detail, the UN stabilization force "effectively provided cover for the police to wage a campaign of terror in Port-au-Prince's slums."[24] Todd Howland directs the Robert F. Kennedy Memorial's Center for Human Rights, and has worked with UN peacekeeping missions in Rwanda and Angola. "It's a totally inappropriate solution for the member-states to tell the United Nations to take sides in Haiti, but that's what they've done," he said in early 2006.

> It's simply crazy that the UN was not allowed to do what the UN typically does to bring peace to a country. It needed to bring the parties of the conflict together to discuss how to resolve the underlying conflict. There needed to be a peace process, a peace negotiation. This is the only country in the world where you have a significant UN operation without a peace accord. People can think what they want to about Lavalas. Love them or hate them, it is short-sighted and costly to exclude them from this process. It's not a question of good or bad. Lavalas is the major political force and that's the reality in Haiti.[25]

However many people were killed and arrested, it wasn't enough to stop neighborhoods like Bel Air from protesting the coup and demonstrating in favor of Lavalas. On the first anniversary of the coup, 28 February 2005, thousands of Aristide supporters marched up from the slums to the UN headquarters on John Brown avenue. In full view of foreign correspondents and UN staff, Haitian police fired on the demonstration, killed five of its leaders and wounded dozens more – these and related "police killings poisoned an atmosphere," said the exasperated head of MINUSTAH, "that peacekeepers had been working to improve for two months."[26] After a few peaceful weeks in March during which the UN prevented the PNH from supervising demonstrations, further mass rallies in downtown Port-au-Prince, and further PNH killings, followed on 24 March (at least two demonstrators killed), 27 April (at least five demon-strators killed) and 18 May (at least two more dead).[27] As many as thirty people may have been killed in a series of police raids on Bel Air over four days, starting 3 June.[28] By that stage, however, the chief focus of both the PNH and the UN had shifted to somewhere else – Cité Soleil.

THE ASSAULT ON CITÉ SOLEIL

Of all the Port-au-Prince slums, Cité Soleil has an exceptional status. Packed with around 300,000 inhabitants, it is by far the largest single neighborhood in the entire country. Built on low-lying, reclaimed (and regularly flooded) land on the water's edge, a few kilometers north and west of downtown, it's relatively easy to cut it off from the rest of the city. Infrastructure is almost non-existent. As of 2006 there are virtually no public schools and indeed almost no government facilities of any kind, other than a lone hospital. There is no longer any regular police presence. Unlike Bel Air, many residents of Cité Soleil are relatively recent arrivals, refugees from a barren countryside that can no longer support them. They are Haiti's poorest of the poor. Regular jobs are extremely scarce, and nowhere are the immediate pressures of survival so intense. Compared with other poor neighborhoods in the capital, therefore, it is more difficult to separate political commitments in Cité Soleil from brutal economic necessities. Once many hundreds of Cité residents lost their public sector jobs in March 2004, some of them began to starve. Absolute destitution and permanent vulnerability have predictable social consequences, some of which discourage close international attention.[29] Only two foreign human rights workers (Anne Sosin and Judy DaCruz) undertook sustained work in Cité Soleil in the post-coup years, and they are both careful to point out that in the Cité the distinction between political and criminal gangs is often artificial.[30]

It was not Cité Soleil's high level of criminality, however, that made it a source of particular concern for the de facto authorities in 2004. In many respects, Cité Soleil provides the elite with a useful way of containing the human damage caused by the way they rule the country – it ordinarily serves as a fairly secure holding pen for the people who have suffered most from the effects of Haiti's class war. By the same token, however, once the mechanics of domination had to shift from straightforward military dictatorship to democratic polyarchy, the existence of a place like Cité Soleil became a serious problem. As the Boulos brothers understood very well in the 1990s, no other single district contains so many registered voters – at least 5 percent of the entire national electorate. No other district can mobilize so many people so quickly.

Lavalas leaders in Cité Soleil can (and frequently do) turn out thousands of people for a demonstration at a moment's notice. No other district has such a high public profile: because it's the poorest, largest and most violent of Haiti's popular neighborhoods it's guaranteed a certain amount of regular media coverage, and intrepid international NGOs like Doctors Without Borders go out of their way to retain a prestigious foothold in the Cité.

No other district, more to the point, contains so many militant Aristide supporters. No doubt some of this support is opportunistic. The imperatives of survival rarely encourage an immaculate idealism, and though its practical resources were severely limited, Aristide's government offered unprecedented resources and hope for the Cité. In addition to providing crucial public sector jobs, the Lavalas government built a substantial public park and renovated the main market square. It improved and paved the main road that runs through the center of the Cité, and developed the port that lies at its end. It built scores of new housing units and took over the running of Boulos' Saint Cathérine hospital. In some ways the symbolic gestures counted for more: Aristide was the first president to make regular trips to the Cité, to speak to its inhabitants as equals, to invite its representatives to his house and to the National Palace. Although there are some disaffected ex-Lavalassians in Cité Soleil as there are anywhere else, by and large it remains Lavalas through and through.

As with Bel Air, in 2004 the most immediate problem with Cité Soleil, as far as the government and international community was concerned, was its robust capacity to defend itself. "Around here," observes Bobby Duval, "if you don't mobilize and demand a better life for yourself, you'll just be forgotten and will fall through the cracks."[31] Towards the end of February, while Philippe's rebels encountered little organized resistance in many parts of the country, Lavalas militants (and Selavi alumni) in Cité Soleil like Dred Wilme or Billy "Prezidan" were undaunted. Both of Billy's parents were killed by FRAPH. "Guy Philippe can't come here," Billy told the *Miami Herald* on 24 February. "If Philippe comes, he dies. The police are afraid. But we are not. We have the power. Philippe says he's got 200 [men]. You know how many people are waiting for him here? We've got 2,000. If Cité Soleil says 'no more', it's over."[32] Once Aristide had been abducted, under the pressure of paramilitary incursions Cité Soleil turned into something of a semi-armed camp. "We are not going to wait for them to come and kill us," Billy told the *New York Times* on 3 March; "we'll take care of Guy Philippe, you'll see." Another militant, Paul Virel, remembered the legacy of Chamblain and FRAPH from the first coup. "The gift we received from FRAPH was pigs eating the bodies of our brothers and sisters," he said. "Mothers would wake up in the morning to find their sons dead. FRAPH will never come here again. We would rather die stopping them than let them come back."[33] Sure enough, over the next few months hundreds of Cité residents died defending their neighborhood. In the spring of 2004 informal self-defense brigades sprang up throughout the district, and soon both the police and their paramilitary allies from Pétionville were obliged to retreat. Cité Soleil became a no-go area for anyone sympathetic to the coup.

The fact that Cité Soleil was capable of fighting back, the fact that it was one of the few places where the police were generally afraid to go, also meant that it was also one of the few places where Lavalas activists were relatively safe. After they lost their jobs, it became a refuge for scores of OP activists and former public sector employees who were high on the list of the IGH's list of political targets.[34]

In March 2004, the new Latortue government had a clear choice. It could have devoted a small fraction of its new international aid to the continuation of a version of Aristide's social and educational programmes. It could have expanded on his efforts to create additional jobs for Cité residents. It could have spent modest sums on water and electricity provision, or garbage disposal. Alternatively, it could fire most of the Cité's public sector workers, abandon the Lavalas literacy project, suspend all social programmes, isolate the local economy, confine thousands of people in permanent unemployment while allowing private sector importers to quadruple the prices of basic foodstuffs – and then send in a combination of turncoat gang-members, death squads, CIMO police and UN troops to deal with the consequences. The decision to opt for the latter course had already been made, presumably, long before Latortue returned to his country in March. The private-sector troika of Boulos, Baker and Apaid, together with their associates in various quasi-official security forces, was hard at work softening up parts of Cité Soleil as early as mid–2003, if not before.

As we saw in chapter seven, until the mid-1990s people like the Boulos, Apaid and Baker families had been free to make liberal use of FAdH troops to "maintain order" in the slums that border the factories they own along the capital's industrial belt. Ever since Aristide abolished FAdH in early 1995, they've had to rely on less formal arrangements. Cité Soleil is not the sort of place that is easily penetrated by external infiltration. The only option, in the end, was to try to buy off some of the local gang leaders. The industrialist Reginald Boulos had attempted to use his wealth and patronage to nourish a base of political support in the Cité for years.[35] Through to the early 2000s, however, anti-FL money didn't go very far in Cité Soleil, and by the summer of 2003 the unpopular Labanye was the only gang leader willing to accept it. Well-placed sources confirm that Apaid promised Labanye and his family visas to the US and paid him tens of thousands of dollars, though since neither party seems to have kept receipts definitive proof will be hard to come by.[36] It's no secret, however, that from mid–summer 2003 Labanye regularly received substantial amounts of money to share out with his followers, and that from then on, Labanye's gang was never troubled by the police or by anti-FL paramilitaries.[37]

Apaid's recruitment of Labanye was a significant breakthrough in the elite's assault on the popular movement in Port-au-Prince. All along, the real target of much of the hype about Lavalas "chimères" was the fact of their relative unity and organization under Aristide. Even after Labanye had been bought off by Apaid and Boulos, even after the violence between Labanye and Dred Wilme in October 2003, by the end of the year Aristide was able to unite the groups against their common political enemies. At the massive pro-government rally of 7 February 2004, Labanye and Dred stood shoulder to shoulder with all the other group leaders, and right through to 29 February 2004 Labanye himself – under heavy pressure from members of his own gang – helped to man the defensive barricades at Tabarre.[38] Once Aristide was out of the picture, however, this strategic unity quickly evaporated. In late March 2004 Apaid arranged a meeting in his office with the Cité's main leaders. Labanye, Tupac, Billy and Amaral all went along, though not Dred, who was never prepared to negotiate with Aristide's enemies. Eléonore Senlis went to the meeting as well, along with French members of the interim occupation force. "It was pointless," she remembers. "It served only to confirm Billy and Amaral's contempt for Apaid, and to make them miss the Aristide days."[39] Apaid himself told Thomas Griffin's investigation team that he asked all of the Cité Soleil gang leaders "to agree to disarm, and only Labanye agreed. Apaid admitted that since Labanye's agreement, he has directed the police to protect Labanye's life, and 'not to arrest him, but to work with him.' Labanye deserves special treatment, he said, 'because he is a witness to the others refusing to disarm.' "[40] Shortly after this meeting an arrest warrant was issued for the "bandit" Dred Wilme, who went into hiding in lower Delmas.[41]

It's easy to understand Baker and Apaid's enthusiasm for vigorous law and order. Apaid's main factory employs thousands of workers and stands right on the edge of Cité Soleil. The Baker family owns half a dozen factories in the same area, and five of them suffered fire damage in the two years running up to Charles Baker's decision to stand as the main pro-business candidate in the 2006 presidential elections. While denying the existence of any "class divide in Haiti," Baker told a journalist the day before those elections that "overwhelming force," combined with "order, discipline and work," was the only solution to the country's predicament.[42]

Through to March 2005, Labanye's gang (with PNH support) was the elite's preferred vehicle for delivering this solution. So long as Aristide was in power, Labanye's capacity to disrupt the FL's power base in lower Cité Soleil was very limited. But with Aristide gone, the running battles that had been taking place off and on since the previous autumn intensified, and by September 2004 the combination of the mass firings of public sector workers, paramilitary attacks and Labanye's relentless disruption made life in the Cité almost impossible to endure. Lavalas leaders like Amaral Duclona and Lamarre Augustin are adamant that they did everything possible to negotiate with representatives of the new government and the private sector, that they were determined to pursue forms of peaceful resistance and sustain non-violence protests against the coup, and that it was the combination of government aggression along with Labanye's provocation that condemned the Cité to take defensive measures which led in turn to the development of a situation resembling martial law.[43] As Griffin observed towards the end of that year, the lack of any constructive intervention from the de facto government or UN together with the ceaseless "anarchy appears to have made leaders and heroes out of the young men who perpetrate violence best."[44]

In Cité Soleil as in Bel Air, a dramatic threshold was crossed on the day of the fateful pro-Aristide demonstration on 30 September 2004. As thousands of people calling for a return of the elected government marched out from lower Cité Soleil to join their comrades downtown, they were intercepted en route by Labanye's gang in Boston; the firefight left group leader Tupac (Winston Jean-Bart) and several other FL militants dead. His younger brother and fellow gang-leader Billy (James Petit Frère) was also badly wounded in the ensuing violence and then arrested while recovering in hospital – it appears that Billy later escaped from prison during the February 2005 jailbreak, only to be shot and killed by police as he tried to make his way back to Cité Soleil.[45] That left Dred Wilme and Amaral Duclona as the two most prominent leaders of pro-FL armed groups, ranged against the alliance of Labanye, the PNH/UN and the paramilitaries. On 14 December 2004, a major MINUSTAH incursion into Cité Soleil gave the government a strategic foothold in the area for the first time, killing two or three people in the process. All through the autumn of 2004 and spring of 2005 Labanye and his allies put relentless pressure on the residents of the lower Cité. Many hundreds of houses were destroyed along the main north-south road of Bois Neuf (which residents subsequently renamed Boulevard Dred Wilme), and the entire area remains a wasteland to this day. Every entrance to the Cité was sealed off with massive barricades and heavily armed checkpoints. Schools inside lower Cité Soleil were closed, markets were suspended, the police station was torched, and the hospital was shut down for three full months. The only way in and out was by boat. Supplies of food and water grew desperately short. All through the long months of the siege atrocities were committed on both sides, and the violence had a traumatizing effect on the social and political fabric of the neighborhood.

If the de facto government's aim was to confirm in both the local and the national mind the confusion of Lavalas activists and brutal gangsters then the assault it launched on Cité Soleil in the autumn of 2004 was at least partially successful. An alumnus of Aristide's home for street kids, an employee (until the March 2004 layoffs) of the National Port Authority and a life-long Lavalas loyalist, much of Dred Wilme's world was shaped by systematic political violence. Members of his group were no doubt guilty of many crimes, and it would be naïve to present him or his followers as high-minded altruists.[46] If Latortue was unable to squash Lavalas resistance to the coup, he succeeded in criminalizing some of it.

It would be quite wrong, however, to try to downplay the insistently political dimension of the struggle for survival that coalesced around Dred, Amaral and their associate Lamarre Augustin. Eléonore Senlis knew Dred Wilme as well as any outsider, and of all the armed leaders in the Cité she describes him as "the most effectively organized and the most loyal to Aristide. He saw Aristide as the true representative of the people and he remained completely devoted to him, even once it was clear that this loyalty would lead to his death. As a leader he was both charismatic and implacable; his ambition was to rebuild the whole of Cité Soleil in the image of Lafanmi Selavi, and he was prepared to defend this project against its enemies by all available means."[47] As Dred himself explained in an interview on NY radio in April 2005, Haiti's ruling

bourgeoisie have never done anything to benefit the people of Cité Soleil. They want the people to be their slaves [. . .]. We have been living for one year now under this de facto government which is destroying the country. 95 percent of the people from the masses who were working government jobs have been fired. Children cannot go to school. Students cannot advance in their studies. We are wondering just how far this crisis will be allowed to go. All of this is why we are in the streets, demonstrating and demanding the physical return of President Jean-Bertrand Aristide to Haiti immediately. This is the only issue the people are interested in today.[48]

It's people like Dred and Amaral who have always suffered the brunt of political repression in Haiti. While they too have blood on their hands, it would be wrong to underestimate the courage of the Lavalas activists who have defended their families against successive waves of paramilitary attack since the late 1980s. Although opinions and affiliations vary from neighborhood to neighborhood, it would be wrong to downplay the degree to which local residents applaud their leaders as resistance fighters, as the only people able and willing to protect them from the outright predation of their enemies. "I know this is hard for people outside Haiti to understand," confirms Guy Delva, "but in Cité Soleil the people with weapons are not seen as criminals or bandits, but as people who are protecting the population. They see that when MINUSTAH or the Haitian police come they kill people, and the gangs do what they can to defend them. I can confirm that when you speak to them, most people in Cité Soleil say they saw Dred Wilme as a leader, as someone who defended their community, they didn't see him as a bandit."[49] Bobby Duval is hardly an advocate for armed struggle, but like the vast majority of the kids he works with, he acknowledges Dred Wilme as "our Robin Hood," as a contemporary version of the anti-US resistance fighter Charlemagne Péralte.[50] People closer to the sharp end of class struggle in lower Port-au-Prince emphatically agree. Dred was "truly admired by the people of Cité Soleil," insist OP militants Belizaire Printemps and Elias Clovis, who shrug off allegations of brutality in the independent media. "In Haiti, as a rule, when you defend the interests of the people you are treated as a criminal, whether your name is Dessalines, Péralte or Wilme."[51]

When then a combination of Dred's resistance and internal betrayal allowed his gang to triumph over Labanye in March 2005, there was consternation in Pétionville and rejoicing on the streets of lower Cité Soleil. Latortue publicly mourned Labanye's death, and with good reason. With Labanye dead and his gang dispersed, the de facto government would now have to take care of unfinished business itself. From now on, the attacks on FL supporters in Cité Soleil would have to be conducted first by the police or its paramilitary allies, and later by armoured UN columns. As the inter-gang violence subsided the IGH also needed a new pretext to justify its policy of counter-insurgency. Conveniently, in the spring of 2005 Port-au-Prince was traumatized by a mysterious and unprecedented spate of kidnappings.[52] Although they almost never ended in bloodshed, the abrupt rise in abductions contributed to a spiralling fixation with security all over Port-au-Prince (and may have helped discourage a budding alliance of student leaders and FL militants). Places like Pétionville which had hitherto suffered few direct consequences of February 2004 suddenly seemed vulnerable, and kidnapping became an obsessive source of public concern. In June 2005 the PNH arrested at least half a dozen of its own members on suspicion of kidnapping. Although reliable evidence is again hard to come by, well-placed sources have traced a significant fraction of the kidnappings to people with the most obvious interest in justifying new investments in the provision of neo-military forms of security, including members of the former military and associates of Gérard Latortue's security chief, ex-Gang Unit officer Youri Latortue.[53] On 27 May 2005, in his capacity as President of the Haitian chamber of Commerce and Industry, Reginald Boulos met with Latortue's police chief Leon Charles and used the pretext of rising insecurity to back up his demand that the IGH help "the business community to form their own private security firms and arm them with automatic weapons,"; he was candid enough to admit that "if they don't allow us to do this then we'll take our own initiative and do it anyway". On 30 May, Boulos' friend Charles Baker denounced the UN on Radio Métropole for offering nothing more than "protection for the armed bandits," i.e. Lavalas militants.[54]

By the spring of 2005 Dred's group had become so powerful that the police could no longer set foot in Cité Soleil. The job of breaking its grip on the Cité fell to the far better equipped UN troops. For most of 2004, MINUSTAH soldiers had managed to resist what their commander General Augusto Heleno Ribeiro condemned in December as the "extreme pressure (from the US, France and Canada) to use violence."[55] As the IGH ran out of options this pressure increased, and in the spring of 2005 MINUSTAH took on a more directly military role. In Cité Soleil, MINUSTAH's Jordanian troops in particular will be long remembered for their readiness, whenever they felt threatened, to open fire on anything that moved. If you visit just about any side-street in the Cité, residents will show you bullet holes in their shacks that they say came from MINUSTAH machine guns. At one point during the MINUSTAH campaign in Cité Soleil, admitted one UN official, UN troops were firing an average of 2,000 rounds of ammunition a day.[56]

On 22 June, the UN Security Council agreed to enlarge its invasion force to the extraordinary level of 9,300 men. On June 23 an increasingly frustrated Roger Noriega told the *Herald* that "as a longtime observer of Haiti, it is abundantly clear to me [. . .] that Aristide and his camp are singularly responsible for most of the violence and for the concerted nature of the violence" in post-coup Haiti. He urged UN troops "to take a more 'proactive role' in going after armed pro-Aristide gangs" and to overcome Aristide's latest attempt to "terrorize the Haitian people and deny them good government."[57] The UN did what it was told. On 6 July 2005, a full-scale military operation mounted by around 400 MINUSTAH troops (combined with the betrayal of one of Dred's confidants) finally succeeded in killing the most wanted man in Haiti, along with four of his closest associates and an uncertain number of Cité residents – perhaps 30 people in all.[58] Guy Delva "saw seven bodies in one house alone, including two babies and one older woman in her 60s," and around twenty of the twenty-seven people who chose to risk public treatment for gunshot wounds at the local MSF clinic were women and children. On the same day, a PNH attack on Bel Air may have left another ten people dead; perhaps twelve more killings followed a couple of days later.[59]

The death of Aristide's most militant supporter in Cité Soleil marked a significant advance in the basic strategy of demonize, divide and rule that has shaped government policy towards the slums of Port-au-Prince ever since February 2004. Dred's elimination, predictably, did not serve to limit but to multiply the number of weapons and armed groups in the poorer parts of Port-au-Prince. By the time the UN launched its next series of military raids in Cité Soleil, in December 2006, the elite's ongoing effort to conflate residual political resistance with criminality pure and simple had born considerable fruit.

In the short term, however, the 6 July offensive proved to be something of a Pyrrhic victory for Latortue's government. Dred's resistance had forced the IGH/UN to have recourse to levels of violence that even the world's most independent media found difficult to disguise. Many thousands of Cité Soleil residents turned out for Dred's funeral, and he quickly became the district's most famous martyr. "We will always keep Dred Wilme alive in our memory," said his successor Amaral, who with the support of hundreds of gang members immediately picked up where his mentor left off.[60] The IGH/UN kept up its campaign of counter-insurgency all through the summer – in the most notorious of several brutal incidents, on 20 August 2005, in the middle of a soccer match attended by around 6,000 people in the Grand Ravine section of the Martissant district in western Port-au-Prince, at least eight people were hacked or shot to death by members of the anti-FL gang Lame Tima-chete, working in collusion with the PNH.[61] In the autumn of 2005, the Cité Soleil hospital continued to treat scores of gunshot victims every month.[62] Despite months of open warfare, however, MINUSTAH's attempt to bludgeon the Cité into submission was no more successful than those of the police or the paramilitaries before them. Anarchic violence was starting to break out all over the city, and even bourgeois neighborhoods were no longer safe. The situation threatened to get entirely out of control. The guardians of international capital were not pleased. By the end of the summer of 2005, in short, it was becoming more and more difficult to delay the moment that the pro-coup forces had been dreading all along – the election of a constitutional successor to Aristide.

THE ELECTIONS OF FEBRUARY 2006

On the first day of January 2005, Roger Noriega reassured the world that "US efforts to help Haiti are on track": "we are on the right path toward helping Haiti become a more prosperous and truly democratic society."[63] A few months later it was already plainly impossible to keep up this pretense. "The summer of 2005 was absolute hell in every way," remembers Father Rick Freshette. "All of the seams were coming apart, and there was no control anywhere."[64] By the end of 2005, some parts of the country had been pushed to the brink of open rebellion. In January 2006, the *New York Times* described Latortue's Port-au-Prince as "virtually paralyzed by kidnappings, spreading panic among rich and poor alike. Corrupt police officers in uniform have assassinated people on the streets in the light of day. The chaos is so extreme and the interim government so dysfunctional that voting to elect a new one has already been delayed four times."[65]

After the July 2005 attacks on Cité Soleil the period in which the use of naked force was both politically acceptable and strategically effective started to draw to a temporary close. Sooner or later, the 2004 coup and its consequences would have to risk validation by popular vote. Preparations for the election of the IGH's replacement began in earnest in the summer of 2005. The registration of presidential candidates was completed by 15 September, and after several delays the election itself finally took place on 7 February 2006. The list of hopefuls included many of the leading players of the post-coup era, including CD leaders Leslie Manigat, Evans Paul, Himmler Rébu and Luc Mésadieu, Dany Toussaint, G184 magnate Charles Baker and FLRN leader Guy Philippe. Aristide was long gone and FL seemed safely broken by the de facto government's repression. Surely this was an election that even the old democratic opposition might be able to win.

What was supposed to happen in February 2006 is clear enough. These elections were supposed to clear up the controversy surrounding 2004 once and for all. With Aristide out of the picture, they were supposed to confirm that his violent and illegal expulsion had actually been a victory for democracy. With the Lavalas grassroots in tatters, they were supposed to give the true friends of pluralism and civil society that democratic mandate they had so long been denied. There should have been a smooth transition from the Latortue government to a similarly-minded administration run by a proper capitalist like Charles Baker, or at least a veteran of the Democratic Convergence like ex-president Professor Leslie Manigat. The need for heightened security would ensure that Aristide's most militant supporters could continue to be barricaded in a few demoralized slums. The Fanmi Lavalas organization was either to be excluded from the process altogether, or at least "integrated" into the system like a more conventional political party.

As it turned out, at least this last expectation was indeed partly (though just temporarily) fulfilled. According to John Joseph Jorel and Paul Christian, when FL leaders met at the Aristide Foundation in August 2005, they decided that it would only participate in the elections if they could run Aristide's close associate Father Gérard Jean-Juste as their new presidential candidate.[66] Jean-Juste had been a prominent figure in the pro-democracy movement both in Haiti and in the Haitian-American communities in the US for decade. A staunch Aristide loyalist and protected like Aristide before him by his status as a popular parish priest (of the Saint Claire church in Petite Place Cazeau, on the edge of Delmas), after the coup he was one of the very few high-profile Lavalassians who could afford to remain in the public eye. On 13 October 2004, a few days into the October assault on Bel Air and Cité Soleil, he was beaten and arrested by a group of masked policemen at his church, in the midst of his regular bi-weekly soup kitchen that feeds hundreds of local children.[67] He spent the next six weeks crammed into a fetid national penitentiary cell with eighteen other men. Undaunted, like his comrades in Bel Air Jean-Juste continued to hold firm to a simple and widely-held set of demands: "Insist that we return to constitutional order in Haiti. Demand freedom for all political prisoners. Respect the human rights of everyone. Pledge to respect the vote of the people. Advocate for the return of President Aristide so he can finish his electoral mandate through February 2006."[68] Jean-Juste stuck to his message after his release from prison on 29 November and by the spring of 2005 it was clear that he represented a significant political threat to the Latortue project. In July Gousse had the good sense to block Jean-Juste's candidacy in advance by having him imprisoned again, on the absurdly implausible charge of complicity in the murder of journalist Jacques Roche (at a time when Jean-Juste wasn't in the country). He was only released, on medical grounds, in January 2006. "Everyone was for Jean-Juste" recalls Samba Boukman, "and that's why he was put in prison."[69]

Frustrated, the FL leadership then split into two camps. In September a couple of former senators were somehow persuaded to adopt Aristide's old opponent Marc Bazin as their candidate. Two other formerly influential figures in the party decided to present themselves as candidates in their own right, in open defiance of the decision taken by the party as a whole and made public by the organization's national representative, Jonas Petit.[70] The rest of the leadership, including all those who enjoy genuine grassroots support, decided that the party should now boycott the election unless Latortue agreed to free the political prisoners and allow FL exiles to return. At the same time, however, many pro-Lavalas OPs joined progressive peasant groups in pressing Aristide's old protégé René Préval (who relied on but never officially joined FL itself) to make a last-minute candidacy. After leaving office in 2001, Préval had devoted himself to the improvement of his hometown of Marmelade, turning it into something of a model of sustainable development, complete with a solar-powered computer center, electric street lamps, a Cuban-staffed health clinic and a Taiwan-sponsored agricultural cooperative. Mindful of what happened to Neptune and Jean-Juste, Préval kept a remarkably low profile all through the post-coup period, and his decision to stand seems to have caught the whole political establishment by surprise. The pro-coup candidates, convinced that their only serious rival (Fanmi Lavalas) was more or less out of the race, continued to devote most of their energy to competing amongst themselves. In the space of a few short weeks, Préval's supporters cobbled together an ad hoc political coalition made up of a couple of small and regional parties (notably the Parti Louvri Barye, and Efò ak Solidarite pou Konstwi yon Altènativ Nasyonal Popilè/ Koordinasyon Resistans Grandans) which they dubbed *Lespwa*, or "hope." After discussing the pros and cons of a boycott, the FL *baz* threw themselves energetically behind Préval's campaign, leaving the pro-Bazin camp hopelessly isolated.[71] This way the FL organization could officially abstain from the election while encouraging its individual members to vote for the twin-brother or *marassa d'Aristide*. A vote for Préval, explains Gérard Jean-Juste, was "a vote for the continuity of Lavalas" and "an absolute rejection of the February 2004 coup." The decision to back Préval was also a carefully strategic move. "We knew what we were up against and were careful not to play our hand too early. You have to be tactical, use different strategies, multiply your alliances and organizations – otherwise forget it."[72]

Like every credible analyst of the election, Ronald Saint-Jean points out that "the majority of Haitian people voted for Préval as a way of voting for the return of Aristide. 90 percent of the people who voted for Préval are partisans of Lavalas."[73] Although Préval has less of a direct link to the FL *baz* in a place like Bel Air than did Aristide, virtually the entire neighborhood voted for him in February 2006. "For us, Préval is the same as Aristide," explains Samba Boukman.[74] "Almost every FL member chose to support Préval," says SOPUDEP's Real Dol, and "we put all our organization and our strength behind him."[75]

Much to the horror of the traditional elite, the Lavalas stratagem worked like a charm. Before Préval's candidacy was announced, re-members Fonkoze's Anne Hastings, "people had become very fatalistic, there was a total disregard of the elections and no sense that they were anything important." In the summer of 2005, ordinary Fonkoze members "spoke openly of how people were prepared to sell their signature for various petitions." Préval's participation transformed the situation completely, and although he was effectively prevented from campaigning by the IGH his candidacy quickly acquired an unstoppable momentum; "on the day of the elections itself it was unbelievable, people were so excited and enthusiastic."[76] True to form, a group of around thirty intellectual veterans of the destabilization campaign (including Cary Hector and Laënnec Hurbon) recognized the danger, and issued a desperate call for the old democratic opposition to unite in opposition to Préval. CD luminary Micha Gaillard warned his colleagues that Préval "symbolised a return to the [Lavalassian] past [. . .]. It would be infantile not to oppose him with a single centrist candidate."[77] A group of nine Convergence leaders (Evans Paul, Charles Baker, Luc Mésadieu, Hubert de Ronceray, Leslie Manigat, Serge Gilles etc.) duly formed a "Group of Democratic Agreement," promising that if the election went to a second round they would pool their votes on behalf of the most popular non-Préval candidate. During the last days of the campaign, pro-elite and pro-army candidates Charles Baker and Guy Philippe assured visiting reporters that they "had a vast invisible support that would wipe out Préval's challenge."[78]

As grassroots FL activists began to invest their full political power in Préval's campaign, the de facto government and its backers did everything they could to avoid the inevitable outcome.[79] In the first weeks of 2006, Charles Baker and his G184 associates put new pressure on the UN to crack down still more aggressively on Cité Soleil and the other neighborhoods whose mobilization might decide the election. The resistance mounted over the previous year by people like Dred and Amaral had made the MINUSTAH campaign so politically damaging, however, that by January 2006 the great powers were no longer willing to approve the full-on assault that Baker and Boulos demanded. Tensions between MINUSTAH and the PNH had already developed into occasionally open conflict, especially in the wake of the police shootings on 28 February 2005. (During a follow-up demonstration in Bel Air on 4 March, for instance, UN troops directly blocked the police from supervising the event, prompting Gousse to lodge an official complaint.[80]) As the UN found itself forced to take on more of a policing role, morale in MINUSTAH began to flag. After the 6 July operations, the MINUSTAH commander General Ribeiro resigned and was replaced by a more hard-nosed Brazilian general, Urano Teixera da Matta Bacellar. On 7 January 2006, however, the day after a tense meeting with Boulos and Apaid, Bacellar was found shot dead in his room at the Hotel Montana – an alleged though incomprehensible "suicide" that stunned everyone who knew him, including his wife. For reasons that remain mysterious, the results of a Brazilian autopsy and investigation were never released. According to a pair of Canadian reporters, "Bacellar reportedly disagreed with plans to invade Cité Soleil upon viewing footage of the collateral damage and deaths following a previous raid into Cité Soleil on 6 July 2005."[81] Although no proof is likely to emerge, as Kim Ives suggests it may be that "Bacellar was killed because like Ribeiro he too was reluctant to act more forcefully against Cité Soleil, Bel Air, and other neighborhoods."[82] A week later, on 16 January, Andy Apaid helped organize a G184 rally in support of Charles Baker's candidacy and renewed UN incursions into the Cité; it was only attended by a few hundred people.

Boulos announced plans for another futile private-sector "strike." In his desperation to get MINUSTAH to deal with the Lavalas "bandits" once and for all, Boulos even went on air to announce his willingness to set up a pre-emptive fund on behalf of the innocent victims who might be killed or injured in any renewed assault on the Cité.[83]

The green light for a repeat of 6 July that Boulos and Apaid were looking for never came, however, and the Cité Soleil *baz* were free to organize a series of massive (and non-violent) pro-Préval rallies in the run-up to 7 February. Both in Bel Air and the Cité, an FL commitment to non-violence held strong in the face of repeated provocations.[84] As Patrick Elie insists, it was "precisely the mobilization of people like Samba and Amaral that eventually allowed the February 2006 elections to take place."[85] Once it was clear that the elections would proceed without paramilitary disruption, the spate of kidnappings that had plagued Port-au-Prince for the previous six months came to an almost immediate stop. By the time Cité Soleil's armed groups announced their readiness to accompany Cité voters and to protect them during their long and potentially dangerous walk to the polls, the outcome of the election was as good as settled.[86] Latortue's officials did what they could to limit the damage. Whereas Préval's own government had provided over 10,000 voter registration centers for the last presidential elections, in 2000, Latortue now set up less than 500, in sites carefully chosen to disadvantage pro-Lavalas neighbourhoods. Only 52,000 voting cards were distributed in Cité Soleil, where the total number of people of voting age is probably closer to 150,000 (more to the point, according to the CEP's official records, only 30,000 votes from the Cité were ever counted).[87] In 2000, some 12,000 polling stations were distributed all across the country; in 2006, a much smaller number were concentrated in just 800 voting centers, again situated in such a way as to marginalize undesirable voters. There was no polling station in or even near Cité Soleil, for instance, so many thousands of Cité residents got up well before dawn on 7 February and spent the entire day walking and waiting in huge lines to cast their ballots. Well before they were due to open at 6 a.m., the queues outside some voting centers already stretched for hundreds of yards. The American reporter Ben Ehrenreich describes what happened when, hours later, some of these centers failed to open.

> Convinced that they had been robbed of their opportunity to vote, thousands waiting at polls on the outskirts of Cité Soleil took to the streets and marched on the National Palace. It is misleading to call them

marches and equate them with our own desultory spectacles of protest: they were eruptions. Haitians ran through the streets, waving torn-off branches in the air. They sang Préval's name, and rained curses on the interim government. They screamed with rage and danced with joy. This was a people roused from slumber, suddenly conscious of its power. The polls eventually did open. Thousands waited for hours to vote in vast, stifling rooms, crammed shoulder to shoulder and belly to back. All day, of the dozens I spoke to, only four people admitted to having voted for anyone other than Préval.[88]

The turnout was huge, on a par with 1990 and 2000, around 65 percent. By 9 February, with a quarter of the votes counted and in keeping with reliable exit polls, it was announced that Préval was leading the field with 62 percent, comfortably ahead of Manigat with 11 percent. It would be hard to imagine a more resounding rejection of the 2004 coup, or a more disastrous result for the Franco-American alliance.

What happened next also came as no great surprise. On 11 February, the electoral council abruptly lowered Préval's tally to just 49.6 percent, and early on the morning of 13 February, it was estimated at a mere 48.7 percent. This was about 22,000 votes short of the 50 percent majority a candidate needs in order to win in a single round of voting. The de facto authorities made little effort to conceal their hand. Tens of thousands of valid votes, mainly cast for Préval, turned up in a Port-au-Prince garbage dump, and in Préval strongholds all over the country thousands of ballots were recorded as mysteriously "missing". CEP officials began noting large numbers of null and blank ballots. No less than 91,000 votes (4.3 percent of the total) were recorded as blank, and another 155,000 (7.4 percent) deemed invalid. "It's clear that many blank votes were inserted into the ballot," argues Guy Delva, "so as to try to dilute Préval's percentage and thus force a second round."[89] If the election could be pushed to a second-round run-off, perhaps the democratic opposition could regain its IRI-era "unity," reorganize itself around a single candidate and win the day after all. Roger Noriega and his colleagues in Canada and France urged the CEP to defy Préval's "violent mobs" and to confirm his total as just under 50 percent.[90]

In response, tens of thousands of Aristide and Préval supporters overwhelmed Port-au-Prince with well-organized demonstrations. The *New York Times* noted that "angry protests paralyzed cities across the country."[91] On the afternoon of 13 February, thousands of angry voters streamed up all the way from Cité Soleil to demand publication of the results from the electoral council at its headquarters in the exclusive Montana Hotel; several hundred demonstrators also grabbed the opportunity to take a quick swim in the Montana's pool, before leaving the hotel and its rattled guests undisturbed. Barricades burned all over Port-au-Prince. "If Préval hadn't won," says Father Freshette, "this place would have blown up like a powder-keg."[92] Like other foreign observers, Reed Lindsay was impressed by the power and discipline of the demonstrations: "When Préval said 'lift the roadblocks' then immediately, all over the city, the roadblocks were lifted, just like that."[93]

Nothing short of blatant electoral fraud had allowed the CEP to postpone the announcement of Préval's victory. Under severe popular pressure, the council decided to abandon an indefensible position, and on 15 February voted 8 to 1 to divide the number of so-called "blank" ballots proportionately among the candidates. As CEP member Patrick Féquière admitted, "We had to do something: we could have just told Préval he got 48.76 percent, but when he contests the results all of this mess is going to come out – the blank votes, the missing votes", etc.[94] (The CEP's director Jacques Bernard, who resisted the compromise, took the usual route to safety and was welcomed in Miami.) The CEP decision was just enough to nudge Préval's proportion over the requisite 50 percent mark, giving him a marginal victory in the first round. It was also enough, no doubt, to leave the impression that this was again a "tainted" or "compromised" election, should the need for another corrective round of democracy enhancement arise.[95] As the acting US ambassador Tim Carney candidly put it on 19 February, if in the judgement of the US Préval "doesn't perform, yes it [the electoral settlement] could weaken him" – though "if he does perform, nobody will remember it."[96] Independent observers put Préval's actual share of the vote as somewhere between 62 percent and 70 percent.[97]

On behalf of the democratic opposition (and true to his old *option-zéro* form) an outraged Manigat denounced the CEP's decision as a "tragedy" and an "electoral coup d'état," before reminding his fellow citizens that a "dog must not return to its vomit."[98]

Elections on their own are hardly an adequate expression of genuine democracy, of course, but occasionally the raw numbers speak for themselves. When the 2006 results were published, the fiction of popular support for the 2004 coup finally dissolved altogether. Even according to the biased official figures, pro-coup candidates were uniformly crushed. Leslie Manigat attracted some of the OPL's liberal-professional constituency and scored 12.4 percent (to Préval's official 51 percent); Baker's prominence on the rightwing edge of the business community, coupled with the opportunistic support of the MPP, gained him 8.2 percent. Most other pro-coup and "social democratic" candidates made hardly any impact at all. The evangelical Luc Mésadieu won 3.3 percent, the OPL's Paul Denis won 2.6 percent, and KID's Evans Paul (now fronting the "Alliance Démocratique" coalition) 2.5 percent. The overtly pro-army candidates did worst of all: Guy Philippe tallied 1.9 percent and Dany Toussaint just 0.4 percent, slightly ahead of Himmler Rébu with 0.2 percent. As for the faked "FL" candidacy of Marc Bazin, it garnered no more than 0.7 percent of the vote.

After February 2006, no-one could continue to deny the single most obvious feature of Haitian politics after the expulsion of Duvalier: every free presidential election since 1986 – in 1990, 1995, 2000 and now 2006 – has been won, by overwhelming margins, either by Aristide or by the person Aristide chose as his first prime minister and successor. Through all the vagaries of the past twenty years, neither the people nor their priorities have changed. In 2006 Préval was canny enough to gather several small and scattered political groupings into his tactfully "pluralist" Lespwa coalition, but "like everyone else," insists Radio Solidarité's Venel Remarais, "Préval knows perfectly well that it was the Lavalas masses who won him the election."[99]

PRÉVAL'S SECOND ADMINISTRATION

Préval's re-election was a major victory for ordinary Haitians, in open defiance of the full might of their foreign and domestic enemies. Short of re-electing Aristide himself – an option blocked, as Aristide himself was the first to accept, by the Haitian constitution – there was nothing that the Haitian people could have done to demonstrate more emphatically their rejection of the 2004 coup and all its implications. Rarely have the pretensions of "democracy promotion" been deflated with such determination and panache. Like recent elections in Bolivia, Brazil, Chile, Ecuador, and Venezuela, Préval's victory in 2006 dealt another resounding blow to the neo-conservative agenda in Latin America.

It is of course too early to say whether Préval's new administration will be allowed to live up to its political potential. Unlike 1996, in 2006 Préval has the considerable advantage of coming immediately after an experience of catastrophic failure: even the *pays amis d'Haïti* (the US, France and Canada) can see that they have little to gain, in the short-term, by driving Préval's administration into the ground. In the summer of 2006, the donors pledged Préval's government a sizeable (though still largely theoretical) $750 million in aid for the next fiscal year, which allowed him to announce significant levels of social investment, to pacify some of the most dangerous elements in the ex-military (by paying out some more of their disputed back-pay) and to mollify a few of the most embittered ex-public sector workers in the slums (by agreeing, in principle, to restore some "competent" workers to their jobs). More importantly, in the spring of 2007 trilateral discussions with Venezuela and Cuba led to a whole raft of concrete commitments, including subsidized oil imports and investments in health care, electricity and other infrastructure projects worth around $250 million.[100] Around the same time, Préval announced an ambitious range of long-term initiatives in education, literacy, road-building and tourism. In its November 2006 report, the Economist Intelligence Unit remained optimistic that Préval's government will continue to "enjoy strong support from the foreign governments and multilateral agencies engaged in the country, as well as the goodwill, at least for the time being, of the majority of Haitians."[101]

But Préval's room to maneuver is again extremely limited. The most obvious drawback of Préval's pluralist and multi-party approach, in 2006 as in 1997–2000, is its vulnerability to factional opposition in the national legislature. Lespwa provided a useful platform for electing a president, but a lack of time and deliberate IGH repression helped to prevent it from gaining a parliamentary majority.[102] Although in the legislative elections of April 2006 anti-coup parties (Lespwa, FL and PONT) gained a small edge in the Senate, some 55 of 99 seats in the chamber of Deputies were won by a combination of pro-coup and pro-army parties. Pending a more disciplined showing in the next parliamentary elections, Préval will find it difficult to pass even mildly contentious legislation. Making the best of a bad situation, he re-appointed his old prime minister Jacques Edouard Alexis to lead an eclectic cabinet that includes five members of the old democratic opposition, but for most of its first year in office this relatively "broad-based" administration was able to accomplish little of substance.[103]

Nevertheless, in spite of Préval's extremely cautious approach, by the end of 2006 both the foreign and domestic enemies of the popular movement were pressing hard for the replacement of Prime Minister Alexis by a still more "moderate" alternative. On a couple of occasions Alexis risked a few words that were critical of US priorities (with respect to rising numbers of criminal deportees and the selective prosecution of its "war on drugs"), and drew predictable diplomatic

fire from Washington. Observers like Kim Ives and Patrick Elie interpreted an increase in criminal and political violence in the last months of
the year as part of an attempt to destabilize the government by forcing it
to clamp down on inner-city neighborhoods dominated by its own most
militant supporters.

The survival of the Préval/Alexis government will depend on its ability
to balance several sets of contradictory demands.

First of all, although Préval was elected by people desperate for an end
to the punitive economic policies they have been obliged to endure for
the past thirty years, foreign pressure has obliged him to retain the neo-
liberal macro-economic priorities he inherited from the Latortue government, along with many of its appointees (departmental representatives, diplomats, judges, PNH commanders and administrators . . .).
Préval is as dependent as any Haitian president on the renewal of foreign
and private sector investment and the goodwill of the IC. Secure in the
knowledge that the poor would support him, in their first months in
office Préval and Alexis went out of their way to woo the liberal wing of
the private sector and the Haitian diaspora, and to avoid giving the great
powers a pretext to undermine them. Although it owes its existence to
the mobilization of the Lavalas *baz*, the Préval administration has made it
quite clear that the persistence of such mobilization is "not a government
priority." Rather than mobilize the poor to press for social change,
explains Préval's chief of staff, the government aims to work with all
sectors to improve the delivery of social services, increase levels of
international investment and to enhance the efficiency and autonomy
of the country's political institutions. In the spring of 2007 it became clear
that Préval was prepared to contemplate a new round of privatisations,
including the sell-off of Haiti's telecommunications company.[104]

In Haiti, as in a few other places, the ongoing replacement of meaningful or empowering democracy with its merely formal or minimalist
substitute "has been accompanied by increasing disillusionment about
democracy" itself.[105] As of early 2007, although most Lavalassians
probably still agreed with Moïse Jean-Charles' view that "as things stand
Préval is the best of our available options," popular disappointment was
palpable.[106] "If you consider what the Préval government has done in the
light of why people turned out to vote in February," observed an editor
of *Haïti Progrès* a year after Préval's election, "then we have to conclude
that so far the government has done nothing at all."[107] With respect to
most of the Lavalas election demands – justice for victims of the coup,
release of the political prisoners, return of the exiles, an end to the

militarized assault on the popular neighborhoods – Préval's position has been either diplomatic or indecisive, depending on your point of view. As part of the deal that saw him win the presidency in the first round, Préval agreed not to push demands for investigations into either the blatant electoral fraud of February 2006 or the coup of 2004. Starting in the summer of 2006 Préval's administration slowly released many of the higher-profile political prisoners arrested by Gousse and Latortue, including Neptune, Privert and Mayette, though for reasons that are never stated (but easy to guess), Aristide remains in exile to this day.[108]

Préval has repeatedly said that there is no constitutional basis for Aristide's exile but he has taken no concrete steps to bring it to an end. Over the course of 2006 the issue became the source of a damaging rift within FL circles between those who continued to press for Aristide's immediate return (notably the people around Jean-Marie Samedy and the Cellule National) and those who preferred to prioritize an initial period of "national reconciliation" under Préval (for instance Moïse Jean-Charles or Samba Boukman). Many prominent figures in Fanmi Lavalas, including Yvon Neptune, interpret Préval's hesitation as damaging and "indefensible."[109] Given the current configuration of forces, however, Préval has little to gain in the short-term by re-asserting a fidelity to Aristide, and it's clear that Bob Manuel and other prominent Préval advisors are keen to avoid the disruption that might accompany the former president's return. Nevertheless, it would be wrong to exaggerate the differences between the two most prominent figures in the Lavalas movement. Guy Delva points out that in most respects, despite "some disagreements on privatization, Préval showed a lot of loyalty to Aristide when he was president in the 1990s, and he is never critical of him in public."[110] In the eyes of most of their supporters, Préval and Aristide clearly remain on the same side of the political divide. Once he was re-elected, Préval made a point of working closely with prominent and unrepentant Aristide loyalists like Moïse Jean-Charles, John Joseph Jorel and Samba Boukman. As Marcus Garcia notes, it is people like Moïse who "represent the majority of the people, they have proved their courage and their worth in the eyes of people; now they need to find ways in which they can establish themselves as credible politicians."[111] "I am a member of Lavalas," Jorel insisted in 2006, and "the return of Aristide remains a priority. Préval offers us a breathing space, an end to the oppression that we have suffered for the past two years. We will accompany Préval so long as he shares our goals, but I am Lavalas and will remain Lavalas, and we are already working towards a Lavalas victory in 2010."[112] Moïse is more direct. "Lespwa itself is nothing, it's just bla bla bla," just a vehicle for an eclectic group of interests seeking to manipulate Préval's popularity among the poor: "We in Lavalas will ride it only so long as it continues in the right direction."[113]

If in late 2006 some of the more militant members of Lavalas came to the conclusion that the government was veering dangerously off-course it was above all as a result of the way it responded to the most damaging legacy of the coup – the persistence of politically manipulated insecurity and violence. As we have seen, once Aristide and his most loyal partisans were out of the way there was little to stop representatives of the private and pro-army sectors from enlisting the services of some of Cité Soleil's armed groups, to complement their employment of ex-soldiers and deported ex-convicts – growing numbers of the latter, Ben Dupuy explains, have "in the space of a couple of years driven Haitian street crime to an entirely new level."[114] The combination of harrowing poverty, economic devastation and rigid social exclusion guarantees a steady and growing pool of recruits for groups like Lame Ti Machete in Martissant (reportedly linked to Youri Latortue, police chief Mario Andrésol, and the OPL's Paul Denis) or Belony's gang of kidnappers in Cité Soleil (also with reported links to Youri Latortue). A year after the Martissant soccer field massacre in August 2005, Lame Ti Machete struck again on 6 July 2006, killing at least a dozen Grand Ravine residents and burning scores of homes in a gruesome night of collective punishment. The leading representative of the victims of these attacks, Esterne Bruner, was himself assassinated on 21 September 2006. A few days later Lame killed another eight people in three nights of violence in Martissant, and the neighboring pro-FL group Baz Grand Ravine answered violence with violence. On 12 October, unidentified gunmen killed eight people and wounded eighteen more in Bel Air. Incidents of rape and sexual violence, meanwhile – always a useful way of goading members of an oppressed population into retaliation – continued in line with post-coup trends.[115]

During the same months the rate of kidnappings rapidly intensified, back up to 2005 levels, until the issue was once again a matter of obsessive public concern. The expansion in new criminal funds fed a corresponding increase in new criminal weapons.[116] Slowly but surely, people like Andy Apaid, Serge Gilles and Youri Latortue put increasing pressure on Alexis to abandon his tentative efforts to "negotiate with the bandits" and to approach the situation in military rather than socio-economic terms. So far, Gilles complained in December 2006, "There's [been] too much carrot and not enough stick; it's urgent that we retake the upper hand."[117] In August the government had launched a new disarmament programme, aimed more or less exclusively at armed groups in Cité Soleil. Préval warned them that they now had only two choices: "either you surrender your weapons within the DDR or you will die."[118] Two months later Préval and Alexis had begun to yield to US and private sector calls for more direct action.[119] Activists in Cité Soleil responded to the increasingly aggressive UN incursions by holding a new series of pro-Aristide and anti-occupation rallies. The crackdown began in earnest on 22 December 2006, when under heavy international pressure Préval reluctantly gave the nod for a full-scale UN assault on the Cité that missed all of its intended targets but left around twenty innocents dead.[120] Further military assaults continued for another two months. In 2007, major raids involving hundreds of UN troops took place on 25 January, 9 February and 21 February, and eventually succeeded in driving out the armed groups led by Evens, Belony, and Amaral. At least another dozen people were killed and scores of suspected gang-members were detained. Belony and Amaral escaped and went into hiding; Evens was arrested on 13 March in Les Cayes, and Belony was caught on 23 April in Saint-Michel de l'Attalaye. In late March Amaral began making tentative moves towards cooperation with the government's disarmament commission.[121]

On their own, the impact of such measures is likely to be ambiguous at best, disastrous at worst. Few Cité residents are likely to miss thugs like Evens or Belony, but given the state of their neighborhood they are entitled to wonder how long it will take before they are replaced.[122] As Georges Honorat points out, "The idea that you can go into Cité Soleil with high calibre weapons and rid the place of its 'bandits' is a complete fantasy."[123] The determination shared by the elite, the UN, and the rest of a security-obsessed IC to respond to severe socio-economic problems with military "solutions" will only serve to amplify the damage that they cause. "The poverty in places like Cité Soleil," Ben Dupuy explains,

> is a direct result of the neo-liberal reconfiguration of the Haitian economy that began in the late 1970s – the result of what many Haitians call the "death plan". The US and the Haitian elite believe that they can manage the consequences of this plan by sending foreign troops to police the neighborhoods populated by those that suffer the worst of its effects. They think they can control rising levels of poverty by shooting at the poor. In Haiti as in various other parts of the world they use the UN to put out the fire, without considering who started it. They do everything possible to avoid the obvious conclusion – that this

poverty, and the violence that accompanies it, is a direct consequence of the neo-liberal plan itself. The only way to reverse it is to put a stop to the plan and undo its effects.[124]

Rather than mobilize the only political force in Haiti that has any chance of engaging with the root causes of the problem – the Lavalas *baz* – Préval has so far chosen (or been obliged) to collude in the ongoing conflation of political resistance and organized crime. Members of Amaral's group no doubt committed their share of crimes, but like Dred's group before them they also commanded considerable political respect. They rid much of the Cité of kidnappers, defended the population against the predations of the paramilitaries and their allies, and were an integral part of Lavalas resistance to the legacy of the coup. Again like Dred before him, Amaral knows from long experience that "If you are fighting to take the people out of poverty, they will always call you a gang leader."[125] It remains to be seen whether the government will work with people like Amaral to establish more effective forms of community-based development and policing, or whether it will continue to approach many of its poorest citizens as virtual enemies of the state.

Meanwhile the criminalization of these citizens continues apace, both in reality and in the political representation of that reality. Behind the demonization of Lavalas lies the demonization of the poor. In the eyes of many elite politicians, the equation of "poor" and "criminal" has never been easier to make. With Lavalas on the defensive, there is little to prevent a predictable cycle from spiralling out of control: more poverty breeds more despair, more despair means more gangs, more gangs commit more crimes, more crimes earn more money, more money pays for more guns, more guns facilitate more crimes . . . Such a development has many uses, for those seeking to justify a restoration of the army on the one hand and to fragment the popular movement on the other.

Three years after Aristide's expulsion, some veterans of the movement find the situation "more discouraging than ever before."[126] The residents of a neighborhood like Bel Air, reports Samba Boukman, are now "constantly intimidated by criminals. People from the private sector provide these criminals with guns, and once they have guns it is difficult to take them away." Nevertheless, he continues, "the majority want peace and food, not guns and violence. The people with weapons are still a small minority, and they live in the midst of the majority. If they are well organized, the majority can prevail. So long as we have a government we can work with then we can turn the situation around."[127]

At the time of writing (in March 2007), there was little popular enthusiasm for a government whose hands were so firmly and so obviously tied by international constraints. Préval's ability to implement progressive policies will depend very largely on developments in Washington, Ottawa and Paris. But Washington's hegemony is not absolute; the fate of Préval's administration will also depend on what happens in Caracas and Havana, and on the strength and organization of the Lavalas base. The very fact that Préval's government still exists is itself proof that the massive operation mounted by the elite and its Franco-American allies to discredit and crush the Lavalas movement has not succeeded. Although in many ways he is likely to remain the prisoner of the elite and the IC, Préval's own fidelity to Lavalas remains strong. Whoever succeeds him will in all likelihood share a similar fidelity. "For the time being I am sure of two things," says PPN activist and broadcaster Prad Jean-Vernet. "Any politician who is openly anti-Lavalas will get nowhere with the bulk of the people, and the next election will be won by someone who has remained loyal to Aristide. The people will not forgive the crimes of February 2004."[128] Despite petty divisions among parts of its leadership, Yvon Neptune remains confident that "Fanmi Lavalas is still in a strong position. The ideas that FL has put forward resonate with a majority of the people, who recognize them as their own. So far we have only made a start, but we haven't failed."[129]

After years of intense repression and infiltration the Fanmi Lavalas hierarchy is in disarray, and the organization may not survive in its current official form. The Lavalas *baz* and their myriad *organisations populaires*, however, remain the most powerful political force in the country. In some way they may be stronger now than they were three years ago. They have survived unprecedented levels of repression. They are less dependent on a single charismatic leader. They are less contaminated by opportunists. They have fewer illusions about what must be done next.

Conclusion

"It is better to err with the people than to be right without them."
(Jean-Bertrand Aristide)[1]

It took almost two decades for Haiti's little ruling class and its imperial patrons to devise a workable way of coping with the end of the Cold War. Like other Cold Warriors in Latin America, Haitian dictators François and Jean-Claude Duvalier preserved the dramatic gap between rich and poor through direct military intimidation. Eventually, however, this intimidation began to provoke a movement of popular protest too powerful to control, and in 1990 the Haitian people were able for the first time to rally behind a president of their own choosing. Once this president began to interfere with the interests of the elite, its army got rid of him in the usual way. What was most unusual about Aristide, however, is that in 1995 he then found a way to get rid of this army in its turn. By the time it won the decisive elections of 2000, Aristide's party threatened to overwhelm both the military and the parliamentary mechanisms of elite resistance, and was finally in a position to push through moderate but significant political change. Deprived of its traditional instrument of repression, Haiti's elite and its foreign allies now had to a develop a more indirect, more humanitarian strategy of containment.

In many ways, the people (first-world diplomats, IFI economists, USAID consultants, IRI mediators, CIA analysts, media specialists, ex-military personnel, security advisors, police trainers, aid-workers, NGO staff . . .) who "spontaneously" developed this strategy are entitled to be pleased with the results of their work. Over the course of a decade or so, they managed to back one of the most popular political leaders in Latin America into a corner from which he couldn't escape. They managed not only to overthrow but also to discredit the most progressive government in Haitian history, and they managed to attack this government in ways that were rarely perceived (by mainstream commentators) as aggressive at all. They managed to disguise a deliberate and elaborate political intervention as a routine contribution to the natural order of things. Ten years after his triumphant return from exile in 1994, Aristide's enemies not only drove him out of office but into an apparently definitive disgrace.

It wouldn't be hard to extract a general destabilization recipe from this most exemplary episode in imperial counter-insurgency. Confronted by a threatening attempt at popular democracy, the Haitian elite and its friends in France and US adopted a predictable but highly effective strategy. They starved the Lavalas government of funds and international credit, obliging it to adopt unpopular economic policies and to cut public sector services and jobs. They developed powerful if not irresistible forms of economic pressure to further impoverish and alienate its supporters. They cast doubt on its democratic legitimacy, equating Haiti's most popular president with the Duvalier and Cédras dictatorships. They secured and supported sympathetic assets within the security forces, and bought off opportunistic elements within the popular movement. They obliged the government's supporters to take defensive measures in the face of paramilitary attack, and then characterized these measures as intolerant of dissent. They presented opposition to the government as diverse and inclusive, and valorized these opponents as the embattled victims of government repression. Taking special care to ensure that the government was attacked from both right (business groups, professional associations, civil society organizations) and left (humanitarian NGOs, human rights groups), they sustained a relentless media campaign to present the government as intractable and authoritarian. After a few years of such coercion, even a tiny military insurgency led by notorious criminals and organized by the most reactionary interests in the country was welcomed by most mainstream observers as a "popular insurrection" against a despotic regime. If in the end even such insurrection wasn't enough to get rid of the despot, who then could blame the great powers when they eventually went in to finish the job on their own?

There is no denying that, under the pressure of such aggression, Aristide and the Lavalas organization made a number of damaging compromises and mistakes. To refuse the demonization of Aristide does not require his deification. Nevertheless, claims that Aristide was too messianic, or that he encouraged violence, or that he was authoritarian or intolerant of dissent, are not just far-fetched – they are almost a literal inversion of the truth. If his government deserves to be blamed for anything, it is for being too tolerant of an opposition that sought to replace it, too conciliatory in its relations with foreign powers that sought to overthrow it, too complacent in the face of a media that criticized it, too hesitant in relation to soldiers who attacked it, too lenient with the opportunists who sought to abuse it. "Even the best of our political leaders," regrets Patrick Elie,

> have underestimated the resilience of the Haitian people and their *will* to hang tough, even under immense pressure. Our politicians need to know that if they pursue a courageous and independent course, a course that risks foreign retribution, then a sizeable minority of powerful individuals will indeed scream in protest and demand that the government back down. But not the majority of the people. The Haitian people are used to enduring enormous hardships, and if they know that they are being asked to endure hardship for the sake of their dignity and autonomy then they will readily endure it. Our leaders need to be more assertive, to be more in tune with the profound feeling of independence that animates the majority of Haitians. It has only ever been the elite who have been willing to cave in to foreign pressure. We need to trust the people's determination to fight for their rights.[2]

If Aristide's government shares some of the responsibility for the debacle of 2004 it is because it occasionally failed to act with the sort of vigor and determination its more vulnerable supporters were entitled to expect. Aristide was right to stand for the presidency in 1990, he was right to engineer the US invasion that allowed for the demobilization of the army in 1995, and he was right to consolidate his supporters through the development of Fanmi Lavalas. But after rapidly emerging as Haiti's most popular political organization, Fanmi Lavalas became too inclusive, too moderate, too indecisive, too undisciplined. After gaining an over-whelming popular mandate for radical change, Aristide's government was too often willing to negotiate with its enemies and too rarely willing to mobilize its friends. Aristide tried to placate opponents that he needed to confront. He may never have drawn the full implications of elite hostility, both in Haiti and abroad: drawn from the beginning into a political war, he tried till the end to govern with the strategies of peace.

How much of this responsibility can be fairly attributed to a government that was unavoidably dependent on foreign aid, that remained profoundly vulnerable to foreign intervention, that presided over a precarious and unstable political system, that had little practical control over its economy or bureaucracy and virtually no control over its own security – these are questions that are likely to divide analysts of the Aristide era for the foreseeable future.

What is more important is the fact that this era, in spite of the astonishing levels of repression it aroused, has indeed opened the door to a new political future. There is little to be gained from judging this opening by the standards of either armed national liberation movements on the one hand or entrenched parliamentary democracies on the other. Over the last twenty years, Lavalas has developed as an experiment at the limits of contemporary political possibility. Its history sheds light on some of the ways that political mobilization can proceed under the pressure of exceptionally powerful constraints.

Aristide was obliged to govern Haiti in the absence of international sympathy, military support, institutional stability or economic independence: he presided over the inauguration of a process of collective empowerment, not its realization. With an absolute minimum of resources, his governments were able to take significant strides in the fields of education, justice and health. These governments helped to initiate a profound political transition, and in the process encountered the obstacles that any such transition must face. Aristide dealt with some of these obstacles (the army, the closure of the traditional political system, the public exclusion of the poor) more effectively than others (the economic, bureaucratic and cultural hegemony of the transnational elite). The task that falls to today's Lavalassians is immense. But in spite of all they have suffered, the circumstances in which they will engage with it are in some ways less adverse today than they were back in 2000 or in 1994.

In the first place, the election of the *marassa d'Aristide* in 2006 confirmed, in the face of intense coercion, an extraordinary continuity of political purpose. In 1990, 1995, 2000 and now again in 2006, the Haitian people have voted consistently and overwhelmingly for much the same principles and much the same people. Although prosecuted with unprecedented resources and undertaken with the full backing of the UN, the US and the rest of the international community, the attempt to break this continuity during the catastrophic interlude of 2004–05 has failed. In the long run the second coup against Lavalas may prove no more successful than the first. Although there is much to rebuild, popular fidelity to the Lavalas project remains durable and strong, and whatever institutional form it takes its momentum will continue to shape Haiti's political future.

Lavalas militants have strengthened their position in that future, moreover, by helping to inspire the collective mobilizations that in recent years have brought left-leaning governments to power all across Latin America. Back in 1816, Haiti's first independence leaders provided crucial logistical support to Simon Bolívar; the leaders of Haiti's second independence struggle presided over one of the hemisphere's only popular political mobilizations in the run-up to its new Bolivarian revolution. After years of crippling international isolation, it is now possible to imagine a more assertively progressive government in Haiti working in direct collaboration with supportive governments in Cuba, Venezuela, Bolivia, Ecuador . . . For many years an empty slogan of the far left, calls for international cooperation at both the grassroots and governmental levels are starting to mean something rather different in 2007 than they did a decade or two ago. Members of Lavalas *organisations populaires* have for many years worked alongside representatives of the more militant PPN; in spite of many obstacles, a stronger version of such a collaboration may well manage to mount and win an anti-imperialist campaign for the presidency in 2010. Damaged by its wars of aggression in Afghanistan and Iraq, the capacity of the US to deter such collaboration is perhaps weaker today than at any time over the preceding century. Just as importantly, the capacity of the US or its allies France and Canada to pose as friends of the Haitian people is for the foreseeable future damaged beyond repair.

Over the last couple of years the Lavalas organization has also begun to confront some of its own internal limitations, by becoming less dependent on Aristide's personal charisma and influence, and by purging itself of many of the opportunists who manipulated this influence in the late 1990s. Although it will take several more years to work through the consequences of the 2004 coup, FL leaders who compromised with the interim government have lost most of their power, and younger grassroots leaders are more prominent now than when their organization was in office. They have learned from Aristide's example as well as from his mistakes. The combination of disciplined resilience and strategic flexibility that won the election of 2006 suggests that parts of this organization may have emerged from the crucible of repression stronger than before. The fact that Lavalas also remains bitterly divisive is a consequence above all of the fact that it was the only large-scale popular mobilization ever to address the massive inequalities of power, influence and wealth which have always divided Haitian society; that Lavalas has so far managed to do little to reduce these inequalities says less about the weakness of the organization than it does about the extraordinary strength, today, of the forces that preserve inequality.

Two centuries ago, it took Haiti's armies several years and immeasurable effort to wrest its first independence from the slave economy controlled by the great colonial powers of the day. The ongoing struggle to win Haiti's independence from the contemporary version of slavery has aroused less spectacular but no less implacable opposition from our postcolonial empires. Now as then, Haiti's liberation struggle has confronted the full range of imperial coercion in its most undiluted and illuminating forms. The first victory was achieved through force of arms over the course of little more than a decade, and it was won by Haitians alone. The second victory will not depend on weapons, it will take longer, and in addition to the remobilization of Lavalas, it will require the renewal of emancipatory politics within the imperial nations themselves.

Afterword

From Flood to Earthquake

Just before 5 p.m. on Tuesday, 12 January 2010, Haiti's capital city and the surrounding area were devastated by the most catastrophic earthquake in the history of the hemisphere. The scale of the destruction was overwhelming. According to the best available estimates, around 200,000 people perished and more than 300,000 suffered horrific injuries, leading to many thousands of amputations. Stories told by the bereaved defy summary. Some 200,000 buildings were destroyed, including around 70 percent of the city's schools. More than half a year after the disaster in which they lost their homes and virtually all their belongings, around 1.5 million people continue to live in makeshift camps with few or no essential services, with few or no jobs, and with few or no prospects of any significant improvement in the near future.[1]

Although the earthquake has no precedent in Haitian history, the factors that magnified its impact, and the responses it has solicited, are all too familiar. They are part and parcel of the fundamental conflict that has structured the last thirty years of Haitian history: the conflict between *pèp la* (the people, the poor) and members of the privileged elite, along with the armed forces and international collaborators who defend them. If the 1980s were marked by the rising flood that became Lavalas, by an unprecedented popular mobilization that overcame dictatorship and raised the prospect of modest yet revolutionary social change, then the period that began with the military coup of September 1991 is best described as one of the most prolonged and intense periods of counter-revolution anywhere in the world. For the last twenty years, the most powerful political and economic interests in and around Haiti have waged a systematic campaign designed to stifle the popular movement and deprive it of its principal weapons, resources and leaders. The January earthquake triggered reactions that carried and that are still carrying such measures to entirely new levels.

So far, this ongoing counter-revolution has been grimly successful. Rarely have the tactics of divide and rule been deployed with such ruthless economy and efficacy as in Haiti 2000–2010. A small handful of privileged families are now wealthier and more powerful than ever before; once the post-quake reconstruction begins in earnest, in early 2011, they are set to become wealthier still. More than a million homeless and penniless people, by contrast, are likely to spend the reconstruction years in a sort of squatters' limbo, as foreign technocrats, multinational executives and NGO consultants decide how best to rebuild their city. The majority of their compatriots will remain destitute and forced to endure the most harrowing rates of exploitation in the hemisphere. The majority also know that if current tendencies prevail, their children, and their children's children, can expect nothing different. Today, with the battered remnants of the Lavalas movement more divided and disorganized than ever before, with the country firmly held in the long-term grip of a foreign "stabilization" force, the majority of Haiti's people have little or no political power. At the time of writing, in late summer 2010, many foreign observers of the Haitian popular movement were struck above all by a widespread sense of resignation and impotence. For the time being, it looks as if the threatening prospect of meaningful democracy in Haiti has been well and truly contained.

In these intolerable circumstances, nothing short of popular remobilization on a massive scale, more powerful, more disciplined, more united and more resolute than before – nothing, in other words, short of the renewal of genuinely revolutionary pressure – holds out any real prospect of significant change for the majority of Haiti's people. Of course, this is precisely the prospect that those who have managed the country's recent political development, and who are managing its post-earthquake reconstruction to this day, are most determined to avoid. Just a few days after the immediate trauma of 12 January, it was already clear that the US- and UN-led relief operation would conform to the three main counter-revolutionary strategies that have shaped the more general course of the island's recent history: (a) It would foreground questions of "security" and "stability," and try to answer them by military or quasi-military means; (b) it would sideline Haiti's own leaders and government, and ignore both the needs and the abilities of the majority of its people; (c) it would proceed in ways that directly reinforce and widen the immense gap between the privileged few and the impoverished millions they exploit. Even a cursory review of the first six months of reconstruction in 2010 should be enough to show that the ongoing application of these strategies is best described as an intensification of the measures that have undercut the power and autonomy of Haiti's people over the two preceding decades.

I

The basic political question in Haiti (as in a few other places), from colonial through post-colonial to neo-colonial times, has always been much the same: How can a tiny and precarious ruling class secure its property and privileges in the face of mass destitution and resentment? In Haiti (as in a few other places), the elite owes its privileges to exclusion, exploitation and violence, and only quasi-monopoly control of violent power allows it to retain them. This monopoly was amply guaranteed by the Duvalier dictatorships through to the mid-1980s, and then rather less amply by the military dictatorships that succeeded them (1986–90). But the Lavalas mobilization threatened that monopoly, and with it those privileges.

As I have tried to show in the main body of this book, what has happened in Haiti since Aristide was first elected in 1990 should be understood first and foremost as the progressive clarification of this basic alternative – democracy or the army. It's not hard to see that unadulterated democracy might one day allow the interests of the numerical majority to prevail, and thereby challenge the position of the elite; in such a situation, only an army, or the equivalent of an army, can be relied upon to guarantee the "security" of the status quo. Crucially, the democratic mobilization that took shape in the 1980s in opposition to dictatorship and neo-liberal "adjustment" was strong enough to overcome and indeed *eliminate* the domestic armed forces arrayed against it. It was able first to uproot Duvalier and his Macoutes (in 1986) and then, after a long army crackdown that killed another thousand people or so, to overcome direct military rule (in 1990). Much of the momentum of this mobilization survived the murderous coup of 1991, and Aristide was finally able, at great cost, to disband the army in 1995. When Aristide then won a second overwhelming mandate in the elections of 2000, the resounding victory of his Fanmi Lavalas party at all levels of government raised the prospect, for the first time in Haitian history, of genuine significant political change in a context in which there was no obvious extra-political mechanism – no army – to prevent it.

In order to avoid this outcome, the main strategy of Haiti's little ruling class all through the past decade has been to redefine political questions in terms of "stability" and "security," i.e. the security of the wealthy, their property and their investments. Mere numbers may well win an election or sustain a popular movement but, as everyone knows, only an army is equipped to deal with insecurity. The abundantly armed "friend of Haiti" that is the United States knows this better than anyone else.

In this context, the defining event of contemporary Haitian politics remains the intervention that was designed to restore long-term "security" by killing off the Lavalas mobilization once and for all: the coup of 2004. If the most popular thing that Aristide ever did was to disband the army that deposed his first government, perhaps the most significant achievement of the 2004 coup was to return effective political control to a military force.

In the absence of an available domestic option, the 2004 coup gave power to a foreign army: first a US-French-Canadian invasion force, and then a UN pacification force. (The next time the people of Haiti had a chance to express their opinion, in the elections of February 2006, the main military and political leaders associated with this coup scraped no more than 1 or 2 percent of the vote.) As anyone could have predicted, Aristide's Fanmi Lavalas, the party elected with a landslide in the last elections to be held in un-occupied Haiti, has been blocked from participating in all subsequent elections, in 2006, in 2009 and now again in 2010. Its leaders have been scattered or imprisoned, and its main spokesman remains in involuntary exile on the other side of the world. If Haiti's international minders succeed in preserving this pattern of exclusion, it looks as if Haitian democracy is now finally set to proceed in line with the imperial expectations that were so rudely thwarted twenty years ago, when the local voters chose the wrong man and the wrong agenda (see above, page 000*).

In and after 2004, the only way to persuade these voters to accept the coup and its consequences – the systematic and explicit reassertion of foreign and elite domination of their country – has been to ram it down their throats. Ever since the coup, Haiti has been under international military occupation. Year after year, from 2004 through to 2010, at an annual cost (at around $600m) larger than the entire national budget during the pre-coup years, thousands of foreign troops have patrolled the country and obliged its people to accept the end of the Lavalas sequence. During these years, the UN authorities behind this extraordinary "stabilization mission" have resorted to levels of violent coercion without parallel in UN operations anywhere else in the world. They have been reinforced by thousands of rearmed and retrained Haitian police, along with thousands more private security guards hired to protect wealthy families, their businesses, and the foreign contractors and NGOs they do business with. Dozens of anti-occupation demonstrations held on the streets of Port-au-Prince during these years have had little or no political effect.

You might have been forgiven for thinking, a year ago, that only an earthquake could loosen this armed grip on the country.

II

Sure enough, one of the first things to wobble on the afternoon of 12 January 2010 was the coercive power of the state. The headquarters of the UN mission collapsed, along with 27 of 28 federal government buildings. Perhaps a fifth of government employees were killed. If a revolution requires paralysis of the state's capacity to suppress popular protest, then as Kim Ives points out, in a sense "the earthquake accomplished half a revolution by literally destroying the Haitian state," leaving popular forces on the one hand and elites forces on the other "scrambling to array their 'alternatives' to fill the void."[2] The US embassy immediately rushed to evacuate its staff, along with a few of the people its government is most determined to protect. For a moment or two, no doubt, the Haitian elite and their international minders must have contemplated the apocalypse: the prospect of mass unrest, in the absence of adequate levels of coercive force. The result was a near-instantaneous military response on a scale rarely if ever matched by a peacetime operation.

In the immediate aftermath of the earthquake, few tried to counter arguments in favor of allowing the US military, with its "unrivalled logistical capability," to take de facto control of the relief operation. Weary of bad press in Iraq and Afghanistan, US commanders also seemed glad of this unexpected opportunity to rebrand their armed forces as angels of mercy. As usual, the Haitian government was instructed to be grateful for whatever help it could get.

That was before US commanders actively began, the day after the earthquake struck, to divert aid away from the disaster zone. As soon as the US Air Force took control of Haitian airspace, on Wednesday 13 January, they explicitly prioritized military over humanitarian flights. Although most reports from Port-au-Prince emphasized remarkable levels of patience and solidarity on the streets, US commanders made fears of popular unrest and insecurity their number one concern. Their first priority was to avoid what the US Air Force Special Command

Public Affairs spokesman (Ty Foster) called another "Somalia effort"[3] – which is to say, presumably, a situation in which a humiliated US army might once again risk losing military control of a "humanitarian" mission.

As many observers predicted, however, the determination of US commanders to forestall this risk by privileging guns and soldiers over doctors and food mainly succeeded in helping to provoke a few occasional bursts of the very unrest they set out to contain. In order to amass a sufficiently large amount of soldiers and military equipment on the ground, the US Air Force diverted plane after plane packed with emergency supplies away from Port-au-Prince. The earthquake took place on Tuesday; among many others, World Food Program flights were turned away by US commanders on Thursday and Friday, the *New York Times* reported, "so that the United States could land troops and equipment, and lift Americans and other foreigners to safety."[4] Many similar flights met a similar fate, right through to the end of the week. Médecins sans Frontières (MSF) alone had to watch at least five planeloads of its medical supplies be turned away.[5] Late on Monday 18 January, MSF "complained that one of its cargo planes carrying 12 tonnes of medical equipment had been turned away three times from Port-au-Prince airport since Sunday," despite receiving "repeated assurances they could land." By that stage one group of MSF doctors in Port-au-Prince had been "forced to buy a saw in the market to continue the amputations" upon which the lives of their patients depended.[6]

While US commanders set about restoring security by assembling a force of some 14,000 Marines, residents in some less secure parts of Port-au-Prince soon started to run out of food and water. On 20 January people sleeping in one of the largest and most easily accessed of the many hundreds of impromptu IDP (internally displaced people) camps, in the Champs Mars area of Port-au-Prince, told writer Tim Schwartz that "no relief has arrived; it is all being delivered on other side of town, by the US embassy."[7] The same day, a full eight days after the quake, Telesur reporter Reed Lindsay confirmed that the impoverished southwestern Port-au-Prince suburb closest to the earthquake's epicenter, Carrefour, still hadn't received any food, aid or medical help.[8] The BBC's Mark Doyle found the same thing in an eastern and less badly affected suburb. "Their houses are destroyed, they have no running water, food prices have doubled, and they haven't seen a single government official or foreign aid worker since the earthquake struck."[9] As a Reuters report confirmed six weeks after the quake, "the 9,000 uniformed UN peacekeepers stationed in Haiti when the quake struck on Jan. 12 were the logical 'first responders' to the disaster," but "none of the peacekeepers appeared to be involved in hands–on humanitarian relief in what emergency medical experts describe as the critical first 72 hours after a devastating earthquake strikes. Their response to the appalling suffering was limited to handling security and looking for looters after the magnitude 7.0 quake leveled much of the capital."[10] This too was business as usual: the countries controlling the UN stabilization mission had always voted against any extension of its mandate to include economic development, and from 2004 through to January 2010 it spent its annual $600m budget almost exclusively on military and security priorities.

On Sunday 17 January, Al Jazeera's correspondent Sebastian Walker summarized what many other journalists had been saying all week. "Most Haitians have seen little humanitarian aid so far. What they have seen is guns, and lots of them. Armoured personnel carriers cruise the streets" and "inside the well-guarded perimeter [of the airport], the US has taken control. It looks more like the Green Zone in Baghdad than a centre for aid distribution."[11] Late on the same day, the World Food Program's air logistics officer Jarry Emmanuel confirmed that most of the 200 flights going in and out of the airport each day were still being reserved for the US military: "their priorities are to secure the country. Ours are to feed."[12] By Monday, 18 January, no matter how many US embassy or military spokesman insisted that "we are here to help" rather than invade, governments as different as those of France and Venezuela had begun to accuse the US of effectively "occupying" the country.[13] "Together with geopolitical control," observed Camille Chalmers a few weeks later, "we believe that the militarization of Haiti responds to what Bush called a 'preventive war' logic. The US fears a popular uprising, because the living standards in Haiti have for so long been intolerable, and this is even more so the case now; they are inhumane. So the troops are getting ready for when the time comes to suppress the people."[14]

The US decision to privilege military over humanitarian traffic at the airport sealed the fate of thousands of people abandoned in the rubble of lower Port-au-Prince and Léogane. In countries all over the world, search and rescue teams were ready to leave for Haiti within 12 hours of the disaster. Only a few were able to arrive without fatal delays – mainly teams, like those from Venezuela, Iceland and China, who managed to land while Haitian staff still retained control of their airport. Some subsequent arrivals, including a team from the UK, were prevented from landing with their heavy moving equipment. Others, such as

Canada's several Heavy Urban Search Rescue Teams, were immediately readied but never sent; the teams were told to stand down, the Canadian Foreign Affairs Minister Lawrence Cannon eventually explained, because "the government had opted to send Canadian Armed Forces instead," forces that subsequently played no significant role in the relief operation.[15]

USAID announced on 19 January that international search and rescue teams, over the course of the first week after the disaster, had managed to save a grand total of 70 people.[16] The majority of these people were rescued in quite specific locations and circumstances. "Search-and-rescue operations," observed the *Washington Post* on 18 January, "have been intensely focused on buildings with international aid workers, such as the crushed UN headquarters, and on large hotels with international clientele."[17] Tim Schwartz spent much of the first post-quake week as a translator with rescue workers, and was struck by the fact that most of their work was confined to places – the UN's Hotel Christophe, the Montana Hotel, the Caribe supermarket – that were not only frequented by foreigners and the elite but that could be snugly enclosed within "secure perimeters." Elsewhere, he observed, UN troops did their best to make sure that rescue workers treated onlooking crowds as a source of potential danger rather than as people in need of assistance.[18] No foreign rescue workers, for instance, were dispatched to the site with perhaps the single highest number of casualties, the Carrefour Palm Apparel factory contracted to the Canadian company Gildan Activewear, which collapsed with hundreds of workers still inside.[19] (Gildan responded to the disaster, within hours, with a reassuring announcement that it would be shifting production to alternative sewing facilities in neighboring countries.[20])

Exactly the same logic condemned yet more people to death in and around Port-au-Prince's hospitals. In one of the most illuminating reports filed from the city, on 20 January *Democracy Now*'s Amy Goodman spoke with Dr. Evan Lyon of Partners in Health/Zanmi Lasante from the General Hospital, the most important medical center in the whole country. Lyon insisted that "there's no insecurity [...]. I don't know if you guys were out late last night, but you can hear a pin drop in this city. It's a peaceful place. There is no war. There is no crisis except the suffering that's ongoing [...]. The first thing that [your] listeners need to understand is that there is no insecurity here. There has not been, and I expect there will not be." On the contrary, Lyon explained, "this question of security and the rumors of security and the racism behind the idea of security has been our major block to getting aid in [...]. In terms of aid relief the response has been incredibly slow. There are teams of surgeons that have been sent to places that were, quote, 'more secure,' that have 10 or 20 doctors and 10 patients. We have a thousand people on this campus who are triaged and ready for surgery, but we only have four working operating rooms, without anaesthesia and without pain medications.[21]

Almost by definition, in post-quake Haiti it seemed that anyone or anything that could not be enclosed in a secure perimeter wasn't worth saving. In their occasional forays outside such perimeters, meanwhile, many Western journalists seemed able to find plenty of reasons for retreating behind them. Lurid stories of looting and gangs soon began to lend "security experts" like the London-based Stuart Page[22] an aura of apparent authority, when he explained to the BBC's gullible "security correspondent" Frank Gardner that "all the security gains made in Haiti in the last few years could now be reversed [...]. The criminal gangs, totaling some 3,000, are going to exploit the current humanitarian crisis, to the maximum degree."[23] Another seasoned BBC correspondent, Matt Frei, had a similar story to tell on 18 January, when he found a few scavengers sifting through the remains of a central shopping district. "Looting is now the only industry here," he said. "Anything will do as a weapon. Everything is now run by rival armed groups of thugs." If Haiti is to avoid anarchy, Frei concluded, "what may be needed is a full-scale military occupation."[24]

Scores of Haitian and Haiti-based correspondents boiled over with indignation in the face of such grotesque misrepresentation. On 17 January, for instance, Ciné Institute director David Belle tried to counter international distortion. "I have been told that much US media coverage paints Haiti as a tinderbox ready to explode. I'm told that lead stories in major media are of looting, violence and chaos. There could be nothing further from the truth. I have traveled the entire city daily since my arrival. The extent of the damage is absolutely staggering [but] NOT ONCE have we witnessed a single act of aggression or violence [. . .]. A crippled city of two million awaits help, medicine, food and water. Most haven't received any. Haiti can be proud of its survivors. Their dignity and decency in the face of this tragedy is itself staggering."[25] As anyone can see, however, dignity and decency are no substitute for security. No amount of weapons will ever suffice to reassure those fortunate few whose fortunes isolate them from the people they exploit.

As far as the people themselves were concerned, however, "security is not the issue," Kim Ives explained soon after the earthquake. "We see throughout Haiti the population themselves organizing themselves into popular committees to clean up, to pull out the bodies from the rubble, to build refugee camps, to set up their security for the refugee camps. This is a population which is self-sufficient, and it has been self-sufficient for many years." While the people who have lost what little they had have done their best to cope and regroup, it's the soldiers sent to "restore order" who provoke confrontation, by treating them as potential combatants. "It's just the same way they reacted after Katrina. The victims are what's scary."[26] "According to everyone I spoke with in the center of the city," confirmed Schwarz around the same time, "the violence and gang stuff is pure BS." The relentless obsession with security, agreed Andy Kershaw, is clear proof of the fact that most foreign soldiers and NGO workers "haven't a clue about the country and its people."[27]

In order to help keep these people where they belong, meanwhile, the US Department of Homeland Security took unprecedented emergency measures to secure the homeland during the first post-quake weeks. Operation Vigilant Sentry made full use of the large naval flotilla the US quickly assembled around Port-au-Prince. "As well as providing emergency supplies and medical aid," noted the *Daily Telegraph*, "the *USS Carl Vinson*, along with a ring of other navy and coast guard vessels, is acting as a deterrent to Haitians who might be driven to make the 681 mile sea crossing to Miami." While Senegal's President Abdoulaye Wade offered "voluntary repatriation to any Haitian that wants to return to [the land of] their origin," American officials confirmed that they would continue to apply their long-standing (and thoroughly illegal) policy with respect to all Haitian refugees and asylum seekers – to intercept and repatriate them automatically, regardless of the circumstances.[28] Over these same weeks, to be on the safe side, the US Air Force took the additional precaution of flying a radio-transmitting cargo plane for five hours a day over large parts of the country, so as to broadcast a recorded message from Haiti's ambassador in Washington. "Don't rush on boats to leave the country," the message said. "If you think you will reach the US and all the doors will be wide open to you, that's not at all the case. They will intercept you right on the water and send you back home where you came from." Not even life-threatening injuries were enough to entitle Haitians to a different sort of American reception.

When the dean of medicine at the University of Miami arrived to help set up a field hospital by the airport in Port-au-Prince, he was outraged to find that most seriously injured people in the city were being denied the visas they would need to be transferred to Florida for surgery and treatment.[29] As of 19 January the State Department had authorized a total of 23 exceptions to its golden rule of immigration. Six months later, moreover, no less than 55,000 Haitians (with family members living in the US) who had *already* been approved to come to the US before the earthquake struck would still be languishing in a legal limbo, because of rigid US adherence to immigration quotas.[30]

With breathtaking cynicism, US President Obama appointed his predecessor George Bush (whose administration was responsible for the 2004 coup in Haiti and whose "relief effort following Hurricane Katrina in 2005 amounted to an ethnic cleansing of many of New Orleans's black population"[31]) to help Bill Clinton front US fundraising for the relief effort. When US ambassador to Haiti Kenneth Merten paid a visit to Washington in mid-February he declared himself satisfied with the work in progress. "I believe that this will be something that people will be able to look back on in the future as a model for how we've been able to sort ourselves out as donors on the ground and responding to an earthquake."[32]

III

As untold thousands of bodies were left to rot in the rubble of Port-au-Prince, in February and March international attention turned to plans for the massive reconstruction process. Almost every credible observer agreed about many of the most urgent things that needed to happen.[33] The recovery had to be Haitian-led. The priority had to be measures that would empower ordinary Haitian people to regain some control over their lives, to gain or regain access to an education, an income, a place to live, a future for themselves and their families. The internationally imposed neo-liberal policies that for decades have devastated the agrarian economy and reduced the state sector to an impotent façade had to be dropped and then forcefully reversed. There had to be massive and systematic investment in essential public services, in all parts of the country. Genuine Haitian sovereignty, popular, economic and political, had to be restored.

Instead, the actual reconstruction process has mainly conformed to precisely the same old tendencies that have made Haiti so vulnerable to natural, economic and political disaster in recent decades. The great majority of Haitian people have been entirely excluded from all meaningful participation in the planning or execution of reconstruction work. Apart from a series of forums that began at the Aristide Foundation in Tabarre in March, there has been little or no attempt to bring "large groups of Haitians together to ask for their opinions, their input, or their stories."[34] Even so-called "civil society" organizations and groups (including PAPDA, ENFOFANM, GARR, SOFA, the MPP and so on), nurtured as part of the anti-Lavalas campaign before and immediately after the 2004 coup, have been shut out of this new phase of Haiti's "transition to democracy."[35] No significant measures have been taken to stimulate the local agrarian economy or to encourage the decentralization of people, resources and investment. The strategic plan drafted in early 2009 by neo-liberal "development" economist Paul Collier and subsequently adopted by the UN's reconstruction team remains geared above all to the exploitation of Haitian poverty, as the most reliable means of generating new profits for the benefit of elite and multinational corporations. The political framework that will force implementation of this plan remains one in which the autonomy of Haiti's people and government is reduced more or less to zero.

One of the most striking features of the relief effort was the almost automatic decision of the "international community" to work through their own agencies and NGOs, rather than the Haitian state or grassroots popular organizations. For every dollar of US aid to Haiti in the first weeks after the disaster, only a single penny was received by the Haitian government.[36] Six months on, of the $1.8 billion for earthquake relief sent to Haiti, Paul Farmer notes, "less than 2.9 percent has so far gone to the government."[37] In February, Haiti's president René Préval and his ministers began to complain more loudly about the way foreign governments and NGOs had taken control of the relief and reconstruction effort. In early March, Préval called on the United States to "stop sending food aid" to Haiti "so that our economy can recover and create jobs."[38] Other Haitian leaders "including Prime Minister Jean-Max Bellerive are not happy with the way the aid money is being delivered," reported the AP on 5 March: "the NGOs don't tell us [. . .] where the money's coming from or how they're spending it."[39] On 27 March, speaking from the main hospital in Port-au-Prince, Partners in Health director Dr. Joia Mukherjee confirmed that in practice international management of relief involved "the real disempowerment of the government. The entire response has bypassed the government in its entirety and this is very worrisome for people in Haiti." At a time when hundreds of millions of dollars were starting to funnel through foreign and NGO agencies, the government still had no access to "funds for general operating costs, like paying people's salaries. For us, the most clear example is the general hospital, [. . .] the *only* public referral hospital in the city – [where] salaries haven't been paid for *4.5 months*. You have doctors and nurses and other staff living in their cars, living on the street, living in tents and they haven't been paid."[40]

The subordinate status of the Haitian people and government was made crystal clear in the run-up to the decisive international donors conference held at the UN's New York headquarters on 31 March 2010. The total amount pledged by conference participants came to the substantial sum of $5.3 billion over eighteen months (with an additional $4.6 billion anticipated, in theory, for subsequent years). Of this $5.3 billion, the only direct support pledged to the Haitian government amounted to just $350 million (i.e. 6.6 percent of the total), set aside to cover unpaid salaries of state employees. The key decision, however, involved the creation of a mainly foreign body to decide on the allocation of these promised billions, the Interim Haiti Recovery Commission (IHRC). The commission is jointly chaired by Haitian Prime Minister Jean-Max Bellerive and former US President (and former Haiti occupier) Bill Clinton. (Original plans for a 24-member board – 11 Haitians along with 13 foreigners representing international financial institutions and the larger donor nations – had to be revised, in the face of subsequent protests, to allow for numerically equal Haitian/foreign representation.) Once plans are approved by this IHRC, another group of foreign technocrats and World Bank officials will then supervise the subsequent spending.[41]

No doubt some degree of centralized investment coordination is better than the debilitating fragmentation that has hitherto prevailed in the Haitian "republic of NGOs," NGOs that even before the earthquake provided around three quarters of local public services. As Bellerive points out, before the IHRC was established, "100 percent of the money pledged to Haiti was decided by the one giving it," so a move toward 50 percent is a step forward of sorts."[42] Nevertheless, there is no disguising the fact that Haitians will serve as the junior partners on this commission, in ways that none of the donor countries themselves would ever contemplate. In the weeks after the UN conference, the largest donors held up initial dis-bursement of the promised billions until a sufficiently cowed Haitian government was prepared to offer formal acknowledgement of its subordination. As Yves Engler explains, "the international community – led by the US, France and Canada – demanded the Haitian parliament pass an 18-month long state of emergency law that effectively gave up government control over the reconstruction."[43] When parliamentary terms expired in Haiti in May 2010, the IHRC took over as the de facto government of the country, and in terms of actual power and influence it will remain in charge well after new legislators are elected in November.

One of the main reasons why the Haitian government is in no position to argue with the terms dictated to it on 31 March is that long-term international insistence on the privatization of publicly owned assets has stripped it of direct control over most of the resources and skills required to maintain some influence over its economy (let alone cope with a full-scale disaster). Transport, construction, education, energy, health care, agriculture, banking – virtually every component of every sector has already been sold off to members of Haiti's tightly integrated business community. State-owned factories of two essential products, flour and cement, were privatized in 1997, during Préval's first administration. A year into his second administration, Préval announced the privatization of Haiti's most valuable state-owned asset, the national telephone company (Téléco), and by mid-2007 almost half of the workforce, some 2,800 employees, had already been laid off. Téléco has been one of the few reliable sources of public revenue and employment in neo-liberal Haiti, and Téléco workers protested the privatization process from start to finish.[44] To no avail; four months after the earthquake, in early May 2010, the government finally sold a majority stake to a subsidiary of the Vietnamese army, for a mere $59 million. (Over these same years, the Irish company Digicel rapidly expanded to take a commanding position in Haiti's substantial and lucrative mobile phone market, and by 2008 it was already generating revenues of more than $250 million.[45])

Today, Patrick Elie notes, "Haiti is the most privatized country in the world. Almost everything that could be privatized here has been, and the only reason prisons have not been privatized is because it is not yet profitable for them to do so."[46] As a result, the Haitian government has lost some essential abilities – the ability to create jobs for large numbers of people, to appropriate needed land and resources, to produce vital construction materials and other goods – precisely at the moment of greatest need. By 2009, 65 percent of Haiti's budget already came from external sources,[47] and such far-reaching dependence breeds far-reaching deference. Although most of Haiti's crippling international debt was slowly forgiven over the course of 2010 (as a result of public pressure the

IMF reluctantly canceled Haiti's outstanding debt of $268 million on 21 July, while simultaneously insisting that urgently needed credit should take the form of a new $60m loan, to which the usual macroeconomic strings will apply), needless to say donor countries have stubbornly refused to acknowledge let alone discuss the several far-reaching ways in which *they* owe money to Haiti, rather than the reverse.[48]

Even in the wake of January 2010, no significant steps have been taken to palliate let alone reverse the neo-liberal privatization process. Even now, the depth and urgency of domestic needs are not enough to overturn the basic "development" model that has been imposed on Haiti for decades: orientation of the country's economy in line with the interests of local sweatshop owners and international consumers, privileging export-oriented agriculture, low-wage jobs, and tourism.[49] Punitive trade measures drove small Haitian farmers out of business and led to the massive population explosion in Port-au-Prince in recent decades; when so little aid materialized in the first weeks after the earthquake, more than half a million people retreated to their villages and farms, or what remains of them. With a little support they might well have stayed there. With modest job creation and credit facilities in the countryside, with small amounts of money for seeds and fertilizer, Jeffrey Sachs pointed out in late January, "Haiti's food production could double or triple in the next few years, sustaining the country and building a new rural economy."[50] But as usual, Haiti's small farmers received little or nothing. Only a paltry $23 million of the UN's initial request for emergency funds was intended for the agrarian sector, and by the end of February the UN admitted that even this money still hadn't been received. "In the countryside," Reed Lindsay observed in early March, "there is no evidence of any humanitarian aid, much less for agriculture."[51] As a result, confirms Mark Schuller, "with no jobs, no aid, no prospects of rural development, nothing to keep people in the provinces, the bulk of this reverse migration was undone, and Port-au-Prince is once again a magnet for those seeking jobs."[52]

IV

Although the rhetoric has recently evolved to take more notice of local sensibilities, over the last several decades the substance of international development policy has remained remarkably consistent. In the immediate aftermath of the earthquake, up in the higher, wealthier and mostly undamaged parts of Pétionville everyone already knew that it's the local residents "who through their government connections, trading companies and interconnected family businesses" would once again pocket the lion's share of international aid and reconstruction money.[53] At the same time, their counterparts in the US, represented by powerful think tanks and lobbyists such as the Heritage Foundation, the American Enterprise Institute or the RAND Corporation, were quick to see that (as RAND's James Dobbins, one of Clinton's former special envoys to Haiti, put it) "this disaster is an opportunity to accelerate oft-delayed reforms," including "breaking up or at least reorganizing the government-controlled telephone monopoly. The same goes with the Education Ministry, the electric company, the Health Ministry and the courts."[54] Of course, Eduardo Almeida of the Inter-American Development Bank admitted in mid-February, there are many "large construction companies who are already contacting us, since the investments are going to be huge; it's going to be attractive for any company."[55] And of course, as an Associated Press reporter would point out five months after the earthquake, "most of the companies seeking work in Haiti won't talk about it, in part to avoid seeming like they are capitalizing on catastrophe,"[56] in part because public distribution of substantial reconstruction funds will only begin in earnest in late 2010.

Some of Haiti's most powerful businessmen, however, have already paired up with multinational logistics and disaster recovery companies in order to take full advantage of the unprecedented influx of development funds. The Vorbe group, for instance, is one of the largest construction and logistics companies in Haiti, run by one of the powerful families that supported the 1991 coup; it has joined with the Alabama-based disaster recovery company DRC, which was awarded more than $100 million in contracts after Katrina (and which was investigated for fraudulent billing after Hurricane Mitch in Honduras). Haitian magnate Gilbert Bigio, likewise, has become a partner of Florida-based AshBritt Inc. AshBritt's CEO Randal Perkins is a prominent and well-connected political donor in the US, whose lobbyists helped him secure a $900m contract for helping clean up post-Katrina New Orleans.[57] By early June, AshBritt had already invested $25 million preparing its Haitian reconstruction operation on the outskirts of Port-au-Prince, in anticipation of substantial government contracts later in the year.[58] Other US companies that have profited from disaster in recent years may well calculate that finding a Haitian partner is an unnecessary expense: Leslie Voltaire, currently serving as a mediator between the Haitian government and the IHRC, reportedly told one local businessman that "only 15 percent of the [reconstruction] contracts will be going to Haitian contractors."[59]

In addition to foreign investors, so far it is mainly foreign-funded NGOs that have benefited the most from Haiti's misfortune. "All of the millions that are coming into Haiti right now are going into the hands of NGOs,"[60] complained Préval in early March, and in the estimation of one veteran social worker (Ruth Derilus), "of all the money they send here, only 10 percent actually makes it to the ground. The rest is spent on foreign experts, hotels, car rentals, hotel conferences."[61] The NGO sector has grown to become a "state within a state," agrees former Prime Minister Jacques-Edouard Alexis: "We've seen the NGOs' performance in Haiti, by experience, and there's been no development"[62]

As anyone who visits Port-au-Prince will readily confirm, there is a "massive gulf between people from the UN and the NGOs, and the people they're here to help."[63] Foreign NGO workers "continue to humiliate and discriminate [against] poor and respected Haitian citizens," regrets Haitian journalist Wadner Pierre, "by assuming they are all dangerous, violent, or savage people, and they do not know anything, not even how to put up a tent."[64] Tim Schwartz is probably the best-placed foreign observer of the NGOs that now control most of what happens in Haiti's "public" sphere. "The NGO sector in Haiti is best described," he writes, "as an uncoordinated mass of organizations de facto unaccountable to any governing or regulatory institution, i.e. no accountants, no auditors, no reviews, and no publication of poor or dishonest performance [. . .]. My own research on this matter suggests that at least 90 percent [of NGOs in Haiti] are rife with corruption, functionally inert, or give money intended for the poor to people who do not need it."[65] Surveying the performance of relief organizations during the first half of 2010, the Disaster Accountability Project was struck by a "shocking lack of transparency,"[66] and in early July, even CARICOM leaders began to speak openly about the ways in which the ever-growing influence of NGOs threatens "to undermine the democratic institutions in Haiti."[67]

Foreign investors and foreign NGOs, needless to say, also tend to need foreign protection to guarantee their security. True to form, once the initial wave of foreign troops began to subside, private, neo-military security companies like Triple Canopy (which took over the Xe/Blackwater security contract in Iraq in 2009) and Overseas Security & Strategic Information began promoting their services.[68] As an Al Jazeera report on a 9–10 March meeting of security companies in Miami explained, firms like GardaWorld, DynCorp and their ilk naturally "see new disaster areas as emerging markets."[69]

Their "humanitarian" counterparts in the UN and in USAID have done everything possible, within the limits of public decency, to facilitate such emergence. During the March donor conference John Holmes, the UN official in charge of Humanitarian Affairs, confirmed the essential development priority, telling the Associated Press that "the best sign that recovery was under way in Haiti would be an uptick in private investment." The president of Haiti's Chamber of Commerce and leading Haitian member of the IHRC (and a prominent supporter of both anti-Aristide coups), Reginald Boulos, reminded donors that a boost of foreign investment would depend on publicly funded "improvements in infrastructure" and "a climate change in the business environment."[70] According to Boulos, the agenda for change includes a reduction in government interference and corruption; what it most definitely doesn't include is any significant improvement in the pay or conditions of Haitian workers.

The year before the March 2010 conference, Boulos was a prominent opponent of a sustained campaign to increase Haiti's pitiful minimum wage to the equivalent of US$5 a day (at a time when in terms of actual purchasing power, Haitian wages have dropped to less than a fifth of their 1980 value). A series of well-organized strikes over the summer of 2009 helped encourage the Haitian legislature to approve the $5 rate; less public sorts of pressure encouraged Préval to overrule parliament and cap the increase at just $3 a day. Soon afterwards, in the autumn of 2009, Préval and the UN's special envoy to Haiti (Bill Clinton) announced plans for a new Free Trade Zone on the outskirts of Port-au-Prince, and Clinton has been drumming up new garment sector business ever since.

There are currently around 25,000 garment-sector workers in Haiti, making T-shirts and jeans for labels like Gildan, Hanes, Gap and New Balance. Factory profit margins average about 22 percent.[71] Canadian garment manufacturer Gildan is one of several companies that expanded production in Haiti after the 2004 coup, reassured by a post-democratic regime that promised a tax holiday and a moratorium on wage increases. In April 2005, CIBC World Markets analyst Ronald Schwarz found that "Gildan's manufacturing is among the most cost-competitive in the industry [. . .]. Gildan's labor costs in countries such as Haiti and Honduras are actually cheaper than those in China."[72] As things stand, companies like Gap (which already indirectly hires around 4,000 Haitian workers) are planning to develop their own made-in-Haiti clothing lines, and Grupo M, a large DR-based contractor whose Haitian operations include work for companies like Levi's and Banana Republic, is planning to double the size of its facilities in Ouanaminthe.[73]

The US-driven recovery strategy for Haiti turns on legislation (the Haiti Hemispheric Opportunity through Partnership Encouragement Act, or HOPE) that promises, over a limited period, US tariff exemptions for clothes assembled in Haiti. Clinton and the UN hope that in the coming years a new round of HOPE legislation will help create tens of thousands of new low-paid jobs. As several seasoned observers have pointed out, the same strategy was first used almost 40 years ago, in partnership with "president for life" Jean-Claude Duvalier.[74] Then as now, the investors promised that the creation of low-paid jobs will somehow lead to more and higher-paid jobs, and thus lift Haiti out of poverty.

The promise is belied, however, by the fact that these same investors and their apologists have always strenuously opposed even modest increases in the wages of Haitian workers, who are now so intensively exploited that a full-time job is no longer adequate for the barest necessities. Previous rounds of investment have in fact led to further real-term reductions in Haitian wages and incomes, and not the reverse: today, without the money sent home to their families by slightly better paid Haitian workers (themselves trapped in many of the most heavily exploitative sectors in North America and the Caribbean) the Haitian economy would collapse overnight. As some investors and their advisors are candid enough to admit, Haiti's most significant "comparative advantage" remains the stark fact that its people are so poor and so desperate that they are prepared to work for no more than a twentieth of the money they might receive for comparable employment in the US.[75] If workers are "barely able to scrape by," as David Wilson argues, "their spending can do little to stimulate job creation either in Haiti or in the region as a whole." Even this pathetically inadequate stimulus, moreover, is unlikely to last longer than the momentary effects of an injection of foreign-funded investment in infrastructure: in the Caribbean region as a whole, the light assembly sector has been shrinking rather than growing, as a result of competition from China and a drop in US demand, with tens of thousands of jobs lost in recent years in the neighboring Dominican Republic alone. The UN/US proposal, in other words, is less a matter of creating new jobs than of temporarily relocating some old ones – moving them from places where the pay is poor to a place where it's frankly obscene.[76] Given his commitment to this old agenda, notes Richard Morse, UN envoy Bill Clinton isn't bringing change or hope to Haiti. "Clinton, along with USAID, the World Bank, the Inter-American Development Bank and the United Nations are bringing more of the same to Haiti: more for the few and less for the many."[77]

In 2002–2003 the Aristide/Neptune government, under exactly the same sort of "investment" pressure, reluctantly and controversially went along with the creation of a World Bank-funded free trade zone on the border of the DR, at Ouanaminthe. In those years, the government was at least able to take the small step of doubling the minimum wage. This time around, as an Al Jazeera report observed in July, post-quake plans for the new zone are proceeding without any discussion of wages at all.[78] The sweatshop owners who were the driving force behind the 2004 coup – Andy Apaid, Charles Baker, and their associates – are now in a more blatantly abusive political position than ever before.

V

For the great majority of Haiti's people, preservation of such a profitable and deferential "business climate" comes at a truly devastating price: the transformation of poverty into misery, the decimation of local food production, and the loss of any government capacity to cope with changes in global food prices or supplies. In the spring of 2008, global food prices soared and many Haitians began to starve. That April, their anger took on a political shape. Hundreds of thousands protested, and the pressure forced Préval's prime minister, Jacques Edouard Alexis, to resign.[79] But in 2010 as in 2008 and previous years, the main response has been to increase rather than reduce reliance on a major source of the problem itself: international food aid. "In 2006/07, the entire budget of the Haitian Ministry of Agriculture was a measly $1.5 million," Robert Fatton notes, "a figure that contrasts sharply with the $69 million spent on the UN World Food Program. Instead of reconstructing its rural sector and promoting domestic food production, Haiti has remained a country of malnourished and hungry people alarmingly dependent on external assistance and charity."[80] If development organizations were "serious about improving agricultural output," Tim Schwarz agrees, "they should stop undermining the local market with foreign produce and instead buy Haitian surpluses, use them in nutritional supplement programs for mothers and children as well as store them for redistribution in lean seasons."[81] Instead, as Schwarz demonstrates in convincing detail in his 2008 book *Travesty in Haiti*, food aid has been deployed systematically and deliberately, from the beginning of its intensive use in the 1980s, to "destroy the Haitian economy of small farmers." Ostensibly humanitarian assistance has transformed the country into a captive market for highly subsidized US surplus production in grains and rice. Much of the support that USAID gives to charities like CARE comes "in the form of food and the requirement is that the food must be sold on the local markets," at prices that undercut the local competition. Schwartz shows that in recent years food aid has increased not just when local harvests are weak, but also in years of local *surplus* – with predictable consequences for Haitian farmers.[82] In 2010, intensification of this predatory policy amounted to little less than full-scale economic sabotage.

Meanwhile, the majority of people affected by the earthquake are obliged to wait for the humanitarian investor-saboteurs to determine the course of their future exploitation. It's likely they will wait for a long time. The 2010 donor conference was the third such conference for Haiti since 2004; it's been difficult if not impossible to verify the actual conversion of pledges into payments in the wake of the first two conferences, and a year after the 2009 conference "only 15 percent of the pledges that were made had actually been met."[83] So far, the 2010 conference fits the same pattern. By mid-summer, only five countries (Venezuela, Brazil, Norway, Estonia and Australia) had contributed to the UN's Haiti Reconstruction Fund, and less than 10 percent of the $5.3 billion pledged in March had actually been paid.[84] So far, the governments of France and the US have paid almost none of the millions they promised. US citizens, by contrast, responded to Haiti's plight with exceptional generosity, paying $1.3 billion to relief-oriented charities.[85] Unfortunately, these charities then opted to keep much of the money for themselves, or for an undetermined future. In May, CBS investigated five of the largest charities: CARE, the American Red Cross, Catholic Relief Services (CRS), the Clinton-Bush Haiti Fund, and the Clinton Foundation Haiti Fund. The last two on the list refused to answer questions, but their websites indicated that they had spent less than 15 percent of the $52m they collected; CARE had spent 16 percent of the $34.4 million it collected, and the Red Cross had spent around a quarter of its $444 million. Two months later, ABC News confirmed that of the $1.138 billion donated to the 23 largest charities, "at least 62.7 percent, $714.3 million, has been allocated for future Haiti relief efforts or is unassigned."

Lack of accessible funding, predictably, translates into a scarcity of discernible improvements "on the ground." All through the spring of 2010, press reports described the incredulity of both local residents and foreign observers as they watched the reconstruction effort proceed with a complacency and incompetence that beggar belief.[86] "Real recovery and reconstruction efforts have yet to begin," a Danish Church Aid worker observed in late June, and "international standards defining what people are entitled to after a disaster are in no way being met."[87] Incredibly, as of late summer 2010, only 2 percent of the rubble has been cleared from the streets of Port-au-Prince.[88] Equally shocking, 98 percent of the 1.5 million people made homeless continue to live in more than a thousand desperately inadequate camps, alternately baked by the tropical sun and flooded by torrential rains. Most of these people still lack a waterproof tent, let alone a transitional shelter capable of withstanding the hurricane winds that batter Haiti most summers, often with devastating effect.[89] An IJDH survey of internally displaced families conducted in July found taht "aid has trickled to a halt in most camps, leaving 75 percent of the families surveyed suffering from systematic undernourishment and 44 percent dependent on untreated water.[90] Rates of rape and violence against women have rapidly increased, and in most camps residents have no access to any sort of legal process or protection, or even any means of communicating with the foreign troops who continue to patrol their city.[91]

Today, Isabeau Doucet writes, "tens of thousands of families are subject to a relentless cycle of exodus, dispersal, and brutality at the hands of the Haitian National police and privately hired armed groups, in violation of Haitian and international law." In some places, "rather than clearing rubble from the streets, bulldozers are plowing over the tents of undesired 'squatters' only to resettle IDPs expelled from elsewhere."[92] Many thousands of the unwilling residents of these camps have been evicted or threatened with eviction by putative private landowners, forcing them to retreat to still more precarious or out-of-the-way locations.[93] The IHRC and the government have been unwilling to oblige other owners to sell land needed for more adequate resettlement camps, or even to oblige putative owners to prove the legitimacy of their titles with deeds or tax records. This too is no surprise since, as the AP reports, the government "appointed Gerard-Emile 'Aby' Brun, president of Nabatec Development, a consortium owned by some of Haiti's most powerful families, to be in charge of relocating the squatter camps in Port-au-Prince."[94] According to BAI (Bureau des Avocats Internationaux) lawyer Mario Joseph, almost "all land in Haiti is controlled by the elite through years of bribery and corruption [. . .]. In as much as 70 percent of forced expulsions, the land claims are disputable,"[95] but "the poor have been excluded from their land for years, and are now excluded from the process determining their rights to lodgings."[96]

In this as in so many other ways, Kim Ives confirms, the aftermath of 12 January reveals that the principal fault-line in Haiti is not geological but one of class. A small handful of rich families own large tracts of land in suburban Port-au-Prince which would be ideal for resettling the displaced thousands [. . .]. However, these same families control the Haitian government and, more importantly, have great influence in the newly formed 26-member Interim Commission to Reconstruct Haiti (IHRC) [. . .]. The IHRC is empowered for the next 18 months under a "State of Emergency Law" to seize land for rebuilding as it sees fit [. . .], but the elite families on this body in charge of expropriations are not volunteering their own well-situated land to benefit Haiti's homeless. As a result, only one major displaced person camp, Corail-Cesselesse, has been built, about 10 miles north of the capital, on a forbidding strip of sun-baked desert situated between Titayen and Morne Cabrit, two desolate zones where death-squads dumped their victims during the anti-Aristide coups.[97]

This "model" camp at Corail-Cesselesse remains the showcase of the reconstruction effort to date, an obligatory stop on the itinerary of every visiting journalist. Corail's tents are laid out in symmetrical rows, and it boasts latrines, showers, and a small clinic. But nothing else: there are no markets, shops or schools within walking distance, and there is no work. "There really is nothing to do," a resident told Mark Schuller. "You can't stay in your tent because of the heat. You can't go outside because of the dust. And you can't leave the camp because there's nothing to do."[98] Camp Corail is little more than a holding pen, and a flimsy one at that: most of its tents collapsed during a storm on the night of 12 July, injuring six people. By that stage, months after their construction was announced, only one of the hundreds of "transitional houses" anticipated for the camp had been built.[99] Camp Corail is itself located on land owned by Nabatec, incidentally, which stands to gain handsomely from both the government's compensation scheme and from an anticipated industrial park planned for the new neighborhood. In this way, Ives concludes, "the bourgeoisie keeps its best land and sells its worst for a huge, guaranteed profit."[100]

Most of the homeless, meanwhile, have no choice but to continue camping on the first patch of earth they were able to find – one camp, for instance, is perched on the strip of concrete, two meters wide, that divides the Route de Carrefour. By early June a grand total of 7,500 people had been moved from the most vulnerable campsites to "planned" resettlement zones, and by the end of July, the UN admitted that only 6,000 of the required 125,000 durable shelters required had been built. At the height of this misery, in July, the UN Mission Chief Edmond Mulet acknowledged that "we have lost the sense of urgency."[101]

VI

As you might expect, there is no such sense of loss among people more directly concerned by the disaster. Perhaps the most striking feature of the whole post-quake period has been the extraordinary hardiness and discipline of the hundreds of thousands of people who have lost their relatives, homes and possessions, and who from day one began to organize themselves into new communities. They have pooled their resources, arranged for the distribution of food and water, improvised informal systems of justice. The camps are the product of desperation, but the unprecedented concentration of people also affords unprecedented opportunities for association and assembly: the same factors that have turned Cité Soleil into a center of popular political power in recent decades have also begun to take effect in Champs de Mars and the other larger camps. "In the camps," Camille Chalmers observed a few weeks after the quake, "people are talking a lot about solidarity, fraternity, mutual aid."[102] In the face of dramatic vulnerability and marginalization, camp residents have also begun to exert some political pressure. "Citizens regularly take to the streets," Beverly Bell wrote in July,

> to demand housing for the displaced, good education, and support of national agricultural production. They have recently protested vio-lence by the UN security mission, non-payment of wages to state workers and teachers and the introduction of toxic Monsanto seeds, among other complaints. Grassroots organizations still meet regularly to develop their strategies for political change, as they have throughout history. Across the country on any given day, small groups perch on broken chairs under tarps in refugee camps, huddle amidst rubble in the courtyards of earthquake-destroyed schools or sweat under thatched-roof gazebos [. . .]. They are developing pressure points for housing rights and protection against rape for those in camps. Some plan information campaigns aimed at sweatshop workers, others programs to politicize youth. The agendas are seemingly endless.[103]

On 22 March, hundreds protested the flying visit of former US presidents Clinton and Bush. On 10 May, several thousand people were dispersed by police tear gas after they converged on the ruins of the national palace, calling for Préval to resign. On 17 May, thousands more of people demonstrated against Préval and the "state of emergency law" passed the previous month, which gave de facto control of Haiti to the foreign-dominated IHRC. UN tear gas, rubber bullets and arrests ended a more militant student demonstration on 24 May,[104] and the next day thousands more people converged on the palace ruins.[105] Hundreds rallied in Port-au-Prince to denounce the UN occupation on 1 June, the day of its sixth anniversary; six weeks later, several thousand marched in celebration of Aristide's birthday, calling for his immediate return.[106] Then on 12 August, residents of a dozen or so IDP camps, threatened with imminent eviction, organized the first of a growing and open-ended series of protests against abuse of their human rights, against the expulsions and against illegitimate land claims.[107]

In the election year of 2010, as in the previous elections of 2000 and 1990, the key political difference remains the division between (a) critics calling merely for a more efficient deployment of reconstruction re-sources and more "reasonable" forms of cooperation with the occupying troops and aid workers, and (b) activists working to rekindle popular mobilization for fundamental political change as the only viable means of regaining national sovereignty and establishing social justice. Spokes-people for the NGOs, the UN, the US and other "friends of Haiti" freely grumble about local inefficiency and corruption, but tend to leave political questions to one side. From this perspective, after all, the fundamental decisions have already been taken, and it only remains to find "willing partners" prepared to carry them out; the only roles left for the Haitian people themselves are those of dignified beneficiaries on the one hand or of resentful "obstacles to reform" on the other. The UN's humanitarian chief, for instance, remains concerned first and foremost with "the potential consequences in terms of both politics and security of large demonstrations in some sensitive places."[108] Stability, i.e. docility, remains the top priority. As the CEPR noted in early June, a review of "the last five Joint Operations and Tasking Centre (JOTC) reports reveals that the MINUSTAH [UN stabilization mission] is still focusing almost solely on security. Combining data from the previous six days, the JOTC reports show that MINUSTAH has undertaken 5,092 security opera-tions, involving 29,537 troops, and 56 maritime patrols. On the other hand, there have been 51 humanitarian assistance missions, involving just 359 troops."[109]

By contrast, activists organizing in and around the BAI and the new coalition PLONBAVIL (National Platform of Base Organizations and

State Victims) focus on the mechanisms of exclusion that have pushed the vast majority of Haiti's citizens to the outer margins of politics. "There is a sort of merging of the Fanmi Lavalas base organizations and former PPN members happening there," Kim Ives observes, "one which has happened without the consent (and maybe somewhat to the chagrin) of the leaders of both parties. It was really an attraction and elopement of the 'bases,' and my sense is that the center of anti-imperialist resistance to the Préval plan and crew was and is really coming out of that crucible. This is where the progressive and revolutionary leadership for this post-quake era is emerging from."[110] Patrick Elie, likewise, stakes everything on a renewal of the popular movement that opened the door to political change in the late 1980s: "I put all my money on our ability, at the level of the grassroots movement, to remobilize the Haitian people, to make them believe, once more, that they are the key players in politics."[111]

Unfortunately, the main institutional legacy of the Lavalas mobilization – Aristide's Fanmi Lavalas (FL) Party – is itself both divided and excluded from the political process. After its landslide election victory in 2000, opposition politicians anticipated that FL might remain hegemonic for "sixty years" (see above, page 75). The second anti-Lavalas coup and its aftermath helped level the political playing field. In 2004 Aristide and many of his ministers were forced into exile; his prime minister, Yvon Neptune, and dozens of other high-level members of FL were imprisoned. In the run-up to the 2006 presidential elections the leading FL candidate, Father Gérard Jean-Juste, was jailed on trumped-up charges and prevented from standing. In August 2007, the country's most prominent human rights activist, Lovinsky Pierre-Antoine, was "disappeared" (and is presumed dead) shortly after he announced his intention to stand as an FL candidate for the senate. Préval's hand-picked Provisional Electoral Commission (CEP) went on to block FL candidates from participating in senate elections in April 2009, on bogus procedural grounds.[112]

In response, FL campaigners and supporters organized a boycott, and only a tiny fraction of the electorate turned out to vote – 11 percent, according to Préval's officials, but less than half that according to his opponents and most observers.[113] In public, US and UN officials condemned the CEP decision and called for the inclusion of all political parties. Curiously, however, when the CEP stuck to its guns the US and the rest of its "international community" quietly abandoned calls for free and inclusive elections, and instead agreed to cover most of the election's costs. Brian Concannon draws attention to the double standard: "all of the international agencies that had criticized the exclusion when it was made, praised the elections when they were held without the participation of FL or over 90 percent of Haitian voters."[114] In November 2009, the CEP again barred FL again (along with several other parties) from registering for legislative elections originally planned for February 2010, despite the fact that FL went out of its way to meet the new procedural requirements invented the previous spring; again the CEP won international support and funding. After the earthquake obliged the CEP to push this next round of elections back to November 2010, they renewed (on 21 July) the exclusion of FL yet again, and again in apparent defiance of US and international recommendations.[115]

As a result, the next Haiti parliament and president will be elected, once more, without the participation of the most popular political organization in the country. So long as the result is an apparent endorsement of the status quo, no doubt these elections too will receive the international stamp of approval in due course.

The FL leadership has made matters worse by indulging in years of sterile post-Aristide infighting. By early 2008, animosity between rival factions had grown so intense that they had become more or less separate organizations, and by the spring of 2009 a number of leaders with grassroots support had defected to Préval's camp. Government harassment coupled with the lack of unity deprives the popular movement of any imminent opportunity to use what Samba Boukman could still call, in 2006, its "greatest weapon" – its ability to win elections. At the time of writing (in September 2010), the presidential election scheduled for November 2010 held out little prospect of significant change. For a brief moment in mid-summer, the singer Wyclef Jean's celebrity candidacy rekindled a brief burst of media interest in Haiti. Some commentators were charmed by his youth and "energy," while others drew attention to his support for the 2004 coup and for neo-liberal policies, his lack of political qualifications, program or experience, and the financial scandals that have plagued the Yele Haiti charity he fronts.[116] The journalist Ansel Herz summed him up best by describing him as Haiti's Sarah Palin: "incoherent, incompetent and in it for himself."[117] Having lived most of his life in the US, Wyclef (along with the formerly Miami-based militant Lavarice Gaudin and a dozen other hopefuls) was declared ineligible to stand in August. The remaining candidates include Préval's former Prime Minister Jacques-Edouard Alexis, Jean-Henri Céant (Aristide's former lawyer and a veteran behind-the-scenes FL operator), and Aristide's last prime minister, the moderate FL loyalist Yvon Neptune – Neptune probably represents the most powerful degree of institutional continuity with the pre-2004 régime, but many in or with the FL base still condemn him as a de facto collaborator with the coup. The two anti-Lavalas coups have gone a long way towards eliminating any residual belief that genuine social change in Haiti might still be possible by formal democratic means. "In all the camps I've visited," writes journalist Isabeau Doucet, "there is no interest in the elections let alone any enthusiasm for any particular candidate."[118] The progressive weekly newspaper *Haïti Liberté* has dismissed the upcoming 2010 election as a "charade" rigged up by the foreign "friends of Haiti" in order to legitimate the occupation, and will not back any of the candidates.[119]

In many ways Lavalas is today less an organization than an idea and a memory, and the lack of adequate organization and leadership leaves the renewal of popular mobilization vulnerable to all kinds of opportunistic manipulation. According to some of the mediators that serve as go-betweens between various political interests and the captive residents of the camps, many of the people who participate in demonstrations for or against the government do so for the sake of (pitifully small) financial reward. "Nobody protests without money in this country," one such mediator told Al Jazeera in July: "the rich people keep us in misery, to make us do whatever they want"[120] – which is to say, more often than not, to do nothing at all. The May 2010 protests, the most substantial since the quake, were endorsed by politicians from all sides of the political spectrum, including veteran Lavalas partisans like René Civil and prominent 2004 coup supporters like Hervé Saintilus, Evans Paul and Himmler Rébu.[121] The most important political question in Haiti today concerns the direction, priorities, and integrity of this incipient protest movement. Along with many of his allies, PLONBAVIL's Yves Pierre-Louis is "very aware of the dangers posed by allowing former putchists into our alliance and demonstrations," while insisting that "the unity and consciousness of the progressive forces in this mobilization are strong."[122]

In the election of 2010, as in the last four presidential elections in Haiti, everything will depend on whether this unity and this consciousness are strong enough to prevail over the vast and diverse array of forces drawn up to oppose them. The earthquake has sharpened and accelerated the basic political choice facing Haiti: either renewal of the popular mobilization in pursuit of equality and justice, or long-term confirmation of the island's current status as a neo-colonial protectorate.

17 September 2010.

Appendix

"One Step at a Time": An Interview with Jean-Bertrand Aristide (20 July 2006)[1]

Peter Hallward: Haiti is a profoundly divided country, and you have always been a profoundly divisive figure. For most of the 1990s many sympathetic observers found it easy to make sense of this division more or less along class lines: you were demonized by the rich, and idolized by the poor. But then things started to seem more complicated. Rightly or wrongly, by the end of the decade, many of your original supporters had become more sceptical, and from start to finish your second administration (2001–2004) was dogged by accusations of violence and corruption. Although by every available measure you remained by far the most trusted and popular politician among the Haitian electorate, you appeared to have lost much of the support you once enjoyed among parts of the political class, among aid-workers, activists, intellectuals and so on, both at home and abroad. Most of my questions have to do with these accusations, in particular the claim that as time went on you compromised or abandoned many of your original ideals.

To begin with though, I'd like quickly to go back over some familiar territory, and ask about the process that first brought you to power back in 1990. The late 1980s were a very reactionary period in world politics, especially in Latin America. How do you account for the remarkable strength and resilience of the popular movement against dictatorship in Haiti, the movement that came to be known as Lavalas (a Kreyol word that means "flood" or "avalanche", and also a "mass of people," or "everyone together")? How do you account for the fact that, against the odds and certainly against the wishes of the US, the military and the whole ruling establishment in Haiti, you were able to win the election of 1990?

Jean–Bertrand Aristide: Much of the work had already been done by people who came before me. I'm thinking of people like Father Antoine Adrien and his co-workers, and Father Jean-Marie Vincent, who was assassinated in 1994. They had developed a progressive theological vision that resonated with the hopes and expectations of the Haitian people.

Already in 1979 I was working in the context of liberation theology, and there is one phrase in particular that remains etched in my mind, and that may help summarize my understanding of how things stood. You might remember that the Conferencia de Puebla took place in Mexico, in 1979, and at the time several liberation theologians were working under severe constraints. They were threatened and barred from attending the conference. And the slogan I'm thinking of ran something like this: *si el pueblo no va a Puebla, Puebla se quedará sin pueblo*. If the people cannot go to Puebla, Puebla will remain cut off from the people.

In other words, for me the people remain at the very core of our struggle. It isn't a matter of struggling for the people, on behalf of the people, at a distance from the people; it is the people themselves who are struggling, and it's a matter of struggling with and in the midst of the people.

This ties in with a second theological principle, one that Sobrino, Boff and others understood very well. Liberation theology can itself only be a phase in a broader process. The phase in which we may first have to speak on behalf of the impoverished and the oppressed comes to an end as they start to speak in their own voice and with their own words. The people start to assume their own place on the public stage. Liberation theology then gives way to a liberation of theology, which can also include liberation from theology. The whole process carries us a long way from paternalism, a long way from any notion of a "saviour" who might come to guide the people and solve their problems. The priests who were inspired by liberation theology at that time understood that our role was to accompany the people, not to replace them.

The emergence of the people as an organized public force, as a collective consciousness, was already taking place in Haiti in the 1980s, and by 1986 this force was strong enough to push the Duvalier dictatorship from power. It was a grassroots popular movement, and not at all a top-down project driven by a single leader or a single organization. It wasn't an exclusively political movement, either. It took shape above all through the constitution, all over the country, of many small church communities or *ti legliz*. It was these small communities that played the decisive historical role. When I was elected president it wasn't a strictly political affair, it wasn't the election of a politician, of a conventional political party. No, it was an expression of a broad popular movement, of the mobilization of the people as a whole. For the first time, the national palace became a place not just for professional politicians but for the people themselves. The simple fact of allowing ordinary people to enter the palace, the simple fact of welcoming people from the poorest sections of Haitian society within the very center of traditional power – this was already a profoundly transformative gesture.

PH: *You hesitated for some time, before agreeing to stand as a candidate in those 1990 elections. You were perfectly aware of how, given the existing balance of forces, participation in the elections might dilute or divide the movement. Looking back at it now, do you still think it was the right thing to do? Was there a viable alternative to taking the parliamentary path?*

JBA: I tend to think of history as the ongoing crystallization of different sorts of variables. Some of the variables are known, some are unknown. The variables that we knew and understood at the time were clear enough. We had some sense of what we were capable of, and we also knew that those who sought to preserve the status quo had a whole range of means at their disposal. They had all sorts of strategies and mechanisms – military, economic, political . . . – for disrupting any movement that might challenge their grip on power. But we couldn't know how exactly they would use them. They couldn't know this themselves. They were paying close attention to how the people were struggling to invent ways of organizing themselves, ways of mounting an effective challenge. This is what I mean by unknown variables: the popular movement was in the process of being invented and developed, under pressure, there and then, and there was no way of knowing in advance the sort of counter-measures it might provoke.

Now given the balance of these two sorts of variables, I have no regrets. I regret nothing. In 1990, I was asked by others in the movement to accept the cross that had fallen to me. That's how Father Adrien described it, and how I understood it: I had to take up the burden of this cross. "You are on the road to Calvary," he said, and I knew he was right. When I refused it at first, it was Monsignor Willy Romélus, whom I trusted and still trust, as an elder and as a counsellor, who insisted that I had no choice. "Your life doesn't belong to you anymore," he said. "You have given it as a sacrifice for the people. And now that a concrete obligation has fallen on you, now that you are faced with this particular call to follow Jesus and take up your cross, think carefully before you turn your back on it."

This then is what I knew, and knew full well at the time. It was a sort of path to Calvary. And once I had decided, I accepted this path for what it was, without illusions, without deluding myself. We knew perfectly well that we wouldn't be able to change everything, that we wouldn't be able to right every injustice, that we would have to work under severe constraints, and so on.

Suppose I had said no, I won't stand. How would the people have reacted? I can still hear the echo of certain voices that were asking, "Let's see now if you have the courage to take this decision, let's see if you are too much of a coward to accept this task. You who have preached such fine sermons, what are you going to do now? Are you going to abandon us, or are you going to assume this responsibility so that together we can move forward?" And I thought about this. What was the best way to put the message of the Gospels into practice? What was I supposed to do? I remember how I answered that question, when a few days before the election of December 1990, I went to commemorate the victims of the ruelle de Vaillant massacre, where some twenty people were killed by the Macoutes on the day of the aborted elections of November 1987. A student asked me: "Father, do you think that by yourself you'll be able to change this situation, which is so corrupt and unjust?" And in reply I said: "In order for it to rain, do you need one or many raindrops? In order to have a flood, do you need a trickle of water or a river in spate?" And I thanked him for giving me the chance to present our collective mission in the form of this metaphor: it is not alone, as isolated drops of water, that you or I are going to change the situation but together, as a flood or torrent, *lavalassement*, that we are going to change it, to clean things up, without any illusions that it will be easy or quick.

So were there other alternatives? I don't know. What I'm sure of is that there was then an historic opportunity, and that we gave an historic answer. We gave an answer that transformed the situation. We took a step in the right direction. Of course, in doing so we provoked a response. Our opponents responded with a coup d'état. First the attempted coup of Roger Lafontant, in January 1991, and when that failed, the coup of September 30th 1991. Our opponents were always going to have disproportionately powerful means of hindering the popular movement, and no single decision or action could have changed this. What mattered was that we took a step forward, a step in the right direction, followed by other steps. The process that began then is still going strong. In spite of everything it is still going strong, and I'm convinced that it will only get stronger. And that in the end it will prevail.

PH: *The coup of September 1991 took place even though the actual policies you pursued once in office were quite moderate, quite cautious. So was a coup inevitable? Regardless of what you did or didn't do, was the simple presence* *of someone like you in the presidential palace intolerable for the Haitian elite? And in that case, could more have been done to anticipate and try to withstand the backlash?*

JBA: Well it's a good question. Here's how I understand the situation. What happened in September 1991 happened again in February 2004, and could easily happen again soon, in the future, so long as the oligarchy who control the means of repression use them to preserve a hollow version of democracy. This is their obsession: to maintain a situation that might be called "democratic," but which consists in fact of a superficial, imported democracy that is imposed and controlled from above. They've been able to keep things this way for a long time. Haiti has been independent for 200 years, and we now live in a country in which just 1 percent of its people control more than half of its wealth. For the elite, it's a matter of us against *them*, of finding a way of preserving the massive inequalities that affect every facet of Haitian society. We are subject to a sort of apartheid. Ever since 1804, the elite has done everything in its power to keep the masses at bay, on the other side of the walls that protect their privilege. This is what we are up against. This is what any genuinely democratic project is up against. The elite will do everything in its power to ensure that it controls a puppet president and a puppet parliament. It will do everything necessary to protect the system of exploitation upon which its power depends. Your question has to be addressed in terms of this historical context, in terms of this deep and far-reaching continuity.

PH: *Exactly so – but in that case, what needs to be done to confront the power of this elite? If in the end it is prepared to use violence to counter any genuine threat to their hegemony, what is the best way to overcome this violence? For all its strength, the popular movement that carried you to the presidency wasn't strong enough to keep you there, in the face of the violence it provoked.*

People sometimes compare you to Toussaint L'Ouverture, who led his people to freedom and won extraordinary victories under extraordinary constraints – but Toussaint is also often criticized for failing to go far enough, for failing to break with France, for failing to do enough to keep the people's support. It was Dessalines who led the final fight for independence and who assumed the full cost of that fight. How do you answer those (like Patrick Elie, for instance, or Ben Dupuy[2]) who say you were too moderate, that you acted like Toussaint in a situation that really called for Dessalines? What do you say to those who claim you put too much faith in the US and its domestic allies?

JBA: Well [*laughs*]. "Too much faith in the US," that makes me smile . . . In my humble opinion Toussaint L'Ouverture, as a man, had his limitations. But he did his best, and in reality he did not fail. The dignity he defended, the principles he defended, continue to inspire us today. He was captured, his body was imprisoned and killed, yes; but Toussaint is still alive, his example and his spirit still guide us now. Today the struggle of the Haitian people is an extension of his campaign for dignity and freedom. These last two years, from 2004 to 2006, they continued to stand up for their dignity and refused to fall to their knees, they refused to capitulate. On 6 July 2005 Cité Soleil was attacked and bombarded, but this attack, and the many similar attacks, did not discourage people from insisting that their voices be heard. They spoke out against injustice. They voted for their president this past February, and this too was an assertion of their dignity; they will not accept the imposition of another president from abroad or above. This simple insistence on dignity is itself an engine of historical change. The people insist that they will be the *subject* of their history, not its object. As Toussaint was the subject of his history, so too the Haitian people have taken up and extended his struggle, as the subjects of their own history.

Again, this doesn't mean that success is inevitable or easy. It doesn't mean we can resolve every problem, or even that once we have dealt with a problem, powerful vested interests won't try to do all they can to turn the clock back. Nevertheless, something irreversible has been achieved, something that works its way through the collective consciousness. This is precisely the real meaning of Toussaint's famous claim, once he had been captured by the French, that they had cut down the trunk of the tree of liberty but that its roots remained deep. Our struggle for freedom will encounter many obstacles but it will not be uprooted. It is firmly rooted in the minds of the people. The people are poor, certainly, but our minds are free. We continue to exist, as a people, on the basis of this initial *prise de conscience*, of this fundamental awareness that we *are*.

It's not an accident that when it came to choosing a leader, this people, these people who remain so poor and so marginalized by the powers that be, should have sought out not a politician but a priest. The politicians had let them down. They were looking for someone with principles, someone who would speak the truth, and in a sense this was more important than material success, or an early victory over our opponents. This is Toussaint's legacy.

As for Dessalines, the struggle that he led was armed, it was a military struggle, and necessarily so, since he had to break the bonds of slavery once and for all. He succeeded. But do we still need to carry on with this same struggle, in the same way? I don't think so. Was Dessalines wrong to fight the way he did? No. But our struggle is different. It is Toussaint, rather than Dessalines, who can still accompany the popular movement today. It's this inspiration that was at work in the election victory of February 2006, that allowed the people to out-fox and out-maneuver their opponents, to choose their own leader in the face of the full might of the powers that be.

For me this opens out onto a more general point. Did we place too much trust in the Americans? Were we too dependent on external forces? No. We simply tried to remain lucid, and to avoid facile demagoguery. It would be mere demagoguery for a Haitian president to pretend to be stronger than the Americans, or to engage them in a constant war of words, or to oppose them for opposing's sake. The only rational course is to weigh up the relative balance of interests, to figure out what the Americans want, to remember what we want, and to make the most of the available points of convergence. Take a concrete example, the events of 1994. Clinton needed a foreign policy victory, and a return to democracy in Haiti offered him that opportunity; we needed an instrument to overcome the resistance of the murderous Haitian army, and Clinton offered us that instrument. This is what I mean by acting in the spirit of Toussaint L'Ouverture. We never had any illusions that the Americans shared our deeper objectives, we knew they didn't want to travel in the same direction. But without the Americans we couldn't have restored democracy.

PH: *There was no other option, no alternative to reliance on American troops?*

JBA: No. The Haitian people are not armed. Of course there are some criminals and vagabonds, some drug dealers, some gangs who have weapons, but the people have no weapons. You're kidding yourself if you think that the people can wage an armed struggle. We need to look the situation in the eye: the people have no weapons, and they will never have as many weapons as their enemies. It's pointless to wage a struggle on your enemies' terrain, or to play by their rules. You will lose.

PH: *Did you pay too high a price for American support? They forced you to make all kinds of compromises, to accept many of the things you'd always opposed – a severe structural adjustment plan, neo-liberal economic policies, privatization of the state enterprises, etc. The Haitian people suffered a great deal under these* *constraints. It must have been very difficult to swallow these things, during the negotiations of 1993–4.*

JBA: Yes of course, but here you have to distinguish between the struggle in principle, the struggle to persist in a preferential option for the poor, which for me is inspired by theology and is a matter of justice and truth, on the one hand, and on the other hand, *their* political struggle, which plays by different rules. In their version of politics you can lie and cheat if it allows you to pursue your strategic aims. The claim that there were weapons of mass destruction in Iraq, for instance, was a flagrant lie. But since it was a useful way of reaching their objective, Colin Powell and company went down that path.

As for Haiti, back in 1993, the Americans were perfectly happy to agree to a negotiated economic plan. When they insisted, via the IMF and other international financial institutions, on the privatization of state enterprises, I was prepared to agree in principle, if necessary – but I refused simply to sell them off, unconditionally, to private investors. I said no to untrammeled privatization. Now that there was corruption in the state sector was undeniable, but there were several different ways of engaging with this corruption. Rather than untrammeled privatization, I was prepared to agree to a *democratization* of these enterprises. What does this mean? It means an insistence on transparency. It means that some of the profits of a factory or a firm should go to the people who work for it. It means that some of those profits should be invested in things like local schools, or health clinics, so that the children of the workers can derive some benefit from their work. It means creating conditions on the micro level that are consistent with the principles that we want to guide development on the macro level. The Americans said fine, no problem.

We all signed those agreements, and I am at peace with my decision to this day. I spoke the truth. Whereas they signed them in a different spirit. They signed them because by doing so they could facilitate my return to Haiti and thus engineer their foreign policy victory, but once I was back in office, they were already planning to renegotiate the terms of the privatization. And that's exactly what happened. They started to insist on untrammeled privatization, and again I said no. They went back on our agreement, and then relied on a disinformation campaign to make it look like it was me who had broken my word. It's not true. The accords we signed are there, people can judge for themselves.[3] Unfortunately we didn't have the means to win the public relations fight. They won the communications battle, by spreading lies and distorting the truth, but I still feel that we won the real battle, by sticking to the truth.

PH: *What about your battle with the Haitian army itself, the army that overthrew you in 1991? The Americans re-made this army in line with their own priorities back in 1915, and it had acted as a force for the protection of those priorities ever since. You were able to disband it just months after your return in 1994, but the way it was handled remains controversial, and you were never able fully to demobilize and disarm the soldiers themselves. Some of them came back to haunt you with a vengeance, during your second administration.*

JBA: Again I have no regrets on this score. It was absolutely necessary to disband the army. We had an army of some 7,000 soldiers, and it absorbed 40 percent of the national budget. Since 1915, it had served as an army of internal occupation. It never fought an external enemy. It murdered thousands of our people. Why did we need such an army, rather than a suitably trained police force? So we did what needed to be done.

In fact we did organize a social programme for the reintegration of former soldiers, since they too are members of the national community. They too have the right to work, and the state has the responsibility to respect that right – all the more so when you know that if they don't find work, they will be more easily tempted to have recourse to violence, or theft, as did the Tontons Macoutes before them. We did the best we could. The problem didn't lie with our integration and demobilization programme, it lay with the resentment of those who were determined to preserve the old status quo. They had plenty of money and weapons, and they work hand in hand with the most powerful military machine in the world. It was easy for them to win over some former soldiers, to train and equip them in the Dominican Republic and then use them to destabilize the country. That's exactly what they did. But again, it wasn't a mistake to disband the army. It's not as if we might have avoided the second coup, the coup of 2004, if we had hung on to the army. On the contrary, if the army had remained in place then René Préval would never have finished his first term in office [1996–2001], and I certainly wouldn't have been able to hold out for three years, from 2001 to 2004.

By acting the way we did we clarified the real conflict at issue here. As you know, Haiti's history is punctuated by a long series of coups. But unlike the previous coups, the coup of 2004 wasn't undertaken by the "Haitian" army, acting on the orders of our little oligarchy, in line with the interests of foreign powers, as happened so many times before, and as happened again in 1991. No, this time these all-powerful interests had to carry out the job themselves, with their own troops and in their own name.

PH: *Once Chamblain and his little band of rebels got bogged down on the outskirts of Port-au-Prince and couldn't advance any further, US Marines had to go in and scoop you out of the country.*

JBA: Exactly. The real truth of the situation, the real contradiction organizing the situation, finally came out in the open, in full public view.

PH: *Going back to the mid-1990s for a moment, did the creation of the Fanmi Lavalas party in 1996 serve a similar function, by helping to clarify the actual lines of internal conflict that had already fractured the loose coalition of forces that first brought you to power in 1990? Why were there such deep divisions between you and some of your erstwhile allies, people like Chavannes Jean-Baptiste and Gérard Pierre-Charles? Almost the whole of Préval's first administration, from 1996 to 2000, was hampered by infighting and opposition from Pierre-Charles and the OPL. Did you set out, then, to create a unified, disciplined party, one that could offer and then deliver a coherent political programme?*

JBA: No, that's not the way it happened. In the first place, by training and by inclination I was a teacher, not a politician. I had no experience of party politics, and was happy to leave to others the task of developing a party organization, of training party members, and so on. Already back in 1991, I was happy to leave this to career politicians, to people like Gérard Pierre-Charles, and along with other people he began working along these lines as soon as democracy was restored. He helped found the Organisation Politique Lavalas [OPL] and I encouraged people to join it. This party won the 1995 elections, and by the time I finished my term in office, in February 1996, it had a majority in parliament. But then, rather than seek to articulate an ongoing relation between the party and the people, rather than continue to listen to the people, after the elections the OPL started to pay less attention to them. It started to fall into the traditional patterns and practices of Haitian politics. It started to become more closed in on itself, more distant from the people, more willing to make empty promises, and so on. As for me I was out of office, and I stayed on the sidelines. But a group of priests who were active in the Lavalas movement became frustrated, and wanted to restore a more meaningful link with the people. They wanted to remain in communion with the people. At this point (in 1996) the group of people who felt this way, who were unhappy with the OPL, were known as *la nébuleuse* – they were in an uncertain and confusing position. Over time there were more and more such people, who became more and more dissatisfied with the situation.

We engaged in long discussions about what to do, and Fanmi Lavalas grew out of these discussions. It emerged from the people themselves. And even when it came to be constituted as a political organization, it never conceived of itself as a conventional political party. If you look through the organization's constitution, you'll see that the word "party" never comes up. It describes itself as an organization, not a party. Why? Because in Haiti we have no positive experience of political parties; parties have always been instruments of manipulation and betrayal. On the other hand, we have a long and positive experience of *organisation*, of popular organizations – the *ti legliz*, for instance.

So no, it wasn't me who "founded" Fanmi Lavalas as a political party. I just brought my contribution to the formation of this organization, which offered a platform for those who were frustrated with the party that was the OPL [which was soon to re-brand itself as the neo-liberal Organisation du Peuple en Lutte], those who were still active in the movement but who felt excluded within it. Now in order to be effective Fanmi Lavalas needed to draw on the experience of people who knew something of politics, people who could act as political leaders without abandoning a commitment to truth. This is the hard problem, of course. Fanmi Lavalas doesn't have the strict discipline and coordination of a political party. Some of its members haven't yet acquired the training and the experience necessary to preserve both a commitment to truth and an effective participation in politics. For us, politics is deeply connected to ethics, this is the crux of the matter. Fanmi Lavalas is not an exclusively political organization. That's why no politician has been able simply to appropriate and use Fanmi Lavalas as a springboard to power. That will never be easy: the members of Fanmi Lavalas insist on the fidelity of their leaders.

PH: *That's a lesson that Marc Bazin, Louis-Gérald Gilles and a few others had to learn during the 2006 election campaign, to their cost.*

JBA: Exactly.

PH: *To what extent, however, did Fanmi Lavalas then become a victim of its own success? Rather like the ANC here in South Africa, it was obvious from the* *beginning that Fanmi Lavalas would be more or less unbeatable at the polls. But this can be a mixed blessing. How did you propose to deal with the many opportunists who immediately sought to worm their way into your organization?*

JBA: I left office early in 1996. By 1997, Fanmi Lavalas had emerged as a functional organization, with a clear constitution. This was already a big step forward from 1990. In 1990, the political movement was largely spontaneous; in 1997 things were more coordinated. Along with the constitution, at the first Fanmi Lavalas congress we voted and approved the program laid out in our *Livre Blanc: Investir dans l'humain*, which I know you're familiar with. This program didn't emerge out of nothing. For around two years we held meetings with engineers, with agronomists, with doctors, teachers, and so on. We listened and discussed the merits of different proposals. It was a collective process. The *Livre Blanc* is not a program based on my personal priorities or ideology. It's the result of a long process of consultation with professionals in all these domains, and it was compiled as a truly collaborative document. And as even the World Bank came to recognize, it was a genuine *program*, a coherent plan for the transformation of the country. It wasn't a bundle of empty promises.

Now in the midst of these discussions, in the midst of the emergent organization, it's true that you will find opportunists, you will find future criminals and future drug-dealers. But it wasn't easy to identify them. It wasn't easy to find them *in time*, and to expel them in time, before it was too late. Most of these people, before gaining a seat in parliament, behaved perfectly well. But you know, for some people power can be like alcohol: after a glass, two glasses, a whole bottle . . . you're not dealing with the same person. It makes some people dizzy. These things are difficult to anticipate. Nevertheless, I think that if it hadn't been for the intervention of foreign powers, we would have been able to make real progress. We had established viable methods for collaborative discussion, and for preserving direct links with the people. I think we would have made real progress, taking small but steady steps.

Even in spite of the aid embargo we managed to accomplish certain things. We were able to invest in education, for instance. As you know, in 1990 there were only 34 secondary schools in Haiti; by 2001 there were 138. The little that we had to invest, we invested it in line with the program laid out in *Investir dans l'humain*. We built a new university at Tabarre, a new medical school. Although it had to run on a shoestring, the literacy program we launched in 2001 was also working well;

Cuban experts who helped us manage the program were confident that by December 2004 we'd have reduced the rate of adult illiteracy to just 15 percent, a small fraction of what it was a decade earlier. Previous governments never seriously tried to invest in education, and it's clear that our program was always going to be a threat to the status quo. The elite want nothing to do with popular education, for obvious reasons. Again it comes down to this: we can either set out from a position of genuine freedom and independence, and work to create a country that respects the dignity of all its people, or else we will have to accept a position of servile dependence, a country in which the dignity of ordinary people counts for nothing. This is what's at stake here.

PH: *Armed then with its program, Fanmi Lavalas duly won an overwhelming victory in the legislative elections of May 2000, winning around 75 percent of the vote. No-one disputed the clarity and legitimacy of the victory. But your enemies in the US and at home soon drew attention to the fact that the method used to calculate the number of votes needed to win some Senate seats in a single round of voting (i.e. without the need for a run-off election between the two most popular candidates) was at least controversial, if not illegitimate. They jumped on this technicality in order to cast doubt on the validity of the election victory itself, and used it to justify an immediate suspension of international loans and aid. Soon after your own second term in office began the winners of these seats were persuaded to stand down, pending a further round of elections. But this was a year after the event; wouldn't it have been better to resolve the matter more quickly, to avoid giving the Americans a pretext to undermine your administration before it even began?*

JBA: I hope you won't mind if I take you up on your choice of verbs: you say that we *gave* the Americans a pretext. In reality the Americans *created* their pretext, and if it hadn't been this it would have been something else. Their goal all along was to ensure that come January 2004, there would be no meaningful celebration of the bicentenary of independence. It took the US fifty-eight years to recognize Haiti's independence, since of course the US was a slave-owning country at the time, and in fact US policy has never really changed. Their priorities haven't changed, and today's American policy is more or less consistent with the way it's always been. The coup of September 1991 was undertaken by people in Haiti with the support of the US administration, and in February 2004 it happened again, thanks to many of these same people.

No, the US *created* their little pretext. They were having trouble persuading the other leaders in CARICOM to turn against us (many of whom in fact they were never able to persuade), and they needed a pretext that was clear and easy to understand. "Tainted elections," it was the perfect card to play. But I remember very well what happened when they came to observe the elections. They came, and they said "very good, no problem." Everything seemed to go smoothly, the process was deemed peaceful and fair. And then as the results came in, in order to undermine our victory, they asked questions about the way the votes were counted. But I had nothing to do with this. I wasn't a member of the government, and I had no influence over the CEP [Provisional Electoral Council], which alone has the authority to decide on these matters. The CEP is a sovereign, independent body. The CEP declared the results of the elections; I had nothing to do with it. Then once I had been re-elected, and the Americans demanded that I dismiss these senators, what was I supposed to do? The constitution doesn't give the president the power to dismiss senators who were elected in keeping with the protocol decided by the CEP. Can you imagine a situation like this back in the US itself? What would happen if a foreign government insisted that the president dismiss an elected senator? It's absurd. The whole situation is simply racist, in fact; they impose conditions on us that they would never contemplate imposing on a "properly" independent country, on a *white* country. We have to call things by their name: is the issue really a matter of democratic governance, of the validity of a particular electoral result? Or is actually about something else?

In the end, what the Americans wanted to do was to use the legislature, the Senate, against the executive. They hoped that I would be stupid enough to insist on the dismissal of these elected senators. I refused to do it. In 2001, as a gesture of goodwill, these senators eventually chose to resign on the assumption that they would contest new elections as soon as the opposition was prepared to participate in them. But the Americans failed to turn the Senate and the parliament against the presidency, and it soon became clear that the opposition never had the slightest interest in new elections. Once this tactic failed, however, they recruited or bought off a few hotheads, including Dany Toussaint and company, and used *them*, a little later, against the presidency.

Once again, the overall objective was to undermine the celebration of our bicentenary, the celebration of our independence and of all its implications. When the time came they sent emissaries to Africa, especially to francophone Africa, telling their leaders not to attend the celebrations. Chirac applied enormous pressure on his African colleagues; the Americans did the same. Thabo Mbeki was almost alone in his willingness to resist this pressure, and through him the African Union was represented. I'm very glad of it. The same pressure was applied in the Caribbean: the prime minister of the Bahamas, Perry Christie, decided to come, but that's it, he was the only one. It was very disappointing.

PH: *In the press, meanwhile, you came to be presented not as the unequivocal winner of legitimate elections, but as an increasingly tyrannical autocrat.*

JBA: Exactly. A lot of the $200 million or so in aid and development money for Haiti that was suspended when we won the elections in 2000 was simply diverted to a propaganda and destabilization campaign waged against our government and against Fanmi Lavalas. The disinformation campaign was truly massive. Huge sums of money were spent to get the message out, through the radio, through newspapers, through various little political parties that were supposed to serve as vehicles for the opposition . . . It was extraordinary. When I look back at this very discouraging period in our history I compare it with what has recently happened in some other places. They went to the same sort of trouble when they tried to say there were weapons of mass destruction in Iraq. I can still see Colin Powell sitting there in front of the United Nations, with his little bag of tricks, demonstrating for all the world to see that Saddam Hussein had weapons of mass destruction. Look at this irrefutable proof! It was pathetic. In any case the logic was the same: they rig up a useful lie, and then they sell it. It's the logic of people who take themselves to be all-powerful. If they decide $1 + 1 = 4$, then 4 it will have to be.

PH: *From My Lai to the Iran-Contras to Iraq to Haiti, Colin Powell has made an entire career along these lines . . . But going back to May 2000: soon after the results were declared, the head of the CEP, Leon Manus, fled the country, claiming that the results were invalid and that you and Préval had put pressure on him to calculate the votes in a particular way. Why did he come to embrace the American line?*

JBA: Well, I don't want to judge Leon Manus, I don't know what happened exactly. But I think he acted in the same way as some of the leaders of the Group of 184. They are beholden to a *patron*, a boss. The boss is American, a white American. And you are black. Don't underestimate the inferiority complex that still so often conditions these relationships. You are black. But sometimes you get to feel almost as white as the whites themselves, you get to feel whiter than white, if you're willing to get down on your knees in front of the whites. If you're willing to get down on your knees, rather than stay on your feet, then you can feel almost as white as they look. This is a psychological legacy of slavery: to lie for the white man isn't really lying at all, since white men don't lie! [*laughs*]. How could white men lie? They are the civilized ones. If I lie for the whites I'm not really lying, I'm just repeating what they say. So I don't know, but I imagine Leon Manus felt like this when he repeated the lie that they wanted him to repeat. Don't forget, his journey out of the country began in a car with *diplomatic* plates, and he arrived in Santo Domingo on an American helicopter. Who has access to that sort of transport?

In this case and others like it, what's really going on is clear enough. It's the people with power who pull the strings, and they use this or that *petit nègre de service*, this or that black messenger to convey the lies that they call truth. The people recruited into the Group of 184 did much the same thing: they were paid off to say what their employers wanted them to say. They helped destroy the country, in order to please their *patrons*.

PH: *Why were these people so aggressively hostile to you and your government? There's something hysterical about the positions taken by the so-called "Democratic Convergence," and later by the "Group of 184," by people like Evans Paul, Gérard Pierre-Charles and others. They refused all compromise, they insisted on all sorts of unreasonable conditions before they would even consider participation in another round of elections. The Americans themselves seemed exasperated with them, but made no real effort to rein them in.*

JBA: They made no effort to rein them in because this was all part of the plan. It's a little bit like what's happening now [in July 2006], with Yvon Neptune: the Americans have been shedding crocodile tears over poor imprisoned Neptune, as if they haven't been complicit in and responsible for this imprisonment! As if they don't have the power to change the situation overnight! They have the power to undermine and overthrow a democratically elected government, but they don't have the power to set free a couple of prisoners that they themselves put in prison [*laughs*]. Naturally they have to respect the law, the proper procedures, the integrity of Haitian institutions! This is all bluff, it's absurd.

Why were the Group of 184 and our opponents in "civil society" so hostile? Again it's partly a matter of social pathology. When a group of citizens is prepared to act in so irrational and servile a fashion, when they are so willing to relay the message concocted by their foreign masters, without even realizing that in doing so they inflict harm upon themselves – well if you ask me, this is a symptom of a real pathology. It has something to do with a visceral hatred, which became a real obsession: a hatred for the people. It was never really about me, it's got nothing to do with me as an individual. They detest and despise the people. They refuse absolutely to acknowledge that we are all equal, that everyone is equal. So when they behave in this way, part of the reason is to reassure themselves that they are different, that they are not like the people, not like *them*. It's essential that they see themselves as better than others. I think this is one part of the problem, and it's not simply a political problem. There's something masochistic about this behavior, and there are plenty of foreign sadists who are more than willing to oblige!

I'm convinced it's bound up with the legacy of slavery, with an inherited contempt for the people, for the common people, for the *niggers* [*petits nègres*] . . . It's the psychology of apartheid: it's better to get down on your knees with whites than it is to stand shoulder to shoulder with blacks. Don't underestimate the depth of this contempt. Don't forget that back in 1991, one of the first things we did was abolish the classification, on birth certificates, of people who were born outside of Port-au-Prince as "peasants." This kind of classification, and all sorts of things that went along with it, served to maintain a system of rigid exclusion. It served to keep people outside, to treat them as *moun andeyo* – people from outside. People under the table. This is what I mean by the mentality of apartheid, and it runs very deep. It won't change overnight.

PH: *What about your own willingness to work alongside people compromised by their past, for instance your inclusion of former Duvalierists in your second administration? Was that an easy decision to take? Was it necessary?*

JBA: No it wasn't easy, but I saw it as a necessary evil. Take Marc Bazin, for instance. He was minister of finance under Jean-Claude Duvalier. I only turned to Bazin because my opponents in Democratic Convergence, in the OPL and so on, absolutely refused any participation in the government.

PH: *You were under pressure to build a government of "consensus," of national unity, and you approached people in the Convergence first?*

JBA: Right, and I got nowhere. Their objective was to scrap the entire process, and they said no straightaway. Look, of course we had a massive majority in parliament, and I wasn't prepared to dissolve a properly elected parliament. What for? But I was aware of the danger of simply excluding the opposition. I wanted a democratic government, and so I set out to make it as inclusive as I could, under the circumstances. Since the Convergence wasn't willing to participate, I invited people from sectors that had little or no representation in parliament to have a voice in the administration, to occupy some ministerial positions and to keep a balance between the legislative and the executive branches of government.

PH: *This must have been very controversial. Bazin not only worked for Duvalier, he was your opponent back in 1990.*

JBA: Yes it was controversial, and I didn't take the decision alone. We talked about it at length, we held meetings, looking for a compromise. Some were for, some were against, and in the end there was a majority who accepted that we couldn't afford to work alone, that we needed to demonstrate we were willing and able to work with people who *clearly* weren't pro-Lavalas. They weren't pro-Lavalas, but we had already published a well-defined political programme, and if they were willing to cooperate on this or that aspect of the programme, then we were willing to work with them as well.

PH: *It's ironic: you were often accused of being a sort of ''monarchical'' if not tyrannical president, of being intolerant of dissent, too determined to get your own way . . . But what do you say to those who argue instead that the real problem was just the opposite, that you were too tolerant of dissent? You allowed ex-soldiers to call openly and repeatedly for the reconstitution of the army. You allowed self-appointed leaders of ''civil society'' to do everything in their power to disrupt your government. You allowed radio stations to sustain a relentless campaign of misinformation. You allowed all sorts of demonstrations to go on day after day, calling for you to be overthrown by fair means or foul, and many of these demonstrators were directly funded and organized by your enemies in the US. Eventually the situation got out of hand, and the people who sought to profit from the chaos certainly weren't motivated by respect for the rights of free speech!*

JBA: Well, this is what democracy requires. Either you allow for the free expression of diverse opinions or you don't. If people aren't free to demonstrate and to give voice to their demands there is no democracy. Now again, I knew our position was strong in parliament, and that the great majority of the people were behind us. A small minority opposed us, a small but powerful minority. Their foreign connections, their business interests, and so on, make them powerful. Nevertheless they have the right to protest, to articulate their demands, just like anyone else. That's normal. As for accusations that I was becoming dictatorial, authoritarian, and so on, I paid no attention. I knew they were lying, and I knew they knew they were lying. Of course it was a predictable strategy, and it helped create a familiar image they could sell to the outside world. At home, however, everyone knew it was ridiculous. And in the end, like I said before, it was the foreign masters themselves who had to come to Haiti to finish the job. My government certainly wasn't overthrown by the people who were demonstrating in the streets.

PH: *Perhaps the most serious and frequent accusation that was made by the demonstrators, and repeated by your critics abroad, is that you resorted to violence in order to hang on to power. The claim is that, as the pressure on your government grew, you started to rely on armed gangs from the slums, so-called "chimères," and that you used them to intimidate and in some cases to murder your opponents.*

JBA: Here again the people who make these sort of claims are lying. As soon as you start to look rationally at what was really going on, these accusations don't even begin to stand up. Several things have to be kept in mind. First of all, the police had been working under an embargo for several years. We weren't even able to buy bullet-proof vests or tear-gas canisters. The police were severely under-equipped, and were often simply unable to control a demonstration or confrontation. Some of our opponents, some of the demonstrators who sought to provoke violent confrontations, knew this perfectly well. The people also understood this. It was common knowledge that while the police were running out of ammunition and supplies in Haiti, heavy weapons were being smuggled to our opponents in and through the Dominican Republic. The people knew this, and didn't like it. They started getting nervous, with good reason. The provocations didn't let up, and there were some isolated acts of violence. Was this violence justified? No. I condemned it. I condemned it consistently. But with the limited means at our disposal, how could we prevent every outbreak of violence? There was a lot of provocation, a lot of anger, and there was no way that we could ensure that each and every citizen would refuse violence. The president of a country like Haiti cannot be held responsible for the actions of its every citizen. But there was never any deliberate encouragement of violence, there was no deliberate recourse to violence. Those who make and repeat these claims are lying, and they know it.

Now what about these *chimères*, the people they call *chimères*? This is clearly another expression of our apartheid mentality, the very word says it all. *Chimères* are people who are impoverished, who live in a state of profound insecurity and chronic unemployment. They are the victims of structural injustice, of systematic social violence. And they are among the people who voted for this government, who appreciated what the government was doing and had done, in spite of the embargo. It's not surprising that they should confront those who have always benefited from this same social violence, once they started actively seeking to undermine their government.

Again, this doesn't justify occasional acts of violence, but where does the real responsibility lie? Who are the real victims of violence here? How many members of the elite, how many members of the opposition's many political parties, were killed by "chimères"? How many? Who are they? Meanwhile everyone knows that powerful economic interests were quite happy to fund certain criminal gangs, that they put weapons in the hands of vagabonds, in Cité Soleil and elsewhere, in order to create disorder and blame it on Fanmi Lavalas. These same people also paid journalists to present the situation in a certain way, and among other things they promised them visas – recently some of them who are now living in France admitted to what they were told to say, in order to get their visa. So you have people who were financing misinformation on the one hand and destabilization on the other, and who encouraged little groups of hoodlums to sow panic on the streets, to create the impression of a government that is losing control.

As if all this wasn't enough, rather than allow police munitions to get through to Haiti, rather than send arms and equipment to strengthen the Haitian government, the Americans sent them to their proxies in the Dominican Republic instead. You only have to look at who these people were – people like Jodel Chamblain, who is a convicted criminal, who escaped justice in Haiti to be welcomed by the US, and who then armed and financed these future "freedom fighters" who were waiting over the border in the Dominican Republic. That's what really happened. We didn't arm the "chimères", it was they who armed Chamblain and Philippe! The hypocrisy is extraordinary. And then when it comes to 2004–2006, suddenly all this indignant talk of violence falls quiet. As if nothing had happened. People were being herded into containers and dropped into the sea. That counts for nothing. The endless attacks on

Cité Soleil, they count for nothing. I could go on and on. Thousands have died. But they don't count, because they are just "chimères," after all. They don't count as equals, they aren't *really* people in their own right.

PH: *What about people in your entourage like Dany Toussaint, your former chief of security, who was accused of all kinds of violence and intimidation?*

JBA: He was working for them! It's clear. From the beginning. And we were taken in. Of course I regret this. But it wasn't hard for the Americans or their proxies to infiltrate the government, to infiltrate the police. We weren't even able to provide the police with the equipment they needed, we could hardly pay them an adequate salary. It was easy for our opponents to stir up trouble, to co-opt some policemen, to infiltrate our organization. This was incredibly difficult to control. We were truly surrounded. I was surrounded by people who one way or another were in the pay of foreign powers, who were working actively to overthrow the government. A friend of mine said at the time, looking at the situation, "I now understand why you believe in God, as otherwise I can't understand how you can still be alive, in the midst of all this."

PH: *I suppose even your enemies knew there was nothing to gain by turning you into a martyr.*

JBA: Yes, they knew that a mixture of disinformation and character assassination would be more effective, more devastating. I'm certainly used to it [*laughs*].

PH: *Along the same lines, what do you say to militant leftwing groups like Batay Ouvriye, who insist that your government failed to do enough to help the poor, that you did nothing for the workers? Although they would appear to have little in common with the Convergence, they made and continue to make many of the same sorts of accusations against Fanmi Lavalas.*

JBA: I think, although I'm not sure, that there are several things that help explain this. First of all, you need to look at where their funding comes from. The discourse makes more sense, once we know who is paying the bills. The Americans don't just fund political groups willy-nilly.

PH: *Particularly not pseudo-Trotskyist trade unionists . . .*

JBA: Of course not. And again, I think that part of the reason comes back to what I was saying before, that somewhere, somehow, there's a little secret satisfaction, perhaps an unconscious satisfaction, in saying things that powerful white people want you to say. Even here, I think it goes something like this: "Yes we are workers, we are farmers, we are struggling on behalf of the workers, but somewhere, there's a little part of us that would like to escape our mental class, the state of mind of our class, and jump up into another mental class." My hunch is that it's something like that. In Haiti, contempt for the people runs very deep. In my experience, resistance to our affirmation of equality, our being together with the people, ran very deep indeed. Even when it comes to trivial things.

PH: *Like inviting kids from poor neighborhoods to swim in your pool?*

JBA: Right. You wouldn't believe the reactions this provoked. It was too scandalous: swimming pools are supposed to be the preserve of the rich. When I saw the photographs this past February, of the people swimming in the pool of the Montana Hotel, I smiled [*laughs*]. I thought that was great. I thought ah, now I can die in peace. It was great to see. Because at the time, when kids came to swim in our pool at Tabarre, lots of people said look, he's opening the doors of his house to riff-raff, he's putting ideas in their heads. First they will ask to swim in his pool; soon they will demand a place in our house. And I said no, it's just the opposite. I had no interest in the pool itself, I hardly ever used it. What interested me was the message this sent out. Kids from the poorer neighborhoods would normally never get to see a pool, let alone swim in one. Many are full of envy for the rich. But once they've swum in a pool, once they realise that it's just a pool, they conclude that it doesn't much matter. The envy is deflated.

PH: *That day in February, a huge crowd of thousands of people came up from the slums to make their point to the CEP (which was stationed in the Montana Hotel), they made their demands, and then hundreds of them swam in the Montana's pool and left, without touching a thing. No damage, no theft, just making a point.*

JBA: Exactly. It was a joy to see those pictures.

PH: *Turning now to what happened in February 2004. I know you've often been asked about this, but there are wildly different versions of what happened in the* *run-up to your expulsion from the country. The Americans insist that late in the day you came calling for help, that you suddenly panicked and that they were caught off-guard by the speed of your government's collapse. On the face of it this doesn't look very plausible. Guy Philippe's well-armed rebels were able to outgun some isolated police stations, and appeared to control much of the northern part of the country. But how much support did the rebels really have? And surely there was little chance that they could take the capital itself, in the face of the many thousands of people who were ready to defend it?*

JBA: Don't forget that there had been several attempts at a coup in the previous few years, in July 2001, with an attack on the police academy, the former military academy, and again a few months later, in December 2001, with an incursion into the national palace itself. They didn't succeed, and on both occasions these same rebels were forced to flee the city. They only just managed to escape. It wasn't the police alone who chased them away, it was a combination of the police and the people. So they knew what they were up against, they knew that it wouldn't be easy. They might be able to find a way into the city, but they knew that it would be hard to remain there. It was a little like the way things later turned out in Iraq: the Americans had the weapons to battle their way in easily enough, but staying there has proved to be more of a challenge. The rebels knew they couldn't take Port-au-Prince, and that's why they hesitated for a while, on the outskirts, some 40 km away. So from our perspective we had nothing to fear. The balance of forces was in our favor, that was clear. There are occasions when large groups of people are more powerful than heavy machine guns and automatic weapons, it all depends on the context. And the context of Port-au-Prince, in a city with so many national and international interests, with its embassies, its public prominence and visibility, and so on, was different from the context of more isolated places like Saint-Marc or Gonaïves. The people were ready, and I wasn't worried.

No, the rebels knew they couldn't take the city, and that's why their masters decided on a diversion instead, on attacks in the provinces, in order to create the illusion that much of the country was under their control, that there was a major insurrection under way. But it wasn't the case. There was no great insurrection: there was a small group of soldiers, heavily armed, who were able to overwhelm some police stations, kill some policemen and create a certain amount of havoc. The police had run out of ammunition, and were no match for the rebels' M16s. But the city was a different story.

Meanwhile, as you know on February 29 a shipment of police munitions that we had bought from South Africa, perfectly legally, was due to arrive in Port-au-Prince. This decided the matter. Already the balance of forces was against the rebels; on top of that, if the police were restored to something like their full operational capacity, then the rebels stood no chance at all.

PH: So at that point the Americans had no option but to go in and get you themselves, the night of 28 February?

JBA: That's right. They knew that in a few more hours, they would lose their opportunity to "resolve" the situation. They grabbed their chance while they had it, and bundled us onto a plane in the middle of the night. That's what they did.

PH: The Americans – Ambassador Foley, Luis Moreno, and so on – insist that you begged for their help, that they had to arrange a flight to safety at the last minute. Some reporters were prepared to endorse their account.[4] On the other hand, speaking on condition of anonymity, one of the American security guards who was on your plane that night told the Washington Post *soon after the event that the US story was a pure fabrication, that it was "just bogus."[5] Your personal security advisor and pilot, Frantz Gabriel, also confirms that you were kidnapped that night by US military personnel. Who are we supposed to believe?*

JBA: Well. For me it's very simple. You're dealing with a country that was willing and able, in front of the United Nations and in front of the world at large, to fabricate claims about the existence of weapons of mass destruction in Iraq. They were willing to lie about issues of global importance. It's hardly surprising that they were able to find a few people to say the things that needed to be said in Haiti, in a small country of no great strategic significance. They have their people, their resources, their way of doing things. They just carried out their plan, that's all. It was all part of the plan.

PH: They said they couldn't send peacekeepers to help stabilize the situation, but as soon as you were gone, the troops arrived straight away.

JBA: The plan was perfectly clear.

PH: I have just a couple of last questions. In August and September 2005, in the run-up to the elections that finally took place in February 2006, there was a lot of discussion within Fanmi Lavalas about how to proceed. In the end, most of the rank and file threw their weight behind your old colleague, your "twin brother" René Préval, but some members of the leadership opted to stand as candidates in their own right; others were even prepared to endorse Marc Bazin's candidacy. It was a confusing situation, one that must have put great strain on the organization, but you kept very quiet.

JBA: In a dictatorship, the orders go from top to bottom. In a democratic organization, the process is more dialectical. The small groups or cells that we call the *ti fanmis* are part of Fanmi Lavalas, they discuss things, debate things, express themselves, until a collective decision emerges from out of the discussion. This is how the organization works. Of course our opponents will always cry "dictatorship, dictatorship, it's just Aristide giving orders." But people who are familiar with the organization know that's not the way it is. We have no experience of situations in which someone comes and gives an order, without discussion. I remember that when we had to choose the future electoral candidates for Fanmi Lavalas, back in 1999, the discussions at the Foundation [the Aristide Foundation for Democracy] would often run long into the night. Delegations would come from all over the country, and members of the *cellules de base* would argue for or against. Often it wasn't easy to find a compromise, but this is how the process worked, this was our way of doing things. So now, when it came to deciding on a new presidential candidate last year, I was confident that the discussion would proceed in the same way, even though by that stage many members of the organization had been killed, and many more were in hiding, in exile or in prison. I made no declaration one way or another about what to do or who to support. I knew they would make the right decision in their own way. A lot of the things "I" decided, as president, were in reality decided this way: the decision didn't originate with me, but with them. It was with their words that I spoke. The decisions we made emerged through a genuinely collective process. The people are intelligent, and their intelligence is often surprising.

I knew that the Fanmi Lavalas senators who decided to back Bazin would soon be confronted by the truth, but I didn't know how this would happen, since the true decision emerged from the people, from below, not from above. And no-one could have guessed it, a couple of months in advance. Never doubt the people's intelligence, their power of discernment. Did I give an order to support Bazin or to oppose Bazin? No, I gave no order either way. I trusted the membership to get at the truth.

Of course the organization is guided by certain principles, and I drew attention to some of them at the time. In South Africa, back in 1994, could there have been fair elections if Mandela was still in prison, if Mbeki was still in exile, if other leaders of the ANC were in hiding? The situation in Haiti this past year was much the same: there could hardly be fair elections before the prisoners were freed, before the exiles were allowed to return, and so on. I was prepared to speak out about this, as a matter of general principle. But to go further than this, to declare for this or that candidate, this or that course of action, no, it wasn't for me to say.

PH: *How do you now envisage the future? What has to happen next? Can there be any real change in Haiti without directly confronting the question of class privilege and power, without finding some way of overcoming the resistance of the dominant class?*

JBA: We will have to confront these things, one way or another. The condition *sine qua non* for doing this is obviously the participation of the people. Once the people are genuinely able to *participate* in the democratic process, then they will be able to devise an acceptable way forward. In any case the process itself is irreversible. It's irreversible at the mental level, at the level of people's minds. Members of the impoverished sections of Haitian society now have an experience of democracy, of a collective consciousness, and they will not allow a government or a candidate to be imposed on them. They demonstrated this in February 2006, and I know they will keep on demonstrating it. They will not accept lies in the place of truth, as if they were too stupid to understand the difference between the two. Everything comes back, in the end, to the simple principle that *tout moun se moun* – every person is indeed a person, every person is capable of thinking things through for themselves. Either you accept this principle or you don't. Those who don't accept it, when they look at the *nègres* of Haiti – and consciously or unconsciously, that's what they see – they see people who are too poor, too crude, too uneducated, to think for themselves. They see people who need others to make their decisions for them. It's a colonial mentality, in fact, and this mentality is still very widespread among our political class. It's also a projection: they project upon the people a sense of their own inadequacy, their own inequality in the eyes of the master.

So yes, for me there is a way out, a way forward, and it has to pass by way of the people. Even if we don't yet have viable democratic structures and institutions, there is already a democratic consciousness, a collective democratic consciousness, and this is irreversible. February 2006 shows how much has been gained, it shows how far down the path of democracy we have come, even after the coup, even after two years of ferocious violence and repression.

What remains unclear is how long it will take. We may move forward fairly quickly, if through their mobilization the people encounter inter-locutors who are willing to listen, to enter into dialogue with them. If they don't find them, it will take longer. From 1992 to 1994 for instance, there were people in the US government who were willing to listen at least a little, and this helped the democratic process to move forward. Since 2000 we've had to deal with a US administration that is diame-trically opposed to its predecessor, and everything slowed down drama-tically, or went into reverse. The question is how long it will take. The real problem isn't simply a Haitian one, it isn't located within Haiti. It's a problem for Haiti that is located outside Haiti! The people who control it can speed things up, slow them down, block them altogether, as they like. But the process itself, the democratic process in Haiti itself, it *will* move forward one way or another, it's irreversible. That's how I understand it.

As for what will happen now, or next, that's unclear. The unknown variables I mentioned before remain in force, and much depends on how those who control the means of repression both at home and abroad will react. We still need to develop new ways of reducing and eventually eliminating our dependence on foreign powers.

PH: *And your own next step? I know you're still hoping to get back to Haiti as soon as possible: any progress there? What are your own priorities now?*

JBA: Yes indeed: Thabo Mbeki's last public declaration on this point dates from February, when he said he saw no particular reason why I shouldn't be able to return home, and this still stands. Of course it's still a matter of judging when the time is right, of judging the security and stability of the situation. The South African government has welcomed us here as guests, not as exiles; by helping us so generously they have made their contribution to peace and stability in Haiti. And once the conditions are right we'll go back. As soon as René Préval judges that the time is right then I'll go back. I am ready to go back tomorrow.

PH: *In the eyes of your opponents, it's clear you still represent a major political threat.*

JBA: Criminals like Chamblain and Philippe are free to patrol the streets, even now, but I should remain in exile because some members of the elite think I represent a major threat? Who is the real threat? Who is guilty, and who is innocent? Again, either we live in a democracy or we don't, either we respect the law or we don't. There is no legal justification for blocking my return. It's slightly comical: I was elected president but am accused of dictatorship by nameless people who are accountable to no-one yet have the power to expel me from the country and then to delay or block my return [*laughs*]. In any case, once I'm finally able to return, then the fears of these people will evaporate like mist, since they have no substance. They have no more substance than did the threat of legal action against me, which was finally abandoned this past week, once even the American lawyers who were hired to prosecute the case realized that the whole thing was empty, that there was nothing in it.

PH: *You have no further plans to play some sort of role in politics?*

JBA: I've often been asked this question, and my answer hasn't changed. For me it's very clear. There are different ways of serving the people. Participation in the politics of the state isn't the only way. Before 1990 I served the people, from outside the structure of the state. I will serve the people again, from outside the structure of the state. My first vocation was teaching, it's a vocation that I have never abandoned, I am still committed to it. For me, one of the great achievements of our second administration was the construction of the University of Tabarre, which was built entirely under embargo but which in terms of its infrastructure became the largest university in Haiti (and which, since 2004, has been occupied by foreign troops). I would like to go back to teaching, I plan to remain active in education.

As for politics, I never had any interest in becoming a political leader "for life." That was Duvalier: president for life. In fact that is also the way most political parties in Haiti still function: they serve the interests of a particular individual, of a small group of friends. Often it's just a dozen people, huddled around their life-long chief. This is not at all how a political organization should work. A political organization consists of its members, it isn't the instrument of one man. Of course I would like to help strengthen the organization. If I can help with the training of its members, if I can accompany the organization as it moves forward, then I will be glad to be of service. Fanmi Lavalas needs to become more professional, it needs to have more internal discipline; the democratic process needs properly functional political parties, and it needs parties, in the plural. So I will not dominate or lead the organization, that is not my role, but I will contribute what I can.

PH: *And now, at this point, after all these long years of struggle, and after the setbacks of these last years, what is your general assessment of the situation? Are you discouraged? Hopeful?*

JBA: No I'm not discouraged. You teach philosophy, so let me couch my answer in philosophical terms. You know that we can think the category of *being* either in terms of potential or act, *en puissance ou en acte*. This is a familiar Aristotelian distinction: being can be potential or actual. So long as it remains potential, you cannot touch it or confirm it. But it *is*, nonetheless, it exists. The collective consciousness of the Haitian people, their mobilization for democracy, these things may not have been fully actualized but they exist, they are real. This is what sustains me. I am sustained by this collective potential, the power of this collective potential being [*cet être collectif en puissance*]. This power has not yet been actualized, it has not yet been enacted in the building of enough schools, of more hospitals, more opportunities, but these things will come. The power is real and it is what animates the way forward.

Notes

INTRODUCTION

1. Inter-American Development Bank, *Haiti: Bank's Transition Strategy, 2005–2006*, 1.
2. Kim Ives, "The Lavalas Alliance Propels Aristide to Power" (1994), 19.
3. Donald E. Schulz, "Whither Haiti?", Strategic Studies Institute, 1 April 1996, 16. In this same report of 1996, Schultz considered the possibility that sometime in the future, Duvalierist ex-military forces might re-emerge "from out of the woodwork" and seek to destabilize the Lavalas regime. He concluded that the "US and the international community would not allow it," and that the new Haitian National Police would help the population to resist it (22); future US policy makers would prove him wrong on both counts.
4. US Department of Justice, *Profile Series: Haiti* (August 1993), 9.
5. "Guns to Doves" [Editorial], *Washington Post*, 10 February 1996.
6. "Haiti's 'New Chapter'" [Editorial], *Washington Post*, 1 March 2004; cf. Adrian Karatnycky, "Fall of a Pseudo-Democrat," *Washington Post*, 17 March 2004.
7. Kevin Sullivan and Scott Wilson, "Aristide Resigns, Flies Into Exile," *Washington Post*, 1 March 2004.
8. Andrew Gumbel, "The Little Priest Who Became a Bloody Dictator Like the One He Once Despised," *Independent*, 21 February 2004.
9. Clara Germani, "Rise and Fall of a 'Haitian Mandela,'" *Christian Science Monitor*, 27 February 2004.
10. Tim Padgett, "Haiti: Rebels in Charge," *Time Magazine*, 1 March 2004.
11. "Haïti en danger," *Le Monde* [editorial], 18 December 2003.
12. Alex Dupuy, *The Prophet and Power* (2007), 168, 2. For a detailed assessment of Dupuy's claims see my "The Violence of Democracy: A Review of Alex Dupuy's *The Prophet and Power*," *Haiti Liberté*, July 2007.
13. Alex Dupuy, *The Prophet and Power*, 165, 157. Readers of a new 2003 edition of the most widely read recent English book on Haiti, an acclaimed travelog by Ian Thomson, likewise learned that "since February 2001 Aristide has been implicated in the grossest human rights abuses, murder and disappearances," and has "created his own private militia known as the *chimères*, similar in kind to the *Tontons Macoutes*" (Thomson, *Bonjour Blanc*, 358–9).

   Michael Deibert provides a book-length version of this Aristide = Duvalier equation in his *Notes from the Last Testament* (2005), and concludes that "the Aristide government deserved to be overthrown as much as any in Haitian history. He took a generation of desperately poor slum children whose heads were filled with idealistic notions about changing their country, put weapons in their hands and turned them into killers" (432). As anyone who has glanced through it will know, Deibert's book provides its readers with everything they need to judge the purpose and accuracy of its claims.

Less far-fetched versions of this emphasis on corruption and disillusionment also condition the interpretations of Lavalas put forward in two of the most widely respected books on recent Haitian politics, by Patrick Bellegarde-Smith and Robert Fatton (see Bellegarde-Smith, *Breached Citadel*, 253–64; Fatton, *Haiti's Predatory Republic*, xiii, 33–4, 88; see also Hyppolite Pierre, *Haiti: Rising Flames from Burning Ashes*, 166–7; Christophe Wargny, *Haïti n'existe pas*, 161–4, 180; Jean-Claude Jean and Marc Maesschalck, *Transition politique en Haïti*, 104–11). Comparison of Duvalier and Aristide is also a central theme underlying Bernard Diederich's new multi-volume study, *Le Prix du sang: la résistance d'un peuple face à la tyrannie* (2005); cf. Diederich, "Au bout du compte, Aristide a causé lui-même sa propre chute," *Alterpresse*, 28 February 2005.

14. Ashley Smith, "Aristide's Rise and Fall," *International Socialist Review*, 35 (May 2004).
15. Lyonel Trouillot, "Ce sont bien les Haïtiens qui ont renversé Aristide," *L'Humanité*, 9 March 2004; Lyonel Trouillot, "In Haiti, All the Bridges are Burned," *New York Times*, 26 February 2004; Christophe Wargny, "Aristide a finalement rejoint le camp des maîtres contre les 'Bossales,'" *Le Monde*, 23 February 2004.
16. Roger F. Noriega, "Haiti at the Crossroads of Democracy," 14 April 2004, http://www.state.gov/p/wha/rls/rm/31411.htm.
17. Jean-Bertrand Aristide, *Théologie et politique*, 103.
18. Gérard Jean-Juste, interview of 25 November 2000, in Melinda Miles with Moira Feeney, *Elections 2000: Participatory Democracy in Haiti* (2001).
19. Duvalier's regime may have killed some 50,000 people, whereas partisans of Aristide's embattled Fanmi Lavalas party can perhaps be held responsible for somewhere between 10 and 30 "political" killings: see above, page 155.
20. Monseigneur Chanoine Albert Dorélien, cited in Katherine Kean's 1994 film *Rezistans*.
21. Patrick Elie and Reed Lindsay, "What Future for Haiti?" (August 2006).
22. Lindsay and Elie, "What Future for Haiti?" (2006); cf. Christopher Marquis, "Latin Allies of the US: Docile and Reliable No Longer," *New York Times*, 9 January 2004.
23. Noam Chomsky, *Necessary Illusions*, 69; cf. Joe Emersberger, Jeb Sprague and Chomsky, "The Godfather and the Small Storekeeper: Chomsky on Haiti," *HaitiAnalysis*, December 2006.
24. Lars Schoultz, *Human Rights and United States Policy toward Latin America*, 7.
25. Yvon Neptune, Interview with Crowing Rooster Arts, Port-au-Prince September 2006.
26. See in particular William Robinson, *Promoting Polyarchy*, 25, 306–11; Nicolas Guilhot, "From Cold Warriors to Human Rights Activists," in his *The Democracy Makers*, 29–69; Anthony Fenton, "Legitimizing Polyarchy" (October 2006); cf. Jonathan Hartlyn et al, eds., *The US and Latin America in the 1990s: Beyond the Cold War*, 2–3, 13; 59–61.
27. In his *Empire's Workshop* (2006), Greg Grandin makes a good case for why the long US assault on Latin America's popular democracies should be understood as the experimental laboratory for the more recent "war on terror." Since as Chomsky notes "Haiti happens to be the leading target of US intervention in the 20th century," the assault on Haiti is perhaps the single most instructive of these various experiments ("Torturing Democracy: Noam Chomsky interviewed by Faiz Ahmad", *ZNet*, 25 January 2003; cf. Chomsky, "The Threat Of A Good Example" (1993)).

28. It goes without saying, I hope, that "arguments from one's own privileged experience are bad and reactionary arguments" (Gilles Deleuze, *Negotiations*, 12).

29. Paolo Freire, *Pedagogy of the Oppressed*, 26.

30. This is a point emphasized by Dawn Raby, in her *Democracy and Revolution: Latin America and Socialism Today* (2006): "Another world is indeed possible, but only if the enormous energy of popular resistance is ultimately directed to achieve political power" (x).

31. Don Bohning, "Defection Hurts Aristide," *Miami Herald*, 17 December 2003; Scott Wilson, "Popular Haitian Lawmaker Worries US," *Washington Post*, 4 March 2002.

32. Aristide in 1987, cited in Wilentz, *The Rainy Season*, 113.

33. Charles Arthur, *Haiti in Focus*, 60; cf. Paul Farmer, *The Uses of Haiti*, 113–14.

34. Interview with Georges Honorat, Port-au-Prince, 20 April 2006.

35. Interview with Bobby Duval, Port-au-Prince, 17 April 2006.

36. In the whole of 2003, the *New York Times* doesn't seem to have published a single substantial article on Haiti. For the *Times'* coverage of 2004 see above, page 117.

37. Interview with Robert Fatton, 9 November 2006.

38. Interview with Carol Joseph, Cap-Haïtien, 14 January 2007.

39. Interview with Alinx Albert Obas (Radyo Etensel), Cap-Haïtien, 14 January 2007.

40. Interview with Patrick Elie, Port-au-Prince, 19 April 2006.

41. Aristide's speech to students, Croix des Bouquets, 4 August 1991, cited in Kim Ives, "1791–1991, Haiti's Second Independence," *The Guardian* [NY], 14 August 1991.

42. One of the reasons why Aristide is so vilified today by groups of disillusioned ex-supporters has to do with the depth of their initial illusions. "When Aristide failed to deliver," says one of the several priests who first backed and then turned against him, "it was almost like there's no point in believing anymore that anyone can deliver" (Interview with Father Rick Freshette, Port-au-Prince, 18 April 2006).

43. Amy Wilentz, "Foreword," Aristide, *Parish of the Poor*, xxi; Wilentz, *The Rainy Season*, 223.

44. Interview with Bobby Duval, Port-au-Prince, 17 April 2006.

CHAPTER 1

1. Aristide, *Parish of the Poor*, 103; Scott Wilson, "Haiti Draws on Past for Its Future," *Washington Post*, 21 November 2003.

2. Haiti's Gini coefficient is measured at a staggering 0.65, compared to 0.59 for the region's next most unequal country, Brazil (and 0.48 for the Philippines). See Pål Sletten and Willy Egset, *Poverty in Haiti* (FAFO, 2004), 9.

3. FAFO, "A Profile of Poverty in Haiti" (2004).

4. Aristide, *Autobiography*, 57.

5. Cited in Allan Nairn, "The Eagle Is Landing," *The Nation* 3 October 1994; cf. Ridgeway, "The Ruling Families," in Ridgeway ed., *The Haiti Files*, 29–34.

6. Fatton, *Haiti's Predatory Republic*, 85; cf. 52.

7. Interview with Ronald Saint-Jean, Port-au-Prince, 11 April 2006.

8. "The underlying reality of Haiti has remained remarkably constant for nearly two centuries," says Mark Danner: "the machinery of power, no matter who controls it, exists to funnel the resources of the country from the many to the few – and it is the pastime of those few to fight over who will control the funnel" (Danner, "Fall of the Prophet," *New York Review of Books*, 2 December 1993).

9. Jacques Roumain, "Analyse Schématique 1932–1934."

10. Insofar as Haiti's ruling class is marked by what Patrick Elie calls a "mulatto syndrome" this isn't so much a matter of race or color as of political and geo-cultural orientation. This syndrome applies to someone "who wants above all to gain the respect of the white father who raped his mother and then abandoned him; rather than love his mother or his siblings, he spends all his energy trying to persuade his father that he looks like him. This is what our elite is all about. It's all about trying to please France or the US, and never a matter of drawing on our own solidarity or strength" (Interview with Patrick Elie, Port-au-Prince, 5 January 2007).

11. Patrick James, "An Inside Look at Haiti's Business Elite," *Multinational Monitor*, January 1995.

12. Robert Muggah, *Securing Haiti's Transition* (October 2005), 6–7.

13. Interview with Samba Boukman, Bel Air, 14 April 2006.

14. See in particular Lisa McGowan, *Democracy Undermined, Economic Justice Denied: Structural Adjustment and the Aid Juggernaut in Haiti* (1997). Cf. Wilentz, *The Rainy Season*, 269–84; Eric Verhoogen, "The US–Haiti Connection: Rich Companies, Poor Workers," *Multinational Monitor* 17: 4 (April 1996); Sasha Kramer, "The Friendly Face of US Imperialism: USAID and Haiti" (October 2005); Michel Chossudovsky, *The Globalization of Poverty and the New World Order* (2003); Barbara Briggs and Charles Kernaghan, "The US Economic Agenda" (January 1994); National Labor Committee, *Haiti After the Coup: Sweatshop or Real Development* (April 1993); Marie Kennedy and Chris Tilly, "Up Against The 'Death Plan'" (March 1996); Anthony Fenton, "Gildan Activewear: Taking Sweatshops to New Depths in Haiti," *ZNet* 24 July 2004. The IMF has spent most of the last couple of decades obliging Haitian governments to cut their public spending; the most recent (November 2006) IMF report on poverty in Haiti recognizes, by contrast, that "massive investments must be made in order to increase the provision of basic services nationwide" (IMF, *Haiti: Interim Poverty Reduction Strategy*, 14).

15. Josiane Georges, "Trade and the Disappearance of Haitian Rice," 2004; Oxfam, "Boxing Match in Agricultural Trade" (November 2002), 10; Oxfam, *Rigged Trade and Double Standards* (2002), 141–2.

16. According to Oxfam, "food aid in rice surged from zero in 1994 to 16,000 tonnes in 1999" ("Boxing Match", 10).

17. Oxfam, *Rigged Rules*, 126; Oxfam, *Rigged Trade and Not Much Aid* (2001), 13.

18. Paul Farmer, "Swine Aid," in Ridgeway ed., *The Haiti Files*, 130–3; cf. Aristide, *Eyes of the Heart*, 14–15. Perhaps 1.3 million pigs were slaughtered; in the wake of this assault on the rural economy, school registration fell by nearly 50 percent.

19. World Bank, "2006 World Development Indicators" (measured in constant US dollars for the year 2000).

20. National Labor Committee, *The US in Haiti: How to Get Rich on 11 Cents an Hour* (1996); cf. Ray Laforest, "Disney and Cutler Want to Cut and Run," *Haïti Progrès* 15: 21 (13 August 1997).

21. Arthur, *Haiti in Focus*, 51.

22. Economist Intelligence Unit, *Haiti: Country Profile 2003*, 24; cf. Carol J. Williams, "Haiti Seeks US Tariff Relief for Garment Industry," *LA Times*, 17 June 2006.

23. Interview with Marie Joseph, Cité Soleil, 15 April 2006.

24. IMF, *Haiti: Interim Poverty Reduction Strategy Paper* (November 2006), 7.

25. Interview with Jonas Petit, Miami 8 April 2006; Kennedy and Tilly, "Haiti in 2001" (November 2001).

26. Cited in Catherine Orenstein, "Aristide, Again" (January 2001).

27. Serge Kovaleski, "A Nation in Need: After 5-Year US Intervention, Democracy in Haiti Looks Bleak," *Washington Post*, 21 September 1999.

28. Anne Street, *Haiti 2004: A Nation in Crisis* (2004); IMF, *Haiti: Interim Poverty Reduction Strategy Paper* (November 2006), 11; Sletten and Egset, *Poverty in Haiti* (2004).

29. "WFP Director Appeals for More Aid to Haiti on his Visit to the Country," *World Food Program*, 15 April 2004.

30. Donald Schulz, "Whither Haiti?" (1996), 12–13.

31. Wargny, "Aristide a finalement rejoint le camp des maîtres," *Le Monde*, 23 February 2004; cf. Bellegarde-Smith, *Breached Citadel*, 124; Alex Dupuy, *Prophet and Power*, 47–8.

32. Interview with Yvon Neptune, Port-au-Prince, 5 January 2007.

33. Robert Fatton, *Haiti's Predatory Republic* (2002); Alex Dupuy, *Prophet and Power* (2007).

34. Lisa McGowan, *Democracy Undermined, Economic Justice Denied* (1997).

35. Fatton, *Haiti's Predatory Republic*, 39.

36. Cited in Tom Reeves, "Still Up Against the Death Plan in Haiti," *Dollars & Sense* (September 2003).

37. Paul Farmer, *The Uses of Haiti*, 56.

38. William Robinson, *Promoting Polyarchy*, 260.

39. Eric Williams, *From Columbus to Castro*, 245.

40. Toussaint in 1797, cited in James, *Black Jacobins*, 160.

41. Laurent Dubois, *Avengers of the New World*, 290–292.

42. Robert Heinl and Nancy Heinl, *Written in Blood*, 74, 110.

43. C.L.R. James, *Black Jacobins*, 288.

44. Robin Blackburn, *The Overthrow of Colonial Slavery*, 258.

45. The first constitution of Haiti (1805) broke abruptly with the whole question of race by identifying *all* Haitians, regardless of the color of their skin, as black – a characterization that included, among others, a substantial number of German and Polish troops who had joined in the fight against Napoleon.

46. See in particular Michel-Rolph Trouillot, "An Unthinkable History: The Haitian Revolution as a Non-Event," in Trouillot, *Silencing the Past*, 70–107.

47. Cited in Bellegarde-Smith, *The Breached Citadel*, 71.

48. Farmer, "Who Removed Aristide?" (2004).

49. Cf. Farmer, *Uses of Haiti*, 74–8.

50. Bellegarde-Smith, *Breached Citadel*, 65; Heinl and Heinl, *Written in Blood*, 118–23. The most recent book on the revolution is circumspect about the scale of the massacres, noting only that "precisely how many perished is difficult to establish." Whites willing to swear an oath renouncing France were allowed to retain their property (Dubois, *Avengers of the New World*, 300).

51. Dessalines, cited in Nicholls, *From Dessalines to Duvalier*, 38.

52. Carolyn Fick, *The Making of Haiti*, 249; World Bank, *Haiti: The Challenges of Poverty Reduction* (August 1998), 4; Sletten and Egset, *Poverty in Haiti* (2004), 19.

53. For more on these developments see Bellegarde-Smith, *Breached Citadel*, 79–97; Alex Dupuy, *Prophet and Power*, 25–8.

54. Cf. Bellegarde-Smith, *Breached Citadel*, 107.

55. US Department of Justice, "Profile Series: Haiti" (1993), 29.

56. Alex Dupuy, *Prophet and Power*, 39.

57. Bellegarde-Smith, *Breached Citadel*, 129.

58. Lisa McGowan, "US Policy in Haiti" (1997); Bellegarde-Smith, *Breached Citadel*, 152.

59. Cited in Elizabeth Abbott, *The Duvaliers*, 299–300.

60. US Colonel Steven Butler, cited in Nairn, "The Eagle is Landing," *The Nation*, 3 October 1994.

61. Cited in Kim Ives, "Father Aristide Sweeps Elections in Haiti," *The Guardian* [New York], 18 December 1990.

62. Joseph Treaster, "Strike Paralyzes the Haiti Capital on Eve of Election," *New York Times*, 17 January 1988; cf. Abbott, *The Duvaliers and Their Legacy*, 342.

63. Cited in Wargny, "Introduction," Aristide, *Dignity*, 11.

64. Cited in Jill Smolowe, "With Friends Like These," *Time Magazine*, 8 November 1993.

65. DOJ, "Profile Series: Haiti" (1993), 31–3; cf. Aristide, *Dignity*, 70–1, 112.

66. Cf. Americas Watch/NCHR, *The Aristide Government's Human Rights Record* (November 1991), 9–10; Alex Dupuy, *Prophet and Power*, 114–15.

67. Concannon, "Lave Men, Siye Atè" (2004), 92.

68. Interview with Belizaire Printemps and Elias Clovis, Port-au-Prince, 23 April 2006.

69. Leonardo and Clodovis Boff, *Introducing Liberation Theology*, 6.

70. Noam Chomsky, in Kean, *Rezistans*, 4.

71. Gustavo Gutiérrez, *A Theology of Liberation*, 65–6; cf. 192–6.

72. Cited in Jean-Pierre Cloutier, "Theologies: Liberation vs. Submission," *The Haiti Times* (spring 1987), http://www.cyberie.qc.ca/jpc/haiti/theology.html.

73. Former captain Lawrence Rockwood in conversation with Brian Concannon in 1997, confirmed in a letter from Rockwood, 18 February 2007.

74. Cited in Nairn, "Behind Haiti's Paramilitaries," *The Nation*, 24 October 1994.

75. Antoine Izméry, cited in Kean, *Rezistans*, 22; Aristide, sermon of 5 July 1987, in Kim Ives, "Renewed Turmoil Jeopardizes US-backed 'Elections' Plan in Haiti," *The Guardian* [NY], 9 July 1987.

76. Aristide, *Dignity*, 88; Aristide, *Autobiography*, 121. "The divine does not exist outside of the human [but . . .] to the degree that our values are divine, the human springs from the divine" (Aristide, *Théologie et politique*, 15–16).

77. Aristide, *Théologie et politique*, 21, 67. "I call liberation theology the Christian impulse that does not separate belief from action" (Aristide, *Dignity*, 103; cf. Wilentz, *The Rainy Season*, 112–13).

78. Aristide, *Autobiography*, 120–1.

79. Ibid., 53.

80. Aristide, "Let the Flood Descend," Radio Haiti-Inter, November 1988, in Aristide, *Parish of the Poor*, 104. Aristide always insisted on the concrete primacy of solidarity – as he said in an interview in March 2001, "We owe each other solidarity. A blow to one is a blow to all. No one should have to feel alone in the face of criminals. Everyone should feel that we are one, so that when a criminal is going to attack one person [. . .], he knows when he attacks one person, he is attacking all those who are around this person. If all Haitians in this country let this message give them strength, insecurity will start to decrease" (Michele Montas, "Interview of President Jean-Bertrand Aristide," Radio Haiti-Inter, 3 March 2001, http://haitisupport.gn.apc.org/Montas.html).

81. Gutiérrez, *A Theology of Liberation*, 251–2.

82. Cited in Ives, "New Terror Campaign Targets the Progressive Church," *The Guardian* [NY], 29 August 1987.

83. Aristide, *Théologie et politique*, 29–30.

84. Interview with Guy Delva, Port-au-Prince, 9 April 2006.

85. Aristide, *Dignity*, 95.

86. Aristide, *In the Parish of the Poor*, 31.

87. Farmer, *Uses of Haiti*, 113.

88. Aristide, *Autobiography*, 128, 126.

89. Ibid., 128. In some memorable pages, Amy Wilentz described the "total concentration and rooted excitement" that gripped the congregation of Saint Jean

Bosco during Aristide's sermons of 1986–8 (Wilentz, *The Rainy Season*, 106, 111–13).

90. Aristide in January 1987, cited in Danner, "The Prophet" (1993).

91. Cited in Tom Block, "Portrait of a Folk-Hero: Father Jean-Bertrand Aristide" (October 1990).

92. Aristide, "Call to Holiness" (1 April 1985), in *Parish of the Poor*, 80.

93. Aristide, "Let the Flood Descend" (November 1988), in *Parish of the Poor*, 106–7.

94. Aristide, *Dignity*, 154; Aristide, *In the Parish of the Poor*, 6; cf. Isabel Hilton, "Aristide's Dream," *Independent*, 30 October 1993.

95. Aristide, *Autobiography*, 140.

96. Aristide in November 1987, cited in Danner, "The Prophet" (1993). In a January 1988 interview with *National Catholic Reporter*, Aristide said, "Elections aren't the answer, elections are a way for those in power to control people. The solution is revolution, first in the spirit of the Gospel: Jesus could not accept people going hungry. It is a conflict between classes, rich and poor. My role is to preach and organize . . .".

97. Aristide, *In the Parish of the Poor*, 9.

98. Ibid., 17. Archbishop Ligondé soon responded on behalf of the church hierarchy by denouncing Aristide as a "socio-Bolshevik" and incipient "dictator" (Archbishop Ligondé, sermon of 1 January 1991, cited in Farmer, *Uses of Haiti*, 133).

99. Aristide, *Autobiography*, 198–9; *Dignity*, 92, 96–7.

100. Aristide, *Théologie et politique*, 90–1; cf. Danner, "Beyond the Mountains," *The New Yorker* 27 November 1989.

101. Aristide, *In the Parish of the Poor*, 12–13. "I have never had a gun but if it should one day become necessary for me to use one in defense of the poorest of the poor against the powerful forces of organized crime, I would not let myself be paralyzed by the fatalist sentiment of an insipid theology" (Aristide, *Autobiography*, 133).

102. Cited in Deibert, *Notes from the Last Testament*, 425.

103. Aristide, *Autobiography*, 106.

104. Aristide 1987, in Wilentz, *The Rainy Season*, 217. Aristide's reflections on defensive violence are anything but abstract. The young men who had adopted him as their leader in 1987 saved his life on several occasions, not least during the assault on Saint Jean Bosco in the September 1988 massacre; some of these young men lynched half a dozen of the September attackers, after the latter went on Haitian television to boast of their exploits and to warn that "where Aristide appears, there we will kill" (Wilentz, *The Rainy Season*, 354, 362). There is a reason why, to this day, police who conduct violent raids on popular neighborhoods often wear masks.

105. Aristide, speech to high school students on 4 August 1991, partially transcribed in Americas Watch/NCHR, *The Aristide Government's Human Rights Record*, 26–8.

106. Dupuy, *The Prophet and Power*, 123–5; Americas Watch/NCHR, *The Aristide Government's Human Rights Record*, 6.

107. Letter from Kim Ives, 26 February 2007.

108. For a more detailed discussion of Aristide's "Père Lebrun" speeches see my "The Violence of Democracy" (2007).

109. Telephone interview with Patrick Elie, 24 February 2007.

110. Interview with Douglas Perlitz, Cap-Haïtien, 12 January 2007.

111. Aristide, *Dignity*, 96.

112. Cf. Wilentz, *The Rainy Season*, 50–3.

113. Aristide, *In the Parish of the Poor*, 27.

114. "Eight Reported Dead as Haitian Troops Fire on Crowd," *New York Times*, 27 April 1986. Aristide was among the protestors and described the attack live on radio,

an incident that immediately "turned him into a national hero" (Wilentz, *The Rainy Season*, 119; cf. Aristide, *In the Parish of the Poor*, 27–30).

115. One of the local landowners who helped organize the massacre at Jean-Rabel boasted on television that his men had killed 1,042 "Communists." Cf. Kim Ives, "Repression Grows as Nation-Wide Revolt Spreads and Deepens," *The Guardian* [NY], 8 August 1987.
116. Cited in Nairn, "The Eagle is Landing," *The Nation*, 3 October 1994; cf. Danner, "Beyond the Mountains," *The New Yorker*, 27 November 1989.
117. Although it helped counter the recent excesses of Duvalierist authoritarianism, the constitution that received overwhelming approval in a plebiscite of 29 March 1987 "tended, with all its checks and balances, to produce a stultifying immobilism that favored the status quo of the dominant classes" (Fatton, *Haiti's Predatory Republic*, 70; cf. John M. Carey, "All Presidencies Are Not Created Equal," *Los Angeles Times*, 23 September 1994).
118. As Wilentz observes, the massacre at ruelle Vaillant "proved what everyone had always known. Without arms, you cannot force an army to change" (Wilentz, *The Rainy Season*, 325). Namphy is said to have applauded the result: "Haiti has only one voter. The army. Ha ha" (cited in Abbott, *The Duvaliers and Their Legacy*, xii).
119. Wilentz, *The Rainy Season*, 234.
120. Brian Concannon Jr., "Lave Men, Siye Atè," 78.
121. Wilentz, *The Rainy Season*, 237.
122. Michel-Rolph Trouillot, *Haiti, State Against Nation*, 222.
123. Ives, "The Lavalas Alliance Propels Aristide to Power" (January 1994), 19.
124. Unnamed Lavalas activist, cited in Kean, *Rezistans*, 19.
125. Cited in William Blum, "Who Will Rid Me of This Turbulent Priest," and NACLA, *Haiti: Dangerous Crossroads*, 45; cf. Wilentz, *The Rainy Season*, 330–1.
126. Aristide, *Autobiography*, 116–17, translation modified.
127. Cited in Farmer, *Uses of Haiti*, 129; cf. "Aristide, The People's Candidate," *Haïti Progrès* 24 October 1990, in Pat Chin ed., *Haiti: A Slave Revolution*, 129–30.
128. Patrick Elie, cited in Ben Ehrenreich, "Haiti's Hope," *LA Weekly*, 12 April 2006.
129. "Aristide announced his candidacy with almost no time left to obtain the necessary nominating signatures. Yet 'the day following his announcement, which was disseminated immediately on dozens of [radio] stations, officials from voter registration sites throughout the country began contacting Port-au-Prince to report they had run out of forms and needed new supplies urgently, as waves of people clamored to register. Voter registration surged by at least another million.' Aristide's success in satisfying the ballot requirements was no small feat in a country with such a poor transportation and communication infrastructure. The grassroots community rallied around Aristide's candidacy and provided the organization necessary to satisfy the nominating requirements and generate a massive popular vote" (DOJ, *Profile Series: Haiti*, 12, citing Robert Maguire).
130. Jean Dominique, in Demme, *The Agronomist* [film], 2002.
131. Interview with Samba Boukman, Bel Air 14 April 2006. Although in 1990 there was some debate about whether the movement should have participated in the elections (rather than pursue a more revolutionary path), the great majority of Lavalassians agree with Gérard Jean-Juste's assessment, that "it was definitely right for Aristide to stand as president in 1990" (Interview with Gérard Jean-Juste, Miami, 7 April 2006).
132. Kim Ives, "Haitians Pour Out Joy and Love at Aristide Inauguration," *Guardian*, 18 February 1991.
133. Danner, "Fall of the Prophet" (1993).
134. Aristide, *Autobiography*, 128.

135. Fatton, *Haiti's Predatory Republic*, 40.

136. Ibid., 83.

137. Ibid., 86–7, 83.

138. David Nicholls, *From Dessalines to Duvalier*, xxx.

139. Cf. Alex Dupuy, *Haiti in the New World Order*, 128–9.

140. Antoine Izméry was well-placed to identify the main financial backers of the 1991 coup, and he didn't hesitate to name the main families involved: Mevs, Nadal, Brandt, Mourra, Accra, Bigio, Haloun, Brunt (Antoine Izméry, in Kean, *Rezistans*, 30–1).

141. Aristide, "It's Not If I Go Back, But When," *Time Magazine*, 1 November 1993.

142. Aristide, "Speech of 27 September 1991," *Haiti Observateur*, http://www.hartford-hwp.com/archives/43a/009.html; cf. Anne-Christine D'Adesky, "Père Lebrun in Context" (1991); Stotzky, *Silencing the Guns in Haiti*, 46–8.

143. Cited in Howard French, "Front-Running Priest a Shock to Haiti," *New York Times*, 13 December 1990.

144. Nina Shea, "Human Rights in Haiti" (1993), 26. Shea's main example of Aristide's apparent encouragement of "mob rule" was the lynching in Les Cayes, just before the 1991 coup, of his critic Sylvio Claude, with the alleged collusion of Aristide's associate Jean-Claude Jean-Baptiste (ibid., 29). Other than a dubious photograph of Jean-Baptiste at the scene sometime after the event, she presents no evidence for the involvement of either Jean-Baptiste or Aristide (or any other member of the government) in the killing.

145. Robert Fatton, cited in Marty Logan, "Class Hatred and the Hijacking of Aristide," Inter Press Service News Agency, 16 March 2004.

146. Aristide in February 1991, cited in Robinson, *Promoting Polyarchy*, 291.

147. Cf. Anthony Maingot, "Haiti and Aristide" (1992), 67–8.

148. Interview with Ramilus Bolivar, Port-au-Prince, 15 January 2007.

149. Had the army not intervened in its own fashion in September 1991, notes Alex Dupuy, "there is little doubt that the four major political blocs in the chamber of Deputies, including the FNCD, would have voted in favor of a censure motion" to remove Préval's government (Dupuy, *Prophet and Power*, 127). Once Aristide had been overthrown, FNCD parliamentarians like Eddy Dupiton and Bernard Sansar-icq became "prominent negotiators for the coup regime" (Marx Aristide and Laurie Richardson, "Haiti's Popular Resistance" [1994], 34, 52n.11).

150. Robert Malval, *L'Année de toutes les dupéries*, 42–3.

151. Cited in Paul Quinn-Judge, "US Reported to Intercept Aristide Calls," *Boston Globe*, 8 September 1994.

152. Cited in Heinl and Heinl, *Written in Blood*, 699.

153. Cited in Briggs and Kernaghan, "The US Economic Agenda" (1994), 40.

154. National Labor Committee, *Haiti After the Coup*, 6; cf. Myrlène Daniel, "Ouvriers: Salaire minimum – Patrons: Avantages maximum?", *Haïti Progrès*, 10–16 July 1991.

155. Interview with Patrick Elie, Port-au-Prince, 19 April 2006.

156. The thirty-man force was known as the SSP (Presidential Security Force); cf. Slavin, "The Elite's Revenge" (1991), 5; Michel Laguerre, *The Military and Society in Haiti*, 5–6.

CHAPTER 2

1. Interview with Brian Concannon, 14 November 2006.

2. Howard French, "Haiti Police Seen as Gaining in Coup," *New York Times*, 13 October 1991.

3. Letter from a veteran US investigator who oversaw covert US activity in Haiti 1991–2000, 23 March 2007.

4. Cf. Human Rights Watch, "The Aristide Government's Human Rights Record," 1 November 1991, http://www.hrw.org/reports/pdfs/h/haiti/haiti91n.pdf; Lee Hockstader, *Washington Post*, 8 October 1991. Mark Danner explains that the army first took control of the radio stations, thereby eliminating "Aristide's most potent weapon – his voice. Now squads of soldiers made their way into the bidonvilles, shooting anyone they saw, firing into the scrapwood hovels. When the people came out into the garishly lit streets, the soldiers shot them down [. . .]. The people, confused, frightened, and disorganized – they had received no *mot d'ordre* from their leader – stumbled into the streets and died. Automatic weapons, ruthlessly employed, had given the lie to Aristide's 'unarmed revolution' " (Danner, "Fall of the Prophet," *New York Review of Books* 2 December 1993; cf. Farmer, *Uses of Haiti*, 154).

5. Steven Horblitt, "Multilateral Policy: The Road Toward Reconciliation" (1993), 70.

6. Heinl and Heinl, *Written in Blood*, 702.

7. Jane Regan, "In the Aftermath of Invasion," *Covert Action Quarterly* (1995).

8. "Torturing Democracy: Noam Chomsky Interviewed by Faiz Ahmad", *ZNet*, 25 January 2003; cf. Noam Chomsky, "Democracy Enhancement: The Case of Haiti," *Z Magazine*, July 2004.

9. Cited in Lee Hockstader, "Haiti's Army Chiefs Defend Overthrow," *Washington Post*, 6 October 1991.

10. See in particular Allan Nairn, "The Eagle is Landing" (3 October 1994); "Our Man in FRAPH" (24 October 1994); "Haiti Under the Gun" (8 January 1996); Kim Ives, "The Unmaking of a President" (1994); Jane Regan, "In the Aftermath of Invasion" (1995).

11. White House Press Secretary Marlin Fitzwater, cited in Kim Ives "The Unmaking of a President" (1994), 16.

12. Tim Weiner, "Key Haiti Leaders Said To Have Been in the CIA's Pay," *New York Times*, 1 November 1993; Weiner, "CIA Formed Haitian Unit Later Tied to Narcotics Trade," *New York Times*, 14 November 1993.

13. Brian Concannon, "Lave Men, Siye Atè," 79–80.

14. Kennet Freed, interview with Philippe Girard, 10 April 2002, in Girard, *The Eagle and the Rooster*, 154n. 27.

15. Nairn, "Our Payroll, Haitian Hit," *The Nation*, 9 October 1995.

16. Nairn, "Behind Haiti's Paramilitaries," *The Nation*, 24 October 1994.

17. Nairn, "Haiti Under the Gun" (1996); cf. Chomsky, "Democracy Restored" (1994).

18. Cited in Nairn, "Haiti Under the Gun" (1996).

19. Bob Shacochis, *The Immaculate Invasion*, 29, cf 133; Stan Goff, *Hideous Dream*, vi, 465.

20. Cf. "Haitian Ex-Paramilitary Leader Confirms CIA Relationship," *New York Times*, 3 December 1995; Catherine Orenstein, "Haitian Refugee," *The Village Voice*, 12 August 1997; David Grann, "Giving 'The Devil' His Due," *Atlantic Monthly*, June 2001.

21. Cf. HRW, "Terror Prevails in Haiti" (1994), 26–34; Gilles Danroc and Daniel Roussière, *La Répression au quotidien en Haiti 1991–1994* (1995).

22. Letter from Eléonore Senlis, 23 March 2007.

23. Amnesty International, "Haiti: On the Horns of a Dilemma: Military Repression or Foreign Invasion?" 23 August 1994.

24. DOJ, *Profile Series: Haiti* (August 1993), 17–18; cf. HRW, *Silencing a People* (February 1993).

25. Kevin Pina, "US Corporate Media Distort Haitian Events," *Black Commentator*, 6 November 2003.

26. Brian Concannon, "Justice in Haiti: The Raboteau Trial," *Human Rights Databank* (December 2000).

27. Jim Mann, "CIA's Plan Would Have Undercut Aristide in 1987–88," *Los Angeles Times*, 31 October 1993; Wilentz, *The Rainy Season*, 114–15.

28. Steven Holmes, "Administration is Fighting Itself on Haiti Policy," *New York Times*, 23 October 1993.

29. Sheldon Rampton, "Hustling for the Junta: PR Fights Democracy in Haiti" (1994).

30. Cited in Danner, "Fall of the Prophet" (1993); cf. Ben Dupuy, "The Attempted Character Assassination of Aristide" (1999).

31. Interview with Patrick Elie, Port-au-Prince 5 January 2007. In August 1993 Jean Dominique observed that "there have been a lot of coups in Haiti, but rarely have there been 4,000 people killed. This was not simply to topple a president: it was something carefully planned to break the backbone of the Haitian people, to kill democracy" (Jean Dominique, in Demme, *The Agronomist*, 2002).

32. Numa, in Kean, *Rezistans*, 72.

33. Letter from Kim Ives, 10 February 2007.

34. In 1993, the musician Richard Morse complained to CIA chief Kambourian that "you can't have stability when 90 percent of the population is against the government. And he responded that 'Repression works. It worked in Russia for 40 years.' And I was quite taken aback to hear this from a high-ranking embassy official!" (Richard Morse, in Kean, *Rezistans*, 81).

35. Letter from a US congressional aide, 30 March 2007.

36. Interview with Yvon Neptune, Port-au-Prince, 5 January 2007.

37. Cited in Wilentz "Foreword," Aristide, *In the Parish of the Poor*, xxi. "By ignoring the existing balance of power, as unfortunate as that may be, do we advance more quickly toward the final goal, toward a just state?" (Aristide, *Dignity*, 107).

38. Aristide, "One Step at a Time" (2006). Patrick Elie was Aristide's chief drug enforcement and security advisor in 1991, and in the weeks following the coup he remembers that his SIN and CIA contacts actively encouraged him to begin organizing a popular militia to fight the coup, even giving him classified information about the army's equipment and supplies; Aristide vetoed any such move, on the assumption that their enemies were only looking for a pretext to intensify their support for the army. Elie eventually came to share his president's point of view. "I no longer believe that the people on their own, faced with M16s and armoured personnel carriers, stood any chance against the army. We had nothing, nothing other than the sheer force of numbers. It's not enough" (Interviews with Patrick Elie, 19 April 2006 and 14 January 2007).

39. Aristide, cited in Ives, "Danger of Foreign Invasion Looms as Noose Around Putchists Tightens," *The Guardian* [NY], 11 November 1991.

40. Chavannes Jean-Baptiste, cited in Rod Paul's film *Failing Haiti* (2005).

41. Camille Chalmers (PAPDA), cited in Jane Regan [Clara James], "Haitian Free Trade Zone" (November 2002).

42. As Aristide admitted, "the job of president requires that I be more cautious at times than I would like" (Aristide, *Dignity*, 102). In 1995 his chief of staff Leslie Voltaire said that Aristide had "learned to cut a deal. He saw how his enemies can take his words and use them against him. Now he is very careful of everything he says" (cited in Julia Preston, "Age of Aristide: Haiti Calmed After a Year," *New York Times* 20 September 1995). A former US ambassador (and outspoken ally of Aristide's government) was more candid: Aristide has "come to understand that too much revolution scares away investors. Small countries can't afford too much

social experimentation" (Robert White, cited in Randolph Ryan, "Aristide's Plans for Reform May Face Opposing Tensions," *Boston Globe* 25 September 1994).

43. Fatton, *Haiti's Predatory Republic*, x, 107; cf. Alex Dupuy, *Haiti in the New World Order*, 34.

44. Jill Smolowe, "With Friends Like These," *Time Magazine*, 8 November 1993.

45. Howard French, "Aristide Seeks More Than Moral Support," *New York Times*, 27 September 1992; French, "U.S. Keeps Eye on Haiti, but Action is Scant," *New York Times*, 8 October 1992.

46. Allan Nairn, in Kean, *Rezistans*, 85.

47. Interview with Patrick Elie, Port-au-Prince, 19 April 2006.

48. Norman Kempster, "US Urges Aristide to Agree to Haiti Plan for Coalition Rule," *Los Angeles Times*, 16 February 1994.

49. French, "Aristide Seeks More Than Moral Support," *New York Times*, 27 September 1992.

50. French, "U.S. Keeps Eye on Haiti," *New York Times*, 8 October 1992.

51. Cf. Juan Gonzalez, in Goodman and Nairn, "Different Coup, Same Paramilitary Leaders," *Democracy Now!*, 26 February 2004.

52. Cited in Kim Ives "The Unmaking of a President," 29.

53. Cited in Jill Smolowe, "With Friends Like These: A Host of Shadowy Figures Is Helping Haiti's Military Rulers Hatch a Plot to Sideline Aristide Permanently," *Time Magazine*, 8 November 1993.

54. Aristide, *Dignity*, 140. The Clinton administration demonstrated just how far they were willing to push Aristide into acquiescence with Cédras when in the spring of 1994 they encouraged him to consider a new Junta proposal for a "balanced" cabinet including Michel François' brother as Minister of Defense and Franck Romain (responsible for the 1988 Saint Jean Bosco massacre) as Minister of the Interior.

55. Nairn, "Behind Haiti's Paramilitaries" (1994); cf. Nairn, "Haiti Under the Gun" (1996).

56. Norman Kempster, "Christopher Ties Haiti Sanctions to Aristide OK of Coalition," *Los Angeles Times*, 24 February 1994; Howard French, "Some in Haiti, Impatient with Aristide, Plan Vote," *New York Times*, 24 February 1994. Few themes are more typical in the independent media's presentation of Aristide than this: "Aristide does not understand compromise [. . .]. His biggest problem is he doesn't listen, he doesn't compromise, he's an egomaniac" (Clara Germani, "Rise and Fall of a 'Haitian Mandela,'" *Christian Science Monitor*, 27 February 2004).

57. "US Must 'Stop the Brutal Atrocities' in Haiti, Clinton Says," *Los Angeles Times*, 16 September 1994.

58. Carter told Cédras and the other coup leaders "they could take four weeks to resign, they would not be charged with any crimes, they could remain in the country if they wished, they could run for the presidency if they wished, they could retain all their assets no matter how acquired. Those who chose exile were paid large amounts of money by the United States to lease their Haitian properties, any improvements made to remain free of charge; two jets were chartered to fly them with all their furniture to the country of their choice, transportation free, housing and living expenses paid for the next year for all family members and dozens of relatives and friends, totalling millions of dollars" (Blum, "Who Will Rid Me of This Turbulent Priest?," 1995).

59. Jane Regan, "In the Aftermath of Invasion" (1995).

60. Amy Wilentz, "Aristide On," *Time Magazine*, 17 October 1994.

61. Jane Regan [Clara James], "Haiti: The Roof Is Leaking," *Z Magazine* (June 1997).

62. Larry Rohter, "Some Aristide Supporters Seek Abolition of Military," *New York Times*, 22 November 1994.

63. Nairn, "The Eagle Is Landing," *The Nation*, 3 October 1994.
64. Lawrence P. Rockwood, telephone interview with Philippe Girard (26 February 2001), in Girard, *The Eagle and the Rooster*, 202. "Behind the scenes," confirms former US Special Forces sergeant Stan Goff, "every intelligence summary we received in 1994 was designed to indoctrinate us, as the occupying force, against Aristide. It was some of the most lurid anti-Aristide propaganda you can imagine. The process of undermining him, and of recruiting future PNH as intelligence assets for the CIA, was already well under way in 1994" (Stan Goff, Interview with Crowing Rooster, Miami June 2006).
65. Letter from Kim Ives, 10 February 2007.
66. See in particular Aristide's inaugural address, 7 February 1991, in Aristide, *Théologie et politique*, 101, 112–14.
67. Douglas Farah, "Aristide Returns to Acclaim in Haiti," *Washington Post*, 16 October 1994.
68. Xabier Gorostiaga, "Geoculture: The Key to Understanding Haiti?" (January 1995); cf. Farmer, *Uses of Haiti*, 324–32.
69. Donald Schulz, "Whither Haiti?" (1996), v.
70. Julia Preston, "Age of Aristide: Haiti Calmed After a Year," *New York Times* 20 September 1995. "Probably the biggest reason for the lack of violence," noted *Time Magazine* that summer, "was Aristide himself. The concerns about his leftist opinions and volatile personality, which have long jangled nerves in Washington, have so far proved groundless" (Kevin Fedark, "Thumbs Up, Halfways," *Time Magazine*, 10 July 1995).
71. Interview with Senatus Willy, Tabarre, 9 January 2007.
72. Cited in Howard French, "Aristide Seeks More Than Moral Support," *New York Times*, September 27, 1992.
73. Cited in John Kifner, "Mission to Haiti: The Homecoming," *New York Times*, 16 October 1994.
74. In an interview he gave on 7 November 1994, Aristide acknowledged that the restoration of constitutional rule "has been a slow process. Could it have been faster? The presidential palace was totally sacked. There was no telephone, no water, no desks or chairs. Nothing. To be able to communicate, to meet with people has been extremely difficult and complex, for both infrastructural and security reasons. I can't create too much tension for the US Army with public appearances or with my movements [. . .]. In addition, the FRAPH and the Tontons Macoutes still have a lot of weapons [. . .]. I'll be able to move more freely once we've guaranteed a minimum of security" (Xabier Gorostiaga, "Geoculture: The Key to Understanding Haiti?").
75. Nairn, "Different Coup, Same Paramilitary Leaders," *Democracy Now!* 26 February 2004.
76. Jose De Cordoba, "US Considers Case Against Aristide," *Wall Street Journal*, 2 April 2004.
77. Aristide, *Dignity*, 47.
78. Aristide, *Eyes of the Heart*, 16–17.
79. Catherine Orenstein, "An Interview with Jean-Bertrand Aristide," *Tikkun* (May 1998); Aristide, *Eyes of the Heart*, 49.
80. The elite, Brahimi explained, should "know two things: that political changes are inevitable, but that, on the ideological, economic front, they have the sympathy of Big Brother, capitalism" (cited in HSG, *Haiti Briefing* 25, September 1997).
81. Interview with Bobby Duval, Port-au-Prince, 17 April 2006.
82. HAC, *Hidden from the Headlines* (2003).
83. Axel Peuker (a World Bank official who was party to the 1994 accords), cited in Nairn, "Aristide Banks on Austerity" (1994).

84. "Protests Erupt Across Haiti as Leaders Push Austerity," *New York Times*, 17 January 1997.

85. IMF/World Bank, "Haiti's Strategy of Social and Economic Reconstruction," 22 August 1994, reprinted in *Multinational Monitor*, August 1994, http://multinationalmonitor.org/hyper/mm0894.htmlhaiti.

86. "Aristide actually pulled one over on Cédras" interim government with the 1994 amnesty. He issued a decree, but it only applied to the coup d'état on 30 September itself, not the crimes committed afterwards. The IC never bothered to really read the decree, so it was happy. The human rights community lambasted Aristide for being soft on the coup criminals, but he couldn't defend himself, for fear of tipping off the IC. In the end, we did prosecute the coup criminals, and none even bothered to invoke the amnesty" (Letter from Brian Concannon, 29 November 2006).

87. Interview with Patrick Elie, Port-au-Prince, 19 April 2006; cf. Aristide, *Dignity*, 106–7. It's also important to remember, as Alex Dupuy points out, that the cuts in social services that generally accompany neo-liberal structural adjustment would arguably be less painful in Haiti than in say Ortega's Nicaragua or Manley's Jamaica, since in Haiti "the government had never provided services or subsidies to the poor or the working and peasant classes, and any reforms in the public sector would affect primarily the prebendary state officials, the clientelistic civil servants, and the extended macoute network that siphoned off public resources for their [own] benefit" (Alex Dupuy, *Prophet and Power*, 120).

88. Tod Robberson, "Aristide Selects Business Leader for Prime Minister," *Washington Post* 25 October 1994; cf. Catherine Manegold, "Aristide Chooses a Premier who has Free-Market Ideas," *New York Times*, 25 October 1994.

89. Larry Rohter, "Haiti's Prime Minister Resigns after Disputes over Economy," *New York Times*, 14 October 1995; Rohter, "Privatizations Start Feud in Haiti," *New York Times*, 19 October 1995.

90. Dan Coughlin, "Haiti: Behind Aristide's Angry Words," InterPress Service, 21 November 1995; cf. Douglas Farah, "Haiti's Nascent Prospects Turn Suddenly Bleak," *Washington Post*, 26 November 1995.

91. Larry Rohter, "Haiti's Prime Minister Resigns After Disputes Over Economy," *New York Times*, 14 October 1995. Writing in 2004, veteran analyst Melinda Miles recognized that the main reason for Aristide's removal is that "he did not effectively implement the structural adjustment program in Haiti" (Miles, *Emergency Haiti Observation Mission 23 March–2 April 2004*, 31).

92. Naomi Klein, "6/7: The Massacre of the Poor that the World Ignored," *Guardian*, 18 July 2005.

93. Lisa McGowan, *Democracy Undermined, Economic Justice Denied* (1997).

94. Cited in Larry Rohter, "Split Between Aristide and His Successor Imperils Haiti's Governing Party," *New York Times*, 12 May 1996.

95. Rohter, "Testing Fragile Democracy, Haiti Votes," *New York Times*, 26 June 1995.

96. Schulz, "Haiti: Will Things Fall Apart?" (1998); cf. Michael Norton, "Aristide Supporters Win Elections Hands Down," AP, 5 October 1995.

97. "Election Campaign in Haiti Splits Allies," *New York Times*, 23 June 1995.

98. Cali Ruchala, "The Struggle for Haiti: An Interview with Hyppolite Pierre," *Sobaka*, 21 February 2004.

99. Jane Regan, "In the Aftermath of Invasion" (January 1995); cf. Christophe Wargny, "Le Président Aristide sous haute surveillance," *Le Monde diplomatique* (November 1994).

100. Cf. Regan, "In the Aftermath of Invasion" (1995).

101. HSG Briefing 12 (April 1995), cited in Robinson, *Promoting Polyarchy*, 311.

102. Brian Atwood (USAID), cited in Jane Regan [Clara James], "Haiti: The Roof Is Leaking" (1997).
103. James, "An Inside Look at Haiti's Business Elite" (1995).
104. Cited in Nairn, "Aristide Banks on Austerity" (1994).
105. IMF in 1995, cited in US Network for Global Economic Justice, "Corporate Welfare in Haiti: Fifty Years Is Enough," http://www.50years.org/factsheets/haiti.html.
106. Campaign for Labor Rights, "Garment Production in Haitian Export Processing Zones," 8 August 1998.
107. Ives, "The Fall of the Empire's Ushers," Haïti Progrès 20: 52 (12 March 2003).
108. Julia Preston, "Age of Aristide: Haiti Calmed After a Year," New York Times, 20 September 1995.
109. Jean-Germain Gros, "Haiti's Flagging Transition" (1997), 97–98; cf. Andrew Reding, "Let Mr. Aristide Stay in Office," Journal of Commerce, 12 December 1995, http://www.worldpolicy.org/globalrights/carib/1995–1212-JOC.html. In an interview published two days after his return to Haiti in October 1994, Aristide announced that "I intend, and have always intended, to leave power at the end of my constitutional term. I have no interest in remaining past that time, no matter how I have spent the years of my presidency. As Haiti's first freely elected President, I feel it is my duty to observe strictly the letter as well as the spirit of the constitution. In leaving office and handing over power to a new freely elected President, I will have completed my mission, and that is all I ever wanted" (Amy Wilentz, "Aristide On," Time Magazine, 17 October 1994).
110. Interview with Laura Flynn, 18 December 2006; cf. Kim Ives, "The Fall of the Empire's Ushers," Haïti Progrès 20: 52 (12 March 2003).
111. Larry Rohter, "President-to-Be Of Haiti Faces Tough Agenda," New York Times 17 December 1995. As Concannon explains, the relationship between Aristide and Préval was always complex. "Aristide was the clear leader of Lavalas, and Préval was his protégé, so Préval had an obvious political debt. They shared a common political perspective. But Préval had his own priorities for policy, and wanted to make his own mark. Aristide, being much more charismatic, cast a big shadow. They also have different styles: Aristide is more comfortable with direct confrontation with his opponents, and likes to inspire his supporters. Préval tends to avoid or defuse conflict, and is more low key" (Letter from Brian Concannon, 14 November 2006).
112. Cited in Larry Rohter, "Surprise in Haiti: A Listless Presidential Race," New York Times, 15 December 1995.
113. Aristide, Eyes of the Heart, 31, 15; cf. "The Pitfalls of a Compromise: Privatization Moving, Elections Not," Haïti Progrès 17: 9 (19 March 1999).
114. Larry Rohter, "Growing Gap Between Old Allies Creates New Obstacles for Haiti," New York Times, 29 March 1997; cf. "Aristide lance une violente attaque contre le plan néo-liberal," Haïti en Marche, 17 June 1997.
115. 'Protests Erupt Across Haiti as Leaders Push Austerity," New York Times, 17 January 1997.
116. Interview with Yvon Neptune, Port-au-Prince, 5 January 2007.
117. Ibid.
118. Larry Rohter, "Haiti's Premier Quits, Saying Aristide Forces Undermined Him," New York Times, 10 June 1997. "Two members of former president Jean-Bertrand Aristide's Fanmi Lavalas party, Fourel Celestin and Joseph Yvon Feuillé, obtained the majorities needed to secure the Senate seats for the southeast and southern departments respectively. A second round of voting to decide the remaining 7 seats was postponed indefinitely. Inter-party disputes left the legislature in gridlock until January 1999" (Political Database of the Americas, "Haiti: 1997 Legislative Elections Results," http://pdba.georgetown.edu/Elecdata/Haiti/97legis.html).

119. Bellegarde-Smith, *Breached Citadel*, 256; cf. Donald Schulz, "Haiti: Will Things Fall Apart?" (1998).

120. Larry Rohter, "Political Feuds Rack Haiti," *New York Times*, 18 October 1998.

121. David Gonzalez, "Civilian Police Force Brings New Problems in Haiti," *New York Times*, 26 November 1999.

122. Elizabeth Rubin, "Haiti Takes Policing 101," *New York Times Magazine*, 25 May 1997.

123. Larry Rohter, "Haiti's 'Little Kings' Again Terrorize its People," *New York Times*, 25 August 1996. As Concannon noted in 2004, "Although it has been demobilized for over eight years, the army is still recognized by Haiti's Constitution. In September 2003, Parliament began the process of amending the Constitution to formally abolish the army. Although both houses voted overwhelmingly in favor of abolition, the Senate's vote, which was unanimous with two abstentions, has been called into question" on the grounds that there was no quorum, because seven seats remained empty (Brian Concannon, "Lave Men, Siye Atè," 98n.79). The seats were empty since the opposition to FL refused to participate in the elections needed to fill them, after the controversy surrounding May 2000. The two abstentions were Dany Toussaint and Joseph Médard.

124. Nairn, "Haiti Under the Gun" (1996).

125. Steven Dudley, "The Men Behind Haiti's Rebellion," *San Francisco Chronicle*, 29 February 2004.

126. Nairn, "Haiti Under the Gun" (1996).

127. When Goff visited Haiti that same year he met with colleagues from the 3rd US Special Forces group, ODA 344, who had been responsible for training the new presidential guard; they were already boasting that "the guys that we trained will be the guys that lead the next coup" (Stan Goff, Interview with Crowing Rooster, Miami June 2006).

128. Dan Coughlin, "Haitian Lament: Killing Me Softly," *The Nation*, 1 March 1999.

129. Cf. Laurie Richardson, "Disarmament Derailed" (1996), 11–14.

130. Larry Rohter, "America's Habit of Force in Haiti," *New York Times*, 17 September 1996.

131. Larry Rohter, "US is Recruiting American Police to Join U.N. Force in Haiti," *New York Times*, 2 October 1996; letter from Michelle Karshan, 29 January 2007.

132. Sam Skolnik, "Separating Cops, Spies" *Legal Times*, 1 March 1999; cf. *Haïti Progrès* 16: 51 (10 March 1999), *Haïti Progrès* 13: 48 (21 February 1996).

133. HRW, "HAITI, Security Compromised: Recycled Haitian Soldiers on the Police Front Line" (March 1995); cf. Girard, *The Eagle and the Rooster*, 235–6.

134. "Army Leaders Forced Out by Aristide", *New York Times*, 22 February 1995.

135. Interview with Laura Flynn, 18 December 2006; cf. Ben Dupuy, "The Character Assassination of Aristide," 1999. A veteran US analyst involved in the investigation of Durocher-Bertin's murder told me in March 2007 that the only significant piece of evidence linking it to the National Palace was deliberately rigged. On the day she was killed US eavesdroppers intercepted a phone call from Joseph Médard to Dany Toussaint, instructing him to look out for a car that was roughly similar to the one used by Bertin – in fact, however, Médard's call was prompted by a tip-off from an advance party of US Secret Service personnel who were in Haiti to prepare for Clinton's imminent visit, and the car Médard was describing belonged instead to someone they had identified as a potential assassin – FRAPH deputy commander Jodel Chamblain. A seven-month FBI investigation into Durocher-Bertin's murder failed to identify her killer.

136. Larry Rohter, "Aristide Urges U.N. to Disarm Thugs in Haiti" *New York Times*, 29 March 1995.

137. Jane Regan, "In the Aftermath of Invasion" (1995). "Rather than disarm the Haitian army and its paramilitary assistants as promised in writing to the Aristide government, or purge the human rights violators," Regan observed, "the US is now in effect overseeing a kind of massive School of the Americas for the entire Haitian armed forces."

138. Brian Concannon, "Lave Men, Siye Atè", 84.

139. Rohter, "Haiti's 'Little Kings' Again Terrorize Its People", *New York Times*, 25 August 1996.

140. Irwin Stotzky, *Silencing the Guns in Haiti*, 40, 45.

141. Regan, "In the Aftermath of Invasion" (1995).

142. Rohter, "Haiti's 'Little Kings,'" *New York Times*, 25 August 1996.

143. Ibid.

144. Rohter, "U.N. Troops to Leave Haiti As Feeble as They Found It," *New York Times*, 4 December 1997.

145. Griffin, *Haiti Human Rights Investigation* (November 2004), 36.

146. Patrick Elie, "Taking Us to Democracy Like Cattle to a Killing House," 14 December 2005.

147. Elizabeth Rubin, "Haiti Takes Policing 101," *New York Times magazine*, 25 May 1997.

148. Rubin, "Haiti Takes Policing 101," *New York Times magazine*, 25 May 1997. "Many judges work two jobs just to survive and often release accused criminals almost as soon as they are arrested, either for bribes or out of fear of retaliation. 'When it happens often enough,' Denizé says, 'the policeman tends to say: "What's the use? He's going to walk tomorrow." Or he tends to be fearful: 'I arrest him today and he could be shooting at me tomorrow'" (ibid). At least 18 police officers were killed in 1999 (OAS/UN International Civilian Mission in Haiti, *Human Rights Review*, October–December 1999, http://www.un.org/rights/micivih/rapports/hrr99q4.html).

149. Rohter, "Support Is Waning for Haiti's US-Trained Police," *New York Times* 24 December 1995. Eighteen months later, Rohter noted that "many Haitians express irritation with the police, calling them brutal, corrupt and imperious" (Larry Rohter, "Wave of Violence Unsettles Nerves in Haiti," *New York Times*, 24 March 1997).

150. HRW, "The Human Rights Record of the Haitian National Police" (January 1997).

151. Cited in Rohter, "Haiti Paralysis Brings a Boom In Drug Trade," *New York Times*, 27 October 1998.

152. Letter from Jeb Sprague, 13 December 2006; David Gonzalez, "Civilian Police Force Brings New Problems in Haiti," *New York Times*, 26 November 1999.

153. Charles Lane, "Cop Land," *New Republic*, 29 September 1997, cited in Fatton, *Haiti's Predatory Republic*, 173.

154. Letter from Frantz Gabriel, 17 December 2006.

155. Sources close to Aristide claim that Jean Lamy was probably killed by Dany Toussaint or someone working for Toussaint, "under orders from the Company." Kim Ives argues that although Toussaint certainly had a hand in his departure, "Manuel's downfall was primarily his own doing and due to his class position. As a result of his dealings with the anti-Lavalas bourgeoisie, his conflicts with the Lavalas base groups like the JPP and the TKL, a number of very arrogant remarks he made, and the gas that Toussaint poured on the fire, Manuel became a real target of popular ire, and that is why Préval finally told him it was time for him to leave the country" (Letter from Kim Ives, 14 December 2006).

156. Jean Dominique, "Does Dany Toussaint Take God's Children for a Bunch of Wild Ducks?", Radio Haiti-Inter, 19 October 1999.

157. Andrew Reding, "Haiti in Peril – Ex-Police Chief's Deadly Drive for Power," *Pacific News Service*, 8 January 2002.

158. The American priest and doctor Father Rick Freshette has worked in Haiti since the late 1980s, and remembers that "there were no Protestant sects until the Catholic church started siding with the poor." Now there are around 450 of them – a distracting, divided mass of rival factions, sharing only their hatred for Catholicism, their enthusiasm for the US and their indifference to the material conditions of life before death (Interview with Father Rick Freshette, Port-au-Prince, 18 April 2006).

CHAPTER 3

1. Roger Noriega, "Interview by Chris Bury of Nightline," 1 March 2004, http://www.state.gov/p/wha/rls/rm/30143.htm.

2. Interview with Venel Remarais, Port-au-Prince, 18 April 2006.

3. Melinda Miles with Moira Feeney, *Elections 2000: Participatory Democracy in Haiti* (2001).

4. "Haiti Awaits Results of Sunday's Elections," CNN, 22 May 2000; cf. Michael Dobbs, "Haitians Flood Polls in Peaceful Vote," *Washington Post*, 22 May 2000.

5. Alex Dupuy, *Haiti in the New World Order*, 172.

6. Charles Arthur, *Haiti in Focus*, 69. The FL election program is a substantial 180-page book, entitled *Investir dans l'humain* (1999).

7. See in particular Béatrice Pouligny, "Haïti: Deux ou trois raisons d'espérer," *Libération*, 13 February 2001, and Fatton, *Haiti's Predatory Republic*, 144–7.

8. Interview with Ramilus Bolivar, Port-au-Prince, 15 January 2007.

9. Cited in Jean-Michel Caroit, "Haïti : la deuxième chance d'Aristide," *Le Monde*, 30 May 2000.

10. Cited in Deibert, *Notes from the Last Testament*, 115.

11. Roger Noriega, testimony to Congress 3 March 2004, cited in Scott Wilson, "Top Haitian Rebels Pledge to Disarm," *Washington Post* 4 March 2004. The Jamaican commentator John Maxwell understood perfectly well what was going on: the "irregularities in the elections of a few senators [were] a fact of much slighter significance than the irregularities in the [2000] election of President Bush. In Haiti, there was absolutely no question of who was the people's choice. But in the case of Haiti these 'irregularities' now assume transcendental importance, and are cause for the world to condemn Haiti to starve in obscene misery" (John Maxwell, "Racist Antecedents of US Haiti Policy," *The Jamaica Observer*, 7 January 2004).

12. Frances Kerry, "Aristide Has No Future," Reuters, 27 November 2002.

13. OAS, *The Election Observation Mission in Haiti* (December 2000), 2.

14. Henry Carey, "Not Perfect, But Improving," *Miami Herald*, 12 June 2000.

15. Cited in Melinda Miles with Moira Feeney, *Elections 2000* (February 2001).

16. Letter from Brian Concannon, 29 November 2006; cf. "Haiti Stands Firm Against International Threats," *Haïti Progrès* 18: 15 (28 June 2000); Miles, "Elections and 2004," Haiti Reborn/Quixote Center (August 2003). The CEP's argument is disputed by the US State Department and opponents of FL (see in particular James Morrell, "Snatching Defeat from the Jaws of Victory," Center for International Policy, August 2000).

17. OAS, *The Election Observation Mission in Haiti* (December 2000), 3.

18. Ibid, 53–7.

19. Cf. Heinl and Heinl, *Written in Blood*, 684–5.

20. Léon Manus to Orlando Marville 6 June 2006, *Haïti Progrès* 18: 12 (7 June 2000).

21. Manus, "Declaration", 21 June 2000, cited in Fatton, *Haiti's Predatory Republic*, 117.

22. "Un Grand Rassemblement des vendus en République Dominicaine," *Haïti Progrès* 20: 41 (25 December 2002).

23. Christopher Marquis, "France Seeks UN Force in Haiti," *New York Times*, 26 February 2004. (In reality, of course, Aristide only began "ruling by decree" in January 2004.)

24. Miles with Feeney, *Elections 2000: Participatory Democracy in Haiti* (2001); cf. Miles, "The Corruption of Democracy," in *Let Haiti LIVE*, 142–5.

25. Interview with Anne Hastings, Port-au-Prince, 24 April 2006.

26. Cited in Farmer, *Uses of Haiti*, 99.

27. Sletten and Egset, *Poverty in Haiti* (2004), 20.

28. [US] House International Relations Committee, "Gilman, Helms and Goss Issue Statement on Haitian Election," 8 December 2000.

29. Michele Wucker, "Haiti: So Many Missteps" (Spring 2004).

30. "US Deals Blow to Aristide," AP, 6 February 2001.

31. Interview with Timothy Pershing, Pétionville, 17 April 2006.

32. By the end of 2003, the Haitian government had "paid $30 million in back interest but was still waiting for the first disbursement" (Scott Wilson, "Armed Attacks Increase Pressure on Haitian leader," *Washington Post*, 19 November 2003).

33. Marguerite Laurent, "Haiti: Matters to Investigate" (2006), http://www.marguer-itelaurent.com/law/matterstoinvestigage.html.

34. Jeffrey Sachs testifying before Congress, in Nicolas Rossier's film *Aristide and the Endless Revolution* (2005).

35. Anne Street, *Haiti: A Nation in Crisis*, 4.

36. Jeffrey Sachs testifying before Congress, in Rossier's *Aristide* (2005).

37. Cf. IMF, "Haiti – Letter of Intent, Memorandum of Economic and Financial Policies," Port-au-Prince 10 June 2003.

38. Chossudovsky, "The Destabilization of Haiti," 29 February 2004.

39. World Bank, "2006 World Development Indicators"; cf. UN Food and Agriculture Organization, http://www.fao.org/es/ESS/yearbook/vol_1_2/pdf/Haiti.pdf.

40. Street, *Haiti: A Nation in Crisis*, 4, referring to United Nations Development Program, *La Situation économique et sociale d'Haïti en 2002* (UNDP, 2002).

41. Statement issued by Oxfam, Christian Aid and ActionAid in December 2003, cited in Anne Street, *Haiti: A Nation in Crisis*, 4.

42. Interview with Jonas Petit, Miami, 8 April 2006.

43. The three most important of the dozens of small parties or "particles" that made up the Convergence Démocratique were the OPL (led by Pierre-Charles), MO-CHRENA (a rightwing evangelical party led by Luc Mésadieu, supported with funds from American Protestant groups), and Espace de Concertation (itself a coalition of several smaller parties funded by European social democratic parties, notably KONAKOM, led by Victor Benoît and Micha Gaillard, and PANPRA, led by Serge Gilles; both KONAKOM and PANPRA are heavily dependent on funding and support from European social democratic parties, in particular the French Socialist Party).

44. Amy Wilentz, "Coup in Haiti," 22 March 2004.

45. Cf. Alex Dupuy, "Who is Afraid of Democracy in Haiti? A Critical Reflection," *Haiti Papers* 7 (Trinity College Haiti Program, June 2003), 5–6.

46. Max Blumenthal, "Did the Bush Administration Allow a Network of Right-Wing Republicans to Foment a Violent Coup in Haiti?", *Democracy Now* 20 July 2004, http://www.democracynow.org/article.pl?sid=04/07/20/1327215.

47. Cited in "Canadian Officials Initiate Planning for Military Ouster of Aristide," *Haïti Progrès* 20: 51 (5 March 2003).

48. Cited in Jessica Leight, "Haiti: Waiting for Something Bad to Happen," *Dissident Voice*, 12 February 2004.

49. Cf. Michael Norton, "Aristide Pledges Diverse Rule," AP, 28 November 2000.
50. Michael Norton, "Haiti Government Urged to Resign," AP, 21 June 2000.
51. Fatton, *Haiti's Predatory Republic*, 147.
52. "Résolution de la journée d'ouverture des États Généraux," *Haiti Online*, 29 January 2001, cited in Fatton, *Haiti's Predatory Republic*, 164 n.23.
53. Cited in Deibert, *Notes from the Last Testament*, 131.
54. "Marc Bazin reçu en audience par le président élu," *Métropole Haiti*, 5 December 2000, cited in Fatton, *Haiti's Predatory Republic*, 145.
55. "Summit Leaders Urge Haiti Reform," *BBC News*, 22 April 2001, http://news.-bbc.co.uk/1/hi/world/americas/1291640.stm.
56. Cited in Dupuy, *Prophet and Power*, 153.
57. Luigi Einaudi, Assistant Secretary General of the OAS, cited in Michelle Karshan, "What's Next: Haiti Policy Analysts Weigh In," Haiti Action Committee, 16 December 2002.
58. "Frustration Boils Over," *The Economist*, 30 November 2003.
59. Jeffrey Sachs, "Don't Fall for Washington's Spin on Haiti," *Financial Times*, 1 March 2004.

CHAPTER 4

1. Lawrence Pezzullo in September 1994, cited in Chomsky, "Democracy Restored," *Z Magazine*, November 1994.
2. Lawrence Pezzullo, "Haiti's Lessons for U.S. Leaders," *The Baltimore Sun*, 10 November 2002; Pezzullo, "U.S. Must Take Lead in Developing Peaceful Transition Plan," *Miami Herald*, 15 December 2002.
3. Stan Goff, "Beloved Haiti: A (Counter) Revolutionary Bicentennial," 14 February 2004.
4. Cf. Wilentz, "Haiti's Occupation," *The Nation*, 19 April 2004.
5. Concannon, "Lave Men, Siye Atè," 91.
6. Ron Howell, "US Political Maneuvering Behind the Ouster," *New York Newsday*, 1 March 2004.
7. Fatton, "A War Waged on the Aristide Regime," *Socialist Worker*, 5 March 2004, http://www.socialistworker.org/2004–1/489/489_02_Fatton.shtml.
8. Walt Bogdanich and Jenny Nordberg, "Democracy Undone: Mixed US Signals Helped Tilt Haiti Toward Chaos," *New York Times*, 29 January 2006.
9. Frances Kerry, "Aristide Has No Future," Reuters, 27 November 2002. Carney's HDP colleague Ira Lowenthal developed the implications of this position in a 31 October 2003 editorial in the *Miami Herald*, in which he accused Aristide of trampling on "every basic constitutional precept protecting this suffering nation from the re-emergence of one-man rule, kleptocracy and repression."
10. Denis Paradis, interview with CBS News, 22 March 2005. Michel Vastel exposed part of what was agreed at Meech Lake in an article published in February 2003. According to Vastel, Paradis and his colleagues defined this "responsibility to protect as follows: When a population greatly suffers from the consequences of a civil war, an insurrection, state repression or the failure of its policies, and when the state in question is not willing or capable of putting an end to these sufferings or to avoid them, international responsibility to protect takes precedence over the principle of non-intervention" (Michel Vastel, "Il faut renverser Aristide," *L'Actualité*, 28 February 2003; cf. Anthony Fenton, "Interview With Denis Paradis on Haiti Regime Change," *The Dominion*, 15 September 2004).

11. Kim Ives, "US Policy Towards Haiti Promotes Economic Instability," *The Progressive Media Project*, 6 November 2002.

12. Letter from Jonas Petit, 14 December 2006.

13. USAID Democracy and Governance Program, Program Data Sheet 521–005 (2003), http://www.usaid.gov/pubs/cbj2003/lac/ht/521–005.html.

14. "USAID/OTI Haiti Field Report", August 2005, cited in Sasha Kramer, "USAID and Haiti" (2005). At some point between August 2005 and November 2006 this passage was cut from the online version of this USAID report; USAID official Katherine Donohue explained that "the language originally used had been mis-interpreted" (Letter from Donohue, 4 December 2006).

15. See IFES, "Haiti", http://www.ifes.org/haiti.html; cf. Concannon, "An Prensip," *Truthout*, 4 May 2005.

16. Griffin, *Haiti Human Rights Investigation* (November 2004), 21.

17. Ibid. 21–2.

18. COHA, "The IRI: Promulgating Democracy of Another Variety," 15 July 2004.

19. Allen Weinstein in 1991, cited in William Blum, "Trojan Horse: The National Endowment for Democracy," *Rogue State* (2000), http://www.thirdworldtraveler.com/CIA/National percent20EndowmentDemo.html.

20. Eva Golinger, *The Chavez Code*, 64–5.

21. Max Blumenthal, "The Other Regime Change," *Salon.com*, 16 July 2004.

22. Stanley Lucas, *Radio Tropicale*, 8 February 2001.

23. Heinl and Heinl, *Written in Blood*, 689.

24. Prosper Avril, *An Appeal to History: The Truth About a Singular Lawsuit* (1999), 291–4.

25. Kim Ives, "Class Analysis of a Crisis," *Haïti Progrès* 20: 37 (27 November 2002).

26. Wilentz, *The Rainy Season*, 206.

27. Gérard Gourgue, "De L'Ouverture des États Généraux," 7 February 2001.

28. Walt Bogdanich and Jenny Nordberg, "Democracy Undone: Mixed US Signals Helped Tilt Haiti Toward Chaos," *New York Times* 29 January 2006). Bogdanich and Nordberg's useful exposé has its limitations: although critical of Noriega and Lucas, they are much more forgiving of the (comparatively) "dovish" ambassador Dean Curran, who sought only to isolate and bankrupt the regime, rather than overthrow it by force.

29. Ibid. Back when the destabilization campaign was actually under way, Evans Paul took a slightly different line, regularly insisting that "no compromise is possible with [Aristide's] regime" (in Gary Younge, "Haitian President Urged to Quit to End Violence," *Guardian*, 21 January 2004).

30. For more information see Max Blumenthal, "Did the Bush Administration Allow a Network of Right-Wing Republicans to Foment a Violent Coup in Haiti?", *Democracy Now!*, 20 July 2004.

31. "For the CIA and the State Department, the FLRN and Guy Philippe are to Haiti what the KLA and Hashim Thaci are to Kosovo" (Chossudovsky, "The Desta-bilization of Haiti," *Global Research*, 29 February 2004).

32. Bogdanich and Nordberg, "Democracy Undone," *New York Times*, 29 January 2006.

33. Cf. Anthony Fenton, "US Gvt. Channels Millions through National Endowment for Democracy to Fund Anti-Lavalas Groups in Haiti," *Democracy Now!*, 23 January 2006.

34. "Piatre Massacre: NCHR Can Finally Salute an Indictment Report Fourteen Years Later," NCHR 4 February 2004; "Background and Analysis on the May 28th Confrontation at Champs de Mars," *Haïti Progrès* 17: 18 (21 July 1999).

35. This is a point that is powerfully made, in different ways and among many others, by

William Robinson in his *Promoting Polyarchy* (1996) and by Nicolas Guilhot in his *The Democracy Makers* (2005).

36. Atlas Economic Research Foundation, http://www.atlasusa.org/V2/main/page.php?page_id=408&box=.
37. Jean Saint-Vil, "Haiti's 'Ambassador' to Canada," *ZNet*, 9 July 2005.
38. Deibert, *Notes from the Last Testament*, 309.
39. "Un Grand Rassemblement des vendus," *Haïti Progrès* 20: 41 (25 December 2002).
40. Interviews with Emmanuel Bélimaire and Nazaire Saint-Fort (State University students), Port-au-Prince April 2006.
41. Tom Reeves, "Haiti's Disappeared," *ZNet*, 5 May 2004.
42. "184 Institutions: The Macouto-Bourgeoisie's New Offensive," *Haïti Progrès* 20: 45 (22 January 2003).
43. Cited in National Labor Committee [Charles Kernaghan], *Haiti After the Coup: Sweatshop or Real Development* (1993).
44. Andréa Schmidt and Anthony Fenton, "Andy Apaid and Us," *ZNet*, 19 October 2005; cf. Campaign for Labor Rights, "Garment Production in Haitian Export Processing Zones," 8 August 1998.
45. "André Apaid: Gare à la provocation!" *Haïti Progrès* 21: 35 (12 November 2003); "The February 29th Coup d'état," *Haïti Progrès* 22: 2 (24 March 2004).
46. Tom Reeves, "Letter to the Editor," *Dollars & Sense*, March 2004.
47. Cited in Yves Engler, "NGOs and Haiti," *ZNet*, 7 January 2006.
48. Fatton, *Haiti's Predatory Republic*, 150–1.
49. Ibid., 180.
50. Sauveur Pierre-Etienne (OPL), speaking at a 16 October 2000 CD press conference, cited in "Is a Coup d'état Looming?", *Haïti Progrès* 18: 31 (18 October 2000).
51. Interview with Laurie Richardson, Pétionville, 24 April 2006; cf. Farmer, *Uses of Haiti*, 335.
52. Interview with Robert Fatton, 10 November 2006.
53. Chavannes Jean-Baptiste, interview with Michael Deibert November 2000, in Deibert, *Notes from the Last Testament*, 127; cf. 263–5.
54. Deibert, *Notes from the Last Testament*, 127; cf. Reeves, "The Puzzling Alliance of Chavannes Jean-Baptiste and Charles Henri Baker," *Counterpunch*, 1 March 2006.
55. Chavannes Jean-Baptiste, "MPP Speaks to the New Dimension of the Haitian Crisis," 24 February 2004, http://www.grassrootsonline.org/weblog/mpp.html.
56. Hallward, "Insurgency and Betrayal: An Interview with Guy Philippe," *Haiti Analysis*, 23 March 2007.
57. Tom Reeves, "Haiti's Disappeared" (2004); cf. Reeves, "The Puzzling Alliance of Chavannes Jean-Baptiste and Charles Henri Baker," *Counterpunch*, 1 March 2006.
58. Chavannes Jean-Baptiste, "MPP Speaks to the New Dimension of the Haitian Crisis" (2004).
59. Bogdanich and Nordberg, "Democracy Undone," *New York Times*, 29 January 2006.
60. See for instance US House of Representatives, "Gilman Supports Haiti Civil Society Dialogue," 18 January 2001; Ministère Français des Affaires Etrangères, "Point de Presse," 7 February 2001.
61. Anthony Fenton and Derrick O'Keefe, "Canada in the Haitian Coup," *Seven Oaks Magazine* 21 September 2004; cf. Fenton and Engler, *Canada in Haiti* (2005).
62. For a full list of the recipients see HSG, "European Union Funding for Members of the Group of 184," 11 November 2003.
63. Interview with Anne Hastings, Port-au-Prince, 24 April 2006.
64. Patrick Elie, "A Coup Made Long in Advance," 17 October 2004.
65. Cited in Kim Ives, "The Unmaking of a President" (1994), 21.

66. Anne Street, *Haiti: A Nation in Crisis* (2004), 18.

67. Griffin, *Haiti Human Rights Investigation* (November 2004), 29.

68. Charles Arthur, "Haiti," in the International Press Institute's *World Press Freedom Review 2005*.

69. http://www.wehaitians.com.

70. For more details on some of these stations see http://www.radiovision2000.com; http://www.signalfmhaiti.com; http://www.metropolehaiti.com/metropole/apropos.phtml.

71. Sony Bastien (owner of Radio Kiskeya), interview with Isabel Macdonald February 2006, in Macdonald, "Covering the Coup" (2006), 100.

72. Patrick Elie, "A Coup Made Long in Advance," 17 October 2004.

73. Kevin Pina and Father Gérard Jean-Juste, "Who Really Killed Jean Dominique and Jacques Roche?", KPFA 13 April 2006.

74. Patrick Elie, "A Coup Made Long in Advance," 17 October 2004. I return to Dominique's assassination in chapter seven.

75. Sony Bastien, interview with Isabel Macdonald, December 2005, cited in Macdonald, "Covering the Coup," 97–8. Many of the anti-FL student demonstrators who spoke with Macdonald confirmed the point. According to GRAFNEH's Claude Joseph, for instance, "It could be that we were hundreds in the street. When we heard about it on the media, we would hear 'hundreds of thousands'" (ibid. 98).

76. "The February 29th Coup d'état Against President Jean-Bertrand Aristide," *Haïti Progrès* 22: 2 (24 March 2004). An AHP article of 15 December 2003 gives a long and revealing list of false stories promoted by the independent media in the previous couple of weeks – for instance, that an anti-government activist Jean-Robert Lalanne had been shot by pro-government militants, that Paul Raymond and René Civil had fled into exile, that a student had been killed by FL thugs, that more FL thugs had looted a police weapons warehouse in Delmas 2, that still more thugs had forced Boukman Eksperyans singer Théodore Beaubrun and other anti-government protestors to go into hiding, or that on the morning of 15 December itself "there were anti-government demonstrations from Pétionville all the way to Canapé-Vert [whereas] in reality all that was evident were several flaming tires in the road that were quickly removed by the police" ("Radio Stations Resume Broadcast; Concerns of Dis-information Raised," AHP, 15 December 2003).

77. Kevin Pina, "Haiti's Cracked Screen," *Black Commentator*, 15 January 2004.

78. Jacqueline Charles, "Diplomats Puzzled by Claim Migrants Use Haiti to Enter US," *Miami Herald*, 25 April 2003.

79. Lally Weymouth, "Haiti vs. Aristide," *Washington Post*, 18 December 1992.

80. Cf. Robert Lawless, *Haiti's Bad Press* (1992); Catherine Orenstein, "Haiti in the Mainstream Press: Excesses and Omissions" (1993); Jack Lule, "News Values, News Strategies: The *New York Times* in Haiti 1994–1996" (1996).

81. "Haiti's Disappearing Democracy," *New York Times*, 28 November 2000. The same theme is taken up in a further *Times* editorial, three years later: "Aristide was once hailed as Haiti's democratic champion. Now, his second presidency is declining into despotism . . ." ("Haiti's Descent," *New York Times*, 5 February 2004).

82. Carol J. Williams and Paul Richter, "Violence in Haiti Abates, but not the Tension," *Los Angeles Times*, 29 February 2004.

83. "The World at One," BBC Radio 4, 8 March 2004.

84. Jean-Michel Caroit, "En toute impunité, les 'chimères' font régner la terreur en Haïti," *Le Monde*, 11 April 2000.

85. Caroit, "Haïti: la deuxième chance d'Aristide," *Le Monde* 30 May 2000; Caroit, "Haïti ou le calvaire de la misère absolue," *Le Monde*, 8 February 2001. Cf. Philippe Broussard, "Les Déçus d'Aristide," *Le Monde* 30 January 2002.

86. Caroit, "Haïti prépare le bicentenaire de son indépendance et réclame des réparations financières à Paris," *Le Monde*, 7 October 2003; Caroit, "Les Violences politiques et la contestation s'amplifient à Haïti," *Le Monde*, 8 October 2003.

87. Caroit, "En Haïti, la presse indépendante est harcelée," *Le Monde*, 11 October 2003.

88. Caroit, "La Société civile s'organize face au président Aristide," *Le Monde*, 12 October 2003.

89. Caroit, "La Loi des milices en Haïti," *Le Monde*, 5 November 2003.

90. Caroit, "Haïti s'enfonce dans le chaos, à la veille du bicentenaire," *Le Monde*, 4 December 2003.

91. Caroit, "Après des mois de répression, les Haïtiens réclament le départ de leur président," *Le Monde*, 17 December 2003.

92. "Haïti en danger," *Le Monde* [Editorial], 18 December 2003.

93. Ibid.

94. Laënnec Hurbon, "Le Bicentenaire d'Haïti," *Le Monde*, 30 December 2003.

95. Caroit, "Aristide, du prophète au dictateur," *Le Monde*, 9 January 2004.

96. Jean-Hebert Armengaud, "Du bidonville à la villa de luxe," *Libération*, 31 December 2003.

97. Patrick Sabatier, "Compensation," *Libération*, 31 December 2003; "Anarchie," *Libération*, 24 February 2004.

98. Hassane Zerrouky, "Jean-Bertrand Aristide, de la théologie de la libération à la dictature," *L'Humanité*, 1 March 2004.

99. François Hauter, "Guy Philippe bluffe les Américains," *Le Figaro*, 16 March 2004.

100. "Minimalist Diplomacy," *Washington Post*, 26 February 2004; "Haiti's 'New Chapter,'" *Washington Post*, 1 March 2004.

101. "Failure of Will," *Guardian*, 28 February 2004; Estanislao Oziewicz, "20,000 Protest in Haiti's Capital," *Globe and Mail*, 22 January 2004; cf. Adrian Hamilton, "Why it is Wrong to Wash our Hands of Haiti," *Independent*, 26 February 2004; Richard Lezin Jones, "Haiti's Neighburs Are Pressing Aristide for Reforms," *New York Times*, 29 January 2004. Rod Paul's anti-Lavalas film *Failing Haiti* begins with a similar premise: "In 2004," runs the opening line, "Aristide was forced from power, and the international community was obliged to step in."

102. Donald Rumsfeld, quoted on PBS New Hour, "Haiti: A Fractured Nation," 16 February 2004.

103. "Débarquement," *Libération*, 1 March 2004.

104. Elaine Sciolino, "US and France Set Aside Differences in Effort to Resolve Haiti Conflict," *New York Times*, 3 March 2004.

105. Cf. Heather Williams, "Haiti as Target Practice: How the US Press Missed the Story," *CounterPunch*, 1 March 2004.

106. See for instance Jane Regan, "Haiti: In Bondage to History?", *NACLA Report on the Americas* (January 2005), 4–7.

107. Peter Dailey, "The Fall of the House of Aristide," *New York Review of Books*, 13 March 2003; "Haiti's Betrayal," *New York Review of Books*, 27 March 2003. Kim Ives subjects Dailey's work to a withering point-by-point rebuttal in "The Fall of the Empire's Ushers: Review of a Review," *Haiti Progrès* 20: 52 (12 March 2003).

CHAPTER 5

1. Edward Cody, "Haiti Torn by Hope and Hatred As Aristide Returns to Power," *Washington Post*, 2 February 2001.

2. Robert Fatton, "A War Waged on the Aristide Regime," *Socialist Worker*, 5 March 2004.

3. Allan Nairn, "Haiti Under the Gun" (1996).

4. Andrew Reding, "Haiti: An Agenda for Democracy" (1996).

5. "Is a Coup d'état Looming?", *Haïti Progrès* 18: 31 (18 October 2000).

6. Cited in Susannah Nesmith, "Rebel Chief Says he is a Servant of his Nation," *Miami Herald*, 28 February 2004.

7. Cf. Cody, "Haiti Torn by Hope and Hatred," *Washington Post*, 2 February 2001.

8. See for instance Susannah Nesmith, "Rebel Chief Says he is a Servant of his Nation," *Miami Herald*, 28 February 2004; Jane Regan, "Rebel Leadership United in Mission: To Push Aristide Out," *South Florida Sun-Sentinel*, 24 February 2004.

9. Human Rights Watch, "Haiti: Recycled Soldiers and Paramilitaries on the March," 27 February 2004.

10. "Ex-Police Chief Says He Would Back Coup in Haiti," AP, 10 May 2003.

11. Nesmith, "Rebel Chief Says he is a Servant of his Nation," *Miami Herald*, 28 February 2004.

12. Walt Bogdanich and Jenny Nordberg "Democracy Undone: Mixed US Signals Helped Tilt Haiti Toward Chaos," *New York Times*, 29 January 2006; cf. Deibert, *Notes*, 366.

13. Sue Montgomery, "Mastermind Tells How Plot Evolved," *Montreal Gazette*, 9 March 2004. In a fine demonstration of his political credibility, after this interview "Mr. Arcelin dropped by the Montana Hotel in Port-au-Prince to say goodbye, introducing himself at the front desk as the Canadian ambassador."

14. Fatton, "A War Waged on the Aristide Regime," *Socialist Worker*, 5 March 2004.

15. Cited in Nairn, "The Eagle Is Landing," *The Nation*, 3 October 1994.

16. Michael Niman, "Our Nasty Little Racist War in Haiti" (2004), 4.

17. David Adams, "Anatomy of a Ragtag Rebellion," *St Petersburg Times*, 12 April 2004.

18. Robert Muggah, *Securing Haiti's Transition* (October 2005), 14; cf. Luis Barrios, "U.S. Special Forces Trained and Armed Haitian Anti-Aristide Paramilitaries in D.R.," *Democracy Now!*, 7 April 2004.

19. Patrick Elie, "A Coup Made Long in Advance," 17 October 2004. Stan Goff has investigated the development of the FLRN, and spoken to Dominican customs agents who facilitated the rebels' passage back and forth across the border, and with the retired Dominican general Nobel Espejo. Espejo suggested that from late 2000 Haitian rebels may have been trained along with Dominican soldiers in a military base near Constanza. As Goff insists, "The Dominican government does not do anything militarily that the United States does not allow it to do [. . .]. None of this could have happened without the complicity of the United States, without the facilitation by the United States, without the funding and support of the United States" (Stan Goff, "The Invasion of Haiti," 19 May 2004).

20. "Attacks Raise Fears in Haiti of Uprising by Ex-Soldiers," Reuters, 14 August 2001; cf. "Que voulaient les assaillants?", *Haïti Progrès* 19: 20 (1 August 2001).

21. "Former Haitian Officers Seeking Asylum," *Miami Herald*, 3 August 2001.

22. Himmler Rébu, cited in "Attacks Raise Fears in Haiti of Uprising by Ex-Soldiers," Reuters, 14 August 2001.

23. Fatton, *Haiti's Predatory Republic*, pp. 184–5, 206–7; cf. "Haitian Police Charged with Treason, Killings," Reuters, 9 August 2001.

24. As far as the police were concerned, explains Concannon, "everyone in the PNH knew it was an inside job, and that there would be more attacks and killings if the plotters were not outed. But the infiltration was so widespread that loyal officers did not know who they could trust. Both leaders and rank and file felt it was safer to keep their heads down and hope they weren't in the wrong place when the next attack came, than it was to stick their neck out and investigate the bad apples" (Letter from Brian Concannon, 14 November 2006).

25. OAS, "Report of the Commission of Inquiry Into the Events of December 17, 2001," at http://www.oas.org/OASpage/Haiti_situation/cpinf4702_02_eng.htm. One of the attackers was arrested, former FAdH sergeant Pierre Richardson. At a 19 December 2001 press conference he said he had attended meetings to plan the "coup d'état" in Santo Domingo, run by Philippe and Nau, and said the assailants had been expecting back-up (which never materialized) organized by ex-army officers Guy François and Prosper Avril.

26. Cited in Deibert, *Notes from the Last Testament*, 174.

27. International Tribunal on Haïti, *Preliminary Report of the Commission of Inquiry October 6 to 11, 2005*, 3–4.

28. "Multi-Front Strategy Seeks to Oust Aristide Before 2004," *Haïti Progrès* 21: 2 (26 March 2003).

29. HSG, "Armed Group in Control of Pernal, Murders Deputy-Mayor," 14 December 2003.

30. Chamblain, cited in Steven Dudley, "The Men Behind Haiti's Rebellion," *San Francisco Chronicle*, 29 February 2004.

31. "Aristide Warns More Haitians Will Become Boat People," AP, 24 February 2004.

32. Cited in Bogdanich and Nordberg, "Democracy Undone," *New York Times*, 29 January 2006.

33. Bogdanich and Nordberg, "Democracy Undone," *New York Times*, 29 January 2006.

34. "Multi-Front Strategy Seeks to Oust Aristide Before 2004," *Haïti Progrès* 21: 02 (26 March 2003).

35. Kevin Sullivan, "US Marines Fortify Haiti Embassy," *Washington Post*, 24 February 2004.

36. Michael Christie, "Alarm at Haiti PM's 'Unholy Alliance' with Rebels,'" Reuters, 22 March 2004.

37. Hallward, "Insurgency and Betrayal: An Interview with Guy Philippe," *Haiti Analysis*, 23 March 2007. According to well-placed business sources in Cap-Haïtien, supporters of Philippe's Front included some foreign investors as well, notably the Canadian mining company Saint Geneviève Resources, which had long been looking for leverage to overcome local Lavalas opposition to their investments in north-eastern Haiti (cf. "Locals Halt Gold Drilling in Haiti," Reuters, 4 July 1997).

38. Guy Philippe, interview with Isabel Macdonald, Pétionville, December 2005.

39. Hallward and Philippe, "Insurgency and Betrayal" (2007).

40. Perhaps the most incriminating confessions were made during a broadcast of the programme "Ranmasse," on Radio Caraïbes, in the autumn of 2004; cf. Pierre-Antoine Lovinsky, "Le Coup d'État continue," *Hayti.Net*, 18 January 2007.

41. Hallward and Philippe, "Insurgency and Betrayal" (2007).

42. Roger Noriega, "Remarks on Haiti," 30 October 2002, http://www.state.gov/p/wha/rls/rm/14823.htm.

43. Interview with Yvon Neptune, 20 March 2007.

44. Jane Regan, "Haiti Reports Clashes with Armed Men in the Mountains," *Miami Herald*, 17 March 2003.

CHAPTER 6

1. Interview with Patrick Elie, Port-au-Prince, 5 January 2007.

2. Interview with Steve MacIntosh, Cap-Haïtien, 11 January 2007.

3. Interview with Patrick Elie, Port-au-Prince, 5 January 2007.

4. IMF, *Haiti: Interim Poverty Reduction Strategy Paper* (November 2006), 12.

5. Interview with Marcus Garcia, Port-au-Prince, 20 April 2006.

6. Scott Wilson, "Armed Attacks Increase Pressure on Haitian Leader," *Washington Post*, 19 November 2003.

7. Yvon Neptune, Interview with Crowing Rooster Arts, Port-au-Prince, September 2006.

8. I draw here mainly on the more detailed summaries of these achievements provided by the Haiti Action Committee pamphlets, *We Will Not Forget: The Achievements of Lavalas in Haiti* (2005) and *Hidden from the Headlines* (2003).

9. Anne Street, *Haiti: A Nation in Crisis* (2004), 16.

10. HAC, *We Will Not Forget*, 5.

11. Schulz, "Haiti: Will Things Fall Apart?" (1998), quoting William G. O'Neill, "No Longer a Pipe-Dream? Justice in Haiti" (1997).

12. Lafanmi Selavi was established in 1988. It provided a home for hundreds of orphans and street kids, and was a regular target of anti-Lavalas violence and infiltration. After Aristide's return in 1994, the creation of Radio Timoun was followed by the establishment of Tele Timoun, along with a new Montessori school. In 1999, the shelter for boys was closed when, in the wake of repeated threats and attacks, a sit-in staged by a group of disgruntled and unemployed Lafanmi alumni turned violent; the residential component of Lafanmi was then turned into a large health clinic. The entire complex was torched after the February 2004 coup, and as of early 2007 the buildings remained an empty shell.

13. For an analysis of Manley's Jamaica that is full of resonance for Haiti under Aristide see Evelyn and John Stephens, *Democratic Socialism in Jamaica* (1986).

14. Cf. Tom Reeves, "Still Up Against the Death Plan in Haiti" (2003).

15. "All governments, Aristide's like the others, have used revenues from the Teleco and other state companies to finance programmes that provide them with a certain political advantage. It's a customary practice," one that is geared to this or that constituency: what is unusual about Aristide is that he had the urban poor as his main constituency (Interview with Guy Delva, Port-au-Prince, 25 April 2006).

16. Cited in Farmer, *Uses of Haiti*, 150.

17. Interview with John Joseph Jorel, Port-au-Prince, 15 April 2006; Interview with Jean-Marie Samedy, Port-au-Prince, 15 January 2007.

18. Interview with Bobby Duval, Port-au-Prince, 17 April 2006.

19. Raby, *Democracy and Revolution*, 238.

20. Interview with Maude Leblanc and Georges Honorat, Port-au-Prince, 20 April 2006.

21. Interview with Lamarre Augustin, Cité Soleil, 15 April 2006.

22. Interview with Ramilus Bolivar, Port-au-Prince, 15 January 2007

23. See for instance Jeb Sprague's interview with Moïse Jean-Charles, "A Lavalas Mayor in Hiding," *Left Turn*, July 2006.

CHAPTER 7

1. Tet Kole interview of 12 April 2000, in Melinda Miles, *Elections 2000* (2001).

2. Patrick Elie in February 2006, cited in Ehrenreich, "Haiti's Hope," *LA Weekly*, 12 April 2006.

3. Cf. Fatton, *Haiti's Predatory Republic*, 121–2.

4. Interview with Patrick Elie, Port-au-Prince, 19 April 2006.

5. For an anti-Lavalas account of these appointments see Deibert *Notes from the Last Testament*, 314–16, and Deibert, "Reply to Justin Podur," *ZNet*, 16 February 2006.

6. Rosny Mondestin, "Haiti: The Premises of a Low-Intensity Dictatorship" (April 2001), forwarded to the Corbett listserve by Stanley Lucas on 17 April 2001.

7. "We had advance warnings of both the 28 July and 17 December 2001 coup attempts, and the names of people in the PNH and USGPN who were involved" (Letter from Brian Concannon, 14 November 2006).

8. Hallward and Philippe, "Insurgency and Betrayal" (2007).

9. "De Facto Prime Minister's Nephew and Security Chief Running Guns and Drugs," *Haïti Progrès* 23: 6 (20 April 2005).

10. Letter from Frantz Gabriel, 17 December 2006.

11. Jim DeFede, "A Marked Man," *Miami New Times*, 28 August 1997; Jean-Michel Caroit, "En Haïti, 'chimères' et partisans de l'ancien président Aristide tentent de s'organiser," *Le Monde*, 11 March 2004.

12. See in particular Scott Wilson, "Popular Haitian Lawmaker Worries US," *Washington Post*, 4 March 2002.

13. Deibert, *Notes from the Last Testament*, 361–2. Concannon recalls that "in the legislative elections of May 2000, Toussaint technically ran on the Lavalas ticket, but that was not always apparent – he didn't appear to campaign on or for the ticket, or to help out other candidates. I would expect that by October 1999 both sides knew their paths were diverging" (Brian Concannon, letter of 14 November 2006).

14. Hallward and Philippe, "Insurgency and Betrayal" (2007).

15. Tristram Korten, "Guns & Haiti," *Miami New Times* 15 April 2004; Caroit, " 'Chimères' et partisans de l'ancien président Aristide tentent de s'organiser," *Le Monde*, 11 March 2004; cf. Sprague, Joseph and Concannon, "The Jean Dominique Investigation – Seven Years Later," *HaitiAnalysis*, 3 April 2007.

16. Don Bohning, "Defection Hurts Aristide," *Miami Herald*, 17 December 2003.

17. Interview with Ben Dupuy, 16 February 2007.

18. Oriel Jean, interview with Kim Ives, Miami 30 March 2007. Oriel was replaced by Barthélémy Valbrun in July 2003 but continued to exercise significant influence behind the scenes.

19. Interview with Yvon Neptune, 20 March 2007.

20. The history of this arrangement goes back to 1994. When the US allowed Aristide to return to Haiti in 1994, they provided him with diplomatic security. This task was soon taken over by a team of security guards led by David Johnson, a veteran of the US Army's Protective Services Unit. When Johnson joined the private US company Steele Foundation in 1998, Steele took on the contract to provide protection for Préval and Aristide, and Johnson remained the commanding officer of the Steele detachment through to February 2004. Retention of Steele's services was controversial, and their presence was often cited by Aristide's critics as proof that he was becoming paranoid and aloof. Aristide's chief legal counsellor insists, however, that Steele was the best available choice. "The US always wanted us to rely on Haitian security, so they could buy them off when they needed to. Look at Youri Latortue. If you had a choice between Youri as your security or the Steele Foundation, which would you pick? Steele performed well until the last month. The alternatives were probably worse. Other foreign contractors were no more reliable and would have been more expensive" (Ira Kurzban, letter of 4 March 2007). A senior member of Aristide's Steele detail also defends its contribution to the government's survival. "We were solid, we were independent, we were not corruptible. Nobody messed with us. Nobody tried to buy us off. Whatever skullduggery might be going on in the National Palace, they still had to reckon with *les blans* down the corridor, and this made everyone think twice. Aristide was definitely glad to have us around, I know it. We were always reliable and above the fray. Given the way things were and the kinds of pressure the government was

under, I don't think that any Haitian security team could have retained the same sort of independence" (Interview with a senior member of Aristide's Steele Foundation security detail, 21 March 2007).

21. Interview with a senior member of Aristide's Steele Foundation security detail, 21 March 2007.

22. Janice Stromsem and Joseph Trincellito, "Building the Haitian National Police," *Haiti Papers* 6 (April 2003). Neptune shrugs off accusations of corruption in his government. "Corruption has always existed in Haiti," Neptune explains. "It was institutionalized under Duvalier. We Haitians were raised in an environment of corruption; there may be a few exceptional people who rise above it, but it's very widespread, and you can only change this very slowly. The economic elite has built its fortune on corruption. Many bureaucrats are corrupt. In a country as poor as Haiti people have very little choice. Given this context, corruption doesn't surprise or bother me very much; it's deeply rooted in Haitian history, and we need to create mechanisms to deal with it gradually. It will take a couple of generations. Simply to denounce some current instances of corruption isn't very helpful. We have to take the realities of Haitian history and society into account, and be very practical, and very patient. People of my generation should stop thinking that serious social change will take place in Haiti during our lifetime. We need to accept this, if we are to take genuine steps forward towards a new future" (Interview with Yvon Neptune, Port-au-Prince, 5 January 2007).

23. Interview with Yvon Neptune, Port-au-Prince, 5 January 2007.

24. Paul DeRienzo, "Haiti's Nightmare: The Cocaine Coup and The CIA Connection" (April 1994).

25. Ihosvani Rodriguez, "Jury Acquits Haiti's Ex-Drug Chief," *South Florida Sun Sentinel*, 8 October 2005.

26. Cf. Jay Weaver, "Aristide's Former Security Chief Was US Informant, Attorney Alleges," *Miami Herald* 25 May 2004; Jay Weaver, "Jury: Haitian Smuggled Drugs," *Miami Herald*, 22 July 2005.

27. Larry Lebowitz, "Drug Dealer Accuses Aristide," *Miami Herald*, 26 February 2004; these denials were confirmed in interviews with the people involved, except for Kétant's denial which was reported by Florida-based journalist David Adams in an interview on 19 March 2007.

28. "Americans and Haitians Work Together to Bring in Drug Trafficker Jacques Kétant," AHP, 18 June 2003. Another round of drug-related arrests took place in the autumn of 2003, leading to the extradition of Eliobert Jasme, Carlos Ovalle and Eddy Aurélien.

29. Steven Dudley, "Drug Allegation Gave US Leverage on Aristide," *Boston Globe*, 1 March 2004.

30. See for instance Ann W. O'Neill, "Affidavits Portray Haiti as a Chaotic Drug Haven," *South Florida Sun-Sentinel*, 20 June 2004; Nancy San Martin, "US Aids Aristide Inquiry in Haiti," *Miami Herald*, 24 July 2004.

31. Interview with Ramilus Bolivar, Port-au-Prince, 15 January 2007.

32. David Adams, "US Officials Explore Whether Drug Corruption Went All the Way to the Office of Former President Jean-Bertrand Aristide," *St Petersburg Times*, 3 April 2004; Cali Ruchala, "Haiti, Target Aristide: US Drug Probe Misfires," *Sobaka*, 9 August 2005. Cf. Charles Arthur, "Raising the Stakes: Haiti: Between Mayhem and Decertification" (July 2001); Larry Rohter, "Haiti Paralysis Brings a Boom In Drug Trade," *New York Times*, 27 October 1998.

33. Interview with Patrick Elie, Port-au-Prince, 19 April 2006.

34. Ira Kurzban, cited in David Adams, "Taint of Drugs Reaching Haiti's Upper Echelons," *Saint Petersburg Times*, 3 April 2004.

35. Jay Weaver, "Haiti Drops Lawsuit Alleging Aristide Theft," *Miami Herald*, 6 July 2006.

36. "Un Grain de riz dans la machine," *Haïti en Marche*, 26 January 2002; "Rice Scandal Rocks Aristide's Party," *Haïti Progrès* 19: 47 (6 February 2002). Asked about the significance of the rice and other scandals over 2001–04, Marcus Garcia keeps things in perspective. "Yes of course there was some corruption, but it wasn't very important; compared to what we're used to it was no big deal" (Interview with Marcus Garcia, Port-au-Prince 20 April 2006).

37. Cali Ruchala, "Blood and Ashes," *Sobaka*, 17 January 2003, http://www.diacritica.com/sobaka/2003/blood.html.

38. Interview with Fonkoze's Anne Hastings, Port-au-Prince 24 April 2006. According to lawyer Mario Joseph, "Aristide's support for co-operatives never had anything to do with the co-operative banks. As far I know, Aristide never did or said anything at all to encourage people to deposit money in the so-called cooperative banks" (interview with Mario Joseph, Port-au-Prince, 24 April 2006).

39. Alex Dupuy, *Prophet and Power*, 201, 101. For the time being, notes Jean-Marie Samedy, "There is no getting round the power of the bourgeoisie in Haiti, it's inescapable" (Interview with Jean-Marie Samedy, Port-au-Prince, 15 January 2007).

40. See for instance "Aristide Embraces Free Trade Zones," *Haïti Progrès* 20: 4 (10 April 2002); "Zones Franches: Cession du Térritoire National?", *Haïti Progrès* 20: 7 (1 May 2002); Jane Regan [Clara James], "Haitian Free Trade Zone" (November 2002); Jane Regan, "Workers Fight for Rights in Free Trade Zone," IPS, 27 July 2004. The first factory at the first of the new free trade zones opened for business in August 2003; as of July 2003, 54 peasant farmers and their families had been moved off their land (Jacqui Goddard, "Farmers Forced Out as Global Brands Build Haiti Free-Trade Area," *The Sunday Times*, 6 July 2003).

41. Interview with Ben Dupuy, 16 February 2007.

42. Cf. "Workers Fight for Rights on Orange Plantation," *Haïti Progrès* 19: 9 (16 May 2001); Charles Arthur, "Bitter Fruit," *New Internationalist* 341 (December 2001); "Guacimal: Neo-liberal Repression," *Haïti Progrès* 20: 13 (12 June 2002).

43. Charles Arthur, "Open Letter to Jeb Sprague," HSG, 3 January 2006. According to one of his cousins, FL mayor Sévère accepted around $14,000 from Guacimal owner Jacques Novella to repress Guacimal peasant's union and imprison their leaders ("Haitian Government Supports Big Landowners in Clash with Peasants," *Haïti Progrès* 20: 12 [6 June 2002]). As Brian Concannon notes, the conflict between workers and the Guacimal management was complicated by a further conflict between local and migrant workers; in order to protect some of their customary rights, some of the former resisted the organizing efforts of the latter (Letter from Concannon, 30 November 2006).

44. Interview with Robert Fatton, 10 November 2006.

45. Interview with Yvon Neptune, Port-au-Prince, 5 January 2007; Interview with Moïse Jean-Charles, Cap-Haïtien, 12 January 2007.

46. AW/NCHR, *The Aristide Government's Human Rights Record* (1991), 2.

47. Amnesty International, "Haiti: Human Rights Abuses on the Rise," 8 October 2003.

48. Tom Griffin, "Summary Report of Haiti Human Rights Delegation – March 29 to April 5" (2004).

49. Human Rights Watch annual reports are published on their website, at http://hrw.org/doc/?t=pubs.

50. HRW, "Haiti: Aristide Should Uphold Rule of Law," 14 February 2004.

51. HRW, "Haiti: International Forces Must Assert Control," 3 March 2004.

52. Amnesty International press release, "Haiti: Last Chance to End Cycle of Violence," 21 June 2004.

53. In 2000, according to Amnesty International's annual reports, "a number of electoral candidates, party members and their relatives were killed, most by unidentified assailants," as was journalist Jean Dominique. There were also "several reports of unlawful killings by police; most of the victims were criminal suspects." In 2001, journalist Brignol Lindor was killed "by a mob which included members of a pro-FL organization," and AI refers to "several killings of alleged criminal suspects by police or crowds carrying out 'popular justice' " but identifies only one such victim (Mackenson Fleurimon, who "on 11 October was reportedly shot dead by the police in the Cité Soleil neighborhood of Port-au-Prince"). In 2002, "at least five people were reportedly killed" in confrontations between members of opposing parties, and seven people (three of whom are identified as FL supporters) appear to have been either executed or "disappeared." AI also refers to two other killings in 2002: the shooting of Christophe Lozama, a pro-FL justice of the peace, and the assassination of a bodyguard protecting Michèle Montas, the widow of Jean Dominique. In 2003, two protestors (one pro- and one anti-government) died in a clash in Cap-Haïtien, in April; another pro-FL protestor died in September at a demonstration in Port-au-Prince, and on 22 December "two people were reportedly killed and six wounded when shots were fired at demonstrators and police fired back." Also in 2003, gang leaders Amiot Métayer and Rodson "Colibri" Lemaire were killed by unidentified assailants, and perhaps nine people died in violent skirmishes between their gangs and the PNH.
    A reviewer who managed to work his way through the whole of Deibert's *Notes from the Last Testament* (2005) says that it identifies at least 212 political killings during the years 2001–04, attributing "44 to Lavalas, 43 to the PNH, 24 to Labanye's gang [in Cité Soleil], 13 to Wilme's gang [also in Cité Soleil]," and the remainder to the opposition or unidentified assailants (Justin Podur, "A Dishonest Case for a Coup," *ZNet*, 16 February 2006).

54. Interviews with the author, spring and autumn of 2006.

55. Brian Concannon, "Lave Men, Siye Atè," 85–86. Although she is more sensitive to the purely criminal dimension of some of the gang violence that divided Cité Soleil in 2004–05, Anne Sosin – the most knowledgeable foreign human rights worker to work in Port-au-Prince from 2004 through 2007 – agrees with the gist of Concannon's analysis. Yes there were occasional abuses, but "It was nothing compared to what happened in 2004–06 or 1991–94" (Interview with Anne Sosin, Port-au-Prince, 11 April 2006).

56. Chidi Anselm Odinkalu, "Why More Africans Don't Use Human Rights Language" (1999); cf. Badiou, *Ethics* (1993).

57. Scott Wilson, "Gadfly's Killing Tests Haiti's Justice System," *Washington Post*, 7 December 2000.

58. Interview with Guy Delva, Port-au-Prince 9 April 2006.

59. See for instance Ana Arana, "Haiti: The Case of Jean Léopold Dominique," Inter American Press Association, January 2001; Reporters without Borders, "Who Killed Jean Dominique?", 25 March 2001.

60. HAC, *Hidden from the Headlines: The US War Against Haiti* (2003).

61. Ronald Saint-Jean, *A propos du "Génocide de la Scierie"*, 13–14.

62. NCHR/POHDH, "Massacre in Scierie (St. Marc)," 2 March 2004.

63. NCHR, "La Scierie Genocide: NCHR Advocates for the Organization of a Model Trial," 30 March 2004.

64. Anthony Fenton, "Canada's Growing Role In Haitian Affairs," *ZNet*, 21 March 2005.

65. Ronald Saint-Jean, *A propos du "Genocide de la Scierie": Exiger de la NCHR toute la vérité* (2004); cf. Kevin Skerrett, "Faking Genocide in Haiti," *ZNet*, 23 June 2005.

66. Guy Delva, "UN Says Former Haitian PM Jailed Illegally," Reuters, 4 May 2005.

67. Christian Heyne et al., "Thierry Fagart on La Scierie," *HaitiAnalysis*, 22 February 2007; cf. Brian Concannon et al., "Petition to the Inter-American Commission on Human Rights," IJDH, 20 April 2005.

68. Duncan Campbell, "*Lancet* Caught up in Row over Haiti Murders," *Guardian*, 8 September 2006. The controversy concerned the fact that one of the report's co-authors, Athena Kolbe, had under another name (Lynn Duff) spent a couple of years volunteering for the Lafanmi Selavi orphanage and radio station, in the mid-1990s. The report's methodology and findings were carefully peer-reviewed and approved by the *Lancet*'s editorial staff. Cf. Joe Emersberger, "Discrediting the *Lancet* Study on Haiti," *ZNet*, 2 October 2006.

69. Media Lens, "Haiti – The Traditional Predators: Human Rights, Media Silence and *The Lancet*," 11 September 2006. Guy Delva, head of SOS Journalistes and as impartial a figure as any in the Haitian press, is the first to confirm a comparable shift in the local media bias. Delva told Griffin's team in late 2004 that "If a journalist was arrested during Aristide's government, there would be a public uproar from print and radio journalists. Now, said Delva, when a journalist is arrested, 'the newspapers and radio stations applaud'" (Griffin, *Haiti Human Rights Investigation*, 29). The difference in coverage illustrates the distinction that Noam Chomsky and Edward Herman make, as part of the "propaganda model" they propose for understanding the western media, between "worthy and unworthy victims." "A propaganda system will consistently portray people abused in enemy states as worthy victims, whereas those treated with equal or greater severity by its own government or clients will be unworthy" (Chomsky and Herman, *Manufacturing Consent*, 37).

70. Roger Noriega, "Haiti at the Crossroads of Democracy," State Department, 14 April 2004; cf. David Usborn, "Haiti's Despot Aristide Stirs Up People's Revolution," *Independent*, 13 January 2004.

71. NCHR, "The Return in Full-Force of the Attaché Phenomenon: NCHR Cries Out," 2 September 2003.

72. White House Press Secretary Marlin Fitzwater, 6 Oct. 1991, cited in Kim Ives, "The Unmaking of a President," 16.

73. Chavannes Jean-Baptiste, "MPP Speaks to the New Dimension of the Haitian Crisis," *Grassroots International*, 24 February 2004.

74. See in particular Deibert, *Notes from the Last Testament*, 166–7; 279–80.

75. See for instance Alex Dupuy, *The Prophet and Power*, 143–144, 156; cf. Dailey, "The Fall of the House of Aristide" (2003); Fatton, *Haiti's Predatory Republic*, 29, 151; Jean and Maesschalck, *Transition politique en Haiti*, 104–11.

76. Cf. Stan Goff, "Beloved Haiti," 14 February 2004.

77. Interview with Jean-Marie Samedy, Port-au-Prince, 15 January 2007.

78. Letter from Kim Ives, 11 February 2007.

79. Regan, "In the Aftermath of Invasion" (1995); for more on Boulos and the CDS see Nairn, "Behind Haiti's Paramilitaries" (1994); John Canham-Clyne and Worth Cooley-Prost, "U.S. AID Go Home!", *In These Times*, 8 January 1996; Catherine Maternowska, *Reproducing Inequities* (2006).

80. This summary is based on interviews with John Joseph Joel and Jean-Marie Samedy, January 2007, and with Amaral Duclona, Lamarre Augustin and Samba Boukman, April 2006, and on letters from Kevin Pina, 13 and 22 February 2007.

81. Letter from Patrick Elie, 16 December 2006.

82. "Demonstrations Escalate," AHP, 11 January 2004. As Isabel Macdonald demonstrates in detail, the death of the anti-FL victim, student Maxime Deselmour, was

given full and sympathetic coverage in the press; the death of the pro-FL victim, Louvoi Petit, was "completely ignored" (Macdonald, "Covering the Coup," 67).

83. Interview with Reed Lindsay, Port-au-Prince, 12 April 2006.

84. Cf. "Rival Leader Challenges Aristide to Arrest Him," *Miami Herald*, 25 March 2001.

85. Kevin Pina, "Rolling Haiti Back to Colonialism," *ZNet*, 21 September 2004.

86. As Reding pointed out a decade ago, so long as "Haiti lacks a functioning judicial system [. . .], the development of which will require foreign assistance, Haitians will continue to resort to the vigilantism that so offends foreign sensibilities" (Andrew Reding, "Haiti: An Agenda for Democracy" [1996]).

87. Interview with Ronald Saint-Jean, Port-au-Prince, 11 April 2006.

88. Michael Deibert, "Human Rights, Not Politics, Should be Priority for Haiti," *Blogspot*, 12 September 2006; Alex Dupuy, *The Prophet and Power*, 162.

89. Interview with Anne Sosin, Port-au-Prince, 11 April 2006; a similar point was emphasized by Jacklin Saint Fleur, Judy DaCruz and Reed Lindsay, in conversations and correspondence with the author, April–September 2006.

90. Charles Arthur, "Murder in the Caribbean: How Does Haiti Compare?", *Alter-Presse*, 3 February 2006.

91. Interview with Guy Delva, Port-au-Prince, 25 April 2006.

92. Interview with Robert Fatton, 10 November 2006.

93. Kim Ives, letter of 14 December 2006.

94. Interview with Belizaire Printemps, Port-au-Prince, 23 April 2006.

95. Frantz Gabriel, letter of 17 December 2006.

96. Interview with John Joseph Joel, Port-au-Prince, 15 January 2007.

97. Eléonore Senlis, letter of 19 March 2007. "When people say that Aristide armed the people in Cité Soleil and elsewhere," says *Haïti Progrès'* Georges Honorat, "I have to laugh. Aristide didn't arm the '*chimères*,' though a few of them were already armed. I remember that in 1994–1996, American troops would often make a point of stopping their jeeps in popular neighborhoods, and of leaving them wide open and stuffed with weapons, while they went off for a drink a few hundred yards away. They would wait for kids to come along and pick up the guns and ammunition, it was perfectly obvious what was going on. On a couple of occasions I was right there, and people called me over and said look Georges, here's a weapon – and I said be careful, they're arming you so that you will later fight amongst yourselves" (Interview with Georges Honorat, Port-au-Prince, 20 April 2006).

98. According to a well-documented *Small Arms Survey* report of 2005, there may be as many as 210,000 small arms in circulation in Haiti today. Around 20,000 are registered to the police and perhaps 13,000 are in the hands of "non-state armed groups" (including ex-FAdH, common criminals, and pro-Lavalas gangs), but "Haitian civilians and homeowners – particularly upper-middle-class households – own by far the majority of the estimated national stockpile: up to 170,000 weapons" (Muggah, *Securing Haiti's Transition* [October 2005], 6–7).

99. Patrick Elie, "A Coup Made Long in Advance," 17 October 2004.

100. Jane Regan [Clara James] "Haiti: The Roof Is Leaking" (1997).

101. Jean Saint-Vil, "Time to Stop Resisting Haiti's Resistance," *Corbett List*, 29 November 2002; cf. Reeves, "Still Up Against the Death Plan in Haiti" [September 2003]).

102. Cf. Tracy Kidder, "The Trials of Haiti," *The Nation*, 27 October 2003.

103. Clément François, cited in "Behind Aristide's Fall," *Socialist Worker*, 12 March 2004; cf. Miles, *Elections 2000* (2001).

104. According to the PPN's Maude Leblanc, "Tet Kole never really recovered from the assassination of Father Jean-Marie Vincent in 1994, and over the following decade it

lost a lot of influence" (Interview with Maude Leblanc, Port-au-Prince, 20 April 2006).

105. Stan Goff, "A Brief Account of Haiti," BRC-NEWS, October 1999.

106. Letter from Charles Arthur, 5 April 2004.

107. Wargny, "The Country That Doesn't Quite Exist," *Le Monde Diplomatique* (July 2000).

108. Fatton, *Haiti's Predatory Republic*, 182.

109. Tom Reeves obtained a leaked copy of the Gallup polls; cf. Reeves, "Haiti's Disappeared" (May 2004).

110. Letter from Eléonore Senlis, 27 March 2007.

111. Cited in "Fair Elections Must Be Haiti's Next Milestone," *Miami Herald*, 4 January 2004.

112. "Polls Close in Haiti," BBC News, 26 November 2000.

113. Daniel Lak, "Poverty and Pride in Port-au-Prince," BBC Radio 4, 20 March 2004; cf. Lak, "Haiti's Warning for Nepal: What We Saw in Haiti was Gunboat Diplomacy in the Name of Democracy," *Nepal Times*, 186 (4 March 2004).

114. Robert Fatton, "A War Waged on the Aristide Regime," *Socialist Worker*, 5 March 2004.

115. Stan Goff, "The Invasion of Haiti," 19 May 2004.

CHAPTER 8

1. "Au Revoir Aristide," *The Times* 1 March 2004; cf. "Aristide's Thugs Crush Hopes of People's Revolution with Beatings and Intimidation", *Independent*, 13 February 2004.

2. Stan Goff, "A Journal of Aristide's Inauguration (2001)", in Goff, "Beloved Haiti", 14 February 2004.

3. Fatton, *Haiti's Predatory Republic*, 145.

4. [Kim Ives], "Multi-Front Strategy Seeks to Oust Aristide Before 2004," *Haïti Progrès* 21: 2 (26 March 2003); Pina, "US Plots Régime Change in Haïti," *Black Commentator*, 15 May 2003. See in particular Pina's four-part series of articles on the impending coup in the *Black Commentator*, October–December 2003.

5. Thomas Wiens and Carlos Sobrado, *Haiti: The Challenges of Poverty Reduction* (World Bank, 1998), cited in Anne Street, *Haiti*, 18.

6. Engler and Fenton, *Canada in Haiti*, 48; Interview with Anne Hastings, Port-au-Prince, 24 April 2006.

7. Cf. Paul Farmer, *Never Again*, 151–153.

8. "A Friend to Haitians," *Washington Post*, 17 January 2004.

9. Arthur, *Haiti in Focus*, 48; cf. 33–4.

10. Cf. Briggs and Kernaghan "The US Economic Agenda" (1994), 39.

11. Laurie Richardson, "Feeding Dependency, Starving Democracy: USAID Policies in Haiti," *Grassroots International*, 6 March 1997.

12. Arundhati Roy notes, for instance, that the boom of charitably funded NGOs in India "coincided with the opening of India's markets to neo-liberalism," with the downsizing of the Indian state, with the dramatic reductions in public spending and with the still more dramatic "blunting of political resistance." The "real contribution of NGOs is that they defuse political anger and dole out as aid or benevolence what people ought to have by right. They alter the public psyche. They turn people into dependent victims [. . .]; the greater the devastation caused by neo-liberalism, the greater the outbreak of NGOs" (Roy, "Public Power in the Age of Empire," *Socialist Worker*, October 2004, http://www.socialistworker.co.uk/article.php4?article_id=2910).

13. USAID Democracy and Governance Program, Program Data Sheet 521–005 (2003).
14. Laurie Richardson, "Feeding Dependency, Starving Democracy: USAID Policies in Haiti," *Grassroots International*, 6 March 1997.
15. Interviews with Jacklin Saint-Fleur and Anne Sosin, Cité Soleil, 15 April 2006.
16. Interview with Jacklin Saint-Fleur, Cité Soleil, 15 April 2006. "NGOs live off the poverty in Haiti, it isn't really in their interest to reduce it" (Interview with Anne Sosin, Port-au-Prince, 11 April 2006).
17. Nicolas Guilhot, *The Democracy Makers*, 6.
18. Ibid., 7, 11–14.
19. By mid-1996, he recalls, Patrick Elie started wondering what had happened to the assortment of liberal-professional "revolutionaries and professors" who had once played a role in the struggle against Duvalier. He realised that almost all of them had been absorbed in various NGOs, where "they are comfortable, well-paid, and have the impression that they are continuing to pursue the revolution . . ." (Interview with Patrick Elie, Port-au-Prince, 19 April 2006).
20. "Someone who comes to Haiti with an open mind, who is willing to visit the poorer neighborhoods and talk to the people who live in them, can often gain a better understanding of the country in around a week, than do many foreign NGO employees who come for a couple of years, and who from the beginning approach the country like hostile occupied territory" (Interview with Jacklin Saint-Fleur, Cité Soleil, 15 April 2006).
21. The demonstration "contre la vie chère" held in the capital on 26 July 2006, for instance, was attended by perhaps 20 people. Groups like PAPDA do not make any serious attempt to organize support in the popular neighborhoods, where their pro-coup stance guarantees them a hostile reception for the foreseeable future.
22. Helen Spraos, "Aristide's Failures," letter to the *Guardian*, 3 March 2004.
23. "Christian Aid's Position on the Current Crisis in Haiti," Christian Aid, 3 March 2004.
24. Spraos, "What Now for Haiti?", Christian Aid, 4 March 2004.
25. Charlotte Haines Lyon and Lisane André (GARR), "The Cost of Radicalism," Christian Aid 13 July 2004; "Christian Aid's Position on the Current Crisis in Haiti," 3 March 2004; Spraos, "What Now For Haiti?", 4 March 2004.
26. Reeves, "Haiti's Disappeared" (2004); cf. Miles, "Emergency Haiti Observation Mission" (2004), 14.
27. Interview with Guy Delva, Port-au-Prince, 9 April 2006.
28. Interview with Anne Sosin, Port-au-Prince, 11 April 2006. Before helping to found an organization dedicated to stopping violence against women (Vizyon Dwa Ayisyen), Anne Sosin worked with SOFA for a few months, in 2003. In a letter explaining her decision to cut her links with the organization, she drew attention to its inability to "negotiate the tension that exists between organizational management and popular representation. Like many civil society organizations in Haiti, SOFA is led by educated, French-speaking women from the Haitian middle class, and has become politically aligned with the elite political movement." As most of the original SOFA activists left to join less reactionary organizations, Sosin notes that SOFA fell back on its elite connections to beef up its international profile. SOFA's extreme hostility to Aristide "was not derived from a vote of a dwindling membership, but rather reflects the sentiments of a small handful of paid leaders" (cited in Reeves, "Haiti's Disappeared" [2004]).
29. See for instance Kevin Murray (director of Grassroots International), "Haiti: A Way Forward?" *Peacework Magazine*, May 2004, http://www.afsc.org/pwork/0405/040512.htm.
30. Nicolas Guilhot, *The Democracy Makers*, 4.

31. See for instance Camille Chalmers, "The Neo-Liberal Agenda in Haiti," *Haïti Progrès* 20: 16 (3 July 2002).

32. "PAPDA and Women's Organizations Denounce Violent Acts in Response to 17 December Coup Attempt," PAPDA 26 December 2001 (forwarded to the Corbett List by the Haiti Support Group).

33. Marc Arthur Fils-Aimé, Camille Chalmers, André Wainright [PAPDA], "PAPDA Demands the Immediate Resignation of Jean-Bertrand Aristide," 27 January 2004. Similar positions were endorsed by an influential coalition of Canadian aid agencies and trade unions, the Montréal-based Concertation Pour Haiti.

34. "PAPDA, NCHR and CONAP Demonstrate," AHP, 26 April 2004; cf. Yves Engler, "NGOs and Haiti," *ZNet*, 7 January 2006.

35. Interview with Ronald Saint-Jean, Port-au-Prince, 11 April 2006.

36. "Election Victory for the Haitian People," *Haiti Support Group Briefing* 57 (April 2006), 1. PAPDA paused here to ask a question it had answered rather differently two years before: "What kind of social contract can be built on the refusal to recognize the popular will as expressed at the ballot box?" (1).

37. For background on BO and trade union politics in Haiti see Charles Arthur, "Haiti's Labor Movement in Renaissance" (June 2003).

38. "Collective Bargaining Contract Signed at the Ouanaminthe CODEVI Free Trade Zone," Batay Ouvriye, 15 December 2005.

39. Interview with Paul Philomé and Yannick Etienne, Port-au-Prince, 19 April 2006.

40. If you ask BO how many workers they represent they prefer not to answer, saying that they do not try to recruit members and that the numbers who participate in meetings or demonstrations varies with the circumstances (Interview with Paul Philomé, Port-au-Prince 19 April 2006). CTH officials are perplexed: "We don't really know what BO does, or who they are" (Interview with Loulou Chéry, Port-au-Prince, 24 April 2006).

41. PPN's Georges Honorat doesn't understand why BO is so bitterly divisive. "We're all more or less on the same side," he points out, "we all support the workers and the peasants, yet we can hardly agree on a minimal platform" (Interview with Georges Honorat, Port-au-Prince, 20 April 2006).

42. "It's not enough to be right, you need to be right with and alongside the people" (Interview with Patrick Elie, Port-au-Prince, 19 April 2006).

43. Interview with Belizaire Printemps, Port-au-Prince, 23 April 2006.

44. Mario Pierre, "Batay Ouvriye, *Haïti Progrès*, Jeb Sprague and the War Against Haitian Workers," *Indybay*, 3 January 2006.

45. BO, "Batay Ouvriye Statement on the Haitian Situation Today," 20 December 2003.

46. BO, "Statement on the Situation," March 2004.

47. Interview with Paul Philomé, Port-au-Prince, 19 April 2006; BO, "Open Letter to the Minister of Social Affairs Concerning the Application of the Minimum Wage," *Le Nouvelliste*, 24 June 2003.

48. Paul Philomé, statement in a public meeting held March 2004, cited in Jeb Sprague, "Supporting a Leftist Opposition to Lavalas," 21 November 2005.

49. "Mario Pierre Responds," WBAI Radio, 22 February 2006.

50. Yvon Neptune, cited in Reeves, "Still Up Against the Death Plan in Haiti" (2003).

51. Interview with Guy Delva, Port-au-Prince, 9 April 2006.

52. Sprague, "Batay Ouvriye's Smoking Gun: The $100,000 NED Grant," *Haïti Progrès* 23: 43 (4 January 2006); Sprague, "Failed Solidarity: The ICFTU, AFL-CIO, ILO and ORIT in Haiti," *Labor Notes*, May 2006.

53. "If PPN had received this sort of money, BO would have been the first to say it's a total catastrophe, that it proves Ben Dupuy was working for the CIA" (Interview with Georges Honorat, Port-au-Prince, 20 April 2006).

54. For instance, through to the middle of 2002 the PPN often called, rightly or wrongly, "for the formation of a popular alternative front" in opposition both to FL and the CD. But once it became clear that such calls had become a luxury that no opponent of the CD and its paymasters could afford, the PPN paper *Haïti Progrès* shifted the focus of its coverage towards a critical defense of the constitutional government. Guy Delva's reporting evolved in a similar way.

55. Charles Arthur and Peter Hallward, "Debate on Haiti Today: Moving on, Making Progress?", Institute for the Study of the Americas, University of London, 13 November 2006. Arthur's hostility to Fanmi Lavalas also leads him on occasion to distort his analysis. One of his preferred arguments for demonstrating that Aristide's government was anti-worker and anti-poor, for instance, is a claim that during the negotiations held in the spring of 2003 that led to an increase in the minimum wage, the government proposed a sum (70 gourdes) *smaller* than that apparently proposed by the employers themselves (72 gourdes). If true, such a proposal would indeed be difficult to explain away as a painful but necessary concession to the imperial might of USAID and the IMF. But it isn't true. Trade union participants in these wage negotiations deny it categorically (Interview with Belzin Jacques, Port-au-Prince 24 April 2006; cf. Quixote Center, *Haiti Emergency Observation* [2 April 2004], 27), as do Guy Delva and Marcus Garcia and every other credible analyst I've been able to consult. It isn't true, and it isn't plausible: to my knowledge, no group representing employers and business leaders ever tried to use this altogether exceptional instance of wage generosity to their political advantage. I can find no trace of it in the online record of anti-FL propaganda. Arthur's only evidence is his insistence that the government press officer Michelle Karshan failed to deny the story back in 2003; Karshan herself disputes this, saying "I didn't know anything about what the other sectors might have agreed to, but I don't believe for a second that the 'employers had agreed on 72 gourdes'" (Interview with Michelle Karshan, 21 November 2006).

    Haiti's minimum wage is woefully inadequate, this much is uncontroversial. But Aristide was the first president to make an increase of the minimum wage a political priority, and he raised it on several occasions in the face of vigorous domestic and IFI/USAID opposition. In March 2003 as much as in 1991 or 1995, the employers fought tooth and nail to keep wages as low as possible. Meanwhile the number of jobs which might be affected by anything like a minimum wage had declined dramatically since the late 1980s. In my opinion, Aristide's critics downplay the intense pressure he was under to avoid action that might lead to further job losses and capital flight.

56. "IDB Approves $176.9 Million in Soft Loans for Haiti," IDB, 13 November 2003.

57. Robert Maguire, "Aristide's Fall: The Undemocratic U.S. Policy in Haiti," 27 February 2004.

58. Over the course of 2003, observed the IMF, the Haitian "authorities have started to implement measures to stabilize the economy and initiate key reforms. Following several important corrective actions in the fiscal and monetary areas, they have embarked on a one-year program that aims at consolidating the initial stabilization gains, clearing external payment arrears, and starting key structural reforms – thereby establishing a track record of economic policy implementation that could be a basis for a PRGF [poverty reduction and growth facility] program" (IMF, *Haiti: Staff-Monitored Program* [August 2003], 4; cf. 9–10).

59. "South Africa: Government Defends Mbeki's Plan to Attend Haitian Bicentennial Fete," BBC Monitoring Service, 18 December 2003; Michael Ottey, "Haiti's Bicentennial," *Miami Herald*, 2 January 2004.

60. Michael Ottey, "Haiti's Bicentennial: Supporters Swarm to Aristide," *Miami Herald*, 2 January 2004. Writing in the *New York Times*, Lydia Polgreen somehow managed to describe the bicentennial crowd as "small"; a few days later the paper acknowledged this "imprecise" description was the result of "an editing error" (*New York Times*, 6 January 2004).

61. "Elections," AHP, 5 October 2003.

62. "Political Situation, Elections," AHP, 21 October 2003.

63. It's well worth comparing what happened that day with perhaps the most significant of the so-called civil society protests that preceded it, an elite rally against "insecurity and anarchy" that took place back on 28 May 1999. The May 1999 rally was organized by the Haitian chamber of Commerce and various IRI- and USAID-funded groups (soon to be repackaged as members of the G184), and heavily publicized by their friends and relations in the independent press. Its chief spokesman was Olivier Nadal, a businessman notorious for his contempt for the *peuple*, his role in the 1990 Piatre massacre and his support for the 1991 coup. As the day of the rally approached, popular organizations close to FL lined up to denounce Nadal and his corporate associates. "All those who participated in the coup d'état," said FL spokesman Yvon Neptune, "who financed the coup d'état, who beat down the people resisting the coup d'état, who are trampling and strangling the people, these are the different categories of people who have launched, organized and financed this demonstration [. . .]. They are the agents of death and destruction of the Haitian people. They should be behind bars" (cited in "'Anti-Violence' Demonstration Sparks Clash," *Haïti Progrès* 17: 11 [2 June 1999]). The rally itself was closed down by the police after a small handful of participants clashed with a much larger group of Aristide supporters. As *Haïti Progrès* explained, "The reactions to this event – like so many things in Haiti – were split down class lines. The organizers of the event and most middle class and wealthy Haitians were horrified and outraged by the spectacle [. . ., but] among ordinary Haitians there was a barely disguised glee and sense of satisfaction" ("Background and Analysis on the May 28th Confrontation at Champs de Mars," *Haïti Progrès* 17: 18 [21 July 1999]).

64. Economist Intelligence Unit, *Country Report January 2004: Dominican Republic, Haiti*, 40–1. Back in February 2001 the *Economist* already recognized that "the opposition mostly represents the upper-middle class and intellectual elite," whereas "FL, by contrast, is a tightly-run and powerful movement" with "deep roots in Haiti's poorest communities" ("Another Half-Chance for Aristide and Haiti," *The Economist*, 8 February 2001).

65. "Haitian Bourgeoisie's Protests End as Fiascos," *Haïti Progrès* 21: 36 (19 November 2003).

66. Cited in Kevin Murray, "Haiti: A Way Forward?" (May 2004).

67. Cali Ruchala, "Two Days: Two Crucial Events that Led to Lavalas' Collapse," *Sobaka's Communiqué* 3 (spring 2004); cf. Jean-Michel Caroit, "Après des mois de répression, les Haïtiens réclament le départ de leur président," *Le Monde*, 18 December 2003.

68. "Intellectuals and Artists Engage in a Struggle Against the Status Quo," *Alterpresse*, 23 November 2003.

69. Letter from Anne Sosin, 16 December 2006.

70. Ruchala, "Two Days" (2004).

71. Cited in Richard Jones, "Haiti's Neighbors Are Pressing Aristide for Reforms," *New York Times*, 29 January 2004.

72. Letter from Marie Carmel Paul-Austin, 9 August 2008. Was Aristide himself personally involved in the conflict at the university? "Up to a point yes," says Paul Austin. "He organized meetings with the different sectors – the students the

professors, and some of the heads of faculty. But his decisions were taken without genuine consultation" (ibid).

73. Ruchala, "Two Days" (2004).

74. Marie Carmel Paul-Austin, "5 décembre 2003 . . . Un an déjà!" (document dated 5 December 2004, sent by letter to the author).

75. Deibert, *Notes from the Last Testament*, 371.

76. "Protest and Violence at the State University on December 5," AHP, 5 December 2003.

77. Interview with Dr. Marie-Antoinette Gauthier, Pétionville, 9 January 2007.

78. Brian Concannon, "Analysis of *Ordonnance de clôture* in December 5, 2003 case" (21 April 2006); interview with Georges Honorat, Port-au-Prince, 20 April 2006.

79. Griffin, *Haiti Human Rights Investigation* (November 2004), 22.

80. Anne-Marie Issa, interview with Macdonald December 2005, in Macdonald, "Covering the Coup," 99.

81. Jacklin Saint-Fleur (director of the Cité Soleil hospital), for instance, knows of several cases of medical students who, in exchange for visas to the US, falsely alleged that they had been victims of FL violence and received death threats. Such allegations were then used to draw other students out to rally together in solidarity and to protest the government. By January at least two of these students had received their visas, apparently through the personal intercession of Andy Apaid (Interview with Jacklin Saint-Fleur, Cité Soleil, 15 April 2006).

82. "Opposition and Pro-Government Demonstrators Violently Clash," AHP, 11 December 2003.

83. Interview with Belizaire Printemps and Elias Clovis, Port-au-Prince, 23 April 2006.

84. As the *New York Times* explained on 29 January 2004, "Experts say Aristide's ouster is unlikely as long as he has the support of the national police. As for another possible resolution to the crisis, Mr. Aristide's resignation, experts say that is even more remote. 'Aristide is a real hard head,' Professor Marc Prou [University of Massachusetts] said. 'He's not going anywhere' " (Jones, "Haiti's Neighbors Are Pressing Aristide for Reforms," *New York Times*, 29 January 2004).

CHAPTER 9

1. Scott Wilson, "Armed Attacks Increase Pressure on Haitian Leader," *Washington Post*, 19 November 2003.

2. "Violence in Cité Soleil,"AHP, 3 November 2003.

3. Although they were not yet in any position to affect the balance of power, the autumn of 2003 did witness the emergence of several other anti-FL gangs in various other districts of Port-au-Prince. On 1 November 2003, for instance, Radio Signal FM broadcast calls to rebellion issued by the Carrefour-based Front des Jeunes pour Sauver Haiti (FROJESHA). FROJESHA appealed to members of the former army to help them overthrow the government. "As for us, we shall start shooting. We shall start shooting at everything that exists so that we can overthrow Aristide" ("Group Says it has Weapons, Seeks 'Civil War' to Overthrow Aristide," *BBC Monitoring Unit*, 1 November 2003).

4. Brian Concannon, "Justice in Haiti: The Raboteau Trial," *Human Rights Databank* 7: 4 (December 2000).

5. Cf. Charles Arthur, " 'Jean Tatoune' and 'Cubain': A Chronology," Haiti Support Group 2005.

6. Kevin Pina, "US Corporate Media Distort Haitian Events," *Black Commentator* 6 November 2003. Concannon adds that "Amiot Métayer was always someone who

played both sides," even back in 1994 (Concannon, "UN Supports Death Squads: On the Justice of Impunity in Haiti," *Flashpoints Radio* 16 May 2005).

7. When he came to comment on the implementation of OAS resolution 822, Noriega singled Amiot Métayer out for special mention, in relation to the "politically motivated crimes" attributed to the FL administration (Noriega, "Remarks on Haiti," State Department 30 October 2002). As Concannon observes, "Although Tatoune had been actually convicted and sentenced for murder, and Métayer had no serious allegations against him before the Haitian courts, the US and its allies in Haiti continuously chastised the Haitian government for not arresting Métayer, but rarely if ever mentioned Tatoune." Concannon also points out that the OAS case against Métayer consisted of nothing other than the single-sentence assertion that he had been "identified as one of those who attacked" Mesadieu's house. Neither the police nor any witness corroborated the claim, and the charges against Métayer were dropped in the summer of 2002 when his accusers withdrew their complaint (Brian Concannon, "Lave Men, Siye Atè," 88–9).

8. Cited in Jane Regan [Clara James], "The Raboteau Revolt" (December 2002).

9. Cf. Deibert, *Notes from the Last Testament*, 353–4.

10. Amy Wilentz, "Haiti: A Savior Short on Miracles," *Los Angeles Times* 12 October 2003; Jane Regan, "Former Haitian Allies Become Enemies," *Christian Science Monitor* 16 October 2003.

11. Griffin, *Haiti Human Rights Investigation* (November 2004), 22.

12. Letter from Frantz Gabriel, 17 December 2006; cf. Philip Agee, *Inside the Company: CIA Diary* (1975).

13. Interview with Ben Dupuy, 16 February 2007.

14. Letter from Amy Wilentz, 25 February 2007.

15. Letter from Patrick Elie, 16 December 2006.

16. After he broke out of prison in August 2002, Brian Concannon explains, "Mr. Métayer was, for good reason, wary of the police and the government. He would not go anywhere outside of Raboteau alone without several armed men with him for protection. Then on 21 September Odonel Paul somehow convinced Métayer to leave with him, alone. Métayer knew Paul, who was notoriously untrustworthy. He would not have left alone with him without a very good reason. The best explanation I have heard is that Paul convinced Métayer to participate in some activity, such as a drug deal, that involved a lot of money, that would have had to have been shared with bodyguards if they came. None of the 'political' explanations account for why Métayer would have gone out alone with Paul. It is possible that Paul used the drug ruse, which was made credible by previous transactions, to lure Métayer out to be killed for political purposes. But I find it unlikely that Lavalas officials would have ordered the killing, because of the easily foreseeable fallout. Mr. Paul's employment with the Ministry of Interior and other government offices does not by itself establish a link to top government officials, because he did not have a position of responsibility, and it is well-known that he put his own interests first" (Letter from Brian Concannon, 14 November 2006).

17. Wargny, *Haïti n'existe pas*, 157–8.

18. Paraphrased in "Amiot Métayer Murdered; Protests in Gonaïves Continue," AHP, 29 September 2003.

19. Deibert claims that during a raid on 2 October, police killed eleven people in "an atrocious repeat of the 1994 Raboteau massacre" (Deibert, *Notes from the Last Testament*, 355). The Associated Press provided a different version of what happened that day, based largely on anti-FL radio reports whose own reliability is doubtful: "Police trying to raid Raboteau touched off a gunfight that killed five men in the

Haitian city of Gonaïves, radio stations reported. Officers went on the offensive Thursday, a day after protestors torched the police station [. . .]. Five people were shot and killed in nearby slums, including two motorbike taxi drivers trying to flee the firefight, two radio stations reported" (Michael Norton, "Police Raid Leaves Five Dead in Haiti," AP, 3 October 2004).

20. Cited in "Situation in Gonaïves," AHP, 27 October 2003.

21. "Opposition in Gonaïves Promises a Massacre: Violence Begins," AHP, 6 January 2004.

22. Jones, "Haiti's Neighbors Are Pressing Aristide for Reforms," *New York Times*, 29 January 2004; DeNeen L. Brown, "In Haiti, Two Sides and Bloodshed Between," *Washington Post*, 3 February 2004.

23. Kirk Semple, "Haiti's New Cabinet and Rebels Hit the Road," *New York Times*, 21 March, 2004. The *New York Times* interpreted Latortue's speech as "sending a clear message of stability" (ibid.).

24. Griffin, *Haiti Human Rights Investigation* (November 2004), 22.

25. Joel Deeb, a Haitian-American arms dealer who has reportedly brokered deals with Youri Latortue since the 29 February 2004 ouster of President Jean-Bertrand Aristide, called Youri Latortue a drug-smuggling "Kingpin," with "close ties" to paramilitary leader Guy Philippe (Anthony Fenton, "Have the Latortues Kidnapped Democracy in Haiti?," *ZNet*, 26 June 2005).

26. "The Haiti Support Group Hails Recent Progress in the Struggle Against Impunity," HSG, 27 March 2002.

27. Thierry Oberlé, "Les Narcotraffiquants font main basse sur Haïti," *Le Figaro*, 21 December 2004.

28. Fenton, "Have the Latortues Kidnapped Democracy in Haiti?," *ZNet*, 26 June 2005.

29. Cf. "De Facto Prime Minister's Nephew and Security Chief Running Guns and Drugs," *Haïti Progrès* 23: 6 (20 April 2005). "Youri Latortue was well-placed," Charles Arthur confirms, "to get heavily involved in whatever went on in Gonaïves in the 2003–5 period" (Letter from Charles Arthur, 2 October 2006).

30. Letter from Anthony Fenton, 17 December 2006.

31. "Senator Latortue Denies Lavalas Accusations of Destabilization," Radio Métropole, 15 November 2006 (via BBC Worldwide Monitoring Service).

32. Interview with Reed Lindsay, Port-au-Prince, 22 April 2006.

33. Scott Wilson, "Two Haitian Towns Retaken," *Washington Post*, 10 February 2004.

34. Wilson, "Armed Attacks Increase Pressure on Haitian Leader," *Washington Post*, 18 November 2003.

35. "Situation in Gonaïves," AHP, 3 November 2003.

36. Hallward and Philippe, "Insurgency and Betrayal," *HaitiAnalysis*, 23 March 2007.

37. Wilson, "Rival Militias May Determine Haiti's Future," *Washington Post*, 12 February 2004.

38. Michael Norton, "Haitian Uprising Unites Onetime Enemies," AP, 10 February 2004.

39. Hallward and Philippe, "Insurgency and Betrayal," *HaitiAnalysis*, 23 March 2007.

40. Jane Regan, "Rebel Leadership United in Mission," *South Florida Sun-Sentinel*, 24 February 2004.

41. Wilson, "Armed Attacks Increase Pressure on Haitian Leader," *Washington Post*, 18 November 2003.

42. See for instance Michael Ottey, "Rebels Attack Cops Sent to Gonaïves," *Miami Herald*, 9 February 2004.

43. Kevin Sullivan, "Haitian Rebels Eye Capital," *Washington Post*, 26 February 2004.

44. Lydia Polgreen, "Amid Fear and Chaos, Haitian City Goes On," *New York Times*, 15 February 2004; cf. Michael Norton, "Exiled Paramilitaries Join Haiti Rebels," AP, 16 February 2004.

45. Jane Regan, "In Haiti, Shift from Disjointed Rebellion to Wider Uprising," *Christian Science Monitor*, 23 February 2004.

46. Cited in Jane Regan, "Rebel Leadership United in Mission," *South Florida Sun-Sentinel*, 24 February 2004; cf. Trenton Daniel, "Notorious Figures Return from Exile to Aid Gangs," *Miami Herald*, 15 February 2004.

47. "The February 29th Coup d'état Against President Jean-Bertrand Aristide and the Role of the United States in the Coup," *Haïti Progrès* 22: 2 (24 March 2004); cf. Wilson, "Forces Close in on Key Haitian City," *Washington Post*, 15 February 2004.

48. "Police in Haiti's Second City Retreat into Station," AP, 19 February 2004.

49. "Haitian Official Appeals For Help to End Revolt," AP, 18 February 2004.

50. Michael Ottey, "Three Gang Leaders Hatched Plot for a Revolt," *Miami Herald*, 15 February 2004.

51. Scott Wilson, "Aristide's Supporters Fighting Back," *Washington Post*, 11 February 2004.

52. Michael Norton, "40 Dead as Haitian Rebels Take 11 Towns," *Guardian*, 10 February 2004.

53. Jane Regan, "Haiti Rebels Angry but Disorganized," *Christian Science Monitor*, 13 February 2004.

54. Scott Wilson, "Rival Militias May Determine Haiti's Future," *Washington Post*, 12 February 2004.

55. Marika Lynch, "Town Taken from Rebels Feels Heat of Reprisal," *Miami Herald*, 24 February 2004.

56. Lydia Polgreen, "Weakened Haitian Police Forces Overwhelmed by Rebel Violence," *New York Times*, 22 February 2004.

57. Polgreen, "Amid Fear and Chaos, Haitian City Goes On," *New York Times*, 15 February 2004.

58. Norton, "Exiled Paramilitaries Join Haiti Rebels," AP, 16 February 2004; cf. Tom Reeves, "US Double Game in Haiti," *ZNet*, 16 February 2004.

59. Carol Williams, "Contempt Unites All Kinds in Haiti," *Los Angeles Times*, 15 February 2004.

60. Trenton Daniel, "Rebel Force Small But Intense," *Miami Herald*, 22 February 2004.

61. Cited in Rod Paul, *Failing Haiti* (2005).

62. Tony Smith, "Rebel Soldiers Take Control of Haiti's Central Plateau," *New York Times*, 20 February 2004.

63. Trenton Daniel and Michael Ottey, "Police Won't Fire on Rebels, Aristide Says," *Miami Herald*, 12 February 2004.

64. Stan Goff, "Beloved Haiti," 14 February 2004. Kim Ives makes the same point. "Aristide should have heeded the advice told him several times in the months leading up to the coup to 1) arm the people and 2) train and equip a counter-insurgency force to face off with the rebels. Either because he was afraid of the US/French response to such a step or had a naïve trust in the unarmed people's power to resist, Aristide never made a move other than giving some money and maybe a few weapons to some urban popular organizations. But it was a disorganized, halting, fitful and sporadic response where discipline, clarity, boldness and decisiveness were necessary" (Letter from Kim Ives, 14 December 2006).

65. Scott Wilson, "Forces Close In on Key Haitian City," *Washington Post*, 15 February 2004.

66. "Scenes of Horror in Haiti Battles," AP, 8 February 2004.

67. "Police in Haiti's Second City Retreat into Station," AP, 18 February.

68. Wilson, "Cap-Haïtien Falls to Rebels," *Washington Post*, 23 February 2004; cf. Paisley Dodds, "50 Marines Arrive in Haiti," AP, 23 February 2004.

69. Lydia Polgreen and Christopher Marquis, "Aristide's Foes Given 24 Hours to Study Plan," *New York Times*, 24 February 2004.

70. Paisley Dodds, "50 Marines Arrive in Haiti," AP, 23 February 2004.

71. Lieutenant Colonel Acacio, cited in "International Forces in Haiti," Reuters, 18 March 2004.

72. Peter Bosch, "Key Haitian City Falls as Rebels Aim for Capital," *Miami Herald*, 23 February 2004.

73. Tim Collie, "Port-au-Prince Calm but Tense while Awaiting Rebels," *South Florida Sun-Sentinel*, 24 February 2004. Reuters correspondent Michael Christie had observed a similar pattern in rebel-controlled Saint-Marc back on 8 February: "Residents looked on nervously, refusing to be identified by name. 'People are scared. The ones who are out in the street aren't scared, because they're the ones with the guns,' said one man" (Christie, "Armed Revolt In Haiti Spreads to More Cities," Reuters, 9 February 2004).

74. Interview with Douglas Perlitz, Cap-Haïtien, 12 January 2007.

75. Kevin Sullivan and Peter Slevin, "Haitian Leader Appeals for Foreign Security Aid," *Washington Post*, 25 February 2004. Fort Liberté is another example. "On 19 February 2004, the rebels attacked the jail in Fort Liberté, near the border [. . .]. Jacques Édouard, the jail supervisor, said he was forced to release 73 prisoners, including convicted murderers. Some prisoners joined the rebels, while others took over the city, robbing residents and burning homes until the United Nations arrived a month later, said Andrea Loi Valenzuela, a United Nations worker there" (Bogdanich and Nordberg "Democracy Undone," *New York Times*, 29 January 2006).

76. Scott Wilson, "Rival Militias May Determine Haiti's Future," *Washington Post*, 12 February 2004.

77. Tim Collie, "A Nation in Tatters," *South Florida Sun-Sentinel*, 22 February 2004.

78. Muggah, *Securing Haiti's Transition* (October 2005), 10; Brian Concannon, "Complaint to the Inter-American Commission on Human Rights," 2 February 2006. Rather than terminate the embargo after 1994, the US amended its wording so as to allow exceptions to be considered on a "case by case basis".

79. "In 2001 the government leased and later bought an ex-military helicopter, a Huey converted for civilian use, from a Connecticut company called Hummingbird. Although we bought it perfectly legally, and signed the relevant papers with the Federal Aviation Administration, in late 2003 the US government suddenly invoked their old embargo – the embargo they'd imposed on the Cédras government, but that they never lifted once democracy was restored – in order to prevent us getting the parts we needed to repair it. By this stage the rebels were shooting at us on a regular basis; I'd say that by the end of 2003 there were already around 30 bullet holes in the cockpit. The Americans suddenly said that because it had once been a military vehicle, we weren't entitled to use it. But they never said this before, back when we bought the damn thing" (Interview with Frantz Gabriel, Pétionville, 9 January 2007).

80. NCHR, "The Return in Full-Force of the Attaché Phenomenon: NCHR Cries Out," 2 September 2003; cf. Pina, "Propaganda War Intensifies against Haiti," *Black Commentator*, 30 October 2003.

81. "The evidence I've seen," says Concannon, "indicates that a significant part of the police, but far less than a majority, was pro-coup. The majority supported the constitution, but were not willing to risk their lives to prevent an overthrow. Loyal officers were reluctant to even talk about organizing against the coup, because they could not be sure of anyone else. So only the putchists trusted each other, and everyone else was trying to get through the day alive. When the tide changed, many

officers went with it to save themselves" (Letter from Brian Concannon, 14 November 2006).

82. Jane Regan, "In Haiti, Shift from Disjointed Rebellion to Wider Uprising," *Christian Science Monitor*, 23 February 2004; Tony Smith, "Rebel Soldiers Take Control of Haiti's Central Plateau," *New York Times*, 20 February 2004.

83. Letters from Frantz Gabriel and Patrick Elie, 17 December 2006.

84. Kevin Sullivan, "Haitian Rebels Eye Capital," *Washington Post*, 26 February 2004.

85. "Former Senator Toussaint Called to Court for Threats," AHP, 22 January 2004. On 15 January Dany Toussaint was quoted as saying that "opposition demonstrators would not hesitate to kill and burn whomever [among the political opposition] should choose to go ahead and negotiate with President Aristide [. . .]. Toussaint also affirmed that he has good relations with the United States" ("Dany Toussaint Raises Spectre of Palace Invasion," AHP, 15 January 2004).

86. Trenton Daniel, "Ex-Police Chief Back for Old Role: Another Ghost from Haiti's Horrible Past Has Emerged from the Power Vacuum Left by Jean-Bertrand Aristide," *Miami Herald*, 3 March 2004. According to FL spokesman Jonas Petit, on the day of Aristide's expulsion Dany Toussaint was the person who coordinated the police operation to retake control of the streets of Port-au-Prince (Interview with Jonas Petit, Miami 8 April 2006).

87. Nancy San Martin, "Shock and Grief Are Shared by Many in Capital," *Miami Herald*, 1 March 2004.

88. Letter from Frantz Gabriel, 17 December 2006.

89. Scott Wilson, "A City Smolders as Night Falls," *Washington Post*, 1 March 2004; cf. Scott Wilson and Kevin Sullivan, "Rebels Enter Haiti Capital In Triumph; Signs Surface of Reprisals Against Aristide Loyalists," *Washington Post*, 2 March 2004.

90. Tony Smith, "Rebel Soldiers Take Control of Haiti's Central Plateau," *New York Times*, 20 February 2004.

91. In mid-November, Yvon Neptune told Wilson "that there are links between some elements of these armed groups with the opposition on every level – financial as well as political [. . .]. We're trying to show that this is all a pretext for not wanting to participate in elections" (Scott Wilson, "Armed Attacks Increase Pressure on Haitian Leader," *Washington Post*, 18 November 2003).

92. Carol Williams, "Militants Force Haiti Opposition to Abort March," *Los Angeles Times*, 13 February 2004.

93. Scott Wilson, "Armed Attacks Increase Pressure on Haitian Leader," *Washington Post*, 18 November 2003.

94. Michael Christie, "Armed Revolt in Haiti Spreads To More Cities," Reuters, 9 February 2004.

95. Carol Williams, "Marines Land in Haiti to Protect US Embassy," *Los Angeles Times*, 23 February 2004.

96. Wilson, "Aristide Supporters Halt Protest," *Washington Post*, 13 February 2004.

97. "Violence Spreads in Haiti; Toll Is Put at 41," AP, 10 February 2004.

98. Wilson, "Rival Militias May Determine Haiti's Future," *Washington Post*, 12 February 2004.

99. Kevin Sullivan, "US Marines Fortify Haiti Embassy," *Washington Post*, 24 February 2004.

100. Carol Williams and Paul Richter, "Chaos Erupts in Haitian Capital," *Los Angeles Times*, 28 February 2004.

101. Polgreen, "Aristide's Foes," *New York Times*, 26 February 2004.

102. Juan Tamayo, "When Aristide Leaves, Revolt Ends, Rebel Says," *Miami Herald*, 23 February 2004.

103. "Rebel Uses Internet to Check World Pulse," CNN, 29 February 2004.

104. Trenton Daniel, "Tough Rebel Both Feared and Loved," *Miami Herald*, 20 February 2004.

105. Paisley Dodds and Ian James, "Thousands Cheer Aristide Ouster," AP, 1 March 2004.

106. Cited in Keith Jones, "Haiti: Thousands March in Port-au-Prince Against US-backed coup," *WSWS*, 6 March 2004.

107. "Re-Establishing the Army," AHP, 9 March 2004; "New Haitian Government," *AHP*, 17 March 2004; "Haiti's Troika of Terror," *Black Commentator*, 29 March 2004.

108. Cited in DeNeen L. Brown, "In Haiti, Two Sides and Bloodshed Between," *Washington Post*, 3 February 2004.

109. Michael Ottey and Jacqueline Charles, "Opposition Rejects Talks with Aristide," *Miami Herald*, 6 February 2004.

110. Peter Slevin and Scott Wilson, "Aristide Offers to Share Power; Haitian Opposition Demands Resignation," *Washington Post*, 22 February 2004.

111. Roger Noriega, "Haiti at the Crossroads of Democracy," State Department, 14 April 2004.

112. Slevin and Wilson, "Aristide Offers to Share Power," *Washington Post*, 22 February 2004.

113. "Haiti: A Fractured Nation," PBS, 16 February 2004.

114. Peter Bosch, "Key Haitian City Falls," *Miami Herald*, 23 February 2004.

115. Slevin and Wilson, "Aristide Offers to Share Power," *Washington Post*, 22 February 2004.

116. Polgreen, "Aristide's Foes," *New York Times*, 26 February 2004.

117. Williams, "Aristide Appeals to World for Aid," *Los Angeles Times*, 25 February 2004.

118. Slevin and Wilson, "Aristide Offers to Share Power," *Washington Post*, 22 February 2004.

119. Smith, "Haitian Leader Warns of Exodus and Appeals for Help," *New York Times*, 25 February 2004. The opposition's refusal supposedly "surprised Bush administration officials, who had drafted the power-sharing plan and seemed confident of their ability to deliver opposition support" (Christopher Marquis, "Aristide's Foes Rule Out Plan to Share Power," *New York Times*, 25 February 2004).

120. Roger Noriega, "Interview by Chris Bury of *Nightline*," 1 March 2004.

121. Kim Ives, "Aristide Betrayed by the US as Parliamentarians Block his Return," *The Guardian* [NY], 8 October 1991.

122. Aristide, *Autobiography*, 143.

123. Ibid. and Aristide cited in Rossier, *The Endless Revolution* (2005). "We refuse what the 'developed' countries call 'aid', beginning with the US. In our view these countries are themselves *under*-developed – they are undeveloped in the *human* sense" (Aristide, cited in Demme, *The Agronomist*, 2002).

124. Michael Dash, cited in Dionne Jackson Miller, "Aristide's Call for Reparations from France Unlikely to Die," Inter Press Service News Agency, 12 March 2004.

125. Scott Wilson, "Haiti Draws on Past for Its Future," *Washington Post*, 21 November 2003.

126. Jacqueline Charles, "Aristide Pushes for Restitution from France," *Miami Herald*, 18 December 2003; cf. Heather Williams, "A Coup for the Entente Cordiale! Why France Joined the US in Haiti," *CounterPunch* 11: 4 (16 February 2004), 6; Gérard Lehmann, *Haïti 2004*, 59–64.

127. Jooneed Khan, "Washington menace Port-au-Prince," *La Presse*, 23 September 2003.

128. Caroit, "Haïti prépare le bicentenaire de son indépendance," *Le Monde*, 7 October 2003.

129. Letter from Eléonore Senlis, 23 March 2007.

130. Jean-Michel Caroit, "La société civile s'organise face au président Aristide," *Le Monde*, 12 October 2003; cf. Philippe Broussard, "Les Deçus d'Aristide," *Le Monde*, 30 January 2002. Serge Gilles spent twenty-five years in exile in France, from 1961 to 1986; in the 2006 presidential election he got 2.6 percent of the vote. According to Philippe and Ravix, it was Gilles himself who coordinated the FLRN assault on the Peligre dam in May 2003.

131. Yves Eudes, "L'Opposition refuse tout compromis," *Le Monde*, 3 January 2004.

132. Régis Debray, *Rapport du comité indépendant de réflexion et de propositions sur les relations franco-haïtiennes* (January 2004), 91, 13.

133. Debray, *Rapport*, 5, 53. Writing in *Libération* on the eve of Haiti's bicentenary, Patrique Sabatier struck the typical note when he denounced Aristide's restitution claim as the raving of a "delirious megalomaniac," the fantasy of "a despot intoxicated by the populist and xenophobic rhetoric he uses to hoodwink his own people" (Patrick Sabatier, leader, *Libération*, 31 December 2003).

134. Debray, *Rapport*, 11, 35, 12, 52–4.

135. Jean-Michel Caroit, "Comment la France a préparé son retour en Haïti," *Le Monde*, 15 April 2004; Claude Ribbe, *Aristide, un an après* [film], February 2005.

136. Interview with Georges Honorat, Port-au-Prince, 20 April 2006.

137. "French Consider Haiti Peace Force," BBC News, 17 February 2004.

138. Dominique de Villepin, cited in Christopher Marquis, "France Seeks U.N. Force in Haiti," *New York Times*, 26 February 2004.

139. Nancy San Martin, "France Wants Aristide Out," *Miami Herald*, 26 February 2004.

140. Nancy San Martin, "Aristide: I Won't Quit," *Miami Herald*, 27 February 2004.

141. "Minimalist Diplomacy," *Washington Post*, 26 February 2004. Conspiracy theorists are free to ponder the fact that in 2002, France apparently mounted an international military exercise on the island of Marie-Galante to simulate an operation in a fictional "sovereign francophone nation in the Caribbean." The staging of the operation envisaged a "weak and corrupt state whose mafioso degeneration has [. . .] favored the development of militias" beyond its control, and whose "under-equipped and poorly paid police force has been unable to stop the north of the island from falling under the control of insurgents." The scenario even anticipated violence against the university rector . . . (François-Xavier Guillerm, "Cinq nations manoeuvrent à Marie Galante," in *France–Antilles* 1 March 2002, reprinted in *Haïti-Progrès* 21: 39 [10 December 2003]).

142. Elaine Sciolino, "The Aristide Resignation: The Allies; US and France Set Aside Differences in Effort to Resolve Haiti Conflict," *New York Times*, 3 March 2004; cf. Sabatier, "Débarquement," *Libération*, 1 March 2004; Jean-Michel Caroit, "Comment la France a préparé son retour en Haïti," *Le Monde*, 15 April 2004.

143. Guy Delva, "Haiti Drops 'Ridiculous' $22 Billion Claim," Reuters, 17 April 2004.

144. Slevin and Wilson, "Aristide Offers to Share Power," *Washington Post*, 22 February 2004.

145. "Haitian Official Appeals For Help to End Revolt," AP, 18 February 2004; "Foreigners Leave Haiti as Unrest Persists," AP, 20 February 2004.

146. Frank Davies And Jacqueline Charles, "Greater Strife Could Fill a Post-Aristide Vacuum," *Miami Herald*, 28 February 2004.

147. Lest anyone forget where the US government stood regarding its international obligations to grant asylum to refugees fleeing political persecution, on 25 February George Bush reminded reporters that "I have made it abundantly clear to the Coast Guard that we will turn back any refugee that attempts to reach our shore" (cited in Christopher Marquis, "France Seeks U.N. Force in Haiti," *New York Times*, 26 February 2004).

148. Cited in Marquis, "Aristide Flees After a Shove from the US," *New York Times*, 1 March 2004.

149. "Rebels Take Crossroads Town Near Haiti's Capital," AP, 27 February 2004.

150. Shawn McCarthy et al., "Canada Assailed for Failing to Step in and Save Aristide," *Globe and Mail*, 2 March 2004.

151. Amnesty International, "Haiti: Rebels, Like Government Forces, Must Respect Human Rights," 23 February 2004; cf. AI, "Haiti: Perpetrators of Serious Past Abuses Re-Emerge," 16 February 2004.

152. George Gedda, "Powell Questions Aristide Tenure in Haiti," AP, 26 February 2006.

153. "US Questions Aristide's 'Fitness' to Govern Haiti," AFP, 28 February 2004.

154. For a more detailed analysis of what happened on the night of 28/29 February 2004 see Hallward, "Did He Jump or Was He Pushed?" (forthcoming 2007).

155. Les Cayes fell to a "new rebel group" on Thursday 26 February ("Rebels Take Crossroads Town Near Haiti's Capital," AP, 27 February 2004).

156. Peter Slevin and Mike Allen, "Former Ally's Shift in Stance Left Haiti Leader No Recourse," *Washington Post*, 1 March 2004.

157. Ambassador Foley, cited in David Adams, "Aristide's Last Days," *Saint Petersburg Times*, 28 February 2006, and in Rod Paul's 2005 film *Failing Haiti*. It's not clear how we are meant to reconcile Powell and Foley's apparent astonishment with the general State Department view quoted by the *New York Times* the day after his departure – "it was as if Aristide was the last guy in the world to figure out that the country would be better off were he to relinquish power" (cited in Christopher Marquis, "Aristide Flees After a Shove from the US," *New York Times*, 1 March 2004).

158. Roger Noriega, "Interview by Chris Bury of Nightline," State Department, 1 March 2004.

159. Cited in David Adams, "Aristide's Last Days," *Saint Petersburg Times*, 28 February 2006.

160. Ibid.

161. Amy Goodman, "Colin Powell's Former Chief of Staff Col. Wilkerson on Haiti: Defends U.S. Role in Ouster of President," *Democracy Now!*, 22 November 2005.

162. "US Ambassador Says Haiti's Aristide Was Sad and Passive, Not Combative About Ouster," AP, 13 April 2004.

163. Adams, "Aristide's Last Days," *Saint Petersburg Times*, 28 February 2006. David Johnson is currently the head of the Steele Foundation's "Special Projects."

164. Slevin and Wilson, "Aristide's Departure: The US Account," *Washington Post*, 3 March 2004.

165. "Press Briefing by White House Press Secretary Scott McClellan," 1 March 2004. In response to the natural question, "Why did President Aristide contact the United States about his decision to resign and not the OAS or the U.N.?", McClellan explained, "He talked to Ambassador Foley. His office talked to Ambassador Foley. Q: Why the US and why not one of the international agencies that's been working – MR. McCLELLAN: Well, I think for the reasons that I stated, that he wanted to make sure that his family – he and his family would be protected, his property would be protected. For the reasons that I stated.
Q: Couldn't those other agencies have protected him?
MR. McCLELLAN: You would have to ask – you can ask him."

166. Colin Powell, "Powell Responds to Aristide Allegations," CNN, 1 March 2004.

167. Lydia Polgreen And Tim Weiner, "Seeing New Beginning, Bush Sends Marines to Restore Order" *New York Times*, 29 February 2004.

168. Elaine Sciolino, "The Aristide Resignation: The Allies; US and France Set Aside Differences in Effort to Resolve Haiti Conflict," *New York Times*, 3 March 2004.

169. "Haiti: On the Brink," PBS Newshour, 26 February 2004.
170. "Aristide: Haitian Killers like those of 9/11," CNN, 26 February 2004. The CNN interviewer Judy Woodruff told Aristide that "you sound remarkably calm for someone at the center of such a terrible, terrible situation in your country right now. [Aristide:] Yes, I am. You know why I am? Because I am sure that what I'm doing is the right thing."
171. "CNN Late Edition with Wolf Blitzer", 29 February 2004, http://transcripts.cnn.com/TRANSCRIPTS/0402/29/le.00.html.
172. Trenton Daniel, "Appeals for Calm Bring Respite," *Miami Herald*, 29 February 2004.
173. Oriel Jean, interview with Kim Ives, Miami, 30 March 2007.
174. "When I tried to reach him again in the evening I was unable to get through. Someone answered the telephone who was not the usual person at his home and in a gruff manner said he could not speak now. In light of our earlier conversation and his desire to speak with me again, I was quite surprised" (Ira Kurzban, letter of 4 March 2007).
175. Nancy San Martin, "Rebels Get Out; Marines Roll In," *Miami Herald*, 4 March 2004.
176. Peter Eisner, "Aristide Back in Caribbean Heat; Before Arriving in Jamaica, Haitian Details 'Coup' by US," *Washington Post*, 16 March 2004.
177. This transcription is edited and compiled from interviews that I did with Frantz Gabriel in Pétionville in January 2007, and from interviews that Gabriel did with Crowing Rooster in Miami, in June 2006.
178. Interview with a senior member of Aristide's Steele Foundation security detail, 21 March 2007.
179. Interview with Mildred Trouillot Aristide, Pretoria, 20 July 2006.
180. Interview with David Adams, 19 March 2007.
181. Letter from Brian Concannon, 27 March 2007. After trying to translate the key passage of the letter as "tonight I am resigning in order to avoid a bloodbath," the State Department was obliged to hire Kreyol expert professor Bryant Freeman to provide a more accurate translation. Freeman pointed out that Aristide's letter never said, "I am resigning," and that its actual meaning was more evasive: "Thus, if this evening it is my resignation which can prevent a bloodbath, I agree to leave . . ." (Jennifer Byrd, "KU Prof Asked to Translate Aristide's Statement," *Lawrence Journal-World*, 11 March 2004).
182. "Lawyer: Aristide Can't Use Telephone," *Miami Herald*, 3 March 2004; Jeff Koinange, "Aristide's Guest Privileges Pared in Exile," CNN, 6 March 2004.
183. "Aristide and His Bodyguard Describe the U.S. Role in his Ouster," *Democracy Now!*, 16 March 2004.
184. "President Aristide Says 'I Was Kidnapped,' 'Tell the World it is a Coup,'" *Democracy Now!*, 1 March 2004.
185. "South Africa Rejects Washington's Claim Aristide Was Denied Asylum," *Democracy Now!*, 2 March 2004.
186. Erin Mobekk and Anne Street, "Disarmament, Demobilization and Reintegration" (ActionAid, October 2006), 6.
187. Lydia Polgreen And Tim Weiner, "Seeing New Beginning, Bush Sends Marines to Restore Order," *New York Times* 29 February 2004; cf. "Haiti's 'New Chapter'," *Washington Post*, 1 March 2004.
188. Elaine Sciolino, "The Aristide Resignation," *New York Times*, 3 March 2004.
189. Slevin and Wilson, "Aristide's Departure: The US Account," *Washington Post*, 3 March 2004. Deibert repeats most of this account in his *Notes from the Last Testament*, 411–13.

190. Interview with Aristide, CNN Tonight, 1 March 2004, http://transcripts.cnn.com/TRANSCRIPTS/0403/01/ldt.00.html. Aristide insisted on the imminent threat of violence again in what would prove to be his most detailed account of what happened on 28/29 February, on 5 March. He said that US military personnel took control of his house and then explained three things. "First that all the American security agents who have contracts with the Haitian government [must] either leave immediately to go to the United States, or they fight to die. Secondly, they told me the remaining 25 of the American security agents hired by the Haitian government who were to come in on the 29th of February as reinforcements were under interdiction, prevented from coming. Thirdly, they told me the foreigners and Haitian terrorists alike, loaded with heavy weapons, were already in position to open fire on Port-au-Prince. And right then, the Americans precisely stated that they will kill thousands of people, that it will be a bloodbath, and that the attack is ready to start" (Aristide, "Aristide Details Last Moments In Haiti," Pacific News Service, 5 March 2004).

191. Jeff Koinange, "Aristide's Guest Privileges Pared in Exile," CNN, 5 March 2004.

192. Roger Noriega, "Interview by Chris Bury of Nightline," 1 March 2004.

193. "Press Briefing by White House Press Secretary Scott McClellan," 1 March 2004.

194. Richard Boucher, "US Department of State Daily Press Briefing," 4 March 2004; cf. Thalif Deen, "US, France Block UN Probe of Aristide Ouster," Inter Press Service, 13 April 2004.

195. Donald Rumsfeld, "Pentagon Press Briefing", 1 March 2004.

196. "It is unfortunate," Kofi Annan wrote, "that in its bicentennial year, Haiti had to call again on the international community to help it overcome a serious political and security situation." Rather than make any sort of inquiry into the circumstances of his expulsion, Annan simply noted that "early on February 29, Mr Aristide left the country." Like the rest of the IC, Annan hoped that the toppling of the constitutional government by the great powers would offer Haiti "a peaceful, democratic and locally-owned future" (UNSC, Report of the Secretary-General on Haiti [16 April 2004], 31, 3).

197. Letter from Eléonore Senlis, 30 March 2007.

198. According to Neptune, when he spoke to Aristide around 1 a.m. he said only "I'm trying to undo something." A couple of hours later they spoke again and Aristide said, without further explanation, "Yvon in the situation I am now I feel like a prisoner. It's up to you. If you decide to stay you stay, if you decide to go you go." Aristide "didn't describe to me the pressure that he was under," says Neptune, "and it's clear that at the last minute he didn't tell me everything about what he was up against. But this isn't a reproach. It was obvious that the governments of the US and France were closing in, and I accept that in certain circumstances a political leader is entitled to decide that there is some information that he should keep to himself, if he feels it might alter or confuse certain things. Aristide was a very popular leader, he had a lot of responsibility, and he had on his shoulders the weight of what was happening to the country. He was responsible for what was happening, and might happen, to the vast majority of his supporters" (Interview with Yvon Neptune, 20 March 2007).

199. Interview with Patrick Elie, 3 March 2007.

200. Kevin Sullivan and Peter Slevin, "Haitian Leader Appeals For Foreign Security Aid," Washington Post, 25 February 2004.

201. Tim Collie and Jane Regan, "Rebels Close in on Port-au-Prince," South Florida Sun-Sentinel, 28 February 2004; cf. Tim Collie, "Aristide Backers Brace for Fight as Haitian Rebels Advance," South Florida Sun-Sentinel, 27 February 2004.

202. John-Thor Dahlburg, "Aristide's Supporters See a Friend of the Poor," Los Angeles Times, 29 February 2004.

203. Nancy San Martin, "Rebels" Aim: Choke, Take Port-au-Prince," *Miami Herald*, 28 February 2004.

204. Trenton Daniel, "Appeals for Calm Bring Respite; Mayhem in Haiti's Capital Ends as the President Tells Backers to Stop Attacks," *Miami Herald*, 29 February 2004.

205. Scott Wilson and Kevin Sullivan, "US Puts Blame for Crisis on Aristide; Thousands in Haiti Rally for President," *Washington Post*, 29 February 2004.

206. Interview with Patrick Elie, Port-au-Prince, 19 April 2006.

207. Tim Weiner and Lydia Polgreen, "Rebels Enter Haitian Capital; US and French Troops Arrive," *New York Times*, 1 March 2004. "The United States soldiers are like us," Philippe added. "We're brothers."

208. Jane Regan, "Haitian Rebels out of Loop," *Christian Science Monitor*, 27 February 2004.

209. AP, "Rebels Take Crossroads Town Near Haiti's Capital," *New York Times*, 27 February 2004.

210. Tim Collie and Jane Regan, "Rebels Close In on Port-au-Prince," *South Florida Sun-Sentinel*, 28 February 2004.

211. Guy Philippe, interview with Isabel Macdonald, Pétionville, December 2005.

212. Carol. J. Williams, "Doubts Linger on Aristide's Exit," *LA Times*, 1 March 2005.

213. Powell, "Powell Responds to Aristide Allegations," CNN, 1 March 2004; David Lazarus, "Watching Aristide's back," *San Francisco Chronicle*, 12 March 2004.

214. Interview with a senior member of Aristide's Steele Foundation security detail, 21 March 2007.

215. Jamaican foreign minister K.D. Knight later confirmed that he spoke to both Aristide and Powell on Saturday. He told Powell that the police supplies "would be passing through Jamaica from South Africa [. . .], that all was in place, and that [the equipment] would arrive about 5:30 p.m. on the Sunday [29 February]" (Balford Henry, "No Repercussions Likely from US over UN Security Council Seat," *Jamaica Observer*, 16 July 2006; cf. "South Africa Admits Sending Weapons to Haiti," BBC Caribbean, 5 March 2004).

216. Although vigorously denied by Powell and Foley, this point has been amply investigated by Aristide's lawyer Ira Kurzban, the *Miami Herald*'s investigative reporter Juan Tamayo and well-connected analysts like Robert Fatton. According to Fatton, "Steele reinforcements were already on their way," before their arrival was blocked by officials in the State Department (Interview with Robert Fatton, 10 November 2006). A senior member of Aristide's Steele team confirmed this to me in March 2007. "In response to a request from the Haitian government Steele had recruited some extra security guards, in Miami, and in late February I know they were ready to fly out to join us. But it didn't happen, I don't know why." Once aboard the plane to Bangui, Steele's commanding officer David Johnson told Frantz Gabriel that the reinforcements were intercepted by "the personal order of Colin Powell himself" (Frantz Gabriel, letter of 17 December 2006). When directly asked whether any Steele personnel might have been "delayed in coming down and adding to the contingent around the president," Steele CEO Kurtz refused to comment (Amy Goodman and Kenneth Kurtz, "Head of U.S. Security Firm that Guarded Aristide Speaks Out," *Democracy Now!*, 2 March 2004).

217. In 2004 as in 1991, this was a controversial decision. As one veteran Lavalassian told me in March 2007, "By the end of February 2004 Aristide was still in a strong position as regards his popularity and the determination of the people in Port-au-Prince, but he wasn't in a strong position in terms of the loyalty of his inner circle, especially regarding security, and he had failed to make effective contingency plans for a violent confrontation. With 500 trained and motivated people we could have made mincemeat of Guy Philippe, and dealt with the state of emergency in an

orderly and organized way. But this just isn't something you can improvise. You've got to be prepared."

218. Nancy San Martin, "Shock and Grief Are Shared by Many in Capital," *Miami Herald*, 1 March 2004.

219. Mark Stevenson, "Day of Horror, Hope in Haiti as Dawn Brings Aristide's Departure," *South Florida Sun-Sentinel*, 1 March 2004.

220. Interview with Belizaire Printemps and Elias Clovis, Port-au-Prince, 23 April 2006.

221. Nancy San Martin, "US Troops Deployed to Haiti," *Miami Herald*, 29 February 2004.

222. Mark Stevenson, "Day of Horror," *South Florida Sun-Sentinel*, 1 March 2004.

223. Trenton Daniel, "Ex-Police Chief Back for Old Role," *Miami Herald*, 3 March 2004.

224. Nancy San Martin, "Shock and Grief," *Miami Herald*, 1 March 2004.

225. Dodds and Ian James, "Thousands Cheer Aristide Ouster as Rebels Roll into Capital," AP, 1 March 2004.

226. Scott Wilson, "A City Smolders as Night Falls," *Washington Post*, 1 March 2004.

227. Lydia Polgreen and Tim Weiner, "Seeing New Beginning, Bush Sends Marines to Restore Order," *New York Times*, 29 February 2004. Cf. Tom Griffin, "Summary Report of Haiti Human Rights Delegation – March 29 to April 5" (April 2004).

CHAPTER 10

1. In February 2004, more than 200 foreign journalists arrived to cover the insurgency and its consequences (Carlos Lauria and Jean-Claude Chery, "Haiti: Taking Sides," *Committee to Protect Journalists*, 26 July 2004, http://www.cpj.org/Briefings/2004/haiti_7_04/haiti_7_04.html).

2. Lydia Polgreen, "Haitian Forces Battling Uprising Report Retaking 3 Towns," *New York Times*, 11 February 2004.

3. "Rebels Take Crossroads Town Near Haiti's Capital," AP, 27 February 2004.

4. AP 15 February 2004, cited in Tom Reeves, "US Double Game In Haiti," *ZNet*, 16 February 2004.

5. Mark Stevenson, "Day of Horror, Hope in Haiti as Dawn Brings Aristide's Departure," *South Florida Sun-Sentinel*, 1 March 2004; Scott Wilson and Kevin Sullivan, "Rebels Enter Haiti Capital in Triumph; Signs Surface of Reprisals against Aristide Loyalists," *Washington Post*, 2 March 2004.

6. Cited in Polgreen and Weiner, "Rebel Says He Is in Charge," *New York Times*, 3 March 2004.

7. Cited in Tim Weiner and Lydia Polgreen, "Facing New Crisis, Haiti Again Relies on US Military to Keep Order," *New York Times*, 7 March 2004.

8. Tim Collie, "Aristide Leaves Haiti," *South Florida Sun-Sentinel*, 29 February 2004.

9. Interview with Patrick Elie, Port-au-Prince 19 April 2006. Amaral Duclona and other militants in Cité Soleil insist on the same point (interview with Amaral Duclona, Cité Soleil, 12 April 2006).

10. Tim Weiner and Lydia Polgreen, "Rebels Enter Haitian Capital," *New York Times*, 1 March 2004.

11. Ronald Saint-Jean, *A propos du "Génocide de la Scierie"*, 24.

12. Interview with Prad Jean-Vernet, Cap-Haïtien, 12 January 2007.

13. Paisley Dodds, "Cap-Haïtien Scene," AP, 23 March 2004; Michael Christie, "Convicts Rule Haiti Town, Executions Plague Another," Reuters, 23 March 2004. Les Cayes' La Savane slum suffered a similar fate to that of Cité Soleil in Port-au-Prince. "With Aristide gone, La Savane – a hive of stick-framed huts on a spit of land between mangrove and sea – is politically unprotected and cut off from the rest

of the city now" (Joe Mozingo, "Violence, Chaos Stalk Haitian City Les Cayes," *Miami Herald*, 7 March 2004).

14. Griffin, "Summary Report of Haiti Human Rights Delegation," (April 2004), 7–8.

15. Stan Goff and Anthony Fenton, "The Invasion of Haiti," *ZNet*, 19 May 2004.

16. Tom Reeves, "Haiti's Disappeared," *ZNet*, 5 May 2004.

17. On 10 March, the Associated Press – which consistently under-reported the actual amount of violence – estimated that "reprisal killings since Aristide's ouster have left at least 300 dead" ("Haiti's Prime Minister Chosen", AP, 10 March 2004).

18. Steven Dudley, "Paramilitaries Hunt Pro-Aristide Gangs," *Boston Globe*, 2 March 2004.

19. Interview with Lamarre Augustin, Cité Soleil, 15 April 2006.

20. Bill Van Auken, "Reign of Terror Follows US-Backed Coup in Haiti," *WSWS*, 3 March 2004.

21. Griffin, "Summary Report of Haiti Human Rights Delegation" (April 2004), 4.

22. Carlos Lauria and Jean-Claude Chery, "Haiti: Taking Sides," 26 July 2004.

23. Jesus Martin with Amy Goodman, "The Killing of Ricardo Ortega: Witnesses Say U.S. Marines Fatally Shot Spanish Journalist in Haiti," *Democracy Now!*, 22 November 2004.

24. Yvon Antoine was arrested on 22 March 2004, and held on spurious charges relating to both the 7 March shootings and the 5 December 2003 violence at the University. Antoine was eventually acquitted, along with Paul Raymond and Annette Auguste, after a trial on 14 August 2006; no evidence against him was presented during the trial. Three other journalists were killed in 2005: Abdias Jean on 14 January, Robenson Laraque on 20 March, and Jacques Roche on 14 July 2005. Jean was shot by PNH in cold blood in front of several bystanders, after reportedly witnessing a series of public police executions; Laraque was apparently shot by MINUSTAH troops, but his death was never investigated (Interview with Guy Delva, Port-au-Prince 9 April 2006). Some analysts attribute Roche's murder to pro-FL gang leader Nicolas Augudson (a.k.a. General Toutou), and others to anti-FL police informants (Interview with Marcus Garcia, Port-au-Prince, 20 April 2006).

25. Tom Griffin and Amy Goodman, "Hundreds of Corpses Fill Haiti Morgues," *Democracy Now!*, 12 April 2004; cf. Melinda Miles, *Emergency Haiti Observation Mission*, 10; IJDH, *Human Rights Violations in Haiti (February–May 2004)*.

26. Cited in Sullivan and Wilson, "Rebel Claims Control Over Haiti's Security," *Washington Post*, 3 March 2004.

27. Polgreen and Weiner, "Rebel Says He Is in Charge," *New York Times*, 3 March 2004.

28. Polgreen, "US Patrols Start in Haiti, but Residents Remain Wary," *New York Times*, 4 March 2004.

29. "Haiti's Prime Minister Chosen," AP, 10 March 2004. Exactly the same order was given back in 1994 (Farmer, *Uses of Haiti*, 320).

30. Anthony Fenton, "Witch Hunt in Haiti," *ZNet*, 6 April 2004. A few months later, "On July 29th, the Commander of the Canadian Forces contingent in Haiti, Lieutenant Colonel Jim Davis, acknowledged to a well-attended media teleconference call that at least 1,000 people had been killed in Port-au-Prince since February 29. He also acknowledged that occupying forces took part in a massacre of between forty and sixty Lavalas civilians in the neighborhood of Bel Air on March 12" (Fenton, "Were Canadians Involved in a Massacre in Haiti?", *ZNet*, 9 August 2004).

31. Reeves, "Return to Haiti: The American Learning Zone," *CounterPunch*, 14 April 2004.

32. Reeves, "Haiti's Disappeared," *Z Magazine*, 05 May 2004.

33. Letter from Eléonore Senlis, 23 March 2007.

34. Weiner, "US Special Forces in Haiti Seeking Out Rebel Leaders," *New York Times*, 6 March 2004.
35. Cf. Brian Concannon Jr., "Haiti's Regime Change: What the Constitution Says," *Boston Haiti Reporter*, June 2004.
36. OAS, "The Political Decision-Making Process," 4 March 2004.
37. Lydia Polgreen, "New Haitian Prime Minister Arrives," *New York Times*, 11 March 2004.
38. "New Haiti Government Selected," *Guardian*, 17 March 2004.
39. Lindsay, "Peace Despite the Peacekeepers in Haiti" (2006), 34.
40. Interview with Father Rick Freshette, Port-au-Prince, 18 April 2006.
41. Pina, "Rolling Haiti Back to Colonialism," *ZNet*, 21 September 2004; Laura Flynn et al., "Report of the Haiti Accompaniment Project," June 29–July 9, 2004, http://www.haitiaction.net/News/hap6_29_4.html.
42. Interview with Marie-André Saint-Aubin [ActionAid], Port-au-Prince, 20 April 2006; Weiner, "The Price of Rice Soars, and Haiti's Hunger Deepens," *New York Times*, 1 June 2004.
43. In the spring of 2006 there was a partial reconciliation of FL and representatives from various student groups including FEUH, GRAFNEH, Collectif des Étudiants Haïtiens and Plateforme Universitaire (Interview with John Joseph Jorel, Port-au-Prince, 15 April 2006).
44. Jean-Claude Paulvin, cited in Lindsay, "Instability Continues to Wrack Haiti," *Washington Times*, 30 November 2004.
45. Brian Concannon, "Haiti's Political Prisoners Exemplify Challenges of Democratic Transition," *Power and Interest News Report*, 11 September 2006.
46. "Senior US Official Visits Unsettled Haiti," *Miami Herald*, 9 June 2005.
47. Canadian Prime Minister Paul Martin, cited in Lindsay, "Instability Continues to Wrack Haiti," *Washington Times*, 30 November 2004.
48. " 'Unholy Alliance' Reigns in Haiti," AP, 24 March 2004.
49. Cited in "Fanmi Lavalas and the Electoral Commission," AHP, 28 April 2004.
50. Members of Bale Wouze, among others, accused Louis-Gérald Gilles of helping the former FL senator Prince Pierre Sonson (who turned against the government in late 2003) transport weapons to the Artibonite insurgents ("L'Ancien Sénateur contesté Pierre Sonson Prince quitte Haïti pour raison de sécurité," *Alterpresse*, 24 February 2004).
51. Interview with Louis-Gérald Gilles, Port-au-Prince, 13 April 2006.
52. Cited in Weiner, "US Special Forces in Haiti Seeking Out Rebel Leaders," *New York Times*, 6 March 2004.
53. In a candid Bastille-day speech delivered at the French embassy in July 2005, Latortue said he "regretted capitulating to international pressure on his government not to work closely with the former soldiers. If the international community 'had given us a little more freedom to work with the ex-military, so that they could have participated in the struggle against the armed groups, I am more than certain that we wouldn't be in the impasse we are in today [. . .]. I sincerely recognize that this was a mistake. But today, we will not repeat this same mistake again. We will look for our allies where we can find them to fight those who have decided to fight us' " ("Rebels Should Have Had Role in Struggle Against Armed Gangs, Haitian Interim Leader Says," AP, 15 July 2005).
54. Cited in COHA, "Haiti: Smouldering on the Edge of Chaos," 23 September 2004.
55. Tony Smith, "Haitian Leader Warns of Exodus," *New York Times*, 25 February 2004.
56. Tim Weiner and Lydia Polgreen, "Rebels Enter Haitian Capital," *New York Times*, 1 March 2004.

57. Dodds and James, "Rebel Chief Declares Himself Haiti's Leader," AP, 2 March 2004.

58. Carol Williams, "Rebel Leader in Haiti Says His Work Is Done," *Los Angeles Times*, 4 March 2004; Nancy San Martin and Susannah Nesmith, "Rebels Get Out; Marines Roll In," *Miami Herald*, 4 March 2004.

59. Wilson and Sullivan, "Rebels Enter Haiti Capital in Triumph," *Washington Post*, 2 March 2004.

60. Griffin, *Haiti Human Rights Investigation* (November 2004), 14.

61. Interview with Venel Remarais, Port-au-Prince, 18 April 2006.

62. "UN Troops and Haitian Police Kill Two Prominent Former Soldiers After Violent Week," *Haïti Progrès* 23: 5 (13 April 2005).

63. Letter from Ira Kurzban, 2 March 2007.

64. Engler and Fenton, *Canada in Haiti*, 65.

65. Cited in Miles, *Emergency Haiti Observation Mission 23 March–2 April 2004*, 22. According to Lovinsky Pierre-Antoine, "There are 800 former Haitian soldiers who were brought into the National Police by the Latortue regime, and it's this group within the Haitian National Police who carried out most of the crimes committed by the police against the people in the slums" (Darren Ell, "Sovereignty and Justice in Haiti: An Interview with Lovinsky Pierre-Antoine," HIP, 18 February 2007).

66. Patrick Elie, "A Coup Made Long in Advance," 17 October 2004.

67. COHA, "Haiti: Smouldering on the Edge of Chaos," 23 September 2004.

68. Cf. Joe Mozingo, "Presidential Hopefuls Have Drug Ties, Sources in Haiti, U.S. Claim," *Miami Herald*, 23 December 2005.

69. James Gordon Meek, "Interim Haitian Prime Minister Relieved to Leave Office," *New York Daily News*, 10 June 2006.

70. See in particular IJDH, "Human Rights Violations in Haiti (February–May 2004);" Griffin, *Haiti Human Rights Investigation* (November 2004); Laura Flynn et al., "Report of the Haiti Accompaniment Project" (June–July 2004); Harvard Law Student Advocates for Human Rights and Centro de Justiça Global, *Keeping the Peace in Haiti?* (March 2005); International Tribunal on Haïti, *Preliminary Report of the Commission of Inquiry* (October 2005).

71. Griffin, *Haiti Human Rights Investigation* (November 2004), 31.

72. "US Ships Guns to Haiti," AP, 5 August 2005.

73. Reed Lindsay, "US Admits 2,600 Weapons Sent to Haiti," *Scotland on Sunday*, 24 April 2005; Muggah, Robert, *Securing Haiti's Transition* (March 2005), 34. This allegation was later removed in a subsequent version of the report, following US complaints. However Muggah assured journalists at the time that his information was reliable, that Haitian officials had receipts for the shipment dating from November 2004, and that the guns had arrived and were being kept in containers at the port. See also Oxfam, *The Call for Tough Arms Controls* (January 2006), 14.

74. Cited in Reed Lindsay, "Peace Despite the Peacekeepers in Haiti" (2006), 33.

75. Susannah Nesmith, "Top Rebel Wavers on Disarming," *Miami Herald*, 6 March 2004.

76. Polgreen and Weiner, "An Interim President for Haiti Is Sworn In," *New York Times*, 9 March 2004; Stevenson and Dodds, "US Marines Move into More of Haiti," AP, 8 March 2004.

77. Polgreen, "In Rebel City, Guns Are Power and No One Wants to Let Go," *New York Times*, 8 March 2004.

78. Cited in *Black Commentator*, "Haiti's Troika of Terror," *CounterPunch*, 29 March 2004.

79. Keith Jones, "US-led Occupation Force Targets Haiti's Slums," *WSWS*, 20 March 2004.

80. Andrew Buncombe, "Bush Administration 'Broke its Own Embargo to Sell Arms to Haiti Police,'" *Independent*, 17 April 2005.

81. Reed Lindsay, "Arms Amnesty Program Thwarted," *Toronto Star*, 15 January 2006; cf. Amnesty International, "Haiti: Disarmament Delayed, Justice Denied" (July 2005); Oxfam, *The Call for Tough Arms Controls* (January 2006), 15–17. The failure is hardly surprising. "What is being offered to the armed leaders in Cité Soleil?", asked a UN official in 2005. "Death or long-term imprisonment. Why would the people in the armed groups play nice? Their own existence is at stake" (cited in Lindsay, "Peace Despite the Peacekeepers in Haiti", 35). Other observers emphasized a different point, noting that the PNH actively prevented pro-FL gang members from participating in the UN's DDR programme – rather than disarm them, the "government wants to kill them, it's as simple as that" (Interview with Guy Delva, Port-au-Prince 9 April 2006). "If disarmament actually takes place," a Bel Air resident told me, "the police will lose the pretext to invade our neighborhood, to search our houses, to attack us" (Interview with a Bel Air resident, 14 April 2006).

82. Michael Christie, "Haiti Police Begin Rounding up Aristide Associates," Reuters, 14 March 2004.

83. "Les Prisons affichent 'complet,'" *Le Nouvelliste* 5 April 2006; interview with Ronald Saint-Jean, Port-au-Prince, 11 April 2006; International Tribunal on Haïti, *Preliminary Report of the Commission of Inquiry October 6 To 11, 2005*, 16–20.

84. Interview with Ronald Saint-Jean, Port-au-Prince, 11 April 2006.

85. Interview with Evel Fanfan (AUMOHD), 17 April 2006.

86. Griffin, *Haiti Human Rights Investigation* (November 2004), 18–19.

87. Haiti Accompaniment Project, "Human Rights Conditions in Haiti's Prisons" (August 2004); cf. Brian Concannon, "Haiti's Political Prisoners Exemplify Challenges of Democratic Transition" (September 2006).

88. Interview with Guy Delva, Port-au-Prince, 9 April 2006.

89. Laura Flynn et al., "Report of the Haiti Accompaniment Project" (July 2004).

90. Interview with Guy Delva, Port-au-Prince, 9 April 2006.

91. Laura Flynn et al., "Report of the Haiti Accompaniment Project" (July 2004).

92. "Haiti: Powell Should Back Rebel Prosecutions," Human Rights Watch, 5 April 2004. http://hrw.org/english/docs/2004/04/06/haiti8397.htm. When HRW representatives met with Bernard Gousse in March, Gousse told them he "might consider giving Jean Tatoune a reduction in sentence if Tatoune turned himself in to the justice authorities. The reduction could be merited, Gousse claimed, because 'he's fought against two dictatorships'" (ibid.). Along with others convicted for their part in the Raboteau Massacre, Tatoune would get his pardon soon enough, in May 2005.

93. "Justice Scorned in Haiti," *New York Times* 20 August 2004.

94. Sasha Kramer and Zoë Moskovitz, "The Politics of Injustice in Haiti," HIP, 24 August 2004.

95. Amnesty International, "Obliterating Justice, Overturning of Sentences for Raboteau Massacre by Supreme Court is a Huge Step Backwards," 26 May 2005; cf. Concannon, "Justice Dodged in Haiti, Once Again," *CounterPunch*, 18 June 2005.

96. "Speech by Former Ambassador James B. Foley," US Embassy 12 August 2005.

97. Colin Powell, "Press Conference with Interim Prime Minister Gerard Latortue," Port-au-Prince, 1 December 2004.

98. Reed Lindsay, "Haiti Bloodbath that Left Dozens Dead in Jail," *Observer*, 19 December 2004; IJDH, "Report on December 1 Massacre in the Haitian National Penitentiary," 20 December 2004.

99. Lindsay, "Answers as Elusive as Prison Escapees in Port-au-Prince," *New York Newsday*, 22 February 2005.

100. Tim Pelzer, "Ex-soldier Says He Was Asked to Kill Haitian Leader," *People's Weekly World*, 26 March 2005. Pelzer's account is corroborated by Reed Lindsay, who has conducted several interviews with Arnel Belizaire. Belizaire was originally imprisoned in the fall of 2004 when he refused to incriminate FL senator Louis-Gérald Gilles for possessing weapons that belonged to Belizaire himself.

CHAPTER 11

1. "Street Resistance to Occupation Regime Surges," *Haïti Progrès* 22: 30 (6 October 2004); "Pro-Aristide March Turns Violent in Haiti," AP, 30 September 2004.
2. "Lavalas Protests, Violence in Port-au-Prince," AHP, 1 October 2004.
3. International Crisis Group, *A New Chance for Haiti?* (November 2004), 14.
4. Cited in Stevenson Jacobs, "Three Pro-Aristide Politicians Arrested," AP, 3 October 2004.
5. HAC," 'Operation Baghdad' brought to you by AP," 3 October 2004.
6. "National Populist Party Leader [Georges Honorat] Denounces Campaign of Repression," AHP, 6 October 2004; Patrick Elie, "A Coup Made Long in Advance," *ZNet*, 17 October 2004; Interview with Venel Remaris, Port-au-Prince 18 April 2006; Paul Chéry and Keven Skerrett, "A Situation of Terror: Haitian Union Leader on the 2004 Coup," *ZNet*, 4 November 2005.
7. Cited in Griffin, *Haiti Human Rights Investigation* (November 2004), 29.
8. Interview with Jean-Marie, Bel Air 19 April 2006.
9. Kevin Sullivan and Scott Wilson, "Rebel Claims Control Over Haiti's Security," *Washington Post*, 3 March 2004.
10. Lydia Polgreen and Tim Weiner, "An Interim President for Haiti Is Sworn In," *New York Times*, 9 March 2004.
11. "Operation in Bel Air," AHP, 6 October 2004.
12. Interview with Samba Boukman, Bel Air, 14 April 2006.
13. Griffin, *Haiti Human Rights Investigation* (November 2004), 10; cf. Reed Lindsay, "Police Terror Sweeps Across Haiti," *Observer*, 31 October 2004; Lindsay, "Violent Tide vs. Aristide Supporters," *Newsday*, 7 November 2004.
14. Michael W. Brewer, "Haitian Death Squads and Child Murders" (Autumn 2004).
15. Griffin, *Haiti Human Rights Investigation* (November 2004), 43.
16. Reed Lindsay, "Instability Continues to Wrack Haiti," *Washington Times*, 30 November 2004.
17. Griffin, *Haiti Human Rights Investigation* (November 2004), 32–4.
18. Interview with Guy Delva, Port-au-Prince, 9 April 2006; Lindsay, "Police Blamed in Haiti Killings," *Toronto Star*, 15 February 2005.
19. Interview with Samba Boukman, Bel Air, 14 April 2006.
20. Ben Ehrenreich, "Haiti's Hope," *LA Weekly*, 12 April 2006.
21. Oxfam, *The Call for Tough Arms Controls* (January 2006), 11.
22. Athena R. Kolbe and Royce A. Hutson, "Human Rights Abuse and Other Criminal Violations in Port-Au-Prince, Haiti: A Random Survey of Households," *The Lancet* 9538 (2 September 2006).
23. Richard Horton, "This Terrible Misadventure Has Killed One in 40 Iraqis," *Guardian*, 12 October 2006.
24. Harvard Law Student Advocates for Human Rights and Centro de Justiça Global, *Keeping the Peace in Haiti* (March 2005), 1; cf. Reed Lindsay, "Abuse after Aristide's Ouster," *Newsday*, 14 February 2005.
25. Lindsay, "Peace Despite the Peacekeepers in Haiti" (2006), 34.
26. General Augusto Heleno Ribeiro, cited in "A Year after Aristide's Fall, Haiti

Remains in Grip of Poverty, Fear and Political Paralysis," AP, 1 March 2005.

27. Lamar Litz, "Attacks Against Demonstrations in Haiti: A Compilation of Reports," IJDH, 13 September 2005.

28. "There is No Political Persecution in Haiti," HIP, 12 June 2005.

29. As the director of the neighborhood's only hospital points out, "Many people in Haiti have no idea what things are like in Cité Soleil, they never see it, they are terrified to come here" (Interview with Jacklin Saint-Fleur, Cité Soleil, 15 April 2006).

30. Interview with Anne Sosin, Port-au-Prince, 21 April 2006; Interview with Judy DaCruz, Pétionville, 17 April 2006. As Saint-Fleur points out, however, "You can't ask people to give what they don't have" (Interview with Jacklin Saint-Fleur, Cité Soleil, 15 April 2006).

31. Interview with Bobby Duval, Port-au-Prince, 17 April 2006.

32. Nancy San Martin, "Slum's 'Military of Aristide' Set to Take on Rebels," *Miami Herald*, 25 February 2004. "Aristide doesn't have money to do much, but he does his best," continued Billy. "I want to see Aristide finish his five years. I worked for that. I voted for Aristide. Nobody is going to take that away."

33. Lydia Polgreen, "US Patrols Start in Haiti," *New York Times*, 4 March 2004.

34. Reed Lindsay, "Violence in Haiti," *Marketplace* (National Public Radio), 4 January 2006.

35. Back in 1996, Reginald Boulos described Cité Soleil as a political "gold mine: more than 200,000 people living in less than two square miles." But as the *New York Times* went on to note, "community groups that support the Lavalas movement have long been hostile to Dr. Boulos and his organization [the CDS]. During the three brutal years of military dictatorship that preceded Mr. Aristide's restoration to power in October 1994, they accused him of providing information on his clients to the paramilitary thugs who killed hundreds of people in Cité Soleil as well as of supplying jobs and food to some of the most notorious gunmen. Dr. Boulos admits to trying not to antagonize the military regime and its agents, but said it was 'a conscious decision' taken to avoid the shutdown of the hospital and a program that fed 29,000 people" (Larry Rohter, "Quarrel Imperils Health Care in Haiti," *New York Times*, 26 May 1996).

36. Eléonore Senlis accompanied Labanye when he met with Apaid, Gervais Charles (G184 lawyer and head of the Port-au-Prince Bar Association) and a representative of the CEDH at Apaid's office in early October 2003. In exchange for a written statement cataloguing an alleged array of Lavalas misdeeds Labanye was promised passports for himself and his wife Sonia. As a gesture of goodwill Apaid quickly arranged a flight out for Sonia, on 4 November 2003, but he kept Labanye dangling in Cité Soleil. "To be honest," remembers Senlis, "after he got what he wanted I think Apaid was just quietly waiting for Labanye to be bumped off by a member of his own gang, or another gang. And he knew he wouldn't have to wait too long, since Labanye wasn't a very popular chief" (Letter from Eléonore Senlis, 27 March 2007).

37. The police officers interviewed by Griffin's team said that while the police is actively hunting Dred Wilme, "all officers have been directed not to arrest Thomas 'Labanye' Robinson, the Cité Soleil gang leader they know is opposed to the Lavalas movement. According to the officers, the protection order came from Andy Apaid and 'the bourgeoisie' " (Griffin, *Haiti Human Rights Investigation* (November 2004), 37; cf. 3). According to Samba Boukman, during a group interview on Radio Megastar on the afternoon of 7 January 2006, Labanye's former lieutenant Evens Jean reminded Andy Apaid of specific munitions deliveries at specific places and times (Interview with Samba Boukman, Bel Air 14 April 2006).

38. Letter from Eléonore Senlis, 27 March 2007.
39. Ibid.
40. Interview with Andy Apaid, in Griffin, *Haiti Human Rights Investigation* (November 2004), 27.
41. Letter from Eléonore Senlis, 27 March 2007.
42. Ben Ehrenreich, "Haiti's Hope," *LA Weekly*, 12 April 2006.
43. Interview with Amaral Duclona, Cité Soleil, 12 April 2006; Interview with Lamarre Augustin, Cité Soleil, 15 April 2006.
44. Griffin, *Haiti Human Rights Investigation* (November 2004), 7.
45. Michael Deibert, "On September 30th," *Blogspot*, 1 October 2006, http://michaeldeibert.blogspot.com/2006/10/on-september–30th.html.
46. Most members of the armed groups in Cité Soleil "aren't revolutionaries," says Anne Sosin, "they're young men who are the product of their environment, the structural violence that exist in places like Cité Soleil and Bel Air, and many are engaged in criminal activity in order to survive. Most of the time there are simply no viable economic alternatives" (Interview with Anne Sosin, Port-au-Prince 11 April 2006; cf. Interview with Judy DaCruz, Pétionville 17 April 2006). Reporter Reed Lindsay also echoes Sosin's comments: in 2004–05, under the constant pressure of paramilitary aggression, "My sense was that in Cité Soleil parts of the Lavalas movement were being silenced. There were a lot of genuine Lavalas supporters, strong Aristide supporters, who couldn't say or do anything" so long as armed leaders were in charge (Interview with Lindsay, Port-au-Prince, 22 April 2006).
47. Letter from Eléonore Senlis, 24 March 2007.
48. Lakou New York, 'Interview with Dread Wilme,' 4 April 2005, http://www.lakounewyork.com/dreadwilmeentevyou.htm.
49. Interviews with Guy Delva, Port-au-Prince, 9 April 2006 and 25 April 2006.
50. Interview with Bobby Duval, Port-au-Prince, 17 April 2006.
51. Interview with Belizaire Printemps and Elias Clovis, Port-au-Prince 23 April 2006. Kim Ives agrees: "Dred truly was a hero for the people, and he was politically astute, as is his successor Amaral" (Letter from Kim Ives, 14 December 2006).
52. Ginger Thompson, "A New Scourge Afflicts Haiti: Kidnappings," *New York Times*, 6 June 2005.
53. Cf. Amy Goodman and Anthony Fenton, "US Democracy Promotion and Haiti," *Democracy Now!*, 23 January 2006.
54. "There is No Political Persecution in Haiti," HIP, 12 June 2005.
55. Cited in Reeves, "How Bush Brings Freedom to the World," *CounterPunch*, January 29, 2005.
56. Cited in Reed Lindsay, "UN's Feared Blue Helmets Blamed for Haiti Attacks," *Sydney Morning Herald*, 4 February 2006.
57. Pablo Bachelet and Roger Noriega, "Aristide Accused of Fostering Violence," *Miami Herald*, 24 June 2005.
58. Yves Engler, "Haiti After the Coup," *Z Magazine* October 2005; cf. International Tribunal on Haïti, *Preliminary Report of the Commission of Inquiry October 6 To 11, 2005*, 5–8.
59. Naomi Klein, "6/7: The Massacre of the Poor that the World Ignored," *Guardian*, 18 July 2005; Engler, "Haiti After the Coup" (October 2005).
60. "Kevin Pina Interviews the Most-Wanted Man in Haiti: Amaral Duclona," HIP, 1 February 2006.
61. "U.N. to Investigate Haiti Slum Lynchings," Reuters, 25 August 2005; Concannon, "Throwing Gasoline on Haiti's Fires," *Peaceworks*, October 2005; Letter from Anne Sosin, 30 December 2006.

62. Interview with Jacklin Saint-Fleur, Cité Soleil, 15 April 2006.
63. "US Efforts to Help Haiti Are On Track, Says Noriega," US Embassy to Brazil, January 2005.
64. Interview with Father Rick Freshette, Port-au-Prince, 18 April 2006.
65. Walt Bogdanich and Jenny Nordberg, "Democracy Undone," *New York Times*, 29 January 2006.
66. Interviews with John Joseph Jorel, Port-au-Prince 15 April 2006 and Paul Christian, Port-au-Prince, 14 April 2006.
67. "Disturbing the Peace," *Boston Haitian Reporter*, November 2004.
68. Bill Quigley, "Message from a Jailed Priest in Haiti," *Common Dreams*, 18 October 2004.
69. Interview with Samba Boukman, Bel Air, 14 April 2006.
70. Incredibly, notes Jonas Petit, Latortue's CEP immediately accepted Marc Bazin and Louis-Gérald Gilles as FL nominations in the absence of any authorization from FL itself. "The whole thing was a ruse to try to disarm and to divide the organization" (Interview with Jonas Petit, Miami, 8 April 2006).
71. Like many FL activists, Cité Soleil's John Joseph Jorel was initially hesitant about Préval's candidacy. In early September we still "truly believed that Jean-Juste would be able to run, and Préval assured us that in that case he would not stand against him." But once it was clear that the only actual choice was Préval or Bazin, Jorel and his associates threw their considerable influence behind Aristide's former protégé, helping to organize major pro-Préval demonstrations in Cité Soleil and lower Port-au-Prince on 23 October and 3 November (Interview with John Joseph Jorel, Port-au-Prince, 15 April 2006).
72. Interview with Gérard Jean-Juste, Miami, 7 April 2006.
73. Interview with Ronald Saint-Jean, Port-au-Prince, 11 April 2006.
74. Interview with Samba Boukman, Bel Air, 14 April 2006. Reporter Ben Ehrenreich was given access to the voting lists from a Bel Air polling station, which indicated that Préval had won around 92 percent of the local vote (Ehrenreich, "Haiti's Hope," *LA Weekly*, 12 April 2006).
75. Interview with Rea Dol, Port-au-Prince, 18 April 2006.
76. Interview with Anne Hastings, Port-au-Prince, 24 April 2006.
77. Cited in Caroit, "Les anciens opposants craignent un retour au passé," *Le Monde*, 22 November 2005.
78. Duncan Campbell, "A Country at Boiling Point," *Guardian*, 21 February 2006.
79. See in particular Concannon, "Haiti's Elections: Seeing the Forest and the Trees," *CounterPunch*, 3 December 2005, http://www.counterpunch.com/concannon12032005.html; Concannon, "Haiti's Elections: Right Result, For The Wrong Reason," IJDH, 17 February 2006.
80. "Haitian Minister Accuses UN Troops of Violating Mandate," *Business Day*, 9 March 2005.
81. Leslie Bagg and Aaron Lakoff, "Haiti's Elites Pressure the UN," *Haiti Action News*, 18 January 2006.
82. Letter from Kim Ives, 14 December 2006.
83. Interview with Venel Remarais, Port-au-Prince, 18 April 2006.
84. Interview with Samba Boukman, Bel Air, 14 April 2006.
85. Interview with Patrick Elie, Port-au-Prince, 19 April 2006; cf. Bellegarde-Smith, *Breached Citadel*, 203.
86. "Kevin Pina Interviews Amaral Duclona," HIP, 1 February 2006; cf. Tim Collie, "Haitian Gang Leaders Rally Hundreds of Marchers in Capital to Demand Voting Sites," *South Florida Sun-Sentinel*, 2 February 2006.
87. Interview with Paul Christian, Port-au-Prince, 19 April 2006.

88. Ben Ehrenreich, "Haiti's Hope," *LA Weekly*, 12 April 2006.
89. Interview with Guy Delva, Port-au-Prince, 25 April 2006.
90. Roger Noriega, "Rays of Hope for Haiti's Future," *Miami Herald*, 16 February 2006.
91. Ginger Thompson, "Préval's Silence Obscures Bid to Reunite Haiti," *New York Times*, 20 February 2006.
92. Interview with Father Rick Freshette, Port-au-Prince, 18 April 2006.
93. Interview with Reed Lindsay, Port-au-Prince, 12 April 2006; cf. Letta Tayler, "An Uncertain Course in Haiti," *South Florida Sun Sentinel*, 21 February 2006.
94. Cited in Richard Dufour and Keith Jones, "Washington Reluctantly Concedes Préval Is Haiti's President-Elect," *WSWS*, 21 February 2006.
95. Cf. Stevenson Jacobs, "Opponents Could Use Disputed Election Result to weaken Préval," AP, 18 February 2006.
96. Stevenson Jacobs, "American: Haiti Leader Must Perform," AP, 19 February 2006.
97. Interview with Paul Christian, Port-au-Prince, 19 April 2006; Interview with Timothy Pershing, Pétionville, 17 April 2006.
98. Letta Tayler, "An Uncertain Course in Haiti," *South Florida Sun Sentinel*, 21 February 2006.
99. Interview with Venel Remarais, Port-au-Prince, 18 April 2006; cf. Interview with Alinx Albert Obas [Radyo Etensel], Cap-Haïtien, 14 January 2007.
100. Guy Delva, "Venezuelan Leader Cheered by Crowds in Haiti," Reuters, 12 March 2007; "Cuba/Venezuela: De vrais amis," *Haïti Progrès*, 25: 2 (21 March 2007).
101. EIU, *Country Report: Haiti*, November 2006, 3; cf. Jacqueline Charles, "As Haiti Stabilizes, Progress Still Slow," *Miami Herald*, 16 February 2007.
102. Cf. Concannon, "Naje Pou Soti," IJDH, 7 March 2006.
103. Cf. "Un Cabinet ministériel pour tous?" *Haïti Progrès*, 23: 11 (7 June 2006).
104. Interview with Fritz Longchamp (Préval's chief of staff), Port-au-Prince, 3 January 2007.
105. Chomsky, *Hegemony or Survival*, 137.
106. Interview with Moïse Jean-Charles, Cap-Haïtien, 12 January 2007.
107. Interview with Maude Leblanc, Port-au-Prince, 4 January 2007.
108. US interim ambassador Tim Carney was prepared to accept Préval's "contested" election in February 2006 so long as he demonstrated his willingness to cooperate with the US by "reaching out to the opposition, by beginning to move forward with no Aristide in sight." Another western ambassador told the *New York Times* that "We made very clear to Mr. Préval that we see Aristide as a figure of the past, with no place in Haiti's future" (Ginger Thompson, "Préval's Silence Obscures Bid to Reunite Haiti," *New York Times* 20 February 2006; "Haiti's Chance," *Washington Post* 19 February 2006). Prominent figures in the Haitian business community were more direct. "If Préval does try to bring Aristide back," warned Lionel Delatour, "he will not finish his presidency" (Carol Williams, "Aristide's Former Ally May Be Turning Away," *Los Angeles Times*, 20 February 2006).
109. "For me, when Préval says that no Haitian citizen needs a visa in order to come back to his country, this is a cop-out. Aristide is the former president of this country. His house has been ransacked. This is a scandal: it should be immediately restored. The Aristide Foundation for Democracy is a legitimate institution, and so are Radio Timoun, Tele Timoun, the university at Tabarre; their closure is indefensible. This too is a simple matter of democratic principle. Rather than dodge the issue, Préval should instead begin taking the steps that will allow Aristide to return. He should

take steps that will ensure his security, and the security of the people and the ventures he's involved with" (Interview with Yvon Neptune, Port-au-Prince, 5 January 2007).

110. Interview with Guy Delva, Port-au-Prince, 9 April 2006.
111. Interview with Marcus Garcia, Port-au-Prince, 20 April 2006.
112. Interview with John Joseph Jorel, Port-au-Prince, 15 April 2006.
113. Interview with Jean-Charles Moïse, Port-au-Prince, 11 April 2006.
114. By the end of 2006, the US was shipping around 100 convicts to Haiti every month. "These are young Haitian-Americans who grew up in the US, usually in poor black neighborhoods, and who were 'educated,' so to speak, in the American underworld. The US cannot cope with its own catastrophic levels of criminality; its prisons are already stretched to the breaking point. So now they export these casualties of their own social system back to Haiti, a country that doesn't have anything like the police or judicial resources needed to handle them. Most of these people arrive in the country with nothing, with no skills or family ties. What can they do to survive? Of course they do what they know: they turn to drugs and kidnapping, they join armed groups" (Interview with Ben Dupuy, 16 February 2007; cf. "Haiti: Justice Reform and the Security Crisis," ICG, 31 January 2007, 7).
115. Guy Delva, "Haiti Kidnap Wave Accompanied by Epidemic of Rape," Reuters, 9 March 2007.
116. At the time of Aristide's expulsion, estimates Cité Soleil hospital director Jacklin Saint-Fleur, "There were only one or two Galils in the hands of local armed groups; by the end of 2006 there were more than fifty" (Interview with Jacklin Saint-Fleur, Port-au-Prince, 9 January 2007).
117. Cited in Jean-Michel Caroit, "Le chaos règne en Haïti," Le Monde, 27 December 2006; Manuel Roig-Franzia, "In Haiti, Abductions Hold Nation Hostage," Washington Post, 21 February 2007.
118. Préval, "Disarm or Die," Radio Kiskeya 10 August 2006; Guy Delva, "Haiti Tells Gangs to Disarm or Face Death," Reuters, 10 August 2006.
119. "Désarmement: les gangs hésitent à rendre les armes, exigent des garanties," AHP, 21 September 2006; Ives, "The Clashes in Cité Soleil: The UN Fails Haiti, Again," Counterpunch, 24 November 2006.
120. Interview with Guy Delva, Port-au-Prince, 9 January 2007.
121. Marc Lacey, "U.N. Troops Fight Haiti Gangs One Street at a Time," New York Times, 10 February 2007; Jacqueline Charles, "In Haitian Slum, Gangs Retreat but Misery Persists," Miami Herald, 19 February 2007.
122. Guy Delva, "Haiti Slum Residents Enjoy New Peace, Want More," Reuters, 18 April 2007.
123. Interview with Georges Honorat, Port-au-Prince, 4 January 2007.
124. Interview with Ben Dupuy, 16 February 2007.
125. Cited in Tim Collie, "Haitian Gang Leaders Rally Hundreds of Marchers in Capital to Demand Voting Sites," South Florida Sun-Sentinel, 2 February 2006.
126. Interview with Rea Dol, Port-au-Prince, 15 January 2007.
127. Interview with Samba Boukman, Port-au-Prince, 4 January 2007.
128. Interview with Prad Jean-Vernet, Cap-Haïtien, 12 January 2007.
129. Interview with Yvon Neptune, Port-au-Prince, 5 January 2007.

CONCLUSION

1. Cited in Slavin, "Elite's Revenge" (1991), 6.
2. Interview with Patrick Elie, Port-au-Prince, 5 January 2007.

AFTERWORD

I'm grateful to Roger Annis, Isabeau Doucet and Kim Ives for their comments on an initial draft of the afterword.

1 Peter Beaumont, "Haiti Earthquake: Six Months On," *Guardian*, 10 July 2010. Two of the most usefully consolidated sources of information about post-quake Haiti are the CEPR's invaluable "Haiti Relief and Reconstruction Watch" (http://www.cepr.net/index.php/relief-and-reconstruction-watch/) and the Canada Haiti Action Network website (http://canadahaitiaction.ca/).

2 Kim Ives, "How the Earthquake Has Affected Haiti's National Democratic Revolution and International Geopolitics," talk delivered at the University of Aberdeen, 12 March 2010.

3 Quoted on BBC Radio 4, *Ten O'clock News*, 16 January 2010.

4 Ginger Thompson and Damien Cave, "Officials Strain to Distribute Aid to Haiti as Violence Rises," *New York Times*, 17 January 2010.

5 "Médecins Sans Frontiéres Says Its Plane Turned Away from U.S.-run Airport," *Daily Telegraph*, 19 January 2010

6 Giles Whittell and Jacqui Goddard, "America Sends Paratroopers to Haiti to Help Secure Aid Lines," *The Times*, 20 January 2010.

7 Email from Tim Schwartz, 20 January 2010.

8 Reed Lindsay, *Honor and Respect Foundation Newsletter*, 20 January 2010; cf. Luis Felipe Lopez, "Town at Epicenter of Quake Stays in Isolation," *Miami Herald*, 17 January 2010.

9 BBC Radio 4, *Ten O'clock News*, 18 January 2010.

10 Tom Brown, "Haiti Aid Effort Marred by Slow UN Response," *Reuters*, 26 February 2010.

11 "Disputes Emerge over Haiti Aid Control," *Al Jazeera*, 17 January 2010. Roger Annis notes the resemblance of the Canadian relief effort to its more prominent US counterpart. "The principal Canadian government response to the earthquake was to dispatch two Canadian warships loaded with nearly 2,000 soldiers and sailors. They arrived offshore from Léogâne and Jacmel on Jan. 19 and 20. At the time, this was touted by the government as a major earthquake relief operation. But as the Mar. 12 *Halifax Chronicle Herald* later reported, the ships carried relatively few earthquake relief supplies and equipment. They were instead loaded with military personnel and supplies. The military operations performed only peripheral aid and supply tasks. The medical teams the ships brought did not perform a single surgery, according to a study by John Kirk and Emily Kirk in April (www.counterpunch.-org/kirk04012010.html). When the ships departed six weeks after arriving, they took with them their vital air traffic control and heavy lift equipment" (Annis, "Canada's Failed Aid," *Haïti Liberté*, 4 August 2010).

12 Ginger Thompson and Damien Cave, "Officials Strain to Distribute Aid to Haiti as Violence Rises," *New York Times*, 17 January 2010.

13 Chris McGreal and Esther Addley, "Haiti Aid Agencies Warn: Chaotic and Confusing Relief Effort Is Costing Lives," *Guardian*, 18 January 2010.

14 Camille Chalmers, cited in Beverly Bell, "Haiti: 'Post-Disaster Needs Assessment' – Whose Needs? Whose Assessment?" *Other Worlds*, 26 February 2010.

15 Don Peat, "HUSAR Not Up to Task, Feds Say: Search and Rescue Team Told to Stand Down," *Toronto Sun*, 17 January 2010.

16 USAID, www.usaid.gov/helphaiti/index.html, accessed on 20 January 2010.

17 William Booth, "Haiti's Elite Spared from Much of the Devastation," *Washington Post*, 18 January 2010.

18 Tim Schwarz, phone call with the author, 18 January 2010; cf. Tim Schwartz, "Is this Anarchy? Outsiders Believe this Island Nation Is a Land of Bandits. Blame the NGOs for the 'Looting'," *NOW Toronto*, 21 January 2010.

19 Meg Laughlin, "At Stricken Haitian Factory: Prayers for the Dead and New Jobs," *St. Petersburg Times*, 13 February 2010.

20 Ross Marowits, "Gildan Shifting T-shirt Production Outside Haiti to Ensure Adequate Supply," *Canadian Press*, 13 January 2010.

21 "With Foreign Aid Still at a Trickle, Devastated Port-au-Prince General Hospital Struggles to Meet Overwhelming Need," *Democracy Now!*, 20 January 2010.

22 Stuart Page is chairman of Page Group, www.pagegroupltd.com/aboutus.html.

23 Gardner then explained that, with the police weakened by the quake, "Thousands of escaped criminals have returned to areas they once terrorized, like the slum district of Cité Soleil [...]. Unless the armed criminals are re-arrested, Haiti's security problems risk being every bit as bad as they were in 2004" (BBC Radio 4, *Six O'Clock News*, 18 January 2010). In fact, when some of these ex-prisoners tried to re-establish themselves in Cité Soleil in the week after the quake, local residents promptly chased them out of the district on their own (see Ed Pilkington and Tom Phillips, "Haiti Escaped Prisoners Chased Out of Notorious Slum," *Guardian*, 20 January 2010; Tom Leonard, "Scenes of Devastation Outside Port-au-Prince 'Even Worse'," *Daily Telegraph*, 21 January 2010).

24 BBC television, *Ten O'Clock News*, 18 January 2010. An extreme instance of the quasi-military emphasis on security led to an armed police response to a failed prison breakout in Les Cayes on 19 January, killing between 12 and 19 inmates and wounding another 40 (Deborah Sontag and Walt Bogdanich, "Escape Attempt Led to Killings of Unarmed Inmates," *New York Times*, 22 May 2010).

25 David Belle, Ciné Institute, 17 January 2010.

26 "Journalist Kim Ives on How Western Domination Has Undermined Haiti's Ability to Recover from Natural Devastation," *Democracy Now!*, 21 January 2010. Ives illustrated the way such community organizations work with an example from the Delmas 33 neighborhood. "A truckload of food came in the middle of the night unannounced. It could have been a melee. The local popular organization was contacted. They immediately mobilized their members [. . .]. They lined up about 600 people who were staying on the soccer field behind the [Matthew 25] house, which is also a hospital, and they distributed the food in an orderly, equitable fashion. They were totally sufficient. They didn't need Marines. They didn't need the UN. [. . .] These are things that people can do for themselves and are doing for themselves." Cf. Ansel Herz, "As Aid Efforts Flounder, Haitians Rely on Each Other," IPS 15 January 2010.

27 Andy Kershaw, "Stop Treating these People like Savages," *Independent*, 21 January 2010.

28 Bruno Waterfield, "US Ships Blockade Coast to Thwart Exodus to America," *Daily Telegraph*, 19 January 2010; 'Senegal Offers Land to Haitians,' *BBC News*, 17 January 2010.

29 James C. McKinley Jr., "Homeless Haitians Told Not to Flee to United States," *New York Times*, 19 January 2010.

30 Cf. "The US Should Welcome Haitians In," *Washington Post*, 29 January 2010; "President Obama Could Rapidly Aid Haitian Immigration Seekers," *Washington Post*, 26 June 2010.

31 John Pilger, "The Kidnapping of Haiti," *New Statesman*, 28 February 2010.

32 Cited in Reed Lindsay, "Haiti's Excluded," *The Nation*, 11 March 2010.

33 See for instance, Mark Schuller, "Haiti's Resurrection: Promoting Human Rights," *Huffington Post*, 5 April 2010; Robert Fatton Jr., "Toward a New Haitian State," *The Root*, 9 February 2010; Tim Schwartz, "Program of Development in Interest of Impoverished Haitians," 7 March 2010; Yves Engler, "The Political Roadblocks to Haiti's Reconstruction," *Counterpunch*, 16 July 2010; Paul Farmer, "Testimony to the Congressional Black Caucus: Focus on Haiti," 27 July 2010; Melinda Miles, "Haiti's Answer for Six Months and Sixty Years," *Let Haiti Live*, 12 August 2010.

34 Laura Flynn, "'We Want our Voices to be Heard': Democracy in Haiti's Earthquake Zone," *Haiti Action*, 3 May 2010.

35 "Haitian NGOs Decry Total Exclusion from Donors' Conferences on Haitian Reconstruction," IJDH, 18 March 2010.

36 Martha Mendoza, "Haiti Gets a Penny of Each US Aid Dollar," AP, 27 January 2010.

37 Paul Farmer, "Testimony to the Congressional Black Caucus: Focus on Haiti," 27 July 2010.

38 Kim Ives, "Haiti Reconstruction: Factories, not Fields," *NACLA* 43:3 (May 2010).

39 Jonathan Katz, "Criticism Grows on How Money Is Spent in Haiti," AP, 5 March 2010.

40 "Partners in Health's Medical Director and Director of Advocacy and Policy Urge Donor Countries to Support the Haitian Government," Partners in Health, 27 March 2010, www.pih.org, accessed 31 March 2010.

41 Kim Ives, "For $10 Billion in Promises, Haiti Surrenders Its Sovereignty," *Haïti Liberté*, 31 March 2010.

42 Interviewed by Sebastian Walker, "Haiti: Six Months On," *Faultlines*, Al Jazeera English, 12 July 2010.

43 Yves Engler, "The Political Roadblocks to Haiti's Reconstruction," *Counterpunch*, 16 July 2010.

44 Jeb Sprague and Wadner Pierre, "Haiti: Workers Protest Privatization Layoffs," *IPS*, 24 July 2007.

45 "Denis O'Brien's Digicel Is Upwardly Mobile in Haiti," *Irish Times*, 20 June 2008.

46 Isabeau Doucet, "The Drama of Haiti's Internally Displaced," Part Two, *Haiti Liberté*, 25 August 2010.

47 Yasmine Shamsie, "Export Processing Zones: The Purported Glimmer in Haiti's Development Murk," *Review of International Political Economy*, October 2009, cited in Regan Boychuk, "The Vultures Circle Haiti at Every Opportunity, Natural or Man-made," *MR Zine*, 2 February 2010.

48 Cf. Bill Quigley, 'Why the US Owes Haiti Billions – The Briefest History," *Huffington Post*, 17 January 2010; Naomi Klein, "Haiti: A Creditor, Not a Debtor Nation," *The Nation*, 12 February 2010. The earthquake did at least provide an occasion to put restitution of the old French debt (see above, page 000) back on the agenda, in a manner of speaking, when in July an audacious Yes Men-style prank announcing French intentions to repay the money they extorted over the course of the nineteenth century attracted some prominent supporting signatures and considerable attention in the press. See "M. Sarkozy, rendez à Haiti son argent extorqué," *Libération*, 16 August 2010; Kim Willsher, "France Urged to Repay Haiti Billions Paid for Its Independence," *Guardian* 15 August 2010.

49 Ashley Smith, "The 'Shock Doctrine' for Haiti," *Socialist Worker*, 8 February 2010. To anticipate some of the implications of a new "tourist boom" in Haiti, see Polly Patullo, *Last Resorts: The Cost of Tourism in the Caribbean* (NY: Monthly Review Press, 1996).

50 Jeffrey Sachs, "Haiti's Road to Recovery," *Guardian*, 31 January 2010.

51 Reed Lindsay, "Haiti's Excluded," *The Nation*, 11 March 2010.

52 Mark Schuller, "Rained Out? Opportunities in Haiti Washing Away," *Huffington Post*, 21 July 2010.

53 William Booth, "Haiti's Elite Spared from Much of the Devastation," *Washington Post*, 18 January 2010.

54 James Dobbins, "Skip the Graft," *New York Times*, 17 January 2010; cf. Isabel MacDonald, "Same Old Interests Have Plan for 'New Haiti'," *The Indypendent*, 29 January 2010.

55 Quoted in Avi Lewis, "Haiti: The Politics of Rebuilding," *Fault Lines*, Al Jazeera English, 12 February 2010.

56 Ben Fox, "Foreign Firms in Haiti Ready for Construction Boom," AP, 7 June 2010.

57 Martha Brannigan and Jacqueline Charles, "US Firms Want Part in Haiti Cleanup," *Miami Herald*, 8 February 2010; cf. Jacqueline Charles, "Groups Jockey for Role in Haiti Revival," *Miami Herald*, 9 March 2010.

58 Ben Fox, "Foreign Firms in Haiti Ready for Construction Boom," AP, 7 June 2010.

59 Kim Ives, "Only 15 percent for Haitians: Interim Commission Prepares to Dole Out Reconstruction Contracts," *Haïti Liberté*, 16 June 2010.

60 Cited in Jacqueline Charles, "Groups Jockey for Role in Haiti Revival," *Miami Herald*, 9 March 2010.

61 Cited in Reed Lindsay, "Haiti's Excluded," *The Nation*, 11 March 2010.

62 Interviewed in Sebastian Walker, "Haiti: Six Months On," *Fault Lines*, Al Jazeera English, 12 July 2010.

63 Sebastian Walker, "Haiti: Six Months On," 12 July 2010.

64 Wadner Pierre, "Haiti Post-Earthquake: Discrimination and Prejudice," *The Dominion* weblogs, 24 June 2010.

65 Tim Schwartz, "How to Save the NGO Sector from Itself," 10 March 2010.

66 *Report On Transparency of Relief Organizations Responding to the 2010 Haiti Earthquake*, Disaster Accountability Project, 12 July 2010.

67 Peter Richards, "Flooded with NGOs, Haiti Looks to Fall Presidential Polls," IPS, 7 July 2010.

68 Cf. Anthony Fenton, "Haiti: Private Contractors 'Like Vultures Coming to Grab the Loot'," IPS, 19 February 2010; Bill Quigley, "Mercenaries Circling Haiti," *Haïti Liberté*, 3 March 2010; Martha Brannigan, "Haiti Rebuilding Summit Under Way in Miami," *Miami Herald*, 10 March 2010.

69 Rob Reynolds, "Al Jazeera Reports on the Haiti 'Summit' for Private Contractors," Al Jazeera, 10 March 2010.

70 Jonathan Katz, "Private Investment Key to Haiti's Future," AP, 1 April 2010.

71 Jonathan Katz, "Post-Quake Haiti's Economic Revival: Is Low-Paying Garment Industry the Answer?" AP, 21 February 2010; Ashley Smith, "The 'Shock Doctrine' for Haiti," *Socialist Worker*, 8 February 2010.

72 Carolyn Leitch, "Analysts Upsize Gildan Targets," *Globe and Mail*, 12 April 2005, cited in Regan Boychuk, "The Vultures Circle Haiti at Every Opportunity, Natural or Man-made," *MR Zine*, 2 February 2010.

73 Sean Gregory, "Entrepreneur Manufactures a Haitian Recovery," *Time*, 3 May 2010; Sebastian Walker, "Haiti: Six Months On," *Fault Lines*, Al Jazeera English, 12 July 2010.

74 See for instance Kim Ives, "Who Will Lead Haiti Reconstruction?" *Haïti Liberté*, 24 March 2010.

75 "Due to its poverty and relatively unregulated labor market," Paul Collier writes, "Haiti has labor costs that are fully competitive with China, which is the global benchmark. Haitian labor is not only cheap, it is of good quality. Indeed, because the garments industry used to be much larger than it is currently, there is a substantial pool of experienced labor" available for use (Collier, "Haiti: From Natural Catastrophe to Economic Security: A Report for the Secretary-General of the United Nations," January 2009, www.focal.ca/pdf/haiticollier.pdf).

76 David Wilson, "'Rebuilding Haiti' – the Sweatshop Hoax," *MR Zine*, 4 March 2010.

77 Richard Morse, "Haiti: Stuck in a Trap," *Huffington Post*, 28 March 2010. As Morse

points out, "Importing cheap rice and sugar were concepts sold to Haitians by Haitian economist Leslie Delatour during the mid to late 1980's. It was called Chicago economics: free markets. The concept destroyed rural production and incentives in Haiti and sent an additional 2 million people to go live in Port-au-Prince [. . . Today,] lobbying is still taken care of by a Delatour, Leslie's younger brother Lionel. Right now the younger Mr. Delatour is looking to attract more people out of the countryside and into the city with his HOPE2 garment bill, which is the crux of Haiti's economic future if Mevs, Soros, Boulos, Ban Ki Moon and Bill Clinton get their way. Mr. Delatour is also busy trying to funnel reconstruction monies to brother Patrick Delatour, Minister of Tourism and reconstruction 'expert,' and sister-in-law Elizabeth Delatour Préval who has helped turn the Haitian government, led by husband President Rene Préval, into a lobby machine for Haiti's elite families" (ibid.).

78 Sebastian Walker, 'Haiti: Six Months On', *Faultlines*, Al Jazeera English, 12 July 2010.

79 Nazaire St. Fort and Jeb Sprague, 'Anti-Hunger Protests Rock Haiti', *NACLA*, 25 April 2008; cf. Nazaire St. Fort and Jeb Sprague, 'Once-Vibrant Farming Sector in Dire Straits', *IPS*, 4 March 2008.

80 Robert Fatton Jr., "Toward a New Haitian State," *The Root*, 9 February 2010; Caroline Preston and Nicole Wallace, "6 Months after Earthquake, Haiti Struggles to Rebuild," *The Chronicle of Philanthropy*, 8 July 2010.

81 Tim Schwartz, "Program of Development in Interest of Impoverished Haitians," 7 March 2010. By the spring of 2010, even Bill Clinton could see that his own neo-liberal assault on Haitian farmers, in the 1990s, had been counter-productive. "It may have been good for some of my farmers in Arkansas, but it has not worked. It was a mistake," Clinton admitted to the Senate Foreign Relations Committee on 10 March (Katz, "With Cheap Imports, Haiti Can't Feed Itself," AP, 20 March 2010).

82 Tim Schwartz, *Travesty in Haiti* (Charleston: Booksurge, 2008), 108, 94.

83 "Partners In Health's Medical Director and Director of Advocacy and Policy Urge Donor Countries to Support the Haitian Government," Partners In Health, 27 March 2010, www.pih.org, accessed 31 March 2010; cf. Annis, "Canada's Failed Aid," *Haïti Liberté*, 4 August 2010.

84 Isabel Macdonald, "Where's Haiti's Bailout?" *Huffington Post*, 12 July 2010.

85 Caroline Preston and Nicole Wallace, "6 Months After Earthquake, Haiti Struggles to Rebuild," *The Chronicle of Philanthropy*, 8 July 2010.

86 See for instance Kathie Klarreich, "Haiti Relief: Anger, Confusion as Authorities Relocate Homeless," *Christian Science Monitor*, 20 April 2010; CBS Evening News, "Relief Efforts 'Certainly Not Good Enough,'" 22 April 2010.

87 E. Thomas Johnson, "Haitians Still Wait for Recovery," *LA Times*, 25 June 2010.

88 Tamara Lush, "Just 2 Percent of Quake Debris in Haiti Cleared", AP, 11 September 2010.

89 Mark Weisbrot, "Washington and International Donors Have Failed Haiti," *Sacramento Bee* (CA), 13 August 2010; cf. Katie Kane, "A Country 'Forgotten,'" *The Missoulian*, 6 June 2010; Mark Schuller, "Haiti's Resurrection: Promoting Human Rights," *Huffington Post*, 5 April 2010.

90 " 'We've Been Forgotten": Conditions in Haiti's Displacement Camps Eight Months After the Earthquake," 23 September 2010, pp. 1–2, http://ijdh.org/archives/14633.

91 See in particular BAI, "Our Bodies Are Still Trembling: Haitian Women's Fight Against Rape," IJDH, 27 July 2010.

92 Isabeau Doucet, "The Drama of Haiti's Internally Displaced," part one, *Haïti Liberte*, 11 August 2010. Needless to say, when the IHRC finally met on 17 August to rattle off an initial round of reconstruction targets and plans, "there was no mention of the humanitarian disaster and human rights violations suffered daily by 1.7 million

internally displaced, many of whom have not yet received emergency supplies after seven months" (Doucet, "IHRC Promises Millions for 'Sustainable Development,'" *Haïti Liberté*, 18 August 2010).

93 Ansel Herz, "Haut-Turgeau, Haiti: The Camp that Vanished and the Priest Who Forced Them Out," IPS, 9 March 2010; Herz, "Displaced Fear Expulsion from Makeshift Camps," IPS, 8 April 2010. Cf. "Forced IDP Relocations," *TransAfrica Forum*, 12 April 2010; IAT, "Vanishing Camps at Gunpoint," 14 July 2010. "Though there are some programs to relocate people back to their homes," Sasha Kramer points out, "the majority of displaced people were renters with uncertain property rights and 50 percent of the buildings in Port-au-Prince are now uninhabitable. Most of the camps are located on private property and pressure to relocate has been intense and at times violent. With nowhere else to go, many families are forced to endure terrible conditions and human rights violations only to sleep under a leaky tarp" (Sasha Kramer, "Haiti 6 Months Later; Frozen in Time," *Our Soil*, 12 July 2010).

94 Jonathan Katz, "Fights Over Land Stall Haiti Quake Recovery," AP, 11 July 2010.

95 Cited in Doucet, "The Drama of Haiti's Internally Displaced," Part One, *Haïti Liberte*, 11 August 2010.

96 Milinda Miles, "Haiti Earthquake Survivors to Peacefully Demonstrate to Call Attention to the Horrific Conditions in Camps," *Let Haiti Live*, 12 August 2010.

97 Kim Ives, "Six Months Later: Land Ownership at the Crux of Haiti's Stalled Reconstruction," *Haïti Liberte*, 14 July 2010; cf. "Sean Penn on Haiti Six Months after the Earthquake," *Democracy Now!*, 13 July 2010.

98 Mark Schuller, "Rained Out? Opportunities in Haiti Washing Away," *Huffington Post*, 21 July 2010.

99 Melinda Miles, "Rain and Weeping at Camp Corail," *Let Haiti Live*, 30 July 2010; Edward Cody, "Despite 'all that money,' More than 1 Million Haitians Remain Displaced by January Earthquake," *Washington Post*, 22 August 2010.

100 Kim Ives, "Six Months Later: Land Ownership at the Crux of Haiti's Stalled Reconstruction," *Haïti Liberté*, 14 July 2010.

101 Cited in Sebastian Walker, "Haiti: Six Months On," *Fault Lines*, Al Jazeera English, 12 July 2010.

102 Interviewed in Avi Lewis, "Haiti: The Politics of Rebuilding," *Fault Lines*, Al Jazeera English, 12 February 2010.

103 Beverly Bell, "'We've Lost the Battle, but We Haven't Lost the War:' Haiti Six Months After the Earthquake," *The Wip*, 12 July 2010.

104 Ansel Herz, "UN Clash with Frustrated Students Spills into Camps," *IPS*, 25 May 2010.

105 Yves Pierre-Louis, "Broad Mobilization Against Préval Continues," *Haïti Liberté*, 19 May 2010.

106 Randall White, "Thousands in Haiti March on Aristide's Birthday," *Haiti Action*, 16 July 2010.

107 Doucet, "The Drama of Haiti's Internally Displaced," part two, *Haïti Liberté*, 25 August 2010.

108 Reed Lindsay, "Haiti's Excluded," *The Nation*, March 11, 2010; cf. Ansel Herz, "Looking More and More Like a War Zone," *IPS 30 March 2010*.

109 "MINUSTAH Continues to Prioritize Security over Relief," CEPR, 2 June 2010.

110 Kim Ives, letter to the author, 25 May 2010.

111 Quoted in Sebastian Walker, "Haiti: Six Months On," *Fault Lines*, Al Jazeera English, 12 July 2010.

112 The final FL list of candidates was endorsed by the party leader (Aristide) by fax, but at the last minute the CEP invented a new requirement, knowing FL would be unable to meet it: Aristide, still exiled in South Africa and denied entry to Haiti, would have to

sign the list in person. In the 2006 elections, by contrast, several former FL senators claimed to represent FL without the endorsement of either Aristide or the membership, and the CEP made no objection (Jeb Sprague, "Fanmi Lavalas Banned, Voter Apprehension Widespread," *IPS*, 17 April 2009; cf. IJDH, "International Community Should Pressure the Haitian Government for Prompt and Fair Elections," 30 June 2010; Ira Kurzban, "Unfair and Undemocratic," *Miami Herald*, 8 September 2010).

113 Wadner Pierre, "Empty Streets, Empty Boxes: Haitians Reject Manipulated Election," *HaitiAnalysis*, 30 June 2009.

114 IJDH, "International Community Should Pressure the Haitian Government for Prompt and Fair Elections," 30 June 2010.

115 "Haiti's Leader Rejects US Election Proposals," Reuters, 30 June 2010; Wadner Pierre, "Haiti Gears Up for Polls – Again, Sans Lavalas," *IPS*, 30 July 2010.

116 Cf. Kevin Edmonds, 'The Assault on Haitian Democracy,' *NACLA*, 23 August 2010.

117 Ansel Herz, "Stay in the States: Incompetent, Egotistical Wyclef Jean Offers Only False Hope for Haiti," *New York Daily News*, 7 August 2010. "The very fact that he is taken seriously" in the foreign press when he has no qualifications of the job, adds Robert Fatton, is another indication of the fact that the US tends to "look at the typical Haitian population as a bankrupt kind of species" (cited in Tamara Lush, "Haiti Ruling Ends Wyclef Jean's Run for President," AP, 21 August 2010).

118 Isabeau Doucet, letter to the author, 16 September 2010.

119 "Notre position sur la conjoncture politique," *Haïti Liberté*, 11 August 2010; English translation at canadahaitiaction.ca/content/haiti-libert%C3%A9-editorial-political-situation-upcoming-election. "The CEP and Préval have excluded the most popular political party, Fanmi Lavalas, and are trying to corrupt its members," argues Yves Pierre-Louis, but "the masses remain attached to Jean Bertrand Aristide as their national representative [. . .]. The priorities of [their] mobilization are to demand the resignation of René Préval and the CEP, to form a transitional political power capable of organizing inclusive elections [. . .], and to get rid of the international community's imposed occupation forces" (Yves Pierre-Louis, interview with Isabeau Doucet, Port-au-Prince, 17 Sept 2010).

120 Carlos Jean-Charles, interviewed in Sebastian Walker, "Haiti: Six Months On," *Fault Lines*, Al Jazeera English, 12 July 2010.

121 Kim Ives, "With Strange Bedfellows: Mobilization Against Préval Gains Momentum," *Haïti Liberté*, 12 May 2010.

122 Quoted in Kim Ives, 'With Strange Bedfellows', *Haïti Liberté*, 12 May 2010; cf. Yves Pierre-Louis, 'Broad Mobilization Against Préval Continues',*Haïti Liberté*, 19 May 2010.

APPENDIX

1. Jean-Bertrand Aristide has been living in exile in South Africa since 31 May 2004. This interview was conducted in French, in Pretoria, on 20 July 2006; it was translated and edited by Peter Hallward. An abbreviated version of the interview appeared in the *London Review of Books* 29: 4 (22 February 2007), http://www.lrb.co.uk/v29/n04/hall02_.html.

2. Interview with Patrick Elie, Port-au-Prince, 19 April 2006; Ben Dupuy, "The Class Dynamics of Haiti's Freedom Struggle" (September 2004).

3. The text of the Paris accords was published in the August 1994 issue of *Multinational Monitor*, http://multinationalmonitor.org/hyper/mm0894.html#haiti.

4. See for instance Michael Deibert, *Notes from the Last Testament*, 410–13.

5. Peter Eisner, "Aristide Back in Caribbean Heat," *Washington Post*, 16 March 2004.

Bibliography

(not including newspaper articles)

Abbott, Elizabeth. *Haiti: The Duvaliers and Their Legacy*. New York: McGraw-Hill, 1988.

Agee, Philip. *Inside the Company: CIA Diary*. Harmondsworth: Penguin Books, 1975.

Americas Watch/NCHR. *The Aristide Government's Human Rights Record*. 1 November 1991. http://www.hrw.org/reports/pdfs/h/haiti/haiti91n.pdf.

Amnesty International "Haiti: On the Horns of a Dilemma: Military Repression or Foreign Invasion?" 23 August 1994. http://www.amnestyusa.org/countries/haiti/document.do?id=73C713226595BEEC802569A6006051E8.

———. "Haiti: Still Crying Out for Justice" (1998). http://web.amnesty.org/library/Index/ENGAMR360021998?open&of=ENG-HTI.

———. "Haiti: A Worrying Increase in Violence Against the Police Force," 18 October 1999. http://web.amnesty.org/library/Index/ENGAMR360061999?open&of=ENG-HTI.

——— "Haiti: Disarmament Delayed, Justice Denied," 28 July 2005. http://web.amnesty.org/library/index/engamr360052005.

Aristide, Jean-Bertrand. *In the Parish of the Poor: Writings from Haiti*. Maryknoll, NY: Orbis Books, 1990.

———. *Théologie et politique*. Montréal: CIDIHCA, 1992.

———. *An Autobiography*. Maryknoll, NY: Orbis Books, 1993.

———. *Dignity*. Charlottesville: University Press of Virginia, 1996.

———. *Eyes of the Heart: Seeking a Path for the Poor in the Age of Globalization*. Monroe ME: Common Courage Press, 2000.

Arthur, Charles. "Bitter Fruit." *New Internationalist* 341 (December 2001), http://www.newint.org/issue341/bitter.htm.

———. *Haiti in Focus: A Guide to the People, Politics and Culture*. London: Latin American Bureau, 2002.

———. "Haiti's Labor Movement in Renaissance." *International Union Rights* 10: 2 (June 2003). http://www.haitisupport.gn.apc.org/fea_campaign_index.html.

———. "Walking the Tightrope." David Dadge, ed. *Silenced: International Journalists Expose Media Censorship*. NY: Prometheus Books, 2005. 273–93.

Avril, Prosper. *An Appeal to History: The Truth About a Singular Lawsuit*. USA: Universal Publishers, 1999.

Badiou, Alain. *Ethics: An Essay on the Understanding of Evil*, trans. Peter Hallward. London: Verso, 2001.

Bellegarde-Smith, Patrick. *Haiti: The Breached Citadel*. Toronto: Canadian Scholars' Press, 2004.

Blackburn, Robin. *The Overthrow of Colonial Slavery 1776–1848.* London: Verso, 1988.

Blum, William. "Who Will Rid Me of This Turbulent Priest? Haiti 1986–1994." *Killing Hope: U.S. Military and CIA Interventions since World War II.* Monroe, ME: Common Courage Press, 1995. Online at http://www.thirdworldtraveler.com/Blum/Haiti_KH.html.

Blumenthal, Max. "The Other Regime Change." *Salon* 16 July 2004. http://dir.salon.com/story/news/feature/2004/07/16/haiti_coup/print.html.

Boff, Leonardo, and Clodovis Boff. *Introducing Liberation Theology*, trans. Paul Burns. Tunbridge Wells: Burns and Oates, 1987.

Briggs, Barbara and Charles Kernaghan. "The US Economic Agenda: A Sweatshop Model of Development." *NACLA Report on the Americas* 27: 4 (January 1994): 37–40.

Chin, Pat, et al., eds. Haiti: A Slave Revolution. New York: International Action Center, 2004.

Chomsky, Noam, and Edward S. Herman. *Manufacturing Consent: The Political Economy of the Mass Media.* NY: Pantheon Books, 1988.

Chomsky, Noam. *Necessary Illusions: Thought Control in Democratic Societies.* Boston: South End Press, 1989.

————. "The Threat Of A Good Example." *What Uncle Sam Really Wants* [1993], chapter I: 6. http://www.zmag.org/chomsky/sam/sam–1–6.html.

————. *Year 501: The Conquest Continues.* Boston: South End Press, 1993.

————. "Democracy Enhancement: The Case of Haiti." *Z Magazine* July 1994. http://www.zmag.org/zmag/articles/chomdemenh2.htm.

————. "Democracy Restored." *Z Magazine* November 1994. http://www.zmag.org/zmag/articles/chomdemrest.htm.

Chomsky, Noam, Paul Farmer and Amy Goodman, eds. *Getting Haiti Right this Time: The US and the Coup.* Monroe ME: Common Courage Press, 2004.

Concannon Jr., Brian. "Justice in Haiti: The Raboteau Trial." *Human Rights Databank* 7: 4 (December 2000). http://www.hri.ca/tribune/viewArticle.asp?ID=2580.

————. "Lave Men, Siye Atè: Taking Human Rights Seriously." Melinda Miles and Eugenia Charles, eds. *Let Haiti LIVE: Unjust US Policies Towards its Oldest Neighbor.* Coconut Creek FL: Educa Vision 2004. 75–98.

————. "Haiti's Political Prisoners Exemplify Challenges of Democratic Transition," *Power and Interest News Report*, 11 September 2006. http://www.pinr.com/report.php?ac=view_

————. "Haiti's Elections: Right Result, for the Wrong Reason." IJDH 17 February 2006. http://www.ijdh.org/articles/article_recent_news_2–17–06.htm.

Coughlin, Dan. "Haitian Lament: Killing Me Softly." *The Nation* 1 March 1999. http://www.thenation.com/docprint.mhtml?i=19990301&s=coughlin.

Council on Hemispheric Affairs (COHA). "Haiti: Waiting for Something Bad to Happen." COHA 13 February 2004. http://www.coha.org/NEW_PRESS_RELEASES/New_Press_Releases_2004/04.07_Haiti_Waiting.htm.

————. "The International Republican Institute: Promulgating Democracy of Another Variety". COHA 15 July 2004. http://www.coha.org/2004/07/15/the-international-republican-institute-promulgating-democracy-of-another-variety/.

————. "Haiti: Smouldering on the Edge of Chaos." COHA 23 September 2004. http://www.coha.org/2004/09/23/haiti-smoldering-on-the-edge-of-chaos/.

Cromwell, David, and David Edwards. "Bringing Hell to Haiti." *Dissident Voice* 1 March 2004. http://www.dissidentvoice.org/Mar04/Edwards0301.htm.

Dailey, Peter. "The Fall of the House of Aristide." *New York Review of Books* 13 March 2003. http://www.nybooks.com/articles/16126.

Danner, Mark. "Beyond the Mountains," *The New Yorker* 27 November 1989.

————. "Haiti on the Verge." *New York Review of Books* 4 November 1993. http://www.markdanner.com/nyreview/110493_Haiti_on_the_Verge.htm.

Danroc, Gilles and Daniel Roussière, eds. *La Répression au quotidien en Haiti 1991–1994*. Paris: Karthala, 1995.

Debray, Régis. *Rapport du comité indépendant de réflexion et de propositions sur les relations franco-haïtiennes.* Paris: Ministère des Affaires Étrangères, 28 January 2004. http://www.diplomatie.gouv.fr/fr/IMG/pdf/rapport_haiti.pdf.

Deibert, Michael. *Notes from the Last Testament: The Struggle for Haiti.* New York: Seven Stories Press, 2005.

Deleuze, Gilles. *Negotiations, 1972–1990*, trans. Martin Joughin. New York: Columbia University Press, 1995.

Deleuze, Gilles, and Félix Guattari. *A Thousand Plateaus: Capitalism and Schizophrenia*, trans. Brian Massumi. Minneapolis: University of Minnesota Press, 1987.

Department of Justice [US]. *Profile Series: Haiti* [pr/hti/93.001] (August 1993). http://www1.umn.edu/humanrts/ins/haiti93.pdf.

DeRienzo, Paul. "Haiti's Nightmare: The Cocaine Coup and the CIA Connection." *The Shadow* 32 (April 1994). http://globalresearch.ca/articles/RIE402A.html.

Dewind, Josh and David H. Mckinley III. *Aiding Migration: The Impact of International Development Assistance on Haiti.* Boulder, CO: Westview Press, 1988.

Diederich, Bernard. *Le Prix du sang: la résistance d'un peuple face à la tyrannie.* Port-au-Prince: Editions Antillia, 2005.

Dubois, Laurent. *Avengers of the New World: The Story of the Haitian Revolution.* Cambridge: Harvard University Press, 2004.

Dupuy, Alex. *Haiti in the World Economy: Class, Race, and Underdevelopment since 1700.* Boulder: Westview Press, 1989.

————. *Haiti in the New World Order: The Limits of the Democratic Revolution.* Boulder: Westview Press, 1997.

————. *The Prophet and Power: Jean-Bertrand Aristide, the International Community and Haiti.* New York: Rowman & Littlefield, 2007.

Dupuy, Ben. "The Attempted Character Assassination of Aristide." *Project Censored* (1999). http://www.thirdworldtraveler.com/Global_Secrets_Lies/Aristide_CharacAssass.html.

————. "The Class Dynamics of Haiti's Freedom Struggle." *Socialism and Liberation Magazine* 1: 2 (September 2004). http://socialismandliberation.org/mag/index.php?aid=71.

Economist Intelligence Unit. *Country Report: Haiti.* London: EIU, 2003–2006.

Ehrenreich, Ben. "Haiti's Hope: A Tortured Country Searches for a Future." *LA Weekly* 12 April 2006. www.laweekly.com/general/features/haitis-hope/13089/.

Elie, Patrick. "Taking Us to Democracy Like Cattle to a Killing House." *ZNet* 14 December 2005. http://www.zmag.org/content/print_article.cfm?itemID=9329&sectionID=1.

Elie, Patrick, and Anthony Fenton. "A Coup Made Long in Advance." *ZNet* 17 October 2004. http://www.zmag.org/content/showarticle.cfm?ItemID=6439.

Elie, Patrick, and Reed Lindsay. "What Future for Haiti? An Interview with Patrick Elie." *NACLA News* 30 August 2006. http://news.nacla.org/2006/08/30/what-future-for-haiti-an-interview-with-patrick-elie/.

Engler, Yves, and Anthony Fenton. *Canada in Haiti.* Vancouver: Red Publishing, 2005.

Engler, Yves. "Haiti After the Coup." *Z Magazine* 18: 10 (October 2005). http://zmagsite.zmag.org/Oct2005/engler1005.html.

Episcopado Latinoamericano. *Documento de Puebla: III Conferencia General del Episcopado Latinoamericano.* March 1979. http://www.multimedios.org/docs2/d000363/index.html.

Farmer, Paul. *The Uses of Haiti.* Monroe ME: Common Courage Press, 2003.

————. "Who Removed Aristide?" *London Review of Books* 26: 8 (15 April 2004). http://www.lrb.co.uk/v26/n08/farm01_.html.

————. *Never Again: Reflections on Human Values and Human Rights*. University of Utah: The Tanner Lectures, 30 March 2005. www.tannerlectures.utah.edu/lectures/ Farmer_2006.pdf.

Fatton, Robert. *Haiti's Predatory Republic: The Unending Transition to Democracy*. Boulder: Lynne Rienner Publishers, 2002.

Felux, Justin. "Debunking the Media's Lies about President Aristide." *Dissident Voice* 14 March 2004, http://www.dissidentvoice.org/Mar04/Felux0314.htm.

Fenton, Anthony. "Year 201: Imperialists Bring Horror to Haiti." *Left Turn* (2005). http://www.leftturn.org/Articles/Viewer.aspx?id=657&type=M.

————. "Have the Latortues Kidnapped Democracy in Haiti?" *ZNet* 26 June 2005. http://www.zmag.org/content/showarticle.cfm?ItemID=8165.

————. "Legitimizing Polyarchy: Canada's Contribution to 'Democracy Promotion' in Latin America and the Caribbean." *Canadian Dimension* 40: 6 (29 October 2006). www.zmag.org/content/showarticle.cfm?ItemID=11290.

Fick, Carolyn E. *The Making of Haiti: The Saint Domingue Revolution from Below*. Knoxville: University of Tennessee Press, 1990.

Georges, Josiane. "Trade and the Disappearance of Haitian Rice." *Ted Case Studies* no. 725 (June 2004). http://www.american.edu/TED/haitirice.htm.

Girard, Philippe R. *The Eagle and the Rooster: The 1994 US Invasion of Haiti*. Ohio University PhD, August 2002. http://www.ohiolink.edu/etd/send-pdf.cgi?ohiou1035828999.

Goff, Stan. *Hideous Dream: A Soldier's Memoir of the US Invasion of Haiti*. New York: Soft Skull Press, 2000.

————. "Beloved Haiti: A (Counter) Revolutionary Bicentennial." *Counterpunch* 14 February 2004. http://www.counterpunch.org/goff02142004.html.

Golinger, Eva. *The Chavez Code: Cracking US Intervention in Venezuela*. Northampton, MA: Olive Branch Press, 2006.

Gorostiaga, Xabier. "Geoculture: The Key to Understanding Haiti?" *Revista Envío* 162 (January 1995). http://www.envio.org.ni/articulo/1826.

Grandin, Greg. *Empire's Workshop: Latin America, the United States, and the Rise of the New Imperialism*. New York: Metropolitan Books, 2006.

Grann, David. "Giving 'The Devil' His Due." *Atlantic Monthly* June 2001.

Griffin, Thomas M. "Summary Report of Haiti Human Rights Delegation – March 29 to April 5." National Lawyers Guild April 2004. http://www.nlg.org/programs/inter-national/Haiti_delegation_report1.pdf.

————. *Haiti Human Rights Investigation: November 11–21, 2004*. Miami: Center for the Study of Human Rights, University of Miami School of Law, January 2005. http://www.law.miami.edu/cshr/CSHR_Report_02082005_v2.pdf.

Gros, Jean-Germain. "Haiti's Flagging Transition." *Journal of Democracy* [NED] 8:4 (1997): 94–109.

Guattari, Félix. *The Three Ecologies*. London: Athlone Press, 2000.

Guilhot, Nicolas. *The Democracy Makers: Human Rights and International Order*. New York: Columbia University Press, 2005.

Gutiérrez, Gustavo. *A Theology of Liberation: History, Politics, and Salvation* [1971], trans. Sister Caridad Inda and John Eagleson. Maryknoll, NY: Orbis Books, 1988.

Haiti Accompaniment Project [Laura Flynn, Robert Roth and Leslie Fleming]. "Report of the Haiti Accompaniment Project 29 June–9 July 2004." HAC July 2004. http://www.haitiaction.net/News/hap6_29_4.html.

————. "Human Rights Conditions in Haiti's Prisons: Second Report of the Haiti Accompaniment Project 30 July–16 August 2004." HAC August 2004. http://www.haitiaction.net/News/HAP/8_16_4.html.

Haiti Action Committee [Laura Flynn et al.]. *Hidden From the Headlines: The U.S. War Against Haiti*. San Francisco: Haiti Action Committee, 2003, http://www.haitiaction.net/HidFrame.html.

——. *We Will Not Forget: The Achievements of Lavalas in Haiti*. San Francisco: Haiti Action Committee, 2005, http://www.teledyol.net/WWNF/wwnf.pdf.

Hallward, Peter. "Option Zero in Haiti." *New Left Review* 27 (May 2004), 23–47. http://www.newleftreview.net/NLR26102.shtml.

——. "The Politics of Prescription." *South Atlantic Quarterly* 104: 4 (Autumn 2005), 771–91.

——. "One Step at a Time: An Interview with Jean-Bertrand Aristide" [full transcript], *HaitiAnalysis* 18 February 2007. http://www.haitianalysis.com/2007/2/18/%E2%80%98one-step-at-a-time%E2%80%99-an-interview-with-jean-bertrand-aristide.

——. "The Violence of Democracy: A Review of Alex Dupuy's *The Prophet and Power* (2007)." *Haiti Liberté* nos. 1, 2, 3 (July–August 2007).

——. "Insurgency and Betrayal: An Interview with Guy Philippe," *HaitiAnalysis* 23 March 2007. http://www.haitianalysis.com/2007/3/25/insurgency-and-betrayal-an-interview-with-guy-philippe.

——. "Did He Jump or Was He Pushed? Aristide and the 2004 Coup in Haiti." forthcoming 000 June 2007.

Hardt, Michael, and Antonio Negri. *Empire*. Cambridge, MA: Harvard University Press, 2000.

Hartlyn, Jonathan, et al., eds. *The United States and Latin America in the 1990s: Beyond the Cold War*. Chapel Hill: University of North Carolina Press, 1992.

Harvard Law Student Advocates for Human Rights and Centro de Justiça Global. *Keeping the Peace in Haiti? An Assessment of the UN Stabilization Mission in Haiti*, March 2005. http://www.law.harvard.edu/programs/hrp/clinic/documents/Haiti_English_Final.pdf.

Heinl, Robert Debs, and Nancy Gordon Heinl, revised by Michael Heinl. *Written in Blood: The Story of the Haitian People 1492–1995*. Lanham, MD: The University Press of America, 2005.

Horblitt, Steven. "Multilateral Policy: The Road Toward Reconciliation." Georges Fauriol, ed. *The Haitian Challenge: US Policy Considerations*. Washington DC: Center for Strategic and International Studies, 1993.

Human Rights Watch. "Haiti, Security Compromised: Recycled Haitian Soldiers on the Police Front Line." *Human Rights Watch* 7: 3 (March 1995). http://www.hrw.org/reports/1995/Haiti.htm.

——. "The Human Rights Record of the Haitian National Police." *Human Rights Watch* 9: 1 (January 1997). http://www.hrw.org/reports/1997/haiti/Haiti.htm62_1831.

——. "Haiti: Recycled Soldiers and Paramilitaries on the March." HRW 27 February 2004. http://hrw.org/english/docs/2004/02/27/haiti7677.htm.

——. "Terror Prevails in Haiti: Human Rights Violations and Failed Diplomacy." *Human Rights Watch* 6: 5 (April 2004). http://www.hrw.org/reports/pdfs/h/haiti/haiti944.pdf.

IMF. *Haiti: Staff-Monitored Program*, IMF Country Report No. 03/260 (August 2003). http://www.imf.org/external/pubs/ft/scr/2003/cr03260.pdf.

——. "Haiti: Interim Poverty Reduction Strategy Paper," IMF Country Report No. 06/411 (November 2006). http://www.imf.org/external/pubs/ft/scr/2006/cr06411.pdf.

Institute for Justice & Democracy in Haiti. *Human Rights Violations in Haiti (February–May 2004)*. IJDH June 2004. http://www.ijdh.org/articles/article_ijdh-human-rights-violations.html.

Inter-American Development Bank (Barbara Szaszkiewicz et al.). *Haiti: Bank's Transition Strategy 2005–2006*. Inter-American Development Bank November 2004. http://idbdocs.iadb.org/wsdocs/getdocument.aspx?docnum=561125.

International Crisis Group. "A New Chance for Haiti? ICG Latin America/Caribbean Report No. 10." ICG 18 November 2004. http://www.icg.org/home/index.cfm?id=3109&l=1.

————. "Haiti: Justice Reform and the Security Crisis." *Latin America/Caribbean Briefing* no. 14, ICG 31 January 2007. http://www.crisisgroup.org/home/index.cfm?id=4639&l=1

International Tribunal on Haïti [Thomas Griffin, with Ramsey Clark, John Parker, Dave Welsh, Kim Ives, Lawrence Rockwood]. *Preliminary Report of the Commission of Inquiry October 6 to 11, 2005.* http://www.ijdh.org/pdf/COIReport.pdf.

Ives, Kim. "The Unmaking of a President." *NACLA Report on the Americas* 27: 4 (January 1994): 16–29.

————. "US Policy Towards Haiti Promotes Economic Instability." *The Progressive Media Project* 6 November 2002. http://progressive.org/media_1420.

James, C.L.R. *The Black Jacobins; Toussaint L'Ouverture and the San Domingo Revolution* [1938]. London: Penguin, 2001.

James, Clara: see Regan, Jane.

James, Patrick. "An Inside Look at Haiti's Business Elite." *Multinational Monitor* January 1995. http://multinationalmonitor.org/hyper/issues/1995/01/mm0195_10.html.

Jean, Jean-Claude, and Marc Maesschalck. *Transition politique en Haïti: radiographie du pouvoir Lavalas.* Paris: L'Harmattan, 1999.

Jean-Baptiste, Chavannes. "MPP Speaks to the New Dimension of the Haitian Crisis." MPP 24 February 2004. http://www.grassrootsonline.org/weblog/mpp.html.

Karshan, Michelle. "What's Next: Haiti Policy Analysts Weigh in: Putting the Pieces Together." Haiti Action Committee 16 December 2002. http://www.MichelleKarshan.com/page10.html.

Kean, Katherine. *Rezistans* [film]. NY: Crowing Rooster Arts, 1994. (Page numbers refer to an unpublished 90-page typescript.)

Kennedy, Marie and Chris Tilly. "Up Against The 'Death Plan': Haitians Resist US-imposed Economic Restructuring." *Dollars & Sense* March 1996.

————. "Haiti in 2001: Political Deadlock, Economic Crisis." *Dollars & Sense* November 2001.http://www.thirdworldtraveler.com/Haiti/Haiti_2001.html.

Kidder, Tracy. "The Trials of Haiti: Why Has the US Government Abandoned a Country it Once Sought to Liberate?" *The Nation* 277: 13 (27 October 2003).

Kolbe, Athena R. and Royce A. Hutson. "Human Rights Abuse and Other Criminal Violations in Port-Au-Prince, Haiti: A Random Survey of Households." *The Lancet* 9538 (2 September 2006).

Kramer, Sasha. "The Friendly Face of US Imperialism: USAID and Haiti." *CounterPunch* 14 October 2005. http://www.counterpunch.org/kramer10142005.html.

Laguerre, Michel S. *The Military and Society in Haiti.* Knoxville: University of Tennessee Press, 1993.

Lawless, Robert. *Haiti's Bad Press.* Rochester VT: Schenkman Books, 1992.

Lehmann, Gérard. *Haïti 2004, radiographie d'un coup d'État.* The University of Southern Denmark, 2005.

Lindsay, Reed. "Peace Despite the Peacekeepers in Haiti." *NACLA Report on the Americas* 39: 6 (May 2006): 31–6.

Lule, Jack. "News Values, News Strategies: The *New York Times* in Haiti 1994–96" [1996]. http://list.msu.edu/cgi-bin/wa?A2=ind9612c&L=aejmc&T=0&P=9485.

Macdonald, Isabel. "Covering the Coup: Canadian News Reporting, Journalists and Sources in the 2004 Haiti Crisis." MA Dissertation, York University (Canada), preliminary draft, December 2006.

McGowan, Lisa. *Democracy Undermined, Economic Justice Denied: Structural Adjustment and the Aid Juggernaut in Haiti.* Washington: Development Group for Alternative Policies,

January 1997. http://www.developmentgap.org/foriegn_aid/Democracy_Undermined_Economic_Justice_Denied_Structural_Adjustment_&_Aid_Juggernaut_in_Haiti.html.

Maingot, Anthony. "Haiti and Aristide: The Legacy of History." *Current History* February 1992.

Malval, Robert. *L'Année de toutes les dupéries.* Port-au-Prince: Editions Regain, 1996.

Maternowska, M. Catherine. *Reproducing Inequities: Poverty and the Politics of Population in Haiti.* New Brunswick: Rutgers University Press 2006.

Miles, Melinda, with Moira Feeney. *Elections 2000: Participatory Democracy in Haiti.* Haiti Reborn/Quixote Center, February 2001. http://www.quixote.org/hr/election–2000/.

————. "Emergency Haiti Observation Mission 23 March–2 April 2004." Haiti Reborn/Quixote Center, April 2004. www.quixote.org/hr/campaigns/lhl/ob-miss-mar04.php.

Miles, Melinda, and Eugenia Charles, eds. *Let Haiti LIVE: Unjust U.S. Policies Towards Its Oldest Neighbor.* Coconut Creek, FL: Educa Vision, 2004.

Mobekk, Erin, and Anne Street. *Disarmament, Demobilisation and Reintegration: What Role Should the EU Play in Haiti?* ActionAid, October 2006. http://www.actionaid.org/wps/content/documents/Haiti%20report%20–%20english.pdf.

Morrell, James. "Snatching Defeat from the Jaws of Victory." Center for International Policy August 2000. http://www.haitipolicy.org/archives/Publications&Commentary/snatch2.htm.

Muggah, Robert. *Securing Haiti's Transition: Reviewing Human Insecurity and the Prospects for Disarmament, Demobilization, and Reintegration.* Small Arms Survey Occasional Paper no. 14. Geneva: Small Arms Survey, October 2005. http://www.smallarmssurvey.org/files/sas/publications/o_papers_pdf/2005-op14-haiti-eng.pdf. An earlier version of this report was published in March 2005.

Murray, Kevin. "Haiti: A Way Forward?" *Peacework Magazine* May 2004. http://www.afsc.org/pwork/0405/040512.htm.

NACLA, ed. *Haiti: Dangerous Crossroads.* Boston: South End Press, 1995.

Nairn, Allan. "Aristide Banks on Austerity." *Multinational Monitor* July/August 1994. http://multinationalmonitor.org/hyper/mm0894.htmlhaiti.

————. "The Eagle Is Landing: U.S. Forces Occupy Haiti," *The Nation* 3 October 1994.

————. "Behind Haiti's Paramilitaries: Our Man in FRAPH." *The Nation* 24 October 1994.

————. "Haiti Under the Gun: How U.S.-backed Paramilitaries Rule Through Fear." *The Nation* 8 January 1996.

National Labor Committee. *Haiti After the Coup: Sweatshop or Real Development?* New York: National Labor Committee, 1993. http://www.nlcnet.org/campaigns/archive/haiti/Haiticoup.shtml.

———— [Eric Verhoogen]. *The U.S. in Haiti: How to Get Rich on 11 Cents an Hour.* New York: NLC, January 1996. http://www.doublestandards.org/verhoogen1.html.

Neild, Rachel M. *Police Reform in Haiti: The Challenge of Demilitarizing Public Order and Establishing the Rule of Law.* Washington: The Washington Office on Latin America, November 1996.

Nicholls, David. *From Dessalines to Duvalier: Race, Color, and National Independence in Haiti.* New Brunswick NJ: Rutgers University Press, 1996.

Niman, Michael I. "Our Nasty Little Racist War in Haiti." *ArtVoice* 10 June 2004. http://coldtype.net/Assets.04/Niman.04/Niman.20.04.pdf.

Odinkalu, Chidi Anselm. "Why More Africans Don't Use Human Rights Language." *Carnegie Council on Ethics and International Affairs* series 2, no. 1 (5 December 1999). http://www.cceia.org/viewMedia.php/prmID/602.

Orenstein, Catherine. "Haiti in the Mainstream Press: Excesses and Omissions." *NACLA Report on the Americas* 27: 1 (August 1993).

————. "Aristide, Again." *The Progressive* 65: 1 (January 2001). http://www.access-mylibrary.com/coms2/summary_0286–10543078_ITM.

Organization of American States. *The Election Observation Mission in Haiti February to July 2000* [CP/doc. 3383/00]. OAS 13 December 2000. http://www.sap.oas.org/docs/permanent_council/2000/cp_doc_3383_00_eng.pdf.

————. "Report of the Commission of Inquiry into the Events of December 17, 2001." at http://www.oas.org/OASpage/Haiti_situation/cpinf4702_02_eng.htm.

Oxfam. *Rigged Trade and Not Much Aid: How Rich Countries Help to Keep the Least Developed Countries Poor*. London: Oxfam, May 2001. http://www.oxfam.org.uk/what_we_do/issues/trade/downloads/rigged_trade.pdf.

————. *The Call for Tough Arms Controls: Voices from Haiti* (January 2006). http://www.oxfam.de/download/Haiti_Bericht.pdf.

Paul, Rod. *Failing Haiti* [film]. Atlanta: Primary Pictures, 2005.

Pierre, Hyppolite. *Haiti: Rising Flames from Burning Ashes: Haiti the Phoenix*. Lanham, MD: University Press of America, 2006.

Pierre-Antoine, Lovinsky. "Le Coup d'état continue." *Hayti.Net* 18 January 2007. http://www.hayti.net/tribune/index.php?mod=news&ac=commentaires&id=240.

Pina, Kevin. "Is the US Funding Haitian 'Contras?' " *Black Commentator* 36 (3 April 2003). http://www.blackcommentator.com/36/36_guest_commentator.html.

————. "US Plots Regime Change in Haïti." *Black Commentator* 42 (15 May 2003). http://www.blackcommentator.com/42/42_issues.html.

————. "Propaganda War Intensifies against Haiti as Opposition Grabs for Power." *Black Commentator* 62 (30 October 2003). http://www.blackcommentator.com/62/62_haiti_1.html.

————. "US Corporate Media Distort Haitian Events." *Black Commentator* 63 (6 November 2003). http://www.blackcommentator.com/63/63_haiti_2.html.

————. "The Bush Administration's End Game for Haiti." *Black Commentator* 67 (4 December 2003). http://www.blackcommentator.com/67/67_pina.html.

————. "US-Backed Haiti Opposition Emboldened, Student 'Revolt' Unmasked." *Black Commentator* 69 (18 December 2003). http://www.blackcommentator.com/69/69_haiti.html.

————. "Haiti's Cracked Screen: Lavalas Under Siege While the Poor Get Poorer." *Black Commentator* 73 (15 January 2004). http://blackcommentator.com/73/73_haiti_pina.html.

————. "One Man's Democracy, Another Man's Chains: The Untold Story of Aristide's Departure from Haiti." *Black Commentator* 105 (16 September 2004). http://www.blackcommentator.com/105/105_pina.html.

————. *Haiti: "We Must Kill the Bandits"* [film], 2007.

Podur, Justin. "Kofi Annan's Haiti" [review of Michael Deibert, *Notes from the Last Testament*]. *New Left Review* 37 (January 2006). http://newleftreview.org/A2604.

Raby, Dawn Linda. *Democracy and Revolution: Latin America and Socialism Today*. London: Pluto, 2006.

Rampton, Sheldon. "Hustling for the Junta: PR Fights Democracy in Haiti." *PR Watch* autumn 1994. http://www.prwatch.org/prwissues/1994Q3/junta.html.

Reding, Andrew. "Haiti: An Agenda for Democracy." World Policy Institute February 1996. http://www.worldpolicy.org/globalrights/carib/1996-haiti.html.

Reed, Betsy. "Aristide's Financial Bind." *Dollars & Sense* November 1994.

Reeves, Tom. "Still Up Against the Death Plan in Haiti: The Aristide Government is Straightjacketed by Low-Intensity Warfare and Neo-liberal Economic Demands." *Dollars & Sense* 249 (September 2003): 38–45.

————. "Return to Haiti: The American Learning Zone." *Counterpunch* 14 April 2004. http://www.counterpunch.org/reeves04142004.html.

————. "Haiti's Disappeared." *ZNet* 5 May 2004. http://www.zmag.org/content/showarticle.cfm?SectionID=55&ItemID=5467.

————. "How Bush Brings Freedom to the World: The Case of Haiti." *Counterpunch* 29 January 2005. http://www.counterpunch.org/reeves01292005.html.

————. "The Puzzling Alliance of Chavannes Jean-Baptiste and Charles Henri Baker." *Counterpunch* 1 March 2006. http://www.counterpunch.org/reeves03012006 .html.

Regan, Jane. "In the Aftermath of Invasion: A.I.D.ing US Interests in Haiti." *Covert Action Quarterly* 51 (January 1995): 7–58. Online at http://www.hartford-hwp.com/archives/43a/002.html.

————. [Clara James] "Haiti: The Roof Is Leaking." *Z Magazine* (June 1997), http://www.zmag.org/ZMag/articles/june97james.htm

————. [Clara James]. "Haitian Free Trade Zone." *Dollars & Sense*, November 2002.

————. "Haiti: In Bondage to History?" *NACLA Report on the Americas* 38: 4 (January 2005): 4–7.

Richardson, Laurie. "Disarmament Derailed." *NACLA Report on the Americas* 29: 6 (1996), 11–14.

————. "Feeding Dependency, Starving Democracy: USAID Policies in Haiti." *Grassroots International* 6 March 1997. http://www.grassrootsonline.org/haiti_food_-security.html.

Ridgeway, James, ed. *The Haiti Files: Decoding the Crisis.* Washington DC: Essential Books/Azul Editions, 1994.

Robinson, William I. *Promoting Polyarchy: Globalisation, US Intervention, and Hegemony.* Cambridge: Cambridge University Press, 1996.

Rossier, Nicolas. *Aristide and the Endless Revolution* [film]. NY: Baraka, 2005.

Ruchala, Cali. "Two Days: Two Crucial Events that Led to Lavalas' Collapse." *Sobaka's Communiqué* 3 (Spring 2004). http://www.diacritica.com/communique/content/is-suethree/b.html.

Saint-Jean, Ronald. *Pourquoi les Etats-Unis ont-ils planifié le retour du FRAPH?* Port-au-Prince: Editions Séli, 2004.

————. *A propos du "Génocide de la Scierie": Exiger de la NCHR toute la vérité.* Port-au-Prince: CDPH, July 2004.

Saint-Vil, Jean. "Time to Stop Resisting Haiti's Resistance." *Corbett List* 29 November 2002. http://www.hartford-hwp.com/archives/43a/396.html.

Schmidt, Andréa and Anthony Fenton. "Andy Apaid and Us." *ZNet* 19 October 2005. http://www.zmag.org/content/showarticle.cfm?ItemID=8966.

Schoultz, Lars. *Human Rights and United States Policy toward Latin America.* Princeton, Princeton University Press: 1981.

Schulz, Donald E. (US Army War College). "Whither Haiti?" Strategic Studies Institute 1 April 1996. http://www.strategicstudiesinstitute.army.mil/pdffiles/PUB39.pdf.

————. "Haiti: Will Things Fall Apart?" *Parameters: US Army War College Quarterly* 27: 4 (Winter 1997–98): 73–91. http://www.carlisle.army.mil/usawc/Parameters/97winter/schulz.htm.

Shea, Nina. "Human Rights in Haiti." Georges Fauriol, ed. *The Haitian Challenge: US Policy Considerations.* Washington DC: Center for Strategic and International Studies, 1993.

Skerrett, Kevin. "Faking Genocide in Haiti: Canada's Role in the Persecution of Yvon Neptune." *ZNet* 23 June 2005. http://www.zmag.org/content/showarticle.cfm?SectionID=55&ItemID=8142.

Skolnik, Sam. "Separating Cops, Spies." *Legal Times* 1 March 1999.

Slavin, J.P. "Haiti: The Elite's Revenge." *NACLA Report on the Americas* 25: 3 (December 1991): 4–6.

Sletten, Pål, and Willy Egset. *Poverty in Haiti*. Oslo: FAFO, 2004. http://www.fafo.no/pub/rapp/755/755.pdf.

Smith, Ashley. "Aristide's Rise and Fall: The New Occupation of Haiti." *International Socialist Review* 35 (May 2004). http://www.isreview.org/issues/35/aristide.shtml.

Sprague, Jeb. "Supporting a Leftist Opposition to Lavalas: The AFL-CIO's Solidarity Center and the Batay Ouvriye." *MR Webzine* 21 November 2005. http://mrzine.-monthlyreview.org/sprague211105.html.

————. "Failed Solidarity: The ICFTU, AFL-CIO, ILO and ORIT in Haiti," *Labor Notes* May 2006. http://labornotes.org/node/230.

————. "A Lavalas Mayor in Hiding: An Interview with Moïse Jean Charles." *Left Turn*, July 2006. http://www.leftturn.org/?q=node/536.

Stephens, Evelyn Huber, and John D. Stephens. *Democratic Socialism in Jamaica: The Political Movement and Social Transformation in Dependent Capitalism*. Princeton: Princeton University Press, 1986.

Stotzky, Irwin P. *Silencing the Guns in Haiti: The Promise of Deliberative Democracy*. Chicago: University of Chicago Press, 1997.

Street, Anne. *Haiti: A Nation in Crisis*. London: Catholic Institute for International Relations, 2004.

Trouillot, Michel-Rolph. *Haiti, State Against Nation: The Origins and Legacy of Duvalierism*. New York: Monthly Review Press, 1990.

————. *Silencing the Past: Power and the Production of History*. Boston: Beacon Press, 1995.

Verhoogen, Eric. "The U.S.–Haiti Connection: Rich Companies, Poor Workers." *Multinational Monitor* 17: 4 (April 1996). http://multinationalmonitor.org/hyper/mm0496.04.html.

Wargny, Christophe. *Haïti n'existe pas: 1804–2004, deux cents ans de solitude*. Paris: Autrement, 2004.

Williams, Eric. *From Columbus to Castro: The History of the Caribbean 1492–1969*. London: André Deutsch, 1970.

Williams, Heather. "A Coup for the Entente Cordiale! Why France Joined the US in Haiti." *Counterpunch* 11: 4 (16 February 2004).

Wilentz, Amy. *The Rainy Season: Haiti since Duvalier* [1989]. London: Vintage, 1994.

————. "Haiti's Collapse." *The Nation* 278: 8 (1 March 2004). http://www.thenation.com/doc/20040301/wilentz.

————. "Coup in Haiti." *The Nation* 278: 11 (22 March 2004). http://www.thenation.com/doc/20040322/wilentz.

World Bank. *Haiti: The Challenges of Poverty Reduction*. Washington: World Bank, August 1998.

————. "Financing Haiti's Future." World Bank 21 July 2004.

Wucker, Michele. "Haiti: So Many Missteps." *World Policy Journal* 21: 1 (Spring 2004). http://www.worldpolicy.org/journal/articles/wpj04–1/wucker.htm.

Index

wages xxxii, 5, 6–7, 15, 33, 37, 56,
61, 83, 102, 136, 163, 180,
410n.55
Wainwright, Yves André 260
Walt Disney 6
"war on terror" 175, 279, 375n.27
Wargny, Christophe 162, 172,
375n.13
Washington Post xxvii–xxviii, 40, 112,
117, 132, 178, 200, 206, 209,
212, 225, 226, 229, 234, 239,
240, 243–4
water supplies 7
Waters, Maxine 50
We Haitians (website) 109
Werleigh, Claudette 58
Weymouth, Lally 112
White, Robert 90, 377n.42

Widmaier, Herbert 109
Widmaier, Richard 109
Wilentz, Amy xxxvii, 25, 84, 96, 172,
204, 379n.89, 381n.118, 413n.10
Wilkerson, Lawrence 233
Williams, Carol 215
Wilme, Emmanuel "Dred" 201–2,
289, 290–4, 430n.36
Wilson, Scott 209, 214, 216, 220,
226, 247
Women's Affairs, Ministry of 135, 257
women's rights 135, 183–4
World Bank 8, 56, 61, 82, 152, 177,
190, 356
World Food Program 7
World Freedom Press Review 108–9

Zanmi Lasante 9, 133–4, 178